A GUIDE TO WORLD
LANGUAGE DICTIONARIES

A GUIDE TO WORLD LANGUAGE DICTIONARIES

Andrew Dalby

FITZROY DEARBORN PUBLISHERS
CHICAGO • LONDON

Originated and produced in Great Britain by
Library Association Publishing
7 Ridgmount Street
London WC1E 7AE

Library Association Publishing is wholly owned by The Library Association.

Published in the United States of America by
Fitzroy Dearborn Publishers
70 East Walton Street
Chicago, Illinois 60611

First published in the USA and UK, 1998

A Cataloging-in-Publication record for this book is available from the Library of Congress.

ISBN 1-57958-069-6

Cover illustration: *The Building of the Tower of Babel* by the Master of the Duke of Bedford. Shelfmark ADD 18850 fol 17v. By Permission of the British Library.

Typeset by the author.
Printed and made in Great Britain by Bookcraft (Bath) Ltd, Midsomer Norton, Somerset, UK.

CONTENTS

'If questions are on the menu,' said Larensius, 'here is one from me. Tell me, what is a *tetrax*?'

'A kind of bird', said someone – exactly what teachers tell their students in answer to any such question, *a kind of plant, a kind of bird, a kind of mineral.*

'Oh, I know as well as you do, my dear fellow,' said Larensius, 'that the *tetrax* belongs among the birds. There it is in good old Aristophanes: *woodpigeon and magpie, pelican and phlexis, tetrax and peacock.* I want to know if you can cite the word from any other authors.'

Athenaeus 9*c.* AD 200), *The Professors at Dinner* 398b.

INTRODUCTION

This is a guide to the cream among language dictionaries, the ones that are of serious research use and are likely to remain so. I hope it will be helpful to dictionary users around the world – to readers searching for words, their usage and history, in many languages – who want to know the range of information sources that are waiting to be used. It should also help linguists and librarians who need to know the strengths of their own reference shelves and what more is available elsewhere.

There are perhaps five thousand languages in the world. Estimates differ: a figure of ten thousand was recently quoted in the press. In any case, within a unit that most people would recognise as a 'language', there are all kinds of variations – from place to place ('dialects'), from time to time ('periods'), and between formal and informal and spoken and written ('registers'). More than this: every individual's linguistic usage is unique.

All these varieties of languages can be described. A full description entails, at least, a grammar and a dictionary: one description that starts from the structure of the language, and one that starts from its words.

For about half the world's known languages there is probably some kind of published word-list or dictionary. For many of the better-known languages there is a large number of dictionaries to choose from, some of them simply in competition with one another, some dealing with a language variety, some offering different approaches to the same material. The catalogue of a large research library will include many thousands of language dictionaries.

This book is therefore very selective. The aim is to pick out those dictionaries that offer something more than a simple list of words placed alongside brief equivalents ('glosses') in another language. Dictionaries of that kind are indispensable: any student of a foreign language needs them, and for many languages they are all that there is. But any individual dictionary of that kind tends to remain useful only until something better or newer comes along.

By contrast, most of the dictionaries listed here are likely to retain some value whatever else is published in their field. Typically, they not only list the vocabulary but also document it. They cite sources of information, oral or printed, and often quote them at length to show how a word is or was used. They suggest word origins, or discuss them at length with references to earlier scholarly work. They identify the special registers in which a word is used; they date its first or last recorded occurrence, and they supply the evidence to back up the dating.

This makes them among the most compelling of reference books. In many of the dictionaries listed here, every single article reports the results of original research, and each successive letter of the alphabet has taken years of labour to complete. Some, including the *Oxford English dictionary* (**360**), can fairly be described as the greatest single literary enterprises in their language.

The history of dictionaries and word-lists will not be set out in this book (see **6** onwards). It goes back thousands of years, to the clay tablets on which Akkadian scribes wrote bilingual glossaries to help them with their Sumerian. The oldest dictionaries that still come into the terms of reference of this book – as being of current research use for the languages they cover – are over three hundred years old (for example, **654**). Dictionary making is a task *de longue haleine*: some dictionaries begun in this century will, at the current rate of progress, take three hundred years, or even eight hundred years, to complete ... (consider **86**, **1355**, **1432** and **1443** for the prize in this category).

Most dictionaries that belong in this book cover only one or two languages. There have been many multilingual dictionaries, but they naturally tend to be superficial in their treatment of individual languages. I have listed three interesting ones, the oldest, the newest, and the *Polyglotta Africana*, below (**13** onwards). I have also listed below three curious dictionaries of 'stray words' that do not fit under the heading of any single language (**16** onwards): another endlessly fascinating work, *Hobson-Jobson* (**382**), might well have found its place here.

Out of over 2000 languages for which some word-list could be found, only about 275 have headings in this book. Languages covered here include all of those that are important on a world scale, nearly all of those that have a significant written literature, and a selection of others on which really interesting lexicographical work has been done. Selection was not easy. At the edges of the field, many different decisions could have been made: numerous dialect dictionaries, and linguists' or ethnographers' dictionaries of hitherto unknown languages, begged for inclusion. At the centre of the field, I hope I have included all the major and historical dictionaries for all the major languages, excepting only those works entirely in a single language in a non-European script that are likely to be unapproachable by those who are not already familiar with the language concerned. Another volume, of equal size or larger, would be necessary to pick out the best available dictionaries for the other languages of the world.

I have tried not only to list the dictionaries, but also, where they cover similar fields, to bring out their relative strengths and to guide the user through some of their individualities. Many of these dictionaries were the life's work of their compilers. Others have an editorial history of hundreds of years (for example, **796**). Dictionary makers read one another's work – but few of them ever agree on the style, the layout and the readers' aids that make up a perfect dictionary. Therefore this book explores the contents of dictionaries, especially the bigger and more complex ones, picking out the various kinds of help that they offer to users, and giving full page references whenever it will be most useful.

To consult a dictionary one needs to know its alphabetical order. A special feature of this guide is that it tabulates the dictionary alphabetical order of dozens of languages. A glance will show that even among dictionaries using the Latin alphabet, alphabetical order is unexpectedly varied: see **603** for a surprising example.

The purpose of the tables of non-Latin scripts is, likewise, to assist users who need to consult dictionaries in the relevant languages and need help with the alphabetical order. For convenience, transliterations are added – but it is as well to remember that standards for the transliteration of non-Latin scripts vary, and they are generally too complex to set out fully in these tables.

a/á b c cs d e/é f g gy h i/í j k l m n
o/ó ö/ő p q r s sz t ty u/ú ü/ű v w x y z zs

This example (Hungarian) shows how alphabetical order is explained in the tables in this book. An oblique stroke indicates that characters are interfiled: for example, *a* and *á* are interfiled (as if they were the same character) in Hungarian dictionaries. Otherwise all characters and character groups count as separate letters: for example, *cs* counts as a separate single letter and will be found between *c* and *d* in Hungarian dictionaries.

Alphabets are not necessarily the latest that have been officially adopted: they are the ones that users of the dictionaries listed in this book need to know. Several countries have adopted new alphabets recently.

Terminology

There is no need here to define 'language' or 'dialect'. Problematic as these terms are, it is a fact that dictionaries gather around names such as English and Spanish, Australian English and Mexican Spanish. A bibliographer simply works with this fact – following what library classifiers call 'literary warrant'.

Although the term is occasionally used in a different way, most would agree that a 'dictionary' is, by definition, in alphabetical order (though that phrase cannot be properly applied to a script such as Chinese). I have included scarcely any dictionaries that cannot be said to be in alphabetical order of some kind.

In describing dictionaries I use some standard terms frequently.

- A *gloss* is a word's meaning, stated either an an explanation or synonym in its own language, or as a translation into another language.
- A *brief-entry* dictionary, in this guide, is one that simply supplies glosses, without further information or supporting evidence. Brief-entry dictionaries are listed here very selectively, only to the extent that users of the other dictionaries listed will need the support of these. Languages for which nothing more than brief-entry dictionaries are available are, as a general rule, not included at all in this book.
- A *citation*, in this book, is a reference to a text in which the word in question is used. If it is a *precise reference*, to a page or section or chapter number and with a supporting bibliography, so much the better, from many users' point of view, because potential lines of research are opened up by this information. A citation, in this book, is a slightly different thing from a *quotation*, which is an actual extract from the text including the word in question: for most users that is an even better thing than a citation, though it makes for bigger dictionaries!
- A *historical* dictionary, in this guide, is one that the reader can use to trace changes over time in the meaning and usage of words, with the help of precise references to, and often quotations from, texts. This is a laxer definition than the editors of the *Oxford English dictionary* and some of its European counterparts would accept: they like to *see* the dates, and they like a certain arrangement of glosses and quotations.
- Unless otherwise specified, a *supplement*, in this book, is a supplementary alphabetical listing, usually published at the end of a big dictionary or as a separate volume, that supplies 'new' (newly recorded or previously forgotten) words along with additions and corrections to existing entries.

- An *etymological* dictionary is one whose main purpose is to trace the origins of words (see **9**).

Arrangement of entries

Languages are arranged here in alphabetical order. Cross-references in SMALL CAPITALS are given from individual languages to the language families to which they belong, and vice versa. These cross-references will be useful particularly to readers who are pursuing word histories. After exhausting the etymological sources on a single language one often needs to look at those for the language family or sub-group, and to track down those for other single languages in the same group.

The introduction to each language heading also answers such questions as where the language is spoken and in what alphabet it is written. For further information on these topics, see the reference books listed at **1** to **5** and **14**.

Under each language for which more than half a dozen dictionaries are listed, a standard arrangement has been adopted: 1. *Historical dictionaries*, normally those that cover the current or a recent period and also extend some distance into the past; 2. *The modern standard*; 3. *Older periods*, a heading that may well include some historical dictionaries; 4. *Regional forms* or dialects, whether spoken or written or both; 5. *Slang and special vocabularies*; 6. *Etymological dictionaries*, often with a subheading for *Foreign words*. Finally there may be brief entries for *Other works of interest*.

Within each heading or subheading, entries are arranged alphabetically by the first author's or editor's surname, or, if the title page names no author or editor, by the first word of the title.

All the entries for dictionaries and 'other works of interest', beginning with the bibliography that follows this general introduction, are numbered in a single sequence through the book: all numbered cross-references and index entries refer to these numbers and not to page numbers.

Bibliographical details

This section is mainly for bibliographers and librarians: readers should find that the layout of entries is self-explanatory.

Big multi-volume dictionaries are quite difficult to reduce to bibliographical rule. Descriptions here are often selective but they always aim to give names and titles under which works will be found in other catalogues. It is often necessary, when searching in library catalogues for the type of work listed in this book, to hunt for several possible headings – title as well as author/editor; alternative language forms of a title; even, perhaps surprisingly, alternative language forms of an author's name. See **697** (Hebrew) and **1425** (Sorbian) for two authors each of whom has supplied, on a quadrilingual title page, four different spellings of his own name.

The format of entries in this book consists of a description, followed in most cases by one or more notes and a discussion.

Except as stated below, descriptions are based on the title page; information drawn from elsewhere in the book is normally relegated to a note.

The description normally relates to the latest edition of the work that is either complete or still in progress.

In the description, main authors' and editors' names (up to three) and the first or main title are given as they appear on the title page: if they are in a non-Latin script, the original script is given whenever possible. If more than one title appears on the title page, all are given. If the author's name and the first title appear only in a non-Latin script, a transliteration is added in square brackets. If additional main authors or editors are named on the title pages of later volumes, they are added in square brackets.

Information on place of publication, publisher and date is taken from any part of the book. Only the first-named place and publisher are given for any single volume; but for multi-volume sets, if place and publisher change in the course of production, an attempt has been made to list the first, the latest, and others of importance. 'N.p.' means that no place of publication appears. Where no publisher is given in the description, it may be assumed that an associated corporate body (given in the following note) acted as publisher, or that no publisher at all is credited in the book. 'N.d.', or a date in square brackets, means that no date of publication appears in the book.

Place names are generally given in a current English form, if there is one. However, place names that appear on title pages in a minority language have not been altered: thus, at **519**, Ljouwert (not Leeuwarden); at **539**, A Coruña (not Corunna or La Coruña).

Pagination is counted to the last page of text or indexes, ignoring colophons and advertisements. Preliminary pages are normally ignored in the pagination. One ISBN, for a complete copy of the work, is given if available.

A note gives the names of main authors or editors if they do not appear on the title page, and the names of corporate bodies.

Further notes give information first on later uncompleted editions and on supplements, and then on earlier editions, abridged versions and translations. Unchanged reprints are listed here occasionally, when the information might be specially helpful, but not as a general rule. Abridged versions are only listed if they retain some information useful to the serious enquirer, or if they offer something new.

Sometimes the edition statement in the book is questionable (for example, a '2nd edn' may really be a reprint of the first): I use inverted commas to draw the user's attention to this. Unless otherwise indicated, all quotations in inverted commas in the notes and discussion are taken directly from the work that is being described; translations are mine.

The succinct statement in the introduction to the second edition of the *Oxford English dictionary* –

> This new edition of the *Oxford English Dictionary* contains the whole text, unaltered in all essentials, of the twelve-volume first edition, which appeared in 1933 as a reprint of the ten-volume *New English Dictionary on Historical Principles*, itself originally published in parts between 1884 and 1928. It also contains the complete text of the four-volume *Supplement to the Oxford English Dictionary*, published between 1972 and 1986; this superseded the previous *Supplement*, which was issued in 1933 as a companion to the main work –

comes out not quite so readably in this book:

The Oxford English dictionary. Oxford: Clarendon Press, 1989. 20 vols. 2nd edn by J. A. Simpson, E. S. C. Weiner. 0–19–861186–2 …

First edition of the main work: James A. H. Murray, Henry Bradley, W. A. Craigie, C. T. Onions, *A new English dictionary on historical principles, founded mainly on the materials collected by the Philological Society*. 1884–1928. 10 vols in 12.

Corrected re-issue under new title: *The Oxford English dictionary*. 1933. 12 vols.

Introduction, supplement and bibliography [to the 1st edn]: 1933 …

The 1933 supplement was replaced by: R. W. Burchfield, editor, *A supplement to the Oxford English dictionary*. 1972–86. 4 vols;

but that's bibliography!

In the notes, the place of publication and publisher are not repeated unnecessarily. It should normally be assumed that, if not specified, they are the same as those of a preceding edition or of the edition that figures in the main description. Series titles, and names of corporate bodies associated with the book, are given as a note, whether they appear on the title page or elsewhere in the book.

When a dictionary has no English title (or the English title is not a true translation of the main title, for example **1620**), I have tried to give a translated title in square brackets at the beginning of the discussion.

If a work is still in progress, I have tried to include information on the current state of things, usually at the end of the discussion. Here my information depends on the libraries I have used, and is not guaranteed!

Endnote

I am grateful to the libraries used in the course of this work, particularly Cambridge University Library, University College London Library, the London Library, and the Libraries of the Institute of Linguists (at Regent's College) and of the School of Oriental and African Studies. For the languages of South-East Asia I have drawn on material originally included in my *South East Asia: a guide to reference material* (London: Hans Zell, 1993).

I worked in Microsoft Word, and produced the camera-ready copy on an Epson Stylus Color printer. Many of the non-Latin fonts are TrueType fonts from Gamma Unitype (Gamma Productions); others are individually credited. Fonts for many foreign languages are now to be found on the World Wide Web.

My thanks to the London Goodenough Trust, which provided me with a London base while I was working on this book; to Hans Zell, doyen of Third World publishing, who first encouraged me to get to work on it; to Janet Liebster and Helen Carley, of Library Association Publishing, for their support, and Merle Read, for attempting to achieve consistency (any lack of it is my fault, not hers); and to Maureen, who kept me going.

My thanks in advance to readers who tell me of errors, and of dictionaries that ought to have been included here and are not.

St-Coutant, 79120 Lezay, France
June 1998

Works cited in the introduction

Language atlases

I.

Christopher Moseley, R. E. Asher, general editors, *Atlas of the world's languages*. London: Routledge, 1994. 372 pp. 0–415–01925–7.

2.

Stephen A. Wurm, Shirō Hattori, editors, *Language atlas of the Pacific area*. Canberra: Australian Academy of the Humanities, 1981–3. Portfolio of 47 plates and accompanying pages. 0–85883–239–9.

Pacific linguistics, series C, 66–7. Australian National University, Research School of Pacific Studies. 'In collaboration with the Japan Academy.' Cartography by Theo Baumann.

Language surveys

3.

Andrew Dalby, *Dictionary of languages*. London: Bloomsbury, 1998. 701 pp.

4.

Peter T. Daniels, William Bright, editors, *The world's writing systems*. New York: Oxford University Press, 1996. 920 pp. 0–19–507993–0.

5.

Barbara Grimes, editor, *Ethnologue: languages of the world*. Austin, Texas: Summer Institute of Linguistics, 1996. 13th edn. 1–5567–1026–7.

Joseph E. Grimes, Barbara F. Grimes, *Ethnologue language name index*. 1996. 288 pp. 1–5567–1027–5. – *Ethnologue language family index*. 1997. 125 pp. 1–5567–1028–3.

History of lexicography

6.

Rykle Borger, *Altorientalische Lexikographie: Geschichte und Probleme*. Göttingen, 1984.

Nachrichten der Akademie der Wissenschaften in Göttingen, Philologisch-historische Klasse, 1984 part 2.

7.

Robert L. Collison, *A history of foreign-language dictionaries*. London: Deutsch, 1982. 214 pp. 0–233–97310–9.

The language library.

8.

Gregory James, editor, *Lexicographers and their works*. Exeter: University of Exeter, 1989.

Exeter linguistic studies, 14.

9.

Yakov Malkiel, *Etymological dictionaries: a tentative typology*. Chicago: University of Chicago Press, 1976. 144 pp. 0–226–50292–9.

10.

B. G. Misra, editor, *Lexicography in India: proceedings of the First National Conference on Dictionary Making in Indian Languages, Mysore, 1970*. Manasagangotri, Mysore: Central Institute of Indian Languages, 1980. 253 pp.
CIIL conferences and seminars series, 4.

11.

Henri van Hoof, *Petite histoire des dictionnaires*. Louvain-la-Neuve: Peeters, 1994. 129 pp. 90–6831–630–3.
Bibliothèque des Cahiers de l'Institut de Linguistique de Louvain, 77.

12.

Franz Josef Hausmann [and other editors], *Wörterbücher: ein internationales Handbuch zur Lexikographie = Dictionaries: an international encyclopedia of lexicography = Dictionnaires: encyclopédie internationale de lexicographie*. Berlin: De Gruyter, 1989. 3 vols [3355 pp.]. 3–11–009585–8.

Three multilingual dictionaries

13.

Sigismund Koelle, *Polyglotta Africana, or a comparative vocabulary of nearly three hundred words and phrases in more than one hundred distinct African languages*. Graz, 1963. Facsimile reprint with historical introduction by P. E. H. Hair and word index by David Dalby.
Original edn: London, 1854. 188 pp.

A collection of almost 300 words and phrases in well over 100 languages – all collected from freed slaves settled in Sierra Leone. It was criticised by some nineteenth century scholars, but the real test is that Koelle's book was used then and is still used now. For some languages, even now, no better vocabulary exists. Practically all the languages he listed can be identified (though he had never visited the places where they originated).

On its value for research of the history of West African languages see P. E. H. Hair, 'The contribution of early linguistic material to the history of West Africa' in D. Dalby and others, *Language and history in Africa* (New York: Africana, 1971) pp. 50–63, especially p. 56: since the reprint of 1963, many studies in individual languages had appeared in *African language review* and more were expected.

Earlier work is surveyed in P. E. H. Hair, 'Collections of vocabularies of Western Africa before the Polyglotta: a key' in *Journal of African languages* vol. 5 (1966) pp. 208–17.

14.

Michel Malherbe, *Les langages de l'humanité*. Paris: Robert Laffont, 1995. 1735 pp. 2–221–05947–6. Revised by Serge Rosenberg.

1st edn: Paris: Seghers, 1983.

[*The languages of humankind.*] Word-lists of between 300 and 600 words in each of 171 languages.

15.

Hieronymus Megiser, *Thesaurus polyglottus, vel dictionarium multilingue, ex quadringentis circiter tam veteris quam novi (vel potius antiquis incogniti) orbis nationum linguis, dialectis, idiomatibus et idiotismis constans*. Frankfurt am Main, 1603. 832 + 751 pp.

See R. C. Alston, B. Danielsson, 'The earliest dictionary of the known languages of the world' in *English studies presented to R. W. Zandvoort on the occasion of his seventieth birthday* (Amsterdam: Swets & Zeitlinger, 1964. *English studies*, supplement to vol. 45) with reproductions of the list of abbreviations, selected tables and pp. 1–13 of the text.

[*Polyglot dictionary compiled from about four hundred languages, dialects and idioms of the peoples of the world, both ancient and modern (or rather, unknown in classical times).*] Alphabetical under Latin terms. The number of languages listed under each word varies considerably, from about 6 to 60. The work begins with tables of language relationships and an alphabetical list of the 400 language and dialect abbreviations used in the dictionary. The point of the parenthesis in the title is that African and American languages may be counted just as ancient as Latin and Greek, but had only recently become known in Europe.

Three lists of stray words

16.

M. Delafosse, 'Mots soudanais du moyen âge' in *Mémoires de la Société Linguistique de Paris* vol. 18 (1914) pp. 281–8.

[*Medieval Sudanese words.*] Fulani, Soninke, Mandekan, Songhay and other African language words recorded in medieval Arabic sources, 1100–1400.

17.

Georg Friederici, *Amerikanistisches Wörterbuch und Hilfswörterbuch für Amerikanisten*. Hamburg, 1960. 831 pp. 2nd edn.

1st edn: *Amerikanistisches Wörterbuch*. Hamburg: Cram, de Gruyter, 1947. 722 pp. (Universität Hamburg. *Abhandlungen aus dem Gebiet der Auslandskunde*, 53. Reihe B, *Völkerkunde, Kulturgeschichte und Sprachen*, 29.)

This was a reworking of: *Hilfswörterbuch für den Amerikanisten: Lehnwörter aus Indianer-Sprachen und Erklärungen altertümlicher Ausdrücke, Deutsch–Spanisch–Englisch*. Halle: Niemeyer, 1926. (*Studien über Amerika und Spanien, Extra-serie*, 2.)

[*Americanist dictionary.*] A handbook of American vernacular terms that are found in early printed sources on the exploration of America – 'from Eskimo to Patagonian' – and that have resulted in loanwords in European languages. The best-known forms are chosen as headwords, followed by glosses in German, Spanish, English and French as appropriate, or in scientific Latin for flora and fauna. Then follows etymological discussion. The quotations from early sources in several languages are often well worth reading. There is an important bibliography and a single big index of alternate word forms.

18.

Franz Miklosich, 'Die türkischen Elemente in den südost- und osteuropäischen Sprachen (Griechisch, Albanisch, Rumunisch, Bulgarisch, Serbisch, Kleinrussisch, Grossrussisch, Polnisch)' in *Denkschriften der Kaiserlichen Akademie der Wissenschaften, philosophisch-historische Classe*, vol. 34 part 2 (1884) pp. 239–338, vol. 35 (1885) pp. 105–92.

A supplement, larger than the original work, was published in the same serial, in vol. 37 part 1 (1889) pp. 1–88, and as vol. 38 part 1 (1890), 194 pp.

A further supplement: Friedrich von Kraelitz-Greifenhorst, *Corollarien zu F. Miklosich, Die türkischen Elemente in den südost- und osteuropäischen Sprachen (Griechisch, Albanisch, Rumunisch, Bulgarisch, Serbisch, Kleinrussisch, Großrussisch, Polnisch), 1884–1890*. Vienna: Holder, 1911. (*Sitzungsberichte der Kais. Akademie der Wissenschaften in Wien, philosophisch-historische Klasse*, vol. 166 part 4.)

See the reviews of the original work by Th. Korsch in *Archiv für slavische Philologie*, vol. 8 p. 631, vol. 9 pp. 487, 653.

[*The Turkish elements in southeast and east European languages: Greek, Albanian, Romanian, Bulgarian, Serbian, Ukrainian, Russian, Polish.*] Entries are in alphabetical order of Latin transliteration of the Turkish headwords (these are also given in Arabic script). The transliteration naturally differs from the Latin orthography now used for Turkish: note especially *dž* for the sound now written as *c*.

Miklosich's work is informative on Turkish loanwords well beyond the bounds of south-eastern Europe: he cites many forms from Kurdish and Spanish, to take two examples.

Lists of abbreviations: vol. 35 pp. 191–2, vol. 38 part 1 pp. 191–4. Addenda to the first supplement, vol. 38 part 1 pp. 188–91.

ABKHAZ

Abkhaz belongs to the group of North West CAUCASIAN LANGUAGES. It is a minority language of Georgia and the focus of a violent separatist movement.

19.

K. S. Sh'aqryl, V. H. Konj'aria, *Aphsua byzshwa azhwar = Slovar' abkhazskogo iazyka = Ap'xazuri enis lek'sikoni*. Aqua: Alashara, 1986–7. 2 vols.

Sakartvelos SSR Mecnierebata Akademia. D. Gulias Sax. Apxazetis Enis, Literaturisa da Istoriis Instituti.

[*Dictionary of the Abkhaz language.*] Not seen: cited from the Library of Congress catalogue. Apparently a big dictionary of Abkhaz with glosses in Georgian and Russian, published by the Institute for Abkhaz Language, Literature and History of the Georgian Academy.

ACHEHNESE

Achehnese, a language of Indonesia, has two million speakers at the northern tip of Sumatra, where Banda Aceh was once the capital of a Muslim kingdom and an important Indian Ocean trading port.

The closest relatives of Achehnese are the AUSTRONESIAN LANGUAGES of Vietnam, notably Cham. The Arabic alphabet was used traditionally, but published dictionaries adopted the Latin alphabet, which became known here under Dutch rule and is now standard.

20.

Aboe Bakar [and others], *Kamus Aceh Indonesia*. Jakarta: Pusat Pembinaan dan Pengembangan Bahasa, Departemen Pendidikan dan Kebudayaan, 1985. 2 vols [1073 pp.].

Seri K, 85.025.

[*Achehnese–Indonesian dictionary.*] Useful as a fairly large current bilingual dictionary of Achehnese.

21.

A. J. W. Bikkers, *Malay, Achinese, French and English vocabulary alphabetically arranged under each of the four languages*. London: W. H. Allen, 1882. 352 pp.

A very rare work, apparently, and the only sizable Achehnese–English dictionary.

22.

Hoesein Djajadiningrat, *Atjèhsch–Nederlandsch woordenboek met Nederlandsch–Atjèhsch register*. Batavia, 1934. 2 vols.

Some copies are labelled as published at The Hague: Nijhoff. The Dutch–Achehnese index by G. W. J. Drewes, signalled in the title, did not (I think) appear.

[*Achehnese–Dutch dictionary with Dutch–Achehnese index.*] A really encyclopaedic dictionary of what was once a ruling language of northern Sumatra. Based on published and manuscript literature (precise references given) and on oral sources: for earlier dictionaries see vol. 1 p. iv. In the Latin alphabet.

Substantial supplement, vol. 2 pp. 1289–1349.

AFRIKAANS

This GERMANIC language, an offshoot of Dutch, is one of the major languages of South Africa.

Apartheid is an Afrikaans word, 'separateness'. Afrikaans ('Cape Dutch') developed long before the twentieth century heyday of apartheid, and shows heavy influence from Portuguese, Malay, and the Bantu and Khoisan languages of southern Africa.

There is no historical dictionary of the language, though one has been projected (see **25**), and the big dictionary begun by Schoonees (**24**) is becoming more informative historically as it proceeds. The historical dictionaries of South African English (especially **389**) add useful information, since the two languages share some vocabulary.

23.

M. S. B. Kritzinger, P. C. Schoonees, U. J. Cronjé, editors, *Groot woordeboek*. Pretoria: van Schaik, 1986. 1410 pp. 13th edn by L. C. Eksteen. 0–6270–1491–7.

4th edn: 1946. 1320 pp. – 9th edn: 1963. 1340 pp. – 11th edn: 1972. 1639 pp. – 12th edn: 1981. 1623 pp.

[*Big dictionary.*] A two-way Afrikaans–English and English–Afrikaans dictionary. It is rather easier than in most dictionaries to find one's way through the phrases in long articles, as they are sub-arranged in simple alphabetical order by keyword and this keyword is in upper-case italic.

24.

P. C. Schoonees, [F. J. Snijman, chief editors], *Woordeboek van die Afrikaanse taal*. Pretoria: Staatsdrukker, 1950– .

Cover title: *Die Afrikaanse woordeboek.*

[*Dictionary of the Afrikaans language.*] Nine volumes have appeared so far, the latest in 1994: half the alphabet is now covered. In its early volumes this was simply a very large-scale illustrated brief-entry dictionary with no quotations. As Snijman took over the editorship a change began. In vol. 5, **J–Ki**, quotations are given, attributed to authors but without precise references. From vol. 6, full references appear.

Other works of interest

25.

F. J. Snijman, 'Thoughts on a dictionary of Afrikaans on historical principles' in W. Pijnenburg, F. de Tollenaere, editors, *Proceedings of the Second*

International Round Table Conference on Historical Lexicography (Dordrecht: Foris, 1980) pp. 333–47.

AFROASIATIC LANGUAGES

The Afroasiatic or Afrasian or Hamito-Semitic language family may have begun its long development in the region of the Horn of Africa (modern Somalia and Ethiopia) fifteen thousand years ago or more. The branches of the family are the CUSHITIC LANGUAGES, Omotic languages, CHADIC LANGUAGES, BERBER LANGUAGES, Ancient EGYPTIAN and the SEMITIC LANGUAGES.

The Omotic languages, spoken only in Ethiopia, form the least-known branch of Afroasiatic. They include Basketto, Kafa, Wolaytta and others. But Amharic, the national language of Ethiopia, belongs to the Semitic branch of the family.

Afroasiatic (or the Semitic branch of it) has sometimes been thought to be linked with Indo-European and other families in an even more ancient and inclusive family: see 'Proposed wider relationships' under INDO-EUROPEAN LANGUAGES.

Following early work by Marcel Cohen (**28**) and others, the two comparative dictionaries listed here represent very new developments in Afroasiatic research. For a brief review of the two side by side, see John A. C. Greppin in the *Times literary supplement* (1 November 1996). Neither of them, regrettably, has an index of forms cited from the individual Afroasiatic languages.

Comparative dictionaries

26.

Christopher Ehret, *Reconstructing Proto-Afroasiatic (Proto-Afrasian): vowels, tone, consonants and vocabulary*. Berkeley: University of California Press, 1995. 557 pp. 0–520–09799–8.

University of California publications in linguistics, 126.

The comparative word-list, arranged under reconstructed roots, is on pp. 73–478; additional entries, pp. 523–7. There are 1011 numbered entries. English index of meanings, pp. 543–57.

27.

Vladimir E. Orel, Olga V. Stolbova, *Hamito-Semitic etymological dictionary: materials for a reconstruction*. Leiden: Brill, 1995. 578 pp. 90–04–10051–2.

Handbuch der Orientalistik = Handbook of Oriental studies, 1. Abteilung: Der Nahe und Mittlere Osten = The Near and Middle East, 18.

There are 2672 numbered entries, arranged under reconstructed roots. English index of meanings, pp. 557–78.

Other works of interest

28.

Marcel Cohen, *Essai comparatif sur le vocabulaire et la phonétique du chamito-sémitique*. Paris, 1947. 248 pp.

AHOM

Ahom belonged to the TAI LANGUAGES. It was spoken by a conquering band who ruled the lower Brahmaputra valley, modern Assam, for six hundred years from their capital at Sibsagar. Now extinct, Ahom is the language in which the medieval chronicles of Assam are preserved. There are manuscript Ahom–Assamese glossaries, and these form the basis of the only two available printed dictionaries.

Ahom script is much like the Shan alphabet, with an especially close resemblance to its northern, more cursive forms. Like the Ahom language, the script has now fallen out of use, though an Ahom typeface was cast to facilitate the publication of historical manuscripts during the British period.

29.

B. Barua, N. N. Deodhai Phukan, *Ahom lexicons (based on original Tai manuscripts)*. Gauhati: Department of Historical and Antiquarian Studies in Assam, 1964. 205 pp.

An edition of the Ahom–Assamese manuscript glossaries *Barakakot homung puthi* and *Loti amra*, with the addition by the editors of transcriptions and English glosses, arranged in six columns across double-page spreads. The first glossary is in Ahom alphabetical order; the second is arranged thematically and concentrates on plants and animals. Appendices include a guide to the Ahom alphabet.

30.

Golap Chandra Barua, *Ahom–Assamese–English dictionary*. Calcutta: Baptist Mission Press, 1920. 327 pp.

Based on the vocabulary of the Ahom chronicles. Guide to alphabet and pronunciation in preliminary pages.

AINU

The Ainu people of Hokkaido island, Japan, were once unique linguistically, anthropologically and culturally. They are now almost completely assimilated into Japanese society, and their language is on the verge of extinction. Just in time, learned Ainu, Japanese and Western scholars have recorded something of the language and its remarkable oral literature. In three of the four dictionaries listed here, Japanese is the language of scholarship. The fourth, the real pioneering work, is in Russian.

Hattori, editor of the Ainu dialect dictionary (**32**), is also one of the two editors of the *Language atlas of the Pacific area* (**2**).

31.

М. М. Добротворскій, *Аинско-русскій словарь* [M. M. Dobrotvorskii, *Ainsko–russkii slovar'*]. Kazan: Universiteta, 1875. 487 pp.

Ученыя записки И. Казанскаго Университета, 44, supplement.

[*Ainu–Russian dictionary.*]

32.

Hattori Shirō, chief editor, *Ainugo hogen jiten*. 1964. 556 pp.

[*Ainu dialect dictionary.*] The result of a survey of nine Ainu dialects made in the 1950s by a team of scholars under Hattori's direction.

33.

Kubodera Itsuhiko, *Ainugo Nihongo jiten ko = Ainu–Japanese dictionary*. [Sapporo]: Hokkaido Kyoiku Iinkai, 1992. 511 pp.

Hokkaido Kyoikucho Shogai Gakushubu Bunkaka hen.

34.

Nakagawa Hiroshi, *Ainugo Chitose hogen jiten = The Ainu–Japanese dictionary: Chitose dialect*. Tokyo: Sofukan, 1995. 431 pp. 48–8323–078–3.

AKHA

Akha is spoken by mountain-dwellers who live in scattered villages in five countries, China, Vietnam, Laos, Burma and Thailand. It is the main language in the 'southern Loloish' sub-group of SINO-TIBETAN LANGUAGES. There are perhaps two million speakers, far more than most reference books say. The language is known as *Hani* in China, as *Akha* in Thailand: Akha may be regarded as a southern dialect of Hani, and is so regarded in China. The two dictionaries listed here represent the major Thai and Chinese varieties, though Lewis at first 'served as a missionary with the Burma Baptist Convention [and] began learning the language while living in Pangwai, Kengtung State'.

There is no indigenous tradition of literacy: the Latin alphabet is used, in three different orthographies. For a full explanation of these see Lewis (**36**) p. 803.

35.

Paul Lewis, *A ka daw–Ga la pyu daw–Tai daw di sha na li = Akha–English– Thai dictionary*. Chiangrai: Development & Agricultural Project for Akha, 1989. 707 pp.

Earlier version of Lewis's work: Paul Lewis, *Akha–English dictionary*. Ithaca: Cornell University, Department of Asian Studies, 1968. 363 pp. (Southeast Asia Program. *Data paper*, 70. *Linguistics series*, 3.) See the review of this by James Matisoff in *Journal of Asian studies* vol. 28 (1969) pp. 644–5.

I have not seen the 1989 publication, recorded here from the Library of Congress catalogue.

36.

Paul W. Lewis, Bai Bibo [Piu Bo], *Hani–English English–Hani dictionary = Haqniqdoq–Yilyidoq doqlo-soqdaoq*. London: Kegan Paul International, 1996. 837 pp. 0–7103–0564–8.

In association with the International Institute for Asian Studies, Leiden.

This is in the orthography that is standard in China, using final 'consonants' to indicate tones (thus *Haqniq*, in the book title, is the native name of the language itself). In the Hani–English section of the dictionary, alternative Akha forms (from Thai sources) are also given: these are in the Thai Akha orthography.

The Hani people and language, pp. 1–23; bibliography and list of sources, pp. 27–36. The appendices, pp. 803–37, include a comparison of the three orthographies, a specimen text ('The dragon and the son-in-law') in Hani and English, Hani genealogy, names of 56 ethnic groups in China, geographical names, onomatopoeias, terms of endearment, set phrases with the negative, proverbs, riddles, years, months, days, four-syllable elaborate expressions.

AKKADIAN

The most ancient recorded member of the SEMITIC branch of Afroasiatic languages, Akkadian was once a vehicle of empire in Iraq and Syria. Some of the oldest literature in the world survives in clay tablets in Akkadian cuneiform script – including the *Epic of Gilgamesh*, and myths of the Creation and the Flood.

Supplanted by Aramaic and Greek, Akkadian fell from use, and for nearly two thousand years it was a forgotten language. Through the decipherment of Akkadian, in the nineteenth and twentieth centuries, the recorded history of the Middle East has been pushed back thousands of years into the past.

Akkadian is also known as Assyrian and Babylonian: these are most often used as names of the two dialects of later Akkadian that became standard languages of the empires of Assyria and Babylon. They were still spoken and written under Persian and Greek rule, in the last few centuries BC – but by then Aramaic had become the lingua franca of the region.

The cuneiform writing system was not a new invention when it was first applied to Akkadian about 2350 BC. It had already been used for Sumerian, the ancient and unrelated language of the oldest kingdoms of southern Iraq. Later it was used for Hurrian, Urartian, Hittite, Ugaritic, Elamite, Old Persian and several other languages.

The Latin transliteration of Akkadian is standard, and so is the alphabetical order in Akkadian dictionaries:

a b d e g ḫ i j k l m n p q r s ṣ š t ṭ u w z

37.

I. J. Gelb, *Glossary of Old Akkadian*. Chicago: University of Chicago Press, 1957. 318 pp.

Materials for the Assyrian dictionary, 3.
Reprinted: 1973. 0–226–62307–6.

'Presents a picture of the Old Akkadian lexicographical material from the oldest times down to the end of the third dynasty of Ur ... contains words collected for the use of the Assyrian Dictionary [**39**], ordered according to form and rough semantic groupings, with translations.' Includes Akkadian loanwords in Sumerian texts. Entirely in Latin transliteration. The glossary is arranged under consonantal roots; it does not include words that are recorded only as logographs and whose phonetic shape is thus unknown.

38.

G. Howardy, *Clavis cuneorum, sive lexicon signorum Assyriorum linguis Latina, Britannica, Germanica.* Leipzig: Harrassowitz; Copenhagen: Michaelsen, 1904–33. 957 pp.

Later parts published: Copenhagen: Hasselbalch, Gad; London: Humphrey Milford. Sumptibus Instituti Carlsbergici Hauniensis et Ministerii Instructionis Publicae.

[*Key to cuneiform, or a dictionary of Assyrian signs in Latin, English and German.*] The dictionary is on pp. 32–871, arranged in numerical order of signs from 1 to 563. On the left hand pages appear cuneiform signs and combinations in 'autograph'. On facing pages are transliteration, translations, occasional Hebrew cognates and Biblical references. Early (Sumerian and Old Akkadian) words are bracketed.

Order of signs (1 to 563), pp. 2–5; neo-Babylonian to neo-Assyrian key, pp. 5–8; list of phonetic values in sign order, pp. 8–24, with a briefer, clearer abridged list, pp. 26–9; selected phonetic values in Hebrew alphabetical order – a kind of Assyrian alphabet – p. 25; list of classifiers ('determinativa') p. 30. Index of Assyrian words in Latin alphabetical order, pp. 873–957.

39.

A. Leo Oppenheim, editor, *The Assyrian dictionary of the Oriental Institute of the University of Chicago.* Chicago: Oriental Institute, 1956– .

Editorial board: Ignace J. Gelb [and others].

A large-scale historical dictionary. The arrangement of entries is explained on p. v of vol. 6, ḫ, which was the first to be published. The first paragraph of each entry gives the English glosses; the second, in a small font, variants of form and spelling, with citations; the third, detailed discussion of meanings, in English, with quotations in Akkadian and English and precise references; the fourth, the word's origin if known; the last, again in small font, references to modern scholarship.

The dictionary will be complete in 21 volumes: the last (z) is already available, but some gaps remain.

Introduction, by I. J. Gelb, vol. 1 pp. vii–xxiii.

40.

Wolfram von Soden, *Akkadisches Handwörterbuch.* Wiesbaden: Harrassowitz, 1965–81. 3 vols [1592 pp.].

Incorporates lexical materials collected by Bruno Meissner (1868–1947).

[*Concise Akkadian dictionary.*] An Akkadian–German dictionary, the handiest complete dictionary of Akkadian. No quotations of sources, but many citations: abbreviations for source texts, vol. 3 pp. x–xvi. There are no entries under roots, but a list of roots, with cross-references to major relevant entries, appears at the head of each letter of the alphabet.

Supplement, vol. 3 pp. 1541–91, with a few last-minute entries on p. 1592.

ALBANIAN

Albanian forms a separate branch of the INDO-EUROPEAN LANGUAGES, distinct in its development from Greek and its other modern neighbours. It is the national language of Albania and is spoken by large minorities in Serbia and Macedonia, with long-established smaller minorities in Greece and southern Italy.

Two early dictionaries, important in the historical study of Albanian and other Balkan languages, are available in modern editions (**52** and **53**). There is a shortage of detailed dictionaries of the language: Tagliavini's (**49**) is important, but deals with a single dialect spoken outside Albania.

Until early this century, Albanian had scarcely any written literature and no standard orthography. The Latin alphabet was adopted at the Monastir Conference in 1908 in defiance of Albania's Ottoman rulers.

Albanian alphabetical order

a b c ç d dh e ë f g gj h i j k l ll m n nj o p q r rr s sh t th u v x xh y z zh

Historical dictionaries

41.

Stuart E. Mann, *An historical Albanian–English dictionary*. London: Longmans, Green, 1948. 601 pp.

Published for the British Council. Alternate title: *A historical Albanian and English dictionary (1496–1938)*.

For the present this is the only approach to a historical dictionary, and is better than nothing. It indicates source texts by means of an initial letter (bibliography, pp. vii–viii), but gives no quotations, and no precise references. 'Entries not marked with an initial are words gathered from the lips of peasants and others in various parts of Albania during the years 1929–1931, or taken from magazines or pamphlets of no literary importance.'

The modern standard

42.

Angelo Leotti, *Dizionario albanese–italiano*. Roma: Istituto per l'Europa Orientale, 1937. 1710 pp.

[*Albanian–Italian dictionary.*] This big dictionary dates from the short-lived Italian conquest of Albania. Not seen.

43.

Stuart E. Mann, *An English–Albanian dictionary*. Cambridge: Cambridge
University Press, 1957. 434 pp.

Briefer than its Albanian–English counterpart (**41**), and deals with the modern
language only.

44.

Leonard Newmark, editor, *Albanian–English dictionary*. Oxford: Oxford
University Press, 1998. 978 pp. 0–19–864340–3.

At first glance, this is an important contribution to Albanian lexicography. Scientific
Latin glosses are supplied for botanical and zoological terms.

Overview of the form and content of entries, pp. xvi–xxvi; grammatical sketch for
readers of Albanian, pp. xxvii–xlviii; 'extensive aids for recognizing forms encountered
in texts which are not identical to the citation forms in the dictionary,' pp. xlix–lxviii,
this section being largely a key to the identification and deconstruction of suffixes and
word terminations; dialect variation and the standard language, pp. lxix–lxxv, with an
important table of variants which may be found in printed texts.

45.

Jani Thomaj [and others], *Fjalor i gjuhës së sotme shqipe: me rreth 41.000 fjalë*.
Tiranë, 1980. 2273 pp.

Edited by Androkli Kostallarit. Akademia e Shkencave e RPS të Shqipërisë, Instituti i Gjuhësisë dhe i
Letërsisë.

[*Dictionary of the modern Albanian language: 41,000 words.*] The largest available
monolingual dictionary of Albanian.

46.

Abdullah Zajmi [and others], *Fjalor shqip–serbokroatisht = Albansko srpskohrvatski rečnik*. Prishtinë: Instituti Albanologjik i Prishtinës, 1981. 1065 pp.

[*Albanian–Serbo-Croat dictionary.*] Informative on the Albanian of Serbia.

Regional forms

47.

Antonio Bellusci, *Dizionario fraseologico degli albanesi d'Italia e di Grecia:
testo originale nella parlata albanese, traduzione in lingua italiana, inglese e
francese: ricerca sul campo in 115 comunità albanofone*. Cosenza: Centro
Ricerche Socio-culturali 'G. K. Skanderbeg', 1989. 261 pp.

[*An idiomatic dictionary of the Albanian of Italy and Greece, based on fieldwork in
115 Albanian-speaking communities: Albanian–Italian–English–French.*]

48.

Sulejman Drini [and others], *Fjalor fjalësh e shprehjesh popullore*. Prishtinë:
Instituti Albanologjik i Prishtinës, 1982. 317 pp.

[*Dictionary of colloquial idioms and sayings.*] Based on the Geg dialects spoken in the Kosovo Metohija region of Serbia.

49.

Carlo Tagliavini, *L'albanese di Dalmazia: contributi alla conoscenza del dialetto ghego di Borgo Erizzo presso Zara.* Florence: Olschki, 1937. 317 pp.
Biblioteca dell' Archivum romanicum, vol. 2 part 22.

[*The Albanian of Dalmatia: contributions to the knowledge of the Geg dialect of Borgo Erizzo near Zara.*] The major feature, on pp. 67–302, is an important dialect dictionary, with quotations from texts and historical and etymological notes.

Etymological dictionaries

50.

Martin E. Huld, *Basic Albanian etymologies.* Columbus, Ohio: Slavica, 1984. 213 pp. 0–89357–135–0.

A modest but fundamental and necessary gathering and updating of the material that is available on Albanian etymology. A practical, useful etymological dictionary.

51.

Gustav Meyer, *Etymologisches Wörterbuch der albanesischen Sprache.* Strasbourg: Trübner, 1891. 524 pp.
Sammlung indogermanischer Wörterbücher, 3.

[*Etymological dictionary of the Albanian language.*] In a phonetic script: at this date the Arabic and Greek alphabets were generally used for Albanian, and no standard Latin orthography existed. The alphabetical order demands careful study.

'Gustav Meyer … discovered only 400 radical words which were demonstrably of native Indo-European origin. This number can now be multiplied by five at least … he was extremely well-informed linguistically [but produced] a work which might almost be called a Dictionary of Albanian Jargon. Nearly all the modern Greek and Turkish words admitted into his dictionary are not used in Albanian at all, whereas most of the abundant native material of the language was overlooked by Meyer altogether' (Mann, **41**).

Other works of interest

52.

Frang Bardhi, *Fjalor latinisht–shqip.* Prishtinë: Rilindja, 1983. 384 pp. Edited by Engjëll Sedaj.

The author is also known under his Latin name of Franciscus Blanchus. His Latin–Albanian dictionary was first printed in 1635 under the title *Dictionarium latino–epiroticum.*
Another edition: *Le dictionnaire albanais de 1635.* Paris: Geuthner, 1932. Edited by Mario Roques.

53.

Protopeiria: das dreisprachige Wörterverzeichnis von Theodoros Anastasiu Kavalliotis aus Moschopolis, gedruckt 1770 in Venedig: albanisch–deutsch–

neugriechisch–aromunisch. Hamburg: Buske, 1981. 278 pp. 3–87118–466–7.
Edited with new comparative material and indices by Armin Hetzer.
Balkan-Archiv, supplement 1.

AMERIND LANGUAGES

The Amerind language family postulated by Joseph Greenberg (**54**) is highly controversial. There are well over a hundred language families in the Americas whose existence linguists consider has been fully demonstrated: many still believe that more distant links among them are unprovable.

Comparative dictionaries or word-lists exist as yet for relatively few of these smaller families (or branches of Amerind, if that is what they are). Some of the most accessible work is listed below: references to plenty more will be found in Greenberg's bibliography, and in the bibliographies of the works to which he in turn refers. There are separate entries in this book for the following Amerind languages: ARAUCANIAN, AYMARA, Black CARIB, CHEROKEE, CREE, CROW, DAKOTA, GUARANÍ, KLAMATH, MAYAN LANGUAGES, NAHUATL, OJIBWA, QUECHUA.

American language words in early European sources are listed by Friederici (**17**).

Comparative dictionaries

54.

Joseph Greenberg, *Language in the Americas*. Stanford: Stanford University Press, 1987. 438 pp. 0–8047–1315–4.

In large part this is an 'etymological dictionary' (so Greenberg calls it, leading with his chin) of the language families that he considers to form part of Amerind. Entries are arranged in alphabetical order of English meanings. This central section, pp. 181–270, is preceded on pp. 63–180 by little etymological dictionaries of the groupings which he sets up as first-level subdivisions of Amerind. Some of these were already familiar in earlier work by others.

English index to meanings in all these lists, pp. 407–13; index of language and group names, pp. 414–35.

Greenberg's proposed subdivisions of Amerind are listed here with references to the comparative dictionaries that relate to them and to entries elsewhere in this book.
- Macro-Ge.
- Macro-Panoan, see **59**; includes Takanan, **62**.
- Macro-Carib, see **70**.
- Equatorial; includes Arawakan, **55**, **70** (see also Black CARIB), Guahiban **55**, and see GUARANÍ.
- Macro-Tucanoan, see **55**.
- Andean, see **68**; includes ARAUCANIAN, AYMARA, QUECHUA.
- Chibchan-Paezan, see **55**.

- Central Amerind, see **72**; includes Otomanguean, **60**, **65**, **69**, Tanoan and Uto-Aztecan, **57**, **58**, **67** (see also NAHUATL).
- Hokan, see **61**; includes Pomo, **66** Yuman, **71**.
- Penutian; includes KLAMATH, MAYAN LANGUAGES (see also **55**).
- Almosan-Keresiouan; includes Algonquian, **56** (see also CREE), Salish **63**, Wakashan **64**, Siouan (see CROW and DAKOTA), and Iroquoian (see CHEROKEE).

55.
Esther Matteson [and others], *Comparative studies in Amerindian languages.*
The Hague: Mouton, 1972. 251 pp.
Janua linguarum, series practica, 127.

Like Greenberg's work, this includes several 'cognate sets' (the term preferred to 'etymological dictionary' by the more fastidious American linguists, especially when at the stage of research at which it is not yet possible to reconstruct proto-forms). These are arranged in alphabetical order of English meanings, and they include a 'proto-Amerindian' section (pp. 44–89, by Matteson) which contains 974 entries and foreshadows Greenberg's Amerind.

After this come 'cognate sets' for the following smaller family groupings: proto-Chibchan, by Alva Wheeler, pp. 104–8; proto-Mayan, by Frances L. Jackson, pp. 114–18; proto-Tucanoan, by Nathan E. Waltz and Alva Wheeler, pp. 137–49; proto-Guahiban, by Diana R. Christian and Esther Matteson, pp. 154–9; proto-Arawakan and eleven of its sub-groups, twelve lists by Esther Matteson, pp. 171–242.

Sub-groups

56.
George F. Aubin, *A proto-Algonquian dictionary.* Ottawa: National Museum of Canada, 1975. 197 pp.
Canadian Ethnology Service. *Paper,* 29. *Mercury series.*

57.
Lyle Campbell, Ronald W. Langacker, 'Proto-Aztecan vowels. Part III' in *International journal of American linguistics* vol. 44 (1978) pp. 262–79.

Includes collections of 'cognate sets' arranged in alphabetical order of English meanings: 198 Aztecan, pp. 262–9, and 117 Uto-Aztecan, pp. 270–79.

58.
Irvine Davis, 'Numic consonantal correspondences' in *International journal of American linguistics* vol. 32 (1966) pp. 124–40.

Deals with the Plateau Shoshonean or Numic languages, including Comanche and Ute, which belong to the Uto-Aztecan family. A collection of cognate sets, with 185 entries, is on pp. 134–9, arranged in alphabetical order of initial consonants in Comanche. Index of English meanings, pp. 139–40.

59.

Victor Girard, *Proto-Takanan phonology*. Berkeley: University of California Press, 1971. 209 pp. 0–520–09369–0.

University of California publications in linguistics, 70.

Includes a 'Dictionary of proto-Takanan', on pp. 49–138, with 504 entries, arranged under reconstructed proto-Takanan forms, which are considerably revised by comparison with Key's work (**62**). They are followed by a list of 'Loans into Takanan', pp. 138–41. Then follows a 'Proto-Pano-Takanan dictionary', on pp. 161–71, with 116 entries, arranged under reconstructed forms marked with a tentative pair of asterisks ******. Annotated bibliography of work on the Panoan and Takanan languages, pp. 177–206. These are languages of Bolivia, Peru and Brazil.

60.

Sarah C. Gudschinsky, *Proto-Popotecan: a comparative study of Popolocan and Mixtecan*. Baltimore: Indiana University, 1959. 118 pp.

Indiana University publications in anthropology and linguistics. International journal of American linguistics, vol. 25 part 2 supplement. *Memoir*, 15.

On the author see: Eunice V. Pike, *Sarah's life*. Dallas: Summer Institute of Linguistics, 1993. 55 pp. 0–88312–618–4.

Dictionary of PPtn [proto-Popotecan] reconstructions and PMx [proto-Mixtecan] cognates, pp. 60–87; 356 numbered entries, arranged by initial consonant of the reconstructed form. English index, pp. 89–92, followed by separate indexes of cited forms in Ixcatec, Popoloc, Chocho and Mazatec. Concordance between entries and text (i.e. an index of discussions and citations of forms in the dictionary), pp. 113–18.

61.

Karl-Heinz Gursky, 'Der Hoka-Sprachstamm' in *Orbis* vol. 23 (1974) pp. 170–215.

[*The Hoka language stock.*] A study of the Hoka-Subtiaba and Algonkin-Gulf languages. Glossary of cognates, arranged under English meanings, pp. 178–212. Addendum, p. 215. Bibliography, including earlier papers by Gursky subsumed in this, pp. 212–15.

62.

Mary Ritchie Key, *Comparative Tacanan phonology with Cavineña phonology and notes on Pano-Tacanan relationship*. The Hague: Mouton, 1968. 107 pp.

Janua linguarum, series practica, 50.

A dictionary of cognate sets, pp. 52–75, is arranged under English meanings; it is followed by indexes of forms cited from the individual Takanan languages. For later work on this family see Girard (**59**).

63.

Aert H. Kuipers, 'Towards a Salish etymological dictionary' in *Lingua* vol. 26 (1970) pp. 46–72.

64.

Neville J. Lincoln, John C. Rath, *North Wakashan comparative word list.* Ottawa, 1980. 426 pp.

Canadian Ethnology Service. *Paper*, 68. National Museum of Man, *Mercury series*.

65.

Robert E. Longacre, *Proto-Mixtecan.* Bloomington: Research Center, Indiana University, 1957. 195 pp.

Indiana University, Research Center in Anthropology, Folklore, and Linguistics. *Publication*, 5. *International journal of American linguistics*, vol. 23 no. 4 part 3.

'Array of M, C, T cognates', pp. 113–49 (279 entries), followed by separate indexes of cited forms in Mixtec, Cuicatec, Trique and Amuzgo, pp. 159–94.

66.

Sally McLendon, *Proto Pomo.* Berkeley: University of California Press, 1973. 113 pp. 0–520–09444–1.

University of California publications in linguistics, 71.

A study of seven languages formerly spoken between the Pacific coast and the Sacramento valley, California. Glossary of cognates, arranged under English meanings, pp. 65–95; instrumental prefixes, pp. 96–8; index of proto-Pomo reconstructions, pp. 98–110.

67.

Wick R. Miller, *Uto-Aztecan cognate sets.* Berkeley: University of California Press, 1967. 83 pp.

University of California publications in linguistics, 48.

Deals with a major language family 'stretching from the Great Basin into the Valley of Mexico … Not intended to be an etymological study, but rather a collection of some of the material needed for such a study'. Cognate sets, in alphabetical order of English meanings, pp. 17–65; kinship terms, pp. 65–8; numerals, pp. 68–9, a total of 514 entries. Index of reconstructed forms, pp. 71–83. Note the slightly unexpected abbreviations *Azt.* and *Mej.* for the languages now more often called Nahua/Nahuatl and their immediate relatives.

68.

Carolyn Orr, Robert E. Longacre, 'Proto-Quechumaran' in *Language* vol. 44 (1968) pp. 528–55.

This family grouping, comprising AYMARA and QUECHUA, is not accepted by all linguists.

69.

Calvin Ross Rensch, *Comparative Otomanguean phonology.* Bloomington: Indiana University Press, 1976.

70.

Douglas Taylor, *Languages of the West Indies.* Baltimore: Johns Hopkins University Press, 1977. 278 pp. 0–8018–1729–3.

Includes word lists of Arawak and Island Carib (Black Carib) and of the following extinct languages of the West Indies: Karina (Carib), Nepuyo, Sebayo, Taino, Yao.

71.

Alan Campbell Wares, *A comparative study of Yuman consonantism*. The Hague: Mouton, 1968. 100 pp.
Janua linguarum, series practica, 57.

Deals with languages of the southern edge of California state and the northern edge of California Baja. 'Comparative Yuman vocabulary', 501 entries, pp. 77–96, arranged in alphabetical order of English meanings.

72.

Benjamin L. Whorf, George L. Trager, 'The relationship of Uto-Aztecan and Tanoan' in *American anthropologist* vol. 39 (1937) pp. 609–24.

A seminal study of wider relationships among Amerindian languages. Short list of cognates, arranged by reconstructed initial consonants, pp. 619–24 (67 entries).

AMHARIC

Classical ETHIOPIC or Ge'ez, one of the SEMITIC LANGUAGES, has divided into several modern languages. Of these Amharic has become the most important: it is the national language of Ethiopia, with 14 million speakers as a mother tongue and as many again who use it as a second language.

Amharic literature goes back to the royal praise poetry of the fourteenth century.

The Amharic alphabet

The Amharic script is a variant of that used for Ethiopic. There are no separate vowel characters. Instead, each consonant character has seven modifications (the 'seven orders') to denote a following vowel.

The first row below gives one-seventh of the full Amharic alphabet table, showing the consonant letters combined with the vowel *ä*. The second row gives examples of the modifications that are made in a single character to denote the vowels.

The 'first order'

ሀ ለ ሐ መ ሠ ረ ሰ ሸ ቀ በ ተ ቸ ኀ ነ ኘ አ ከ ኸ ወ ዐ ዘ ዠ የ ደ ጀ ገ ጠ ጨ ጸ ፀ ፈ ፐ

h l h m s r s sh k' b t ch h n ny ä k h w ä z zh y d j g t' ch' p' c c f p

'h' with the seven vowels

ሀ ሁ ሂ ሃ ሄ ህ ሆ

hä hu hi ha he hə ho

73.

D. L. Appleyard, *A comparative approach to the Amharic lexicon*. Malibu: Undena, 1977. 67 pp.
Afroasiatic linguistics, vol. 5 part 2.

Etymologies are listed and discussed under semantic groups, and there is no index. Part of the author's London Ph. D. thesis, *The Semitic basis of the Amharic lexicon* (1975).

74.

Carl Hubert Armbruster, *Initia amharica = An introduction to spoken Amharic*. Cambridge: Cambridge University Press, 1908–20. Part 1 to part 3 vol. 1.

Part 1 is an Amharic grammar. Part 2 is an English–Amharic vocabulary; part 3 is an Amharic–English vocabulary, of which only the first volume was published.

75.

Ignazio Guidi, *Vocabulario amarico–italiano*. Rome: Casa Editrice Italiana, 1901. 915 pp.

Followed by: *Supplemento*. Rome: Istituto per l'Oriente, 1940. 267 pp. With the assistance of Francesco Gallina, Enrico Cerulli.

[*Amharic–Italian dictionary*.] A relatively detailed bilingual dictionary with some references to scholarly literature (abbreviations, pp. xi–xiii). Additions and corrections, pp. 899–915.

76.

Thomas Leiper Kane, *Amharic–English dictionary*. Wiesbaden: Harrassowitz, 1990. 2 vols [2351 pp.]. 3–447–02871–8.

The Amharic is in Ethiopic script and in transliteration. Kane's dictionary is modestly described as 'basically a compilation of the existing lexicons' by Guidi, Baeteman, Armbruster, Amsalu Aklilu, Leslau and others (these sources are credited by initials) – but actually it contains much new material too. Interesting discussion of the problems of Amharic lexicography, pp. vii–ix.

77.

Wolf Leslau, *English–Amharic context dictionary*. Wiesbaden: Harrassowitz, 1973. 1503 pp. 3–447–01482–2.

An interesting experiment in lexicography, clearly laid out. Every English word is illustrated by one or more Amharic sentences, accompanied by an English translation: see the full explanation, pp. vii–xi. Discussion of variant spellings in Amharic, pp. xi–xiii: in this work the spellings chosen tend to be the etymological ones. Amharic is in Ethiopic script only, not in transliteration.

ARABIC

Arabic is a SEMITIC LANGUAGE, and thus a member of the Afroasiatic family. It is also one of the great languages of the world, with as many as 165 million native speakers.

Arabic may be the descendant of the language of the 'proto-Sinaitic' inscriptions of about 1500 BC. The first record of Arabic apart from this is in inscriptions from various parts of Arabia beginning about a thousand years later and continuing for several centuries. This is 'pre-classical' Arabic, leading up to the poetry of the pre-Qur'anic period and the Qur'an itself, the holy book of Islam.

The importance of Arabic in the modern world goes back to its position as the language of the Qur'an, the language of a conquering religion. Its wide geographical range and long history have produced a great variety of modern dialects, which compete for status with 'modern standard Arabic' (in essence, the language of classical Arabic literature). MALTESE, in origin an Arabic dialect like many others, is the only one that happens to have achieved the status of a standard language.

This book lists only a small selection of Arabic dictionaries, the ones that are most approachable by those relatively unused to reading Arabic. Further information can be found through the bibliographies of many of the recent dictionaries listed below, and particularly those of **103** and **105**. The order of entries in Arabic dictionaries usually represents a compromise between strict alphabetisation and an arrangement by three-letter roots, a pervasive feature of the structure of the language: for discussion see Shivtiel's paper in **105**.

Included below are several useful dictionaries of modern regional dialects. Some have been the subject of long study by European scholars, notably the colloquials of Egypt, Syria and Algeria and Tunisia. Others, like those of Mauretania, Nigeria and Yemen, are arousing new interest now. The Arabic of medieval Spain (Andalusi) is also a growing field of study. In addition to the works listed here, note Johnstone's information (**1429**) for Oman, and the *Dictionary English–Tigrigna–Arabic* (**1553**) for Eritrea.

For Arabic loanwords in other languages see Serra (**827**), Pellegrini (**1257**) and Steiger (**1258**).

The Arabic script

ي و ه ن م ل ك ق ف غ ع ظ ط ض ص ش س ز ر ذ د خ ح ج ث ت ب ا

a b t t̲ j ḥ kh d d̲ r z s š ṣ ḍ ṭ ẓ ʿ gh f q k l m n h w y

In this table the full form of each individual letter is shown, arranged from left to right to match the transliterations in the second row. But Arabic is written and read from right to left, and much-simplified forms of some letters are used in normal writing and printing when they are joined into words.

Historical dictionaries

78.

Régis Blachère, Claude Denizeau, Moustafa Chouémi, [Charles Pellat,]
Dictionnaire arabe–français–anglais (langue classique et moderne) = *Arabic–French–English dictionary* = الكامل. Paris: Maisonneuve et Larose, 1964– .

Vol. 4 adds to the French title: *Al-kâmil, dictionnaire arabe–français–anglais (langue classique et moderne)*.

[*Arabic–French–English dictionary of the classical and modern language.*] A spacious dictionary. It is based on textual sources but no precise citations are given, at least in the early volumes. The last part I have seen, published in 1988, is part 46, belonging to vol. 4 and taking the coverage into ح, the fifth letter of the Arabic alphabet. In practice the emphasis is on the classical language.

The modern standard

79.

N. S. Doniach, editor, *The Oxford English–Arabic dictionary of current usage*. Oxford: Clarendon Press, 1972. 1392 pp. [0–19–864312–8.]

A brief-entry dictionary. The Arabic is in Arabic script only.

80.

Götz Schregle, *Arabisch–deutsches Wörterbuch*. Wiesbaden: Steiner, 1981– .
Deutsche Morgenländische Gesellschaft. Orient-Institut, Beirut.

[*Arabic–German dictionary.*] In the traditional way, Arabic words are filed under consonantal roots. This is a large-scale dictionary of modern usage, drawing on a corpus of 200,000 extracts from modern writing, but with no precise references to texts.

It is to be complete in two large volumes. Vol. 2 part 3/4, published 1992, is the last I have seen: coverage has reached ق , twenty-first letter of the alphabet.

81.

Hans Wehr, *Arabisches Wörterbuch für die Schriftsprache der Gegenwart: arabisch–deutsch*. Wiesbaden: Harrassowitz, 1985. 1452 pp. '5th edn', revised by Hans Wehr and Lorenz Kropfitsch. 3–447–01998–0.
1st edn: 1952. The 2nd, 3rd and 4th editions were reprints of this. – *Supplement zum Arabischen Wörterbuch für die Schriftsprache der Gegenwart*. 1959.
An independently revised edition is available in English: Hans Wehr, *A dictionary of modern written Arabic (Arabic–English)*. Wiesbaden: Harrassowitz, 1979. 1301 pp. '4th edn', edited by J. Milton Cowan. 3–447–02002–4.
1st English edn: 1961. 1110 pp. Edited by Cowan, it was 'an enlarged and improved version of *Arabisches Wörterbuch für die Schriftsprache der Gegenwart* [which] includes the contents of the *Supplement zum Arabischen Wörterbuch für die Schriftsprache der Gegenwart* and a collection of new additional material.'

[*Dictionary of the modern Arabic written language.*] The Arabic is in Arabic script and in transliteration. There are numerous set phrases and brief examples. All added material in the English editions (about 16,000 new items in all) is said to have been derived 'from primary sources', but no references are given.

Older periods

Classical Arabic

82.

E. Fagnan, *Additions aux dictionnaires arabes*. Alger: Carbonel, 1923. 193 pp.

[*Additions to Arabic dictionaries.*] Includes citations, sometimes in generous number, from classical Arabic texts.

83.

Edward William Lane, *An Arabic–English lexicon, derived from the best and the most copious Eastern sources*. London, 1863–93. Vol. 1 [8 parts; 3064 pp.].
Parts 6–8 edited by Stanley Lane-Poole, the author's great-nephew.
Reprinted: Beirut: Librairie du Liban, 1968.
See: E. W. Lane, 'Über die Lexicographie der arabischen Sprache' in *Zeitschrift der Deutschen Morgenländischen Gesellschaft* vol. 3 (1849) pp. 90–108.

A dictionary of classical Arabic 'compiled from the writings of upwards of one hundred Arabic lexicographers': on these sources see part 1 pp. xi–xxii, with a chronological list, p. xxx, and abbreviations, p. xxxi. The principal authority is the eighteenth century *Taj al-'Arus* of Murtada al-Zabidi.

'Nearly twenty years have elapsed since I commenced this work ... For seven years, in Cairo, I prosecuted my task on each of the work-days of the week, after an early breakfast, until within an hour of midnight, with few and short intervals of rest, (often with no interruption but that of a few minutes at a time for a meal, and half an hour for exercise,) except on rare occasions when I was stopped by illness, and once when I devoted three days to a last visit to the Pyramids.' For a memoir of Lane and his work see part 5, pp. v–xxxix.

Lane would not print a list of errata – 'I have generally found them to be such as any one qualified to make a profitable use of my work may easily discover and rectify without my aid' (Postscript to the Preface, 1869) – but Lane-Poole did, part 6, p. xli.

Vol. 1 was to contain 'all the classical words and significations commonly known to the learned among the Arabs'; the projected vol. 2 'those that are of rare occurrence and not commonly known'. Vol. 2 never appeared; Dozy's work (**88**) helps to fill the gap. On the basis of Lane's completed manuscript the publication of vol. 1 in full form reached as far as ﺟ , leaving only the last two letters of the alphabet to be done. The 'Supplement' (part 8 pp. 2973–3064) rounds off the alphabet, simply on the basis of Lane's notes and drafts and not continuing the translation of the old lexicons – which had in any case been published in Arabic by that time. 'The great value of Mr Lane's work lies not so much in his translations from standard works of Arabic lexicography, as in the comments and explanations ...' (S. Lane-Poole in the 'Postscript' to part 8).

'This marvellous work in its fullness and richness, its deep research, correctness, and simplicity of arrangement, far transcends the lexicon of any language ever presented to the world' (Badger, **87**).

84.

Jörg Kraemer, editor, *Theodor Nöldekes Belegwörterbuch zur klassischen arabischen Sprache*. Berlin: De Gruyter, 1952–4. Parts 1–2 [no more published].

[*Theodor Nöldeke's citation dictionary of the classical Arabic language.*] Glosses in German and English, followed by many citations and a few brief quotations from classical literature. Abbreviations and bibliography: pp. vi–xxiii. Covers the letter **A** only.

85.

F. Steingass, *The student's Arabic–English dictionary*. London: Allen, 1884. 1242 pp.

A brief-entry dictionary, with Arabic in both script and transliteration. Tends towards simple alphabetical order (see pp. iii–xiii for full explanation).

86.

Manfred Ullmann, *Wörterbuch der klassischen arabischen Sprache*. Wiesbaden: Harrassowitz, 1957– .
Deutsche Morgenländische Gesellschaft.
Vorläufiges Literaturverzeichnis zum zweiten Band (Lam). 1979. 76 pp. [*Preliminary bibliography for vol. 2 (L)*.]

[*Dictionary of the classical Arabic language*.] A very large-scale dictionary of pre-classical and classical Arabic, with numerous quotations from literature from the fourth century to the tenth. Entries are arranged strictly by consonantal roots (on the alphabetical order see vol. 1 p. xix), so you have to be confident with Arabic to find your way about. Quotations are not in script but in Latin transliteration (and they are not translated); headwords are in both script and transliteration, and are followed by German and English glosses. Note the very lengthy additions and corrections to vol. 1, pp. 520–82; index of foreign words cited in the etymologies in vol. 1, pp. 583–6.

The *Wörterbuch der klassischen arabischen Sprache* begins with **K**, for a reason I have not fathomed, and is still working through the next letter, **L**, which has run into three volumes. The 2400 pages so far published equate to 70 of Steingass's dictionary (**85**), and unless publication speeds up it will take several centuries to complete.

Post-classical Arabic

87.

George Percy Badger, *An English–Arabic lexicon*. London: Kegan Paul, 1881. 1224 pp.

Arabic is in Arabic script only, but with vowel pointing to assist with pronunciation. There are numerous example phrases, given both in English and in Arabic.

88.

R. Dozy, *Supplément aux dictionnaires arabes*. Leiden: Brill, 1881. 2 vols.
The '2nd edn', 1927, and the '3rd edn', 1967, are reprints of the first.

[*Supplement to Arabic dictionaries*.] Compiled out of notes from the reading of post-classical and modern Arabic texts. Sources include also the writings of European travellers and scholars: list of authors cited, vol. 1 pp. xvii–xxix, followed by a list of works that turned out to be useless, pp. xxix–xxx! There are many citations and quotations, for some of which French translations are given; there is also discussion of variant and erroneous forms.

Regional forms

Algeria and Tunisia

89.

Marcelin Beaussier, *Dictionnaire pratique arabe–français, contenant tous les mots employés dans l'arabe parlé en Algérie et en Tunisie, ainsi que dans le style épistolaire, les pièces usuelles et les actes judiciaires* = كتاب اللغتين العربية والفرنساوية . Algiers: Bouyer, 1871. 764 pp.

[*Practical Arabic–French dictionary, containing all the words used in the spoken Arabic of Algeria and Tunisia as well as those of the language of correspondence, popular plays and the law courts.*] Well printed from the author's clear, regular handwriting. 16 pages of additions and corrections at end. List of abbreviations, pp. 1–2.

Egypt

90.

Martin Hinds, El-Said Badawi, *A dictionary of Egyptian Arabic: Arabic–English* = السعيد بدوي ، مارتن هايندس معجم اللغة العربية المصرية عربي–انكليزي . Beirut: Librairie du Liban, 1986. 981 pp. [1–85341–003–9.]

A concise dictionary of modern usage, with examples. 'The focus is on Cairo and the phonological frame is that of Cairo and the Delta, to the exclusion of Upper Egypt where the phonology is markedly different; Alexandria, too, has been denied the closer attention that it clearly deserves' (Preface). Very brief etymologies for about two thousand loanwords (see pp. xiii–xiv, with further references there). Arabic is given in Arabic script and in the International Phonetic Alphabet: example phrases are in the International Phonetic Alphabet (and English translation) only.

91.

Socrates Spiro, *Arabic–English dictionary of the modern Arabic of Egypt*. Cairo: Elias' Modern Press, 1923. 518 pp. 2nd edn.

1st edn: *An Arabic–English vocabulary of the colloquial Arabic of Egypt*. 1895.

A brief-entry dictionary giving one-word etymologies for recent loanwords.

92.

Socrates Spiro, *An English Arabic vocabulary of the modern and colloquial Arabic of Egypt*. Cairo: Elias' Modern Press, 1929. 325 pp. 3rd edn.

1st edn: 1897? 2nd edn: 1906?

Arabic glosses are given in Arabic script and in Latin transliteration. Lists of numerals, weights and meansures, the provinces of Egypt: pp. viii–xiii.

93.

Charles Vial, *L'égyptien tel qu'on l'écrit: glossaire établi d'après un choix d'oeuvres littéraires égyptiennes contemporaines*. Le Caire: Institut Français d'Archéologie Orientale, 1983. 382 pp.
Textes arabes et études islamiques, 18.

[*Egyptian as it is written: a glossary derived from a selection of contemporary Egyptian literature.*] Egyptian words and expressions with French glosses, all entries including at least one quotation from modern Egyptian Arabic literature, with precise references. Quotations are given both in Arabic and in French translation. Bibliography of sources, pp. xv–xix; index of French meanings, pp. 339–82.

Mauritania

94.

Catherine Taine-Cheikh, *Dictionnaire hassaniyya français: dialecte arabe de Mauritanie*. Paris: Geuthner, 1988– .

[*Hassaniya–French dictionary: the Arabic dialect of Mauritania.*] A large-scale bilingual dictionary in which Arabic is given in phonetic transcription and in Arabic script. Six volumes have appeared, reaching to ص , fourteenth letter of the alphabet.

Morocco

95.

A.-L. de Premare [and others], *Langue et culture marocaines. Dictionnaire arabe–français établi sur la base de fichiers, ouvrages, enquêtes, manuscrits, études et documents divers*. Paris: L'Harmattan, 1993– .

[*Moroccan language and culture. An Arabic–French dictionary based on manuscript collections, published and unpublished texts, research papers, fieldwork, etc.*] Headwords appear in Arabic script and phonetic transcription, sub-arranged under triliteral roots. Numerous phrases are provided as examples: these are in phonetic script and French translation. Abbreviations at end of articles give sources used, including earlier dictionaries. A guide to abbreviations appears in each volume.

Publication is rapid: the ninth volume, the latest, takes the coverage to غ , nineteenth letter of the alphabet, and to the word مغيوئة 'provocative'.

Nigeria

96.

Alan S. Kaye, *Nigerian Arabic–English Dictionary*. Malibu: Undena, 1986. 90 pp.
Bibliotheca Afroasiatica, 2.
Note also: Alan S. Kaye, *A dictionary of Nigerian Arabic*. Malibu: Undena, 1982. (*Bibliotheca Afroasiatica*, 1.)

A brief-entry dictionary in Latin transcription, in Latin alphabetical order. The earlier work of 1982 is an English–Nigerian Arabic dictionary.

Spain

97.

F. Corriente, *A dictionary of Andalusi Arabic*. Leiden: Brill, 1997. 623 pp. 90–04–09846–1.

Handbuch der Orientalistik = Handbook of Oriental studies, 1. Abteilung, der Nahe und Mittlere Osten = The Near and Middle East, 29.

Note also: F. Corriente, *El léxico árabe andalusí según P. de Alcalá (ordenado por raíces, corregido, anotado y fonémicamente intepretado)*. Madrid: Departamento de Estudios Árabes e Islámicos, Universidad Complutense de Madrid, 1988. 259 pp. [*The Andalusian Arabic vocabulary according to Pedro de Alcalá, arranged under roots, corrected and annotated, with phonemic interpretations.*]

A dictionary of the Arabic of medieval Spain, entirely in Latin transliteration. Headwords are in consonantal form, and are followed by English glosses and by numerous citations and brief quotations (list of sources, pp. xiii–xvii) in transliterated Arabic with vowels. An excellent dictionary, though some may find the lack of Arabic script irritating. There is much attention to etymology; indexes of cited forms by language, pp. 581–623.

Corriente's 1988 work was a rearrangement of the vocabulary of Pedro de Alcalá's *Arte para ligera mente saber la lengua arauiga* [*Easy lessons in the Arabic language*] and *Vocabulista arauigo en letra castellana* [*Arabic word-list in Spanish transliteration*] (Granada, 1505), primary sources for the late medieval Arabic of Andalusia.

Syria, Lebanon, Palestine

98.

A. Barthélemy, *Dictionnaire arabe–français: dialectes de Syrie: Alep, Damas, Liban, Jérusalem*. Paris: Geuthner, 1935–54. 943 pp.

[*Arabic–French dictionary of the dialects of Syria, including Aleppo, Damascus, Lebanon and Jerusalem.*] A big dictionary of modern usage. Entries are filed under roots, which appear in the left column, in Arabic script. Otherwise everything is in a phonetic script, including example phrases: explanation of the phonetics, pp. vii–ix. Additions, pp. 921–40.

Yemen

99.

Peter Behnstedt, *Die nordjemenitischen Dialekte*. Wiesbaden: Reichert, 1985– .

Jemen-Studien, 3.

[*The North Yemeni dialects.*] In Latin transliteration. The dictionary is in Arabic alphabetical order and is arranged under consonantal roots. References to sources.

Part 1, published in 1985, is an atlas of the dialects (226 pp.). Part 2 is the beginning of the dictionary, covering ﺍ–ﺩ, the first eight letters of the alphabet (1992. 400 pp.).

100.

Moshe Piamenta, *Dictionary of post-classical Yemeni Arabic*. Leiden: Brill, 1990–91. 2 vols [541 pp.].

A highly detailed, well-documented dictionary of the vernacular vocabulary and idiom of medieval and modern Yemen, based on manuscripts, printed material, and oral collections, with quotations (in Arabic script and with English translation) and precise references: list of sources, vol. 1 pp. xv–xxiv. Includes the Judaeo-Arabic of Yemen. Important as an ethnographical source.

Slang and special vocabularies

101.

Henri Grosset-Grange, *Glossaire nautique arabe ancien et moderne de l'océan Indien (1975)*. Paris: CTHS, 1993. 217 pp.

Comité des Travaux Historiques et Scientifiques. *Mémoires de la Section d'Histoire des Sciences et des Techniques*, 5. Edited by Alain Rouaud; preface by Michel Mollat du Jourdin.

[*Arabic nautical glossary of the Indian Ocean, ancient and modern.*] Includes bibliographical references (pp. 211–15). Text in French and romanized Arabic.

Foreign words

102.

Asya Asbaghi, *Persische Lehnwörter im Arabischen*. Wiesbaden: Harrassowitz, 1988. 286 pp. 3–447–02757–6.

[*Persian loanwords in Arabic.*] A brief listing, often simply referring to earlier authorities. Headwords are in Arabic and in Latin transliteration.

103.

Erich Prokosch, *Osmanisches Wortgut im Ägyptisch-Arabischen*. Berlin: Schwarz, 1983. 141 pp. 3–922968–23–6.

Islamkundliche Untersuchungen, 78.

[*Turkish vocabulary in Egyptian Arabic.*] The alphabetical listing, in Latin alphabetical order, is on pp. 37–141. Note the bibliography – a handy source of information on Arabic etymology – on pp. 22–9.

104.

Erich Prokosch, *Osmanisches Wortgut im Sudan-Arabischen*. Berlin: Schwarz, 1983. 75 pp. 3–922968–29–5.

Islamkundliche Untersuchungen, 89.

[*Turkish vocabulary in Sudan Arabic.*] Arranged like its companion work (**103**). The alphabetical listing is on pp. 43–75.

Other works of interest

105.

K. Dévényi, T. Iványi, A. Shivtiel, editors, *Proceedings of the Colloquium on Arabic Lexicology and Lexicography (CALL) part 1, Budapest, 1–7 September 1993.* Budapest, 1993–4. 2 vols.

The Arabist: Budapest studies in Arabic, 6/7, 11/12. Note especially Avihai Shivtiel, 'Root-dictionary or alphabetical dictionary: a methodological dilemma', vol. 1 pp. 13–25.

ARAMAIC

One of the SEMITIC LANGUAGES, Aramaic was once a major international language of the Middle East. It was the language of administration in the Persian Empire, 2500 years ago.

Aramaic soon afterwards became the standard language of Judaism and Jewish scholarship, having replaced Hebrew as the everyday speech of Palestine. It is from this period that most Aramaic literature comes, and most of it is in Hebrew script.

'Chaldaean' is an old-fashioned term for Biblical Aramaic. By tradition SYRIAC is the name used for the forms of Aramaic that were written, mostly by Christians, in Syriac script. Modern Aramaic, still spoken in some districts of Syria, Iraq, Turkey and Azerbaijan, has also been called 'Syriac', 'Assyrian' and 'Chaldaean': for Mandaic, one modern form of the language, see the dictionary by Drower and Macuch (**1504**).

Aramaic studies are compartmentalised, and published dictionaries reflect this. The earliest recorded Aramaic, in inscriptions, is counted with other 'West Semitic' dialects (**1370**). There are thorough dictionaries of Old Testament Aramaic, usually combined with Biblical Hebrew (**703** onwards) but also separately (**110** below). There are important dictionaries of Jewish scholarly Aramaic, again combined with Hebrew (e.g. **111, 112**). More recently, scholars have attempted to separate out the Aramaic vocabulary (e.g. **116**) and there are plans for a large-scale general dictionary of early Aramaic (see **118**).

Modern regional forms

106.

Arthur John Maclean, *A dictionary of the dialects of vernacular Syriac as spoken by the eastern Syrians of Kurdistan, north-west Persia, and the plains of Mosul, with illustrations from the dialects of the Jews of Zakhu and Azerbaijan, and of the western Syrians of Ṭūr Abdin and Maʿlūla.* Oxford: Clarendon Press, 1901. 334 pp.

In Syriac script and Latin transcription. List of dialects with abbreviations, pp. ix–xi.

Eastern

107.

ורדה שילה מילון עברי-ארמי-אשורי בלהג יהודי זאכו [Vardah Shiloh, *Milon*
'Ivri–Arami–Ashuri be-lahag Yehudé Zakho]. Jerusalem: Shiloh, 755 [1994/5?].
2 vols.

[*Hebrew–Assyrian Aramaic dictionary of the Jews of Zakhu.*] A dictionary of the
Aramaic of the modern 'Assyrians', entirely in Hebrew script.

Western

108.

Gotthelf Bergsträsser, *Glossar des neuaramäischen Dialekts von Ma'lūla.*
Leipzig: Brockhaus, 1921.
Abhandlungen für die Kunde des Morgenlandes, vol. 15 part 4.

[*Glossary of the modern Aramaic dialect of Ma'lūla.*] A daunting little work, offset
printed from the author's handwritten fair copy. Cites printed sources (abbreviations, p.
v). Headwords are in transliteration, in consonantal form. There are indexes of Aramaic
and Arabic forms cited.

Older periods

109.

Joannes Buxtorfius, *Lexicon chaldaicum, talmudicum et rabbinicum*. Leipzig:
Schaefer, 1866–75. 2 vols [1328 pp.]. New edition by Bernardus Fischerus.
Originally published: Basle, 1639. Edited by Johannes Buxtorfius filius. – 6th edn: *Johannis Buxtorfi Lexicon*
Hebraicum et Chaldaicum. London, 1646. – 7th edn: 1663.

[*Biblical Aramaic, Talmudic and Rabbinic dictionary.*] In Hebrew script, with Latin
(and occasionally German) glosses: generous quotations from the literature, in Aramaic
with Latin translations. List of earlier lexicographers and glossators, vol. 1 pp. ix–xiii.

Biblical

110.

Ernestus Vogt, editor, *Lexicon linguae Aramaicae Veteris Testamenti, docu-*
mentis antiquis illustratum. Rome: Pontificium Institutum Biblicum, 1971. 192 pp.

[*Dictionary of the Aramaic language of the Old Testament, illustrated from early*
documents.] A glossary of the small parts of the Old Testament that were written in
Aramaic and not Hebrew. List of non-Biblical texts quoted, pp. 9*–11*.

Post-Biblical

111.

Gustav Dalman, *Aramäisch–neuhebräisches Handwörterbuch zu Targum, Talmud und Midrasch.* Frankfurt am Main: J. Kauffmann, 1922. 457 + 120 pp. 2nd edn.

1st edn: 1901.

[*Concise Aramaic and Late Hebrew dictionary of the Targum, Talmud and Midrash.*] A brief-entry dictionary in Hebrew script, vowel-pointed. There are some citations of sources, but no quotations. The second pagination, 120 pp. at end, consists of: G. H. Händler, *Anhang zum Aramäisch–neuhebräischen Wörterbuch von Gustaf H. Dalman: Lexikon der abbreviaturen* [*Supplement: dictionary of abbreviations*]; J. Kahan, *Verzeichnis der Mischna-Abschnitte* [*Index of passages from the Mishnah*].

Note the bibliography of recent contributions to Aramaic lexicography, mainly of the realia of classical Palestine, on p. iii of the first edition.

112.

Marcus Jastrow, *A dictionary of the Targumim, the Talmud Babli and Yerushalmi, and the Midraschic literature.* London: Trübner, Luzac, 1886–1903. 2 vols [1736 pp.].

Several reprints, including: New York: Choreb, 1926. 2 vols in 1.

'Covers a period of about one thousand years, and contains Hebrew and Aramaic elements in about equal proportions.' The Hebrew and Aramaic are in Hebrew script, vowel-pointed. Each entry begins with a brief etymology in brackets – often simply *(b.h.)* 'Biblical Hebrew'. There are many citations and brief quotations, with precise references.

Supplement, pp. 1706–21; index of Biblical passages for which Talmudic and Midrashic interpretations are quoted in the dictionary, pp. 1722–36.

113.

Jacob Levy, *Neuhebräisches und chaldaisches Wörterbuch über die Talmudim und Midraschim.* Leipzig: Brockhaus, 1875–89. 4 vols [22 parts].

Supplemented by: Jacob Levy, Lazarus Goldschmidt, *Nachträge und Berichtigungen zu Jacob Levy, Wörterbuch über die Talmudim und Midraschim.* Berlin: Harz, 1934. Various paginations.

[*Later Hebrew and Aramaic dictionary to the Talmudim and Midrashim.*] Numerous quotations and citations from the literature; glosses and discussion in German. Selective index of cited passages, vol. 4 pp. 684-741. Many additions and corrections are scattered through the volumes: these are cumulated and replaced by the supplementary volume by Levy and Goldschmidt (see note above).

114.

Friedrich Schulthess, *Lexicon syropalaestinum.* Berlin: Reimer, 1903. 226 pp.

Reprinted: *Lexicon syropalaestinum = Wörterbuch der christlich-syrischen Sprache aus den biblischen Büchern und syrisch-palästinensischen Schriften des Frühmittelalters zusammengestellt.* Amsterdam: APA-Oriental Press, 1979. 90–6023–263–1.

[*Syrian-Palestinian dictionary.*] Schulthess's work is more compact than Schwally's (**115**), with less discussion and more citations from the texts.

115.

Friedrich Schwally, *Idioticon des christlich palästinischen Aramaeisch.* Giessen: Ricker, 1893. 134 pp.

[*Dialect dictionary of Christian Palestinian Aramaic.*] A short Aramaic–German dictionary with comparative emphasis. The Aramaic is in Syriac script. There are two sequences: the first, with Aramaic headwords, is of the native vocabulary (pp. 1–102); the second is of Greek and Latin loanwords, with headwords in Greek followed by the Aramaic form. Many entries cite Greek equivalents, the texts dealt with (list, pp. 9–10) being mainly translations from Greek.

116.

Michael Sokoloff, *A dictionary of Jewish Palestinian Aramaic of the Byzantine period.* Ramat-Gan: Bar-Ilan University Press [1990]. 823 pp. 965–22–6101–7. *Dictionaries of Talmud, Midrash, and Targum*, 2.

A very important new dictionary of 'the Aramaic dialect spoken and written by Jews, mainly in Palestine, during the Byzantine period (3rd century CE – Arab Conquest) and for some time afterward … Together with Christian Palestinian Aramaic [see **114**] and Samaritan Aramaic, JPA forms the western branch of Middle Aramaic, which has survived to the present day in the dialect of Maʻlūla [see **108**]' (Introduction).

Deals with the language of some Targumic, Midrashic and Talmudic texts. There are many citations and quotations. Replaces Jastrow (**112**) with regard to this period and region (Jastrow also covers other Aramaic dialects, and includes Hebrew to the extent that it occurred in Aramaic texts).

Abbreviations and list of source texts, pp. 8–28; index of sources cited and quoted in the entries, an important aid to research, pp. 597–820. Additions, pp. 821–3.

Foreign words

117.

Daniel Sperber, *A dictionary of Greek and Latin legal terms in Rabbinic literature = Milon le-munahim mishpatiyim shebe-sifrut Hazal ha-she'ulot mi-Yevanit ve-Latinit.* Ramat-Gan: Bar-Ilan University Press, 1984. 226 pp. *Dictionaries of Talmud, Midrash, and Targum*, 1.

Other works of interest

118.

Comprehensive Aramaic Lexicon Project newsletter. Baltimore, 1985– .

ARAUCANIAN

This AMERIND language of Chile and Argentina is known to its own speakers, the 300,000–strong Mapuche, as Mapudungun. It has no close linguistic relatives.

119.

E. Erize, *Diccionario comentado mapuche–español araucano, pehuenche, pampa, picunche, rancülche, huilliche.* Buenos Aires: Cuadernos del Sur, 1960. 550 pp.

Some catalogues give a different imprint: Bahía Blanca: Editorial Yepun, 1960.
Reviewed in Jorge A. Suárez, 'Problemas de lexicografía hispano-india' in *Romance philology* vol. 7 (1963–4) pp. 155–69.

[*Annotated Mapudungu and Spanish dictionary.*] A two-way dictionary: Mapudungu–Spanish, pp. 45–430; Spanish–Mapudungu, pp. 433–550. Important bibliography, pp. 27–42. The title lists the several alternative names for Araucanian and its dialects.

ARDHAMAGADHI

Ardhamagadhi is the classical language of the Jain scriptures, and is one of the Middle INDO-ARYAN languages. It is known in two forms. One, found in the earliest sutras, is roughly contemporary with PALI. The other, dating from around the sixth century AD and now known from Buddhist dramatic texts, may be based on the spoken language of Awadh, in northern India, at that period. Ardhamagadhi has long been extinct as an everyday spoken language

120.

Ratnachandraji, *An illustrated Ardha-Magadhi dictionary, literary, philosophic, and scientific, with Sanskrit, Gujraïi, Hindi, and English equivalents, references to the texts & copious quotations* = रत्नचन्द्रजी | सचित्र अर्ध—मगधी कोष. [Ajmer?:] S. S. Jaina Conference, 1923–38. 5 vols.

Introduction by A. C. Woolner. The title page of vol. 5 reads: *The remaining part of Ardha-Magadhi quadrilingual dictionary, or, Maharashtri and Deshya Prakrit dictionary* = परिशिष्ट अर्ध—मगधी कोष.
Reprinted: Varanasi: Amar Publication, 1988. 81–217–0046–9.

A brief-entry dictionary in which all the Indian languages, even Gujarati, are in Devanagari script: the Sanskrit, serving rather as an etymological indication than as a gloss, is in brackets. One, or occasionally more than one, citation is provided to the Jain scriptures, but there is scarcely any quotation (in spite of the promise of the title) or discussion. Vol. 5 is a supplementary sequence.

The author's name appears on vol. 1 as 'Shatadvani the Jaina Muni Shri Ratnachandraji Maharaj', and with variations later.

ARMENIAN

Armenian forms a separate branch of the INDO-EUROPEAN LANGUAGES, one that has been established south of the Caucasus for at least two thousand years. There are two million speakers, in Armenia (formerly a Soviet republic), in Iran, and in a world-wide diaspora. The eastern dialects form the basis of the modern standard language of Armenia, while outside Armenia the western dialects are best known: bilingual dictionaries based on both these standards are listed below.

The major Armenian dictionary, though it is hard for non-Armenians to use, is the etymological dictionary by Adjarian (**127**).

The Armenian alphabet

ԱԲԳ ԴԵ Զ Է Ը Թ Ժ Ի Լ Խ Ծ Կ Հ Ձ Ղ Ճ Մ Յ Ն Շ Ո Չ Պ Ջ Ռ Ս Վ Տ Ր Ց Ւ Փ Ք Օ Ֆ

ա բ գ դ ե զ է ը թ ժ ի լ խ ծ կ հ ձ ղ ճ մ յ ն շ ո չ պ ջ ռ ս վ տ ր ց ւ փ ք օ ֆ

a b g d e z ē ə t' ž i l x c k h j ł č m y n š o č' p j ŕ s v t r c' w p' k' ō f

The Armenian script was invented by Meshrop Mashtots' in 405 AD, specifically so that Christian literature could be translated into the local language from Syriac and Greek.

The modern standards

121.

Հ. Ա. Ասմանգուլյանի, Մ. Ի. Հովհաննիսյանի *Անգլերեն–Հայերեն*
բառարան [H. A. Asmangulyani, M. I. Hovhannisyani *Angleren–Hayeren*
baŕaran] = H. A. Asmangulian, M. I. Hovhannisian, editors, *English–Armenian*
dictionary. Yerevan: Hayastan, 1984. 1143 pp.

A brief-entry dictionary in modern Eastern Armenian with about 30,000 entries.

122.

M. Bedrossian, *New dictionary Armenian–English* = Մատութեալ Պետրսեան,
Նոր բառգիրք Հայ–Անգլիարէն. Venice: St. Lazarus Armenian Academy,
1875–9. 786 pp.

An early Western Armenian brief-entry dictionary which is still regularly reprinted.
List of proper names, pp. 765–86.

123.

Армянско–русский словарь [*Armyansko–russkii slovar'*] = *Հայ–Ռուսերէն*
բառարան. Yerevan: Izdatel'stvo Akademii Nauk Armyanskoi SSR, 1987. 724 pp.
E. G. Galstyan, chief editor. Haykakan SSH Gitutyunneri Akademia, Lejvi Institut.

[*Armenian–Russian dictionary.*] The largest modern bilingual dictionary out of
Armenian.

124.

Մեսրոպ Կ. Գույումճեան, *Ընդարձակ բառարան Անգլիերէն Հայերէն*
[Mesrop K. Gouyoumcean, *Enghardzak baṙaran Anglierene Hayeren*] = Mesrob
G. Kouyoumdjian, *A comprehensive dictionary English–Armenian*. Cairo:
Sahag-Mesrob, 1961. 1411 pp.

A Western Armenian bilingual dictionary. I have seen a Beirut reprint (Doniguian,
1981).

125.

Մեսրոպ Կ. Գույումճեան, *Ընդարձակ բառարան Հայերէն Անգլիերէն*
[Mesrop K. Gouyoumcean, *Enghardzak baṙaran Hayerene Anglieren*] = Mesrob
G. Kouyoumdjian, *A comprehensive dictionary Armenian–English*. Cairo:
Sahag-Mesrob, 1950. 1150 pp.

A Western Armenian bilingual dictionary, with many appendices: trade terms, pp.
897-928 and abbreviations pp. 928-30; names of countries, p. 944; anatomical and
medical terms, pp. 945-83; musical terms, pp. 984-99; military terms, pp. 1000-1033;
philosophy and psychology, pp. 1034-49; legal and political terms, pp. 1050-76;
architecture, pp. 1077-84; names of animals, pp. 1136-46; and others. I have only seen a
Beirut reprint (Atlas Press, 1970).

Older periods

126.

Ռ. Ս. Ղազարյան, Հ. Մ. Ավետիսյան, *Միջին Հայերենի բառարան* [R.
S. Ghazaryan, H. M. Avetisyan, *Mijin Hayereni baṙaran*]. Erevan: Erevani
Petakan Hamalsaran, 1987– .

[*Middle Armenian dictionary.*] Entirely in Armenian. Vol. 1, the only one I have
seen, covers the first fifteen letters of the alphabet. Etymologies of loanwords are given
in brackets, and a single textual source is cited for each word.

Etymological dictionaries

127.

Հր. Աճառյան, *Հայերեն արմատական բառարան* [Hr. Ačaṙyan, *Hayeren
armatakan baṙaran*]. Erevan: Erevani Hamalsarani Hratarakč'ut'iwn, 1971–9. 4
vols. New edn.

1st edn: Հ. Աճառեան, *Հայերէն արմատական բառարան* = Р. Ачарян, *Этимологический коренной
словарь армянского языка* = H. Adjarian, *Armenisches etymologisches Wörterbuch*. 7 vols. 1926–35.
See M. Minassian, 'A. Meillet et l'adaptation inachevée du *Dictionnaire etymologique arménien* d'Adjarian' in
Revue des études arméniennes vol. 13 (1978/9). Meillet died in 1936 before he could complete his French
adaptation, which remains unpublished.

[*Armenian etymological dictionary.*] Entirely in Armenian, with references both to
Armenian texts (bibliography, vol. 1 pp. 30–58) and to scholarship and etymological
dictionaries in other languages (abbreviations, pp. 59–62 and 27–9). In citing forms in

other languages Adjarian used Greek, Latin, Arabic, Georgian, Hebrew, Syriac and even cuneiform scripts, but, mercifully, he added a transliteration of the cuneiform!

The first edition is harder to use, being an offset reproduction from the author's difficult Armenian handwriting. In early volumes, moreover, the print quality was poor and the paper not opaque enough.

128.

Jost Gippert, *Iranica armeno-iberica = Studien zu den iranischen Lehnwörtern im Armenischen und Georgischen.* Vienna: Verlag der Österreichischen Akademie der Wissenschaften, 1993. 2 vols. 3–7001–2110–5.

Österreichische Akademie der Wissenschaften, philosophisch-historische Klasse. *Sitzungsberichte*, 606. *Veröffentlichungen der Kommission für Iranistik*, 26.

[*Studies on the Iranian loanwords in Armenian and Georgian.*] A discursive dictionary arranged in alphabetical order under Iranian original forms, known or reconstructed. Discussion ranges into numerous other languages: Syriac, Hebrew and Georgian (but not Armenian) scripts are used. Abbreviations, vol. 1 pp. 351–6, and bibliography pp. 357–82; numerous separate indexes, pp. 383–448, including indexes of texts cited and of words cited. The second volume, subtitled *Materialien*, consists of numerous further quotations of texts keyed to the headwords of vol. 1: a German translation is sometimes but not always given.

129.

John A. C. Greppin, 'An etymological dictionary of the Indo-European components of Armenian' in *Bazmavep* no. 141 (1983) pp. 235-323.

Not seen.

ASLIAN LANGUAGES

This group of 'aboriginal' AUSTROASIATIC LANGUAGES of the Malay Peninsula includes Sengoi (or Semai), which has about 20,000 speakers, Temiar, Orang Benua and others with smaller numbers.

130.

Geoffrey Benjamin, 'Austroasiatic subgroupings and prehistory in the Malay Peninsula' in *Austroasiatic studies* ed. Philip N. Jenner and others (Honolulu: University Press of Hawaii, 1976) pp. 37–128.

Includes (pp. 101–26) 'Aslian comparative vocabulary' with a concordance to the earlier word-lists in W. W. Skeat, C. O. Blagden, *Pagan races of the Malay Peninsula* (London: Macmillan, 1906).

ASSAMESE

Its origin in the Brahmaputra valley of north-eastern India made Assamese the easternmost of all the Indo-European languages, at least until the colonisations and migrations of the last two centuries. It belongs to the INDO-ARYAN branch of the family. There are about twelve million speakers in the Indian state of Assam, where Assamese is the language of administration, education and the press.

Assamese script

অ আ ই ঈ উ ঊ এ ঐ ও ঔ

a ā i ī u ū e ai o au

ক খ গ ঘ ঙ চ ছ জ ঝ ঞ টঠ ড ঢ ণ ত থ দ ধ ন প ফ ব ভ ম য র ল ৱ শ ষ স হ

k kh g gh ṅ c ch j jh ñ ṭ ṭh ḍ ḍh ṇ t th d dh n p ph b bh m y r l v ś ṣ s h

131.

হেমচন্দ্র বৰুৱাৰ হেকোষ = Hemchandra Barua, *Hema kosha; or, An etymological dictionary of the Assamese language*. N.p., 1900. 972 pp.
Edited by P. R. Gurdon, Hemchandra Gosain. 'Published under the authority of the Assam Administration.'

A brief-entry dictionary in the etymological orthography which had by 1900 regained its predominance for Assamese. Essentially this is a monolingual Assamese dictionary, to which brief English glosses have been added. Example phrases are given both in Assamese (Assamese script only) and in English. The brief etymologies that are offered are weighted towards Indo-Aryan, Sanskrit (সং·), English and 'Mahomedan' origins, sidelining Sino-Tibetan influences.

132.

Miles Bronson, *A dictionary in Assamese and English*. Sibsagar: American Baptist Mission Press, 1867. 609 pp.

Uses the experimental phonemic (as we would now call it) orthography of the American Baptist Mission, which was abandoned later in the nineteenth century. Vocabulary 'culled from the lips of the people' (Gurdon, **131**).

133.

চন্দ্রকত্ত অভিধান = *Chandrakanta abhidhan: a comprehensive dictionary of the Assamese language with etymology and illustrations of words with their meanings in Assamese and English*. Guwahati: Guwahati Biswabidyalaya, 1987. 922 pp. 3rd edn by Maheswara Neog.
1st edn: 1933. Asam Sahitya Sabha. – 2nd edn: 1962. 1044 pp.

A modern brief-entry dictionary that aims to cover both Old and Modern Assamese. Brief etymologies.

AUSTROASIATIC LANGUAGES

The Austroasiatic language family extends widely across south and south-east Asia, but only two members of it – Khmer and Vietnamese – are ruling languages of modern nation states. Otherwise, Austroasiatic language speakers form minorities – some of them lowland peoples, others hill-dwellers – from India to southern China, Vietnam and the Malay peninsula.

The Austroasiatic languages that have separate entries in this book are: ASLIAN LANGUAGES, BAHNAR, HO, KHASI, KHMER, MON, MUNDARI, PALAUNG, SANTALI, VIETNAMESE, WA LANGUAGES. There are plenty of other members of the family, with numbers of speakers ranging from a few hundred to several hundred thousand, but for most of them no good dictionaries are to be found.

Vietnamese and the regional language Muong are the two members of the very distinctive Viet-Muong group studied by Thompson (**135**). Kharia, the language which formed the starting-point for Pinnow's study, is actually one of the minor languages of the Munda group, spoken in central India: Mundari, Santali and Ho are better-known members of this group.

Parkin (**136**), Pinnow (**134**) and Zide (**137**) provide useful bibliographical guides.

Comparative dictionaries

134.

Heinz-Jürgen Pinnow, *Versuch einer historischen Lautlehre der Kharia-Sprache*. Wiesbaden: Steiner, 1959. 514 pp.

[*Towards a historical phonology of the Kharia language.*] A numbered sequence of reconstructions from proto-Munda and proto-Austroasiatic runs through the book, interspersed with discussion. Each entry gives German (always) and English (usually) and French (occasionally) glosses, with scientific Latin for flora and fauna, and then modern cognates. English index, pp. 491–5, followed by indexes of forms cited from the individual Austroasiatic languages, pp. 490–514. Oddly, there is no German index. Full and important bibliography, pp. 459–89.

For additional etymologies see: S. Bhattacharya, 'Some Munda etymologies' in *Studies in comparative Austroasiatic linguistics* ed. Norman H. Zide (The Hague: Mouton, 1966); R. Shafer's review of Pinnow in *Word* vol. 16 (1960) pp. 424–33; R. Shafer, *Studies in Austroasian: II* (*Studia orientalia* vol. 3 no. 5) (Helsinki, 1965).

135.

Lawrence C. Thompson, 'Proto-Viet-Muong phonology' in *Austroasiatic studies* ed. Philip N. Jenner and others (Honolulu: University Press of Hawaii, 1976) pp. 1113–1203.

Includes a comparative glossary, pp. 1163–97.

Other works of interest

136.

Robert Parkin, *A guide to Austroasiatic speakers and their languages*. Honolulu: University of Hawaii Press, 1991. 213 pp. 0–8248–1377–4.
Oceanic linguistics special publications, 23.

137.

Norman Zide, 'The Munda languages' in Franz Josef Hausmann [and other editors], *Wörterbücher: ein internationales Handbuch zur Lexikographie = Dictionaries: an international encyclopedia of lexicography = Dictionnaires: encyclopédie internationale de lexicographie* (Berlin: De Gruyter, 1989) pp. 2533–47.

AUSTRONESIAN LANGUAGES

An extensive language family spoken by very large numbers from Madagascar eastwards to Easter Island, and from Taiwan southwards to New Zealand.

The greatest language diversity is to be found in the relatively small space of Taiwan, although there the 'aboriginal' Austronesian languages of the highlands (FORMOSAN LANGUAGES) are giving way to Chinese. Taiwan must be the place from which, in a series of seaborne migrations, the people who spoke early Austronesian languages migrated, eventually spreading across the Indian and Pacific Oceans. Austronesian languages appear to be related to some language groups of mainland southern China, making up a larger family, the AUSTRO-TAI LANGUAGES.

Apart from the Formosan languages, the following members of the Austronesian family have entries in this book: ACHEHNESE, BALINESE, BARE'E, BATAK LANGUAGES, BIKOL, BUGIS, CEBUANO, CHAM, CHAMORRO, FIJIAN, GAYO, GORONTALO, HAWAIIAN, HILIGAYNON, IBAN, ILOCANO, JAVANESE, MADURESE, MAGINDANAON, MAKASAR, MALAGASY, MALAY, MANGGARAI, MAORI, PANGASINAN, RHADÉ, ROTI, SAMOAN, SANGIR, SUNDANESE, TAGALOG, TONGAN, TONTEMBOAN, TORAJA. The most important internationally is Malay (which includes Indonesian and Malaysian); the Austronesian language with the largest number of native speakers is Javanese.

The important comparative dictionary edited by Tryon (**141**) gives an up-to-date view of historical work on this language family. Dempwolff (**138**) was a pioneer of Austronesian studies. The series *Pacific linguistics* contains many dictionaries and glossaries of Austronesian languages, in most cases forming the best available sources for the languages concerned. Full lists of the series appear at the end of each published volume: see **1254** for an example.

Comparative dictionaries

138.

Otto Dempwolff, *Austronesisches Wörterverzeichnis*. Berlin: Reimer, 1938. 192 pp.
Zeitschrift für eingeborenen Sprachen, Beiheft, 19. Otto Dempwolff, *Vergleichende Lautlehre des austronesischen Wortschatzes*, 3.

[*Austronesian word-list.*] The main dictionary is arranged under reconstructed proto-Austronesian forms, with a brief listing of modern reflexes of these, pp. 11–164; language abbreviations, p. 10; German index of meanings, pp. 165–92.

139.

Lawrence A. Reid, editor, *Philippine minor languages: word lists and phonologies*. Honolulu: University of Hawaii Press, 1971. 239 pp. 0–87022–691–6.
Oceanic linguistics special publication, 8.

140.

W. A. L. Stokhof, editor, *Holle lists: vocabularies in languages of Indonesia*. Canberra: Australian National University, Research School of Pacific Studies, 1980–87. 11 vols in 20.
Pacific linguistics, series D, 17, 28, 35, 44, 49–53, 59–62, 66, 69, 71, 74–6. *Materials in languages of Indonesia.*

Publication from manuscripts in the Museum Nasional, Jakarta, of 234 surviving word-lists from those collected for K. F. Holle in the late nineteenth century, translating a standard set of up to 1546 words into about 250 languages of Indonesia. Vol. 1 includes the master list with Bahasa Indonesia, Dutch and English indexes: the remaining volumes are arranged regionally. Vol. 11 ends with an index to language and dialect names for the set, and an index to maps. Contents of set, vol. 11 p. 349.

141.

Darrell T. Tryon, editor, *Comparative Austronesian dictionary: an introduction to Austronesian studies*. Berlin: Mouton De Gruyter, 1995. 4 parts in 5 vols. 3–11–012729–6.
Assistant editors: Malcolm D. Ross, Charles E. Grimes, Adrian Clynes, K. A. Adelaar.

Part 1 (2 vols): Introduction; 'The Austronesian languages' and 'Some current issues', by Tryon and Ross, both largely concerned with language classification, pp. 5–120; 'Listing of Austronesian languages', pp. 121–279, by Barbara F. Grimes, Joseph E. Grimes, and editors, based on the Cornell-SIL Language Archive which is also the basis of *Ethnologue* (**5**). Introductions to the 80 selected languages whose word lists form the basis of the dictionary, pp. 283–964. 'Select Austronesian bibliography', by Lois Carrington and Charles E. Grimes, pp. 965–1103. 'A glossary of Austronesian reconstructions', by R. David Zorc, proto-Austronesian–English with an English–proto-Austronesian index by Ross, pp. 1105–97.

The dictionary forms parts 2 to 4 and is arranged in classified order. Each entry begins with English meaning and then gives the 80 language equivalents for this in a standard order; notes are keyed to these. The notes point out, for example, if a particular word is a loanword, thus breaking the cognate set.

The lists of general abbreviations, and of the three-letter upper-case language abbreviations that are used throughout the book, are repeated at the head of each volume.

AUSTRO-TAI

A postulated family relationship linking the AUSTRONESIAN LANGUAGES, Kadai languages, TAI LANGUAGES, MIAO and YAO was first proposed by Paul Benedict, and has now become the linguistic orthodoxy, though some still dispute it. The once generally accepted link between Tai and Sino-Tibetan languages is correspondingly out of favour: in truth there had never been much evidence for it beyond a number of close word resemblances between Tai languages and Chinese, which Benedict and others would attribute to early borrowing.

The Kadai languages are the least-known of this family. The name was applied by Benedict in 1942 to a group of minority languages of Hainan and southern China, including Li, Kelao and others, with no more than a few hundred speakers apiece.

Benedict calls his family grouping *Austro-Thai*. Some others omit the *h*, because by Western linguists *Thai* is used as the name of the national language of Thailand, *Tai* as that of a linguistic group. In a recent book (**143**) Benedict claims to have found historical links between Japanese, on the one side, and the Austro-Tai grouping which he had previously explored, on the other.

142.

Paul K. Benedict, *Austro-Thai language and culture, with a glossary of roots.*
[New Haven:] HRAF Press, 1975. 490 pp. 0–87536–323–7.
Foreword by Ward H. Goodenough.

The glossary is on pp. 219–427, arranged in alphabetical order of English meanings: it forms a comparative dictionary of the apparently shared element in the vocabulary of these language families. The very lengthy 'Introduction to glossary' includes glossary entries for pronouns, pp. 202–10, and numerals, pp. 211–18. List of language abbreviations (indispensable), pp. xviii–xxiv.

The volume includes (pp. 438–63) a reprint of Benedict's 'Thai, Kadai and Indonesian: a new alignment in south east Asia' first published in *American anthropologist* vol. 44 (1942) pp. 576–601. It thus contains all of Benedict's most seminal work on the Austro-Thai relationship. For up-to-date views on the subject see Peter S. Bellwood, 'Austronesian prehistory in southeast Asia: homeland, expansion and transformation' in *The Austronesians: historical and comparative perspectives* ed. P. Bellwood, J. J. Fox, D. S. Tryon (Canberra: Australian National University, Research School of Pacific and Asian Studies, Department of Anthropology, 1995) pp. 96–111.

143.

Paul K. Benedict, *Japanese/Austro-Tai*. Ann Arbor: Karoma, 1990. 276 pp. 0–89720–078–0.
Linguistica extranea. Studia, 20.

The main feature is a glossary of 'cognate sets' – words or roots apparently shared by Japanese and the Austro-Tai family – arranged in alphabetical order under English meanings on pp. 161–264. There are no indexes.

AVESTAN AND OLD PERSIAN

Avestan is the language of the Zoroastrian scriptures, and is one of the oldest recorded forms of the IRANIAN LANGUAGES – close to, but identifiably different from, Old Persian. It is long extinct as a language of everyday speech, but it is still used in ritual.

Traditionally Avestan has been written in its own script, which is close to that sometimes used for middle Persian (Pehlevi) texts.

Western scholars usually prefer to use a Latin transcription, which has its own very special alphabetical order:

a ā ə e o å a̦ i ᵢy u ᵤv k g x č ĵ t d θ ṭ p b f ŋ ń n m y v r s z š ž h ħ xᵛ

The transcription used for Old Persian is much simpler than this.

144.

Christian Bartholomae, *Altiranisches Wörterbuch*. Strasbourg: Trübner, 1904. 2000 columns.

Followed by: C. Bartholomae, *Zum altiranischen Wörterbuch: Nacharbeiten und Vorarbeiten*. 1906. 287 pp. (*Indogermanische Forschungen*, vol. 19, supplement.)
The main work and supplement were reprinted together as: *Altiranisches Wörterbuch; zusammen mit den Nacharbeiten und Vorarbeiten*. Berlin: De Gruyter, 1979. 1999 columns + 287 pp. 3–11–000104–7.

[*Old Iranian dictionary.*] A concise dictionary of the literature in Avestan and the inscriptions in Old Persian as then known, with German glosses and with numerous brief quotations from the texts, some of which (but not all) are also given in German translation. Entries are preceded by *j.* 'jungAwestisch' (late Avestan); *p.* 'altPersisch' (Old Persian); or *g.* 'gāθisch-Awestisch' (Avestan of the gathas, i.e. of the genuinely ancient stratum of the Avesta). A dotted circle symbol, not explained, seems to me to distinguish attested forms from reconstructed ones. For other symbols see p. xxxii.

Even though it is is entirely in transliteration, this dictionary must have been a printer's and proofreader's nightmare: see the alphabet set out above.

145.

Walther Hinz, *Altpersischer Wortschatz*. Leipzig: Brockhaus, 1942. 160 pp.
Abhandlungen für die Kunde des Morgenlandes, vol. 27 part 1.

[*Old Persian vocabulary.*] A concordance to the words on Old Persian inscriptions with precise references, parsing and German glosses. In transcription (the cuneiform alphabet and its transliteration, pp. 11–16). List of inscriptions, pp. 1–10; bibliography, pp. 17–39.

146.

Kavasji Edalji Kanga, *A complete dictionary of the Avesta language, in Guzerati and English* = કવશજી એદલજી કાંગા, અવસ્ત ભાષાની સંપૂર્ણ ફરҲંગ. Bombay, 1269/1900. 611 pp.
Printed at the Education Society's Steam Press.

Originating in the Parsee community, for which the Avesta is a sacred text, this concise dictionary uses traditional Avestan script. Glosses are in English and Gujarati. There are precise references to the source texts (titles in Avestan script: chapter and section numbers in Gujarati numerals!).

147.

Bernfried Schlerath, *Awesta-Wörterbuch: Vorarbeiten*. Wiesbaden: Harrassowitz, 1968. 2 vols.

[*Avesta dictionary: groundwork.*] A useful supplement to the existing dictionaries. Vol. 1 (264 pp.) is a bibliography, arranged in the order of the Avesta text, of scholarly literature bearing on the text and its vocabulary. Vol. 2 (199 pp.) is a concordance of repetitions and of variants within the canonical texts.

AYMARA

Aymara is an AMERIND language of Bolivia and Peru. It has about two million speakers. Many are bilingual in Quechua (and an increasing number trilingual in Spanish). Aymara and Quechua have interacted for so many centuries that it is uncertain whether the similarities between them result simply from borrowing or from a single origin in a postulated 'proto-Quechumaran' language (see **68**). Hardman-de-Bautista (**148**) is a critical review of dictionaries and lexicographical work on Aymara.

148.
Martha J. Hardman-de-Bautista, 'Aymara lexicography' in Franz Josef Hausmann [and other editors], *Wörterbücher: ein internationales Handbuch zur Lexikographie = Dictionaries: an international encyclopedia of lexicography = Dictionnaires: encyclopédie internationale de lexicographie* (Berlin: De Gruyter, 1989) pp. 2684–90.

149.
Thomas A. Sebeok, 'Materials for an Aymara dictionary' in *Journal de la Société des Américanistes* vol. 40 (1951) pp. 89–151.

AZERI

Azeri is a TURKIC language, closely related to Turkish, its neighbour to the west. There are perhaps fourteen million speakers, nearly half of them in independent Azerbaijan (formerly a Soviet republic), most of the rest in north-western Iran.

The Azeri alphabet

A B C Ç D E Ə F G H X İ I J K L M N O Ö P Q R S Ş T U Ü V Y Z

a b c ç d e ə f g h x i ı j k l m n o ö p q r s ş t u ü v y z

Azeri has been written in Cyrillic and in Arabic scripts. Arabic is still the standard in Iran. In independent Azerbaijan the Latin alphabet has recently been adopted as standard, in a version that differs only slightly from Turkish.

150.
Bihzad Bihzadi, *Farhang-i Azarbayajani–Farsi*. Tehran: Intisharat-i Dunya, 1369 [1990]. 1142 pp.
    [*Azeri–Persian dictionary.*] Reflecting the usage of Persian Azerbaijan.

151.

Г. Гусеинов, *Азербаиджанско–русский словарь* [G. Guseinov, editor,
Azerbaidzhansko–russkii slovar']. Baku, 1939.

[*Azeri–Russian dictionary.*] The Azeri is in the Latin alphabet, as used officially for
Azeri in the USSR between 1923 and 1939.

152.

Ә. Ә. Оручов, *Азәрбаjчан дилинин изаһлы луғати* [A. A. Orujov,
Azarbaijan dilinin izahly lughati] = *Толковый словарь азербаиджанского
языка*. Baku: Azarbaijan SSR Elmlar Akademiiasy Nashriiiaty, 1966– .
Azarbaijan SSR Elmlar Akademiyasy. Nizami adyna Adabiyat va Dil Institutu.

[*Explanatory dictionary of the Azeri language.*] I know of three volumes of this
large-scale monolingual dictionary of Azeri.

153.

М. Т. Тағыев, *Азәрбаjчанjа-русjа луғат* [M. T. Taghyev, chief editor,
Azarbaijania–rusia lughat] = *Азербаиджанско–русский словарь*. Baky: Elm,
1986– .
Azarbaijan SSR Elmlar Akademiyasy.

[*Azeri–Russian dictionary.*] In progress: I know of two volumes.

BACTRIAN

A Middle IRANIAN language, spoken in cities of the Silk Road in the first millennium AD.

154.

G. Djelani Davary, *Baktrisch: ein Wörterbuch auf Grund der Inschriften,
Handschriften, Münzen und Siegelsteine*. Heidelberg: Groos, 1982. 306 pp. 3–
87276–270–2.

[*Bactrian: a dictionary on the basis of inscriptions, manuscripts, coins and seals.*]
The dictionary, pp. 146–303; index of fragmentary words, pp. 304–6. Text of Bactrian
inscriptions with transliteration, pp. 53–144. Alphabet table, p. 52; bibliography, pp. 17–
36. Bactrian script, handwritten, is used throughout.

BAHNAR

A minority AUSTROASIATIC language of Vietnam, with about 85,000 speakers.

155.

Paul Guilleminet, R. P. Jules Alberty, *Dictionnaire bahnar–français*. Paris,
1959–63. Vols 1–2 [pp. 1–991; no more published].
Publications de l'Ecole Française d'Extrême-Orient, 40.

[*Bahnar–French dictionary.*] An ambitious work of which only the alphabetical
section has appeared, in two volumes. It was to have been followed by a classified list of

classifiers, of onomatopoeias etc., of descriptive adjectives, and of pejoratives; then by an illustrated dictionary of technical terms in various fields.

BAI

Bai is a language of Yunnan, in south-western China, known in older literature as *Minchia* or *Pai*. Its family relationship is uncertain because it has been so extensively influenced by neighbouring languages and particularly by Chinese: Bai speakers, numbering nearly a million, are culturally hardly distinguishable from the Chinese of Yunnan. It is most often classed in the Tibeto-Burman branch of SINO-TIBETAN LANGUAGES (**158**), yet Benedict (**142,** p. 135) considers it remotely related to the Austro-Tai family and not Sino-Tibetan at all.

Bai may first occur in historical records as *Pai Man*, one of the two languages of the old kingdom of Nanchao for which there is a word-list in the Chinese historical text *Man Shu* (**157**). There are other word-lists, but no full dictionary as yet.

156.
François Dell, *La langue bai: phonologie et lexique*. Paris: Editions de l'Ecole des Hautes Etudes en Sciences Sociales, 1981. 169 pp. 2–7132–0417–8.
Matériaux pour l'étude de l'Asie moderne et contemporaine. Etudes linguistiques, 2.
[*The Bai language: phonology and vocabulary.*] Bibliography, pp. 143–8.

157.
Giok Po Oey, Gordon H. Luce, translators, *The Man Shu: book of the southern barbarians*. Ithaca: Cornell University, Department of Far Eastern Studies, 1957. 116 pp.
Cornell University, Southeast Asia Program. *Data paper*, 44.

158.
Wen Yu, 'A study of the synonyms in the Min-chia language' in *Studia serica* vol. 1 (1940/41).
Included in the 1949 selective reissue of this volume, on pp. 67–84.
The author's conclusion is that the oldest and fundamental word in each synonym group is of Tibeto-Burman origin. The work is in Chinese, with summary and (1949) addenda in English.

BALINESE

Like nearly all the other languages of Indonesia, Balinese belongs to the family of AUSTRONESIAN LANGUAGES. It has about three million speakers. The civilisation of Bali is highly distinct: it is the easternmost survivor of the chain of high Hindu cultures that once spread across south east Asia and the Malay Archipelago.

The hierarchies of this eastern Hinduism are displayed more clearly in Balinese than in any other language. Balinese has very distinct 'formal' (*basa madia*) and 'informal' (*basa ketah*) registers, which speakers switch between as necessary. *Basa singgih* is the most elevated of all and consists very largely of words borrowed from Javanese. On the registers see Kersten (**161**).

Balinese is traditionally written in a form of the *kawi* alphabet, historically used for Javanese as well: in fact the Hindu literature of Java survived to be rediscovered in modern times in Balinese manuscripts, and van der Tuuk's dictionary (**163**) is a reminder of the long symbiosis between these two neighbouring cultures.

The script is of Indic origin. Only 18 characters are needed for native Balinese words: others are used for Javanese and Sanskrit loanwords.

The modern standard

159.

I Wayan Warna, editor, *Kamus Bali–Indonesia*. Denpasar: Dinas Pengajaran Propinsi Daerah Tingkat I Bali, 1990. 2nd edn.

1st edition by the Panitia Penyusun Kamus Bali–Indonesia: 1978. 651 pp.

[*Balinese–Indonesian dictionary.*] There are 15,000 entries, 30,000 sub-entries, according to Kersten. Not seen.

160.

Kamus Indonesia–Bali. Jakarta: Departemen Penelitian dan Kebudayaan, 1975. 221 pp.

Balai Penelitian Bahasa Singaraja; Pusat Pembinaan dan Pengembangan Bahasa.

[*Indonesian–Balinese dictionary.*] About 20,000 brief entries.

161.

J. Kersten, *Bahasa Bali*. Ende: Nusa Indah, 1984. 646 pp.

The first part is a grammar of Balinese in Indonesian, a revised translation of: J. Kersten, *Balische grammatica*. The Hague, 1948. 102 pp.

[*The Balinese language.*] The larger part of this work, pp. 133–646, is a Balinese–Indonesian dictionary of modern colloquial Balinese, with about 7500 entries. Many fairly long examples are given, with Indonesian translations.

The linguistic registers of Balinese, with a table of words that differ in the various registers, pp. 16–29.

Older periods

162.

C. Clyde Barber, *A Balinese–English dictionary*. Aberdeen: Aberdeen University Library, 1979. 2 vols (809 pp.). 0–9505322–3–1.

Alternate title: *A dictionary of Balinese–English.*

About 32,000 brief entries: photocopied from typescript. A dictionary of the literary language, 'a translation into English and a complete rearrangement of R. van Eck's *Eerste proeve van een Balineesch–Hollandsch woordenboek* (Utrecht, 1876) supplemented from other sources', e.g. van der Tuuk (**163**). Thus based on already-published material, which it renders much more conveniently accessible. No precise definitions are given for flora and fauna. Balinese appears in romanization: 'I have used throughout a mechanical transliteration of the beautiful native script, not the modern roman orthography now often used in Bali.' Note that **ng** and **ny** are treated as single letters, filing between **n** and **o**. The script, vol. 1 pp. vii–ix. Addenda, pp. 782–809.

163.

H. N. van der Tuuk, *Kawi–Balineesch–Nederlandsch woordenboek*. Batavia, 1897–1912. 4 vols.

Uitgegeven ingevolge Gouvernements-Besluit van 14 Februari 1893, no. 3.

[*Old Javanese and Balinese–Dutch dictionary.*] Arranged in the order of the 18 letters of the traditional Balinese alphabet, into which the remaining homophonous letters of the old *kawi* alphabet are simply interfiled. No alphabet table is provided. About 40,000 entries, many very lengthy. Balinese script for headwords, followed by transliteration. This is a dictionary of the traditional bilingual Javanese–Balinese culture of Bali, and largely based on Balinese manuscripts of old and middle Javanese literary texts, to which references are given. List of abbreviations, mostly of sources, on preliminary pages 5–15.

Published after the author's death, van der Tuuk's Javanese and Balinese dictionary is a vast and erudite work – but considered to be seriously flawed as a tool for scholars of either language. Indigenous Balinese words are glossed in Dutch. Javanese words are not: sometimes their traditional Balinese glosses are given, but these are not necessarily acceptable to students of Javanese. See Zoetmulder and Robson (**843**) for further comment.

BALTIC LANGUAGES

A small group of INDO-EUROPEAN LANGUAGES, closely related to the Slavonic group: some consider that the two were at first a single branch, Balto-Slavic, and that is the logic behind the reconstructions in Trautmann's dictionary (**165**). The three Baltic languages are LATVIAN, LITHUANIAN and the extinct OLD PRUSSIAN.

164.

René Lanszweert, *Die Rekonstruktion des baltischen Grundwortschatzes*. Frankfurt am Main: Lang, 1984. 188 pp. 3–8204–7927–9.

Europäische Hochschulschriften. Reihe 16, Slawische Sprachen und Literaturen, 30.

[*Reconstruction of the basic Baltic vocabulary.*] In alphabetical order of English meanings, pp. 1–180. Entries give full citations of the scholarly literature (bibliography, pp. 181–8). There is no index of cited forms in Lithuanian, Latvian or other languages.

165.

Reinhold Trautmann, *Baltisch-Slavisches Wörterbuch*. Göttingen: Vandenhoeck & Ruprecht, 1923. 382 pp.

Göttinger Sammlung indogermanischer Grammatiken und Wörterbücher.

Reprinted 1970.

[*Balto-Slavic dictionary.*] In German in Fraktur type (but linguistic forms in italic). Headwords, marked with ⊙, are reconstructed proto-Balto-Slavic forms (note that not all would now agree that a unitary Balto-Slavic stage existed). These are followed in this order by Baltic, Slavonic and other Indo-European cognates. Bibliography, pp. 377–82. There is no list of abbreviations of language names: note *li.* Lithuanian; *oftli.* East Lithuanian; *le.* Latvian; *akfl.* Old Church Slavonic; *fkr.* Serbo-Croat; *ai.* 'Old Indian', i.e. Sanskrit.

BALUCHI

Baluchi, one of the modern IRANIAN LANGUAGES, has about four million speakers. It is a regional language of south-western Pakistan and south-eastern Iran, and also one of the 'national languages' of Afghanistan. It has coexisted for many centuries with a Dravidian language, BRAHUI, and the two quite unrelated languages have influenced one another extensively.

166.

Wilhelm Geiger, *Etymologie des Balūčī.* München: Verlag der K. Akademie, 1891. 49 pp.

[*Etymology of Baluchi.*]

BARE'E

Bare'e or Pamona is an AUSTRONESIAN language of central Celebes. There are about 100,000 speakers.

167.

N. Adriani, *Bare'e woordenboek met Nederlandsch–Bare'e register.* Leiden: Brill, 1928. 1074 pp.
Bataviaasch Genootschap van Kunsten en Wetenschappen.

[*Bare'e–Dutch dictionary with Dutch–Bare'e index.*] Lengthy entries, with some etymological notes on cognates in related languages. Addenda, pp. 985–94; Dutch–Bare'e section, pp. 995–1074.

BASHKIR

Bashkir is a TURKIC language, spoken by a population of about a million Muslims most of whom live in the self-governing republic of Bashkortostan in European Russia, in the western valleys of the Urals.

Bashkir alphabetical order

а б г д ҙ ж з и й к ҡ л м н ң о ө п р с ҫ т у ф х һ ш ы э ә

168.

Словарь башкирского языка [*Slovar' bashkirskogo yazyka*] = *Bashqort teleneng huthlege.* Moscow: Russkii Yazyk, 1993. 2 vols. 5–20–001089–6.
Edited by Biishev A. Gh. and others. Rossiia Fandar Akademiiahy, Ural Bulege. Bashqortostan Ghilmi Uthage, Tarikh Tel ham Athabiat Instituty.

[*Dictionary of the Bashkir language.*] A monolingual dictionary of modern usage.

169.

К. З. Ахмеров, *Русско–башкирский словарь* [*K. Z. Akhmerov, Russko–bashkirskii slovar'*]. Moscow, 1964. 985 pp.
Edited by N. K. Dmitriev.
Earlier version: N. K. Dmitriev, K. Z. Akhmerov, J. G. Baishev, *Russko–bashkirskii slovar'*. 1948. 958 pp.

[*Russian–Bashkir dictionary.*]

170.

Z. G. Uraqsin, editor, *Bashqortsa–russa huthlek* = *Башкирско-русский словарь*. Moscow: Russkii Yazyk, 1996. 863 pp. 5–20–002354–8.
Rossiia Fandar Akademiiahy, Ofo Ghilmi Uthage. Bashqortostan Fandar Akademiiahy, Gumanitar Fandar Bulege, Tarikh Tel ham Athabiat Instituty.

[*Bashkir–Russian dictionary.*] 32,000 entries.

BASQUE

Unique among the languages of Europe, Basque has no known relatives. Now spoken by about 700,000 people in northern Spain and south-western France, Basque was one of the earliest European languages to cross the Atlantic: French explorers found that the Amerindians of the St Lawrence River already knew the language, which they had learnt from adventurous Basque fishing crews. Basque has been the focus of research since the sixteenth century.

171.

Manuel Agud, Antonio Tovar, *Diccionario etimológico vasco*. San Sebastián: Diputación Foral de Guipúzcoa, 1989– .
Anejos del Anuario del Seminario de Filología Vasca "Julio de Urquijo".

[*Basque etymological dictionary.*] This extensive etymological dictionary will be complete in about twelve volumes.

172.

Gorka Aulestia, *Basque–English dictionary*. Reno: University of Nevada Press, 1989. a108 + 558 pp. 0–87417–126–1.
The Basque series.

A comprehensive brief-entry dictionary, including some example sentences which are drawn from a corpus (see pp. a102–a106) but are not individually attributed. Dialect origin is indicated: *C* Common, *U* Unified Basque, *G* Guipuzcoa, *B* Biscayan, *L* Labourdin, *LN* Low Navarrese, *Z* Souletin (Zuberoan). Unified Basque or *Euskera Batua* is a twentieth century development.

173.

Gorka Aulestia, Linda White, *English–Basque dictionary*. Reno: University of Nevada Press, 1990. 397 pp. 0–87417–156–3.

The Basque series.

Similar to its companion but with no example sentences. The indications of dialect origin remain.

174.

R. Ma. de Azkue, *Diccionario vasco–español–francés*. Bilbao: Gran Enciclopedia Vasca, 1969. 2 vols. New edn.

1st edn: Bilbao, 1905–6. 2 vols. – Reprint of the 1st edn, with an introduction by Luis Michelena: Bilbao: Euskaltzaindia, 1984. 1219 pp. 84–85479–27–0.

Abridged version: Arbelaitz, *Diccionario castellano–vasco y vasco–castellano de voces comunes a dos o más dialectos, extraído del diccionario mayor de R. Ma. de Azcue y con su autorización*. Bilbao: Gran Enciclopedia Vasca [1978?]. 357 pp. 84–24–80758–8.

[*Basque–Spanish–French dictionary.*] A major dictionary in its time, with glosses in Spanish and French. Includes quotations, with precise references (list of sources, vol. 1 pp. ix–xiii), and indication of dialect variation (abbreviations for dialects, vol. 1 pp. v–vi.).

The 1969 reprint includes a supplement of new entries, much briefer than those in the main part, vol. 2 pp. 491–590.

175.

Martin Löpelmann, *Etymologisches Wörterbuch der baskischen Sprache: Dialekte von Labourd, Nieder-Navarra und La Soule*. Berlin: De Gruyter, 1968. 2 vols [1356 pp.].

[*Etymological dictionary of the Basque language: Labourdin, Lower Navarre and La Soule dialects.*] A remarkably comprehensive dictionary with over 30,000 concise entries. The text is reproduced from typescript. There are 4 loose pages of corrections.

176.

Luis Michelena, *Diccionario general vasco = Orotariko euskal hiztegia*. Bilbao: Real Academia de la Lengua Vasca, 1987– . 84–27–11493–X.

[*General Basque dictionary.*] At least eight volumes have appeared of this large-scale modern dictionary of Basque.

177.

Plácido Múgica Berrondo, *Diccionario vasco–castellano*. Bilbao: Mensajero [1981?]. 2 vols. 84–27–11269–6.

[*Basque–Spanish dictionary.*] A comprehensive current bilingual dictionary of Basque.

BATAK LANGUAGES

This group of closely related AUSTRONESIAN LANGUAGES has well over three million speakers in the highlands of central Sumatra, in Indonesia. The Batak group consists of seven main languages or dialects: Alas, Karo Batak (600,000 speakers), Dairi or Pakpak, Simalungun, Toba Batak (2,000,000 speakers), Angkola and Mandailing (together 750,000 speakers).

The indigenous Batak culture was literate, with an unusual angular alphabet of Indic origin: this is still used in magical and ceremonial contexts. Otherwise Batak is now written in the Latin alphabet, like Indonesian.

178.

H. J. Eggink, *Angkola- en Mandailing-Bataksch–Nederlandsch woordenboek*. Bandung: Nix, 1936. 260 pp.

Verhandelingen van het Koninklijk Bataviaasch Genootschap van Kunsten en Wetenschappen, vol. 72 part 5.

[*Batak (Angkola and Mandailing)–Dutch dictionary.*] Lengthy entries, with idioms and other examples.

179.

M. Joustra, *Karo-Bataksch woordenboek*. Leiden: Brill, 1907. 244 pp.

[*Karo Batak dictionary.*] Batak script followed by Latin transliteration and Dutch gloss.

180.

J. H. Neumann, *Kamus bahasa Karo-Batak–Belanda = Karo-Bataks– Nederlands woordenboek*. Medan: Varekamp, 1951. 343 pp.

Lembaga Kebudajaan Indonesia. Koninklijk Bataviaasch Genootschap van Kunsten en Wetenschappen.

[*Karo Batak–Dutch dictionary.*] Latin alphabet only. Compact and informative, with numerous examples. Gives taxonomic names in glosses for plants and animals.

Described as a revision of Joustra (**179**).

181.

Tindi Radja Manik, *Kamus bahasa Dairi Pakpak–Indonesia*. Jakarta: Pusat Pembinaan dan Pengembangan Bahasa, Departemen Pendidikan dan Kebudayaan, 1977. 333 pp.

[*Dairi Pakpak–Indonesian dictionary.*] Much fuller than most other dictionaries in this series. Typically, long entries are given in which various meanings are illustrated and references cited (including van der Tuuk's dictionary, **182**, and numerous manuscript texts). In spite of its brevity, this is a true historical dictionary.

182.

H. N. van der Tuuk, *Bataksch–Nederduitsch woordenboek*. Amsterdam: Muller, 1861. 551 pp.

[*Batak–Dutch dictionary.*] A dictionary of Toba Batak with frequent reference to the other related languages. Batak script is used for headwords and in examples throughout. With 30 beautiful colour plates illustrating technical terminology.

183.

Joh. Warneck, *Toba-Batak–Deutsches Wörterbuch, mit einem Register Deutsch–Batak*. The Hague: Nijhoff, 1977. 332 pp. 90–247–2018–4.

New edition with additions by Joh. Winkler; edited by R. Roolvink. The index is by K. A. Adelaar.
1st edn: 1906.

[*Toba Batak–German dictionary, with a German–Batak index.*] Latin alphabet. Arranged under roots: in this language of complex affixation some forms may be difficult to find. For words recognisable as loanwords a brief etymology is given. The German–Batak index is on pp. 291–332.

BELORUSSIAN

One of the less-known SLAVONIC LANGUAGES, Belorussian is the national language of Belarus, formerly a Soviet republic and now an independent state. There are about 7,500,000 speakers. Until Soviet times Belorussian or 'White Russian' was considered nothing more than a local dialect of Russian. Even now many Belorussians regard Russian as their main language.

The Belorussian version of the Cyrillic alphabet is easily recognisable. It uses I i (in place of Russian И и) for *i* and Ў ў for *w*. Until the early twentieth century, under Polish influence, some Catholic Belorussians wrote their language in the Latin alphabet.

184.

К. К. Атраховіч (Кандрат Крапіва), *Беларуска-рускі слоўнік* [K. K. Atrakhovich (Kandrat Krapiva), *Belaruska–ruski slounik*] =
К. К. Атрахович (Кондрат Крапива), *Белорусско-русский словарь*. Minsk: Vydavetstva Belaruskaya Savetskaya Entsyklapedyya, 1988–9. 2 vols.

Earlier edn, under pseudonym of Kandrat Krapiva: 1962. 1048 pp.

On the author, a major figure in Belorussian literature, see Yanka Kazeka, *Kandrat Krapiva: krytyka-biyagrafichny narys*. Minsk, 1965. 166 pp.

[*Belorussian–Russian dictionary.*] A bilingual dictionary into Belorussian, the largest available.

185.

Этымалагічны слоўнік беларускай мовы [*Etymalahichny slounik belaruskai movy*]. Minsk: Navuka i Tekhnika, 1976– .

[*Etymological dictionary of the Belorussian language.*] Not seen: cited from *Walford's guide to reference material* vol. 3 (6th edn: London: Library Association Publishing, 1995). Six volumes had appeared up to 1990.

186.

Тлумачальны слоўнік беларускай мовы [*Tlumachal'ny slounik belaruskai movy*]. Minsk: Galounaya Redaktsyya Belaruskai Sovetskai Entsyklapedyi, 1977–84. 5 vols.

[*Explanatory dictionary of the Belorussian language.*] A large-scale dictionary of modern Belorussian which gives plenty of attributed quotations from literature (list of works cited, vol. 1 pp. 14–24) but no precise references.

BEMBA

One of the Bantu languages of the NIGER-CONGO family, Bemba has nearly two million speakers in Zaire and Zambia. It is the main lingua franca of the Zambian Copperbelt.

187.

The White Fathers' Bemba–English dictionary. [Lusaka:] White Fathers, 1991. 829 pp. [New edn.]

1st edn: *Bemba–English dictionary*. Chilubula : White Fathers, 1947. 1505 pp.
2nd edn: *The White Fathers' Bemba–English dictionary*. London: Longmans, Green, 1954. 829 pp. Published for Northern Rhodesia and Nyasaland Joint Publications Bureau.

BENGALI

One of the most important INDO-ARYAN LANGUAGES, Bengali has about 110 million speakers in mainly Muslim Bangladesh and over 50 million in mainly Hindu West Bengal, one of the states of India. There is also a worldwide Bengali diaspora. The total number of speakers is at least 180 million.

The small selection of dictionaries listed here includes two dialect dictionaries, covering West Bengal and Bangladesh (**193, 194**), Sukumar Sen's classic etymological dictionary (**195**), and modern Bengali–English dictionaries from both Bangladesh and West Bengal. For older dictionaries see the 'Bibliography of Bengali dictionaries, 1743–1867' by Bhattacharya (**196**).

Bengali script

অ আ ই ঈ উ ঊ এ ঐ ও ঔ

a ā i ī u ū e ai o au

ক খ গ য ঙ চ ছ জ ঝ ঞ টঠ ড ঢ ণ ত থ দ ধ ন প ফ ব ভ ম য র ল শ ষ স হ

k kh g gh ṅ c ch j jh ñ ṭ ṭh ḍ ḍh ṇ t th d dh n p ph b bh m y r l ś ṣ s h

The Bengali alphabet is one of the local developments of India's early Brahmi. Like the others, it has numerous conjunct characters for doubled and adjacent consonants. When this alphabet is used for Sanskrit texts, the symbol ব serves for both *b* and *v*.

Historical dictionaries

188.

হরিচরণ বন্দ্যোপাধ্যায়, *বঙ্গীয় শব্দকোষ* [Haricaran Bandyopadhyay, *Bangiy sabdakos*]. New Delhi, 1969. 2435 pp. New edn?

1st edn: Calcutta, 1933–44. 105 parts [3276 pp.].

[*Bengali dictionary.*] A concise monolingual historical dictionary with many brief quotations from literary sources.

The modern standard

189.

Mohammad Ali, Mohammad Moniruzzaman, Jahangir Tareque, editors, *Bangla Academy Bengali–English dictionary*. Dacca: Bangla Academy, 1994. 878 pp. 984–0–73140–8.

Compilers: Latifur Rahman, Jahangir Tareque.

A bilingual dictionary based on the Bangladesh standard.

190.

Sailendra Biswas, *Samsad English–Bengali dictionary*. Calcutta: Sahitya Samsad, 1980. 1354 pp. 5th edn by Birendramohan Dasgupta.

1st edn: 1959. – Successively revised by Subodhchandra Sengupta, Sudhangshukumar Sengupta.

Intended for Bengali-speaking users, this dictionary gives a generous allowance of synonymous glosses followed by a brief etymology of the English word. Meanings are arranged historically rather than by frequency of use.

191.

জ্ঞানেন্দ্রমোহন দাস, *বাঙ্গালা ভাষার অভিধান* [Jñanendramohan Das, *Bangala bhasar abhidhan*]. Calcutta: Sahitya Samsad, 1979. 2 vols [2318 pp.]. New edn.

1st edn: Allahabad, 1323 [1916]. 1577 pp. Alternate title: *Dictionary of the Bengali language, pronouncing, etymological and explanatory with appendices*. – 2nd edn: 1937.

[*Dictionary of the Bengali language.*] The classic monolingual dictionary of Bengali, with brief etymological notes in brackets. Taxonomic names in scientific Latin for flora and fauna.

Older periods

192.

Sir Graves Champney Haughton, *A dictionary, Bengálí and Sanskrit, adapted for students of either language, to which is added an index, serving as a reversed dictionary*. London: Parbury, Allen & Co., 1833. 2 vols [2851 columns or pages].

Reprint: *A dictionary, Bengali–Sanskrit–English*. Delhi: Caxton Publications, 1987. 81–85066–00–0.

The most useful of the older Bengali–English dictionaries, important for the classical language of literature.

Regional forms

193.

Asitkumar Bandyopadhyay, chief editor, *Añcalik Bamla bhasar abhidhan* = *Dictionary of dialectal Bengali language*. Calcutta: Kalikata Bisvabidyalaya, 1991– .

A large-scale dictionary of which vol. 1 covers the first three letters of the Bengali alphabet, **A–I**.

194.

Purva Pakistani añcalik bhasa abhidhan. Dacca: Bangla Academy.

[*Dictionary of the dialects of East Pakistan.*] Not seen.

Etymological dictionaries

195.

Sukumar Sen, *An etymological dictionary of Bengali, c. 1000–1800 A.D.*
Calcutta, Eastern Publishers [1971]. 2 vols [968 pp.].

Entirely in Latin transliteration, but in Indic alphabetical order. The first date refers to the *Caryapada* poems, of uncertain date but certainly preceding 1100: Sen had edited these important texts.

Frequently used abbreviations include *Td.* 'tadbhava', *Ts.* 'tatsama'. Few if any of the words treated here are loans from Sino-Tibetan languages, and relatively few from Arabic or Persian.

Other works of interest

196.

Jatindra Mohan Bhattacharya, *Bangla abhidhan granthur paricay, 1743–1867*.
Calcutta: University of Calcutta, 1970.

BERBER LANGUAGES

This important branch of the AFROASIATIC LANGUAGES is to be found north and south of the Sahara. Berber languages are not spoken by a majority in any country, and are now overshadowed by Arabic, French and others. They extend from northern Mauritania to the oases of western Egypt.

Berber languages include Tamashek (Tuareg), with a million speakers in Niger, Mali and other countries; Kabyle with up to two million speakers in Algeria; Rifia, with up to two million speakers, Algeria and Morocco; Tamazight and Tashelhet, sometimes known as Shluh or Chleuh, with several million speakers in Morocco.

197.

Ghubayd agg-Alawjeli, *Awgalel temajeq–tefrensist* = Ghoubeïd Alojaly, *Lexique touareg–français*. København: Akademisk Forlag, 1980. 284 pp. 87–500–1988–0.

Edited with introduction and morphological tables by Karl-G. Prasse.

> [*Tuareg–French dictionary.*]

198.

Charles-Eugène Foucauld, *Dictionnaire touareg–français*. [Paris:] Imprimerie Nationale de France, 1951–2. 4 vols.

> [*Tuareg–French dictionary.*] The largest available dictionary of any Berber language.

199.

E. Ibañez, *Diccionario rifeño–español*. Madrid: Instituto de Estudios Africanos, 1949.

> [*Rifia–Spanish dictionary.*] With grammatical notes and extensive bibliography.

200.

Hugo Schuchardt, *Die romanische Lehnwörter im Berberischen*. Vienna, 1918. 82 pp.

Sitzungsberichte der Kais. Akademie der Wissenschaften in Wien, philosophisch-historische Klasse, vol. 188 part 4.

On the author, an important figure in the study of language mixture and creoles, see: Klaus Lichem, Hans Joachim Simon, editors, *Hugo Schuchardt, Gotha 1842–Graz 1927: Schuchardt-Symposium 1977 in Graz: Vorträge und Aufsätze*. Vienna: Österreichische Akademie der Wissenschaften, 1980. 314 pp. (*Sitzungsberichte, philosophisch-historische Klasse*, 373. *Veröffentlichungen der Kommission für Linguistik und Kommunikationsforschung*, 10.)

> [*The Romance loanwords in Berber.*]

201.

Miloud Taïfi, *Dictionnaire tamazight–français: parlers du Maroc central*. Paris: L'Harmattan-Awal, 1992. 879 pp.

> [*Tamazight–French dictionary: dialects of central Morocco.*]

BIKOL

Bikol has three million speakers in the Philippine provinces of southern Luzon – a region unofficially referred to as *Bicolandia*. Bikol is closely related to Tagalog, the *de facto* national language, whose homeland is just to the north. Like all other Philippine languages except English and Spanish, Bikol belongs to the AUSTRONESIAN language family.

202.

Malcolm Warren Mintz, José del Rosario Britanico, *Bikol–English dictionary = Diksionáriong Bíkol–Inglés*. Quezon City: New Day, 1985. 555 pp. 971–10–0212–4.

Earlier version: *Bikol dictionary*. Honolulu: University of Hawaii Press, 1971. 1012 pp. 0–87022–528–6. (*PALI language texts: Philippines.*)

Indicates origin of loanwords from European and Chinese languages. Includes an English–Bikol section, pp. 57–212. Bikol dialects, p. 3; sound system and grammar, pp. 4–46.

BODO

Bodo, one of the SINO-TIBETAN LANGUAGES, has about a million speakers in northern Assam, where it is the focus of a separatist movement.

203.

Moniram Mochari, editor, *Bodo–English dictionary*. N.p.: Bodo Catholic Youth Association, 1985. 510 pp.

BRAHUI

Brahui, a major language of western Pakistan, is an astonishing survival – utterly different from the Iranian languages that surround it. There is no doubt that Brahui belongs to the family of DRAVIDIAN LANGUAGES of south India, though it is separated from the nearest of them by many hundreds of miles.

The speakers of Brahui and Baluchi have long lived side by side. Brahui is heavily influenced by Baluchi and by Sindhi, languages in which many Brahui speakers are necessarily bilingual. Literacy is normally in one or other of these two languages: there is no tradition of written literature in Brahui.

204.

Denys De S. Bray, *The Brahui language*. Calcutta, Delhi, 1909–34. 2 vols.
The second volume, published by the Manager of Publications, Delhi, contained parts 2 and 3.

Part 1, Introduction and grammar; part 2, The Brahui problem; part 3, Etymological vocabulary.

'The major description of the language, superseding all earlier work ... Bray, of the Indian Civil Service, had been stationed as political officer in the Khanate of Kalat for four years ... The vocabulary [gives] copious examples of usage and etymologies of all words for which Bray could find them (Dravidian, Iranian, Indo-Aryan). For this volume Bray had gone through all the previous records of the language and had taken account of everything recorded' (M. B. Emeneau, 'Brahui language studies' in his *Language and linguistic area*, Stanford: Stanford University Press, 1980, p. 316). For a much more critical assessment of Bray's etymological work see Rossi (**205**), pp. ix–xiii.

205.

Adriano V. Rossi, *Iranian lexical elements in Brāhūī*. Naples, 1979. 360 pp.
Istituto Universitario Orientale, Seminario di Studi Asiatici. *Series minor*, 8.

'Some fifty copies of the typescript in its "prehistoric" Italian redaction had been circulated among scholars', according to the preface.

This work serves as an etymological supplement to Bray (**204**). It consists of a series of lists followed by an alphabetical Brahui index (pp. 341–360). Since there is no table of contents, the lists are summarised here: A, p. 3, words borrowed from Baluchi; B, p. 61, with uncertain Baluchi etymologies; C, p. 81, from other Iranian languages; D, p. 85, unclear whether from Baluchi or other Iranian languages; E, p. 91, words shared with Baluchi or other languages where the direction of borrowing is uncertain; F, p. 119, not attested in other Iranian languages but possibly borrowed from them; G, p. 153, falsely thought to be borrowed from Iranian languages; H, p. 158, unclear whether from Persian or Baluchi or from non-Iranian languages; I, p. 297, unclear whether from Baluchi or from Indo-Aryan languages.

BRETON

Breton is the CELTIC language of north-western France. It has half a million speakers.

Historical dictionaries

206.

Roparz Hemon, *Geriadur istorel ar brezhoneg* = *Dictionaire historique du breton.* Quimper, Plomelin: Preder, 1979– . 2nd edn.

1st edn: 1958–79. 36 parts.

[*Historical dictionary of Breton.*] The revised edition of this major historical dictionary has now reached part 31 and page 1984, covering **A–Mouch**. Entries have a brief French gloss followed by a generous selection of quotations from sources. Quotations are not fully translated, but sometimes additional glosses are added to help the reader. Bibliography of sources, pp. 19–30.

The modern standard

207.

Remon Ar Porzh, *Geriadur brezhoneg–saozneg gant skouerioù* = Raymond Delaporte, *Breton–English dictionary with examples.* [Lesneven:] Mouladuriwhere Hor Yezh, 1986– .

I have seen three volumes, covering the letters **A–G**.

208.

Francis Favereau, *Dictionnaire du breton contemporain* = *Geriadur ar brezhoneg a-vremañ.* Morlaix: Skol Vreizh, 1993. 1357 pp. 2–903313–65–2.

[*Dictionary of contemporary Breton.*] A brief-entry two-way dictionary of French and Breton. Breton pronunciation is given in the International Phonetic Alphabet. Important for its numerous indications of dialect variation (list of dialects, p. xi) and for its attributions to sources (though not usually with precise references: list of sources, p. xv). Many spelling and pronunciation varieties are given, with cross-references, but the treatment of pronunciation variants under headwords is sometimes so abridged as to be confusing.

209.

Roparz Hemon, *Geriadur brezhoneg gant skoueriù ha skeudennoù.* Kergleuz: An Here, 1995. 1232 pp. 2–86843–152–6.

[*Breton dictionary with examples and illustrations.*] A concise, fervently monolingual dictionary, with a generous number of brief examples but not attributed quotations. Taxonomic names for flora and fauna are easy to pick out in a sans-serif italic font. Breton pronunciation is given in the International Phonetic Alphabet.

Hemon's first Breton–French dictionary was published as long ago as 1943.

210.

F. Vallée, *Grand dictionnaire français–breton, suivi du 'Supplément'*. Glomel: Association Bretonne de Culture, 1980. 814 +176 pp.

Combined reprint of the first edition: Rennes, 1931, and the supplement: La Baule, 1948.

[*Big French–Breton dictionary with supplement.*] The supplement drew further on oral sources and redressed a previous neglect of materials from the Vannetais dialect. Relatively brief entries, but with some citations of sources and some indications of dialect variation, especially in the supplement.

Older periods

211.

Emile Ernault, *Glossaire moyen breton*. Paris: Bouillon, 1895–6. 2 vols. 2nd edn.

H. Arbois de Jubainville, *Etudes grammaticales des langues celtiques*, vol. 2.

Reprinted: Marseille: Laffitte Reprints, 1976. 2 vols in 1 [833 pp.].

The first edition appeared as part of Ernault's edition of *Le mystère de Sainte Barbe* (Nantes: Société des Bibliophiles Bretons, 1885–7. *Archives de Bretagne*, 3).

[*Middle Breton glossary.*]

212.

Claude Evans, Léon Fleuriot, *A dictionary of Old Breton, historical and comparative, in two parts = Dictionnaire du vieux breton*. Toronto: Prepcorp, 1985. 2 vols [574 pp.]. 0–9692225–0–5.

Vol. 1 was first published as: Léon Fleuriot, *Dictionnaire des gloses en vieux breton*. Paris: Klincksieck, 1964. 372 pp.

A detailed, discursive explanatory dictionary of the glosses in old Breton manuscripts, some of which take a good deal of explaining. Full references to sources are given, and cognates in other Celtic languages are cited. Indexes in each Celtic language, pp. 341–72. Vol. 2, the new part, repeats the headwords of vol. 1 and gives a suggested phonemic rendering, French translation, English translation, references to further literature, afterthoughts and cross-references. In vol. 2 a new set of abbreviations is used, this time English-based, including one rather startling change: 'Old Welsh forms', formerly abridged as *f.v.g.* (*forme vieille galloise*) in vol. 1, have now been appropriated as *obr2* ('Old Breton 2'). On this detail see vol. 1 pp. 13–16 and vol. 2 preliminary pages 1–2.

Etymological dictionaries

213.

Christian J. Guyonvarc'h, *Dictionnaire étymologique du breton ancien, moyen et moderne: origine et histoire des mots*. Rennes: Ogam-Celticum, 1973– .
Celticum, 27– . *Ogam–Tradition celtique*, supplement.

[*Etymological dictionary of old, middle and modern Breton: word origins and history.*] I have only seen parts 1–6, **A–Amleal**, of this potentially important large-scale etymological dictionary: there may have been more, since the libraries I have used have had difficulty getting books from this publisher. Entries include full discussion of changes of form and meaning, with references to printed and manuscript sources. Part 1 is the introduction, including a list of Breton dictionaries, pp. 22*–24*.

214.

Victor Henry, *Lexique étymologique des termes les plus usuels du breton moderne*. Rennes: Plihon & Hervé, 1900[–1903]. 350 pp.
Bibliothèque bretonne armoricaine, 3. Issued as a supplement to *Annales de Bretagne* vols 15–18 (1900–1903).

[*Etymological dictionary of the commonest words of modern Breton.*]

BUGIS

Bugis or Buginese has about three million speakers in the southern peninsula of the spider-like island of Sulawesi (Celebes) in Indonesia. It belongs to the AUSTRONESIAN language family.

Bugis script: the 19 characters

ka ga nga nka pa ba ma mpa ta da na nra ya ra la wa sa a ha

Like neighbouring Makasar, Bugis has traditionally been written in Lontara script, derived from the ancient Brahmi alphabet of India.

FONT: BUGISA BY ANDI MALLARANGENG AND JIM HENRY

215.

B. F. Matthes, *Boegineesch–Hollandsch woordenboek met Hollandsch–Boeginesche woordenlijst*. The Hague: Nijhoff, 1874. 1180 pp.

[*Bugis–Dutch dictionary with Dutch–Bugis glossary.*] A large-scale historical dictionary: script followed by romanisation in the main sequence. In the Dutch–Bugis section, pp. 914–1120, the script alone is given. List of boat terms, pp. 1159–69.

BULGARIAN

One of the SLAVONIC LANGUAGES, Bulgarian forms part of a dialect continuum that also includes Macedonian and the eastern Serbian dialects. With 8,500,000 speakers, it is the national language of Bulgaria and is spoken by substantial minorities in Ukraine and Moldova.

Gerov's classic dictionary (**216**) is now being replaced, as far as modern Bulgarian is concerned, by a new work edited by Cholakova and others (**217**). A big etymological dictionary (**220**) is still in progress: it was begun by V. Georgiev, a historical linguist well known internationally.

The Bulgarian alphabet

АБВГДЕЖЗИЙКЛМНОПРСТУФХЦЧШЩЪЬЮЯ

а б в г е ж з и й к л м н о п р с т у ф х ц ч ш щ ъ ь ю я

a b v g d e zh z i y k l m n o p r s t u f kh ts ch sh sht ă ' yu ya

Historical dictionaries

216.

Найден Геров, *Речник на българския език* [Naiden Gerov, *Rechnik na bălgarskiya ezik*]. Sofiya: Bălgarski Pisatel, 1975–8. 6 vols.

First published: Найденъ Геровъ, *Рѣчникъ на българскій языкъ*. Plovdiv: Săglasie, 1895–1904. 5 vols. – Preliminary version: *Блъгарскій рѣчникъ*. St Petersburg, 1856. Vol. 1 [127 pp.].

[*Dictionary of the Bulgarian language.*] A monolingual dictionary of usage, in the older form of the Cyrillic script, with a few attributed quotations from literature, especially from poetry, but no precise references. Taxonomic names for flora and fauna are in Latin italics.

The 1856 edition covered only the first three letters of the alphabet. The 1975–8 edition is a reprint of that of 1895–1904, but with a new sixth volume, a supplement of 336 pages: in this, all entries are supported by precise references to texts.

217.

Речник на българския език [Rechnik na bălgarskiya ezik]. Sofiya: Izdatelstvo na Bălgarskata Akademiya na Naukite, 1977– .

Edited by Kristalina Cholakova and others. Bălgarska Akademiya na Naukite, Institut za Bălgarski Ezik.

[*Dictionary of the Bulgarian language.*] So far eight volumes have appeared, covering **A–L**, of this major dictionary of modern Bulgarian in which each entry gets a brief gloss followed by several lengthy quotations. For loanwords only, a line in small type at the end of the entry gives the etymology – users unfamiliar with Cyrillic script should remember that the frequently occurring *Typ.* is to be read 'Turkish'.

The modern standard

218.

Английско—български речник [Angliisko-bălgarski rechnik] = *English–Bulgarian dictionary*. N.p.: Elpis, 1996. 1279 pp.

Edited by Diana Batsova and others.

Claiming 90,000 entries, this is the biggest and newest English–Bulgarian dictionary, with very poor paper and binding.

219.

Т. Атанасова, *Българско—английски речник* [*Bălgarsko-angliiski rechnik*] = T. Atanassova [and others], *Bulgarian–English dictionary*. Sofiya: Izdatelstvo Nauka i Izkustvo, 1990. 2 vols.

Earlier edition: 1988.
Shorter version: 1975. 1021 pp. Reprinted with addenda: 1980. 1050 pp. Reprinted: 1983.

Etymological dictionaries

220.

Вл. Георгиев, *Български етимологичен речник* [V. Georgiev and other editors, *Bălgarski etimologichen rechnik*]. Sofiya: Izdatelstvo na Bălgarskata Akademiya na Naukite, 1962– .

[*Bulgarian etymological dictionary.*] Five volumes have so far appeared of this large-scale etymological dictionary, covering **А–Пускам**. Citations of other etymological dictionaries and of Bulgarian source materials, with discussions of word history in Bulgarian and in related languages. Two more volumes are to be expected. The current editor is Ivan Duridanov.

221.

Стефан Младенов, *Етимологически и правописен речник на българския книжовен език* [Stefan Mladenov, *Etimologicheski i pravopisen rechnik na bălgarskiya knizhoven ezik*]. Sofiya: Danov, 1941. 704 pp.

[*Etymological and historical dictionary of the Bulgarian literary language.*]

Foreign words

222.

Alf Grannes, *Turco-Bulgarica: articles in English and French concerning Turkish influence on Bulgarian*. Wiesbaden: Harrassowitz, 1996. 320 pp. 3–447–03819–5.

Contains a series of glossaries of Turkish loanwords in Bulgarian, classified by source and type.

BURMESE

One of a recognised Burmese-Lolo group of SINO-TIBETAN LANGUAGES, Burmese is the national language of Burma and the predominant language in coastal and central Burma, where, about a thousand years ago, it replaced the little-known Pyu language and began to supplant Mon. There are over twenty million speakers.

Apart from the Burmese–English dictionary by Judson (**225**), there is a more modern alternative listed at PALI (**1177**).

Burma and *Burmese* are English approximations to the colloquial Burmese name for the speakers, their country and their language, which is *Bamā*. The stress falls on the final long *ā*, hence the old-fashioned English rendering *Burmah*. In Burmese formal speech and writing *Myanmā*, not *Bamā*, is correct. *Myanmar*, the form at present encouraged in English and French, is a misspelling of this formal and official name.

The Burmese alphabet

Burmese script is Indian in origin. Its rounded shapes are well-adapted for writing with a stylus on palm leaves: straight strokes would split the leaf. Latin transliterations of Burmese vary greatly (see **231**).

The thirty-three characters

က ခ ဂ ဃ င စ ဆ ဇ ဈ ဉ ဋ ဌ ဍ ဎ ဏ တ ထ ဒ ဓ န ပ ဖ ဗ ဘ မ ယ ရ လ ဝ သ ဟ ဠ အ

k kh g gh ng c ch z zh ny ṭ ṭh ḍ ḍh ṇ t th d dh n p ph b bh m y y l w th h ḷ a

The thirty-three characters are given in dictionary order (but some dictionaries begin with the vowel character, အ: more information at **223**).

The twelve vowels shown with က k

က ကာ ကိ ကီ ကု ကူ ကေ ကဲ ကော ကို ကား ကံ

ka kā ki kī ku kū kè ké kò kó ka: kã

There are many more than twelve possible vowel-tone combinations with each character – but these are the twelve that schoolchildren chant as they learn to read and write, beginning with *k* as given here and running through each character in turn. The same vowel combinations, with each character in turn, are used in numbering manuscript pages from 1 to 396.

FONT: *SUU KYI BURMA* BY SOE PYNE

Historical dictionaries

223.

J. A. Stewart, C. W. Dunn, Hla Pe [and others], *A Burmese–English dictionary.* Parts 1–6 [no more published]. [London: School of Oriental and African Studies] 1940–81. 0–7286–0092–7.

Parts 1–2 'under the auspices of the University of Rangoon'; parts 3–6 published by the School of Oriental and African Studies.

See: Hla Pe, 'A short history of *A Burmese–English dictionary*, 1913–1963' in C. D. Cowan, O. W. Wolters, editors, *Southeast Asian history and historiography: essays presented to D. G. E. Hall*. Ithaca: Cornell University Press, 1976, pp. 86–99.

Compilation was begun by the Burma Research Society in 1925. This is a large-scale work modelled on the *Oxford English Dictionary*, with many examples of usage, covering written Burmese from the fifteenth century. It was abandoned before reaching the end of the first letter of the alphabet (which, in the sequence adopted here, is အ).

The alphabetical order adopted, placing the vowels at the beginning, not at the end, of the sequence was Judson's (compare **225**): it marked a break with Burmese tradition in favour of that of India, because the vowels come first in Indian alphabets. 'Judson's alphabetical order has a major practical defect. Words beginning with အ [a] come first. But အ is a living prefix allowing the formation of a deverbative from *any* Burmese verb.

To begin with အ means arranging all deverbatives ahead of all parent verbs, and it is precisely this that has slowed down Stewart's dictionary – an outstanding work none the less, with precise and detailed glosses and numerous citations' (Bernot, **230**, vol. 1 p. 11).

The chequered history of the project is outlined in the memoir by a major contributor, Hla Pe, cited above.

The modern standard

224.

မြန်မာ အဘိဓာန် အကျဉ်းချုပ် *[Myanma abidan akyin-gyok]*. Rangoon, 1982–[1985?]. 5 vols.

A preliminary edition of the အ to ဃ section appeared in 1978.

[*Big Burmese dictionary.*] A modern encyclopaedic dictionary of the Webster kind, entirely in Burmese, illustrated with line drawings. About 37,000 entries.

225.

The Judson Burmese–English dictionary. Rangoon: American Baptist Mission Press, 1921. 1123 pp.

[4th edn,] revised by Rev. F. H. Eveleth. – Later reprinted as: *Judson's Burmese–English dictionary*. Rangoon: Baptist Board of Publications, 1953, with a 'Preface to the Centenary edition' by F. G. Dickason. Several other reprints can be found.

1st edn: Moulmein: American Mission Press, 1852. This was prepared for the press by E. A. Stevens, who added some terms (particularly for flora and fauna) in square brackets.

2nd edn: A. Judson: *A dictionary, Burmese and English*. Rangoon: American Baptist Mission Press, 1883. 783 pp. 'Preface to the second edition' by Edward O. Stevens, son of the editor of the first edition. Appendices: 'A grammar of the Burmese language' by A. Judson, pp. 657–704 [this was also issued separately: 1883. 52 pp.]; Geographical names, Burmese and foreign, pp. 707–37; Scripture proper names (from a manuscript by Judson), pp. 740–80; Hebrew and Greek loanwords used in the Burmese Bible, pp. 781–2.

[3rd edn:] *Judson's Burmese–English dictionary*. Rangoon, 1893. Revised and enlarged by Robert C. Stevenson, Burma Commission. 1194 pp. Burmese proverbs, aphorisms and quaint sayings, pp. 1189–94. See the review of this 1893 edition: R. F. St. Andrew St. John: 'The new Burmese dictionary' in *Journal of the Royal Asiatic Society* (July 1894) pp. 556–8.

The earliest version of Judson's material had been published as: *A dictionary of the Burman language with explanations in English: compiled from the manuscripts of A. Judson, D. D. and of other missionaries in Burmah*. Calcutta: Thacker, 1826. 411 pp.

With about 27,500 entries the 1921 edition of Judson is still in many ways the best complete Burmese–English dictionary. It includes the following appendices: notes (brief encyclopaedic entries for Buddhist concepts) pp. 1062–99; Buddhist proverbs and quaint sayings, pp. 1100–04; formal and colloquial phraseology contrasted, pp. 1105–11; antonyms, pp. 1112–23.

226.

Judson's English and Burmese dictionary. Rangoon: American Baptist Mission Press, 1901. 928 pp.

5th edn. Subsequent editions are reprints of this, e.g. the 'unabridged tenth edition': Rangoon: Baptist Board of Publications, 1966. 928 pp.

1st edn: A. Judson, *A dictionary, English and Burmese*. Moulmein, 1849. 589 pp.

The latest, fifth, substantive edition results from successive revisions and enlargements by Rev. E. O. Stevens, Dr Francis Mason, Rev. F. H. Eveleth and Miss Phinney. Judson's English–Burmese dictionary, with only about 20,000 concise entries, is a smaller work than his Burmese–English dictionary, and is now for most practical purposes superseded.

227.

Maung Ba Han, *The university English–Myanmar dictionary*. Rangoon: Win Literature, 1995–1996. 3 vols [2238 pp.].

Previous edn: Maung Ba Han, *The university English–Burmese dictionary*. Rangoon: Hanthawaddy Press, 1951–66. 10 parts [2292 pp.].

A vast work by a scholar well versed in both languages (Barrister of Lincoln's Inn; Professor Emeritus of Law, Rangoon). About 80,000 entries, many of some length and complexity, with lively examples: the best available English–Burmese dictionary.

228.

The Khit Pyin English English Burmese dictionary. Rangoon: Moe Wai, 1960. Multiple paginations.

Compiled by Sun Htoo editorial staff.

This does not match Maung Ba Han's dictionary (**227**) in size, but it is still a massive work.

Some of the space is taken up, as indicated by the title, in the provision of English as well as Burmese definitions of headwords. The English is far from infallible (e.g. **auxilliary**) and many headwords are of doubtful value (e.g. **availably**).

229.

Phonetic pronouncing new method English–Myanmar dictionary. Rangoon, 1995. 2 vols [2057 pp.].

Not seen: noted from the Library of Congress catalogue.

230.

Denise Bernot, editor, *Dictionnaire birman–français*. Paris: SELAF, 1978–92. 15 vols.

Langues et civilisations de l'Asie du Sud-Est et du monde insulindien, 3. Published with the support of the Centre National de la Recherche Scientifique.
Compiled by Denise Bernot, Jean-Pierre Sribnai and Daw Yin Yin Myint.

[*Burmese–French dictionary*.] A large-scale dictionary, reproduced from typescript of gradually improving legibility, with plenty of illustrations. The total number of entries is around 35,000, many of them quite lengthy. Phonetic transcriptions are given; taxonomic names are provided for flora and fauna. Ends with the vowel characters (see the quotation at **223** above).

Other works of interest

231.

John Okell, *A guide to the romanization of Burmese*. London: Royal Asiatic Society, 1971. 69 pp.

James G. Furlong fund, 27.

CARIB

Black or Central American Carib is an Arawakan language and thus perhaps one of the AMERIND language family. It has about a hundred thousand speakers in Honduras, Belize and Guatemala. It is to be distinguished from Carib of Venezuela, which is a Cariban, not an Arawakan language.

232.
John J. Stochl, Román Zúñiga, *A dictionary of Central American Carib*. Belize, 1975. 3 vols.
Belize Institute of Social Research and Action.

CATALAN

Catalan is one of the ROMANCE LANGUAGES descended from Latin. After a period of severe discrimination it is now recognised as one of the official languages of Spain. There are about 6,500,000 speakers. The great historical dictionary by Alcover and Moll (**233**) is evidence of the persistence of Catalan studies through the difficult Franco period; the new encyclopaedia (**243**) demonstrates the effort and investment now being devoted to the language and its culture.

Historical dictionaries

233.
Antoni Mª Alcover, Francesc de B. Moll, *Diccionari català–valencià–balear: inventari lexicogràfic i etimològic de la llengua catalana en totes les seves formes literàries i dialectals, recollides dels documents i textos antics i moderns, i del parlar vivent al Principat de Catalunya, al Regne de València, a les Illes Balears, al departament Francès dels Pirineus Orientals, a les Valls d'Andorra, al marge oriental d'Aragó i a la ciutat d'Alguer de Sardenya.* Palma de Mallorca, 1930–62. 10 vols.
2nd edn of vols 1–2: 1968, 1964.

   [*Catalan–Valencian–Balearic dictionary: a lexical and etymological inventory of the Catalan language in all its literary and dialectal forms, collected from early and modern documents and texts and from the living speech of the Principality of Catalonia, the Kingdom of Valencia, the Balearic Islands, the French department of Pyrénées Orientales, the Valls d'Andorra, the eastern marches of Aragon and the Sardinian city of Alghero.*] 'Enormously rich' (Malkiel, **9**). A very large-scale dictionary combining historical quotations for many words with an indication of dialect variation (as indicated in the title) and a generous listing (without quotations or citations) of the modern scientific and technical vocabulary. The quotations are in a narrow sans-serif face. Many entries end with the subheading *FON.*, which introduces variant pronunciations from the dialects, and *ETIM.*, which gives etymologies for selected words. The dictionary includes illustrations, mainly in the fields of natural history and folklore.

Bibliography, vol. 1 pp. xxix–lxxviii.

234.

A. Griera, *Tresor de la llengua, de les tradicions i de la cultura popular de Catalunya*. Barcelona: Catalunya, Rodríguez, 1935–47. 14 vols.

[*Treasury of Catalan language, traditions and popular culture.*] Not a full dictionary of the language, but giving interesting quotations from folk poetry and indications of dialect variation.

The modern standard

235.

Jesús Giralt i Radigales, editor, *Diccionari de la llengua catalana*. Barcelona: Enciclopèdia Catalana, 1993. 2080 pp. New edn. 84–7739–615–9.

1st edn: Joan Carreras i Martí, editor, *Diccionari de la llengua catalana*. Barcelona, 1982. 1679 pp. 84–8519–446–2.

[*Dictionary of the Catalan language.*] A concise monolingual dictionary of modern usage, with numerous brief example phrases but no attributed quotations.

236.

S. Oliva, A. Buxton, editors, *Diccionari anglès–català*. Barcelona: Enciclopèdia Catalana, 1985. 1109 pp.

[*English–Catalan dictionary.*]

237.

S. Oliva, A. Buxton, editors, *Diccionari català–anglès*. Barcelona: Enciclopèdia Catalana, 1986. 842 pp.

[*Catalan–English dictionary.*]

238.

Jordí Vigué i Viñas, editor, *Diccionari castellà–català*. Barcelona, 1985. 1341 pp.

[*Spanish–Catalan dictionary.*] The largest available bilingual dictionary into Catalan.

Older periods

239.

Mariano Aguiló i Fuster, *Diccionari Aguiló: materials lexicogràfics aplegats per Mariano Aguiló i Fuster*. Barcelona, 1918–34. 8 vols.

Edited by Pompeu Fabra, Manuel de Montoliu.

[*The Aguiló dictionary: lexicographical materials collected by Mariano Aguiló i Fuster.*] A collection of materials on early Catalan.

240.

José Balari i Jovany, *Diccionario Balari: inventario lexicográfico de la lengua catalana*. Barcelona [1925]. 410, 196 pp.

Edited by Manuel de Montoliu.

[*The Balari dictionary: an inventory of the Catalan vocabulary.*] A posthumous publication of research on the early language, covering the letters **A–E** only.

Etymological dictionaries

241.

Joan Coromines [Juan Corominas], *Diccionari etimològic i complementari de la llengua catalana*. Barcelona: Curial, 1980–91. 84–7256–173–9.

With the collaboration of Joseph Gulsoy, Max Cahner.

[*Etymological and supplementary dictionary of the Catalan language.*] A very large-scale dictionary of the history of the Catalan vocabulary, dealing in detail with changes of form and meaning as well as with origins. Many words come in for very lengthy discussion, e.g. **ver** 'true', vol. 9 pp. 129–140. There are cross-references for derivatives and other words not covered in alphabetical order.

Bibliography, vol. 1 pp. xv–xliii; abbreviations, vol. 1 pp. xliv–xlvii.

242.

Francesc de B. Moll, 'Suplement català al Diccionari romànic etimològic' in *Anuari de l'Oficina de Lingüística i Literatura* vols 1–4, 1928–31.

Intended as a supplement to the 1911 edition of Meyer-Lübke (**1256**).

[*Catalan supplement to the Romance etymological dictionary.*]

Other works of interest

243.

Jordi Carbonell, editor, *Gran enciclopèdia catalana*. Barcelona: Edicions 62, Enciclopèdia Catalana, 1969–83. 15 vols. 84–300–5511–8.

Supplement 1: 1983. Supplement 2: 1989. Supplement 3: 1993.

CAUCASIAN LANGUAGES

The linguistic diversity of the mountainous Caucasus region, between the Black Sea and the Caspian, is astonishing. There are two separate families of languages spoken here that have no clear demonstrated links elsewhere in the world. Languages belonging to the Indo-European, Mongolian and Turkic families are also spoken in the region.

One of the families confined to the Caucasus is that of the KARTVELIAN LANGUAGES (including Georgian). There is a separate entry for these. The other is the North Caucasian family, dealt with here. Its three branches are:

- West or North West Caucasian, including ABKHAZ, CIRCASSIAN and others.
- Nakh or North Central Caucasian, including Chechen and Ingush.

- East or North East Caucasian or Dagestanian, including Avar, the Andi languages, Dargwa, the Dido languages, Lak, Lezghian and some others, most of them spoken in the Russian republic of Dagestan. None of these has a separate entry here, but some multilingual word-lists and dictionaries are listed below. Ancient HURRIAN, spoken three thousand years ago in eastern Anatolia, was probably an East Caucasian language.

Trubetzkoy's demonstration (**245**) that the three branches are to be regarded as a single family is now confirmed by the work of Nikolayev and Starostin (**244**).

North Caucasian as a whole

244.

S. L. Nikolayev, S. A. Starostin, *A North Caucasian etymological dictionary.* Moscow: Asterisk Publishers, 1994. 1406 pp. + 3½ inch disk.

The first comparative dictionary offering systematic reconstructions. Entries are filed under reconstructed forms in alphabetical order (table, pp. 3–4) though with a systematic error in filing caused by a computer program. The dictionary, pp. 200–1110. Indexes by language, pp. 1111–1376; index of English meanings, pp. 1377–1406. Abbreviations for languages, pp. 23–8. Bibliography, pp. 29–38. Important intrroduction, pp. 38–199.

245.

N. Trubetzkoy, 'Nordkaukasische Wortgleichungen' in *Wiener Zeitschrift für die Kunde des Morgenlandes* vol. 37 (1930) pp. 76–92.

[*North Caucasian lexical correspondences.*]

East Caucasian

246.

Сравнительно-историческая лексика дагестанских языков [*Sravnitel'no-istoricheskaya leksika dagestanskikh yazykov*]. Moscow, 1971. 296 pp.
By Saida M. Gasanova and others.

[*Comparative and historical dictionary of the Dagestanian languages.*] In Russian.

247.

Саид М. Хайдаков, *Сравнительно-сопоставительный словарь дагестанских языков* [Said M. Khaidakov, *Sravnitel'no-sopostavitel'nyi slovar' dagestanskikh yazykov*]. Moscow: Nauka, 1973. 179 pp.

[*Comparative and contrastive dictionary of the Dagestanian languages.*] In Russian, arranged in order of Russian concepts: there is no index of these or of word forms. Deals with '13 languages' and numerous dialects. Abbreviations for languages and dialects, pp. 174–5.

CEBUANO

One of the AUSTRONESIAN LANGUAGES of the Central Philippine group, Cebuano is the best known of the languages of *Visayas*, the group of mountainous islands between Luzon and Mindanao in the Philippines archipelago. There are about 12 million speakers, making Cebuano the second most used language of the Philippines after Tagalog. Speakers customarily call themselves *Bisayaq* ('Visayan') and their language *Binisayaq*. The names *Sebuano* and *Sugbuhanon* are also seen.

248.
John U. Wolff, *A dictionary of Cebuano Visayan*. Ithaca: Cornell University, Department of Asian Studies, 1972. 2 vols [1164 pp.].
Southeast Asia Program. *Data paper*, 87. *Linguistics series*, 6. Linguistic Society of the Philippines.

There are 25,000 entries (and 700 addenda) in this Cebuano–English dictionary, with many example phrases. It is 'meant as a reference work for Cebuano speakers and as a tool for students.' Well printed in small but clear type, unusually for this series.

249.
Rodolfo Cabonce, *An English–Cebuano Visayan dictionary*. Metro Manila: National Book Store, 1983. 1135 pp. 971–08–0052–3.

A massive work by a local parish priest, with about 20,000 entries.

CELTIC LANGUAGES

This branch of the INDO-EUROPEAN language family includes BRETON, CORNISH, GAELIC, IRISH, MANX and WELSH.

'Continental Celtic', the ancient Celtic language of mainland Europe, now extinct, was once spoken in Gaul, part of Spain, south-western Germany, the Danube valley, and even in Galatia in central Anatolia. The two dictionaries listed here are collections of material for the reconstruction of early Celtic languages, particularly Continental Celtic. The only comparative and historical dictionary of Celtic languages was published long ago as part of a series of Indo-European dictionaries, otherwise superseded (**767**). Big etymological and historical dictionaries of Breton and Irish, although not yet complete, compensate for the lack of a good modern comparative Celtic dictionary.

250.
Pierre-Henry Billy, *Thesaurus linguae Gallicae*. Hildesheim: Olms-Weidmann, 1993. 229 pp. 3–487–09746–X.
Alpha-omega, series A, 144.

[*Thesaurus of the Gaulish language.*] Index of source materials for western Continental Celtic, arranged as a dictionary, also covering proper names down to the fifth century AD and personal names to the sixth. The whole work is in Latin, except that glosses are in French. Note the abbreviation *intell.*, 'to be understood as follows ...'. List of sources, mostly Latin with a few Greek, pp. xiii–xxv.

251.

Alfred Holder, *Alt-Celtischer Sprachschatz*. Leipzig: Teubner, 1891–1913. 3 vols [21 parts].

[*Early Celtic vocabulary.*] This was intended as a complete thesaurus, arranged alphabetically, of ancient sources for Celtic words and names, with full quotations. The sources are mainly Greek and Latin texts, with the addition of Celtic coins and inscriptions. There is also a great number of modern place names deriving from early Celtic words. The Latin and Greek are not translated, but some of the early Celtic inscriptions are.

The alphabet is completed at vol. 3 column 464. There are no indexes and no list of abbreviations for source texts, but a general list of abbreviations occupies four unnumbered pages in vol. 1.

A very substantial supplement to vol. 1 occupies vol. 3 columns 465–1280, covering **A–Corbacum** and breaking off abruptly in the middle of the latter entry.

CHADIC LANGUAGES

This branch of the AFROASIATIC language family includes over a hundred minority languages of Chad and northern Nigeria. Only one of them – HAUSA – has a sufficiently large number of speakers to be important on the national and international scale.

252.

Paul Newman, *Chadic classification and reconstructions*. Malibu: Undena, 1977. 42 pp.

Afroasiatic linguistics, vol. 5 part 1.

Note also: P. Newman, R. Maa, 'Comparative Chadic: phonology and lexicon' in *Journal of African languages* vol. 5 (1966) pp. 218–51. – H. Jungraithmayr, K. Shimizu, *Chadic lexical roots: a first evaluation of the Marburg Chadic Word Catalogue*. Berlin: Reimer, 1981.

Comparative word list, in alphabetical order of English meanings, pp. 22–34 (150 entries); list of languages, pp. 35–8.

CHAM

Cham is unusual among AUSTRONESIAN LANGUAGES: it is clearly long established on the Asian mainland, where it was the language of the Hindu kingdom of Champa – founded, some say, in AD 192. When this kingdom fell, as a result of a Vietnamese victory in 1471, many of its people migrated inland. This is the origin of the Cambodian Cham-speaking community, now larger than the one in Vietnam. Islam had been adopted in the fourteenth century and the speakers of Cham are still Muslims. They number a little over 200,000.

The beautiful Cham script is of Indic origin, like the Hindu culture of the old Champa kingdom. It has a history of well over a thousand years, and some Cham speakers in Vietnam still use it. Among Cambodian speakers of Cham, whose Islam has been closer to orthodoxy, Arabic script has been used. Under French rule the Latin alphabet was introduced for both Cham communities.

253.

Etienne Aymonier, Antoine Cabaton, *Dictionnaire cam–français*. Paris: Leroux, 1906. 587 pp.
(*Publications de l'Ecole Française d'Extrême-Orient*, 7.)

[*Cham–French dictionary.*] Essentially a dictionary of the medieval language recorded on inscriptions. Cham script (beautifully cast) and transliteration followed by French glosses. Many example phrases. Taxonomic names are given for flora and fauna.

Complete French index, pp. 533–52; Cham index in romanised alphabetical order, pp. 553–87. Language and script, pp. vii–xxxiv; the alphabet, pp. xviii–xx; order of vowels adopted under each consonant, pp. xxxiii–xxxiv.

254.

Kvoeu-Hor, Timothy Friberg, *Bôh panuaik Chăm = Ngu-vung Chàm = Western Cham vocabulary*. [Huntington Beach, California:] Summer Institute of Linguistics, 1978. 336 pp.
Tu sách Ngôn-ngu dân-tôc thiêu-sô Việt-nam, vol. 21 part 1.

A Cham–Vietnamese–English vocabulary, the best available source for the majority dialect of modern Cham. Most speakers are in Cambodia.

255.

G. Moussay, *Dictionnaire căm–vietnamien–français = Từ-điển Chàm–Việt–Pháp*. Phanrang: Centre Culturel Căm, 1971. 597 pp.

[*Cham–Vietnamese–French dictionary.*] A dictionary of the modern language of Phan-rang and neighbourhood (map of these and other Cham-speaking districts, p. vi).

Tabular format. Cham terms appear in three forms: traditional Cham script (handwritten), standard Latin transliteration of the script, phonetic transcription of the modern pronunciation. Many text boxes giving technical terms.

Script and phonology, pp. ix–xxiii; grammar, pp. xxiv–xxxix. List of Cham villages with Cham and Vietnamese names, pp. 477–91; kinship terms, pp. 493–8; French–Cham index, 43 pp.; Vietnamese–Cham index, 43 pp.; Latin–Cham index of zoological and botanical names, 2 pp.

CHAMORRO

Chamorro, with about 70,000 speakers, is the native language of the island of Guam. It is one of the AUSTRONESIAN LANGUAGES, and is most closely related to those of the Philippines. Chamorro is written in the Latin alphabet.

256.

P. Callistus, *Chamorro-Wörterbuch enthaltend I. Deutsch–Chamorro, II. Chamorro–Deutsch, nebst einer Chamorro-Grammatik und einigen Sprach-übungen*. Hongkong: typis Societatis Missionum ad Exteros, 1910. 172 + 33* pp.

[*Chamorro dictionary, Chamorro–German and German–Chamorro, with a Chamorro grammar and some exercises.*] Compiled by a Capuchin missionary, this work describes a much earlier state of the language than that in Topping's dictionary (**257**). It already had numerous Spanish loanwords. German–Chamorro, pp. 1–86; Chamorro–German, pp. 87–172.

257.

Donald M. Topping, Pedro M. Ogo, Bernadita C. Dungca, *Chamorro–English dictionary*. Honolulu: University Press of Hawaii, 1975. 336 pp. 0–8248–0353–1.

A brief-entry dictionary with some examples of usage. Taxonomic names are given for flora and fauna. 'Spelled according to the principles adopted by the Marianas Orthography Committee in February 1971'. English–Chamorro index, pp. 219–336.

CHEROKEE

Cherokee belongs to the Iroquoian family of AMERIND LANGUAGES, as was first observed by Benjamin Smith Barton (*New views of the origin of the tribes and nations of America*, 1797), though the Cherokee were not one of the original Five Nations of the Iroquois. There are still about 10,000 speakers of the language.

258.

Durbin Feeling, *Cherokee–English dictionary*. Tahlequah: Cherokee Nation of Oklahoma, 1975. 355 pp.

Edited by William Pulte, in collaboration with Agnes Cowen and the Dictionary Committee.

An outline of Cherokee grammar, by Pulte and Feeling, is on pp. 235–355.

259.

J. T. Alexander, *A dictionary of the Cherokee Indian language*. Sperry, Oklahoma, 1971. 359 pp.

Not seen.

The Cherokee syllabary

D	a	R	e	T	i	Ꮵ	o	Ꮎ	u	i	v
S	ga	Ᏺ	ge	y	gi	A	go	J	gu	E	gv
Ꮕ	ka		ke		ki		ko		ku		kv
W	ta	Ꮦ	te	Ꮧ	ti		to	S	tu	Ꮬ	tv
Ꮮ	da	Ꮥ	de	Ꮧ	di	V	do		du		dv
Ꮸ	ha	Ꮲ	he	Ꮯ	hi	Ꮶ	ho	Ꮁ	hu	Ꮵ	hv
W	la	Ꮳ	le	Ꮅ	li	G	lo	M	lu	Ꮑ	lv
Ꮉ	ma	Ꮊ	me	H	mi	Ꮽ	mo	Ꮍ	mu		
Ꮎ	na	Ꭺ	ne	Ꭽ	ni	Z	no	Ꮷ	nu	Ꮕ	nv
Ꮀ	hna										
G	nah										
Ꮖ	qua	Ꮹ	que	Ꮗ	qui	Ꮺ	quo	Ꮾ	quu	Ꮛ	quv
Ꮂ	sa	Ꮷ	se	Ꮅ	si	Ꮝ	so	Ꮜ	su	R	sv
Ꮝ	s										
Ꮅ	dla	L	dle	C	dli	Ꮧ	dlo	Ꮭ	dlu	P	dlv
Ꮪ	tla		tle		tli		tlo		tlu		tlv
G	tsa	V	tse	Ir	tsi	K	tso	Ꮪ	tsu	Ꮳ	tsv
Ꮝ	wa	Ꮺ	we	Ꮻ	wi	Ꮼ	wo	Ꮽ	wu	Ꮾ	wv
Ꮿ	ya	Ᏸ	ye	Ᏹ	yi	Ᏺ	yo	Ᏻ	yu	B	yv

In 1821 a Cherokee, Sequoyah, devised a syllabic script for his native language, quite independent of all others though with characters that resemble Roman ones. This came at just the right time to be used by the first missionary to the Cherokee, Samuel Worcester, who began his work in 1825 and published translations and religious texts in the script. It was widely used for a century or more. Fewer Cherokee know the script now.
FONT: *CHEROKEE.TTF* BY JOSEPH LOCICERO IV

CHINESE

Chinese belongs to the family of SINO-TIBETAN LANGUAGES. It is in fact a whole branch of the family, one that has developed apart from its relatives for several thousand years.

Chinese is the standard language of China, sometimes known as 'Mandarin' and *Putonghua*. It is also a group of regional languages of China – some of them, including Cantonese and Hokkien, well known outside China too – which all share the same written form, though their spoken forms have diverged well beyond the point of mutual intelligibility.

There is little lexicographical work on the regional languages of China – or, at least, little that is accessible to scholars not fully familiar with Chinese script (but see **266**, **267** and **270**). Linguistic reconstruction within the Chinese group of languages is reflected in Karlgren's work; beyond this one must look to recent work on the SINO-TIBETAN family as a whole.

The 'etymology' of Chinese written characters (**269**) is a study in its own right, linked to but certainly not identical with the etymology of the spoken vocabulary. Wieger's work (**272**) is thus arranged as a series of 'etymological lessons', followed by listings of other kinds – but it lacks a table of contents.

This book lists only a selection of the more accessible dictionaries of Chinese. There is a full bibliography by Yang (**273**).

The modern standard

260.

Dictionnaire français de la langue chinoise. Paris: Institut Ricci, 1990. 1135 + 186 pp.

Prepared by the Institut Ricci. Parallel title in Chinese.

[*French dictionary of the Chinese language.*] A concise dictionary arranged phonetically and sub-arranged by character. Each compound word or phrase is given both in Chinese script and in Wade transliteration. Phonetic headings group all relevant characters and also give the four standard Latin transliterations – and Chinese phonetic script, which is not to be found in other dictionaries listed here. Character indexes, second pagination pp. 63–186; phonetic concordances, second pagination pp. 40–62.

261.

Ge Chuan-gui [and others], *A new English–Chinese dictionary.* Seattle: University of Washington Press, 1988. 1770 pp. Revised and enlarged edn. 0–295–96609–2.

1st edn: Hong Kong: Joint Publishing Co., 1975.

A brief-entry dictionary into Chinese. Chinese glosses are in script only, without indication of pronunciation. The new edition is a reprint of the first with a supplement of new and revised entries.

262.

R. H. Mathews, *A Chinese–English dictionary.* Cambridge, Massachusetts: Harvard-Yenching Institute, 1943. 1250 pp. 'Revised American edition', revised by M. Y. Wang, Y. R. Chao.

Alternate title: *Mathews' Chinese–English dictionary.*
Accompanied by: *Revised English index.* 186 pp. This includes errata to the main volume, pp. 185–6.
1st edn: Shanghai: China Inland Mission, 1931. 1232 pp. Compiled for the China Inland Mission. –
Accompanied by: *English index.* 185 pp.

Arranged phonetically under the Wade transliteration, sub-arranged by character. The revised edition claims about 15,000 revisions and corrections but retains the original pagination.

263.

И. М. Ошанин, *Большой китайско-русский словарь* [I. M. Oshanin, editor, *Bol'shoi kitaisko–russkii slovar'*]. Moscow, 1983–4. 4 vols.

Akademiya Nauk SSSR, Institut Vostokovedeniya.
Earliest version: *Китайско-русский словарь* [*Kitaisko–russkii slovar'*]. 1955. – 3rd edn: 1959.

[*Big Chinese–Russian dictionary.*] The biggest bilingual dictionary of Chinese. Vol. 1 consists of various guides and appendices including a list of geographical names, pp. 20–62; chronological charts, pp. 63–172; weights and measures, pp. 173–82; indexes of characters, pp. 183–552. Vols 2–4 are the main dictionary, in character order under a total of 15,505 character headings: a very full listing of compound words and phrases, with all entries in both Chinese script and Pinyin. Additions and corrections, vol. 4 pp. 1055–64.

264.

Wu Jingrong, editor-in-chief, *The Pinyin Chinese–English dictionary*. Beijing, Hong Kong: Commercial Press, 1979. 976 pp. 0–273–08454–2; 0–471–27557–3.
Parallel title in Chinese.

Arranged phonetically under the Pinyin transliteration of Chinese words. The detailed arrangement is by successive first syllables, subdivided according to script character (summary list of characters in the same order, pp. 32–7) – thus in a sense the arrangement might be said to be 'etymological' or by root. Anyway it is easier to use than I find it to describe. Under each character, compound words appear in their Pinyin form.

'Radical index', pp. 13–31; appendix of older complex forms with modern simplified versions, pp. 948–55; concordance of Pinyin and Wade transliterations, pp. 957–9. List of geographical names, pp. 961–71.

265.

Yu T'ang Lin, *Lin Yutang's Chinese–English dictionary of modern usage*. Hong Kong: Chinese University of Hong Kong, 1972. 1720 pp.

The author is better known to many by the alternative arrangement of his name, Lin Yutang. His dictionary has main headings for over 8,000 unsimplified characters (listed on pp. xxxiii–lxvi): these include all of the 3,000 'selected by the International Press Institute'. Characters are arranged by the author's patented system, which is explained on the inside front cover. Entries give Chinese script followed by the *Gworyuu Romatzyh* transliteration, the least popular nowadays of the standard romanisations. A concordance between this and the Wade and Yale systems appears on pp. xxvi–xxviii. There is no concordance with Pinyin, which is scarcely mentioned at all, for ideological reasons.

Regional forms

266.

R. T. Cowles, *The Cantonese speaker's dictionary*. Hong Kong: Hong Kong University Press, 1965. 1318 + 232 pp.

The main section is in romanisation (Meyer–Wempe system); the second pagination is an index by characters.

267.

Ernest John Eitel, *A Chinese–English dictionary in the Cantonese dialect*. Hong Kong: Kelly & Walsh, 1910. 1417 pp. New edition, revised and enlarged by Emmanuel Gottlieb Genähr.

1st edn: 1877.

Arranged phonetically by Cantonese pronunciation. The 731 syllables (table of these with typical character forms, pp. v–viii) are sub-arranged by the nine tones that Eitel distinguishes (list and symbols, p. xii). The characters are in general those of Mandarin, except for those marked *V.* 'vulgar', but many compound words and phrases are unknown in Mandarin. Entries are classed *Cl.* 'classical', *Co.* 'colloquial', *Mi.* 'mixed'.

268.

F. M. Savina, *Guide linguistique de l'Indochine Française*. Hong Kong: Société des Missions-Etrangères, 1939. 2 vols [1198 pp.].

[*Linguistic guide to French Indochina.*] An eight-language glossary in tabular format, covering French, Vietnamese, Tho (a Tai language), Man (Yao), Miao, Cantonese, Hoclo (a Chinese language of Hainan), and Mandarin, in alphabetical order of the French entries. Includes Sino-Vietnamese forms and corresponding Chinese characters: note the 107–page supplement at the end of vol. 1, which completes these.

Appendix to vol. 2: Chinese characters for foreign and Chinese place names, for French Christian names, and for the 60–year cycle and year divisions. As regards Tho, Miao and Yao, the work is based on bilingual dictionaries that Savina had published earlier.

Etymological and historical dictionaries

269.

Chang Hsüan, *The etymologies of three thousand Chinese characters in common usage*. Hong Kong: Hong Kong University Press, 1968. 960 pp.

See the review by Paul Serruys in *Journal of Chinese linguistics* vol. 1 (1973) pp. 479–92.

270.

Bernhard Karlgren, *Analytic dictionary of Chinese and Sino-Japanese*. Paris: Geuthner, 1923. 436 pp.

Reprinted: New York: Dover, 1974. 0–486–26887–X.

Tabular format; each character is followed by pronunciations in *M* 'Mandarin', *C* 'Cantonese' and *A* 'Ancient Chinese' of about AD 600, followed by the meaning and, often, historical and etymological discussion.

271.

Bernhard Karlgren, *Grammata Serica recensa*. Stockholm, 1957. 332 pp.

Bulletin of the Museum of Far Eastern Antiquities, 29.

Note also: Avishai Gil, *Index of characters (arranged by order of radicals) to Bernhard Karlgren's "Grammata serica recensa"*. Cambridge: [Gil,] 1974. 92 pp.

Earlier version of the main work: Bernhard Karlgren, *Grammata Serica: script and phonetics in Chinese and Sino-Japanese*. 1940. 471 pp. (*Bulletin of the Museum of Far Eastern Antiquities*, 12.)

[*The Chinese script: revised.*] 1260 numbered entries for syllable forms, with lettered sub-entries for different characters (thus distinguishing both homophones and historical changes in character forms). Entries are arranged in inverse alphabetical order, i.e. in order of rhymes. This is because Karlgren's great work is based on his own systematic reconstruction of the phonetic structure of 'Archaic Chinese' of pre-Han Dynasty times, drawing largely on the rhyming system of the *Book of odes*. It is fundamental to research both in the history of Chinese and in Sino-Tibetan comparative studies.

The older version, *Grammata Serica*, has important introductory matter which is not repeated in *Grammata Serica recensa*.

Although it is a dictionary of Archaic Chinese, *Grammata Serica recensa* is hard to consult as such – one needs to be able to predict Karlgren's phonetic reconstruction. Gil's index is therefore important.

Other works of interest

272.
Léon Wieger, *Chinese characters: their origin, etymology, history, classification and signification: a thorough study from Chinese documents*. Peking: Catholic Mission Press, 1927. 820 pp. 2nd edn, enlarged and revised according to the 4th French edn.
Reprinted: New York: Paragon, Dover, 1965. 0–486–21321–8.
1st edn: 1915. Translated into English by L. Davrout. Original French title: *Caractères chinois*.

273.
Paul Fu-mien Yang, *Chinese lexicology and lexicography: a selected and classified bibliography*. Hong Kong: Chinese University Press, 1985. 361 pp.
Parallel title in Chinese.

CHOKWE

Chokwe is one of the Bantu languages of the NIGER-CONGO family. It is spoken in Angola, Zaire and Zambia, in the upper Kasai valley and along the left bank tributaries of this river, by a total of perhaps a million speakers.

274.
Adriano Barbosa, *Dicionário cokwe–português*. Coimbra: Instituto de Antropologia, Universidade de Coimbra, 1989. 750 pp.
Publicações do Centro de Estudos Africanos, 11.
[*Chokwe–Portuguese dictionary.*]

CHUVASH

Chuvash is a TURKIC language that differs strongly from its relatives and is widely separated from most of them geographically. It is spoken in European Russia.

Chuvash: older alphabetical order

а е ы и/i у о ÿ ӑ ĕ й в к л љ м н њ п р ҏ с ç т т̌ ъ ф х ш

Current alphabetical order

аӑбвгдеĕёжзийклмнопрсҫтуўфхцчшщъыьэюя

Chuvash is written in a form of the Cyrillic alphabet that has been several times remodelled, most recently in 1938: Ashmarin's great dictionary (**275**) is in the older spelling.

Historical dictionaries

275.

Н. И. Ашмарин [N. I. Ashmarin], *Thesaurus linguae tchuvaschorum = Словарь чувашского языка = Б̌аваш сӑмахӗсен кӗнеки.* Kazan', Cheboksary, 1928–50. 17 vols.

Vols 1–2 [А–ашшĕ-ҫурри] were reprinted with an introduction by Gerhard Doerfer. Bloomington: Indiana University Press, 1968. (Indiana University. *Uralic and Altaic series*, 70i–ii.)

[*Dictionary of the language of the Chuvash people.*] The best and most comprehensive of Chuvash dictionaries. Chiefly a dictionary of citation and usage, giving sometimes a page or more of examples from books, newspapers and other sources. In vols 1–16 the older Chuvash orthography is used, and is accompanied by a phonetic transcription in Cyrillic for many words. There is frequent citation of dialect words and parallels. Vols 1–2 also have definitions in Latin followed by the Russian equivalents. Vol. 17 uses the post-1938 orthography and has no additional phonetic transcription.

The novice will require some practice to use the dictionary, because all derived words are given after the main entry, thus sometimes disrupting the alphabetical order. (Annotation adapted from J. R. Krueger, *Chuvash manual*, Bloomington: Indiana University, 1961.)

Ashmarin (1870–1933) was the greatest scholar of the Chuvash language. He also published a major two-volume grammar. Vol. 17 of the present dictionary includes a biography of Ashmarin, as well as a guide to abbreviations of source citations.

The modern standard

276.

И. А. Андреев, Н. П. Петров, *Русско—чувашский словарь = Вырӑсла—чӑвашла словарь* [I. A. Andreev, N. P. Petrov, editors, *Russko–chuvashskii slovar'*]. Moscow: Sovetskaya Entsiklopediya, 1971. 893 pp.

Earlier version: И. А. Андреев, Н. К. Дмитриев, *Русско—чувашский словарь* [I. A. Andreev, N. K. Dmitriev and others, *Russko–chuvashskii slovar'*]. Moscow, 1951. 896 pp.

[*Russian–Chuvash dictionary.*] 40,000 entries.

277.

H. Paasonen, *Csuvas szójegyzék.* Budapest, 1908. 244 pp.

A Nyelvtudományi Közlemények kötetének melléklete, 37–38.
Later published in a Chuvash–Turkish version: H. Paasonen, *Çuvaş sözlügü*. Istanbul: Horoz Basimevi, 1950.
218 pp.

[*Chuvash dictionary.*] A Chuvash–Hungarian–German glossary (with Hungarian and German indexes) of the texts in Paasonen's *Gebräuche und Volksdichtung der Tschuwassen* ed. E. Karahka, M. Räsänen (Helsinki: Société Finno-Ougrienne, 1949) [*Customs and oral poetry of the Chuvash*]. Important for its etymological information. The Hungarian glosses are more complete than the German. The Chuvash is in Latin script.

278.

М. Я. Сироткин, *Чӑвашла-вырӑсла словарь* = *Чувашско–русский словарь.*
[M. Ya. Sirotkin, editor, *Chuvashsko–russkii slovar'*.] Moscow, 1961. 630 pp.

[*Chuvash–Russian dictionary.*] Includes a grammatical sketch by N. A. Andreev.

279.

М. И. Скворцов, *Чӑвашла-вырӑсла словарь* = *Чувашско–русский словарь*
[M. I. Skvortsov, editor, *Chăvashla–vyrăsla slovar'*]. Moscow: Russkii Yazyk, 1982. 712 pp.
Compiled by I. A. Andreev and others.

[*Chuvash–Russian dictionary.*] About 40,000 entries. A good concise bilingual dictionary with some illustrations of technical, botanical and zoological terms. The illustrations are captioned in Chuvash and Russian.

Regional forms

280.
Л. П. Сергеев, *Диалектологический словарь чувашского языка* [L. P. Sergeev, *Dialektologicheskii slovar' chuvashskogo yazyka*]. Cheboksary, 1968. 104 pp.
Nauchno-issledovatel'skii Institut pri Sovete Ministrov Chuvashskoi ASSR.

[*Dialect dictionary of the Chuvash language.*]

Etymological dictionaries

281.
В. Г. Егоров, *Этимологический словарь чувашского языка* [V. G. Yegorov, *Etimologicheskii slovar' chuvashskogo yazyka*]. Cheboksary, 1964. 355 pp.
Nauchno-issledovatel'skii Institut pri Sovete Ministrov Chuvashskoi ASSR.

[*Etymological dictionary of the Chuvash language.*]

CIRCASSIAN LANGUAGES

Circassian, a dialect group including Adyge, Cherkess and Kabardian, belongs to the North West CAUCASIAN LANGUAGES. There are about one and a half million speakers, including a gradually declining number in Turkey, to which many Circassians fled to escape Russian conquest in 1864.

282.

М. Л. Апажев, Б. М. Карданов, *Кабардинско—русский словарь* [M. L. Apazhev, B. M. Kardanov, *Kabardinsko–russkii slovar'*]. Nal'chik, 1957. 576 pp.
Kabardino-Balkarskii Nauchno-Issledovatel'skii Institut.

[*Kabardian–Russian dictionary.*]

283.

Gábor Bálint-Illyés (Szentkatolnai), *Lexicon cabardico–hungarico–latinum.* Cluj: Typographeo Gutenbergiano Kolozsvariensi, 1904. 611 pp.

[*Kabardian–Hungarian–Latin dictionary.*]

284.

Амин К. Шагиров, *Этимологический словарь адыгских (черкесских) языков* [Amin K. Shagirov, *Etimologicheskii slovar' adygskikh (cherkesskikh) yazykov*]. Moscow: Nauka, 1977. 2 vols.

[*Etymological dictionary of the Adyghian (Circassian) languages.*] 1564 numbered entries in a Cyrillic-based phonetic script (table, with Latin equivalents, vol. 1 p. 39). Glosses are in Russian. Index of Russian meanings, vol. 2 pp. 163–78; indexes by language, pp. 179–223. Bibliography, vol. 1 pp. 40–51; abbreviations for language names, pp. 52–3.

COPTIC

Under Greek and Roman domination, a Greek alphabet was adopted for the native language of Egypt. For EGYPTIAN written in this new script the name Coptic is used. This AFROASIATIC language survived many centuries of Islamic rule. It is now no longer anyone's mother tongue, but is still used in rituals of the Coptic church.

Coptic literature includes Christian poetry and prose (some of it translated from Greek) as well as Gnostic and Manichaean texts. Known texts are increasing in number as more are discovered in papyri.

The Coptic alphabet

ⲁ ⲃ ⲅ ⲇ ⲉ ⲍ ⲏ ⲑ ⲓ ⲕ ⲗ ⲙ ⲛ ⲝ ⲟ ⲡ ⲣ ⲥ ⲧ ⲩ ⲫ ⲭ ⲯ ⲱ ϣ ϥ ϩ ϫ ϭ ϯ

a v gh dh e z ē th i k l m n x o p r s t w ph kh ps ō sh f ch h j g ti

The Coptic alphabet is usually printed, as here, in a more florid style than Greek. At the end of the sequence are seven extra characters representing sounds unknown in Greek. These extra symbols are adapted from the demotic form of Egyptian script.

The strange filing order of Coptic dictionaries takes some getting used to. Aspirated and unaspirated consonants are interfiled. An initial vowel is counted, but other vowels are ignored in filing. The digraphs *ei* and *ou* each count as a single letter. Since these two digraphs may represent either consonants (y, w) or vowels (i, u), they are sometimes counted and sometimes ignored in filing. The difficulties are so great that Kasser (**286**) and Černý (**288**) both provide page references to Crum (**285**) for their entries, though all three works follow the same filing order.

The classical language

285.

Walter E. Crum, *A Coptic dictionary*. Oxford: Clarendon Press, 1939. 953 pp.

Note R. Kasser: 'Compléments morphologiques au dictionnaire de Crum' in *Bulletin de l'Institut Français d'Archéologie Orientale* vol. 64 (1966) pp. 19–66. – Gérard Roquet, *Toponymes et lieux-dits égyptiens enregistrés dans le Dictionnaire copte de W. E. Crum*. Cairo: Institut Français d'Archéologie Orientale [1973]. 41 pp. (*Bibliothèque d'études coptes*, 10.)

This Coptic–English dictionary covers words of Egyptian and of unidentified origin: some early Greek loanwords have crept in. Etymologies are not provided: for these see Westendorf (**287**) or Černý (**288**). Within its terms of reference this is the major citation dictionary of Coptic.

Entries are highly abridged. They begin by listing variant forms: dialects are identified as *A*chmîmic, *B*ohairic, *F*ayyûmic, *O*ld Coptic, *S*ahidic; *S̄* means 'Sahidic with Fayyûmic tendency', and so on. English glosses are then followed by source references, often with example phrases, which are given with an English translation. Greek equivalents and occasionally Arabic are provided, naturally enough, since many source texts are translated from one or other language.

Additions and corrections, pp. xv–xxiv. Greek and Arabic indexes at end.

'No doubt much water will flow beneath the bridges of the Isis and the Lez before a Coptic scholar finds time and courage to do afresh the work done by Crum ... [He] had access to such a vast number of unpublished texts that we still come across citations from Coptic Biblical versions, given by him with a simple reference to the scriptural passage, which we are quite unable to trace to a known manuscript, the cited reading not occurring in texts quoted by Vaschalde, listed by Till, held by Pierpont Morgan, or otherwise available to us' (Kasser, **286**).

286.

Rodolphe Kasser, *Compléments au dictionnaire copte de Crum*. Cairo: Institut Français d'Archéologie Orientale, 1964. 135 pp.

Bibliothèque d'études coptes, 7.

[*Supplement to Crum's Coptic dictionary.*] In French. Entries that are revisions or enlargements of those of Crum (**285**) have a page and column reference to the earlier work.

Addenda, p. 115–16; abbreviations, pp. 117–31. Remarks on alphabetical order, pp. viii–ix; on the dialects, pp. x–xiv.

287.

Wolfhart Westendorf, *Koptisches Handwörterbuch*. Heidelberg, 1965–77. 679 pp.

[*Concise Coptic dictionary.*] The most complete dictionary. Gives German glosses and brief etymologies, but very few source references or examples. The German index, pp. 576–631, turns this into a two-way Coptic and German dictionary. Separate indexes of words from Egyptian, Demotic, Greek, Arabic, Hebrew, Aramaic, Akkadian, Berber, Bedauye (Beja) and some other languages cited in the etymologies.

Etymological dictionaries

288.

Jaroslav Černý, *Coptic etymological dictionary*. Cambridge: Cambridge University Press, 1976. 384 pp. 0–521–07228–X.

Covers only a limited range of Coptic words, but serves as an important etymological and bibliographical supplement to Crum (**285**). Černý gives Egyptian forms and Arabic and Hebrew cognates, but very few from other Afroasiatic languages. Bibliographical citations are often preceded by ^{H} 'hieroglyphic' or ^{D} 'demotic'. Both hieroglyphic and demotic scripts are used (with romanisation) alongside Arabic, Hebrew, Syriac and Greek (without romanisation).

Appendix of geographical names, pp. 343–58. List of Coptic words in Crum for which no etymologies are given (i.e. of uncertain origin), pp. 359–69. Language indexes, pp. 370–84.

289.

Werner Vycichl, *Dictionnaire étymologique de la langue copte*. Louvain: Peeters, 1983. 520 pp. 2–8017–0197–1.

Preface by Rodolphe Kasser. Accompanied by a loose sheet of additions and corrections.
Earlier uncompleted version: Rodolphe Kasser with Werner Vycichl, *Dictionnaire auxiliaire, étymologique et complet de la langue copte*. Geneva, 1967– . (*Ecrits et idiomes de l'Egypte et du Proche-Orient.*)

[*Etymological dictionary of the Coptic language.*] Far stronger in the essential Afroasiatic field than Černý (**288**). There is full discussion of etymologies; contesting views are set out clearly, with bibliographical references. Hebrew, Arabic and even Egyptian (hieroglyphic) forms are given both in original script and in transliteration.

General bibliography, pp. xiii–xxi. List of abbreviations for Coptic dialects used here and in other standard works, pp. xi–xii.

Other works of interest

290.

Alexander Boehlig, *Ein Lexikon der griechischen Wörter im Koptischen: die griechisch-lateinischen Lehnwörter in den koptischen manichäischen Texten*. Munich: Robert Lerche, 1954. 39 pp.

Studien zur Erforschung des christlichen Aegyptens, 1.
2nd edn, with a two-page comment on a review by P. E. Kahle in *Theologische Literaturzeitung* (1954) pp. 484–6.
1st edn: 1953.

291.

Alexander Boehlig, *Die griechischen Lehnwörter im sahidischen und bohairischen Neuen Testament*. Munich: Robert Lerche, 1954. 427 pp.

Accompanied by: *Register und Vergleichstabellen zu Heft 2*. 1954. 121 pp.
Studien zur Erforschung des christlichen Aegyptens, 2, 2a.

292.

Eugène Dévaud, *Etudes d'étymologie copte*. Fribourg, 1922. 68 pp.

CORNISH

The native speech of Cornwall, one of the CELTIC LANGUAGES, is closely related to Welsh and Breton. Cornwall was conquered by the Saxons in 936, but the language, without any official status, survived in daily use for nearly a thousand years after that date. The last native speaker of Cornish, John Davey of Zennor, died in 1891. A revival of the language is taking place – based on early written records, since there is no continuous spoken tradition. The published dictionaries result from this revival movement.

293.

Ken George, *Gerlyver Kernewek kemmyn: an gerlyver meur Kernewek–Sowsnek = Cornish–English dictionary*. [Hayle:] Cornish Language Board, 1993. 338 pp. 0–907064–07–9.

[*Common Cornish dictionary: the big Cornish–English dictionary.*] 'Common Cornish' is the standardised revived form of the language. The dictionary is intended as 'prescriptive rather than descriptive' but, usefully, gives the date at which each word is first recorded in Cornish and other historical information, including source texts for some rarer words (see explanations on pp. 13–15). These historical details are in curly brackets {}. Then follows a gloss, followed again by etymologies in square brackets, and then Welsh and Breton cognates. Further notes on forms and origin are sometimes given in small font. An important contribution to Celtic lexicography.

294.

Ken George, *Gerlyver Kernewek kemmyn: dyllans servadow, Sowsnek–Kernewek*. N.p.: Kesva an Taves Kernewek, 1995. 76 pp.

[*Common Cornish dictionary: provisional edition, English–Cornish.*] The Cornish Language Board's English–Cornish dictionary is far more laconic than its companion: it is a computer-produced inversion of the latter with some additional editing. Abbreviations are not fully explained (see the Cornish–English dictionary, pp. 16–17).

295.

R. Morton Nance, *Gerlyver noweth Kernewek–Sawsnek ha Sawsnek–Kernewek*. Trywolsta: Dyllansow Truran, 1990. 213 + 200 pp. [1–85022–055–7.]
Spine title: *A new Cornish dictionary.*
One-volume reprint, with addenda, of *A new Cornish–English dictionary* (St Ives: Federation of Old Cornwall Societies, 1938) and *A new English–Cornish dictionary* (Marazion, 1952).

[*A new Cornish–English and English–Cornish dictionary.*] A brief-entry dictionary but with some indications of source texts: abbreviations are listed at the end of the preliminary pages. The addenda, on pp. 210–13 of the first pagination, consist of 'new words' that were first included in Nance's abridged *Cornish–English dictionary* of 1955.

296.
R. Williams, *Lexicon Cornu-Britannicum = A dictionary of the ancient Celtic language of Cornwall, in which the words are elucidated by copious examples from the Cornish works now remaining, with translations in English.* Llandovery: Roderic, 1865. 400 pp.
Supplemented by: W. Stokes, *A Cornish glossary*. London: Trübner, 1870. 114 pp. – J. Loth, *Remarques et corrections au Lexicon Cornu-Britannicum de Williams*. Paris: Bouillon, 1902. 70 pp.

Still interesting for its quotations; also gives cognate forms in Welsh, 'Armoric' (Breton), Irish, Gaelic and Manx. Not seen: entry based on *Walford's guide to reference material* vol. 3 (6th edn: London: Library Association Publishing, 1995).

CREE

Cree belongs to the Algonquian family of AMERIND LANGUAGES. There are about 70,000 speakers, most of them in Canada. Cree is usually written in the Latin alphabet; a syllabary, invented in the 19th century, is still in occasional use.

297.
Leonard Bloomfield, *Cree–English lexicon*. New Haven: Human Relations Area Files, 1984. 2 vols [319 leaves].
Unfinished work by an important figure in twentieth-century linguistics.

298.
R. Faeries, *A dictionary of the Cree language*. Toronto, 1938. 530 pp.

CROW

Crow is a Siouan language, perhaps to be assigned to the wider AMERIND family, with about 5000 speakers in the US state of Montana.

299.
Robert H. Lowie, *Crow word lists: Crow-English and English-Crow vocabularies*. Berkeley: University of California Press, 1960. 411 pp.
Companion work: Robert H. Lowie, *Crow texts*. Berkeley, 1960. 550 pp.

CUSHITIC LANGUAGES

This branch of the AFROASIATIC LANGUAGES is to be found in north-eastern Africa, from Sudan to Tanzania. It includes Afar, Beja, OROMO, SOMALI and many others less well-known than these.

300.
Christopher Ehret, *The historical reconstruction of southern Cushitic phonology and vocabulary*. Berlin: Reimer, 1980. 470 pp.

Kölner Beiträge zur Afrikanistik, B, 5.

Southern Cushitic includes Iraqw and other little-known languages of Tanzania. See also C. Ehret, 'Proto-Cushitic reconstruction' in *Sprache und Geschichte in Afrika* vol. 8 (1987) pp. 7–180.

301.

Bernd Heine, *The Sam languages: a history of Rendille, Boni and Somali*. Malibu: Undena, 1978. 93 pp.
Afroasiatic linguistics, vol. 6 part 2.

This sub-group of Cushitic includes Somali and two minority languages of Somalia. Comparative vocabulary, pp. 51–78; English–proto-Sam word-list, pp. 81–93.

302.

Grover Hudson, *Highland East Cushitic dictionary*. Hamburg: Buske, 1989. 424 pp. 3–87118–947–2.
Kuschitische Sprachstudien = Cushitic language studies, 7.

The Highland East Cushitic sub-group includes Gedeo, Hadiyya, Kembata, Sidamo and other languages of Ethiopia. There may be as many as five million speakers of these languages in total.

303.

Hans-Jürgen Sasse, *The consonant phonemes of proto-East-Cushitic (PEC): a first approximation*. Malibu: Undena, 1979. 67 pp.
Afroasiatic linguistics, vol. 7 part 1.

The East Cushitic group includes Afar, Oromo, Somali and the Highland East Cushitic languages listed above.

CZECH

Czech belongs to the SLAVONIC branch of the Indo-European language family. It is the national language of the Czech Republic – until recently united with the speakers of the very closely related Slovak in Czechoslovakia – and has about twelve million speakers.

Czech uses the Latin alphabet with many diacritical marks: these are ignored in determining alphabetical order.

The modern standard

304.

H. T. Cheshire, L. Klozner, A. Srámek [and others], *Česko–anglický slovník = Czech–English dictionary*. Prague: Otto, 1933–5. 2 vols.

Still the largest Czech–English dictionary – there are many smaller more recent ones. Makes excellent use of example phrases. Corrections, vol. 2 pp. 1021–2.

305.

Karel Hais, Břetislav Hodek, *English–Czech dictionary = Velký anglicko–český slovník*. Prague: Academia, 1984–5. 3 vols [2843 pp.].

Makes generous use of examples.

306.
Příruční slovník jazyka českého. Prague: Státní Pedagogické Nakladatelství, 1935–57. 8 vols.
Ceské Akademie Věd a Umění; Ceskoslovenská Akademie Věd.

[*Concise dictionary of the Czech language.*] This work grew massively in the course of production, and no longer meets the usual definition of conciseness! A dictionary of modern Czech, in which glosses (in italics) are illustrated by quotations from named authors (final list, vol. 8 pp. v–xv) but without precise references.

307.
Slovník české frazeologie a idiomatiky. Prague: Academia Praha, 1994. 2 vols.
Edited by František Čermák and others.

[*Dictionary of Czech phrases and idioms.*] A dictionary of common phrases and idioms, alphabetical under keywords, most often nouns. Mainly in Czech, but some articles give equivalents in *A*, English; *N*, German; *F*, French; *R*, Russian. Vol. 2 completes the alphabet and contains a 'Concept index' (pp. 373–596) and a final essay by Čermák. Expansion of a smaller work under the same title published in 1988.

Older periods

308.
Jan Gebauer, *Slovník staročeský*. Prague: Unie, 1901–16. Vols 1–2 [no more published].
Vol. 2 edited by E. Smetánka. – Reprinted: Prague: Academia, 1970.

[*Old Czech dictionary.*] A concise historical dictionary of Old Czech with quotations of Latin and Czech sources, for which precise references are given (bibliography and abbreviations, vol. 1 pp. ix–xxix). The two published volumes cover **A–Netbalivost**, breaking off abruptly in the course of the latter entry.

309.
Staročeský slovník. Prague: Academia, 1977– .
Accompanied by: Jaromír Bělič, editor, *Uvodní stati, soupis pramenů a zkratek*. 1968. 130 pp. [*General introduction, list of sources and abbreviations.*]

[*Old Czech dictionary.*] Entirely in Czech, with numerous quotations from early literature. On a considerably larger scale than Gebauer (**308**), this new dictionary has sensibly been scheduled to deal first with the parts of the alphabet that were *not* covered by Gebauer, using his unpublished materials alongside new research. Thus it began with **N** and has so far almost completed three volumes, reaching **Povolánie** in 1994.

Etymological dictionaries

310.
Václav Machek, *Etymologický slovník jazyka českeho*. Prague: Academia, 1968. 866 pp. 2nd edn.
Prace Ceskoslovenské Akademie Ved, Sekce jazyka a literatury, 6.

1st edn: *Etymologický slovník jazyka českeho a slovenského*. 1957. 627 pp.

[*Etymological dictionary of the Czech language.*] A very useful concise etymological dictionary with a generous collection of cognates in other Slavonic languages. Abbreviations, including bibliography of scholarly works and of other etymological dictionaries, pp. 19–32.

The second edition omits 'Slovak' from the title, with the implication that Slovak deserves its own etymological dictionary. Slovak still comes first, in each entry, in the listing of cognates from other Slavonic languages.

Foreign words

311.

Věra Petráčková, Jiří Kraus, editors, *Akademický slovník cizích slov*. Prague: Academia Praha, 1995. 2 vols [834 pp.]. 80–200–0497–1.

[*Academic dictionary of foreign words.*] An extensive dictionary of foreign words in Czech; about 50,000 entries. A brief indication of etymology is given. Many terms are highly specialised or technical.

DAKOTA

Dakota or Sioux is a Siouan language, perhaps to be assigned to the wider AMERIND family, still spoken by about 20,000 people in southern Manitoba (Canada) and some north central states of the USA.

312.

Stephen R. Riggs, *A Dakota–English dictionary*. Washington, 1890. 665 pp.

Edited by J. Owen Dorsey. *Contributions to North American ethnology*, 7.

DANISH

Danish belongs to the GERMANIC branch of Indo-European languages, and is a descendant of OLD NORSE. There are about 5,500,000 speakers in Denmark and in Greenland (where Danish and Inuit are the two official languages).

Until the nineteenth century Danish was the official language of Norway, and until 1944 of Iceland.

Danish alphabetical order

a b c d e f g h i j k l m n o p q r s t u v/w x y z æ ø å

V and **W** are usually interfiled. **Q** occurs only in foreign words.

Historical dictionaries

313.

H. Juul-Jensen [and other editors], *Ordbog over det danske sprog, grundlagt af Verner Dahlerup*. Copenhagen: Gyldendal, 1918–56. 28 vols.

Det Danske Sprog- og Litteraturselskab.

Foreløbig liste over forkortelser, Liste over forkortelser. 1918–1939. 3 vols. These lists of abbreviations, to which loose supplements were issued, are now superseded by vol. 28 of the main work.

Supplement. 1992– .

[*Dictionary of the Danish language, founded by Verner Dahlerup.*] This large-scale historical dictionary, known as *ODS*, covers Danish from 1700 to 1955, and contains about 2,500,000 citations and many quotations, mostly relatively brief. There is some use of hieroglyphic symbols for special vocabularies, e.g. ✝ 'bird names'. Vol. 28 is a supplementary volume giving abbreviations for source texts, pp. 11–87, and other abbreviations, pp. 91–3, and also containing a history of the work, with list of editors and sub-editors, pp. 99–113.

The main work adhered, throughout, to the older variant of Danish orthography, without the letter *Å*.

The supplement, begun in 1992, will be on a considerable scale: vols 1–2, so far published, cover **A–Dozer**. Additions to *ODS* articles are marked +. Other articles are new, mostly dealing with new twentieth century vocabulary. Additional list of sources, vol. 1 pp. li–lxi.

314.

Pia Riber Petersen, *Nye ord i dansk, 1955–75*. Copenhagen: Gyldendal, 1984. 678 pp.

[*New words in Danish, 1955–75.*] A considerable selection of new vocabulary, with quotations mainly from journalism and recent fiction. List of sources, pp. 673–7; very comprehensive indexes, pp. 547–670, including indexes by prefix and suffix, by origin of loanwords, and by date of first appearance.

The modern standard

315.

B. Kjærulff Nielsen, *Engelsk–dansk ordbog*. Copenhagen: Gyldendal, 1991. 1203 pp. New edn.

1st edn: 1964. 1294 pp. This was followed by: *Tillæg til B. Kjærulff Nielsen, Engelsk–dansk ordbog*. 1974. 87–00–78971–2. [*Supplement.*]

[*English–Danish dictionary.*] United States usage is noted with the abbreviation *US*; some brief examples of usage are included, preceded by *Ex*. The sans-serif **S** marks slang terms.

316.

Hermann Vinterberg, C. A. Bodelsen, *Dansk–engelsk ordbog*. Copenhagen: Gyldendal, 1990. 1473 pp. 3rd edn by Viggo Hjørnager Pedersen. 87–00–25801–6.

Gyldendals store ordbøger. Cover title: *Dansk engelsk.*
1st edn: 1966.

[*Danish–English dictionary.*] A compact work, but with careful explanations of variant meanings. Where there is no equivalent English word and the gloss is an explanation rather than a translation, it is given in square brackets, e.g. '**Overboer** [person living in the flat above]'. Intended mainly for Danish users.

Older periods

317.

Otto Kalkar, *Ordbog til det aeldre danske sprog (1300–1700).* Copenhagen: Thiele, 1881–1907. 4 vols.

Followed by: *Nachträge.* 1908–18. [*Supplement.*] – *Kilde-fortegnelse.* 1925. [*List of sources.*]
Reprinted with the supplement and a revised list of sources: 1976. 6 vols.

[*Dictionary of the older Danish language, 1300–1700.*] Uneven because of changes of plan and lack of finance. Essentially a glossary of words not to be found in modern Danish, with quotations and precise references to source texts.

Regional forms

318.

J. C. S. Espersen, *Bornholmsk ordbog.* Meisenheim am Glan: Hain, 1908. <171> + 512 pp.

Reprinted: Copenhagen: Rosenkilde og Bagger, 1975. Det Kgl. Danske Videnskabernes Selskab.

[*Bornholm dialect dictionary.*] The dictionary cites few sources but is useful etymologically for its collections of cognate forms from other Germanic languages. Includes a grammar, by Vilh. Thomsen and Ludv. F. A. Wimmer, pp. <1>–<149>.

319.

Christian Molbech, *Dansk dialect lexikon, indeholdende ord, udtryk og talemaader af den danske almues tungemaal i Rigets forskiellige landskaber og egne.* Copenhagen, 1841. 696 pp.

On the author see Morten Borup, *Christian Molbech.* Copenhagen, 1954. 469 pp.

[*Danish dialect dictionary, including words, phrases and idioms of Danish vernacular speech from the various provinces and districts of the Kingdom.*]

320.

Ømålsordbogen: en sproglig-saglig ordbog over dialekterne på Sjælland, Lolland–Falster, Fyn og omliggende øer. Copenhagen: Reitzel, 1992– . 87–7421–744–5.

Institut for Dansk Dialektforskning, Københavns Universitet. *Universitets-jubilæets Danske Samfunds skrifter,* 518, etc.
Accompanied by: *Tillægsbind.* 1992. 66 pp. and 26 maps.

[*Dictionary of the island dialects: a linguistic and enthnographic dictionary of the dialects of Zealand, Lolland, Falster, Fyn and neighbouring islands.*] An important dialect dictionary, but poorly designed. Quotations, often in the International Phonetic

Alphabet, are in a very narrow italic font, and, if proverbial, are spaced out – thus quite uncomfortable to the eye. Entries are under normalised Danish forms and begin with a list of local pronunciations, sub-arranged by islands: *S*, Zealand; *L*, Lolland including Falster and Mön; *F*, Fyn including Taasing, Langeland, Ærö. The *Tillægsbind* or supplementary volume gives detailed explanations with a list of place name abbreviations, pp. 38–48, and of sources, pp. 49–66.

321.
Peter Skautrup, chief editor, *Jysk ordbog*. Aarhus: Universitetsforlaget, 1970– .
Aarhus Universitet. Institut for Jysk Sprog- og Kulturforskning.

[*Jutland dialect dictionary.*] A large-scale dialect dictionary of the mainland dialects, with word maps and quotations from printed and oral sources. The quotations, some of which are in phonetic script, are in large font, the glosses smaller. I have seen only four parts of vol. 1, which contain entries from **A–Ankel**: the latest appeared in 1979.

Etymological dictionaries

322.
Niels Åge Nielsen, *Dansk etymologisk ordbog*. Copenhagen: Gyldendal, 1966. 481 pp.
Gyldendals røde ordbøger.

[*Danish etymological dictionary.*] Highly compressed, with numerous abbreviations (list of these, pp. xiii–xix). Still there is room for the essential cognate forms and for occasional citations of the scholarly literature.

DINKA

One of the NILO-SAHARAN LANGUAGES, Dinka has about 1,250,000 speakers in the upper Nile valley in southern Sudan.

323.
Arthur Nebel, *Grammatica e dizionario dinka*. Bologna: Editrice Missionaria Italiana, 1978. 563 pp.

[*Dinka grammar and dictionary.*] Glosses in Italian. Italian–Dinka section, pp. 25–329.

DOGRI

Dogri, with 1,300,000 speakers, is the language of the formerly autonomous state of Jammu, now part of Indian Kashmir. It is an INDO-ARYAN language, and once had its own local script, resembling the Gurmukhi script that is used for Panjabi. Dogri is now written in Devanagari script, as is Hindi.

324.
रामनाथ शास्त्री | दोगरी डिक्शनरी [Ramnath Śastri, chief editor, *Dogri dikśanri*].
Jammu: J & K Academy of Art, Culture, & Languages, 1979–89. 6 vols.

[Dogri dictionary.]

DRAVIDIAN LANGUAGES

The compact Dravidian language family is made up of languages of southern and central India, in addition to one that is spoken on the borders of Pakistan and Afghanistan.

The interrelationship of the southern and south central Dravidian languages (notably the four state languages, KANNADA, MALAYALAM, TAMIL and TELUGU) has long been clear to Indian and European scholars. A link between these and the more northerly and more obscure languages, including Kurukh, Kui, Kuvi and Malto, was first recognised by Francis Whyte Ellis in 1816. Later BRAHUI, and the long-extinct ELAMITE, have been brought into the picture.

325.

T. Burrow, M. B. Emeneau, *A Dravidian etymological dictionary*. Oxford: Clarendon Press, 1984. 853 pp. 2nd edn. 0–19–864326–8.
1st edn: 1961. 609 pp. – Followed by a supplement in 1968, and by: T. Burrow, M. B. Emeneau, 'Dravidian etymological notes' in *Journal of the American Oriental Society* vol. 92 (1972) pp. 397–418, 475–91.

Fastidiously, 'the dictionary does not contain proto-Dravidian reconstructions' – yet it is still arranged as if it did, in Indian alphabetical order of what the reconstructions would have been! See the table of phonetic correspondences, with starred forms (proto-Dravidian) in column 1, on pp. xii–xiii. Entries are headed simply by numerals: these are followed by lists of cognates, often accompanied by quite long lists of meanings, in a standard order of languages. True etymological notes are few, appearing at the end of entries, preceded by /. Words that are certainly loans from Indo-Aryan languages are excluded.

Indexes by language, pp. 515–771 (see note on alphabetical order at the beginning of each index); index of English meanings, pp. 773–816; index of taxonomic names for flora, pp. 817–23. Concordance of entry numbers with those of Burrow and Emeneau's previous works, pp. 824–53.

Some challenging problems for the etymological lexicographer have here been discussed clearly and dealt with as effectively as possible, in Malkiel's view (**9** pp. 62–3).

326.

M. B. Emeneau, T. Burrow, *Dravidian borrowings from Indo-Aryan*. Berkeley: University of California Press, 1962. 121 pp.
University of California publications in linguistics, 26.

Fills the gap in their *Dravidian etymological dictionary* (**325**). A supplement will be found in the second edition of the latter work, pp. 509–14.

327.

David W. McAlpin, *Proto-Elamo-Dravidian: the evidence and its implications*. Philadelphia: American Philosophical Society, 1981.
Transactions of the American Philosophical Society, vol. 71 part 3.

DUTCH

Dutch, a GERMANIC language with about 20 million speakers, is the national language of the Netherlands and one of the two official languages of Belgium. AFRIKAANS, in South Africa, an offshoot or creole of Dutch, remains as a reminder of the former world-wide range of the language, which used to be spoken also in Indonesia (the former Dutch East Indies) and is still an official language of Suriname (the former Dutch Guiana).

There is a long history of research on Dutch and its vocabulary (**344, 346**). The existing historical dictionaries are to be joined by a new, large-scale 'Dictionary of Early Middle Dutch' (**345**), in which the vocabulary of twelfth and thirteenth century poetry will be highlighted. Late middle Dutch is more fully covered by Verwijs and Verdam (**334**); modern Dutch, dealt with exhaustively by the *Woordenboek der nederlandsche taal* (**328**) is usually counted as beginning in the seventeenth century.

Historical dictionaries

328.

M. de Vries, L. A. te Winkel [and others], *Woordenboek der nederlandsche taal.* The Hague: Nijhoff, Koninginnegracht, 1864– .

Jan A. N. Knuttel, Cornelis H. A. Kruyskamp, editors, *Supplement.* The Hague: Nijhoff, 1956. Vol. 1 [2334 columns]. This contains supplementary entries **A–Azursteen** followed by addenda, columns 2305–34.

H. A. Kruyskamp, *Bronnenlijst.* 1943. 144 pp. [*List of sources.*] Supplemented by: A. J. Persijn, *Bronnenlijst: tweede aanvilling.* 1966. 58 pp.

A reduced size reprint of vols 1–25 with the two 'Lists of sources' and the *Supplement* was published: The Hague: Koninginnegracht, 1993.

A. Moerdijk, *Handleiding bei het Woordenboek der nederlandsche taal (WNT).* 1994. 307 pp. 90–12–08027–4. (*Aan het woord*, 8.)

P. G. J. van Sterkenburg, *Het Woordenboek der nederlandsche taal: portret van een taalmonument.* 1992. 253 pp. 90–12–08008–8. [*Portrait of a linguistic monument.*]

[*Dictionary of the Dutch language.*] The great Dutch dictionary is now almost complete, the main sequence making up 27 numbered volumes in 38 physical volumes and reaching from **A** to **Zitdag**. Vol. 29 will be the last.

It is not surprising to observe significant changes in aim over the 130 years of publication. The oldest sections (parts of letters **A, G, O**) are organised as a prescriptive dictionary of modern usage, though already with additional historical information. In sections compiled from about 1880 onwards the dictionary emeges as more truly historical in its purpose, explicitly covering Dutch from 1500 to the date of compilation. In the final tranche, entries **V–Z**, a closing date of 1921 has been established, thus excluding the new words and usages of later twentieth century writing.

Typographically the dictionary is hard going, though the font is a bit bigger in later volumes than it is in earlier ones. In its long, dense paragraphs only a || symbol marks off glosses from quotations. These quotations are long and generously chosen, with precise references to sources.

Moerdijk's *Handleiding*, published in 1994, gives important and full explanations of the arrangement of the dictionary and of individual entries. Van Sterkenburg's *Portret* is a historical outline of the development of the dictionary: more briefly see van Sterkenburg (**346**) pp. 51–101.

The modern standard

329.

G. Geerts, H. Heestermans, Cornelis Kruyskamp, editors, *Van Dale: groot woordenboek der nederlandse taal*. Utrecht: Van Dale Lexicografie, 1992. 3 vols [3897 pp.]. 12th edn. 90–6648–411–X.

Van Dale en de nieuwe spelling. 1996. 31 pp. [*Van Dale and the new orthography.*] This appendix is accompanied by three coloured pages of new spellings, one to be stuck into each volume.

1st edn, by I. M. Calisch, N. S. Calisch: 1864. – 2nd edn, by J. H. van Dale: 1872. – 11th edn: 1984. 3 vols [3730 pp.].

Shorter edition: Piet van Sterkenburg, Willy J. J. Pijnenburg, editors, *Van Dale: groot woordenboek van hedendags Nederlands*. Utrecht, 1984. 1569 pp. 90–6648–104–8. (*Van Dale woordenboeken voor hedendaags taalgebruik.*)

On the dictionary's publisher and early editor see P. G. J. van Sterkenburg, *Johan Hendrik van Dale en zijn opvolgers*. Utrecht: Van Dale Lexicografie, 1983. 95 pp. 90–6648–901–4. [*Johan Hendrik van Dale and his successors.*]

[*Van Dale big dictionary of the Dutch language.*] A concise dictionary of modern usage. Numerous example phrases but very few attributed quotations. Separate dictionary of foreign words and phrases, vol. 3 pp. 3745–842. Layout of entries, vol. 1 pp. xlvi–xlviii; abbreviations, pp. xlix–liii; index of entries for prefixes, suffixes etc., pp. liv–lvii.

330.

W. Martin, G. A. J. Tops, *Van Dale groot woordenboek Engels–Nederlands*. Utrecht: Van Dale Lexicografie, 1989. 1654 pp. 2nd edn. 90–6648–123–4.

Van Dale woordenboeken voor hedendaags taalgebruik.

See the review (of this and **331**) in *Van taal tot taal*, December 1991.

1st edn: 1984. 1594 pp.

[*Van Dale big English–Dutch dictionary.*] I suspect many users' eyes glaze over at the complex symbols and numbered sub-headings used in this and its companion (below). Still they are the best and fullest bilingual dictionaries available.

331.

W. Martin, G. A. J. Tops, *Van Dale groot woordenboek Nederlands–Engels*. Utrecht: Van Dale Lexicografie, 1991. 1691 pp. 2nd edn. 90–6648–127–7.

Van Dale woordenboeken voor hedendaags taalgebruik.

1st edn: 1986. 1560 pp.

For an evaluation of the concise version of this dictionary see Geart van der Meer, 'Grammar, construction information and collocations in active bilingual dictionaries: a comparison and assessment of *Wolters' Nederlands-Engels* and *Van Dale handwoordenboek Nederlands-Engels*' in *Leuvense bijdragen*, 1997 no. 1.

[*Van Dale big Dutch–English dictionary.*] The English is sometimes rather quaint.

Older periods

332.

M. de Vries, *Middelnederlandsch woordenboek*. The Hague: Nijhoff, 1864–5. Parts 1–2 [no more published].

[*Middle Dutch dictionary.*] Covers **A–Anxt**, with numerous quotations. De Vries's work was to be replaced, at greater length, by that of Verwijs and Verdam (**334**).

333.

A. C. Oudemans, *Bijdrage tot een middel- en oudnederlandsch woordenboek, uit vele glossaria en andere bronnen bijeengezameld*. Arnhem: van Marle, 1870–80. 7 vols.

[*Contributions to a Middle and Old Dutch dictionary, collected from numerous glossaries and other sources.*] Still interesting as a collection of lengthy quotations from early literature.

334.

E. Verwijs, J. Verdam, [F. A. Stoett,] *Middelnederlandsch woordenboek*. The Hague: Nijhoff, 1882–1952. 11 vols.

Vol. 10 consists of two supplementary works with separate title pages: Willem de Vreese, *Tekstkritiek van J. Verdam in het Middelnederlandsch woordenboek*. 1927–9. 96 pp. [*Index to Verdam's contributions to text criticism in the dictionary.*]; W. de Vries, G. I. Lieftinck, *Bouwstoffen*. Completed 1952. 555 pp. [*Materials.*] This is an important guide to the printed and manuscript sources for Middle Dutch.

Vol. 11: A. A. Beekman, *Aanvullingen en verbeteringen op het gebied van dijk- en waterschapsrecht, bodem en water, aardrijkskunde, enz.* 1941. 600 columns. [*Additions and corrections in the field of land and water engineering and law, geography, etc.*]

Abridged version: Jacob Verdam, *Middelnederlandsch handwoordenboek*. The Hague: Nijhoff, 1932. 812 pp. 2nd edition. This is not a full revision: only the entries **Sterne–Z** were rewritten, on the basis of later volumes of the main work, by C. H. Ebbinge Wubben. (1st edn: 1911.)

J. J. van der Voort van der Kleij, editor, *Verdam Middelnederlandsch handwoordenboek: supplement*. Leiden: Nijhoff, 1983. 354 pp. 90–247–9130–8.

[*Middle Dutch dictionary.*] The main alphabetical sequence occupies vols 1–9 and was completed in 1929. The compressed layout, with its very small print and its inconspicuous || separating off the glosses from the quotations, resembles the layout of the *Woordenboek der nederlandsche taal* (**328**). Note that **Z** is interfiled with **S**. Entries are given under normalised West Flemish forms (for discussion see Pijnenburg, **345**, p. 170) but there are many cross-references for variant spellings.

History of the work, by J. W. Muller, vol. 9 pp. v–xxii: see also van Sterkenburg (**346**) pp. 103–13.

Van der Voort van der Kleij's *Supplement* actually serves as a supplement to the main work as well as to the *Handwoordenboek*. It contains no quotations but very numerous highly abridged citations from sources. Bibliography of sources, pp. 339–54.

335.

P. G. J. van Sterkenburg, *Een glossarium van zeventiende-eeuws Nederlands*. Groningen: Wolters-Noordhoff, 1977. 270 pp. 2nd edn. 90–01–81210–4.

1st edn: *Een glossarium van zeventiende-eeuws Nederlands: voorafgegaan door Enige aspecten uit de geschiedenis van de Nederlandse lexicografie*. Groningen: Tjeenk Willink, 1975. 152 pp.

[*A glossary of seventeenth century Dutch.*] A brief-entry glossary of early modern Dutch. The first edition was prefaced by historical notes on the history of Dutch lexicography.

Regional forms

336.

L.-L. de Bo, *Westvlaamsch idioticon*. Bruges: Gailliard, 1873. 1488 pp.

[*West Flemish dialect dictionary.*] Many, though not all, words are illustrated by quotations, often of folk poetry.

337.

Walter de Clerck, *Nijhoffs zuid nederlands woordenboek*. The Hague: Nijhoff, 1981. 854 pp. 90–247–9096–4.

[*Nijhoff's South Dutch dictionary.*] A dictionary of modern Belgian ('Flemish') words and usages, with long quotations from twentieth century Belgian authors. Appendices: cross-references for variant forms, p. 673; French loanwords, p. 679; list of words that are also found in the *Woordenboek der nederlandsche taal* (**328**), p. 685; 'list of synonyms', in effect a Dutch–Flemish glossary and index, p. 692. Bibliography of sources, pp. 845–54.

338.

H. C. M. Ghijsen, *Woordenboek der Zeeuwse dialecten*. The Hague: Van Goor, n.d. 3 parts [1232 pp.].
Zeeuwse Vereniging voor Dialectonderzoek.

[*Dictionary of the Rhine delta dialects.*] Entries concentrate on geographical variation. Abbreviations of place names, pp. xi–xiii; maps of selected isoglosses, pp. xiv–xxviii. Entries are under imitative spellings – note that the initial apostrophe ', which represents a 'missing *h*' in contrast with standard Dutch pronunciation, interfiles with *h* in the alphabetical order. Plenty of illustrations for agricultural and ethnographic items. Additions and corrections, pp. 1208–16. List of contributors, pp. 1218–31.

Slang and special vocabularies

339.

Hans Heestermans, editor, Piet van Sterkenburg, John van der Voort van der Kleij, *Erotisch woordenboek*. Baarn: T. Rap, 1977. 274 pp. 90–6005–135–1.

[*Erotic dictionary.*] Quite a lot fatter, for some reason, than the rest of the series of specialised dictionaries from this publisher. Bibliography, pp. 239–74.

Etymological dictionaries

340.

Jan de Vries, *Nederlands etymologisch woordenboek*. Leiden: Brill, 1971. 977 pp.
Shorter version: J. de Vries, F. de Tollenaere, *Etymologisch woordenboek*. Utrecht: Het Spectrum, 1991. 449 pp. 90–274–2947–2. Revised edn. – 1st edn: 1958.

[*Dutch etymological dictionary.*] Relatively lengthy and discursive articles, concentrating on the older vocabulary of Dutch. A second paragraph, indented, often deals with more speculative and distant origins. Addenda, pp. 881–5. Indexes of Germanic words cited in the articles, pp. 886–977, including an index of Dutch words for which no alphabetical entry appears, pp. 916–40.

341.

Franck's etymologisch woordenboek der nederlandsche taal. The Hague: Nijhoff, 1912–29. 897 pp. 2nd edn, revised by N. van Wijk.

B. van Haeringen, *Supplement* to the 2nd edn: 1936. 235 pp. A 1949 reprint of the main work was issued in a single volume with this supplement.

1st edn of the main work: Johannes Franck, *Etymologisch woordenboek der nederlandsche taal.* 1892. 1228 pp.

[*Franck's etymological dictionary of the Dutch language.*] Concise entries packed with Germanic and Indo-European cognates. Indexes of German and Dutch forms cited, pp. 849–97. The 1936 supplement has a separate index of all forms from Germanic languages that are cited in it.

342.

P. A. F. van Veen, *Etymologisch woordenboek: de herkomst van onze woorden.* Utrecht: Van Dale Lexicografie, 1990. 895 pp.

[*Etymological dictionary: the origin of our words.*] About 36,000 very compressed entries – a high number for an etymological dictionary, due partly to the great variety of loan words in Dutch, partly to the full coverage here of scientific words and compounds. The index of languages of origin, pp. 847–90, is useful but is cut to the bone: only one language is allowed per entry, either the one from which Dutch borrowed, or the one from which all European languages borrowed. Index of eponyms, pp. 890–93.

Foreign words

343.

R. Dozy, *Oosterlingen: verklarende lijst der nederlandsche woorden, die uit het Arabisch, Hebreeuwsch, Chaldeewsch, Perzisch en Turkisch afkomstig zijn.* The Hague: Nijhoff, 1867.

[*Easterners: glossary of Dutch words of Arabic, Hebrew, Aramaic, Persian and Turkish origin.*]

Other works of interest

344.

D. Geeraerts, G. Janssens, *Wegwijs in woordenboeken: een kritisch overzicht van de lexicografie van het Nederlands.* Assen: van Gorcum, 1982. 149 pp. 90–232–1926–0.

345.

Willy J. J. Pijnenburg, 'The *Dictionary of early middle Dutch (DEMD)*: the sources, their area and chronology' in W. Pijnenburg, F. de Tollenaere, editors, *Proceedings of the Second International Round Table Conference on Historical Lexicography* (Dordrecht: Foris, 1980) pp. 149–75.

The dictionary itself, known in Dutch as *Vroegmiddelnederlands woordenboek*, has not yet begun to appear. The intention is to cover the period 725–1300.

346.

P. G. J. van Sterkenburg, *Van woordenlijst tot woordenboek: inleiding tot de geschiedenis van woordenboeken van het Nederlands*. Leiden: Brill, 1984. 212 pp. 90–04–07304–3.

Index of titles discussed, pp. 208–12.

EDO

A regional language of Nigeria, with about 1,250,000 speakers, and the major member of the Edoid branch of NIGER-CONGO LANGUAGES. Edo was the language of the Benin empire and is also known as *Benin* and *Bini*.

347.

Ben Ohiomamhe Elugbe, *Comparative Edoid: phonology and lexicon*. [Port Harcourt]: University of Port Harcourt Press, 1989. 253 pp. 978–232–112–5.

Delta series, 6.

A study of the vocabulary of Edo and closely related languages. Bibliography, pp. 246–53.

EGYPTIAN

Egyptian represents a separate branch of the AFROASIATIC LANGUAGES, coordinate with Semitic, Berber, Chadic and others. It has a special distinction as the oldest recorded form of any linguistic family that still survives: this is because Sumerian, which was recorded even earlier than Egyptian, has no surviving relatives.

The oldest hieroglyphic Egyptian texts date to before 3000 BC – over five thousand years ago. When the various forms of hieroglyphic script gave way, under Greek influence, to a Greek-based alphabet, the resulting new form of Egyptian is conventionally treated as a different language, COPTIC. In this form Egyptian remained a living language, among Christians in Egypt, until a few hundred years ago.

The transliteration of Egyptian has been standardised for many years. The alphabetical order in Egyptian dictionaries is also standard:

ꜣ ỉ ꜥ w b p f m n r h ḥ ḫ ẖ s ś š ḳ k g t ṯ d ḏ

Hieroglyphic texts

348.

E. A. Wallis Budge, *An Egyptian hieroglyphic dictionary: with an index of English words, king list, and geographical list with indexes, list of hieroglyphic characters, Coptic and Semitic alphabets, etc.* London: Murray, 1920. 1356 pp.

Reprinted: New York : Dover Publications, 1978. 2 vols [1314 pp.]. 0–486–23615–3.

A concise dictionary with selective quotations: these are in hieroglyphic script only. Headwords are in Budge's non-standard transliteration with vowels. Progress of Egyptology, with a history of earlier dictionaries, pp. v–xlv. Numerous appendices, including an English index, pp. 1067–1255.

Not universally praised. People still use it; for those who know German, however, Hannig (**351**) is now preferable.

349.

Adolf Erman, Hermann Grapow, editors, *Wörterbuch der aegyptischen Sprache.* Leipzig: Hinrichs; Berlin: Akademie-Verlag, 1925–63. 12 vols.

The twelve volumes are organised as follows: 5 volumes of the main dictionary, published 1926–31. 5 corresponding volumes of *Belegstellen* [*Quotations and references*], published 1940–53 (note that the first of these was marked 'vol. 6 part 1'. It replaced an earlier typeset section of citations, which was issued with vol. 1 part 1 of the main dictionary in 1925). Vol. 6, *Deutsch–Aegyptisches Wörterverzeichnis* [*German–Egyptian index*], 1950. Vol. 7, reverse index by W. F. Reineke, 1963.

There have been several reprints of individual volumes. The whole set was reprinted: Stuttgart: Kunst und Wissen, 1982. 12 vols. 3–87953–045–9.

[*Dictionary of the Egyptian language.*] Almost the whole work is printed from calligraphy. The main dictionary is set out in four columns: transliteration (giving the alphabetical order, see above); hieroglyphic form; gloss in German with reference or quotation (if there is only one of these to give) or reference number; compounds and phrases in hieroglyphic script. If a reference number is given, this is keyed to the corresponding volume of *Belegstellen.*

The quotations and references, thus separated out from the main dictionary, are partly typeset and partly printed from calligraphy: only for vol. 2 is the latter method used exclusively. The method saves space but makes the search for references more complex.

Vol. 6 is arranged as follows: German–Egyptian alphabetical index, pp. 1–194; key to this in topic order, pp. 195–211; then a series of indexes of Coptic, Arabic, Akkadian, Hebrew and Greek words cited in the dictionary.

350.

Raymond O. Faulkner, *A concise dictionary of Middle Egyptian.* Oxford: Griffith Institute, 1962. 327 pp. [0–900416–32–7.]

David Shennum, *English–Egyptian index to Faulkner's Concise dictionary of Middle Egyptian.* Malibu: Undena, 1977. 178 pp. (*Aids and research tools in Ancient Near Eastern studies*, 1.)

Deals with Egyptian 'from the Heracleopolitan period to the end of the Eighteenth Dynasty'. Intended for students, but gives references to texts and also to some modern scholarly literature (abbreviations, pp. xii–xvi).

351.

Rainer Hannig, *Die Sprache der Pharaonen: großes Handwörterbuch Ägyptisch–Deutsch (2800–950 v. Chr.)*. Mainz: Philipp von Zabern, 1995. 1412 pp. 3–80531–771–9.

Kulturgeschichte der antiken Welt, 64.

[*The language of the Pharaohs: big concise Egyptian–German dictionary, 2800–950 BC.*] Important introduction on script and transliteration, pp. xxiii–lix. Glossaries including gods, kings, weights and measures, abbreviations, place names, pp. 1183–1412. Lists and indexes of characters, pp. 1025–1182. Twenty pretty maps, lettered in hieroglyphic scipt only, at end of volume.

352.

Roger Lambert, *Lexique hiéroglyphique*. Paris: Geuthner, 1925. 445 pp.

[*Hieroglyphic dictionary.*] In the author's handwriting, in four columns.

353.

Leonard H. Lesko, editor, *A dictionary of late Egyptian*. Berkeley, Providence: B. C. Scribe Publications, 1982–90. 5 vols.

A brief-entry dictionary to the Egyptian of the nineteenth to twenty-first dynasties, clearly laid out in 4 columns: transliteration, English gloss, precise source references, hieroglyphic forms. Numerous compound words and phrases are included (indented under the main headword) but there are no quotations of usage. Some references to scholarly literature. Abbreviations, vol. 1 pp. xiii–xix, supplemented in later volumes.

Vol. 5 is an English–Egyptian index.

354.

Dimitri Meeks, editor, *Année lexicographique 1977[–1979]*. Paris, 1980–82. 3 vols.

[*Lexicographical year.*] This was an annual guide, in the usual alphabetical order, to new text publications and scholarly work that were relevant to Egyptian lexicography.

Demotic texts

355.

Wolja Erichsen, *Demotisches Glossar*. Copenhagen, 1954. 712 pp.

[*Demotic glossary.*]

Special vocabularies

356.

Dilwyn Jones, *A glossary of ancient Egyptian nautical titles and terms*. London: Kegan Paul International, 1988. 294 pp. 0–7103–0284–3.

Studies in Egyptology.

Foreign words

357.

James E. Hoch, *Semitic words in Egyptian texts of the New Kingdom and Third Intermediate Period*. Princeton: Princeton University Press, 1994. 572 pp.

ELAMITE

An ancient language of southern Iran, believed by some to be distantly related to the DRAVIDIAN LANGUAGES. Early inscriptions from the region are in hieroglyphs, which are undeciphered. Then a cuneiform script was developed, an offshoot of the Sumerian type. Elamite ceased to be written, and became extinct, over two thousand years ago.

358.

Walther Hinz, Heidemarie Koch, *Elamisches Wörterbuch*. Berlin: Reimer, 1987. 2 vols [1392 pp.]. 3–496–00923–3.

Deutsches Archäologisches Institut, Abteilung Teheran. *Archäologische Mitteilungen aus Iran*, Ergänzungsband 17.

In Latin transliteration, with no table of characters. A major dictionary, with references, serving as an index to the corpus of Elamite texts; includes proper names, and gives German glosses (but some words remain unexplained).

The alphabetical order is A, B/P, D/T, E, G/K/Q, H, I, L, M, N, R, S, Š, U, W, Y, Z, and is made more complicated by the fact that prefixes (*h. f. hh.* and others) are ignored in filing. Sumerograms are capitalised and are interfiled with phonetic spellings.

List of abbreviations, mainly of source texts, pp. 1317–31. Important bibliography of Elamite studies AD 1711–1986, in chronological order, pp. 1332–68.

ENGLISH

English belongs to the GERMANIC branch of Indo-European languages. It has more than two hundred million speakers in the United States, fifty million in Britain and many hundreds of millions elsewhere in the world.

Numerically, United States and neighbouring Canadian speakers now dominate the English-speaking community, and increasingly set an international standard for the language. Historically, English is the language of England, established there as a result of migrations of early Germanic speakers in the fifth and sixth centuries. Its development in England is conventionally divided into Old English (or Anglo-Saxon, to about 1100: **365** onwards); Middle English (to about 1500, strongly influenced by French: **369** onwards) and Modern English (**360** and see **413**).

English spread to Wales, Scotland and Ireland, where regional standard forms exist (Anglo-Welsh, Scots, Anglo-Irish: **383** onwards; see **412**) as well as local dialects. Regional standards and local dialects are also to be found in several countries where English-speaking colonisation and imperial rule have implanted English as a local medium of communication (**371** onwards). There are many creole and pidgin languages based on English, but few of these have full dictionaries: see **376, 380, 391, 395**.

Only a selection of modern dictionaries can be listed here: among fuller lists note Hulbert's (**415**), with Barnhart's historical survey (**414**).

Historical dictionaries

359.

Samuel Johnson, *A dictionary of the English language*. London, 1755. 2 vols.

Several reprints, e.g.: London: Times Books, 1979. 2 vols in 1. 0–7230–0228–2. But many smaller books exist, with titles such as 'Johnson's dictionary', which are not to be confused with the real work.

See Gertrude E. Noyes, 'The critical reception of Johnson's Dictionary in the later eighteenth century' in *Modern philology* vol. 52 (1954/5) pp. 175–191. – Allen Reddick, *The making of Johnson's dictionary 1746–1773*. Cambridge: Cambridge University Press, 1990. 249 pp. 0–521–36160–5.

Johnson, a major figure in eighteenth-century English literature, set a pattern for later dictionaries in many languages, with his brief etymologies (now naturally superseded by later work) and his well-chosen, fairly long, literary quotations. These are attributed to authors, but without precise references. Quotations from prose or verse are given for most general words but not for the technical vocabulary. The dictionary is spaciously laid out; verse is set line for line.

360.

The Oxford English dictionary. Oxford: Clarendon Press, 1989. 20 vols. 2nd edn by J. A. Simpson, E. S. C. Weiner. 0–19–861186–2.

Also published in compact format: *The compact Oxford English dictionary*. 1991. – Also on CD-ROM: *The Oxford English dictionary, second edition, on compact disc*. 0–19–861260–5. – Note: Donna Lee Berg, *A user's guide to the Oxford English dictionary*. Oxford: Oxford University Press, 1991. 71 pp.

Supplemented by: John Simpson, Edmund Weiner, editors, *Oxford English dictionary additions series*. Oxford: Clarendon Press, 1993– .

Abridged edn of the main work: Lesley Brown, editor, *The new shorter Oxford English dictionary on historical principles*. 1993. 2 vols [3801 pp.]. 0–19–861134–X.

1st edn of the main work: James A. H. Murray, Henry Bradley, W. A. Craigie, C. T. Onions, *A new English dictionary on historical principles, founded mainly on the materials collected by the Philological Society*. 1884–1928. 10 vols in 12.

Corrected re-issue under new title: *The Oxford English dictionary*. 1933. 12 vols.

Introduction, supplement and bibliography [to the 1st edn]: 1933. Includes corrigenda, list of spurious words, bibliography of sources. The complete corrected re-issue and supplement were also published together in compact format: *The compact edition of the Oxford English dictionary: complete text reproduced micrographically*. Oxford: Oxford University Press, 1971. 2 vols.

The 1933 supplement was replaced by: R. W. Burchfield, editor, *A supplement to the Oxford English dictionary*. Oxford: Clarendon Press, 1972–86. 4 vols. This new supplement was also published in compact form as: *The compact edition of the Oxford English dictionary: complete text reproduced micrographically*, vol. 3. 1987. 1412 pp. 0–19–861211–7.

Abridged edition of the older work: William Little [and other editors], *The shorter Oxford English dictionary*. 1933. – 2nd edn: 1936. – 3rd edn: 1944. – Reprint with additions: 1973.

See: Hans Aarsleff, 'The early history of the Oxford English dictionary' in *Bulletin of the New York Public Library* vol. 66 (1962) pp. 417–439. – On the creator and first editor of the dictionary see: K. M. Elisabeth Murray, *Caught in the web of words: James A. H. Murray and the Oxford English dictionary*. New Haven: Yale University Press, 1977. 386 pp. Also published: Oxford: Oxford University Press, 1979.

The *Oxford English dictionary* is familiarly known as 'the *OED*' (formerly '*NED*', and to members of the Philological Society 'the Society's dictionary'). The history of the dictionary is outlined in vol. 1 pp. xxxv–lxi (see also references above).

Key to conventions, vol. 1 pp. lxii–lxiv; abbreviations, pp. lxvi–lxviii. A full and clear explanation of the layout of entries is in the *User's guide*, which accompanies copies of the compact and CD-ROM versions.

For over a hundred years the *OED* has been an essential item of equipment for those who work on English literature and history. It has also exerted enormous influence on the planning and layout of other English and foreign-language historical dictionaries – including even the Grimms' *Deutsches Wörterbuch* (**562**), which had itself helped to inspire the *NED* but was completed only long afterwards.

The original edition was completed after Herculean labour with the issuing of an introduction, supplement and bibliography in 1933. Practically everything in that first supplement was incorporated in the new four-volume supplement of 1972–86 (which, for the first time, admitted the existence of certain 'four-letter words'). All this material – along with a small selection of about 5000 further new words – then went into the second edition of 1989. So the second edition is a significant improvement on the first: the whole vocabulary now appears in a single alphabetical order, with a few additions and corrections, and with pronunciations (in round brackets) now in the International Phonetic Alphabet. A careful explanation of how the original materials were combined is given in vol. 1 pp. xii–xxi.

Based on a reading programme undertaken by hundreds of volunteers, the *OED* is a well-documented history of all the words that have formed part of English writing since 1150 – a very long period by comparison with many other historical dictionaries. It contains over 500,000 entries. It is also a vast fund of literary and documentary references, nearly 2,500,000 of them: until recently the user could trace these only under the headwords that they had been chosen to illustrate, but the CD-ROM version of the dictionary allows unrestricted searching.

A third edition, fully revised and updated, is now in preparation. Meanwhile an almost-annual supplement has begun to appear. The three volumes of the *Additions series* contain supplements to existing entries alongside new ones. Each of these volumes covers the alphabet **A–Z**. Some newly identified usages are traced back to the seventeenth century, e.g. **skelf** 'splinter', or even the fourteenth, e.g. **shut** 'narrow alley-way'. From vol. 2 onwards, each volume of the *Additions series* contains a cumulative index.

It is important to understand the limitations of the *OED*. Since the basic requirement for inclusion (sometimes relaxed) was five occurrences in printed sources, it is a dictionary of written (and, in essence, of published) English – not of the ordinary spoken language, still less of local dialects or of slang and argot, unless these happen to break into literary sources. It does not deal with old English and only selectively with middle English. Although overseas varieties of English were not excluded, they are covered sketchily. A series of specialised historical dictionaries, listed below, helps to fill these gaps.

361.

William George Smith, *The Oxford dictionary of English proverbs*. Oxford: Clarendon Press, 1935. 644 pp.

Introduction and index by Janet E. Heseltine.

Also of use: G. L. Apperson, *English proverbs and proverbial phrases; a historical dictionary*. London: Dent, 1929. 721 pp.

Proverbs are entered under first word (even if it is **A** or **The**): the index, pp. 613–44, is essential. Sometimes a brief explanation or gloss is given – not always, if the author felt the meaning did not need explaining. The quotations are the main feature: they show successive forms of each proverb along with contexts, dated, with precise references to sources. No bibliography of sources – but the bibliography of the *OED* (**360**) will serve.

The modern standards

362.

Stuart Berg Flexner, editor, *The Random House unabridged dictionary of the English language*. New York: Random House, 1994. 2550 pp. 'Revised and updated 2nd edn.' 0–679–42917–4.

1st edn: 1967. 2059 pp. – 2nd edn: *The Random House dictionary of the English language: the unabridged edition*. 1987. 2478 pp.

This has more proper names than its competitors, making it something of an encyclopaedic dictionary on the Larousse model.

363.

Philip Babcock Gove, editor, *Webster's third new international dictionary of the English language, unabridged*. Springfield, Massachusetts: Merriam-Webster, 1961. 2662 pp. [0–8777–9201–1.]

1st edn: *Webster's new international dictionary of the English language*. 1909. 2620 pp. – 2nd edn: 1934. 3210 pp. Earliest versions: Noah Webster, *A compendious dictionary of the English language*. Hartford, 1806. 408 pp. – *An American dictionary of the English language*. New York, 1828. 2 vols.

See: Eva Mae Burkett, *American dictionaries of the English language before 1861*. Metuchen: Scarecrow Press, 1979. 292 pp. 0–8108–1179–0. – Herbert C. Morton, *The story of Webster's Third: Philip Gove's controversial dictionary and its critics*. Cambridge: Cambridge University Press, 1994. 332 pp. 0–521–46146–4. There is a review of Morton's work by Anthony Quinton in the *Times literary supplement* (21 April 1995).

The 1961 edition aroused lasting and intemperate controversy, demonstrating the market potential for a large-scale 'conservative' or prescriptive dictionary, a market which *The American Heritage dictionary* (**364**) duly tried to attract.

364.

William Morris, editor, *The American Heritage dictionary of the English language*. Boston: Houghton Mifflin, 1992. 2140 pp. 3rd edn. 0–395–44895–6.

1st edn: 1969. 1550 pp.

Includes an appendix, 'Indo-European roots' by Calvert Watkins (cf. **772**). Notes on prescriptivism and 'politically correct' vocabulary, by Geoffrey Nunberg, pp. xxvi–xxx.

Older periods

Old English

365.

John R. Clark Hall, *A concise Anglo-Saxon dictionary*. Cambridge: Cambridge University Press, 1960. 432 + [20] pp. 4th edition by Herbert D. Meritt.

1st edn: 1894. 2nd edn: 1916. 3rd edn: 1931. The 4th edn is a reprint of the 3rd with a 20–page supplement.

A brief glossary, but with one highly abridged precise reference to literature (no quotation) for most entries. Sometimes useful for its references – marked off by square brackets and inverted commas – to entries in *OED* (**360**) under which Anglo-Saxon words are dealt with.

366.

C. W. M. Grein, *Sprachschatz der angelsächsischen Dichter*. Heidelberg: Winter, 1912–14. 897 pp. 2nd edn by J. J. Köhler, F. Holthausen.

Germanische Bibliothek. 1, Sammlung germanischer Elementar- und Handbücher. 4. Reihe, Wörterbücher, 4. 1st edn: 1864.

[*Vocabulary of the Anglo-Saxon poets.*] An Anglo-Saxon to Latin (or sometimes German!) dictionary. Proper names, pp. 856–71. Abbreviations, p. 872. Supplement, by Holthausen, pp. 873–97.

367.

Ferdinand Holthausen, *Altenglisches etymologisches Wörterbuch*. Heidelberg: Winter, 1932–4. 428 pp.

Germanische Bibliothek. 1, Sammlung germanischer Elementar- und Handbücher. 4. Reihe, Wörterbücher, 7. Reprinted: 1963.

See also: Alfred Bammesberger, *Beiträge zu einem etymologischen Wörterbuch des Altenglischen: Berichtigungen und Nachträge zum Altenglischen etymologischen Wörterbuch von Ferdinand Holthausen*. Heidelberg: Winter, 1979. 155 pp. 3–533–02799–6. (*Anglistische Forschungen*, 139.)

[*Old English etymological dictionary.*] In general this is a very concise etymological dictionary, tracing Old English words only as far back as proto-Germanic. Abbreviations, pp. 414–16. Supplement, pp. 417–28.

Bammesberger' work is a series of comments and corrections on Holthausen, alphabetically arranged, with references to further scholarly work. Abbreviations, pp. 142–6; bibliography, pp. 147–55.

368.

T. Northcote Toller, editor, *An Anglo-Saxon dictionary based on the manuscript collections of the late Joseph Bosworth*. Oxford: Clarendon Press, 1882–98. 1302 pp. [0–19–863101–4.]

T. Northcote Toller, *Supplement*. 1921. – Supplement reissued, with revised and enlarged addenda by Alistair Campbell: 1972. 753 + 68 pp. [0–19–863112–X.]

Earliest version of the main work: Joseph Bosworth, *A dictionary of the Anglo-Saxon language*. London: Longman, 1838. 721 pp.

A concise dictionary with very numerous short quotations, for which English translations are given; Bosworth-Toller acts as a selective index of Old English literature. Glosses are given in English: where a direct descendant of the Old English word can act as a gloss, this appears in small capitals. Latin glosses are added, on the basis of translated texts and manuscript glosses. The supplement is particularly full for **A–H** and fullest of all for **G**, a relic of the uneven state of the original work (see Toller's 1921 preface). Place names are covered in the original dictionary, but no new ones are added to the supplement and addenda.

Middle English

369.

Hans Kurath [and other editors], *Middle English dictionary*. Ann Arbor: University of Michigan, 1952– .

Plan and bibliography. 1954. 105 pp. Layout, with general list of abbreviations, pp. 3–14; bibliography of sources, with abbreviations for these, pp. 23–105. The bibliography itself makes use of a further list of abbreviations, see pp. 18–22.
Plan and bibliography, supplement 1. 1984. 0–472–01002–6. Contains additions and errata.

A large-scale historical dictionary, intended to deal fully with middle English, which is covered in the *OED* (**360**) relatively briefly. The set now covers **A–Tyxtest**, and will finally amount to about 15,000 pages. The typeface is now much improved on that of early parts, which were reproduced from reduced-size typescript.

Entries give alternative forms and spellings (which are cross-referenced), then glosses at great length. These are followed by many long quotations for each meaning in turn, arranged in date order. Quotations are not translated. Dates are often preceded by *a* 'before', *c* 'about'.

370.

Francis Henry Stratmann, *A Middle-English dictionary, containing words used by English writers from the twelfth to the fifteenth century*. Oxford: Clarendon Press, 1891. 708 pp. New [4th] edn by Henry Bradley.

1st edn: *A dictionary of the English language of the XIII, XIV and XV centuries*. Krefeld, 1864–67. – 2nd edn: *A dictionary of the Old English language, compiled from writings of the XII. XIII. XIV. and XV. centuries*. 1871–3. 594 pp. – 3rd edn: 1878-81. 661 pp.

A very concise dictionary. Following the Middle English headword appear Old English forms and Germanic (or other) cognates, modern English gloss, and references to selected texts – but scarcely any quotations. Addenda, pp. 704–8.

Regional standards and dialects

Australia and New Zealand

371.

S. J. Baker, *New Zealand slang: a dictionary of colloquialisms*. Christchurch: Whitcombe & Tombs [1941?].

Not seen. H. W. Orsman's *The dictionary of New Zealand English: a dictionary of New Zealandisms on historical principles* (Oxford: Oxford University Press, 1998. 965 pp.) has just been announced.

372.

Edward E. Morris, *Austral English: a dictionary of Australasian words, phrases and usages, with those Aboriginal-Australian and Maori words which have become incorporated in the language and the commoner scientific words that have had their origin in Australia*. London: Macmillan, 1898. 525 pp.

Title on running heads: *Australasian dictionary*.
Reprinted with foreword by H. L. Rogers as: *A dictionary of Austral English*. Sydney: Sydney University Press, 1972. 0–424–06390–5.

A concise dictionary with single and occasionally multiple long quotations to illustrate most entries, with full bibliographical references. Remains useful, not least for its coverage of New Zealand. The author was able to cite, under **Swagger**, a newspaper reference to his own work – and he laid claim, in square brackets, to the lexicographer's right to have the last word:

> 1896. 'The Champion,' Jan. 4, p. 3, col. 3: '*He* [Prof. Morris] *says that 'swagger' is a variant of 'swagman'. This is equally amusing and wrong.*' [Nevertheless, he now says it once again.]

373.

W. S. Ramson, editor, *The Australian national dictionary; a dictionary of Australianisms on historical principles*. Melbourne: Oxford University Press, 1988. 814 pp. 0–19–554736–5.

Abridged edition: Joan Hughes, editor, *Australian words and their origins*. 1989. 662 pp. 0–19–553087–X. This retains at least one quotation, sometimes several, for each word.

The aim of this dictionary was similar to that of several dictionaries of regional English. It covers 'words and meanings of words which have originated in Australia, which have a greater currency here than elsewhere, or which have a special significance in Australia because of their connection with an aspect of the history of the country'. Layout is very similar to that of the *OED* (**360**). Pronunciation is given between oblique strokes; etymological notes are in square brackets. Quotations, relatively brief, are arranged in date order under each meaning.

Selective bibliography of sources, pp. 765–814; abbreviations, pp. xiv–xv.

374.

G. Simes. *A dictionary of Australian underworld slang*. Melbourne: Oxford University Press, 1993. 225 pp. 0–19–553499–9.

375.

G. A. Wilkes, *A dictionary of Australian colloquialisms*. [Melbourne:] Oxford University Press Australia, 1996. 426 pp. 4th edn. 0–19–553798–X.

1st edn: 1978. – 2nd edn: 1985. – 3rd edn: 1990.

An enjoyable short dictionary with long and often amusing quotations. Phrases are entered under keywords, with cross-references.

The Bahamas

376.

John A. Holm, Alison Watt Shilling, *Dictionary of Bahamian English*. Cold Spring, New York: Lexik House, 1982. 228 pp. 0–936368–03–9.

A dictionary of 'the words Bahamians use when talking informally', including words originating in the Bahamas or now used there with special forms or meanings. Entries are under normalised English spelling, and include numerous quotations from dialect collections and literature. Etymologies and notes on non-Bahamian usage are in square brackets. List of informants, pp. xx–xxii; abbreviations, pp. xxiv–xxv; bibliography, pp. xxix–xxxvii. There are some encyclopaedic entries for folklore concepts, consisting partly of cross-references; a list of these entries can be found in the table of contents.

Canada

377.

Walter S. Avis, editor-in-chief, *A dictionary of Canadianisms on historical principles*. Toronto: Gage, 1967. 927 pp.

Follows closely the model of Mathews (**394**): a few illustrations enliven the pages of this scholarly historical dictionary. Rather lengthy, readable quotations. Bibliography of sources, pp. 881–927.

378.

G. M. Story, W. J. Kirwin, J. D. A. Widdowson, editors, *Dictionary of Newfoundland English*. Toronto: University of Toronto Press, 1982. 625 pp. 0–8020–5570–2.

A readable historical dictionary of the local spoken and written vocabulary where it differs from standard English, with long quotations and precise references. A well-organised bibliography: chronological list, pp. xxxv–lii; alphabetical index, with titles of periodicals, pp. liii–lviii; list of dialect collections, pp. lix–lxvi; alphabetical index of collectors and contributors, pp. lxvii–lxxii; abbreviations, pp. lxxiii–lxxvii.

The Caribbean

379.

Richard Allsopp, *Dictionary of Caribbean English usage*. Oxford: Oxford University Press, 1996. 697 pp. 0–19–866152–5.

See the author's brief memoir 'Cataloguing the Caribbean' in *English today* vol. 13 no. 3 (1997) pp. 37–8.

A concise dictionary of the written English of the Caribbean. Intended for educational use, it excludes most usages considered 'wrong' locally, but cites oral as well as written sources, with precise references for the latter. 'Citation codes' (i.e. bibliography of sources), pp. 627–66. Etymological notes in heavy square brackets; pronunciation (International Phonetic Alphabet) in light square brackets.

The 'French and Spanish supplement' on pp. 669–97 is in fact an important quadrilingual English–scientific Latin–Caribbean French–Caribbean Spanish glossary of local flora and fauna.

380.

F. G. Cassidy, R. B. Le Page, editors, *Dictionary of Jamaican English.*
Cambridge: Cambridge University Press, 1980. 509 pp. 2nd edn. 0–521–22165–X.
1st edition: 1967. 489 pp.

A concise dictionary, on the *OED* model, of Jamaican creole and of the local spoken English from 1655 to modern times, based on written and oral sources, with brief, precisely attributed quotations. Headwords are normalised English spellings for words that have appeared in writing: these are capitalised, with cross-references for variants. Headwords for words known only from oral sources are in lower case. Supplement, pp. 491–509, incorporating the brief supplement that appeared on pp. lxv–lxxii of the first edition. Layout, pp. xii–xv; bibliography, in chronological order, pp. xvii–xxix; abbreviations, including dictionaries and glossaries cited, pp. xxx–xxxv.

The vocabulary gathered here was seen by one linguist as 'an abstract ideal type, a composite of all non-standard features, a combination which is actually spoken by few if any Jamaicans ... I am sure that Cassidy is the only living Jamaican familiar with all the fifteen thousand "Jamaicanisms" contained in it. I would not have wanted Bailey, Cassidy and Le Page to do otherwise, for ... the idealized extreme variety had to be described ...' (David DeCamp in *Pidginization and creolization of languages* ed. Dell Hymes, Cambridge: Cambridge University Press, 1971, p. 350). Jamaican creole, with over two million speakers, is one of the most important of the daughter languages of English.

England

381.

Joseph Wright, editor, *The English dialect dictionary, being the complete vocabulary of all dialect words still in use, or known during the last two hundred years.* London: Frowde, 1898–1905. 6 vols.

Vol. 6 has several paginations. It completes the alphabet, **T–Z**, and provides a supplement and a major bibliography of sources, which is arranged geographically with an alphabetical index. After this, with a separate title page: Joseph Wright, *The English dialect grammar.* Oxford: Frowde, 1905. 187 pp. This grammar is a fearsomely laconic work, so packed with examples that the word index to it (a significant supplement to the dictionary) takes up more than half of the space, pp. 83–187.

A dictionary of words known to have been in use in English dialects in the eighteenth or nineteenth centuries and not simply part of standard English. Standard English words that have a different meaning in dialects are also covered. Entries appear under a normalised English spelling, and are followed by a geographical listing of variant forms, followed by glosses and cross-references. Then, in a smaller typeface, quotations follow, most of them from dialect glossaries and texts, but some taken from literary sources. Occasional etymological notes, and some quotations from non-dialectal English literature, are given in square brackets.

Wright dealt mainly with English dialects, but a fair number of Scottish collections and a few Welsh, Irish and 'Colonial' are also cited.

India

382.

Henry Yule, A. C. Burnell, *Hobson-Jobson: a glossary of colloquial Anglo-Indian words and phrases, and of kindred terms, etymological, historical, geographical and discursive*. London: Murray, 1903. 1021 pp. New edn by William Crooke.

Reprinted: London: Routledge & Kegan Paul, 1985. 0–7100–2886–5. Reprinted as: *Hobson-Jobson: the Anglo-Indian dictionary*. Ware: Wordsworth, 1996. 1–85326–363–X.
1st edn: 1886.

'My first endeavour in preparing this work has been to make it accurate; my next to make it – even though a Glossary – interesting' (Yule). No one with an interest in history or language can fail to find *Hobson-Jobson* interesting. It is a historical dictionary of words current in 'Anglo-Indian' and on the Eastern trade routes, from the sixteenth to the end of the nineteenth century. Illustrative quotations, in date order, are drawn from travel narratives and other literature in numerous languages: those in Arabic and other Asian languages are given in translation. In the 2nd edition Crooke added a few entries and some further quotations, and corrected some etymologies.

Entries are under Anglicised (sometimes laughably Anglicised) Victorian spellings. Where words remain current at all, a different spelling has usually come into use by now, but the index, pp. 967–1021, offers many alternatives.

Difficult to classify in the terms of this Guide, *Hobson-Jobson* might as well have been placed under 'Foreign words' (see **407–411**), since most of the words it deals with are of Asian origin – or among the multilingual dictionaries (see **13–15**), since its word histories and its quotations are relevant to Portuguese, French, medieval Latin, Persian, Arabic and Urdu studies as well as to English. It is unique in English lexicography.

The catch-title is only partly explained by the relevant entry:

HOBSON-JOBSON, s. A native festal excitement ... This phrase may be taken as a typical one of the most highly assimilated class of Anglo-Indian *argot* ... peculiar to the British soldier and his surroundings ... an Anglo-Saxon version of the wailings of the Mahommedans as they beat their breasts in the procession of the *Moharram* – "*Yâ Hasan! Yâ Hosain!*"

For further help see Yule's preface, p. ix, which concludes: 'At any rate, there it is.'

Ireland

383.

C. I. Macafee, editor, *A concise Ulster dictionary*. Oxford: Oxford University Press, 1996. 405 pp. 0–19–863132–4.

© The Ulster Folk and Transport Museum. – See the review in the *Times literary supplement*, 1 November 1996, which backhandedly praises the dictionary as a 'folk-life project' and 'an antiquarian paradise'. 'The argot of the current conflict [has] rigorously been excluded.'

Based on materials collected in the 1950s and now in the Ulster Dialect Archive. No citations or quotations, but some important etymological notes. Taxonomic names are given for flora and fauna, and there are many line-drawings. Intended partly for school use.

384.

Diarmaid Ó Muirithe, *A dictionary of Anglo-Irish: words and phrases from Irish in the English of Ireland*. Blackrock: Four Courts Press, 1996. 240 pp. 1–85182–197–X.

Irish headwords appear here in standard Irish spelling (thus *whiskey* appears under **Uisce beatha**). Alternative spellings are given in the body of entries, and there is an index of these on pp. 211–40. Some brief quotations, or at least citations, are given for every entry. List of oral sources, pp. 17–20; printed sources, pp. 205–10.

385.

Richard Wall, *A dictionary and glossary of the Irish literary revival*. Gerrards Cross: Smythe, 1995. 137 pp. 0–86140–359–2.

Entries are under a selected normalised English spelling, with many cross-references for variants. Uses 'quotations from the works of all the major and a number of the minor writers who were active in the fifty-year period, 1889–1939'.

Scotland

386.

William A. Craigie, A. J. Aitken, J. A. C. Stevenson, *A dictionary of the older Scottish tongue from the twelfth century to the end of the seventeenth*. Chicago: University of Chicago Press; Aberdeen: Aberdeen University Press; Oxford: Oxford University Press, 1931– .

'*DOST*' has now reached part 44 in vol. 8, covering **s(c)hake–s(c)hot**, published 1996. It is a historical dictionary giving very numerous brief quotations, very precisely referenced. Brief etymologies are given in square brackets. Bibliography of sources, vol. 3 pp. xiii–xxxii, followed by later supplementary lists. Entries include numerous alternative spellings. There is a volume index of these in each of vols 1–3; for vol. 4 onwards, cross-references are given in the main alphabetical sequence.

387.

William Grant, David D. Murison, editors, *The Scottish national dictionary, designed partly on regional lines and partly on historical principles, and containing all the Scottish words known to be in use or to have been in use since c. 1700*. Edinburgh: Scottish National Dictionary Association, 1931–76. 10 vols. [0–08–030361–7.]

Reprint in compact format: *The compact Scottish national dictionary*. Aberdeen: Aberdeen University Press, 1986. 2 vols. [0–08–034518–2.]

'The dictionary offers or suggests valuable material for the scientist, the linguist and the literary man' [*sic*]. Its layout is pleasantly spacious. At first the majority of quotations came from literary sources; in later volumes they were drawn predominantly from journalism and from dialect collections. They are arranged by county and by date; verse is set line for line. 'The Association took over all the material gathered by the Scottish Dialects Committee ... collecting unrecorded dialect idioms, words, meanings and pronunciations.'

Supplement to the dictionary, vol. 10 pp. 325–535; supplements of personal names, pp. 299–307; place names that have local forms, pp. 307–11; abbreviations of Scottish relevance, p. 323; scientific words with Scottish connections, pp. 575–91. List of fairs and markets, pp. 311–5; currencies, weights and measures, pp. 316–17.

Abbreviations used in the dictionary, vol. 10 pp. 318–22; bibliography of sources, pp. 537–74; list of correspondents and informants, vol. 10 pp. v–ix. The coda is taken from Barbour's *Bruce*:

> For gude begynnyng and hardy,
> And it be followit wittely,
> May ger oftsiss unlikly thing
> Cum to full conabill endyng.

388.

Mairi Robinson, editor-in-chief, *The concise Scots dictionary*. Aberdeen: Aberdeen University Press, 1985. 820 pp. 0–08–028491–4.

A brief-entry dictionary with no examples and no quotations: a bit boring, in fact, but notable for its careful datings, based on the *OED* (**360**) and the two larger Scottish dictionaries (**386**, **387**). Numerous cross-references for variant spellings.

South Africa

389.

A dictionary of South African English on historical principles. Oxford: Oxford University Press, 1996. 825 pp. 0–19–863153–7.
In association with the Dictionary Unit for South African English. Managing editor, Penny Silva.

Distinguished, among the many offspring of the *OED* (**360**), for its relatively long entries with generously selected quotations. There are naturally numerous loanwords from Afrikaans and from Khoisan languages; '|| precedes any item not fully assimilated into South African English.' List of abbreviations, pp. xxviii–xxix; selective bibliography of sources, pp. 811–25.

390.

Jean Branford, *A dictionary of South African English*. Cape Town: Oxford University Press, 1991. 412 pp. 4th edn. 0–19–570595–5.
1st edn: 1978.

On a smaller scale than the *Dictionary of South African English* (**389**) but with long and well-chosen explanatory quotations, for which precise references are given. Some entries on grammatical points, with cross-references, marked by a black square (see pp. xvi–xvii). List of sources, pp. 394–412. Enjoyable.

Suriname

391.

J. C. Focke, *Negerengelsch woordenboek*. Leiden: van den Heuvell, 1855.

[*Negro-English dictionary.*] A dictionary of the English-based creole of Suriname (Dutch Guiana). The language is now known as Sranan.

United States

392.

Frederic G. Cassidy, chief editor, *Dictionary of American regional English*. Cambridge, Mass.: Belknap Press, 1985– .

Review of vol. 2, alongside vol. 2 of the *Random House historical dictionary of American slang* (**398**) in the *Times literary supplement* (4 February 1998).

'*DARE*' is a large-scale dialect dictionary based on oral collections and on literature; alongside other United States dialects of English it includes Gullah, the creole of the Sea Islands and the Georgia coast. Most entries are under normalised American English spellings. Entries are arranged historically, like the *OED* (**360**), with dates and geographical abbreviations standing out well in bold face. Many word maps. The layout is a particularly neat variant on the *OED* model.

Huge list of informants, vol. 1 pp. lxxxvi–cli. Abbreviations, vol. 3 pp. xi–xv. Geographical abbreviations consist of state names often preceded by compass point designations, e.g. *csKY* 'central southern Kentucky'.

Vols 1–3, published to date, cover **A–O**.

393.

Sir William A. Craigie, James R. Hulbert, editors, *A dictionary of American English on historical principles*. Chicago: University of Chicago Press, 1936–44. 20 parts in 4 vols [2552 pp.].

The aim was to exhibit 'clearly those features by which the English of the American colonies and the United States is distinguished from that of England and the rest of the English-speaking world'. Covers American English, on the basis of published texts, down to 1900 (but for words established before that deadline some later quotations were allowed, down to 1925). Using small but clear type for quotations, this is a very capacious dictionary, modelled on the *OED* (**360**). * marks a word or meaning recorded in English before 1600; *ƚ* a word that originated in the United States; || an 'individualism', a nonce-word or at any rate one that was known from only a single citation.

394.

Mitford M. Mathews, *A dictionary of Americanisms on historical principles*. Chicago: University of Chicago Press, 1951. 1946 pp.

Also published: London: Cumberlege, 1951. 2 vols [1946 pp.].

Designed to supplement, and often to correct, the *OED* (**360**) and the *Dictionary of American English* (**393**), this is a concise historical dictionary, with plenty of quotations, of words and expressions that originated in the United States. It includes terms for flora and fauna that have different meanings in the United States and Britain. Numerous illustrations by Irvin Studney. Bibliography, pp. 1913–46.

Vanuatu

395.

Terry Crowley, *An illustrated Bislama–English and English–Bislama dictionary.* Port Vila: Pacific Languages Unit and Vanuatu Extension Centre, University of the South Pacific, 1990.

Bislama (the older form of the name is *Beach-la-Mar*) is a pidgin based on English. It is the lingua franca of Vanuatu, a former British possession in the south Pacific, and is closely related to Tok Pisin, the pidgin of Papua New Guinea.

Slang and special vocabularies

396.

Gregory R. Clark, *Words of the Vietnam War: the slang, jargon, abbreviations, acronyms, nomenclature, nicknames, pseudonyms, slogans, specs, euphemisms, double-talk, chants, and names and places of the era of United States involvement in Vietnam.* Jefferson, North Carolina: McFarland, 1990. 604 pp. 0–89950–465–5.

Includes Vietnamese terms and proper names found in English narratives of the war. Amusing but difficult to read because of the heavy use of jargon in the definitions.

397.

J. S. Farmer, [W. E. Henley,] *Slang and its analogues, past and present. A dictionary, historical and comparative, of the heterodox speech of all classes of society for more than three hundred years, with synonyms in English, French, German, Italian, etc.* [London:] 'Printed for subscribers only,' 1890–1904. 7 vols.
A revised edn of vol. 1 is recorded: 1903–9.
Reprinted: New York, Kraus Reprint, 1965. 7 vols in 3. – Reprinted with an introduction by Theodore M. Bernstein: [New York] Arno Press [1970]. 7 vols in 1.
For the anonymously published *Vocabula amatoria*, counted as vol. 8 of this set, see **495**.

Spacious, informal, enjoyable entries giving a gloss (sometimes rather coyly) with historical notes and foreign (especially French) equivalents. Most entries, but not all, have quotations from sources, often long and informative. There are often cross-references to a main article under which English, French, German, and a few Italian and Spanish synonyms are gathered: these foreign terms were to be indexed in separate volumes, which did not appear except for *Vocabula amatoria* (**495**).

This work deals with the 'four-letter words' (though these are not, of course, truly slang) and offers exhaustive lists of synonyms and foreign equivalents for them.

398.

J. E. Lighter, editor, *Random House historical dictionary of American slang.* New York: Random House, 1994– .

Review of vol. 2, alongside vol. 2 of the *Dictionary of American regional English* (**392**) in the *Times literary supplement* (4 February 1998).

Closely modelled on the *OED* (**360**), this is probably at present the best and fullest historical dictionary of slang in any language. It is based largely on literary sources, but uses oral collections too. Critical bibliography of other dictionaries, vol. 1 pp. xli–xlvii; guide to arrangement of entries, vol. 2 pp. xi–xxii; abbreviations, vol. 2 pp. xxv–xxviii.

Vols 1–2 cover **A–O**, so the third volume will presumably complete the set.

399.

Eric Partridge, *A dictionary of slang and unconventional English*. London: Routledge, 1984. 1400 pp. 0–7100–9820–0. 8th edition by Paul Beale.

1st edn: 1937. – 2nd edn: 1938. – 3rd edn: 1949. – 4th edn: 1951. – 5th edn: 1961. 6th edn: 1967. – 7th edn: 1970. In these two editions the supplement was issued as a second volume. Abridged edn: *A dictionary of historical slang*. Harmondsworth: Penguin, 1972. 1065 pp. 0–14–051046–X. Abridged by Jacqueline Simpson. (*Penguin reference*.) This was also published as: *The Routledge dictionary of historical slang*. London: Routledge, 1973. 1065 pp. 0–7100–7761–0. The abridged edition retains datings and a few references to sources.

The 8th edition at last combines the growing supplement with the original material in a single alphabetical order, also incorporating later work by Partridge up to his 'last suggestion for a new entry, a mere six weeks before his death at the age of 85 on 1 June 1979'. This is a very concise dictionary with century datings, localisations (*Aus.*; *prisons' coll.*), references to other dictionaries, and a few quotations (but no precise references). Entries from many registers and from many historical periods, with some discussion of synonyms and their contrasting usages. Appendix of encyclopaedic entries on some special jargons and argots, pp. 1373–1400.

The problem with slang dictionaries is that heavy jocular expressions, unfunny even when first written, get enshrined here for ever. Partridge, like Farmer (**397**), was too hospitable to such expressions. Older editions also included entries for 'solecisms, malapropisms, illiteracies', but Beale has cut most of these.

400.

Eric Partridge, *A dictionary of the underworld*. London: Routledge, 1950. 804 pp.

Reprinted as: *The Wordsworth dictionary of the underworld*. Ware: Wordsworth, 1995. 1–85326–361–3.

Very important dictionary of cant, tracing the history of many words back to the tramps and vagabonds of Elizabethan England. Very brief citations of sources: no precise references. So condensed that it is hard to read, but worth the effort. Supplement, pp. 789–804.

401.

J. Redding Ware, *Passing English of the Victorian era: a dictionary of heterodox English, slang, and phrase*. London: Routledge [1909]. 271 pp.

'It may be hoped that there are errors on every page, and also that no entry is "quite too dull".' Not dull, and not entirely superseded by any other dictionary.

402.

Gordon Williams, *A dictionary of sexual language and imagery in Shakespearean and Stuart literature*. London: Athlone Press, 1995. 3 vols [1616 pp.]. 0–485–11393–7.

See the amusing and full review by Glyn Maxwell, 'Her privates we' in the *Times literary supplement* (21 April 1995): 'Given the nature of the age in question, Gordon Williams's dictionary could only have been broader in scope had he elected to confine himself to the imagery and language of, say, Life.'

Etymological dictionaries

403.

Clarence L. Barnhart, editor, *The Barnhart dictionary of etymology*. N.p.: Wilson, 1988. 1284 pp.

A readable, though concise, etymological and historical dictionary, naturally with some emphasis on the American variant of English, and with careful datings. About 30,000 entries. By far the best available etymological dictionary of English, the only one that stands comparison with modern equivalents in major foreign languages.

404.

Ernest Klein, *A comprehensive etymological dictionary of the English language, dealing with the origin of words and their sense development*. Amsterdam: Elsevier, 1966–7. 2 vols.

Reprinted in one volume: 1971. 844 pp. 0–444–40930–0.

Important for its coverage of scientific and technical terms, but lacks datings. About 50,000 very brief entries.

405.

C. T. Onions, G. W. S. Friedrichsen, R. W. Burchfield, editors, *The Oxford dictionary of English etymology*. Oxford: Clarendon Press, 1966. 1025 pp.

Good but highly condensed: no concessions to the casual user.

406.

Walter W. Skeat, *An etymological dictionary of the English language*. Oxford, 1909. 4th edn.

1st edn: 1879–82. – 2nd edn: 1883. – 3rd edn: 1897.

Note Skeat's 'Complete index to the notes on English etymology' in *Transactions of the Philological Society* (1903/6) pp. 373–8. This indexes his later work, published in papers in the *Transactions of the Philological Society* and partly in his *Notes on English etymology* (Oxford: Clarendon Press, 1901).

Skeat's preface has been quoted against him: 'In very difficult cases, my usual rule has been not to spend more than three hours over one word. During that time, I made the best I could of it, and then let it go.' Not reliable, but occasionally useful for its lists and indexes: prefixes and suffixes, pp. 732–7; homonyms, 737–48; doublets, pp. 748–51; language of origin (a selective index), 751–76.

Foreign words

407.

J. F. Bense, *A dictionary of the Low-Dutch element in the English vocabulary.*
London: Oxford University Press, 1926–[1939]. 5 parts [663 pp.].

A major, scholarly, etymological and historical dictionary of Dutch loanwords in English, many of very ancient standing, with close attention to forms and meanings and careful dating. Supplement, pp. 616–37; corrigenda, pp. 661–3. Symbols and abbreviations, pp. xii–xiv; bibliography (in its final form), pp. 638–60.

408.

Gerard M. Dalgish, *A dictionary of Africanisms: contributions of sub-Saharan Africa to the English language.* Westport, Connecticut: Greenwood Press, 1982. 203 pp. 0–31323585–6.

Reproduced from neat typescript. Almost all entries are supported by quotations (indented), mostly from the African or international press. Entries end with an etymology in square brackets.

409.

C. A. M. Fennell, editor, *The Stanford dictionary of Anglicised words and phrases.* Cambridge: Cambridge University Press, 1892. 826 pp.
'Published in accordance with the bequest of J. F. Stanford.'

Deals with loanwords that arrived in English 'since the introduction of printing'. There are 12,798 entries. 'Anglicised' may mean 'borrowed and wholly or partly naturalised; used without naturalisation; familiarised by frequent quotation.' Examples of these three categories: **Potato, Amour, Revenons à nos moutons**. This is a historical dictionary with dated quotations and precise references, based on the reading of 'several hundred' sources. Still interesting, though the *OED* (**360**) often has more quotations and earlier datings.

410.

John Orr, *Old French and modern English idiom.* Oxford: Blackwell, 1962. 160 pp.

The main section (chapter 5, pp. 30–147) is a dictionary of modern English usages and phrases which are calques of old French. This is followed by a brief list of English proverbs with old French analogues. Generous quotations of old French texts throughout: bibliography of these, pp. 156-60.

411.

J. Alan Pfeffer, Garland Cannon, *German loanwords in English: an historical dictionary.* Cambridge: Cambridge University Press, 1994. 381 pp. 0–521–40254–9.

The dictionary (5380 entries) is on pp. 133–353; it includes many modern loanwords usually counted as Graeco-Latin, on the proper grounds that they were adopted in English as a result of having been devised and used in German. 'Supplementary loanwords', pp. 359–78 (mostly not fully naturalised: see p. xxxiv).

Other works of interest

412.
A. J. Aitken, 'On some deficiencies in our Scottish dictionaries' in W. Pijnenburg, F. de Tollenaere, editors, *Proceedings of the Second International Round Table Conference on Historical Lexicography* (Dordrecht: Foris, 1980) pp. 33–56.

413.
R. Bailey, 'Progress toward a dictionary of early modern English 1475–1700' in W. Pijnenburg, F. de Tollenaere, editors, *Proceedings of the Second International Round Table Conference on Historical Lexicography* (Dordrecht: Foris, 1980) pp. 199–226.
Work was begun in 1927 by Charles C. Fries of the University of Michigan. Bailey gives the draft entry for **Sonnet** as an example. The original scheme was important for including quotations from contemporary grammarians and literary theorists, like *Le français classique* (**471**) but on a very large scale.

414.
Clarence L. Barnhart, 'American lexicography, 1945–1973' in *American speech* vol. 53 (1978) pp. 83–140.

415.
J. R. Hulbert, *Dictionaries, British and American*. London: Andre Deutsch, 1968. 109 pp. 'Revised edn.'
The language library.
1st edn: 1955. 107 pp.

ESTONIAN

One of the URALIC LANGUAGES, Estonian is most closely related to neighbouring Finnish: their territories are separated by the Gulf of Finland. There are just over a million speakers of Estonian in the now-independent republic of Estonia, which has also a large Russian-speaking minority.

Estonian alphabetical order

a b c č d e f g h i j k l m n o p q r s š z ž t u v w õ ä ö ü x y

c, q, w, x and *y* occur only in foreign loanwords that keep their original foreign spellings. *č, f, š* and *ž* are used for non-native sounds in foreign loanwords that have been respelt the Estonian way.

The modern standard

416.
Eesti kirjakeele seletussõnaraamat. Tallinn: Valgus, 1988– .
Edited by E. Raiet and others. Eesti NSV Teaduste Akadeemia, Keele ja Kirjanduse Instituut.

[*Explanatory dictionary of the Estonian literary language.*] A monolingual dictionary of modern Estonian illustrated by example sentences and quotations, both of which appear in italics. No precise references are given, but attributed quotations are distinguished with a black dot •. So far publication has reached vol. 4 part 3, and **A– Põgusus** is covered.

417.

Eesti õigekeelsuse-sõnaraamat. Tartu, 1925–37. 3 vols [1719 pp.].

Eesti Kirjanduse Selts. Edited by J. V. Veski, E. Muuk and others.
1st edn: *Eesti keele õigekirjutuse-sõnaraamat.* 1918.

[*Estonian standard dictionary.*] Initially edited by Johannes Voldemar Veski, this is an officially sponsored monolingual dictionary designed to be the standard authority on written Estonian. In this and other works Veski extended the resources of Estonian, drawing on dialect vocabulary and making new compounds; 7000 neologisms are credited to him personally.

418.

Paul F. Saagpakk, *Eesti–inglise sõnaraamat = Estonian–English dictionary.* New Haven: Yale University Press, 1982. 1180 pp. 0–300–02849–0.

With an introduction by Johannes Aavik. *Yale linguistic series.*

A concise bilingual dictionary with full treatment of compound words. Aavik's introduction is actually a grammar, pp. xxxvii–lxxviii; it is followed by Saagpakk's article 'Linguistic innovation in Estonian', pp. lxxix–lxxxvii, and by paradigms, pp. lxxxix–cxi. These are numbered, 1–594, and the entries in the dictionary itself are keyed to them.

419.

J. Silvet, *Eesti–inglise sõnaraamat = Estonian–English dictionary.* Tallinn: Kirjastus "Eesti Raamat", 1965. 508 pp.

Reprint or new edition: Tallinn: Valgus, 1989. 508 pp. 5–440–00035–6.

[*Estonian–English dictionary.*] A brief-entry dictionary intended for Estonian users. Both editions were also published in North America.

420.

J. Silvet, *Inglise–eesti sõnaraamat.* Tallinn: Valgus, 1989. 2 vols. '3rd edn.'

1st edn: *An English-Estonian dictionary = Inglise-eesti sõnaraamat.* Tartu, 1939–40. 7 parts [1205 pp.]. – '2nd edn': Vadstena, 1946. 1205 pp.

[*English–Estonian dictionary.*] A brief-entry dictionary. I have not seen the earlier editions, cited here from the British Library catalogue.

Regional forms

421.

Eesti murrete sõnaraamat. Tallinn: Eesti Keele Instituut, 1994– .

Edited by Anu Haak and others.

[*Estonian dialect dictionary.*] A large-scale project which still has far to go.

422.

Valdek Pall, *Väike murdesõnastik =Краткий диалектный словарь*. Tallinn: Valgus, 1982–9. 2 vols.

Eesti NSV Teaduste Akadeemia Keele ja Kirjanduse Instituut.

[*Little dialect glossary.*] A brief-entry dictionary whose main feature is a list of districts where each word is used. Abbreviations for place names, vol. 1 pp. 9–10.

ETHIOPIC

Ethiopic or Geᶜez, the classical language of Ethiopia, is a SEMITIC language, parent of Amharic and some other modern languages of Ethiopia. It is most closely related to Arabic and to the South Arabian dialects. It first occurs in inscriptions of the first few centuries AD, especially in fourth century inscriptions from Axum, now in Eritrea. Ethiopic was still the language of literature, religion and official documents in the nineteenth century, but now retains only some religious uses.

As the vehicle of a classical Christian civilisation of the interior of Africa Ethiopic first caught the interest of European scholars in the sixteenth century. There is a long history of research on the language.

The Ethiopic alphabet

The distinctive Ethiopic script was developed from an alphabet used for an early South Arabian language.

In this script, which is written from left to right, the original consonant signs are modified in a fixed pattern to indicate one of seven following vowels. Thus, unlike the other writing systems used for Semitic languages, that of Ethiopic represents the sounds of the language fairly fully. The 'first order' is of consonants followed by the vowel ä.

The 'sixth order' may represent either the vowel ə or the absence of a vowel: the same ambiguity exists in the scripts of some modern Indian languages.

The 'first order'

ሀ ለ ሐ መ ሠ ረ ሰ ቀ በ ተ ኀ ነ አ ከ ወ ዐ ዘ የ ደ ገ ጠ ጸ ፀ ፈ ፐ

h l ḥ m š r s k' b t ḫ n ʼ k w ä z y d g t' p' c z f p

'h' with the seven vowels

ሀ ሁ ሂ ሃ ሄ ህ ሆ

hä hu hi ha he hə ho

423.

Gabriele da Maggiora, *Vocabolario etiopico–italiano–latino*. Asmara: Scuola Tipografica Francescana, 1953. 578 pp.

[*Ethiopic–Italian–Latin vocabulary.*]

424.

Chr. Fr. Augustus Dillmann, *Lexicon linguae Aethiopicae cum indice latino.*
Leipzig: Weigel, 1865. 1522 + 64 columns.
Reprinted: New York: Ungar, 1955.
Note also: Sylvain Grébaut, [Roger Schneider,] *Supplément au Lexicon linguæ æthiopicæ de August Dillmann (1865) et édition du lexique de Juste d'Urbin (1850–1855).* Paris: Imprimerie Nationale, 1952. 521 pp.

[*Dictionary of the Ethiopic language, with a Latin index.*] Dillmann's work is based largely on the vocabulary of the Ethiopic translations of the Bible, though many other texts are also quoted. Quotations are in Ethiopic script and are often accompanied by the Greek equivalents that they originally served to translate. Glosses are in Latin. Latin–Ethiopic index, columns 1435–1522.

The final 64 columns contain a separate work: Werner Munzinger, *Vocabulaire de la langue tigré.* The Tigré is in Ethiopic script with Latin transliteration. Arabic equivalents are sometimes supplied: glosses are usually in French, occasionally in German.

Grébaut's *Supplement* has a curious structure, but may be useful occasionally. The main section, pp. 1–390, forms an edition of Juste d'Urbin's unpublished Ethiopic glossary of 1850–55: all entries are included, whether or not they duplicate Dillmann. Interfiled with them are Grébaut's own additions to Dillmann (luckily identifiable as such without too much difficulty). This section is followed by corrections and additions by Grébaut himself (pp. 391–8 and 446–90) and by some notes on Juste d'Urbin's glossary by Roger Schneider (pp. 399–443).

425.

Wolf Leslau, *Comparative dictionary of Ge'ez (classical Ethiopic), Ge'ez–English, English–Ge'ez, with an index of the Semitic roots.* Wiesbaden: Harrassowitz, 1987. 813 pp. 3–447–02592–1.
Bibliography, pp. xxvii–xlix.

426.

Wolf Leslau, *Concise dictionary of Ge'ez (classical Ethiopic).* Wiesbaden: Harrassowitz, 1989. 247 pp. 3–447–02873–4.

427.

Hiob Ludolf, Johann Michael Wansleben, *Lexicon æthiopico–latinum, ex omnibus libris impressis, nonnullisque manuscriptis collectum; et cum docto quodam Æthiope relectum.* London: apud Thomam Roycroft, 1661. 559 columns and various paginations.

[*Ethiopic–Latin dictionary, compiled from all published texts and numerous manuscripts, and revised in consultation with a learned Ethiopian.*] Ludolf's work was far ahead of its time: he was one of the greatest of Semitic scholars.

ETRUSCAN

Etruscan is the ancient language of what is now Tuscany, in central Italy. Supplanted by Latin, it became extinct in the first century AD. Only short texts are known in the language, and it has not been fully deciphered. In spite of many conjectures, it has not yet been shown to be related to any other known language.

428.

Massimo Pallottino, *Thesaurus linguae Etruscae*. Rome: Consiglio Nazionale delle Ricerche, 1978– .

> [*Thesaurus of the Etruscan language.*] Vol. 1, which is all that has appeared – in four parts so far – consists of various alphabetical arrangements of the known vocabulary.
>
> The most important part is the *Indice lessicale*, published in 1978. This contains a main dictionary derived from texts in the Etruscan alphabet (but transliterated), pp. 41–375; then supplementary sections: words from texts in other alphabets, pp. 379–91; list of texts that cannot be confidently divided into words, pp. 395–6; fragmentary words, pp. 397–408; Etruscan glosses from Greek and Latin texts, pp. 415–18. Abbreviations for source texts, pp. 13–16; list of texts not used, pp. 411–12.
>
> Supplements 1 and 2 to the *Indice lessicale* were published in 1984 and 1991.
>
> Another part of vol. 1 is: Leone Fassani, *Ordinamento inverso dei lemmi*. This reverse index appeared in 1985.

EVEN

Even (Lamut) has about 20,000 speakers. It is a Tungusic language – member of a small and obscure language group of north-eastern Asia. The only other Tungusic language with an entry in this book is MANCHU.

429.

В. И. Цинциус, Л. Д. Ришес, *Русско-евенский словарь* [V. I. Cincius, L. D. Rišes, *Russko–evenskii slovar'*]. Moscow, 1952.

> [*Russian–Even dictionary.*] Not seen: cited from Sinor (**1599**).

430.

Gerhard Doerfer, Wolfram Hesche, Hartwig Scheinhardt, *Lamutisches Wörterbuch*. Wiesbaden: Harrassowitz, 1980. 1181 pp.

> [*Even dictionary.*] A bilingual dictionary into German.

431.

Harry Halén, editor, *Westlamutische Materialien, aufgezeichnet von Arvo Sotavalta*. Helsinki: Suomalais-Ugrilainen Seura, 1978. 212 pp.
Suomalais-Ugrilaisen Seuran toimituksia, 168.

> [*Materials in western Even, recorded by Arvo Sotavalta.*] This consists mainly of an Even–German dictionary of the western dialect.

FAROESE

Faroese is a GERMANIC language, a descendant of the OLD NORSE spoken by the Vikings who colonised the Faroe Islands in the ninth and tenth centuries. Once despised by the Danish rulers of the islands, Faroese is now the language of the press and of local government and education. There are about 50,000 speakers.

Faroese alphabetical order

a á b d ð e f g h i í j k l m n o ó p r s t u ú v y ý æ ø

432.

Hjalmar P. Petersen, editor, *Donsk–føroysk orðabók*. Tórshavn: Føroya Fróðskaparfelag, 1995. 879 pp. 3rd edn. 99918–41–51–2.

1st edn: Jóhannes av Skarði, *Donsk–føroysk orðabók*. 1967.
2nd edn: Jóhannes av Skarði, J. H. W. Poulsen, *Donsk–føroysk orðabók*. 1977.

[*Danish–Faroese dictionary.*] Danish spelling rules, pp. 852–65; Faroese spelling rules, pp. 866–73.

433.

M. A. Jacobsen, Chr. Matras, *Føroysk–donsk orðabók = Færøsk–dansk ordbog*. Tórshavn: Føroya Fróðskaparfelag, 1961. 521 pp. 2nd edn by Chr. Matras.

Accompanied by: J. H. W. Poulsen, *Eykabind*. 1974. [*Supplement*.]

[*Faroese–Danish dictionary.*]

434.

Annfinnur í Skala, Jonhard Mikkelsen, Zakarias Wang, *Ensk–føroysk orðabók*. Hoyvík: Stiðin, 1992. 669 pp.

Reprinted with minor corrections 1993.

[*English–Faroese dictionary.*]

435.

G. V. C. Young, Cynthia R. Clewer, *Føroysk–Ensk orðabók = Faroese–English dictionary, with Faroese folk-lore and proverbs and a section by W. B. Lockwood on Faroese pronunciation*. Peel, Isle of Man: Mansk-Svenska Publishing Co., 1985. 684 pp. 0–907715–22–2.

A useful brief-entry dictionary, essentially a reworking of Jacobsen and Matras's dictionary combined with Poulsen's supplement (**433**).

FIJIAN

This is a group of AUSTRONESIAN languages, with about 350,000 speakers in the Fijian island group.

436.

A. Capell, *A new Fijian dictionary*. Suva: Government Printer, 1968. 407 pp. 3rd edn.

'Compiled for the Government of Fiji.'

1st edn: Glasgow, 1941. 464 pp. – 2nd edn: 1957.

In origin a reworking of Hazlewood's dictionary (below).

437.

David Hazlewood, *A Fijian and English and an English and Fijian dictionary, with examples of common and peculiar modes of expression and uses of words; also containing brief hints on native customs, proverbs, the native names of natural productions, and notices of the islands of Fiji, and a grammar of the language, with examples of native idioms*. London: Sampson Low, Marston, 1872. 281 + 64 pp. New edn.

Reprinted: New York: AMS Press, 1979. 0–404–14136–6.

1st edn: *A Feejeean and English dictionary*. Vewra, 1850. 349 pp.

FINNISH

Finnish is one of the URALIC LANGUAGES. It has about five million speakers, most of them in Finland.

Karelian, official language of the Russian republic of Karelia, to the east, is usually written in Cyrillic script: it is best regarded as a dialect of Finnish (see **443**). Other Finnish dialects once spoken in Russia (**444** onwards) are extinct or on the way to extinction as their speakers have migrated to Finland en masse.

Finnish alphabetical order

a b c d e f g h i j k l m n o p r s t u v x y z ä ö

The modern standard

438.

Matti Sadeniemi, editor, *Nykysuomen sanakirja*. Porvoo: Söderström, 1953–61. 6 vols.

Suomalaisen Kirjallisuuden Seura.

[*Modern Finnish dictionary.*] A very large-scale dictionary of modern usage, with example sentences but no attributed quotations. Supplement, vol. 8 pp. 777–806. Corrections, vol. 8 pp. 807–9.

The so-called 'new edition' of *Nykysuomen sanakirja* (actually a quite different work under the same title) takes the form of a series of specialised dictionaries of the Finnish vocabulary. Two members of this series are listed here (**449, 451**).

439.

Suomen kielen perussanakirja. Helsinki: Kotimaisten Kielten Tutkimuskeskus, 1990–1994 3 vols. 951–861–433–4.

Edited by Risto Haarala and others. *Kotimaisten Kielten Tutkimuskeskuksen julkaisuja*, 55.

[*Comprehensive dictionary of the Finnish language.*] Strong on the modern technical and scientific vocabulary.

440.

Raija Hurme, Riitta-Leena Malin, Olli Syväoja, *Uusi suomi–englanti suursanakirja = Finnish–English general dictionary*. Porvoo: Söderström, 1984. 1446 pp. 951–0–12157–6.

A copious brief-entry bilingual dictionary.

441.

A. Tuomikoski, A. Slöör, *Englantilais–suomalainen sanakirja = English– Finnish dictionary*. Helsinki: Suomalaisen Kirjallisuuden Seura, 1973. 1100 pp. 6th edn.

1st edn: 1939.

The biggest English–Finnish dictionary.

Regional forms

Finland

442.

Suomen murteiden sanakirja. Helsinki: Kotimaisten Kielten Tutkimuskeskus, 1985– .

Edited by Tuomo Tuomi and others. *Kotimaisten Kielten Tutkimuskeskuksen julkaisuja*, 36.

[*Finnish dialect dictionary.*] Not seen.

Karelia

443.

Karjalan kielen sanakirja. Helsinki: Suomalais-Ugrilainen Seura, 1968– .

Edited by Pertti Virtaranta and others. *Lexica Societatis Fenno-Ugricae*, 16. *Kotimaisten kielten tutkimuskeskuksen julkaisuja*, 25.

[*Karelian dialect dictionary.*] A dialect dictionary of Karelian spoken usage based on research among older informants now in Finland. Glosses in Finnish followed by example sentences. List of place name and other abbreviations, vol. 1 pp. civ–cvi. The dictionary has so far reached vol. 4 and covers **A–P**.

Russia

444.

Juho Kujola, editor, *Lyydiläismurteiden sanakirja*. Helsinki: Suomalais-Ugrilainen Seura, 1944. 543 pp.

Lexica Societatis Fenno-Ugricae, 9.

Jarmo Elomaa, Johanna Laakso, *Lyydiläismurteiden käänteissanasto*. 1986. 150 pp. (*Lexica Societatis Fenno-Ugricae*, 9, 2.)

[*Dictionary of the Lydian dialect.*] Lydian–Finnish dictionary, pp. 1–510; Finnish index, pp. 511–43. The Lydian is in the transcription of the Société Finno-Ougrienne. There is full indication of local dialect variants: list of place name abbreviations, p. ix.

445.

R. E. Nervi, *Inkerosmurteiden sanakirja*. Helsinki: Suomalais-Ugrilainen Seura, 1971. 730 pp.

Lexica Societatis Fenno-Ugricae, 18.

[*Ingerman dialect dictionary.*] Fully documented dictionary from written and oral sources. Additions, pp. 702–10; brief Finnish index, pp. 711–30.

446.

А. В. Пунжина, *Словарь карельского языка: тверские говоры* [A. V. Punzhina, *Slovar' karel'skogo yazyka: tverskie govory*]. Petrozavodsk: Kareliya, 1994. 396 pp. 5–7545–0650–3.

Karel'skii Nauchnyi Tsentr Rossiiskoi Akademii Nauk. Institut Yazyka, Literatury i Istorii.

[*Dictionary of the Karelian language: Tver' dialects: about 17,000 words.*] Tver', formerly known as Kalinin, is close to Moscow in central Russia. A Karelian population migrated to this region in 1617 to escape Swedish rule. With a Russian–Karelian index.

447.

Y. H. Toivonen [and others], *Suomen kielen etymologinen sanakirja*. Helsinki: Suomalais-Ugrilainen Seura, 1955–81. 7 vols [2293 pp.].

Lexica Societatis Fenno-Ugricae, 12.

[*Etymological dictionary of Finnish dialects.*] An etymologically oriented dictionary. List of abbreviations for place names and dialect source materials, vol. 6 pp. 1883–9; other abbreviations, pp. 1890–95.

Vol. 7, *Sanahakemisto*, by Satu Tanner and Marita Cronstedt, consists of indexes to forms cited from other languages (see table of contents) including Karelian, Lydian and others closely related to Finnish.

United States

448.

Pertti Virtaranta, *Amerikansuomen sanakirja = A dictionary of American Finnish*. Turku: Siirtolaisuusinstituutti, 1992. 329 pp. 951–92664–3–7.

Etymological dictionaries

449.

Kaisa Häkkinen, editor, *Etymologinen sanakirja*. Porvoo: Söderström, 1987. 406 pp. 951–0–14050–3.

Nykysuomen sanakirja, 6.

[*Etymological dictionary.*] A discursive dictionary covering a very small number of words (under 2000), with references to scholarly literature but without explicit datings. Bibliography, pp. 400–406; historical introduction, pp. v–xix.

450.

Suomen sanojen alkuperä: etymologinen sanakirja. Helsinki: Suomalaisen Kirjallisuuden Seura, 1992– .

Edited by Erkki Itkonen. *Suomalaisen Kirjallisuuden Seuran toimituksia, 556. Kotimaisten Kielten Tutkimuskeskuksen julkaisuja, 62.*

[*Finnish word origins: an etymological dictionary.*] Two volumes have appeared to date, covering **A–P**. This work is much more concise than Häkkinen's (**449**) and covers a far greater range of the vocabulary: about 8000 entries so far. There are also fuller bibliographical references. Abbreviations, vol. 1 pp. 35–44; bibliography, vol. 2 pp. 9–29.

Foreign words

451.

Kalevi Koukkunen, *Vierassanojen etymologinen sanakirja*. Porvoo: Söderström, 1990. 714 pp. 951–0–13694–8.

Nykysuomen sanakirja, 8.

[*Etymological dictionary of foreign words.*] Very detailed history and datings of the foreign vocabulary, with references to source texts: index of these, pp. 641–55. Bibliography, pp. 662–714.

FORMOSAN LANGUAGES

This group of AUSTRONESIAN LANGUAGES, including Amis, Paiwan, Atayal and some others, is important historically as marking the probable point of departure of the earliest Austronesian migration, some thousands of years ago, the long term result of which has been the spread of Austronesian languages across the Indian and Pacific Oceans. In Taiwan (Formosa) itself, these 'aboriginal' languages are on the way to extinction under the pressure of Chinese.

452.

Raleigh Ferrell, *Taiwan aboriginal groups: problems in cultural and linguistic classification*. Nankang, Taipei, 1969. 446 pp.

(Institute of Ethnology, Academia Sinica. *Monograph*, 17.)

Comparative vocabulary of nineteen languages, pp. 83–418. English index, pp. 79–81.

FRENCH

French belongs to the ROMANCE LANGUAGES, the descendants of Latin. The language has a traceable history of 1,150 years, beginning with the 'Strasbourg Oaths' sworn by the sons of King Louis the Pious in 842 and recorded verbatim by the historian Nithard.

French is the language of a rich medieval literature, including the epic *chansons de geste* and the classic narratives of King Arthur. Old French is usually considered to be the language of the ninth to thirteenth centuries. Middle French, a more fluid concept, is often assigned to the fourteenth and fifteenth centuries; some linguists also include sixteenth century French under this label. 'Classical' French is the consciously purified, intellectually remodelled language of seventeenth century literature. Its influence, exemplified by the French Academy and its dictionary (**457**), has lasted well into the twentieth century: the French that modern authors learnt to write at school is in many ways scarcely different. There is now plenty of research into new developments in the language (for example, **509** onwards).

Dictionary-making in France has a long history (**506, 508**). Modern writers and scholars are well served by large-scale dictionaries, including two monumental one-man works by Littré and Robert (**454, 455**) and an early and highly successful example of computerised lexicography (**456**). Pierre Larousse was the nineteenth-century pioneer of encyclopaedic dictionaries (**459**). There are many bilingual dictionaries: only one is listed below (**461**). Two publishers, Larousse and 'Le Robert', compete nowadays with a range of specialised dictionaries, only a few of which are listed below. The sexual vocabulary of French has been thoroughly studied (**495, 496**), though partly excluded from general dictionaries (**504, 505**).

Dictionaries of Old and Middle French (**465** onwards) begin with the impressive eighteenth-century work (published later) of la Curne de Sainte-Palaye. In this area, and among the etymological dictionaries (**463** onwards), are several extremely scholarly and technical large-scale dictionaries whose completion may lie far in the future. The innovative 'historical dictionary' published by Le Robert is approachable and complete (**500**).

French is the national language of France and one of the official languages of Belgium, Luxembourg, Switzerland and Andorra. Beyond Europe, French is spoken in Quebec (**488, 489**) and elsewhere in Canada, in Louisiana, and as an official or second language in former French territories in Africa (**473**), Madagascar, south east Asia and some Pacific islands. A full dictionary of Quebec French is planned (**507**). After the Norman Conquest French was for two centuries a major language of England, in the form known as Anglo-Norman (**479**): it survived much longer in the phraseology of English law (**480**).

Regional dialects differ strongly from the Paris standard, but are now in decline. The French of Belgium is sometimes called *Wallon* (**474** onwards). The rural dialects of

Switzerland belong to the Franco-Provençal group (**490** onwards), intermediate between French and OCCITAN. A Norman dialect of French is still spoken by some people in Jersey (**486, 487**) and Guernsey (**481**). There is no general dialect dictionary of French: von Wartburg's etymological dictionary (**501**) would partly fill the gap if it were well indexed. The single-region dialect dictionaries of France are not listed here: there are bibliographies of them (**512, 513**).

Créole, a group of languages of mixed origin in which French vocabulary predominates, is spoken on many Caribbean islands (notably Haiti), and on Indian Ocean islands including Mauritius and Réunion (**483** to **485**). In the Seychelles, Creole (*Seychellois, Seselwa*) is an official language (**482**). The stories of Brer Rabbit derive from folk tales originally told in Louisiana Creole.

Historical dictionaries

453.

Dictionnaire historique de la langue française. Paris: Didot, 1858–94. Vols 1–4 [no more published].
Académie Française.

[*Historical dictionary of the French language.*] A dictionary of the classical vocabulary of modern French, so spacious and leisurely that it seems to come from another world. Numerous generously long quotations, weighted in favour of the seventeenth and eighteenth centuries but also from Old and Middle French, interspersed with discursive comments on usage and meaning. Alternative spellings are listed at beginning or end of entries. No cross-references: see the volume indexes, which also mark with an asterisk words that are not in the seventh edition of the *Dictionnaire de l'Académie* (**457**), e.g. **assécher** 'dry up'.

The four published volumes covered **A–azyme**.

454.

Emile Littré, *Dictionnaire de la langue française*. Paris: Jean-Jacques Pauvert, Gallimard, 1956–8. 7 vols.
Includes added material at head of vol. 1: terrifying photograph of Littré (frontispiece); Sainte-Beuve, 'Notice sur M. Littré, sa vie et ses oeuvres', pp. 13–47; Emile Zola, 'Hugo et Littré', pp. 49–55; Ernest Renan's obituary discourse on Littré, pp. 57–72; E. Littré, 'Comment j'ai fait mon *Dictionnaire de la langue française*', pp. 73–113.
Originally published: Paris: Hachette, 1863–73. 2 vols in 4 [2080, 2628 pp.]. (Additions and corrections, vol. 2 pp. 2567–621; bibliography of sources, pp. 2622–8.) This was followed by a *Supplément*: 1877. 375 + 84 pp. The supplement consists of added entries, and, in addition, L. M. Devic's *Dictionnaire étymologique des mots français d'origine orientale (arabe, persan, turc, hébreu, malais [Etymological dictionary of French words of Oriental (Arabic, Persian, Turkish, Hebrew, Malay) origin]*. This is accompanied by language indexes, and had been published separately in 1876.
Original edition reprinted: Monte Carlo, 1956–8. 4 vols. Not seen.
Jacques Baudenau, Claude Bégué, editors, *Littré: dictionnaire de la langue française. Supplément*. Paris, 1983. 533 pp. I have not seen this.

[*Dictionary of the French language.*] The republication of Littré's great dictionary is not the least of Jean-Jacques Pauvert's contributions to French literature. Although its layout is almost too compact, and it is printed on paper of poor quality, the new edition improves on the original by incorporating the 1873 additions and corrections and the 1877 supplement in the main text. All quotations are now separated off by guillemets, « ». The spelling of headwords is modernised (e.g. **collège** for **collége**).

Littré's dictionary is essentially of modern French from the seventeenth century on. Under each headword, successive meanings are given, accompanied by quotations from literature. A paragraph headed *HIST.* introduces more selective quotations from tenth to sixteenth century writings. *ETYM.* introduces a note on word origins with selected dialect forms.

Bibliography of sources, vol. 7 pp. 1961–76.

455.

Alain Rey, editor, *Le grand Robert de la langue française: dictionnaire alphabétique et analogique de la langue française*. Paris, 1985. 9 vols [9151 pp.]. 2nd edn.

Accompanied by: *Dictionnaire universel des noms propres alphabétique et analogique*. Paris, 1974. 4 vols.
The first edition of the main work was: Paul Robert, *Dictionnaire alphabétique et analogique de la langue française: les mots et les associations d'idées*. Paris: Société du Nouveau Littré, 1953–64. 6 vols [5548 pp.]. This was printed on extremely poor paper: library copies are crumbling.
Supplément to the first edition, edited by Alain Rey and Josette Rey-Debove: 1970. 514 pp.
Concise edition: *Le nouveau petit Robert, 1: dictionnaire alphabétique et analogique de la langue française*. Paris: Dictionnaires Le Robert, 1995. 2552 pp. 2-85036-390-1. '2nd edn, revised.' – 1st edn: *Le petit Robert*. Paris: Société du Nouveau Littré, 1967. 1970 pp. [Edited by Alain Rey.] – 2nd edn: *Le petit Robert, 1: dictionnaire alphabétique et analogique de la langue française*. 1977. 2173 pp. 2–85036–030–9. – Edition under new title, still described as '2nd edn': 1993. 2490 pp. 2–85036–226–3.
The concise edition is accompanied by: *Le petit Robert, 2: dictionnaire universel des noms propres alphabétique et analogique*. Paris: Le Robert, 1991. 1952 pp. 2–85036–074–0. 2nd edn. – 1st edn: 1974. 2016 pp.
For a memoir of his life's work, reproduced from his own handwritten text, see Paul Robert, *Aventures et mésaventures d'un dictionnaire*. Paris: Société du Nouveau Littré, 1970. 149 pp.

[*Alphabetical and semantic dictionary of the French language.*] Entries in *Le Robert* begin with brief etymology and the source and date of the first recorded use of the word; then the range of meanings, illustrated with unattributed (and generally invented) sentences and phrases on the model of the *Dictionnaire de l'Académie* (**457**).

Then follow relatively few, long, well-chosen quotations from literature, with precise references. For each meaning, there are synonyms and cross-references to other entries: this is a major feature of *Le Robert*, carried on into the concise edition. Entries conclude with a list of antonyms and of derived words.

Le petit Robert, the abridged edition, was a model of layout and typography. It retains datings and a few attributed quotations (but no precise references). *Le nouveau petit Robert*, the 'revised 2nd edition' of 1993 onwards, is in a fussier typeface. They include a dates–sources concordance, pp. 2434–6, a two-way dictionary of derivatives of proper names, pp. 2437–60, and a glossary of suffixes, pp. 2461–7.

456.

Paul Imbs, editor, *Trésor de la langue française: dictionnaire de la langue du XIXe et du XXe siècle (1789–1960)*. Paris: Editions du Centre National de la Recherche Scientifique, 1971–94. 16 vols.

For vols 8–16 Paul Imbs was succeeded by the tireless Bernard Quemada, who understandably allows himself to describe **Zzz...** as 'the most longed-for article in the whole dictionary'.

See Gérard Gorcy, 'L'informatisation d' un dictionnaire: l'exemple du *Trésor de la langue française*' in Franz Josef Hausmann and others, editors, *Wörterbücher = Dictionaries = Dictionnaires* (Berlin: De Gruyter, 1990) vol. 2 pp. 1672–8.

[*Thesaurus of the French language: dictionary of the nineteenth and twentieth century language.*] Computerisation allowed the astonishingly rapid completion of one of the largest of historical dictionaries in any language. The layout is excellent. Each spacious article is subdivided by meaning, a paragraph for each, including long quotations from sources (but rather fewer of them from vol. 3 onwards) and observations on usage. Additional paragraphs give stylistic notes, pronunciation, etymology and earlier history (including earlier meanings and citations from older texts). Littré's dictionary (**454**) evidently served as a model. These additional sections are briefer in the volumes edited by Quemada. At the end of many articles *Bbg* introduces a bibliography of research on the word or its meanings.

General bibliography at head of vol. 1, supplemented in each succeeding volume.

The modern standard

457.

Dictionnaire de l'Académie Française. Paris: Hachette, 1932–5. 2 vols [622, 743 pp.]. 8th edn.

Reprinted: Geneva: Slatkine, 1979–82.

9th edn: part 1 (Paris: Imprimerie Nationale, 1986. 2–11–080892–6) covered **A–barattage** in 116 pages. This is replaced by a second '9th edn', vol. 1 (1992. 2–11–081249–4), covering **A–enz** in 834 pp., with 7 green pages at end giving the new spellings that were promulgated in the *Journal officiel* and accepted by the Académie in 1990. No continuation of the 9th edition is promised.

1st edn: 1694. 2 vols [676 + 671 pp.]; revised printing: 1695. 2nd edn: 1718. 3rd edn: 1740. 4th edn: 1762. 5th edn: 1798.

6th edn: Paris: Didot, 1835. 2 vols.

F. Raymond, *Supplément au dictionnaire de l'Académie Française, sixième édition publié en 1835; complément de tous les dictionnaires français, anciens et modernes*. Paris: Barba, 1836. 861 pp. Lists mainly scientific and technical neologisms and foreign loanwords; ends with an entry for the character **&**.

Complément du dictionnaire de l'Académie Française. Paris: Didot, 1842. 1281 pp. 'Published under the direction of a member of the Academy.' Preface by Louis Barré. A much larger collection of neologisms than in the *Supplément* (but not wholly overlapping with it), adding foreign words used in French writings, regional and archaic words.

7th edn: 1878. 2 vols. This reprints the prefaces of the previous six editions. – Reprint of the 7th edn: Geneva: Slatkine, 1994. 2–05–101321–7.

[*Dictionary of the French Academy.*] A dictionary aiming to make authority, not to record usage. Entries are sometimes very lengthy, sub-arranged by meanings: examples are given, but these are normally invented. No citations of authors. The incomplete ninth edition is much stronger in non-standard (colloquial, slang) French than its predecessors, and the supplements to the sixth are useful for obscure and technical nineteenth century terminology.

458.

Jean Dubois, editor, *Lexis: dictionnaire de la langue française*. Paris: Larousse, 1988. 2109 pp. Revised edn.

1st edn: 1975. 1950 pp. 2–03–020285–1. Reissued as *Larousse de la langue française*, 1978, and in an illustrated version in 1979.

[*Lexis: dictionary of the French language.*] Numerous brief citations attributed to named authors. May be regarded as a concise edition of the *Grand Larousse de la langue française* (**460**).

459.

Grand dictionnaire encyclopédique Larousse. Paris: Larousse, 1982–5. 10 vols [11,038 pp.].

Concise edition: *Dictionnaire encyclopédique Larousse.* 1986. 2 vols.

Earliest version: Pierre Larousse, *Grand dictionnaire universel du XIXe siècle.* 1866–76. 15 vols. Supplements were published in 1878, 1886–90.

Other versions include: *Grand Larousse encyclopédique.* 1960–64. 10 vols. Supplements to this were published in 1968, 1975.

[*Big Larousse encyclopaedic dictionary.*] Representative of the encyclopaedic tendency in dictionaries, pioneered in France by Larousse: rich in proper names and in illustrations.

460.

Grand Larousse de la langue française. Paris: Larousse, 1971–8. 7 vols [6730 pp.].

Edited by Louis Guilbert, René Lagane, Georges Niobey.

[*Big Larousse of the French language.*] Essentially a large-scale dictionary of modern usage with some historical information, the Larousse 'of the language' is not too distinct in aim from the dictionaries of Littré (**454**) and Robert (**455**). Includes encyclopaedic entries on linguistics and grammar: for a list of these entries see vol. 7, preliminary page [8].

Detailed linguistic introduction especially on word formation, vol. 1 pp. I–XC; pronunciation and grammar, pp. CXX–CXXVI. Very full bibliography of sources, vol. 7 pp. 6634–730.

461.

J. E. Mansion, *Harrap's new standard French and English dictionary.* London: Harrap, 1972–80. 4 vols. 'Completely revised and enlarged edition' by R. P. L. Ledésert and Margaret Ledésert.

Also published as: J. E. Mansion, *Grand Harrap: dictionnaire français–anglais et anglais–français.* 1981. 4 vols.

1st edn: part 1 (French–English), 1934; part 2 (English–French), 1939. 2nd edn of part 1: 1940. – A supplement (by R. P. L. Ledésert) was added to each part in later issues, and also separately published: supplement to part 1, 1953; to part 2: 1950. 2nd edn of both supplements, 1955; 3rd edn, 1962.

Remains the fullest French and English dictionary, covering current and recent spoken and written styles, rich in phrases and examples (with translations). Pronunciations are given in the International Phonetic Alphabet.

462.

Alain Rey, Sophie Chantreau, *Dictionnaire des expressions et locutions.* Paris: Dictionnaires Le Robert, 1993. 888 pp. '2nd edn revised.' 2–85036–215–8.

Les usuels.

1st edn: 1979. 946 pp. 2–85036–065–1. – 2nd edn: 1988. 1036 pp. 2–85036–067–8.

[*Dictionary of phrases and sayings.*] Entries are filed under keywords: use of the very helpful index, pp. 819–888, is important. One or two quotations exemplify each saying; precise references are given.

Older periods

Old French

463.

Kurt Baldinger, *Dictionnaire étymologique de l'ancien français: DEAF*. Tübingen: Niemeyer, 1974– .

Preliminary edition of part 1, covering **G–garder**: Quebec: Presses de l'Université Laval, 1971. 152 columns. Issued for the 13th Congrès International de Linguistique et de Philologie Romanes, Quebec, August 1971. An inserted note to subscribers, by the French agent, Klincksieck, dated December 1971, promised the publication of 2 parts per year and a finished work in 4 to 5 volumes of about 1000 pages each.

Parts 1–3 'with the assistance of Jean-Denis Gendron and Georges Straka'.

Frankwalt Möhren, *Complément bibliographique 1993*. 638 columns + 47* pp. List of source texts, noting manuscripts and editions, 1–413. Indexes to this list: by date, column 413; by region (dialect), 443; by manuscript collection, 459; by author of text, 525; by modern scholar/editor, 531.

[*Etymological dictionary of Old French.*] A highly technical and detailed etymological dictionary, with numerous references to source texts and to modern scholarship. Entries are arranged under base forms; thus indexes are essential if it is to be fully useful, but, as yet, only an index to parts G1–3 has appeared (published 1974).

So far parts G1 to G9/10 have appeared, the latest in 1995, completing the letter **G** in 1724 columns. For comparison, **G** occupies 805 columns in Tobler-Lommatzsch (**467**), so this promises to be a very big work indeed. Baldinger begins with **G** 'because of the continual references to von Wartburg's dictionary [**501**], which attained its definitive format only with the letter **G**. The present dictionary will deal with **G–Z** and then **A–F**'.

Addenda et corrigenda, columns 1689–1724. List of collaborators and articles on which they worked, part 9/10 pp. v–vii. Bibliography of articles on and reviews of the dictionary, part 9/10 pp. x–xii.

464.

Frédéric Godefroy, *Dictionnaire de l'ancien langue française et de tous ses dialectes du IXe au XVe siècle*. Paris: Vieweg, Bouillon, 1880–1902. 10 vols.

Publié sous les auspices du Ministre de l'Instruction Publique.

Note the review by A. Tobler in *Zeitschrift für romanische Philologie* vol. 5 (1881) p. 147ff.

[*Dictionary of the old French language and of all its dialects, from the twelfth to the fifteenth centuries.*] Very brief glosses but generous exemplification with precise references. The dictionary proper concludes with vol. 8 part 1 (p. 344). *Complément* (briefer, supplementary entries, with some attention to the sixteenth century language) vol. 8 part 2 to vol. 10. The preface to this *Complément* promised a full bibliography of sources, but the promise was not kept.

465.

[Jean Baptiste] la Curne de Sainte-Palaye, *Dictionnaire historique de l'ancien langage françois ou glossaire de la langue françoise depuis son origine jusqu'au siècle de Louis XIV*. Niort: Favre, 1875–82. 10 vols [4829 pp.].

Edited by Louis Favre. Republishes (vol. 1 pp. iv–xii) the *Projet* [*Proposal*] for the dictionary which first appeared in 1756.

One volume of the dictionary itself had been published in 1789, under the title *Glossaire de l'ancienne langue françoise depuis son origine jusqu'au siècle de Louis XIV*. Publication was abandoned and most copies destroyed.

[*Historical dictionary or glossary of the old French language from its origins to the century of Louis XIV.*] The author lived from 1697 to 1781; the manuscript of the dictionary was preserved in the Bibliothèque Nationale. The work centres on the literature of the twelfth to fourteenth centuries, and consists of lengthy entries with numerous citations. Strong in idioms and proverbs.

Vol. 10 pp. 375–94: selected papers by la Curne de Ste-Palaye; final pages 1–24: bibliography of source texts; final pages 26–8: list of works by la Curne de Ste-Palaye.

Also includes (vol. 10 pp. 205–388) a new edition of: Antoine Oudin, *Curiositez françoises pour supplément aux dictionnaires, ou recueil de plusieurs belles propriétés avec une infinité de proverbes et quolibets pour l'explication de toutes sortes de livres* (Paris: Sommaville, 1640. 2nd edn: 1656). This glossary of proverbs and phrases cites no sources. * and *vulg.* are used to mark expressions that were vulgar or obscene. Oudin (1595–1653) served as Royal Interpreter, and taught Italian to King Louis XIV.

466.

Raphael Levy, *Trésor de la langue des juifs français au Moyen Age*. Austin: University of Texas Press, 1964. 237 pp.

[*Thesaurus of the language of French Jews in the Middle Ages.*] A dry glossary, with references to sources. List of these, pp. vii–xix.

467.

[Adolf Tobler, Erhard Lommatzsch,] *Altfranzösisches Wörterbuch*. Berlin: Weidmann; Stuttgart: Steiner, 1925– .

Compiled and edited, from the materials of the late Alfred Tobler, by Erhard Lommatzsch; continued by Hans Helmut Christmann. With the support of the Preussische Akademie der Wissenschaften, and later of the Akademie der Wissenschaften und der Literatur in Mainz.

The latest so far is part 91 (4th part of vol. 11), 1995, covering **vistece–vonjement**.

[*Old French dictionary.*] A very large-scale historical dictionary, usually known as 'Tobler–Lommatzsch'. Meanings are briefly distinguished with (usually German) glosses and illustrated with numerous lengthy quotations: these are not translated. From vol. 11 onwards articles have more references to modern scholarship (including other dictionaries). General bibliographies, not cumulated, at head of each volume.

An obituary of Lommatzsch, who died in 1975: 3 pages and plate at head of vol. 10. References to early reviews of the dictionary, vol. 1 p. iii.

Fifteenth century

468.

Giuseppe di Stefano, *Dictionnaire des locutions en moyen-français*. Montréal: Ceres, 1992. 980 pp. 0–919089–55–0.

Concise edition: Giuseppe di Stefano, Rose M. Bidler, *Toutes les herbes de la Saint-Jean: les locutions en moyen-français*. Montréal: Ceres, 1992. 630 pp. 0–919089–56–9. Bibliography of sources, pp. 611–30.

[*Dictionary of phrases in Middle French.*] An important historical dictionary with long quotations and precise references. Entries are filed under keywords, with no cross-references. Some phrases are merely credited to earlier dictionaries, including Oudin (see **465**).

The catch-title of the concise edition, 'All the herbs of St John's night', i.e. midsummer eve, is clarified by an entry in Greimas and Keane (**469**) under **gauguier** 'walnut tree'.

> *Se une femme veult que son mari ou amy l'aime fort, elle lui doit mettre une feuille de gauguier cueillie la nuit Saint Jehan en son soulier senestre* [If a woman wishes her husband or lover to love her truly, she must place a walnut leaf, picked on St John's night, in his left shoe].

469.

Algirdas Julien Greimas, Teresa Mary Keane, *Dictionnaire du moyen français: la Renaissance*. Paris: Larousse, 1992. 668 pp. 2–03–340322–X.

[*Collection trésors du français.*]

[*Dictionary of Middle French: the Renaissance.*] A glossary of fifteenth century words not surviving in modern French, or whose meaning has changed. Brief information on date of origin and etymology. Glosses are followed by brief quotations, attributed to authors but without precise references.

Notes on vocabulary, phonology, grammar, pp. xiii–xxx; bibliography, pp. xxxi–xli.

Sixteenth century

470.

Edmond Huguet, *Dictionnaire de la langue française du seizième siècle*. Paris: Didier, 1925–67. 7 vols.

[*Dictionary of the French language of the sixteenth century.*] The arrangement resembles that of Tobler-Lommatzsch (**467**): each meaning gets a separate paragraph, with a very brief gloss followed by generous quotations from sixteenth century texts, with precise references. There are numerous cross-references for the spelling variants which are such a feature of the French of this period. List of source texts, vol. 1 pp. lxiii–lxxvii.

Seventeenth century

471.

Gaston Cayrou, *Le français classique: lexique de la langue du XVIIe siècle*. Paris: Didier, 1924. 888 pp. 2nd edn.

Spine title: *Notre français classique.* – 1st edn: 1923. 884 pp.

[*Classical French: dictionary of the seventeenth century language.*] Glossary of words that are no longer used, or have changed their meaning, in modern French. Generous quotations from literature, with precise references. Draws on contemporary grammars and dictionaries to illustrate usage – an unusual and interesting feature. Illustrated survey of seventeenth-century French linguists and lexicographers and their work, plates 23–69 (at end). Symbols and abbreviations, pp. xii–xxviii.

Regional forms

472.

Loïc Depecker, *Les mots de la francophonie.* Paris: Belin, 1990. 399 pp. 2nd edn. 2–7011–1305–9.

1st edn: 1988. 335 pp.

[*Words of the French-speaking world.*] A selection of words and phrases typical of various forms of French from beyond the limits of metropolitan France.

Africa

473.

Inventaire des particularités lexicales du français en Afrique noire. Montreal: AUPELF, 1988. 443 pp. 2nd edn.

1st edn: 1983. 550 pp. 2–920021–15–X. – Earlier incomplete version: 1980. 2–920021–04–4.

Travail réalisé dans le cadre de la table ronde des centres, départements et instituts de linguistique appliquée d'Afrique noire francophone, sous le patronage de l'AUPELF. Equipe du projet IFA: coordonnatrice, Danièle Racelle-Latin; rédacteurs, Jacques Blondé [and others].

See Danièle Racelle-Latin, 'Un inventaire des particularités lexicales du français en Afrique noire: état de la question' in *Le français moderne* vol. 47 (1979) pp. 232–40; Conrad Max Benedict Brann, 'French lexicography in Africa: a three-dimensional project' in *Journal of modern African studies* vol. 20 (1983) pp. 353–9.

[*Inventory of the French regionalisms of black Africa.*]

Belgium

474.

Charles Grandgagnage, *Dictionnaire étymologique de la langue wallonne.* Liège: Oudart, Mayer & Flatau; Brussels: Muquardt, 1845–80. 2 v.

Vol. 2 part 1 appeared in 1850. Vol. 2 part 2, edited by August Scheler, completed the alphabet and added a supplement, an introduction and a glossary of obsolete words.

Reprinted: Brussels: Culture et Civilisation, 1973.

[*Etymological dictionary of the Walloon language.*]

475.

Jean Haust, *Le dialecte wallon de Liège.* Liège: Vaillant-Carmanac, 1927–48. 3 vols.

[*The Walloon dialect of Liège.*] Vol. 2 is the Liégeois–French dictionary: supplementary entries, pp. 713–23, also p. 735, also vol. 3 pp. 488–501. Vol. 3 is a French–Liégeois index.

476.

François Massion, *Dictionnaire de belgicismes*. Frankfurt am Main: Lang, 1987. 2 vols [946 pp.]. 3–82041–206–9.

[*Dictionary of Belgian regional words.*] Bibliography, pp. 924–45.

The Caribbean

477.

Jones E. Mondesir, *Dictionary of St. Lucian Creole*. Berlin: Mouton De Gruyter, 1992. 621 pp. 3–11–012625–7.

Edited by Lawrence D. Carrington. *Trends in linguistics. Documentation*, 7.

A two-way dictionary: part 1, Kwéyòl–English; part 2, English–Kwéyòl. Mondesir, a teacher, spent thirty years compiling this treasury of his native speech, now increasingly used in the media. Numerous examples, but unattributed. Phonetic transcriptions are given where necessary.

478.

Hector Poullet, Sylviane Telchid, Danièle Montbrand, *Dictionnaire des expressions du créole guadeloupéen*. Fort-de-France: Hatier Antilles, 1984. 349 pp. 2–218–06871–0.

[*Dictionary of phrases in Guadeloupe Creole.*] A *Dictionnaire créole guadeloupéen–français* by the same authors was announced as forthcoming in 1989.

England

479.

William Rothwell, Louise W. Stone, T. B. W. Reid, editors, *Anglo-Norman dictionary*. London: Modern Humanities Research Association, 1977–92. 7 parts [889 pp.].

Publications of the Modern Humanities Research Association, 8. 'In conjunction with the Anglo-Norman Text Society.'

See Frankwalt Möhren, 'Unité et diversité du champ sémasiologique: l'exemple de l'Anglo-Norman dictionary' in Stewart Gregory, D. A. Trotter, editors, *De mot en mot: essays in honour of William Rothwell* (Cardiff: University of Wales Press, 1997) pp. 127–46, with other papers in the same volume.

Anglo-Norman is the now-extinct variety of French that was spoken in medieval England. It was the vehicle of a major literature.

The indispensable *Anglo-Norman dictionary* became 'visibly richer and more comprehensive with each succeeding fascicle', but remained far more concise than Tobler–Lommatzsch (**467**): a series of brief glosses followed by brief quotations with precise references (list of works quoted, pp. xv–xxvi). The longer articles are rather easy to get lost in. Note that **U** files immediately after **O**.

480.

J. H. Baker, *Manual of law French*. Aldershot: Scolar Press, 1990. 219 pp. 0–85967–745–1.

Law French was (and even still is) the last gasp of Anglo-Norman.

Very brief entries, but with precise references to law texts: these are heavily abridged in standard legal form. Important introductory matter, pp. 1–39.

Guernsey

481.

M. de Garis, *Dictiounnaire angllais–guernesiais*. Chichester: Phillimore, 1982. 291 pp. New edn. 0–85033–462–4.

1st edn: [St Peter Port:] Société Guernesiaise, 1967.

[*English–Guernsey dialect dictionary.*] With a Guernsey–English section, and with indications of local dialect variation.

The Indian Ocean

482.

Danielle d'Offay, Guy Lionnet, *Diksyonner kreol–franse = Dictionnaire créole seychellois–français*. Hamburg: Buske, 1982. 422 pp. 3–87118–569–8.

Kreolische Bibliothek, 3.

[*Seychelles Creole–French dictionary.*] Shortly after independence, in 1981–2, Creole was declared the first national language of the Seychelles (English and French being the other two) and became the language of primary education.

483.

Philip Baker, Vinesh Hookoomsing, *Diksyoner kreol morisyen = Dictionary of Mauritian Creole = Dictionnaire du créole mauricien*. Paris: L'Harmattan, 1987. 365 pp. 2–85802–973–3.

See Robert Chaudenson, 'A propos de deux dictionnaires du créole mauricien: éléments de "lexicographologie" créole' in *Les créoles français entre l'oral et l'écrit* ed. Ralph Ludwig (Tübingen: Narr, 1989) pp. 111–41. This article compares Baker and Hookoomsing's dictionary with: *Diksyoner kreol angle*. Mauritius: Ledikasyon pou Travayer, 1985.

Note also: Daniel Baggioni, Didier de Robillard, *Ile Maurice: une francophonie paradoxale*. Paris: L'Harmattan, 1990. 185 pp. 2–73840–697–1. (*Espaces francophones*.)

Good, though incomplete, citations from older texts; less strong on modern usage. Notably weak and inconsistent in important technical fields, particularly flora and fauna. The French glosses are very often wrong and are best ignored. A further inconvenience is the use of a new spelling. Nasal vowels are indicated by a superior dot (rather than by the more usual *-n*), and there are other idiosyncrasies. Bibliography, pp. 355–61.

484.

Daniel Baggioni, *Dictionnaire créole réunionnais–français*. [St Denis de la Réunion]: Université de la Réunion, Faculté des Lettres et Sciences Humaines, 1990. 376 pp. 2nd edn. 2–908127–00–9.

1st edn: Daniel Baggioni, *Petit dictionnaire créole réunionnais–français*. St Denis de la Réunion: Université de la Réunion, 1987. 359 pp. 2–905861–02–9.

See Daniel Baggioni, 'Problèmes de normalisation/standardisation du créole réunionnais, à la lumière de deux expériences lexicographiques' in *Les créoles français entre l'oral et l'écrit* ed. Ralph Ludwig (Tübingen: Narr, 1989) pp. 143–52. This compares his own work with: Alain Armand, *Dictionnaire kréol réunioné–français*. Paris: Océan, 1987.

[*Réunion Creole–French dictionary.*]

485.

Robert Chaudenson, *Le lexique du parler créole de la Réunion*. Paris: Champion, 1974. 2 vols [1249 pp.].

[*The vocabulary of the Creole speech of Réunion.*] Bibliography, pp. 1217–36.

Jersey

486.

Frank le Maistre, *Dictionnaire jersiais–français, avec vocabulaire français–jersiais: le parler normand à Jersey*. Jersey: Don Balleine Trust, 1966. 616 pp.

The French–Jersey glossary (pp. 555–615) is by Albert le Carré.

Note also: Albert le Carré, *English–Jersey language vocabulary*. 1972. 80 pp. This contains (pp. 79–80) additions and corrections to le Maistre's *Dictionnaire*.

[*Jersey language–French dictionary, with French–Jersey language glossary: Jersey's Norman dialect.*] A short-entry dictionary, but with many example phrases (not translated) and notes on usage. Pronunciation, pp. xxvii–xxix; verb paradigms, pp. xxx–xxxiii.

487.

N. C. W. Spence, *A glossary of Jersey-French*. Oxford: Blackwell, 1960. 264 pp.

Publications of the Philological Society, 18.

Based on work with oral informants. Includes brief etymological information.

Quebec

488.

Louis-Alexandre Bélisle, *Dictionnaire nord-américain de la langue française*. Montreal: Beauchemin, 1979. 1196 pp. New edn. 2–7616–0013–4.

1st edn: Louis-Alexandre Bélisle, *Dictionnaire général de la langue française au Canada*. Quebec: Belisle, 1957. 1390 pp.

[*North American dictionary of the French language.*] A short-entry illustrated general dictionary of French with some information on Canadian spoken and written usage. Supplement of proper names, pp. 1107–83.

489.

Léandre Bergeron, *Dictionnaire de la langue québécoise*. Montreal: VLB, 1980. 575 pp. [0–82881–092–3.]

Supplement: Léandre Bergeron, *Dictionnaire de la langue québécoise: supplément précédé de la charte de la langue québécoise*. Montreal, 1981. 168 pp. 2–89005–141–2.

Abridged English version: *The Québécois dictionary*. Toronto: Lorimer, 1982.

[*Dictionary of the Quebecois language.*] A glossary of words and usages not found in metropolitan French. Topic index, pp. 527–70.

Switzerland and Franco-Provençal dialects

490.

Antonin Duraffour, *Dictionnaire des patois francoprovençaux*. Paris: Editions du Centre National de la Recherche Scientifique, 1969. 718 pp.

Edited by P. Gardette, Laurette Malapert, Marguerite Gonon. Institut de Linguistique Romane des Facultés Catholiques de Lyon.

[*Dictionary of the Franco-Provençal dialects.*]

491.

L. Gauchat, J. Jeanjaquet, E. Tappolet [and others], editors, *Glossaire des patois de la Suisse romande*. Neuchâtel: Attinger; Geneva: Droz, 1924– .

[*Glossary of the dialects of French-speaking Switzerland.*] Main entries are under standard French forms if any, but all thereafter is in a phonetic script. A historical dictionary with examples drawn from oral usage and from published texts, with translations into standard French. Much information on place names. Subsections headed *HIST.* give etymologies and links with French and other Romance languages. A few cross-references for alternate forms: for further help see the temporary index published as part 51: Pierre Knecht, *Index des formes françaises et latines des tomes I–IV*. 1970. 62 pp.

The latest issue is part 98 (1996), belonging to vol. 7 and covering **fille–flamber**. Vol. 8, for the letter **G**, is also in progress.

For the other big dictionaries of the local languages of Switzerland see **609, 818, 1293**.

492.

W. Pierrehumbert, *Dictionnaire historique du parler neuchâtelois et suisse romand*. Neuchâtel: Attinger, 1926. 764 pp.

A very extensive and informative historical dictionary with quotations and etymological and historical discussion; essentially deals with older local literature, and with the colloquial as recorded in literary sources, thus complementing the vast, still unfinished *Glossaire des patois de la Suisse romande* (**491**), which starts from oral sources.

Supplement, pp. 657–722. Index of place names, pp. 723–31; important bibliography, pp. 733–59.

Slang and special vocabularies

493.

Jacques Cellard, Alain Rey, *Dictionnaire du français non conventionnel*. Paris: Hachette, 1991. 909 pp. 2nd edn. 2–01–016259–5.

1st edn: Paris: Hachette, 1980. 894 pp. 2–01–007382–7.

[*Dictionary of non-standard French.*] A highly readable supplement to general dictionaries, concentrating on slang and jocular expressions from 1880 to 1990. The layout is modelled on that of Robert (**455**), with long quotations, followed by a subsection headed *HIST.* dealing with word origins and dating. Bibliography of sources, pp. 871–84; *glossaire* (topic index), pp. 885–909.

The second edition claims a larger selection of phrases and sayings, partly drawn from: Jacques Cellard, *Ça mange pas de pain.* Paris: Hachette, 1982.

494.

Jean-Paul Colin, Jean-Pierre Mével, *Dictionnaire de l'argot.* Paris: Larousse, 1990. 763 pp. 2–03–340323–8.
[*Collection trésors du français.*]

[*Dictionary of argot.*] Gives glosses with example phrases, followed by references to dated sources (but no actual quotations). *Glossaire français–argot,* pp. 677–726. Bibliography of sources, pp. 728–41. Abbreviations for specialised argots, pp. xxiv–xxv.

495.

[John S. Farmer,] *Vocabula amatoria: a French–English glossary of words, phrases and allusions occuring in the works of Rabelais, Voltaire, Molière, Rousseau, Béranger, Zola and others, with English equivalents and synonyms.* N.p., 1896. 268 pp.
[*Dictionary of slang and its analogues,* 8 (see **397**).]
Reprint, supplying the author's name and with an introduction by Lee Revens: n.p.: University Books, 1966.

[*Sexual words.*] Brief English glosses followed by quotations from a wider range of sources than is suggested in the title. The quotations are not translated.

496.

Pierre Guiraud, *Dictionnaire historique, stylistique, rhétorique, étymologique de la littérature érotique; précédé d'une introduction sur les structures étymologiques du vocabulaire érotique.* Paris: Payot, 1978. 639 pp. 2–228–12040–5.
Le langage de la sexualité, 1. *Langages et sociétés.*
Cover title: *Dictionnaire érotique.*

[*Historical, stylistic, rhetorical and etymological dictionary of erotic literature, with an introduction on the etymological structure of the erotic vocabulary.*]

497.

Lazare Sainéan, *L'argot ancien (1455–1850), ses éléments constitutifs, ses rapports avec les langues secrètes.* Paris: Champion, 1907.
See also Sainéan's *Les sources de l'argot ancien.* 1912. 2 vols.

[*Early argot (1455–1850), its constituents, its links with secret languages.*] Sainéan ferreted out 'countless hidden slivers of lexical material; he had a flair for etymological connections, an intuitive grasp of plausible sequences of events. He had cultivated Rumanian, comparative Romance, and an assortment of Oriental languages. Despite his superb background, commendable accuracy in references and quotations, and exemplary patience, Sainéan often allowed himself to be swayed by emotional and intellectual whims' (Malkiel, **9**, abridged).

Etymological dictionaries

498.

Oscar Bloch, Walther von Wartburg, *Dictionnaire étymologique de la langue française*. Paris: Presses Universitaires de France, 1994. 720 pp. 10th edn.

1st edn: 1932. 2 vols. – 2nd edn: 1950. – 3rd edn, recast by W. von Wartburg: 1960. 674 pp. – 4th edn: 1964. 682 pp. – 5th edn: 1968. 682 pp.

[*Etymological dictionary of the French language.*] An original draft by Bloch was successively revised by von Wartburg on the basis of his gradually accumulating material for the big etymological dictionary (**501**). Entries are arranged alphabetically under modern French words. They give information on parent forms, earliest dating in French, changes of meaning, and derivatives. The work is clear and easy to use; this is a classic of French lexicography. There are cross-references for derivatives, but no indexing.

Most of the changes to the 5th edition concern words of Germanic and Oriental origin. I have not seen the 6th to 9th editions.

499.

Ernst Gamillscheg, *Etymologisches Wörterbuch der französischen Sprache*. Heidelberg: Winter, 1969. 1327 pp. 2nd edn.

1st edn: 1928.

[*Etymological dictionary of the French language.*] Arranged alphabetically under modern French words. Vastly more entries, but also much briefer, than Bloch and von Wartburg (**498**), with some references to scholarly work and controversy. Abbreviations, pp. xix–xxvii. Indexes, by Herta Köster, in alphabetical order of languages or language groups, pp. 909–1317.

500.

Alain Rey, editor, *Dictionnaire historique de la langue française*. Paris: Le Robert, 1992. 2 vols [2387 pp.]. 2–85036–187–9.

Compiled by Alain Rey, Marianne Tomi, Tristan Hurdé, Chantal Tanet.

[*Historical dictionary of the French language.*] A dictionary of the origins, etymology, changes of meaning, changes of usage, and derived forms of French words, with discursive and readable entries aimed at a wide market – an exciting development in lexicography. English has nothing like this. Entries are grouped under base forms with many cross-references. Changes are dated (on the basis of known texts) but the texts are not cited: however, the dates can be linked to texts by way of the chronological index of sources, pp. 2329–79. Diagrams are used to elucidate complex phenomena, e.g. Romance descendants of Latin **caput**, pp. 400–401; meanings of French **chef**, pp. 402–3. There are some encyclopaedic articles on topics connected with language history.

Glossary (linguistic terms), pp. 2309–27; brief bibliography, pp. 2381–3.

501.

Walther von Wartburg, *Französisches etymologisches Wörterbuch: eine Darstellung des galloromanischen Sprachschatzes*. Bonn: Schroeder, Klopp; Basle: Helbing & Lichtenhahn, Zbinden, 1922– .

Continued by Carl Theodor Gossen, 1979–83; Otto Jänicke, 1972–8; Jean-Pierre Chambon.
Accompanied by: *Beiheft: Ortsnamenregister, Literaturverzeichnis, Übersichtskarte.* Tübingen: Mohr, 1950.
135 pp. 2nd edn. (1st edn: Bonn: Klopp, 1929.) – *Supplement* to this, by Margarete Hoffert: Basle, 1957. 54 pp.
See: Eva Büchi, *Les structures du Französisches etymologisches Wörterbuch: recherches
métalexicographiques et métalexicologiques.* Tübingen: Niemeyer, 1996. 593 pp. 3–4845–2268–2 (*Beihefte zur
Zeitschrift für romanische Philologie*, 268.)
On one group of loanwords note: Jan Daeleman, 'Les étymologies africaines du *FEW*' in *Vox romanica* vol. 39
(1980) pp. 104–19.

[*French etymological dictionary: an exposition of the Gallo-Romance vocabulary.*]
This extremely detailed dictionary of French and its dialects is growing in size as it
proceeds: completion is continually receding. **A–Z** were finished in 14 volumes (1922–
61), but the author was unsatisfied with the treatment of words of Germanic origin under
A–F and thereafter withdrew these words to a separate section. *Germanische Elemente*
thus make up the additional volumes 15–17 (1955–69). These were followed by
'Anglicisms' in vol. 18 (1967); 'Oriental words', vol. 19 (1967); 'Loanwords from other
languages', vol. 20 (1968). There is a volume index in each of vols 1–20, but no overall
index.

Vols 21–3 (begun 1965 and still in progress) are compiled by Margarete Hoffert.
Arranged under topics, without indexes, they consist of a challenging ragbag or
thesaurus of words in French and its dialects that are of unknown or uncertain origin.
The challenge has been taken up by Kurt Baldinger, *Etymologien: Untersuchungen zu
FEW 21–23.* Tübingen: Niemeyer, 1988. Vol. 1. 3–4845–2218–6. (*Beihefte zur
Zeitschrift für romanische Philologie*, 218.)

Vols 24–5 (begun 1969 and both still in progress) are a recasting of the letter **A**,
originally covered in vol. 1. This time, since Germanic and other loanwords have been
dealt with separately, only words of Latin and pre-Roman (Celtic, Iberian etc.) origin are
being covered, but at almost ten times the length. **A–atrium** took up 166 pages of vol. 1
but 1356 pages of the new series. An important development is the greater attention to
historical change and to careful dating: the distinction between Old French and Modern
French tended to be all that was noted in the articles at **A–B** in the first edition.

Entries are under original forms, Latin or other. Potentially this work is a treasury of
the French vocabulary and particularly of its dialects, lovingly gathered, carefully
documented and fully discussed; but its usefulness depends largely on thorough
indexing, and it is not surprising that the successive parts of volumes 21–25, which lack
indexes of any kind, have been accumulating for thirty years in the library of University
College London (to take an example) without encountering a single reader.

Foreign words

502.
T. E. Hope, *Lexical borrowing in the Romance languages: a critical study of
Italianisms in French and Gallicisms in Italian from 1100 to 1900.* Oxford:
Blackwell, 1971. 2 vols [782 pp.].

A historical dictionary arranged under successive centuries. The entries emphasise etymology and changes of meaning and usage. Index of Italian loanwords in French, pp. 753–63; of French loanwords in Italian, pp. 763–76.

503.

Josette Rey-Debove, Gilberte Gagnon, *Dictionnaire des anglicismes: les mots anglais et américains en français*. Paris: Le Robert, 1988. 1150 pp. 2nd edn. 2–85036–027–9.

Les usuels.

1st edn: 1981. 1152 pp. 2–85036–034–1.

[*Dictionary of Anglicisms: English and American words in French.*] Bibliography of source texts, pp. 1121–50.

Other works of interest

504.

Domenico D'Oria, 'Les tabous sexuels dans les dictionnaires monolingues français contemporains' in his *Dictionnaire et idéologie* (Fasano: Schena, 1988) pp. 121–173.

First published as a monograph. Lecce: Adriatica Salentina, 1977.

505.

Pierre Guiraud, *Les gros mots*. Paris: Presses Universitaires de France, 1975. 123 pp.

Que sais-je? 1597.

506.

Georges Matoré, *Histoire des dictionnaires français*. Paris, 1967. 278 pp.

507.

Claude Poirier [and others], *Dictionnaire du français québécois: description et histoire des régionalismes en usage au Québec depuis l'époque de la Nouvelle-France jusqu'à nos jours, incluant un aperçu de leur extension dans les provinces canadiennes limitrophes: volume de présentation*. Sainte-Foy: Les Presses de l'Université Laval, 1985. 169 pp. 2–7637–7018–5.

Trésor de la langue française au Québec.

See: Franz Josef Haussmann, 'Autour du TLFQ (Trésor de la langue française au Québec): réflexions sur un nouveau dictionnaire régional' in *Vox romanica* vol. 41 (1982) pp. 181–201. – Lionel Boisvert, Claude Poirier, Claude Verreault, editors, *La lexicographie québécoise: bilan et perspectives: actes du colloque organisé par l'Equipe du Trésor de la Langue Française au Québec et tenu à l'Université Laval, les 11 et 12 avril 1985*. Quebec: Les Presses de l'Université Laval, 1986. 308 pp. 2–7637–7067–3. (*Langue française au Québec*, section 3, vol. 8.)

508.

Bernard Quemada, *Les dictionnaires du français moderne, 1539–1863: étude sur leur histoire, leurs types et leurs méthodes*. Paris: Didier, 1967.

Etudes lexicologiques, 1.

509.

Bernard Quemada, editor, *Matériaux pour l'histoire du vocabulaire français: datations et documents lexicographiques*. Paris: Didier; Klincksieck, 1970– . '2nd series.'

Centre National de la Recherche Scientifique. *Publications du Centre d'Etude du Français Moderne et Contemporain*; Institut National de la Langue Française. *Publications du Trésor général des langues et parlers français.*

Included in the series, which has already reached 44 volumes, are alphabetical, chronological and thematic indexes to vols 1–20 (1988–9. 3 vols) and to vols 21–30 (1992–3. 2 vols).

510.

Bernard Quemada, editor, *Mots nouveaux contemporains*. Paris: Klincksieck, 1993– .

Centre National de la Recherche Scientifique. Institut National de la Langue Française. *Publications du Trésor général des langues et parlers français.*

[*New contemporary words.*] I have seen two volumes in this series, each in alphabetical order. The first is a general collection, the second is specialised: Christiane Tetet, *Les sports de montagne* [*Mountain sports*] (1995).

511.

Bernard Quemada, *Répertoire des dictionnaires scientifiques et techniques monolingues et multilingues 1950–1975*. Paris: Conseil International de la Langue Française, 1978. 590 pp. 2–85319–045–5.

With the assistance of K. Menemencioglu. Centre National de la Recherche Scientifique, Institut de la Langue Française. Trésor des langues et parlers français.

512.

Pierre Rézeau, 'Le dictionnaire dialectal: l'exemple français' in Franz Josef Hausmann [and other editors], *Wörterbücher = Dictionaries = Dictionnaires* (Berlin: De Gruyter, 1990) vol. 2 pp. 1467–75.

513.

Walther von Wartburg, Hans-Erich Keller, Robert Geuljans, *Bibliographie des dictionnaires patois gallo-romans, 1550–1967*. Geneva: Droz, 1969. Revised edn.

Publications romanes et françaises, 103.

1st edn: Walther von Wartburg, *Bibliographie des dictionnaires patois*. Paris: Droz, 1934. (*Publications romanes et françaises*, 8.) – This was followed by: Hans-Erich Keller, J. Renson, *Supplément 1934–1955*. 1955. (*Publications romanes et françaises*, 52.)

FRISIAN

Frisian is a regional language of the north-eastern Netherlands and north-western Germany. It belongs to the GERMANIC branch of Indo-European languages, and has about 750,000 speakers. It is closer to English than any other Germanic language.

Modern national communications threaten the survival of Frisian, particularly of the scattered dialects in Germany. The most stable standard form is the West Frisian of the Netherlands, centring on Leeuwarden.

There is a useful bibliography of Frisian dictionaries by Claes and others (**525**). The greatest dictionary of North Frisian is the six-volume manuscript compiled around 1889 by Moritz Momme Nielsen (or Nissen) and now in Kiel University Library, see **526**.

Modern regional forms

East Frisian

514.

P. Kramer, *Näi Seelter woudeboek = Neues Saterfriesisches Wörterbuch = Nij Seelter Wurdboek = New Saterfrisian dictionary*. Elst, 1992– .

So far vol. 1, covering **A–E**, has appeared, in 490 pages. Reproduced from dot-matrix computer print-out, it is not a pretty book, but it is impressively comprehensive, based on oral and written sources. List of sources, pp. 14–20; other abbreviations, pp. 20–23.

North Frisian

515.

Birgit Kellner, *Deutsch–friesische Wörterliste, Mooringer Mundart, auf der Grundlage des Frasch Uurdebök*. Kiel : Nordfriesische Wörterbuchstelle der CAU Kiel, 1991. 266 pp.

Didactica frisica, 7.

[*German–Frisian glossary of the Mooringer dialect.*] Draws on the *Frasch Uurdebök* of Bo Sjölin, Alistair G. H. Walker and Ommo Wilts (**517**), and on the *Deutsch–friesisches Wörterbuch* of Erk Petersen.

516.

Adeline Petersen [and others], *Freesk Uurdebuk = Friesisches Wörterbuch: Wörterbuch der Wiedingharder Mundart auf der Grundlage eines Manuskripts von Peter Jensen (1861–1939)*. Neumünster: Wachholtz, 1994. 381 pp. 3–529–04618–3.

Edited by the Nordfriesische Wörterbuchstelle der Christian-Albrechts-Universität Kiel.

I have not seen: Peter Jensen, *Wörterbuch der nordfriesischen Sprache der Wiedingharde*. Neumünster: Wachholtz, 1927. 732 pp. – Reprinted: 1967. [*Dictionary of the North Frisian language of the Wiedingharde.*]

[*Frisian dictionary: dictionary of the Wiedingharde dialect on the basis of a manuscript by Peter Jensen.*] Dictionary of a North Frisian dialect spoken close to the Danish border. Very numerous examples, from oral sources, are accompanied by German translations.

517.

Bo Sjölin, Alastair G. H. Walker, Ommo Wilts, *Frasch Uurdebök = Friesisches Wörterbuch: Wörterbuch der Mooringer Mundart auf der Grundlage alter und neuer Sammlungen und Vorarbeiten, sowie unter Mitwirkung von vielen freiwilligen Helfern in der Bökingharde.* Neumünster: Wachholtz, 1988. 276 pp. 3–529–04615–9.

Edited by the Nordfriesische Wörterbuchstelle der Christian-Albrechts-Universität Kiel.

[*Frisian dictionary: dictionary of the Mooringer dialect on the basis of old and new collections and researches and with the cooperation of many voluntary helpers in the Bökingharde.*]

518.

Nann Mungard, *Eilunsfriisk Spraak an Wiis.* Hamburg: Hermes, 1913. 150 pp.

Reprinted as: *Ein inselnordfriesisches Wörterbuch.* Westerland: Verlag für Nordfriesisches Heimatschrifttum, 1974.

[*Island Frisian language and lore.*] A dictionary of the North Frisian of the islands.

West Frisian

519.

Wurdboek fan de Fryske taal = Woordenboek der Friese taal. Ljouwert: Fryske Akademy, De Tille, 1984– . 90–655–3024–X.

Chief editor, K. F. van der Veen. *Fryske Akademy,* 630 [etc.].

[*Dictionary of the Frisian language.*] A large-scale historical dictionary of modern West Frisian, 1800–1975, with careful attention to dialect forms (given in the International Phonetic Alphabet) and many quotations from sources, with precise references. Very rapid publication: the dictionary has already covered **A–Mud** in 13 volumes. List of sources, vol. 1 pp. xxxvi–lxviii. Loose sheets of errata in vols 1 and 2.

520.

J. W. Zantema, [W. Visser,] *Frysk wurdboek: hânwurdboek fan 'e Fryske taal, mei dêryn opnommen list fan Fryske plaknammen, list fan Fryske gemeentenammen.* Ljouwert: Osinga, 1984–5. 2 vols.

Fryske Akademy, 631, 649.

[*Concise dictionary of the Frisian language, including a list of Frisian place names and Frisian parish names.*] A bilingual Frisian and Dutch dictionary (vol. 1, *Frysk–Nederlânsk;* vol. 2, *Nederlânsk–frysk*).

Older periods

521.

Waling Dykstra, *Friesch woordenboek = Lexicon Frisicum.* Leeuwarden: Maijer & Schaafsma, 1896–1911. 4 vols.

[*Frisian dictionary.*] Includes a list of Frisian personal names, by Johan Winkler.

522.

Justus Halbertsma, *Lexicon Frisicum,* **A–Feer.** Deventer, 1874. 1040 pp.

Edited by Tiallingus Halbertsma.

[*Frisian dictionary.*]

523.

Montanus de Haan Hettema, *Idioticon frisicum = Friesch latijnsch–nederlandsch woordenboek uit oude handschriften bijeenverzameld.*
Leeuwarden: Suringar, 1874. 595 pp.

[*Frisian–Latin–Dutch dictionary: materials collected from early manuscripts.*] A concise dictionary but with precise references to sources. List of abbreviations in preliminary unnumbered pages.

524.

Ferdinand Holthausen, *Altfriesisches Wörterbuch.* Heidelberg: Winter, 1985. 191 pp. 2nd edn, revised by Dietrich Hofmann.
Germanische Bibliothek. Neue Folge. 2. Reihe, Wörterbücher.
1st edn: 1925. (*Germanische Bibliothek. 1, Sammlung germanischer Elementar- und Handbücher. 4. Reihe, Wörterbücher,* 5.)

[*Old Frisian dictionary.*] A messy little book in its revised form, with Hofmann's revisions in typescript in a very long sequence on pp. 153–90. They are keyed to the original sequence not by repeating the headwords (as most dictionary supplements do it) but by giving page and line numbers only. It remains necessary to look at Holthausen's two original sequences of additions and corrections, pp. 135–51 and 151–2. There is a small number of references to sources but in general this is simply a brief-entry glossary. Bibliography, pp. xv–xviii and xxiv–xxv.

Other works of interest

525.

F. Claes, P. Kramer, B. van der Veen, *A bibliography of Frisian dictionaries.*
Groningen: Frysk Institút RU, 1984. 24 pp.
Us wurk, vol. 33 part 1.

526.

Claas Riecken, *Wörterbuch im Dornröschenschlaf: zur Entstehung und Anlage des "Nordfriesischen Wörterbuchs" von Moritz Momme Nissen.* Kiel: Fach Friesische Philologie, Christian-Albrechts-Universität; Amsterdam: Stúdzjerjochting Frysk, 1994. 183 pp.
Co-frisica, 15.

FRIULIAN

One of the three so-called Rhaeto-ROMANCE LANGUAGES of the Alps, Friulian is a regional language of north-eastern Italy, spoken in the province of Friuli–Venezia Giulia.

527.

Giorgio Faggin, *Vocabolario della lingua friulana.* Udine: Del Bianco, 1985. 2 vols [1617 pp.].

[*Vocabulary of the Friulian language.*]

528.

Gianni Nazzi, *Dictionnaire frioulan: français–frioulan, frioulan–français*. N.p.:
Ribis, 1995. 525 pp.
With the assistance of Renza Di Bernardo and Sabrina Tossut.
   [*French–Friulian and Friulian–French dictionary.*]

FULANI

Historically the Fulani have been a migrant, pastoral people. With their migrations the
Fulani language, one of the NIGER-CONGO LANGUAGES, has spread widely across the
Western Sudan (the inland plains of West Africa). It may have as many as 15 million
speakers, though it is not the majority language of any single country.

The Fulani alphabet

a b ɓ c d ɗ e f g h i j k l m mb n nd ng nj ŋ ñ o p r s t u w x y ŷ

Fulani is most often written in this variant of the Latin alphabet. The above alphabetical order is adopted by
Osborn (**531**). There is another, quite specific to Fulani, in which the vowels come first, and nasalised
consonants follow immediately after corresponding non-nasalised consonants.

529.

C. A. L. Reichardt, *Vocabulary of the Fulde language*. London: Church
Missionary Society, 1878. 357 pp.

530.

Eldridge Mohammadou, *Lexique fulfulde comparé: parler des Jallinko'en de
l'Ader (Niger central)*. Yaoundé: Ministère de l'Education et de la Culture,
Centre Fédérale Linguistique et Culturel, n.d.
   [*Comparative Fulfulde dictionary: dialect of the Jallinko'en of the Ader, central
Niger.*] Not seen.

531.

Donald W. Osborn, David J. Dwyer, Joseph I. Donohoe Jr, *A Fulfulde
(Maasina)–English–French lexicon: a root based compilation drawn from extant
sources followed by English–Fulfulde and French-Fulfulde listings = Lexique
fulfulde (maasina)–anglais–français*. East Lansing: Michigan State University,
1993. 688 pp. 0–87013–326–8.

532.

Galina Zoubko, *Dictionnaire peul–français*. Osaka: National Museum of
Ethnology, 1995. 552 pp.
Senri ethnological reports, 4.
Zoubko's material was previously published, with Russian as well as French glosses, as: Г. В. Зубко, *Фула–
русско–французский словарь* [*Fula–russko–frantsuzskii slovar'*] = *Kamuusu Pular (Fulfulde)–Riisinkoore–
Farankoore = Dictionnaire peul (fula)–russe–français*. Moscow: Russkii Yazyk, 1980. 600 pp. Edited by
Nialibuli Bureima, Dienga Mamadu.

[*Fulani–French dictionary.*]

533.

Dictionnaire peul–français. Dakar, 1969.

Institut Fondamental d'Afrique Noire. *Catalogues et documents*, 22.

[*Fulani–French dictionary.*] An incomplete work based on the Gaden manuscript at the IFAN, with additional information from oral sources from the Fuuta-Tooro and Fuuta-Dyaloo.

GAELIC

Scottish Gaelic, one of the CELTIC LANGUAGES and historically an offshoot of Irish, spread into Western Scotland from the fourth century onwards. In turn almost overwhelmed by English, Gaelic is now commonly spoken only in some of the western islands and the most isolated parts of the Western Highlands. There are about 80,000 speakers.

Historical dictionaries

534.

Dictionarium Scoto-Celticum = A dictionary of the Gaelic language. Edinburgh: Blackwood, 1828. 2 vols.

Highland Society of Scotland.

Still useful as the only substantial dictionary of Gaelic that cites sources (which include *C.S.* 'common speech'). The etymologies are now considered fanciful, often tracing Gaelic words to Hebrew and Arabic origins.

The modern standard

535.

Edward Dwelly, *The illustrated Gaelic–English dictionary, containing every Gaelic word and meaning given in all previously published dictionaries and a great number never in print before, to which is prefixed a concise Gaelic grammar.* Glasgow: MacLaren, 1920. 1034 pp. 2nd edn.

Reprinted: Glasgow: Gairm Publications, 1988. 1–8719–0128–6. Cover title: *Faclair gaidhlig gubeurla le dealbhan = Dwelly's illustrated Gaelic to English dictionary.* The 3rd to 8th editions are, like this, reprints of the 2nd.

Supplemented by: *Appendix to Dwelly's Gaelic–English dictionary; edited from manuscripts in Dwelly's hand in the National Library of Scotland by Douglas Clyne.* Glasgow: Gairm Publications, 1991. 134 pp. 1–871901–08–7. 'Editing completed and seen through the press by Derick Thomson.'

Note also: Girvan McKay, *English–Gaelic key to Dwelly's Gaelic–English dictionary = Clàr-innsidh beurla gu gàidhlig do'n fhaclair ghàidhlig le dealbhan le Eideard Dwelly.* Glasgow: Gairm Publications, 1975. 22 pp. 0–901771–47–3. (*Gairm publications*, 38.)

1st edn of main work: 'Ewen MacDonald' [i.e. Edward Dwelly], *Faclair gàidhlig le dealbhan.* 1901–11.

All later editions are reprints of the 2nd, though some are labelled '3rd edition'. Dwelly generally follows the spelling of Macbain (**538**). This is a brief-entry dictionary with a total of 675 illustrations, nearly all of them of plants and animals; it gives taxonomic names for plants and birds (but not for fish).

The new supplement, edited by Clyne, offers important additions, discussions and dialect notes related to Dwelly's all-too-concise main work. McKay's English key is not a complete index but it does form a handy brief guide to major sections of the vocabulary.

536.

Malcolm Maclennan, *A pronouncing and etymological dictionary of the Gaelic language: Gaelic–English, English–Gaelic.* Edinburgh: Grant, 1925. 613 pp.
Reprinted: Aberdeen: Aberdeen University Press, 1979. 0–08–025713–5. Spine title: *Gaelic dictionary.*

Essentially a brief-entry dictionary, but the Gaelic–English section (pp. 1–365) gives Irish cognates for the basic vocabulary and marks the origin of loanwords.

537.

An stor-data briathrachais Gaidhlig = The Gaelic terminology database.
Teangue, Isle of Skye: Clo Ostaig, 1993. Vol. 1 [631 pp.]. 1-897873-02-6.

An English-Gaelic dictionary, oddly titled, complete in itself, though it was to be followed by supplements 'in whatever format'. The best available.

Etymological dictionaries

538.

Alexander Macbain, *An etymological dictionary of the Gaelic language.*
Inverness: Mackay, 1911. 412 pp. 2nd edn, revised by Calum MacPharlain.
Reprinted: Glasgow: Gairm Publications, 1982. 0–901771–68–6. (*Gairm publications,* 57.)
1st edn: 1896.

Over 7000 entries, brief but to the point. The 2nd edition incorporates Macbain's 'Further Gaelic words and etymologies' first published in *Transactions of the Gaelic Society of Inverness.* A short biographical note refers to Macbain's 'sudden demise in April 1907, when in the town of Stirling making arrangements with the publisher' for the 2nd edition.

GALICIAN

One of the ROMANCE LANGUAGES, Galician has about three million speakers in the north-western corner of Spain. In early medieval times it could have been said that Portuguese was the southern dialect of Galician. After hundreds of years during which Portuguese has been the language of an independent and expansionist state, while Galician has survived in a regional backwater, the two still resemble one another closely.

The name *Gallegan,* close to the Spanish name for the language, is sometimes used in English.

Historical dictionaries

539.

Diccionario gallego–castellano. A Coruña: Ferrer, Roel, 1913–28. Parts 1–27 [pp. 1–432; no more published].

Real Academia Gallega. The Academy has recently published a short normative dictionary: *Diccionario da lingua galega.* A Coruña: Real Academia Galega, 1990. 822 pp. 84–600–7509–5. Edited by Constantino García. [*Dictionary of the Galician language.*]

  [*Galician–Spanish dictionary.*] A large-scale bilingual dictionary which covers **A–Cativo** and remains incomplete. Quotations from literary sources are given for a minority of words – many of them labelled *C. pop.* 'folk poetry'.

The modern standard

540.

Isaac Alonso Estravís, *Dicionário da língua galega.* Santiago de Compostela: Sotelo Blanco, 1995. 1591 pp. 84–7824–226–0.

Alternate title: *Dicionário Sotelo Blanco da língua galega.*

  [*Dictionary of the Galician language.*] Estravís had previously published a three-volume dictionary under the same title (Madrid, 1986).

541.

Xosé G. Feixó Cid [and others], *Diccionario da lingua galega.* Vigo: Ir Indo, 1986. 3 vols. 84–7680–000–2.

  [*Dictionary of the Galician language.*]

542.

Eladio Rodríguez González, *Diccionario enciclopédico gallego–castellano.* Vigo: Galaxia, 1958–62. 3 vols.

Colección Casa de Galicia, 1. Introduction by R. Otero Pedrayo.

  [*Encyclopaedic Galician–Spanish dictionary.*] A concise dictionary of modern usage with a large number of encyclopaedic entries on topics related to Galician life and folklore.

Etymological dictionaries

543.

Sigrid Buschmann, *Beiträge zum etymologischen Wörterbuch des Galizischen.* Bonn, 1965. 314 pp.

Romanistische Versuche und Vorarbeiten, 15.

  [*Towards an etymological dictionary of Galician.*] An inaugural dissertation.

544.

José S. Crespo Pozo, *Contribución a un vocabulario gallego.* Madrid, 1963. 699 pp.

Continued as: *Nueva contribución a un vocabulario castellano–gallego.* Orense, La Coruña, 1972– . 4 vols.

[Contributions to a Galician dictionary.] Not seen.

GANDA

Ganda was the ruling language of the Kingdom of Buganda and now, with nearly four million speakers, is the majority language of Uganda. It belongs to the Bantu group of NIGER-CONGO LANGUAGES.

545.

John D. Murphy, *Luganda–English dictionary*. Washington: Consortium Press, 1972. 651 pp.

Published for Catholic University of America Press. *Publications in the languages of Africa*, 2.

GASCON

One of the ROMANCE LANGUAGES, Gascon is often regarded as a dialect of Occitan (Provençal), and is spoken in south-western France. It is treated here separately because it is sufficiently distinct from Occitan, even in medieval texts, to require a separate range of dictionaries.

546.

Kurt Baldinger, *Dictionnaire onomasiologique de l'ancien gascon*. Tübingen: Niemeyer, 1975– .

[*Thesaurus of Old Gascon.*] An arrangement of the vocabulary of medieval Gascony in conceptual order, based on manuscripts in Gascon, French and Latin from the region. Draws also on existing lexicographical sources, notably Walther von Wartburg's *Französisches etymologisches Wörterbuch* (**501**). Copious quotations are given from the texts, both literature and documents. The work will gain in usefulness as it grows: eight parts have appeared (641 pp.), containing a total of 1129 entries. The subject area of flora has almost been completed. Each part contains a loose sheet which is an alphabetical index in French.

A similar work dealing with Occitan is also in progress (**1143**).

547.

Simin Palay, *Dictionnaire du béarnais et du gascon modernes (Bassin Aquitain), embrassant les dialectes du Béarn, de la Bigorre, du Gers, des Landes, et de la Gascogne maritime et garonnaise*. Paris, 1980. 1053 pp. 3rd edn.

Bibliothèque de l'Ecole Gastou-Febus.

1st edn 1961–3; 2nd edn 1974. An earlier version of Palay's work had appeared in 1932–4.

[*Dictionary of modern Béarnais and Gascon of the Aquitanian Basin, comprising the dialects of Béarn, the Bigorre, the Gers, the Landes, coastal Gascony and the Garonne valley.*] A concise dictionary of the spoken language of modern Gascony, with example phrases and with an indication of dialect variation (geographical abbreviations, p. xii).

The main text of the 1st edition is repeated in the later ones. A supplement of 2000 new entries in the 2nd edition is superseded by one of 3500 entries in the 3rd edition.

GAYO

An AUSTRONESIAN language of northern Sumatra, with about 200,000 speakers.

548.

G. A. J. Hazeu, *Gajôsch–Nederlandsch woordenboek met Nederlandsch–Gajôsch register*. Batavia, 1907. 1148 pp.

[*Gayo–Dutch dictionary with Dutch–Gayo index.*] An almost encyclopaedic dictionary of a language of northern Sumatra, indicating origins of loanwords, many of which come from Arabic. Dutch–Gajo section, pp. 1059–1129; addenda, pp. 1131–48. Brief grammatical introduction, pp. vii–xvii.

GBE

Gbe is a group of dialects, with several standard forms, belonging to the Kwa branch of NIGER-CONGO LANGUAGES. Until recently these dialects were better known as Ewe (in south-eastern Ghana and Togo) and Fon (in southern Benin). There are about four million speakers.

549.

Diedrich Westermann, *Wörterbuch der Ewe-Sprache*. Berlin, 1905–6. 2 vols.

New edition or reprint: Berlin, 1954. 795 pp. (Deutsche Akademie der Wissenschaften zu Berlin, Institut für Orientforschung. *Veröffentlichung*, 8.)

Note also: Diedrich Westermann, *Gbesela Yeye or English-Ewe Dictionary*. Berlin: Reimer, 1930. 347 pp. New edn. – 1st edn: 1910. 111 pp.

[*Dictionary of the Ewe language.*]

GEORGIAN

Mxedruli: *the Georgian alphabet*

ა ბ გ დ ე ვ ზ ჱ თ ი კ ლ მ ნ ჲ ო პ ჟ რ ს ტ უ ჳ ფ ქ ღ ყ შ ჩ ც ძ წ ჭ ხ ჴ ჯ ჰ ჵ

a b g d e v z ē t i ḳ l m n y o p̣ ž r s ṭ ü u p k ğ q̇ š č c j ç ç̇ x q ǰ h ō

The origin of *Mxedruli* 'warrior script' can be traced to the ninth century. It replaced an older script now known as *asomtavruli*, which is first found in a stone inscription of AD 430. The alphabetical order is that of Greek: additional non-Greek consonant sounds are added towards the end of the sequence. The letter ჳ *ü* is obsolete.

FONT: GEORGIA NET (DEPARTMENT OF INFORMATICS OF THE PARLIAMENT OF GEORGIA)

The best known of the small Kartvelian language family, Georgian is the national language of independent Georgia, in the Caucasus, formerly one of the constituent republics of the Soviet Union. It has about four million speakers. Georgian is the vehicle of an ancient Christian culture and of a literature that goes back to the fifth century AD. For etymological dictionaries, apart from **561** below, see KARTVELIAN LANGUAGES.

Historical dictionaries

550.

სულხან საბა ორბელიანი, *სიტყვის კონა ქართული; romel ars ლექსიკონი*
[Sulxan Saba Orbeliani, *Siṭq̇vis ḳona kartuli; romel ars leksiḳoni*]. Tbilisi, 1965–
6. 2 vols [638 + 655 pp.].

Edited by Ilia Abulaze. *Txzulebani*, vols 4i–ii.

Another edition: Sulxan-Saba Orbeliani, *Leksiḳoni kartuli*; avṭograpiuli nusxebis mixedvit moamzada, gamoḳvleva da ganmarṭebata leksiḳis saziebeli daurto Ilia Abulazem. Tbilisi: Merani, 1991–3. 2 vols. 55–20–00393–9. Sakartvelos Mecnierebata Aḳademia.

[*Bouquet of Georgian words.*] Compiled in 1716 by one of the great figures in Georgian literature, *Siṭq̇vis ḳona kartuli* was first published only in 1884. About 17,000 entries cover texts from the earliest literature to Orbeliani's own day, with references to sources. Arranged partly as a thesaurus 'so that under *horse* are also included words for *stallion, mare, foal, colt, packhorse* etc., though these are also entered at their alphabetical place. Saba does not shrink from including such taboo items as words for the sexual organs and bodily functions' (B. G. Hewitt in *Wörterbücher*, **12**, p. 2416). Entirely in Georgian.

551.

დავით ჩუბინაშვილი, *ქართულ–რუსული ლექსიკონი* = Давит Чубинов,
Гружино–русский словарь [Davit Čubinašvili, *Kartul–rusuli leksiḳoni* = Davit Chubinov, *Gruzhinsko–russkii slovar'*]. St Petersburg: Imp. Akademiya Nauk, 1887. 1780 columns.

Reprinted: Tbilisi: Sabcota Sakartvelo, 1984.

Čubinašvili's first Georgian dictionary was: *Грузинско-русско-французскій словарь*. 1840. 734 pp.
[*Georgian–Russian–French dictionary.*]

[*Georgian–Russian dictionary.*] Based on Orbeliani's work, greatly expanded to include 70,000 entries for terms from old, medieval and modern Georgian texts, with source references. Entries are given under the two or three most useful basic forms of each verb (*masdar* 'verbal noun', first person present, first person aorist if necessary).

The modern standard

552.

არნ. ჩიქობავა, *ქართული ენის განმარტებითი ლექსიკონი* = *Толковый словарь гружинского языка* [Arn. Čikobava, editor, *Kartuli enis ganmarṭebiti leksiḳoni*]. Tbilisi, 1950–64. 8 vols (12,302 pp.).

Akademiya Nauk Gruzhinskoi SSR.

[*Big dictionary of the Georgian language.*] The 'Georgian Academy dictionary'. Over 100,000 entries, with brief quotations from sources for many words, but no precise references. Covers Modern Georgian only. Dialect words are given only if found in literary texts. Up to 20 forms of each verb are given entries in direct alphabetical order:

the 'indirect' prefix *Ó*- has still to be ignored when looking up verb forms. Etymologies for loanwords are given in square brackets; taxonomic names for plants and animals are also in square brackets. Abbreviations, vol. 1 pp. 091–095.

553.

ქ: ლომთათიძე, *რუსულ–ქართული ლექსიკონი* = К. Ломтатидзе, *Русско–грузинский словарь* [K. Lomtatize, chief editor, *Rusul–kartuli leksiḳoni*]. Tbilisi: Sakartvelos SSR Mecnierebata Aḳademiis Gamomcemloba, 1956– .

Sakartvelos SSR Mecnierebata Aḳademia, Enatmecnierebis Insṭiṭuṭi.

Abridged edition: K. Lomtatize, chief editor, *Rusul–kartuli leksiḳoni* = *Russko–gruzhinskii slovar'*. Tbilisi: Sabcota Sakartvelo, 1983. 864 pp.

[*Russian–Georgian dictionary.*] Vols 1–2 cover **A–P**. I have not seen vol. 3, which would complete the set.

554.

Richard Meckelein, *Deutsch–georgisches Wörterbuch* = რიჰარდ მეკელანი, *გერმანლ– ქართული სიტყვარი*. Berlin: De Gruyter, 1937–43. 2 vols [1366 pp.].

Lehrbücher des Seminars für Orientalische Sprachen zu Berlin, 37.

[*German–Georgian dictionary.*] A brief-entry dictionary still useful as a large-scale bilingual dictionary into Georgian.

555.

Richard Meckelein, *Georgisch–deutsches Wörterbuch* = რიჰარდ მეკელანი, *ქართულ–გერმანლი სიტყვარი*. Berlin: De Gruyter, 1928. 656 pp.

[*Georgian–German dictionary.*] A companion to Meckelein's German–Georgian dictionary (**554**), now for most purposes superseded.

556.

Kita Tschenkéli, *Georgisch–deutsches Wörterbuch*. Zürich: Amirani-Verlag, 1965–74. 26 parts [2470 pp.].

Continued after the author's death by Yolanda Marchev, with the help of Lea Flury, Ruth Neukomm and Victor Nosadzé.

[*Georgian–German dictionary.*] In this rather large bilingual dictionary all verb forms are entered under the root – the entry for **svla** 'go' extends to 22 pages. This is useful for the specialist but difficult for others, even Georgians, to use. At the end of each letter of the alphabet, easy to overlook because not distinguished typographically or in the running heads, there is a handy list of verb roots beginning with that letter.

Plenty of examples of usage, in Georgian with German translation. Some information on dialect variation. Abbreviations, part 1 pp. xxxv–xxxviii.

Older periods

557.

ილია აბულაძე *ზველი ქართული ენის ლექსიკონი* = *Словарь древнегрузинского языка* [Ilia Abulaze, *Zveli kartuli enis leksiḳoni*]. Tbilisi: Mecniereba, 1973. 577 pp.

Sakartvelos SSR Mecnierebata Aḳademia, Ḳ. Ḳeḳelizis Saxelobis Xelnacerta Insṭiṭuṭi.

Supplemented by: Z. A. Sardzhveladze, *Zveli kartuli enis leksikoni* ... Tbilisi, 1995. 315 pp. See the review of this by G. A. Klimov in *Voprosy yazykoznaniya* 1996 no. 6 pp. 126–9.

[*Dictionary of the Old Georgian language.*]

558.

E. Cherkesi, *Georgian–English dictionary*. Oxford: Trustees of the Marjorie Wardrop Fund, University of Oxford, 1950. 275 pp.

A brief-entry dictionary of the older language, based on a few classical texts. Verbs are entered under the *masdar* only.

559.

Joseph Molitor, *Glossarium Latinum–Ibericum–Graecum in quattor Evangelia et Actus Apostolorum et in Epistolas catholicas necnon in Apocalypsim antiquioris versionis Ibericae*. Louvain: Secrétariat du Corpus SCO, 1967. 252 pp.

[*A Latin–Georgian–Greek glossary to the older Georgian translation of the four Gospels, the Acts of the Apostles, the Catholic Letters and the Apocalypse.*]

Regional forms

560.

ალ. გლონტი, *ქართულ კილო-თქმათა სიტყვის კონა* [Al. Glonti, editor, *Kartul kilo-tkmata sitqvis kona*]. Tbilisi: Ganatleba, 1984. 798 pp.

[*Dictionary of Georgian dialect words.*] Bibliography, pp. 10–16.

Etymological dictionaries

561.

E. J. Furnée, *Beiträge zur georgischen Etymologie*. Leuven: Peeters, 1982. Part 1 [87 pp.; no more published].

[*Studies on Georgian etymology.*] Chpater 1: East Mediterranean elements in Georgian and Greek; chapter 2: Mediterranean elements in Georgian and in Romance languages; chapter 3: East Mediterranean elements in Georgian with Old European cognates in Indo-European languages; chapter 4: genuine Kartvelian words in Georgian with cognates in Indo-European languages. Each list is in alphabetical order under Georgian words, which are in Latin transliteration. Georgian word index, pp. 83–7.

GERMAN

German belongs to the GERMANIC branch of Indo-European languages. With 120 million speakers, it is the national language of Germany and Austria, one of the four official languages of Switzerland, and is spoken by significant minorities in the United States, Romania, Kazakhstan and several other countries.

In this book, the dialects of northern Germany are dealt with separately at LOW GERMAN.

The makers of German dictionaries have enjoyed experimenting with alphabetical order. Modern dictionaries of the language adopt a simple alphabetical order: note that, in dictionaries, the simple vowels *a o u* and the same vowels with *Umlaut* (*ä ö ü*) are interfiled, although in many other reference books the latter forms are filed as *ae oe ue*. Dictionaries of older periods, and dialect dictionaries, often attempt to reflect the history of German sounds and spelling in a more complex way, interfiling *p* with *b*, *t* with *d*, *k* with *g* and *c* with *z*. The 'Schmellersche System' (see **603**) is more complicated still.

German fonts

𝔄𝔅ℭ𝔇𝔈𝔉𝔊ℌℑℑ𝔎𝔏𝔐𝔑𝔒𝔓𝔔ℜ𝔖𝔗𝔘𝔙𝔚𝔛𝔜ℨ

a b c d e f g h i j k l m n o p q r s t u v w x y z

𝔄𝔅ℭ𝔇𝔈𝔉𝔊ℑℑ𝔎𝔏𝔐𝔑𝔒𝔓𝔔ℜ𝔖𝔗𝔘𝔙𝔚𝔛𝔜ℨ

a b c d e f g h i j k l m n o p q r s t u v w r y z

A B C D E F G H I J K L M N O P Q R S T U V W X Y Z

a b c d e f g h i j k l m n o p q r s t u v w x y z

The two 'Gothic' font families are known as *Fraktur* (lines 1-2) and *Schwabacher* (lines 3-4). Until the 1930s they were typical of German language printing. When quoting single words or longer texts in other languages, printers would normally switch to a Roman font.

Historical dictionaries

562.

Jacob Grimm, Wilhelm Grimm, *Deutsches Wörterbuch*. Berlin: Weidmann; Leipzig: Hirzel, 1852–1958. 16 vols in 32.

Accompanied by a *Quellenverzeichnis* [*Guide to sources*]. 1966–71. 1094 columns. (This replaces the original list of sources in vol. 1 columns lxix–xci. It also supplies a dated list of the published parts of the dictionary, with section editors, pp. 1071–84.)

Reprinted: Munich, 1984.

See Joachim Bahr, 'Das *Deutsche Wörterbuch* von Jacob Grimm und Wilhelm Grimm: Stationen seiner inneren Geschichte' in *Sprachwissenschaft* vol. 9 (1984) pp. 387–455.

Also: Joachim Dückert, editor, *Das Grimmsche Wörterbuch: Untersuchungen zur lexikographischen Methodologie*. Leipzig, 1987.

[*German dictionary.*] This landmark work grew in the course of publication. In the early volumes many words, particularly compounds, are not exemplified; some are merely listed, without even a gloss. Thus the reworking of the letter **A** (see below), when complete, will be about fifteen times the length of the **A** section in the present edition. The letter **G** (including the productive prefix **ge-**) took from 1874 to 1958 to complete: the dictionary's slow progress and gradual huge expansion are well demonstrated in this section alone.

The Grimms' dictionary set the fashion in Germany for the use of roman and italic type (not Fraktur) throughout: italic for glosses, roman for quotations.

563.

Jacob Grimm, Wilhelm Grimm, *Deutsches Wörterbuch: Neubearbeitung.*
Leipzig: Hirzel, 1965– .

Compiled by E. Adelberg and others. 'Edited by the Akademie der Wissenschaften der DDR in collaboration with the Akademie der Wissenschaften in Göttingen.'

[*German dictionary: reworking.*] The new version of the dictionary first planned by the Grimm brothers is now well under way. It will eventually be a very extensive historical dictionary. The longer articles consist of a small-type section giving etymology and variant forms, followed in larger type by the successive meanings of the word (in italic), each supported by numerous attributed quotations (in roman) and dated.

Dates are in a distinctive sans-serif font, with these special abbreviations: *u um* 'about', *n nach* 'after', *v vor* 'before', *h* 'half-century', *A Anfang* 'early', *M Mitte* 'middle', *E Ende* 'late'. As in the original edition, headwords are in upper-case; in these headwords, *SZ* serves as equivalent of the usual German double-*s* symbol *ß*.

Abbreviations, vol. 1 preliminary pages 6–14.

The 'Leipzig workshop' began publication of vol. 1 in 1965 and is now proceeding slowly through vol. 2. The 'Göttingen workshop' began vol. 6 in 1970 and is now working on vol. 8. Parts of the letters **A**, **D–E** are covered by the published volumes.

564.

Lutz Röhrich, *Das große Lexikon der sprichwörtlichen Redensarten.* Freiburg: Herder, 1991–2. 3 vols [1910 pp.]. 3–451–22081–4.

First published as *Lexikon der sprichwörtlichen Redensarten.* 1973. 2 vols. Paperback issue: 1977.

[*The big dictionary of proverbial expressions.*] A scholarly, discursive and illustrated dictionary of proverbs, filed under keywords: far less inclusive than Wander (**566**) but much more informative on those proverbs that are selected for inclusion. Bibliography, pp. 1787–1834; index, pp. 1865–1910.

565.

Keith Spalding, *An historical dictionary of German figurative usage.* Oxford: Blackwell, 1953– .

With the assistance of Kenneth Brooke, Gerhard Müller-Schwefe.

An enjoyable large-scale dictionary in which the origin of expressions is discussed, in English, with frequent references to literary sources. Phrases are filed under keywords: English translations or equivalents are given as glosses. Nearing completion: the last part I have seen is no. 54 (1994). Entries from **A** to **Verwirren** are now completed, in 2584 pages.

566.

Karl Friedrich Wilhelm Wander, editor, *Deutsches Sprichwörter-Lexikon: ein Hausschatz für das deutsche Volk.* Leipzig: Brockhaus, 1867–80. 5 vols.

[*German proverb dictionary: a household treasury for the German people.*] An astonishingly rich compilation. Brief entries are given under keywords (no index), some with attributions to sources, some with historical comments and comparisons with other languages. Includes LOW GERMAN and YIDDISH proverbs. Supplement, vol. 5 columns 685–1824.

Bibliography, vol. 1 pp. xxxi–li. List of contributors, pp. lii–liii.

The modern standard

567.

Günther Drosdowski, editor, *Duden: das große Wörterbuch der deutschen Sprache*. Mannheim: Dudenverlag, 1993–5. 8 vols [4096 pp.]. 2nd edn. 3–411–04732–1.

Review in *Lebende Sprachen*, vol. 41 (1996) no. 1.

1st edn: Mannheim: Bibliographisches Institut, 1976–81. 6 vols [2992 pp.].

[*Big dictionary of the German language.*] A dictionary of modern usage; glosses in italic, followed by invented example phrases, and a few quotations (with precise references), in roman. Non-German users may find this the easiest to use of the three big modern dictionaries (compare **568** and **571**, below), particularly because of its wealth of cross-references for derived forms.

Pronunciation is indicated partly in the International Phonetic Alphabet, partly by conventional signs added to the headword: for an explanation see vol. 1 pp. 9–10. Bibliography of sources, pp. 32–49, 4094; addenda, pp. 4095–6; new German spelling rules, pp. i–xxiv at end of vol. 8.

568.

Ruth Klappenbach, Wolfgang Steinitz, editors, *Wörterbuch der deutschen Gegenwartssprache*. Berlin: Akademie-Verlag, 1961–77. 6 vols [4579 pp.].

A corrected reprint of vol. 1 appeared in 1980.

[*Dictionary of the contemporary German language.*] A large-scale dictionary of modern usage, naturally strong on the East German variant of the standard, with brief quotations from literary sources. Fuller on the basic vocabulary than its competitors; very laconic on compounds. List of country names and their derivatives (including the old official 'people's republic' forms), pp. 4552–6; abbreviations used in the dictionary, pp. 4557–9; sources of quotations, pp. 4559–79.

569.

Hans Schemann, *Deutsche Idiomatik*. Stuttgart: Klett, 1993.

Accompanied by a series of bilingual dictionaries into other European languages, e.g.: Hans Schemann, Paul Knight, *German–English dictionary of idioms = Idiomatik Deutsch–Englisch*. London: Routledge; Stuttgart: Klett, 1995. 1253 pp. 0–415–14199–0. – Hans Schemann, Paul Knight, *English-German dictionary of idioms: supplement to the German-English dictionary of idioms*. London: Routledge, 1997.

[*Dictionary of German idioms.*] An unusually comprehensive listing, based on a corpus of literary sources. Examples are not individually attributed.

570.

Otto Springer, editor, *Langenscheidt's encyclopaedic dictionary of the English and German languages, based on the original work by Prof. Dr. E. Muret and Prof. Dr. D. Sanders = Langenscheidts enzyklopädisches Wörterbuch der englischen und deutschen Sprache, begründet von Prof. Dr. E. Muret und Prof. Dr. D. Sanders.* Berlin-Schöneberg: Langenscheidt, 1962–75. 2 parts in 4 vols [1844 + 2024 pp.].

Also published: London: Hodder & Stoughton.
Earlier version: E. Muret, D. Sanders, *Enzyklopädisches englisch–deutsche und deutsch–englische Wörterbuch.* 1891–1901. 4 vols. Reprints are entitled: *Muret-Sanders enzyklopädisches englisch–deutsche und deutsch–englische Wörterbuch = Muret-Sanders encyclopaedic English–German and German–English dictionary.* In this version the German is in Fraktur type, the English in Roman. Much use is made of pictorial symbols, such as the ominous ☝, gallows, used to denote 'language of the criminal classes'.

Very brief entries with few examples and very curt guidance on usage. The German part is fairly generous in its cross-references for derived forms, e.g. from **gegriffen** to **greifen**. Dictionary of German abbreviations, part 2 pp. 1899–1959. Dictionaries of proper names, giving pronunciations in the respective languages, at end of each part.

571.

Gerhard Wahrig, Hildegard Krämer, Harald Zimmermann, editors, *Brockhaus Wahrig deutsches Wörterbuch.* Wiesbaden: Brockhaus, 1980–84. 6 vols. 3–7653–0312–7.

[*German dictionary.*] A brief-entry dictionary of modern German with generous grammatical and orthographical help. Includes more compound words than its competitors do. Explanation of the format of entries, vol. 1 pp. 9–15.

The family firm of Brockhaus has published dictionaries and encyclopaedias since the early nineteenth century: F. A. Brockhaus's eight-volume *Conversations-Lexikon* appeared in 1809–11.

Older periods

Old High German

572.

E. G. Graff, *Althochdeutscher Sprachschatz, oder Wörterbuch der althochdeutschen Sprache.* Berlin: Nikolai, 1834–42. 6 vols.

[*Old High German linguistic thesaurus, or dictionary of the Old High German language.*] Makes its limited readership work hard, as it is not in any normal version of alphabetical order, not even in the Sanskrit order which some nineteenth century philologists liked. Words are, moreover, grouped under 'roots' (presumed) and other basic forms. There is, however, an alphabetical index in each volume (vol. 1: vowels and semivowels; vol. 2: liquids and nasals; vol. 3: labials; vol. 4: velars including **H**; vol. 5: dentals including **Z**; vol. 6, **S**) and, the saving grace, a full alphabetical index and Latin glossary, by H. F. Massmann, in vol. 6.

Generous references to texts, but no quotations.

573.

Elisabeth Karg-Gasterstadt, Theodor Frings, Rudolf Grosse, editors, *Althochdeutsches Wörterbuch.* Berlin: Akademie-Verlag, 1971– .

Compiled on the basis of the collections bequeathed by Elias von Steinmeyer.

[*Old High German dictionary.*] A very full dictionary, amounting to a fairly comprehensive index of Old High German texts. There is full information on alternate and derived forms, and many long quotations; also quotations from Latin glossaries, which are a major source, and from the Latin originals of texts that are translated from Latin.

Bibliography of sources, vol. 1 pp. ix–xxxiv.

Vols 1 (**A–B**) and 3 (**E–F**) are complete; vols 2 (**C–D**) and 4 (**G–J**) in progress.

574.

Albert L. Lloyd, Otto Springer, *Etymologisches Wörterbuch des Althochdeutschen*. Göttingen: Vandenhoeck & Ruprecht, 1988– .

[*Etymological dictionary of Old High German.*] So far only vol. 1, **A–Bezzisto**, has appeared, in 578 pages. Entries, relatively concise, consist of a series of paragraphs dealing successively with variant forms, origins, cognates, etc., each followed by a paragraph (in a smaller font) of references to scholarship – including many references to other dictionaries.

A separate index volume for vol. 1 was also published in 1988. Reproduced from typescript, it contains separate indexes for each language. A list of these indexes occupies 4 preliminary pages.

575.

Oskar Schade, *Altdeutsches Wörterbuch*. Halle an der Saale, 1872–82. 1446 pp. 2nd edn.

[*Old German dictionary.*] A handy, short-entry dictionary with some references to source texts. Supplement, pp. 1316–1446. List of abbreviations, pp. lxiv–cxv.

576.

Rudolf Schützeichel, *Althochdeutsches Wörterbuch*. Tübingen: Niemeyer, 1969. 250 pp.

[*Old High German dictionary.*] A complete vocabulary of Old High German texts, in the briefest possible form, yet with indication of source texts (no precise references). Abbreviations, pp. vii–xv. It is necessary to check under **B D** for words not found under **P T**. As in other dictionaries of older German, all words beginning with **C** must be looked for under **G** or **K** or **Z**.

Middle High German

577.

Matthias Lexer, *Mittelhochdeutsches Handwörterbuch, zugleich als Supplement und alphabetischer Index zum Mittelhochdeutschen Wörterbuch von Benecke–Müller–Zarncke*. Leipzig: Hirzel, 1872–8. 3 vols.

Reprinted: Stuttgart, 1979.

Abridged edition: *Mittelhochdeutsches Taschenwörterbuch*. Stuttgart, 1981. 504 pp. 3–7776–0359–7. '36th edn', including supplement by Dorothea Hannover, Rena Lippin, Ulrich Pretzel. – 3rd edn: 1885. Many intervening editions are simply reprints.

Note: Erwin Koller, Werner Wegstein, Norbert Richard Wolf, *Neuhochdeutscher Index zum mittelhochdeutschen Wortschatz.* Stuttgart, 1990. 544 pp. 3–7776–0422–4. A Modern German–Middle High German index to the 37th edition of the *Mittelhochdeutsches Taschenwörterbuch.*

Also: Wolfgang Bachofer, Walther von Hahn, Dieter Möhn, *Rückläufiges Wörterbuch der mittelhochdeutschen Sprache: auf der Grundlage von Matthias Lexers Mittelhochdeutschem Handwörterbuch und Taschenwörterbuch.* Stuttgart, 1984. 585 pp. 3–7776–0398–8. Spine title: *Rückläufiges mittelhochdeutsches Wörterbuch.* [*Reverse dictionary of the Middle High German language, on the basis of Matthias Lexer's Concise and Pocket Middle High German dictionaries.*]

On the author see: Horst Brunner, editor, *Matthias von Lexer: Beiträge zu seinem Leben und Schaffen.* Stuttgart: Steiner, 1993. 248 pp. 3–515–06357–9. (*Zeitschrift für Dialektologie und Linguistik, Beihefte, 80.*)

[*Concise Middle High German dictionary, a supplement and an index to Benecke–Müller–Zarncke's Middle High German dictionary.*] Concise entries, in strict alphabetical order, with volume and page references to Benecke-Müller-Zarncke (see next entry). Supplement, vol. 3 second pagination (406 columns).

578.

Mittelhochdeutsches Wörterbuch. Stuttgart: Hirzel, 1990. 4 vols in 5. 3–7776–0466–6.

Compiled using the materials of the late Friedrich Benecke by Wilhelm Müller [and Friedrich Zarncke].
First published: Leipzig: Hirzel, 1854–66. 3 vols in 4.

[*Middle High German dictionary.*] Often referred to as Benecke–Müller–Zarncke, this is a full historical dictionary with glosses in italic followed by numerous quotations in roman, in the Grimm style. Compounds are listed under base forms, hence the need for an index which was for many years fulfilled by Lexer (**577**).

The 1990 edition is a reprint with a new fourth volume (Erwin Koller, Werner Wegstein, Norbert Richard Wolf, *Alphabetischer Index.* 249 pp.), and also with a new guide to abbreviations (including source materials), vol. 1 pp. 8*–33*.

579.

Lorenz Diefenbach, Ernst Wülcker, *Hoch- und nieder-deutsches Wörterbuch der mittleren und neueren Zeit, zur Ergänzung der vorhandenen Wörterbücher insbesondere des der Brüder Grimm.* Basle, 1874–85. 930 pp.

[*High and Low German dictionary of the middle and modern periods, supplementing the available dictionaries, particularly that of the brothers Grimm.*]

580.

Kurt Gärtner [and others], *Findebuch zum mittelhochdeutschen Wortschatz, mit einem rückläufigen Index.* Stuttgart: Hirzel, 1992. 682 pp. 3–7776–0490–9.

[*Finding list for the Middle High German vocabulary, with a reverse index.*] '*Die desolate Situation der mittelhochdeutschen Lexikographie ist wohlbekannt* [The desolate situation of Middle High German lexicography is well known]', the preface begins. This is an index to the glossaries in modern editions of Middle High German texts, and thus a partial author index of the vocabulary.

581.

Bettina Kischstein, Ursula Schultze, *Wörterbuch der mittelhochdeutschen Urkundensprache, auf der Grundlage des Corpus der altdeutschen Originalurkunden bis zum Jahr 1300.* Berlin: Erich Schmidt, 1994– .

[*Dictionary of the language of Middle High German documents, based on the Corpus of old German records to 1300.*] Publication already extends from **A** to **Lônen**, midway through volume 2.

Early Modern High German

582.

Robert R. Anderson, Ulrich Goebel, Oskar Reichmann, editors, *Frühneuhochdeutsches Wörterbuch*. Berlin: De Gruyter, 1986– .

See Robert R. Anderson and others, 'Projekt eines frühneuhochdeutschen Handwörterbuches' in *Zeitschrift für germanistische Linguistik* vol. 5 (1977) pp. 71–94, folllowed by a series of specimen entries in the 1979 volume of the same journal.

Also: Ulrich Goebel, Ingrid Lemberg, Oskar Reichmann, *Versteckte lexikographische Information: Möglichkeiten ihrer Erschliessung dargestellt am Beispiel des Frühneuhochdeutschen Wörterbuchs*. Tübingen: Niemeyer, 1995. 269 pp. 3–484–30965–2. (*Lexicographica, series maior*, 65.)

[*Early New High German dictionary.*] Vols 1 and 2 are complete; vols 3, 4 and 8 are in progress. This covers **A–Beistat** with the letters **I, J** and part of **P**. The preliminary pages of vol. 1 include introduction, list of sources, bibliography.

Regional forms

Austria

583.

Viktor Dollmayr, Eberhard Kranzmayer [and others], *Wörterbuch der bairischen Mundarten in Österreich*. Vienna: Böhlau, 1963– . 3–7001–0550–9.

Alternate title: *Bayerisch-österreichisches Wörterbuch, 1. Österreich*.
Accompanied by: *Beiheft nr. 1: Erläuterungen zum Wörterbuch*. 1971.

[*Dictionary of the Bavarian dialects of Austria.*] A particularly well-planned dictionary covering both oral and local written forms of the language. Deals with the whole of Austria except Vorarlberg, and with bordering districts of Slovenia, Hungary, the Czech Republic and – especially – Italy (see map attached to *Beiheft*).

Entries are under a generalised form with excellent cross-references from alternatives, from standard German and even from taxonomic Latin names. The dictionary is in alphabetical order, but, as with some other German dialect dictionaries, **B** and **P** are interfiled and so are **D** and **T**: so in covering entries from **A–Temper** in 30 parts, the dictionary has not yet reached very far.

Abbreviations, *Beiheft* pp. 5–9; pronunciation, pp. 10–11; bibliography, pp. 12–58.

584.

Jakob Ebner, *Duden Wie sagt man in Österreich? Wörterbuch der österreichischen Besonderheiten*. Mannheim: Bibliographisches Institut, 1980. 252 pp. 2nd edn. 3–411–01794–5.

1st edn: 1969.

[*How do they speak in Austria? Dictionary of Austrian regionalisms.*] Most entries include a quotation from modern Austrian literature or journalism, with a precise reference. Notes on the language, pp. 207–22; list of sources, pp. 223–30; German–Austrian glossary/index, pp. 231–52.

585.

Leo Jutz, *Vorarlbergisches Wörterbuch mit Einschluss des Fürstentums Liechtenstein*. Vienna: A. Holzhausens Nachf., 1955–65. 2 vols.
Edited by the Österreichische Akademie der Wissenschaften.

[*Vorarlberg dialect dictionary, including the Principality of Liechtenstein.*] A relatively brief dictionary which, along with those for Baden and Alsace, completes the coverage of the 'Alemannic' dialects of German. Quotations from oral collections and from literature. Abbreviations, vol. 1, final part, pp. xvii–xxiv.

586.

Matthias Lexer, *Kärntisches Wörterbuch*. Leipzig: Hirzel, 1862. 339 pp.

[*Carinthian dictionary.*] A brief-entry dictionary but with room for examples and quotations, including both medieval and modern texts, and some ethnological explanations and folk poetry. Addenda, pp. 376–7. Annex: 'Christmas games and songs from Carinthia', pp. 274–335. Pronunciation and spelling, pp. vii–xvii; abbreviations, pp. xvii–xviii. Note that **P** is interfiled with **B**, and **T** with **D**.

587.

J. B. Schöpf, *Tirolisches Idiotikon*. Innsbruck: Verlag des Wagner'schen Universitäts-Buchhandlung, 1866. 835 pp.
Completed after the author's death by Anton J. Hofer.

[*Tyrol dialect dictionary.*] A long-entry dictionary with generous examples of usage, explained in German, and with quotations from manuscripts and early and modern printed texts.

588.

Mauriz Schuster, *Alt-Wienerisch: ein Wörterbuch veraltender und veralteter Wiener Ausdrücke und Redensarten der letzten sieben Jahrzehnte*. Vienna: Österreichische Bundesverlag, 1951. 232 pp.

[*Old Viennese: a dictionary of obsolescent and obsolete Viennese expressions and idioms of the last seventy years.*] Brief glosses followed by *A.–* 'origin' and *E.–* 'example'.

589.

Theodor Unger, *Steirischer Wortschatz, als Ergänzung zu Schmellers Bayerischem Wörterbuch*. Graz: Leuschner u. Lubensky's Universitäts-Buchhandlung, 1903. 661 pp.
Prepared for publication by Ferdinand Khull.

[*Styrian vocabulary, a complement to Schmeller's Bavarian dictionary (**603**).*] Sources and other abbreviations, pp. ix–xxiv.

Czech Republic

590.

Heinz Engels, [Otfrid Ehrismann,] editors, *Sudetendeutsches Wörterbuch: Wörterbuch der deutschen Mundarten in Böhmen und Mähren-Schlesien.* Munich: Oldenbourg, 1982– .

Begun by Ernst Schwarz; continued by Franz J. Beranek [and others].

Accompanied by: *Vorläufiges Verzeichnis der Belegorte des Sudetendeutschen Wörterbuchs und ihrer Abkürzungen.* [1989.] 18 pp. [*Preliminary list of place names and abbreviations for them.*]

[*Sudeten German dictionary: dictionary of the German dialects of Bohemia and of Moravia-Silesia.*] Covers German dialects once spoken in what is now the Czech Republic, an area that cuts across five usually recognised German dialect regions. Highly abridged entries, based on oral collections. A few abbreviations are explained by reference to the two maps that came with vol. 1 part 1, but all are listed in the 1989 supplement. Good cross-references, including taxonomic names for plants. So far the dictionary has reached vol. 3 part 1 and covers **A–Daraufscheißen**.

France

591.

Michael Ferdinand Follman, *Wörterbuch der deutsch-lothringischen Mundarten.* Leipzig: Quelle & Meyer, 1909. 571 pp.

Quellen zur lothringischen Geschichte = Documents de l'histoire de la Lorraine, 12. Reprinted 1971.

[*Dictionary of the German dialects of Lorraine.*] A brief-entry dictionary but with local dialect variants (geographical abbreviations, p. xiii) and with some quotations (abbreviations for sources, pp. xv–xvi). In alphabetical order, but **V** and **Uv** are interfiled.

592.

Historisches Wörterbuch der elsässischen Mundart, mit besonderer Berücksichtigung der früh-neuhochdeutschen Periode. Strasbourg: Heitz, 1901. 447 pp.

Based on materials left by Charles Schmidt.

[*Historical dictionary of the Alsatian dialect, with special attention to the Early Modern High German period.*] In good alphabetical order. Bibliography of sources, pp. xi–xv.

593.

E. Martin, H Lienhart, *Wörterbuch der elsässischen Mundarten.* Strasbourg: Trübner, 1899–1907. 2 vols.

[*Dictionary of the Alsatian dialects.*] Deals both with current usage and with early literature, with generous quotations. The alphabetical order is the Schmellersche System (see **603**), and compounds are filed under base form, but there is an index, vol. 2 pp. 968–1160. Addenda, vol. 2 pp. 930–67.

594.

Claude Guizard, Jean Speth, *Dialectionnaire alsacien, français et allemand = Dreisprachiges Wörterbuch*. Mulhouse: Editions du Rhin, 1992. 968 pp. 2–86339–069–4.

[*Trilingual dialect dictionary, Alsatian–French–German.*]

Germany

595.

Luise Berthold, [Hans Friebertshäuser, Heinrich J. Dingeldein,] editors, *Hessen-Nassauisches Wörterbuch*. Marburg: Elwert, 1927– .

Based on materials collected by Ferdinand Wrede.

[*Hesse and Nassau dictionary.*] The main paragraph of each entry gives detailed glosses; a supplementary paragraph in smaller font gives word-form variations and bibliography. Some word maps and illustrations. Abbreviations for place names etc., vol. 3 pp. 922–3.

In its slow and stately progress the *Hessen-Nassauisches Wörterbuch*, which began publication with vol. 2, is now well into vol. 4 and covers **L–Wischen**.

596.

W. Crecelius, *Oberhessisches Wörterbuch*. Darmstadt, 1890–99. 2 vols [951 pp.].

'Based on work by Weigand, Lorenz Diefenbach and Hainebach.'

[*Upper Hesse dialect dictionary.*] Derives from early printed material as well as venerable oral collections. Entries are under normalised German forms. No list of source abbreviations – but see the introduction, pp. i–xl, for information on sources that were used.

597.

Hermann Fischer, *Schwäbisches Wörterbuch*. Tübingen: Laupp, 1901–36. 6 vols in 7.

Collections begun by Adalbert von Keller. Completed by Wilhelm Pfleiderer.

[*Swabian dialect dictionary.*] Entries are filed under normalised German forms; there are very full references to dialect collections. Supplement, vol. 6 part 2 columns 1485–3534. Sources and abbreviations, vol. 6 part 2 columns ix–clxxiv.

598.

Will Hermanns, *Aachener Sprachschatz: Wörterbuch der Aachener Mundart*. Aachen: Mayer, 1970. 596 pp. 3–87519–011–4.

Edited by Rudolf Lantin for the Verein 'Öcher Platt'.

Beiträge zur Kultur- und Wirtschafts-Geschichte Aachens und seiner Umgebung, 1.

[*Aachen vocabulary: dictionary of the Aachen dialect.*] A brief-entry dictionary with entries filed under local word forms in a semi-standardised spelling: but some guidance is offered for consultation from the point of view of standard German. Many quotations, some from oral sources, some attributed to authors (list, pp. xlviii–xlix), some to place names (list, with other abbreviations, p. lii).

599.

Julius Krämer, [Rudolf Post,] *Pfälzisches Wörterbuch*. Wiesbaden: Steiner, 1965– .

Begun by Ernst Christmann. Akademie der Wissenschaften und der Literatur, Mainz, *Veröffentlichungen zur Sprachwissenschaft.*

[*Palatinate dialect dictionary.*] This dictionary is strong in quotations from printed literature; there is also much information on local dialect variation. There are word maps and illustrations, with a list of these in each volume. Abbreviations, including source texts, vol. 1 pp. xxi–xxxv, with two pages of addenda circulated later.

The *Pfälzisches Wörterbuch* has now completed vol. 5 and covers **A–Schw**.

600.

Rudolf Mulch, *Südhessisches Wörterbuch*. Marburg: Elwert, 1965– . 3–7708–0388–4.

Begun by Friedrich Maurer. Hessische Historische Kommission.

[*South Hesse dialect dictionary.*] Many word maps, and much more attention to word form variation than to quotations of examples. There are some (but rather few) quotations from printed literature. Abbreviations, vol. 1 pp. xxv–xl.

Covering **A–Stipps** and now in its fifth volume, the *Südhessisches Wörterbuch* is well on its way to completion.

601.

Josef Müller, *Rheinisches Wörterbuch*. Bonn, Berlin: Klopp, 1928–71. 9 vols.

[*Rhineland dialect dictionary.*] Based on work begun by J. Franck, this is largely a dictionary of the spoken dialects, spanning the border between High and Low German, with some word maps (list of these, vol. 9 columns 1391–4) and many quotations from oral collections, carefully localised. Entries are under normalised German forms if possible, but most quotations are in phonetic script. Supplement, vol. 9 columns 924–1386; full index of prefixes and suffixes, vol. 9 columns 1395–1738;.

Sources and bibliography, vol. 1 pp. vi–x with vol. 9 columns 1387–90.

602.

Ernst Ochs [and others], *Badisches Wörterbuch*. Lahr (Schwarzwald): Schauenburg, 1925– .

[*Baden dialect dictionary.*] Entries are under normalised German forms where possible. Most give at least one literary citation, often with a careful explanation of meaning and usage, followed by one or more quotations from dialect collections (in italic, in a phonetic script). Apart from this the text of vols 1–2, **A–H**, published 1925–74, is entirely in Fraktur. Vol. 3 is in roman, with taxonomic names for flora and fauna picked out in a sans-serif font. The dictionary has grown slightly as it has progressed, now including more citations, both of oral collections and printed texts. References to other dictionaries and modern scholarship are in a small font at the end of entries.

Publication now covers **A–Moste**.

603.

Johann Andreas Schmeller, *Bayerisches Wörterbuch*. Munich: Oldenbourg, 1872–7. 2 vols. 2nd edn by G. K. Frommann.

1st edn: Tübingen, 1827–37.

See Ludwig M. Eichinger, Bernd Naumann, editors, *Johann Andreas Schmeller und der Beginn der Germanistik*. München: Oldenbourg, 1988. 235 pp. 3–486–54551–5.

[*Bavarian dialect dictionary.*] Johann Andreas Schmeller (1785–1852) is blessed for this important, innovative, well-documented historical dictionary of the German of Bavaria.

He is occasionally cursed for the alphabetical order that he invented and adopted, the 'Schmellersche System'. This was praised by Jacob Grimm (*Deutsches Wörterbuch*, **562**, vol. 1 p. xvii) and was adopted by many German lexicographers. It is in use even in one or two dialect dictionaries that are still in course of publication (for example, **609**). Intended to facilitate comparative linguistic research, the filing order of the 'Schmellersche System' works with consonant groups (of which there are many in German) and takes account of vowels only after the consonant groups that follow them. Doubled consonants are counted as single. A dictionary arranged in this way opens with words that begin with a vowel – any vowel – the order of words being determined by the consonants that follow, *ab eb ib ob ub abd ebd ibd* etc.

604.

K. Spangenburg, W. Lösch, editors, *Thuringisches Wörterbuch*. Berlin: Akademie-Verlag, 1966– .

Short version: Karl Spangenburg, *Kleines thuringisches Wörterbuch*. Rudolstadt: Hain, 1994. 383 pp. 3–930215–08–X.

[*Thuringian dialect dictionary.*] Work on Thuringian dialects was begun by V. Michals and continued by H. Hucke. The main dictionary will consist of six volumes, of which vols 4–6, **L–Z**, are complete and vol. 1 is now in progress.

605.

Wörterbuch der obersächsischen Mundarten. Berlin: Akademie-Verlag, 1994– .

Founded by Theodor Frings and Rudolf Grosse; compiled by Gunter Bergmann and others. Sächsische Akademie der Wissenschaften zu Leipzig, Sprachwissenschaftliche Kommission.

[*Dictionary of the Upper Saxon dialects.*] Vols 3–4, covering **L–Z**, have appeared so far.

Poland

606.

Walther Mitzka, *Schlesisches Wörterbuch*. Berlin: De Gruyter, 1962–5. 3 vols [1636 pp.].

[*Silesian dictionary.*] German speakers were expelled from Silesia after 1945. This dictionary of the now dying dialects contains numerous brief entries filed under normalised German forms, which are followed by local pronunciations and variants. Very brief glosses and selective quotations from sources. Many word maps. Geographical origins are indicated by letter–number sigla: list of these, pp. 1582–99;

alphabetical index of place names in their German form, pp. 1601–36 (there is no index or concordance of the modern Polish forms of place names). Sources, pp. 2–12.

Romania

607.
Friedrich Krauss, *Treppener Wörterbuch: ein Beitrag zum Nordsiebenbürgischen Wörterbuch*. Marburg: Elwert, 1970. 1206 columns. 3–7708–0186–5.

[*Treppen dialect dictionary: a contribution to the North Transylvanian dictionary.*] An important treatment of a dialect that is obscure to most: Treppen is now known as Tărpiu, a village in the Romanian department of Bistriţa-Năsăud (the district whose traditional German name is Nösnerland). Entries are under normalised German forms, often very different from the local ones which follow, because 'the Treppen dialect stands out as unusual in its sound pattern even among those of the Nösnerland' (column xi). Thus the entry **Brombeere** actually deals with the local word *brummel* 'blackberry'.

Bibliography and abbreviations, columns xv–xxiv.

608.
Adolf Schullerus [and other editors], *Siebenbürgisch-sächsisches Wörterbuch*. Strasbourg: Trübner; Berlin: De Gruyter; Bucharest: Editura Academiei Române, 1908– .

On the basis of the collections of Johann Wolff. Vols 1–2 and '5i–ii' edited by a committee of the Verein für Siebenbürgischen Landeskunde. Vols. 3–5 edited by Akademie der Sozialistischen Republik Rumänien; vol. 6– edited by Rumänische Akademie.

[*Transylvanian Saxon dictionary.*] A major historical dictionary with numerous quotations from oral sources and from printed literature. Entries are under normalised German forms, with cross-references for local spoken forms (in the International Phonetic Alphabet) in a single alphabetical order. The earlier published sections, particularly **A–F**, have fewer cross-references and more and longer quotations from folk poetry, sometimes with quite lengthy discussion of word history and of ethnographic matters. There is an important bilingual concordance of place names and abbreviations for them, vol. 6 pp. i–xviii.

So far the *Siebenbürgisch-sächsisches Wörterbuch* covers **A–L** and **R–Salarist**. This latter tranche was published in the early years as 'vol. 5 parts 1–2', a numbering made obsolete by the later expansion of the dictionary: the new vol. 5 covers the letter **K**. Vol. 6, for **L**, is the latest so far, having appeared in 1993.

Switzerland

609.
Friedrich Staub, Ludwig Tobler [and others], *Schweizerisches Idiotikon: Wörterbuch der Schweizerdeutschen Sprache*. Frauenfeld: Huber, 1881– .

Antiquarische Gesellschaft in Zürich.

Jan Haltmar, Brigitte Lambrecht-Steimer, Danuta Uhlig-Burbo, *Quellen- und Abkürzungsverzeichnis*. 1980. 155 pp. 3rd edn (1st edn: 1903. 2nd edn: 1951.) [*List of sources and abbreviations.*] Sources, pp. 11–138; general abbreviations, pp. 139–43; place names, pp. 144–51; map, p. 154.

Lotti Arter and others, *Alphabetisches Wörterverzeichnis zu den Bänden I–XI*. 1990. 611 pp. [*Alphabetical word index to volumes 1–11*.] 'It was not foreseen that no index would appear for over a hundred years …' (Preface).

[*Swiss dialect dictionary: dictionary of the Swiss-German language.*] A leisurely work with very lengthy essays on each word, its local uses and its pronunciations, with quotations from oral records and from local literature. The alphabetical order is the Schmellersche System (see **603**) and compounds are filed under base form, but there is at last a sensible index (see above), and from vol. 12 onwards each volume has its own index. The *Schweizerisches Idiotikon* is now in its 15th volume and is nearing completion: it covers **A–Wille**.

For the other big dictionaries of the local languages of Switzerland see **491, 818, 1293**.

United States and Canada

610.

Herfried Scheer, *Die deutsche Mundart der Hutterischen Brüder in Nordamerika*. Vienna: VWGÖ, 1987. 321 pp. 3–85369–691–0.
Beiträge zur Sprachinselforschung, 5.
[*The German dialect of the Hutterite Brethren in North America.*]

Slang and special vocabularies

611.

Ernest Bornemann, *Sex im Volksmund: die sexuelle Umgangssprache des deutschen Volkes: Wörterbuch und Thesaurus*. Reinbek: Rowohlt, 1971. Unnumbered pages.

[*Sex on people's lips: the sexual colloquial of the German people, a dictionary and thesaurus.*] A surprisingly copious brief-entry glossary, which, even so, is only a selection from Bornemann's material, for it is followed by an astoundingly copious thesaurus and an alphabetical index to the thesaurus.

612.

Deutsches Rechtswörterbuch: Wörterbuch der älteren deutschen Rechtssprache. Weimar: Böhlau, 1914– .
Preussische Akademie der Wissenschaften; Akademie der Wissenschaften der DDR; Heidelberger Akademie der Wissenschaften.
Accompanied by: *Quellenheft*. 1912. 87* pp. – *Quellen-Ergänzungsheft*. 1930–70. Pp. 89*–174*. [*Sources. – Additional sources.*]
See: Günther Dickel, Heino Speer, '*Deutsches Rechtswörterbuch*: Konzeption und lexikographische Praxis während acht Jahrzehnten, 1897–1977' in Helmut Henne, editor, *Praxis der Lexikographie* (Tübingen, 1979) pp. 20–37.

[*German law dictionary: dictionary of the older language of German law.*] A very important and astonishingly rich dictionary of legal language. At least one citation, and usually at least one quotation, is given for every word and compound. The dictionary deals with the period from the oldest German legal documents to the end of the eighteenth century, with some even later material. In the earlier volumes, notes and references are in Fraktur type, while headwords, glosses and quotations are in roman.

So far eight volumes have been completed, covering **A–Mahlgenosse**.

613.

Heinz Küpper, *Wörterbuch der deutschen Umgangssprache*. Stuttgart: Klett, 1987. 959 pp. 3–12–570600–9.

Cataloguing-in-publication title: *Pons-Wörterbuch der deutschen Umgangssprache*. Küpper's copious materials had earlier appeared in a series of six volumes, which are not superseded by the 1987 edition. *Wörterbuch der deutschen Umgangssprache*. Hamburg: Claassen, 1955. 421 pp. Includes many obsolete expressions. Standard German–colloquial index, pp. 362–421.

Vol. 2: 1963. 324 pp. '10,000 new entries', with some references to literature. Sources, pp. 15–34.

Vol. 3: 1964. 274 pp. Standard German–colloquial index to vols 1–2, pp. 27–177; index to entries in vols 1–2, pp. 181–270; corrigenda to vols 1–2.

Vol. 4: *Berufsschelten und Verwandtes*. 1966. 291 pp. [*Nicknames for trades and professions etc.*] Standard German–nickname index, pp. 247–91. Sources, pp. 21–41.

Vol. 5: 1967. 377 pp. '10,000 new entries'. Standard German–colloquial index, pp. 325–77. Sources, pp. 8–25.

Vol. 6: *Jugenddeutsch von A bis Z.* 1970. 438 pp. [*Young peoples' German from A to Z.*] Standard German–colloquial index, pp. 391–438. Sources, pp. 11–36.

[*Dictionary of the German colloquial.*] A selective short-entry dictionary, giving about 40,000 entries of mainly current words and phrases collected from all over Germany, each dated to a decade. Abbreviations frequently used include *Halbw.* 'children', *Stud.* 'students', *Sold.* 'soldiers', *Rotw.* 'thieves, criminals'.

614.

Siegmund A. Wolf, *Wörterbuch des Rotwelschen: deutsche Gaunersprache*. Mannheim: Bibliographisches Institut, 1956. 432 pp.

[*Dictionary of Rotwelsch, the German thieves' language.*] A concise historical dictionary: about 7500 entries, with citation of sources (but very few quotations) and some etymological notes. Bibliography, pp. 15–28. Standard German–Rotwelsch index, pp. 355–431.

Etymological dictionaries

615.

Rolf Hiersche, *Deutsches etymologisches Wörterbuch*. Heidelberg: Winter, 1986– .

Germanische Bibliothek.

[*German etymological dictionary.*] On a larger scale than its competitors (below), allowing more room for datings, references, and citations of scholarly literature both on German and on source languages. But publication is slow: only three parts, covering bits of **A** and **D**, have been seen as yet.

616.

Friedrich Kluge, *Etymologisches Wörterbuch der deutschen Sprache*. Berlin: De Gruyter, 1995. 921 pp. 23rd edn, by Elmar Seebold. 3–11–012922–1.

1st edn: Strasbourg, 1883. Successive editors have been: Alfred Götze, from 1910; Alfred Schirmer, from 1951; Walther Mitzka, from 1957. Elmar Seebold was responsible for the 22nd edn, 1989.

There was an English version of the 4th edn: *An etymological dictionary of the German language*. London: Bell, 1891. 446 pp. Translated by John Francis Davis.

'Kluge' has a disputatious readership. See Georg Objartel, 'Zur Geschichte des *Kluge*: Probleme eines etymologischen Wörterbuchs der deutschen Sprache' in *Zeitschrift für germanistische Linguistik* vol. 11 (1983) pp. 268–89. – On the 20th edn see Wolfgang Hoffmann, 'Zum Gebrauchswert etymologischer Wörterbücher: der Lemmata-Bestand von Kluge-Mitzka ([20]1967) und Duden und eine Umfrage unter ihren Benutzern', in *Zeitschrift für germanistische Linguistik* vol. 6 (1978) pp. 31–46.

[*Etymological dictionary of the German language.*] A terse but readable etymological dictionary including the better-established loanwords. Brief bibliography accompanies some entries. Derived forms are entered under headwords, and there are not enough cross-references. 'A classic of high-level popularization' (Malkiel, **9**).

617.

Wolfgang Pfeifer, editor, *Etymologisches Wörterbuch des Deutschen*. Berlin: Akademie-Verlag, 1989. 3 vols [2093 pp.]. 3–05–000626–9.

[*Etymological dictionary of German.*] Very similar in length and style to Kluge (**616**). Few bibliographical references. A useful index of derived words that have no separate alphabetical entry, pp. 2059–93.

Foreign words

618.

Franz Dornseiff, *Die griechischen Wörter im Deutschen*. Berlin: De Gruyter, 1950. 156 pp.

[*Greek words in German.*] Not seen.

619.

E. Eichler, *Etymologisches Wörterbuch der slawischen Elemente im Ostmitteldeutschen*. Bautzen: Domowina, 1965. 189 pp.

Spisy Instituta za Serbski Ludospyt, 29.

[*Etymological dictionary of the Slavic element in East Middle German.*] Quotes and cites source texts among Middle German documents from the eastern reaches of Germany. Index of German meanings, pp. 150–194.

620.

Enno Littmann, *Morgenländische Wörter im Deutschen*. Tübingen: Mohr, 1924. 161 pp. 2nd edn.

1st edn: Berlin: Curtius, 1920.

[*Oriental words in German.*] The 2nd edition includes words of Amerindian origin. The author is most widely known for his German translation of the *Thousand and one nights*, the best in any Western language.

621.

Hans Schulz [and others], *Deutsches Fremdwörterbuch*. Strasbourg: Trübner; Berlin: De Gruyter, 1913–88. 7 vols.

[*Dictionary of foreign words in German.*] A historical dictionary of loanwords from Old High German onwards: includes **Bibliothek** 'library', but not **Bibel** 'Bible', which was already naturalised at the time of the earliest texts. Words are often glossed and exemplified by means of long quotations from the writers who first used them in German, e.g. Heinrich Heine on **Cancan** in 1842. This dictionary grew and grew: vol. 1 covers half the alphabet, **A–K**. The first two volumes are in Fraktur type.

Vol. 7, completed in 1988, includes a bibliography of sources, pp. 1–211; an important 'afterword' or introduction, by Alan Kirkness, pp. 703–835; a bibliography of reviews of the work, pp. 836–7; and the following indexes: alphabetical, pp. 237–335; reverse index, pp. 337–432; chronological index (by date of first recorded use in German), pp. 433–528; index by language of origin, pp. 529–617; by parts of speech, pp. 619–700.

Other works of interest

622.

Franz Claes, *Bibliographisches Verzeichnis der deutschen Vokabulare und Wörterbücher, gedruckt bis 1600*. Hildesheim: Olms, 1977. 256 pp. 3–487–06449–9.

623.

Peter Kühn, *Deutsche Wörterbücher: eine systematische Bibliographie*. Tübingen: Niemeyer, 1978. 266 pp. 3–484–10323–X.

GERMANIC LANGUAGES

The Germanic branch of the INDO-EUROPEAN language family includes the following languages, for all of which individual entries appear in this book: DANISH, DUTCH, ENGLISH, FAROESE, FRISIAN, GERMAN, GOTHIC, ICELANDIC, LOW GERMAN, LUXEMBURGISH, NORN, NORWEGIAN, OLD NORSE, SWEDISH, YIDDISH.

Remarkably enough, in view of the intensity with which Germanic language studies are pursued in Germany and in several other countries, there is no up-to-date comparative dictionary of the Germanic languages: the latest is that by Torp (see **767**). Various partial updatings exist, including Köbler's teaching materials listed below, and some good etymological dictionaries of individual Germanic languages, for example, Kluge's of German (**616**), Lehmann's of Gothic (**633**) and de Vries's of Old Norse (**1154**).

There is a full bibliography of dictionaries of the Scandinavian languages by Haugen (**628**).

Comparative dictionaries

624.

Frank Heidermanns, *Etymologisches Wörterbuch der germanischen Primäradjektive*. Berlin: De Gruyter, 1993. 719 pp. 3–11–01366–X.
Studia linguistica Germanica, 33.

[*Etymological dictionary of Germanic primary adjectives.*] Primary adjectives are those not derived from another part of speech. The dictionary, in alphabetical order of reconstructed forms, pp. 93–697. There is little citation of known forms from the Germanic languages – these are taken for granted – but plenty of discussion, with references to scholarly literature. Index of German meanings, pp. 699–719.

625.

Gerhard Köbler, *Germanisches Wörterbuch*. Gießen: Arbeiten zur Rechts- und Sprachwissenschaft-Verlag, 1982. 581 pp. '2nd edn.'
1st edn: 1980.

[*Germanic dictionary.*]

626.

Gerhard Köbler, *Germanisch–neuhochdeutsches und neuhochdeutsch–germanisches Wörterbuch*. Gießen: Arbeiten zur Rechts- und Sprachwissenschaft-Verlag, 1981. 291 pp. 3–88430–032–6.
Arbeiten zur Rechts- und Sprachwissenschaft, 15. Cover date: 1980.

[*Proto-Germanic–German and German–Proto-Germanic dictionary.*] These are brief word-lists only, compiled as teaching materials.

627.

Elmar Seebold, *Vergleichendes und etymologisches Wörterbuch der germanischen starken Verben*. The Hague, 1970. 571 pp.
Janua linguarum, series practica, 85.

[*Comparative and etymological dictionary of Germanic strong verbs.*] An interesting cross-language study of verb forms in the Germanic languages. Entries are arranged alphabetically under reconstructed proto-Germanic roots, with no index. Bibliography, pp. 11–22; abbreviations of language names, pp. 22–3.

Other works of interest

628.

Einar Haugen, *A bibliography of Scandinavian dictionaries*. White Plains, New York: Kraus, 1984. 387 pp. 0–527–38842–4.

GORONTALO

An AUSTRONESIAN language of northern Sulawesi, with about a million speakers.

629.

Mansoer Pateda, *Kamus bahasa Gorontalo–Indonesia*. Jakarta: Departemen Penelitian dan Kebudayaan, 1977. 338 pp.

[*Gorontalo–Indonesian dictionary.*] One of the largest of a big series of dictionaries of minority languages published by the Indonesian Language and Literature Department.

GOTHIC

Gothic is one of the GERMANIC branch of Indo-European languages. It was the earliest Germanic language to be recorded at length, in the Bible translation of Bishop Ulfilas, made in about AD 350 at the time when Gothic speakers were threatening the stability of the Roman Empire. A Gothic dialect survived in the Crimea until a few centuries ago, but the language is now extinct.

The Gothic alphabet

ᚪᛒᚷᚪᛖᚢᛉᚻᚦᚹᛁᚳᛚᛗᚾᚷᚾᚾᚦᛋᛏᚣᚠᚷᚩᚱ

a b g d e q z h th i k l m n j u p r s t w f ch wh o

FONT: *GOTHIC1.TTF* FROM 'DR BERLIN'S FOREIGN FONT ARCHIVE'

630.

Sigmund Feist, *Vergleichendes Wörterbuch der gotischen Sprache mit Einschluß des Krimgotischen und sonstiger zerstreuter Überreste des Gotischen.* Leiden: Brill, 1939. 710 pp. 3rd edn.

1st edition: *Etymologisches Wörterbuch der gotischen Sprache mit Einschluß des sog. Krimgotischen.* Halle: Niemeyer, 1909. – 2nd edn: 1920–23. 380 pp.

This was a reworking of: Sigmund Feist, *Grundriß der gotischen Etymologie.* Strasbourg: Trübner, 1888.

[*Comparative dictionary of the Gothic language, including Crimean Gothic and other scattered remnants of Gothic.*] On the development and plan of Feist's work see Malkiel (**9**), pp. 28–9.

631.

Gerhard Köbler, *Gotisch–neuhochdeutsches und neuhochdeutsch–gotisches Wörterbuch.* Gießen-Lahn: Arbeiten zur Rechts- und Sprachwissenschaft-Verlag, 1981. 282 pp. 3–88430–033–4.

Arbeiten zur Rechts- und Sprachwissenschaft, 16.

[*Gothic–German and German–Gothic dictionary.*] Brief word-lists only: the main Gothic–German section, pp. 1–139, followed by various appendices; the German–Gothic section, pp. 154–282.

632.

Gerhard Köbler, *Gotisches Wörterbuch.* Leiden: Brill, 1989. 716 pp. 90–04–09128–9.

[*Gothic dictionary.*] Entries give glosses in German and English followed by citations (apparently complete) from the texts. Variant forms are listed, but there are very few quotations of contexts. Appendices: fragmentary words, pp. 657–8; Biblical names, pp. 659–79; Gothic names, pp. 680–707; words from other East Germanic languages, pp. 708–16.

633.

Winfred P. Lehmann, *A Gothic etymological dictionary*. Leiden: Brill, 1986. 712 pp. 90–04–08176–3.

'Based on the third edition of *Vergleichendes Wörterbuch der gotischen Sprache* by Sigmund Feist.' A thorough reworking of Feist's dictionary (**630**) with full discussion of doubtful points and references to modern scholarly literature. Very copious indexes of forms from other languages that are cited in the entries, pp. 417–592; list of these indexes, pp. 415–6.

Comprehensive bibliography, edited by Helen-Jo J. Hewitt, pp. 593–712.

GREEK

Greek, which forms a separate branch of the INDOEUROPEAN LANGUAGES, has for 2,700 years been written in its own alphabetic script, derived from a Near Eastern alphabet which had notations for consonants only. In the Greek alphabet, vowels were written as well – a spectacular advance.

A much earlier stage of the language, usually called Mycenaean, 3,400 years old, was written in the syllabic 'Linear B' script. Linear B is usually transliterated into Latin, as in Chadwick (**639**) and Morpurgo (**641**).

Throughout its recorded history Greek has been the majority language of the Greek peninsula and islands. It is now the national language of Greece and is spoken by minorities in Albania, southern Italy, Georgia and other countries. There are about 11,500,000 speakers.

In its spelling modern Greek looks very like ancient Greek. It is therefore possible to compile a dictionary that covers the whole history of the language from 700 BC to modern times, and this has been done by Dimitrakos (**634**). But the essential dictionary of ancient Greek for the period from 700 BC to AD 550 is Liddell and Scott or 'LSJ' (**646**), supplemented by Lampe (**645**), the latter extending the coverage down to about AD 800. A much larger project, with a long history, is the *Thesaurus linguae Graecae* or '*TLG*', conceived as a complete word index to the vocabulary of all ancient Greek texts (see **650**). The best dictionary into ancient Greek (although this is not its main purpose) is that of Stamatakos (**635**): users who cannot work from modern Greek, as this requires, must fall back on the English–Attic Greek dictionary of Woodhouse (**652**).

Lampe (**645**) and Sophocles (**658**) cover the earlier period of Byzantine literature, down to AD 800 and 1100 respectively. Du Cange (**654**) deals with new words and new meanings, especially administrative and technical, for the whole Byzantine period down to 1453. This last, one of the oldest reference books on any subject that is still of current use, is a Greek–Latin dictionary with Latin–Greek indexes.

Literature in a recognizably modern form of Greek is known from AD 1100. The medieval vernacular is being treated by Kriaras (**656**). There are several brief-entry dictionaries of modern Greek, but the historical dictionary (**660**) still has a long way to go. For many decades there was a fierce dispute over linguistic standards in modern

Greek: the imposition of a *katharévousa* 'purified' standard language eventually became identified with extreme right-wing politics and supporters of the *dhimotikí* 'popular' speech have, perhaps permanently, triumphed.

Users of dictionaries of ancient Greek, such as Liddell and Scott (**646**), have to get to know the varied shapes that regular Greek nouns and verbs can take. Note especially the initial *e-* and the 'reduplication' which are features of past tenses of verbs. These can follow, or merge with, prepositional prefixes: thus for *ébaine* 'he went' one looks up **baíno** 'I go'; for *katébaine* 'he went down' one looks up **katabaíno** 'I go down'.

With modern Greek, users have to be prepared to search for alternative spellings. A recent script reform, ending the redundant distinction between stress accents ´ and ˜ and dropping the other three diacritics (which were irrelevant to modern pronunciation), does not affect the usability of dictionaries.

There are etymological dictionaries of the classical vocabulary by Chantraine (**669**) and Frisk (**670**); there is a periodical, *Glotta*, devoted to the classical Greek vocabulary and its etymology. There is an etymological dictionary of modern Greek by Andriotis (**667**). A useful supplement to these works is a list by Shipp (**677**) of ancient Greek words whose history is elucidated by modern Greek evidence. Ancient and Byzantine texts include several major lexicographical works, including the 'lexicon of Suidas' or 'the *Suda*' (**676**). Note, finally, a bibliography devoted entirely to concordances and dictionaries of the vocabulary of individual ancient authors (**675**).

The Greek alphabet

Α Β Γ Δ Ε Ζ Η Θ Ι Κ Λ Μ Ν Ξ Ο Π Ρ Σ Τ Υ Φ Χ Ψ Ω

α β γ δ ε ζ η θ ι κ λ μ ν ξ ο π ρ σ τ υ φ χ ψ ω

a b g d e z ē th i k l m n x o p r s t y ph ch ps ō

a v gh dh e z i th i k l m n x o p r s t i f kh ps o

The third line gives a transliteration from ancient Greek; the fourth line a transliteration from modern Greek. In both cases, there is much variation in practice.

Historical dictionaries

634.

Δ. Δημητράκου *Μέγα λεξικὸν τῆς ἑλληνικῆς γλώσσης* [D. Dhimitrakos, *Megha lexikon tis ellinikis glossis*]. Athens: Dhimitrakos, 1936–[1952?]. 9 vols [8056 pp.]. Edited by Ioannis S. Zervos.

[*Big dictionary of the Greek language.*] Dhimitrakos is a unique dictionary treating Greek as a single language from 700 BC to the modern period, with well over 300,000 entries: these are relatively brief but often have room for one or two precise references to literature. These extend to the early modern period, and even the ancient ones are not all duplicated in LSJ (**646**) and Sophocles (**658**). Modern citations, by contrast, are not usually attributed: they are often proverbs and clichés, and interesting as such. Dhimitrakos is no substitute for LSJ; however, it has considerable value for later Greek.

Abbreviations of source texts, pp. i–xxx; of grammatical and lexical terms, pp. xxxi–xxxii (these lists repeated in each volume).

The modern standards

635.

Ἰωάννου Δρ. Σταματάκου *Λεξικὸν τῆς νέας ἑλληνικῆς γλώσσης καθαρευούσης καὶ δημοτικῆς, καὶ ἐκ τῆς νέας ἑλληνικῆς εἰς τὴν ἀρχαίαν* [Ioannis D. Stamatakos, *Lexikon tis neas ellinikis glossis katharevousis ke dhimotikis, ke ek tis neas ellinikis is tin arkhean*]. Athens: Finix, 1971. 3 vols [3168 pp.].

[*Dictionary of the modern Greek language, both katharevousa and dhimotiki, and from modern to ancient Greek.*] A large-scale explanatory dictionary of modern Greek, in *katharevousa*; there are entries for both *katharevousa* and *dhimotiki* terms, with generous cross-references between alternative forms and spellings of the latter (*βλ.* = see; *βλ.λ.* = q.v.). There are no citations of sources. Stamatakos also gives ancient Greek synonyms for the modern terms: these are in bold face, preceded by *ἀρχ.*, at the end of relevant entries. About 100,000 entries.

Appendix on the spelling rules of the Athens Academy, pp. 3145–57; glossaries of abbreviations in Greek and Roman scripts, pp. 3158–68.

636.

Μέγα ἀγγλο-ἑλληνικὸν λεξικόν [*Megha anglo–ellinikon lexikon*]. Athens: Odhissefs [1962?]. 4 vols. [0–900834–53–6.]
Edited by Th. N. Tsaveas.

[*Big English–Greek dictionary.*] About 70,000 terms: a dictionary aiming to explain English terms to Greek readers.

637.

W. Crighton, *Μέγα ελληνοαγγλικόν λεξικόν [Megha ellinoanglikon lexikon]* = *Great Greek–English dictionary*. Athens: Eleftheroudakis, 1988. 1681 pp.

Again intended for Greek users, but entries are given for both *katharevousa* and *dhimotiki* terms, thus increasing the usefulness of the work to foreigners.

Older periods

Mycenaean and Cypriot

638.

Francisco Aura Jorro, *Diccionario micénico*. Madrid: Consejo Superior de Investigaciones Científicas, Instituto de Filologia, 1985–93. 2 vols. 84–00–06129–2.
Diccionario griego–español, anejo, 1–2.

[*Mycenaean dictionary.*] In the standard transliteration. Numerous citations and some brief quotations from the tablets, with glosses, discussion, references to scholarship, and lists of classical Greek and other related forms.

The filing order is basically that of the Latin alphabet but allots a separate place to each Linear B sign (**a, a₂, a₃, au** ...) and concludes with the signs for which no agreed transliteration exists (... **18, 22, 34, 35, 47, 49, 56, 64, 65, 82, 83, 89**). No transliteration table.

639.

John Chadwick, Lydia Baumbach, 'The Mycenaean Greek vocabulary' in *Glotta* vol. 41 (1963) pp. 157–271.

Supplemented by: Lydia Baumbach, 'The Mycenaean Greek vocabulary, ii' in *Glotta* vol. 49 (1971) pp. 151–90.

In alphabetical order of classical Greek words (thus providing an alternative approach to that of Morpurgo, **641**). Index of Mycenaean forms, pp. 259–71.

640.

Almut Hintze, *A lexicon to the Cyprian syllabic inscriptions*. Hamburg: Buske, 1993. 235 pp. 3–87548–047–3.

With additional indices compiled by Klaus Boekels. *Lexicographia orientalis*, 2.

In transliteration (table of the Cypriot syllabary, p. 235). Numerous useful indexes.

641.

Anna Morpurgo, *Mycenaeae Graecitatis lexicon*. Rome: Edizioni dell' Ateneo, 1963. 405 pp.

Incunabula graeca, 3.

A reverse index to Morpurgo is provided by M. Lejeune. *Index inverse du grec mycénien*. Paris: CNRS, 1964. 117 pp.

[*Dictionary of Mycenaean Greek.*] A working tool for specialists, this is a complete index to words found on Mycenaean tablets, which had been recently deciphered as early Greek by Michael Ventris. Precise references to source publications, and full information on context, are sometimes followed by notes on possible meanings and links with later Greek words (index of these, pp. 387–404). But many words remained unexplained, and still do. Mycenaean Greek is in the conventional roman transliteration: a table of the original syllabary and ideograms is on pp. xxv–xxxi. Everything else is in Latin, with many unexplained abbreviations: besides easily recognised grammatical terms these include *anthr.* (personal name), *qual. pers.* (title of office or employment), *topon.* (place name).

Classical and Patristic

642.

Francisco R. Adrados, editor, *Diccionario griego–español (DGE)*. Madrid, 1980– . 84–00–06318–X.

Authors include Elvira Gangutia, J. López Facal, Concepción Serrano, R. Bádenas. Consejo Superior de Investigaciones Científicas, Instituto "Antonio de Nebrija".

See: Francisco R. Adrados, 'More on the Diccionario griego–español' in: Hans Henrich Hock, editor, *Historical, Indo-European and lexicographical studies: a Festschrift for Ladislav Zgusta on the occasion of his 70th birthday* (Berlin: Mouton De Gruyter, 1997. *Trends in linguistics, studies and monographs*, 90) pp. 221–31.

[*Greek–Spanish dictionary.*] An important new dictionary on a much larger scale than LSJ (**646**) and covering the whole recorded language from Homer to AD 600, including Christian authors. Bibliography of sources, part 1 pp. xlix–cxxxvii; other abbreviations, pp. cxli–clvi.

Work has reached the fourth letter of the alphabet, covering Α–Διώνυχος in five published parts and 1135 pages. For the Mycenaean supplement see **638**.

643.

Walter Bauer, *Griechisch–deutsches Wörterbuch zu den Schriften des Neuen Testaments und der frühchristlichen Literatur.* Berlin: De Gruyter, 1988. 1796 pp. 6th edn by Kurt Aland and Barbara Aland with Viktor Reichmann.
Institut für neutestamentliche Textforschung.
1st edn: Erwin Preuschen, *Vollständiges Griechisch-Deutsches Handwörterbuch zu den Schriften des Neuen Testaments und der übrigen urchristlichen Literatur.* Gießen, 1908–10. 1184 columns. – 2nd edn: Walter Bauer, editor, *Griechisch-Deutsches Wörterbuch zu den Schriften des Neuen Testaments und der übrigen urchristlichen Literatur.* 1925–8. 1434 columns. – 3rd edn: Berlin: Töpelmann, 1937. 1490 columns. – 4th edn: 1952. – 5th edn: 1958.
A version of the 5th edition is available in English. *A Greek–English lexicon of the New Testament and other early Christian literature*; a translation and adaptation by William F. Arndt and F. Wilbur Gingrich of the fourth revised and augmented edition of Walter Bauer's *Griechish–deutsches Wörterbuch zu den Schriften des Neuen Testaments und der übrigen urchristlichen Literatur.* Chicago: University of Chicago Press, 1979. 900 pp. 2nd edn, revised from Bauer's 5th edn by F. W. Gingrich and Frederick W. Danker. – Note the long review by D. J. Georgacas in *Classical philology* 76, 1981, pp. 153–9. – Some revisions to Arndt and Gingrich must be looked for in: F. W. Gingrich, *Shorter lexicon of the Greek New Testament.* 221 pp. 2nd edn, revised by F. W. Danker. Chicago, 1983. – Note also: John R. Alsop, editor, *An index to the revised Bauer-Arndt-Gingrich Greek lexicon, second edition, by F. Wilbur Gingrich & Frederick W. Danker.* Grand Rapids: Zondervan, 1981. 525 pp.
The first English edition of the dictionary, based on Bauer's 4th edition, was published: Cambridge: Cambridge University Press: Cambridge; Chicago: University of Chicago Press, 1957. 909 pp. – *An index to the Bauer-Arndt-Gingrich Greek lexicon*, a key to that edition, was published: Grand Rapids: Zondervan, 1972. 489 pp.
A complete dictionary of the vocabulary of the New Testament and other texts of about AD 50 to 150, with many precise references and examples, Bauer's work is highly informative on later Greek authors' interpretations of Biblical terms. Proper names are included. Etymologies of loanwords (including many from Hebrew) are given, but there is more on the etymology and semantics of the New Testament vocabulary in Moulton and Milligan (**674**).

644.

Wilhelm Crönert, *Passow's Wörterbuch der griechischen Sprache, völlig neu bearbeitet.* Göttingen: Vandenhoeck & Ruprecht, 1912–13.
[*Passow's dictionary of the Greek language, thoroughly revised.*] Considerably more generous in quotation and citation than LSJ (**646**), though very similar in design. Quotations are not translated. German glosses are given in Schwabacher face.
Only three parts appeared, covering Α–᾽Ανά.

645.

G. W. H. Lampe, editor, *A Patristic Greek lexicon.* Oxford: Clarendon Press, 1961–8. 1616 pp.

The title means 'a Greek–English dictionary of early Christian authors'. 'The user of this work is assumed to have Liddell and Scott [**646**] by its side;' Lampe's work adopts a similar layout and conventions. It deals in untiring detail with new words and special usages in Greek religious texts from about AD 100 to 800, with special attention to theological words and meanings. Extremely useful list of source texts, pp. xi–xlv.

646.

Henry George Liddell and Robert Scott, *A Greek–English lexicon*. Oxford: Clarendon Press, 1925–40. 10 parts [2111 pp.]. 9th edn, revised by Sir Henry Stuart Jones and Roderick Mackenzie.

Parts 2–9 included addenda, eventually cumulated on pp. 2043–2111; part 10 included revised preliminaries. The work was several times reprinted in one volume with these preliminaries and addenda.

The addenda were then incorporated in: E. A. Barber, editor, *H. G. Liddell, Robert Scott, H. Stuart Jones: Greek–English lexicon: a supplement*. 1968. 153 pp. This supplement is included, separately paginated, in reprints of the main work from 1968 onwards.

This has now been replaced by a new cumulated supplement: 1996. 320 pp. 0–19–864223–7. The new supplement is incorporated in the 1996 reprint of the main work.

1st edn: H. G. Liddell, R. Scott, *A Greek–English lexicon based on the German work of Francis Passow*. Oxford, 1843. – 4th edn, 1855 (from here on omitting the name of Passow). – 6th edn, 1869;. – 7th edn, 1883. – 8th edn, 1897.

An American edition 'with corrections and additions, and the insertion in alphabetical order of the proper names occurring in the principal Greek authors, by Henry Drisler' was published: New York: Harper, 1846. 1705 pp. Several reprints to 1876. Passow continued to be credited on the title page of New York editions.

'Liddell and Scott', or 'LSJ', is a complete dictionary of the recorded vocabulary from all Greek texts between 700 BC and 50 AD, and from non-Christian texts to about AD 550: it is complemented, for Greek Christian literature, by Bauer (**643**) and Lampe (**645**). It includes foreign words that occur in its source texts. There are around 200,000 entries: this great number ('the Greeks had a word for it') is explained by the long period covered and by the fact that classical Greek was a free-compounding language and all recorded compounds are included. Based on systematic reading of almost the whole of the literature, by generations of classical scholars, Liddell and Scott gives numerous well-chosen precise references and a generous selection of examples (but the examples are not translated): naturally less exhaustive than the old *Thesaurus* (**650**), it can still serve as a kind of one-volume concept index to Greek literature. The compilers' names are on every classicist's lips: though Alice Liddell, as the inspiration for *Alice's adventures in Wonderland*, is even more famous than her scholarly father.

The work's format is concise in the extreme, with many truncations and abbreviations for grammatical and stylistic terms, literary genres, names of authors and works. One spends much time among the keys to abbreviations and the highly useful lists of source texts, pp. xi–xlviii and supplement pp. vii–xi, learning to use Liddell and Scott fully. The supplements are indispensable especially for their inclusion of words and usages from papyri, inscriptions, and texts in Cypriot and Mycenaean scripts: for example, Διφθεράλοιφος is cited in the main work only on the basis of the ancient lexicon by Hesychius, with his gloss 'schoolmaster (Cypriot dialect)', while in the supplement a citation is given from a Cypriot syllabic text, in which the word is spelt **ti-pe-te-ra-lo-i-po-ne**.

All recorded dialects from the period are included. There are some cross-references for dialect words, and a few for irregular grammatical forms. The origin of derivatives and compounds is indicated when not obvious.

Originally based on Passow's 1831 *Handwörterbuch* (**647**), Liddell and Scott has developed its own character: something of its history can be read in the introduction to the 9th edition. A 10th edition is in preparation.

647.

Franz Passow, *Handwörterbuch der griechischen Sprache.* Leipzig: Vogel, 1841–57. 4 vols. '5th edn', revised and enlarged by Val. Chr. Fr. Rost and others.

Earliest version: Johann Gottlob Schneider, *Kritisches Griechisch–Deutsches Handwörterbuch.* Züllichau, 1797–8. 2 vols.

This was succeeded by: *Johann Gottlob Schneiders Handwörterbuch der griechischen Sprache.* Leipzig, 1819–23. 2 vols. Enlarged by Franz Passow. – '2nd edn': 1825. – '3rd edn': 1827. – '4th edn': Franz Passow, *Handwörterbuch der griechischen Sprache.* Leipzig, 1831. 2 vols.

[*Concise dictionary of the Greek language.*]

648.

Friedrich Preisigke, *Wörterbuch der griechischen Papyrusurkunden, mit Einschluss der griechischen Inschriften, Aufschriften, Ostraka, Mumienschilder usw. aus Ägypten.* Gröbzig in Anhalt, 1925– .

Vols 1–3 were privately published by the author's widow 1925–31. Vol. 4, published in parts 1944–93, and the Supplement published in 1971 in Amsterdam by Hakkert, were edited by Emil Kiessling who also completed vol. 2–3.

[*Dictionary of the Greek papyrus records, also including the Greek inscriptions, graffiti, ostraca, mummy cases etc. from Egypt.*] Vols 1–2 are the original alphabetical dictionary, with glosses in German (Fraktur type) and precise references to source publications. The intention is to provide an index to word occurrences in papyri: vol. 4 begins a supplementary alphabetical sequence taking account of publications after 1925, but has reached only the fifth letter of the alphabet.

The Supplement is an index to entries in both sequences (including those of the second sequence that are not yet published). It includes references to sources, but no glosses.

649.

Bruno Snell [and other editors], *Lexikon des frühgriechischen Epos.* Göttingen: Vandenhoeck & Ruprecht, 1955– .

[*Dictionary of early Greek epic.*] Planned as a complete index to, and historical dictionary of, the vocabulary of the earliest Greek poems in hexameter (*Iliad, Odyssey,* the poems of Hesiod, the *Homeric Hymns,* and some fragments: about 700 to 400 BC). Entries (each signed) are mostly in German, but some of those in recent fascicles are in English, French or Italian: the user has to be a polyglot. Some, especially in vol. 1, are very lengthy, and say almost everything that can be said. They include encyclopaedic entries for proper names. Vol. 1 (**A**) was only completed in 1979; the compilers decided to compress the remainder, and it no longer serves as a complete concordance to the texts, though it is still pretty comprehensive. Vol. 2 (**B–Λ**) was published between 1982 and 1991, and publication has now reached **O**. Entries are subheaded thus: *E* = etymology, *F* = forms, *M* = prosody, *Σχ* = ancient commentaries ('scholia'), *L* = bibliography of modern scholarship, *B* = uses and meanings, *D* = variant readings from papyri.

This work was intended as the first section of a new *Thesaurus Graecae linguae*. It seems unlikely that other sections will now appear, the *TLG* CD-ROM (see **650**) having reduced the need for them.

650.

Thesaurus Graecae linguae ab Henrico Stephano constructus. Paris: Didot, 1831–65. 8 vols in 9. 3rd edition by Carolus Benedictus Hase, Guilielmus Dindorfius, Ludovicus Dindorfius.

1st edn: Paris, 1572. 5 vols. This and the second, compiled by E. H. Barker and others (London: Abraham Valpy, 1819–28; 9 vols) are still occasionally consulted. See the review of the 2nd edn by Blomfield in *Quarterly review* vol. 22 p. 302 ff.

[*Thesaurus of the Greek language compiled by Henri Estienne.*] Intended as a fairly complete index of the vocabulary of all classical Greek texts, organised as a historical dictionary. Useful as it gives far more numerous examples than Liddell and Scott (**646**), but the inevitable result is that articles for common words are almost too unwieldy to search.

In the first and second editions compound words and derivatives are filed not in alphabetical order but as sub-headings under basic forms. There is an alphabetical index in the last volume. This arrangement was so inconvenient that the pirated abridgement by Estienne's assistant Joannes Scapula, *Lexicon graecolatinum novum* (Basle, 1579), which rearranged both base forms and index entries into one alphabet, was popular and ran into many reprints, at least to 1820.

Estienne's plan of a complete dictionary and index was just about realisable for the smaller corpus of literature in classical Latin (see **949**), but could never work for classical Greek so long as printed paper was the medium of publication and the eye was the only search tool. It has now been largely realised, four centuries after Estienne's time, by the new Thesaurus Linguae Graecae project, developed by Theodore F. Brunner at the University of California, Irvine. *Thesaurus linguae Graecae CD-ROM #D* already contains nearly all classical and some early Byzantine Greek texts (an upgrade is expected).

651.

Chr. Abrah. Wahl, *Clavis librorum Veteris Testamenti apocryphorum philologica.* Graz: Akademische Druck- und Verlagsanstalt, 1972. 828 pp. 3–201–00072–8.

Original edn: Leipzig: Barth, 1853. 509 pp.

[*Linguistic key to the apocryphal books of the Old Testament.*] A full dictionary of the Greek vocabulary of the Apocrypha, with references to Hebrew equivalents. The reprint is highlighted in this entry because it contains a collection of supplementary citations from other 'pseudepigraphical' literature of the period, compiled by Johannes Baptista Bauer, badly planned and laid out, wasteful of space, but undeniably useful.

652.

S. C. Woodhouse, *English–Greek dictionary: a vocabulary of the Attic language*. London: Routledge, 1932. 998 pp.

This revised reprint was the first to contain an appendix of proper names, a handy source for their classical spelling and accentuation. – 1st edn: 1910. 1029 pp.

A concise dictionary, intended for English schoolboys learning to write classical Greek prose (*P*) and verse (*V*) and thus restricted to the vocabulary of Attic authors of about 450 to 330 BC. Some references to source texts.

Byzantine, medieval and early modern

653.

Girolamo Caracausi, *Lessico greco della Sicilia e dell'Italia meridionale (secoli X–XIV)*. Palermo, 1990. 635 pp.

Centro di Studi Filologici e Linguistici Siciliani.

[*Dictionary of the Greek of southern Italy and Sicily, tenth to fourteenth centuries.*] Important glossary of regional medieval Greek, including proper names. Italian glosses are followed by references to documents and literary sources, with some brief quotations. Entries end with etymological and historical notes: these are marked off by ||.

654.

Charles du Fresne sieur du Cange, *Glossarium ad scriptores mediae et infimae Graecitatis, in quo Graeca vocabula novatae significationis aut usus rarioris, barbara, exotica, ecclesiastica, liturgica, tactica, nomica, iatrica, botanica, chymica explicantur, eorum notiones et originationes reteguntur*. Lyon: apud Anissonios, 1688. 2 vols [various paginations].

One-volume reprints: Paris, 1943; Graz, 1958.

[*Glossary to authors of middle and low Greek, explaining foreign, religious, military, legal, medical, botanical and chemical terms of new meaning or rare occurrence, revealing their implications and origins.*] This remarkable work is a Greek–Latin historical dictionary of Byzantine neologisms and technical vocabulary (about AD 500 to 1500) with precise references and examples. Main alphabetical sequence, 1794 columns; 'Appendix' (supplement), 214 columns; glossary of symbols and abbreviations, 21 columns. Then list of sources, columns 1–68; corrigenda, 68–70; Latin indexes, 71–101; and more. Du Cange had read a remarkable range of Byzantine literature, much of it available at that time only in manuscript. The references are often difficult to follow up in current editions of texts, but the dictionary remains indispensable.

655.

Στεφάνου ᾽Α. Κουμανούδη *Συναγώγη νέων λεξέων ὑπὸ τῶν λογίων πλασθείσων ἀπὸ τῆς ῾Αλωσέως μέχρι τῶν καθ᾽ ἡμας χρόνων* [Stefanos A. Koumanoudhis, *Sinaghoghi neon lexeon ipo ton loghion plasthison apo tis Aloseos mekhri ton kath' imas khronon*]. Athens, 1900. 2 vols [1166 pp.].

Reprinted in one volume with introduction by K. Th. Dimaras: Athens, 1980.

[*List of neologisms created by writers from the Fall of Constantinople down to our own times.*]

656.

Ἐμμανουήλ Κριαρᾶ *Λεξικὸ τῆς μεσαιωνικῆς ἑλληνικῆς δημώδους γραμματείας, 1100–1669* [Emmanouil Kriaras, *Lexiko tis meseonikis ellinikis dhimodhous grammatias, 1100–1669*]. Thessalonica, 1968– .

[*Dictionary of the written medieval Greek vernacular.*] A large-scale dictionary of medieval and early modern writing in the popular language, Kriaras's well-planned work is now more than half complete in 12 volumes, covering **A–Ο**. Entries give precise references to texts with many quotations and with references to scholarly work: they are entirely in *dhimotiki*, of which Kriaras has been an assiduous supporter. The bibliographies of original sources and modern scholarship in each volume have now been cumulated in vol. 13, which consists of a full bibliography (pp. 17–270) with an index to the introductions (pp. 273–8) and to the considerable mass of additions and corrections in successive volumes (pp. 281–336).

657.

Alfredo Róspide López, Francisco Martín García, *Index popularium carminum*. Hildesheim: Olms-Weidmann, 1997. 199 pp. 3–487–10301–X.

Alpha-omega, series B, 11.

[*Index to the Folk songs.*] A Greek–Spanish glossary and index to the famous collection by N. G. Politis, Ἐκλογαὶ ἀπὸ τὰ τραγούδια τοῦ Ἑλληνικοῦ λαοῦ [*Selections from the folk songs of the Greek* people], Athens, 1914.

658.

E. A. Sophocles, *Greek lexicon of the Roman and Byzantine periods (from BC 146 to AD 1100)*. New York: Scribner, 1887. 1188 pp.

This 'memorial edition', with patriarchal photograph of the author, is a corrected reprint (edited by J. H. Thayer) of the 1st edn, 1870.

Reprinted: New York: Ungar, 1957. 2 vols [1188 pp.].

Brief entries usually limited to a single English gloss and a single (but precise) reference to a source text. Most useful now for the middle Byzantine period, AD 800 to 1100.

Regional forms

659.

Nikolaos Andriotis, *Lexikon der Archaismen in neugriechischen Dialekten*. Vienna: Verlag der Österreichischen Akademie der Wissenschaften, 1974. 705 pp.

Österreichische Akademie der Wissenschaften, Philosophisch-historische Klasse. *Schriften der Balkankommission, Linguistische Abteilung*, 22.

[*Dictionary of ancient survivals in modern Greek dialects.*]

660.

Λεξικὸν τῆς ἑλληνικῆς γλώσσης. Α΄. Ἱστορικὸν λεξικὸν τῆς νέας Ἑλληνικῆς τῆς τε κοινῶς ὁμιλουμένης καὶ τῶν ἰδιωμάτων [*Lexikon tis ellinikis glossis. I.*

Istorikon lexikon tis neas ellinikis tis te kinos omiloumenis ke ton idhiomaton.]
Athens, 1933– .
Edited by A. A. Papadhopoulos and others. Akadhimia Athinon.

[*Dictionary of the Greek language, 1. Historical dictionary of the modern Greek colloquial and the dialects.*] A very large-scale, slow-moving dictionary that has turned out to concentrate largely on the dialects, as noted by Georgacas (**673**), and is extremely useful and interesting on these terms. Precise references are given to source materials, many of them unpublished records by ethnographers and dialectologists: word histories are traced from earlier periods of the language. Prefaces and explanations, contrasting with the subject matter, are in a strongly archaising *katharevousa*.

After a lapse of nearly 30 years part 2 of vol. 4 was published in 1980. Its preliminary pages include a bibliography of sources (supplementing those in previous parts); list of abbreviations of districts and villages, and of grammatical terms; notes on phonetic signs (p. xxxi). The bibliography forms a handy list of single-dialect dictionaries. In view of the variations between dialects it is necessary to study the spelling and choice-of-entry conventions (pp. xxvii–xxviii) carefully.

The last issue I have seen is vol. 5 part 2 (1989), which finally gets the coverage into the fourth letter of the alphabet, reaching **δαχτυλωτός**.

Cyprus

661.

Κωνσταντίνος Γιαγκουλλής, *Λεξικό ετυμολογικό και ερμηνευτικό της Κυπριακής διαλέκτου* [Konstantinos Ghiangoullis, *Lexiko etimologhiko ke ermineftiko tis Kipriakis dialektou*]. Lefkosia, 1994. 186 pp. 9963–555–35–7.
Vivliothiki Kiprion laikon piiton, 54.

[*Etymological and explanatory dictionary of the Cypriot dialect.*] A brief-entry dictionary with short etymologies in square brackets.

662.

Achilleus Kyriakides, *A Greek–English dictionary, with an appendix of Cypriote words.* Athens, 1909. 908 pp.
Previous edn: Nicosia: H. E. Clarke, 1892. 499 pp.

Greece

663.

Θανάση Π. Κοστάκη *Λεξικό της Τσακωνικής διαλέκτου* [Thanasis P. Kostakis, *Lexiko tis Tsakonikis dialektou*]. Athens, 1986–7. 3 vols.

[*Dictionary of the Tsakonian dialect.*] Not seen: cited from *Dictionaries* (**12**).

Italy

664.

Ἀναστάση Καραναστάση *Ἱστορικὸν λεξικὸν τῶν ἑλληνικῶν ἰδιωμάτων τῆς κάτω Ἰταλίας* [Anastasis Karanastasis, *Istorikon lexikon ton ellinikon idhiomaton tis kato Italias*]. Athens: Akadhimia Athinon, 1984– .

[*Historical dictionary of the Greek dialects of Lower Italy.*] On a generous scale, with numerous quotations mainly from oral poetry and prose.

665.

Gerhard Rohlfs, *Lexicon graecanicum Italiae inferioris = Etymologisches Wörterbuch der unteritalienischen Gräzität*. Tübingen: Niemeyer, 1964. 629 pp. 2nd edn.

See the long review by H. and R. Kahane , 'Greek in southern Italy' in *Romance philology* vol. 20 (1967) pp. 404–38; index of entries commented on, pp. 436–8.
1st edn: *Etymologisches Wörterbuch der unteritalienischen Gräzität*. Halle: Niemeyer, 1930.

[*Etymological dictionary of the Greek of southern Italy.*] A comprehensive dictionary of the modern Greek dialects spoken in southern Italy, based on oral collections: there are relatively few citations of texts. Entries are under a normalised Greek form (marked * if unrecorded). Indexes, pp. 589–629.

Turkey

666.

Ἀνθίμου Ἀ. Παπαδόπουλου *Ἱστορικὸν λεξικὸν τῆς Ποντικῆς διαλέκτου* [Anthimos A. Papadopoulos, *Istorikon lexikon tis Pontikis dialektou*]. Athens, 1958–61. 2 vols.

Epitropi Pontiakon Meleton. *Arkheion Pontou*, supplement 3.

[*Historical dictionary of the Pontic dialect.*]

Etymological dictionaries

Modern Greek

667.

Ν. Π. Ανδριώτη *Ετυμολογικό λεξικό της κοινής Νεοελληνικής* [N. P. Andhriotis, *Etimologhiko lexiko tis kinis neoellinikis*]. Thessalonica: Aristotelion Panepistimion, 1983. 436 pp. 3rd edn.

1st edn: 1951. – 2nd edn: 1967.

[*Etymological dictionary of common modern Greek.*] Entirely in Greek, this deals briefly not only with the modern vernacular but also with *katharevousa* terms that are fairly commonly used, most of them direct borrowings from the classical language. There are about 18,000 entries, and useful references to the linguistic literature.

668.

Κ. Δαγγίτση *Ετυμολογικό λεξικό της Νεοελληνικής* [K. Dhangitsis, *Etimologhiko lexiko tis neoellinikis*]. Athens, 1978– .

[*Etymological dictionary of modern Greek.*] Not seen: cited from *Wörterbücher* (**12**).

Ancient Greek

669.

Pierre Chantraine, *Dictionnaire étymologique de la langue grecque. Histoire des mots.* Paris [1968–80]. 4 parts.

Reprinted in 2 volumes.

[*Etymological dictionary of Greek: word history.*] Concentrates, as suggested by the subtitle, on the history of word meanings and derivations within ancient Greek, but also gives their origins, generally following Frisk (**670**) for these. For modern Greek evidence, not fully used by Chantraine and Frisk, see Shipp (**677**).

670.

H. Frisk, *Griechisches etymologisches Wörterbuch.* Heidelberg, 1954–72. 3 vols.

Indogermanische Bibliothek, series 1, division 2.

[*Greek etymological dictionary.*] Concentrates on the Indo-European and other ultimate sources of ancient Greek words. Vol. 3 consists of corrigenda and addenda along with a very useful index of words from other languages that are cited in the entries.

Foreign words

671.

Gustav Meyer, *Neugriechische Studien.* Vienna, 1894–5. 4 parts.

Sitzungsberichte der Philosophisch-historische Classe der Kaiserlichen Akademie der Wissenschaften, vol. 130 parts 4–5, vol. 132 parts 3 and 6.

[*Modern Greek studies.*] Part 1 (vol. 130 part 4; 104 pp.) is a bibliography of modern Greek studies, arranged under topics, with geographical and author indexes. Part 2 (vol. 130 part 5; 103 pp.) is a dictionary of Slavonic, Albanian and Romanian loanwords in modern Greek. Part 3 (vol. 132 part 3; 84 pp.) lists Latin loanwords in modern Greek. Part 4 (vol. 132 part 6) is a dictionary of Romance loanwords in modern Greek, with addenda to parts 1 and 2.

Other works of interest

672.

F. R. Adrados, E. Gangutia, J. Lopez Facal, C. Serrano Aybar, *Introducción a la lexicografía griega.* Madrid, 1977. 280 pp.

Manuales y anejos de Emerita, 33.

673.

D. J. Georgacas, 'An international dictionary of common and cultivated Modern Greek' in *Orbis* vol. 32 (1983: published 1987) pp. 206–22.

674.

James Hope Moulton, George Milligan, *The vocabulary of the Greek Testament illustrated from the papyri and other non-literary sources*. London: Hodder & Stoughton, 1914–29. 835 pp.

Reprinted in compact format, 1930 (705 pp.).

675.

Harald Riesenfeld, Blenda Riesenfeld, *Repertorium lexicographicum graecum: a catalogue of indexes and dictionaries to Greek authors*. Stockholm: Almquist & Wiksell, 1954. 95 pp.

Another issue: 1953. *Coniectanea neotestamentica*, 14.

676.

Suidae *Lexicon* edidit Ada Adler. Leipzig: Teubner, 1928–38. 5 vols.

677.

G. P. Shipp, *Modern Greek evidence for the ancient Greek vocabulary*. Sydney: Sydney University Press, 1979. 655 pp.

GUARANÍ

A member of the Tupí-Guaraní family of AMERIND LANGUAGES, Guaraní has about 3,500,000 speakers in Paraguay.

678.

M. Ricardo Dacunda Díaz, *Gran diccionario de lengua guaraní: vocabulario bilingüe, gramática, sintaxis, cultura guaraní*. Buenos Aires: Ediciones Guairacä, 1987. 511 pp. 950–431–221–7.

[*Big dictionary of the Guaraní language: bilingual dictionary, grammar, syntax, Guaraní culture.*]

679.

Antonio Guasch, Diego Ortiz, *Diccionario castellano–guaraní, guaraní–castellano, sintáctico, fraseológico, ideológico*. Asunción: Centro de Estudios Paraguayos "Antonio Guasch", 1986. 822 pp.

Previously published as: *Diccionario castellano–guaraní y castellano–guaraní*.

[*Spanish–Guaraní and Guaraní–Spanish dictionary of grammar, usage and meaning.*]

680.

Antonio Ortiz Mayans, *Nuevo diccionario español–guaraní, guaraní–español: nombres de la toponimia, de la flora y de la fauna, voces de la mitología, de la leyenda y del folklore; apéndice de voces regionales, un compendio gramatical*. Buenos Aires: Editorial Universitaria de Buenos Aires, 1980. 576 pp.

Earlier edn: 1973. 986 pp.

[*New Spanish–Guaraní and Guaraní–Spanish dictionary, with place names, flora and fauna, words from mythology, legend and folklore; with an appendix of dialect words and a grammatical outline.*]

681.

Christianus Fredericus Seybold, editor, *Lexicon hispano–guaranicum "Vocabulario de la lengua guaraní" inscriptum, a reverendo patre jesuita Paulo Restivo secundum Vocabularium Antonii Ruiz de Montoya anno* MDCCXXII *in civitate S. Mariae Majoris denuo editum et adauctum, sub auspiciis augustissimi domini Petri Secundi Brasiliae imperatoris posthac curantibus illustrissimis ejusdem haeredibus ex unico qui noscitur imperatoris beatissimi exemplari redimpressum necnon praefatione notisque instructum.* Stuttgart: Kohlhammer, 1893. 545 pp.

[*The Spanish–Guaraní dictionary entitled Vocabulario de la lengua guaraní, finally enlarged and published in 1722 by the Reverend Jesuit Father Paulo Restivo on the basis of the Vocabulary of Antonio Ruiz de Montoya, now reprinted under the auspices of Philip II, Emperor of Brazil and with the permission of his successors from the only known copy in the Imperial collection, with a new introduction and notes.*] A modern edition of the early dictionary compiled by Ruiz de Montoya (1585–1652) and revised by Restivo (1658–1741).

GUJARATI

Gujarati, language of the state of Gujarat, has about 45 million speakers in India and across the world. It belongs to the INDO-ARYAN branch of Indo-European languages.

The Gujarati alphabet

અ આ ઇ ઈ ઉ ઊ ઋ એ ઐ ઓ ઔ

a ā i ī u ū ṛ e ai o au

કખગઘઙ ચછજઝઞ ટઠડઢણ તથદધન પફબભમ યરલવ શષસહ

k kh g gh ṅ c ch j jh ñ ṭ ṭh ḍ ḍh ṇ t th d dh n p ph b bh m y r l v ś ṣ s h

The Gujarati script, which is similar to Devanagari but without the headstrokes or 'washing line', was standardised in its present form in the nineteenth century. The usual transliteration is given here.

Historical dictionaries

682.

Maharaja Bhagavatsimhji, editor, ભગવદ્ગોમડંલ [*Bhagavadgomaṇḍal*]. 1944–55. 9 vols.

An encyclopaedic dictionary of Gujarati. 'Quotations of the usages from classical Gujarati works were given at their proper places, and no attempt was spared to give all sorts of derivations. It must be admitted that this big work lacks scientific approach' (K. K. Shastree in Misra, **10**).

The modern standard

683.

M. B. Belsare, *An etymological Gujarati–English dictionary*. Ahmedabad: H. K. Pathak, 1904. 1207 pp. 2nd edn.

'3rd edn' [a reprint]: Ahmedabad: R. M. Shah, 1927. – Also reprinted as: *An etymological Gujarati English dictionary* = ગુજરાતી-અંગ્રેજ ડિકશનરી. New Delhi: Asian Educational Services, 1981.
1st edn: *The Pronouncing and Etymological Gujarati-English Dictionary*. 1895. 846 pp.

Gives very brief etymologies (now often outdated) in square brackets. List of prefixes and suffixes, pp. vi–xi.

684.

પાંડુરંગ ગણેશ દેશપાંડે સર્વાંગી અંગ્રેજ઼-ગુજરાતી કોશ [*Sarvāṅgī Aṅgrejī–Gujrātī koś*] = Pandurang Ganesh Deshpande, *Universal English–Gujarati dictionary*. Bombay: Oxford University Press, 1988. 957 pp. 0–19–561828–9.

A brief-entry English–Gujarati dictionary.

685.

Bhanusukhram Nirgunram Mehta, Bharatram Bhanusukhram Mehta, *The modern Gujarati–English dictionary with etymology, idioms, proverbs, quotations, botanical and other technical terms, etc.* Baroda: Kothari, 1925. 1609 pp.

Over 50,000 entries. They provide many more alternative glosses than does Belsare (**683**), and give attention to literary usage.

686.

સાર્થ ગુજરાતી જોડણીકોશ [*Sārtha Gūjrātī joḍṇīkoś*]. Ahmedabad: Gujarat Vidyapith, 1967. 904 pp. 5th edn.

1st edn: *Gūjrātī joḍṇīkoś*. 1929. 376 pp. – 2nd edn: 1931. – 3rd edn: 1940? – 4th edn: 1949.

[*Practical Gujarati dictionary.*] Aims to prescribe standard spellings: the first edition was a simple list which did no more than this. The second added glosses in Gujarati, the fourth added brief etymologies. The fifth edition has grown to 75,000 entries.

Regional forms

687.

Norihiko Ucida, *A Saurashtra–English dictionary*. Wiesbaden: Harrassowitz, 1990. 279 pp.

Neuindische Studien, 11.

A brief-entry dictionary of Saurashtra, a Gujarati-like language spoken by communities mostly in the state of Tamilnadu in southern India. Brief etymologies, and some citations from printed Saurashtra literature. Entirely in Latin script: the old Saurashtra alphabet is no longer used, and Tamil script, though normal in Saurashtra publications, is unsuited to the phonetics of the language.

Foreign words

688.

છોટુભાઈ રણછોડજી નાયક *ગુજરાતીમાં પ્રચલિત ફારસી શબ્દોનોસાર્થવ્યુત્પત્તિકોશ*

[Chotubhai Ranchodji Nayak, *Gujratimam pracalit Pharsi sabdono sartha vyutpattikos*]. Ahmedabad: Gujarat Yunivarsiti, 1972– .
Gujarat Yunivarsiti prakasan.

A dictionary of Persian loanwords in Gujarati, including many ultimately of Arabic and Turkish origin. Persian source words are in Perso-Arabic script: otherwise all is in Gujarati script. Vol. 3 (1980) took the coverage to **M**: I have not seen later volumes.

GURAGE

A group of dialects spoken in central Ethiopia, belonging to the SEMITIC branch of the Afroasiatic languages. There are perhaps 800,000 speakers in total.

689.

Wolf Leslau, *Etymological dictionary of Gurage (Ethiopic)*. Wiesbaden: Harrassowitz, 1979. 3 vols. 3–447–02041–5.

A very fat work. Vol. 1: individual dictionaries of the twelve Gurage dialects (table of contents, p. vii). Vol. 2: English–Gurage index, a full comparative vocabulary based on vol. 1.

Vol. 3: Etymological section, consisting of an alphabetical dictionary, pp. 1–724 (the alphabetical order is explained on p. x) followed by indexes of Semitic roots, of Arabic loanwords and of Ethiopic roots. Additions and corrections, pp. 725–33, 855–6. Bibliography, pp. xciii–cii.

HAUSA

With 25 million speakers, Hausa is the most widely known of the CHADIC LANGUAGES, a branch of the Afroasiatic family. Once the language of the Empire of Sokoto, it is now spoken in the Northern Region of Nigeria and across most of neighbouring Niger. It is one of the four major languages of Nigeria, alongside Igbo, Yoruba and English.

690.

R. C. Abraham, Malam Mai Kano, *Dictionary of the Hausa language*. [London:] Crown Agents for the Colonies, 1949. 992 pp.
Published on behalf of the Government of Nigeria.
'2nd edn' [reprint with a new preface]: London: University of London Press, 1962. In the reprint Abraham alone is credited as author.

A good though extremely concise dictionary. The Hausa is in the International Phonetic Alphabet, but the alphabetical order is easy to follow. Tones are marked, a major advance in Hausa lexicography, but no explanation is given of the IPA or of the tone marks: for this, one must consult Abraham's grammatical works, e.g. *The language of the Hausa people* (London: University of London Press, 1959), which in any case 'should be in the hands of every user' as Abraham puts it. The 'plan of the dictionary', pp. vii–ix, must be studied carefully as no concessions are made elsewhere to normal human readers. Addenda, pp. 983–92.

691.

G. P. Bargery, *A Hausa–English dictionary and English–Hausa vocabulary*. London: Oxford University Press, 1934. 1226 pp.

Supplemented by: A. Neil Skinner, *Hausa lexical expansion since 1930: material supplementary to that contained in Bargery's dictionary, including words borrowed from English, Arabic, French, and Yoruba.* Madison, Wis.: University of Wisconsin, African Studies Program, 1985. 54 pp.

A large-scale dictionary with many example phrases (in Hausa and English) and with glosses that sometimes stretch to considerable length, for example:

godo ... 2. (a) A woman without a bucket helping the others who have buckets to fill their pots at the well. In return, they fill her pot from their buckets.

English–Hausa section, pp. 1155–1226. Corrections, pp. xlix–liv. 'Notes on the Hausa people and their language', by D. Westermann, pp. ix–xix.

R. C. Abraham, Bargery's assistant, was to write later (**690**): 'My two years' collaboration in Dr Bargery's dictionary of 1934 consisted largely in introducing a coherent grammatical scheme into his work and reducing the millions of loose slips into the form of numbered paragraphs, but in spite of being entrusted with the checking of the whole material, my jurisdiction over rejection of matter was severely limited. For what was sound in that work, however, we must be forever grateful to him.'

692.

P. Newman, R. Ma Newman, *Modern Hausa–English dictionary = Sabon kamus na Hausa zuwa Turanci*. Ibadan: Oxford University Press, 1977. 153 pp. 0–19–575303–8.

Masanan Cibiyar Nazarin Harsunan Nijeriya, Kwalejin Jami'ar Bayero, Kano.
Note also: R. M. Newman, 'Dictionaries of the Hausa language' in *Harsunan Nijeriya* vol. 4 (1974) pp. 1–25.

In standard Nigerian orthography with added diacritics to give full phonemic information. Only 6500 entries.

693.

Roxana Ma Newman, *An English–Hausa dictionary*. New Haven: Yale University Press, 1990. 327 pp. 0–300–04702–9.

Yale language series.
Republication or new edition (not seen): Ikeja: Longman, 1997. 331 pp. 978–139–733–0.

694.

Neil Skinner, *Hausa comparative dictionary*. Cologne: Köppe, 1996. 337 pp. 3–927620–53–X.

Westafrikanische Studien, 11.

Not seen.

HAWAIIAN

Hawaiian belongs to the AUSTRONESIAN language family. There are only about two thousand remaining speakers: English, and Hawaiian English creole, are now the usual languages of the American state of Hawaii.

695.

Lorrin Andrews, *A dictionary of the Hawaiian language, to which is appended an English–Hawaiian vocabulary and a chronological table of remarkable events.* Honolulu: H. M. Whitney, 1865. 559 pp.

Reprinted with an introduction by Terence Barrow. Rutland, Vermont: Tuttle, 1974. 0–8048–1087–7.

696.

Mary Kawena Pukui, Samuel H. Elbert, *Hawaiian dictionary: Hawaiian–English, English–Hawaiian.* Honolulu: University of Hawaii Press, 1986. 572 pp. 0–8248–0703–0.

1st edn in this form: 1971. 402 pp. 0–87022–662–8. 'Updates and combines the third edition of the *Hawaiian–English dictionary* and the first edition of the *English–Hawaiian dictionary.*'
The earlier dictionary was: *Hawaiian–English dictionary.* 1957. 362 pp. – 3rd edn: 1965. 370 pp. –
Accompanied by: *Place names of Hawaii and Supplement to the third edition of the Hawaiian–English dictionary.* 1966. 53 pp.

The Hawaiian–English section is the larger.

HEBREW

Hebrew is a member of the SEMITIC branch of the Afroasiatic language family. It is the language of the Jewish Bible – the Christian Old Testament – and had probably died out as an everyday spoken language in the course of the last centuries BC. By that time Aramaic was the usual language of Palestine.

Hebrew continued to be learnt by Jews as a ritual and scholarly language. In modern times it has been revived, and serves as the national language of Israel, where it has about three million speakers.

This entry includes a few monolingual dictionaries in Hebrew but concentrates on the important bilingual dictionaries, which are more approachable by users who do not read Hebrew easily. With the compartmentalisation of Semitic studies, Clines (**702**) is a groundbreaking attempt to encompass the classical Hebrew language as opposed to the language of a particular corpus – by contrast with the dictionaries listed below under 'Biblical Hebrew', and also by contrast with Hoftijzer and Jongeling (**1370**), who treat Hebrew inscriptions along with other North West Semitic dialects.

The Hebrew alphabet has been used to write many of the other languages of Jewish literature, including Aramaic (which is a Semitic language like Hebrew itself) and YIDDISH and JUDEZMO (which are quite unrelated to Hebrew).

The Hebrew alphabet

The earliest Hebrew alphabet was derived directly from a Phoenician script. The familiar square Hebrew alphabet of classical and modern times developed out of an Aramaic script, itself originally based on Phoenician.

א ב ג ד ה ו ז ח ט י כ ל מ נ ס ע פ צ ק ר ש ת

' b g d h w z ḥ ṭ y k l m n s ġ p ṣ q r š t

Vowels can be fully marked in Hebrew writing by the use of additional signs, but this is normally done only in texts of the Bible, where correct pronunciation is essential for religious reasons. Even when using these vowel signs, no distinction is made between the central vowel ə and the absence of a vowel.

Historical dictionaries

697.

Eliˋezer ben-Yehudah, מלון הלשון העברית הישנה וההרשה [*Milon ha-lashon ha-ˋIvrit ha-yeshanah veha-hadashah*] = Elieser ben Iehuda, *Thesaurus totius Hebraitatis et veteris et recentioris* = Eliezer ben Jehuda, *Gesamtwörterbuch der alt- und neuhebräischen Sprache* = Éliézér ben Yehouda, *Dictionnaire complet de la langue hébraïque ancienne et moderne* = Eliezer ben Yehuda, *A complete dictionary of ancient and modern Hebrew*. Berlin-Schoeneberg: Langenscheidt; Jerusalem: Ben Yehuda; New York: Yoseloff, 1908–59. 16 vols [7945 pp.].

Vols. 15–16 edited by N. H. Tur-Sinai. A 'popular edition' at reduced page size was published: Tel-Aviv: Laˋam, n.d.
Accompanied by: *Prolegomena*. 1940. 280 pp.

A very large-scale dictionary with long quotations from literature, entirely in Hebrew, with precise references to sources. Also gives brief glosses in German, French and English, and taxonomic names for flora and fauna in Latin.

698.

יעקב כנעני אוצר הלשון העברית. [Yaˋaqov Kenaˋani, *Osar ha-lashon ha-ˋIvrit*]. Jerusalem: Massada, 1960–89. 18 vols.

[*Encyclopaedia of the Hebrew language.*] An encyclopaedic brief-entry dictionary, entirely in Hebrew, with brief etymological notes in small type at the end of each entry.

The modern standard

699.

מילון אנגלי-עברי שלם [*Milon ˀangli–ˋivri shalem*] ר. אלקלעי = Reuben Alcalay, *The complete English–Hebrew dictionary*. Tel Aviv: Massada, 1959–61. 4 vols [4270 columns].

A later issue: 1990. 2 vols. This is described as a 'new enlarged edition' but has the same number of columns.

A very copious brief-entry dictionary.

700.

מילון עברי-אנגלי שלם. [*Milon ʾivri–ʾangli shalem*] ראובן אלקלעי = Reuben
Alcalay, *The complete Hebrew–English dictionary*. [Jerusalem]: Massada, 1990.
2932 columns. 'New enlarged edition.'
1st edn: 1964–5. 4 vols [2883 columns].
A brief-entry bilingual dictionary. The Hebrew has vowel pointing.

701.

אברהם אבן-שושן המלון ההדש. [ʾAvraham ʾEven-Shoshan, *Ha-milon he-
hadash.*] Jerusalem: Qiryat-Sefer, 1966–70. 7 vols [3109 pp.].
[*The modern dictionary.*] A brief-entry illustrated dictionary, entirely in Hebrew.

Older periods

702.

David J. A. Clines, editor, *The dictionary of classical Hebrew*. Sheffield:
Sheffield Academic Press, 1993– .
John Elwolde, executive editor.

'Unlike all previous dictionaries of ancient Hebrew this work does not restrict itself
to, or privilege in any way, those ancient Hebrew texts found in the Hebrew Bible ... an
important departure from the tradition.' Within the narrow world of Hebrew studies, this
is indeed innovative. Entries are also unusual in giving relatively long illustrative
quotations, which are accompanied by an English translation. So far three volumes, א–ט,
have appeared. The introduction (vol. 1) includes an interesting discussion of dictionary-
making as applied to classical Hebrew.

The sources, vol. 3 pp. 11–31; abbreviations, vol. 3 pp. 67–9. Supplementary
information, including word frequency and scholarly bibliography, is given in each
successive volume on a letter-by-letter basis.

The work draws on the manuscript of D. Winton Thomas's unpublished revision of
Brown–Driver–Briggs (**703**).

Biblical Hebrew

703.

F. Brown, S. R. Driver, Charles A. Briggs, *A Hebrew and English lexicon of the
Old Testament, with an appendix containing the Biblical Aramaic*. Oxford:
Clarendon Press, 1953. 1127 pp. Reprint 'with many hundreds of corrections' by
G. R. Driver, son of one of the authors.
'Based on the *Lexicon* of William Gesenius [see **704**] as translated by Edward Robinson; edited with constant
reference to the *Thesaurus* of Gesenius as completed by E. Rödiger [1858], and with authorized use of the
latest German editions of Gesenius's *Handwörterbuch über das Alte Testament*.'
Note: Bruce Einspahr, *Index to Brown, Driver & Briggs, Hebrew lexicon*. Chicago: Moody Press, 1977. 456
pp. Revised reprint. 0–8024–4082–7. – 1st edn of this index: 1976.
1st edn of the main work: 1907. – Reprint with additional matter: *The new Brown Driver Briggs Hebrew and
English lexicon of the Old Testament, numerically coded to Strong's Exhaustive concordance, with an
appendix containing the Biblical Aramaic, and with an index*. Lafayette: Associated, 1981. 1118 + 58 pp.

A classic, concise dictionary with numerous citations of scriptural passages but few quotations. Note the use of Fraktur face in abbreviations for the versions of the Bible: ***𝕺*** 'Greek Septuagint', ***𝕱*** 'Hebrew consonantal text', ***𝖊*** 'Syriac', ***𝕿*** 'Aramaic Targum', ***𝖁*** 'Latin Vulgate'. Note also the Greek letter ψ as an abbreviation for Psalms.

Einspahr's index is a complete listing, in computer print-out in tiny type size, of all the entries in Brown–Driver–Briggs that the beginning student might need to consult in reading each successive verse of the Bible, from Genesis to Malachi.

704.

F. H. W. Gesenius, *Hebräisches und aramäisches Handwörterbuch über das Alte Testament.* Berlin: Springer, 1987. 2 vols [517 pp.]. 18th edn, revised by Udo Rüterswörden, Rudolf Meyer, Herbert Donner. 3–540–18206–3.

1st edn: *Hebräisch-Deutsches Handwörterbuch über die Schriften des Alten Testaments, mit Einschluss der geographischen Nahmen und der chaldäischen Wörter beym Daniel und Esra.* Leipzig, 1810–12. 2 vols.
2nd edn: *Neues hebräisch-deutsches Handwörterbuch über das alte Testament mit Einschluss des biblischen Chaldaismus.* Leipzig, 1815. – English version: *A Hebrew and English lexicon to the Old Testament.* 1824. Revised and improved Latin version: *Lexicon manuale Hebraicum et Chaldaicum in Veteris Testamenti libros.* 1833. – An English version, translated by Edward Robinson, appeared in 1836. This, with subsequent revisions to 1854, forms the basis of the later English version by Brown–Driver–Briggs: see **703.**
3rd German edn: *Hebräisches und Chaldäisches Handwörterbuch über das Alte Testament.* 1834.
Another English version: *Gesenius' Hebrew and Chaldee lexicon to the Old Testament Scriptures: numerically coded to Strong's Exhaustive concordance, with an English index of more than 12,000 entries.* 1859. 919 pp. Translated by Samuel Prideaux Tregelles. Reprint: Grand Rapids: Baker Book House, 1979. 0–8010–3736–0.
8th German edn under new title, revised by F. Mühlau and W. Volck: 1878. – 9th edn: 1883. – 11th edn: 1890. – 12th edn, revised by F. Buhl: 1895. – 13th edn: 1899. – 14th edn: 1905. – 15th edn: 1910. 1005 pp. – 16th edn: Leipzig: Vogel, 1915. 1013 pp. – 17th edn (a reprint): 1921.

[*Concise Hebrew and Aramaic dictionary to the Old Testament.*] A completely revised and reset version of this venerable guide to the language of the Old Testament. Generous citations from the Biblical texts, fewer and very brief quotations, but numerous references to the scholarly literature: this category of information was first introduced in quantity by Frants Buhl, in the 14th edition.

Hebrew entries and quotations are in Hebrew script, pointed. Entries begin with German gloss in double inverted commas, sometimes followed by an etymological note. The coverage now includes the Qumran texts (Dead Sea Scrolls), cited as **𝕼.**

705.

Ludwig Koehler, Walter Baumgartner, *Hebräisches und aramäisches Lexicon zum Alten Testament.* Leiden: Brill, 1967–95. 5 vols [1801 pp.]. '3rd edn' by Walter Baumgartner, Johann Jakob Stamm, Benedikt Hartmann.

Followed by: *Supplementband.* 1996. 131* pp. 90–04–10714–2.
English version: *The Hebrew and Aramaic lexicon of the Old Testament.* Leiden: Brill, 1994–6. 3 vols [1364 pp.]. Translation edited by M. E. J. Richardson. 90–04–09700–7.
1st edn of the main work: Ludwig Koehler, Walter Baumgartner, *Lexicon in Veteris Testamenti libros.* Leiden: Brill, 1948–53. 2 parts [1138 pp.]. This was followed by: *Supplementum ad Lexicon in Veteris Testamenti libros.* 1958. 227 pp. The 1st edn, when reprinted together with the supplement in 1958, was described as the '2nd edn'.
See also: L. Koehler, *Vom hebräischen Lexikon; Vortrag gehalten am 31. August zur Gelegenheit der internationalen Alttestamentlertagung in Leiden 1950.* Leiden: Brill, 1950. 19 pp. [*On the Hebrew dictionary: a talk given at the International Old Testament Conference, Leiden, 1950.*]

[*Hebrew and Aramaic dictionary of the Old Testament.*] A completely new dictionary of Biblical Hebrew and Aramaic, not breaking with the Gesenius tradition (as Clines, **702**, does) but giving more explicit attention to word forms and to variations of meaning, with careful and elaborate German glosses. The third edition represents a considerable expansion of the original: more discursive discussion of meanings, and many more references to cognates in Semitic languages. The fifth volume is the Aramaic dictionary.

The Supplement, published in 1996, includes a German–Hebrew index, a German–Aramaic index, and lists of Hebrew and Aramaic proper names.

English glosses, which were given in the first edition, have been dropped: in its place, there is now an English version of the whole work. Richardson's English version adds some references to English Bible translations, and also some additional Akkadian cognates.

In the first edition, introductory matter was given both in German and in a slightly Germanised English, and glosses were in both languages – but the user may be surprised by German-inspired abbreviations in the English glosses, such as *a.* 'and'. Apart from some Arabic cognates, there was no attention to etymology.

706.

שמואל א. ליונסטמם [*Osar lashon ha-Miqra'*] אוצר לשון המקרא. = Samuel E. Loewenstamm, [Menaham Zevi Kaddari,] editors, *Thesaurus of the language of the Bible; complete concordance, Hebrew Bible dictionary, Hebrew–English Bible dictionary*. Jerusalem: Bible Concordance Press, 1957–68. Vols 1–3.
'With the co-operation of Joshua Blau.'

A large-scale dictionary of the language of the Hebrew Bible, mainly in Hebrew but with English glosses. It covered only א–ט (about a third of the alphabet) before publication faltered.

Etymological dictionaries

707.

Ernest Klein, *A comprehensive etymological dictionary of the Hebrew language for readers of English.* Jerusalem: Carta, 1987. 721 pp.
Editor, Baruch Sarel. Alternate title: *Etymological dictionary of the Hebrew language.*

Approachable by those not wholly familiar with Hebrew because of its inclusion of very numerous derived forms as headwords, in simple alphabetical order. Symbols and abbreviations, pp. xvi–xix. Deals fully with loanwords. Provides cognates in Semitic languages for the inherited vocabulary, but offers no proto-Semitic (still less proto-Afroasiatic) reconstructions.

HILIGAYNON

An AUSTRONESIAN language of the Philippines, with over five million speakers. The early dictionary by Mentrida (**709**) assists research into the earlier history of the language.

708.

Cecile Motus, *Hiligaynon dictionary*. Honolulu: University of Hawaii Press, 1971. 305 pp. 0–87022–545–6.

PALI language texts: Philippines.

The only significant modern dictionary.

709.

Alonso Mentrida, *Diccionario de la lengua Bisaya Hiligeceina y Haraya de la Isla de Panay*. Manila: Tomas Oliva, 1841. 827 pp. New edn.

1st edn: 1637. 2nd edn: 1698.

[*Dictionary of the Visayan language, Hiligaynon, of the island of Panay.*] The new edition incorporated a Spanish–Hiligaynon dictionary by Julian Martin (pp. 460–827).

HINDI AND URDU

These are two literary languages originally based on the same spoken dialect – that of Delhi. They belong to the INDO-ARYAN branch of the Indo-European language family.

Hindi (literally 'Indian') is now the dominant native language of India, officially recognised throughout the country and spoken as a mother tongue in several of the most populous northern states. Hindi carries with it Hindu religious culture and the scholarly inheritance of Sanskrit. It is written in the Devanagari script native to northern India.

Urdu (originally 'language of the fort') is the national language of Pakistan, though relatively few speak it as a mother tongue. It is the Muslim form of the language, with numerous loanwords from Arabic and Persian, and it is written in Arabic script.

Varieties of Hindi, or of the Hindi area languages, are spoken in many parts of the world as a result of nineteenth and twentieth century migrations. The total number of speakers is difficult to calculate because of problems of definition – are north Indian languages such as Bhojpuri and Maithili to be counted as dialects of Hindi or as independent languages? Are the widespread Hindi-like languages of the Caribbean and other once-colonial territories to be counted as Hindi, as Bhojpuri or as something else?

Hindi and Urdu are treated together in this book for a practical reason. There are several twentieth-century dictionaries purely of Hindi; however, Platts's great nineteenth-century dictionary (**711**) remains important for both languages and there is nothing at all to supersede it as a large-scale dictionary of Urdu.

There are at least 300 million speakers of Hindi, Urdu and the regional languages that form part of the wider Hindi group. This book lists only the most accessible of Hindi dictionaries – but it is a fact that Hindi lexicography is not well-developed, and no full historical dictionary yet exists.

The Devanagari alphabet for Hindi

The most striking difference between Hindi and Urdu is in their scripts. Urdu uses a form of Arabic script. Hindi is written in the Devanagari alphabet which is also used for Nepali and Marathi and is the usual choice for printing Sanskrit.

अआइईउऊऋ एऐओऔ

a ā i ī u ū ṛ   e ai o au

कखगघङ चछजझञ टठडढण तथदधन पफबभम यरलव शषसह

k kh g gh ṅ   c ch j jh ñ   ṭ ṭh ḍ ḍh ṇ   t th d dh n   p ph b bh m   y r l v   ś ṣ s h

Consonants are combined with a following vowel to make a single character. For a table of the secondary vowel signs see SANSKRIT.

Both standards

710.

हिंदी–उर्दू व्यवहारिक लघु कोश [*Hindī–Urdu vyavaharik laghu koś*]. New Delhi: Kendriy Hindi Nideśalay, 1984. 386 pp.

Dvibhasha kosmala, 3.

[*Concise practical Hindi–Urdu dictionary.*] One of a series of bilingual glossaries of Indian languages. Tabular layout.

711.

John T. Platts, *A dictionary of Urdú, classical Hindí, and English*. London, 1884. 1259 pp.

The original edition was issued successively by two or three publishers. Numerous reprints in Britain (Oxford: Oxford University Press. 0–19–864309–8) and in India.

Headwords are given in Arabic, Devanagari and Latin scripts (sub-headings and phrases in Latin only); they are in the Arabic alphabetical order, appropriate to Urdu. A Hindi user will take a little time to get to know it. A rich collection from oral and printed sources of the vocabulary and usage of the nineteenth-century language, and in some ways still the best concise dictionary today. Etymologies are given in square brackets. Some ethnographical information, but no quotations from literature. Taxonomic names are supplied for flora and fauna.

Additions and corrections, pp. 1255–9.

Hindi

712.

Purshotam Narain Agrawala [and others], *Nalanda current dictionary*. Bhagalpur: Bharat Book Depot [1980?]. 1368 pp. Revised and enlarged by S. A. Nasar, Shri Hari Damodar, Vidya Khandelwal.

A very brief entry English–Hindi dictionary with many technical and scientific terms. Appendix of Indian administrative and legal terminology, English–Hindi, pp. 1337–68.

713.

Nicole Balbi, Jabans K. Balbir, *Dictionnaire général hindi–français =* समन्य हिन्दी–फ्रन्सीसी. Paris: L'Asiathèque, 1992. 1051 pp. 2–901795–46–3.
With the collaboration of Sarasvati Joshi, Niti Srivastava, Vraj Raj Joshi.

[*General Hindi–French dictionary.*]

714.

R. S. McGregor, editor, *The Oxford Hindi–English dictionary.* Oxford: Oxford University Press, 1993. 1083 pp. 0–19–864317–9.

A well laid out, well-printed concise dictionary of modern usage. Headwords are given both in script and in transliteration, in a version which, by omitting silent vowels, reveals pronunciation.

Very brief but useful etymologies are in square brackets: the structure of compound words is clarified in the same way. In the etymologies, *[S.]* by itself indicates a loanword from Sanskrit. A form in square brackets without any language abbreviation is to be taken as a Sanskrit or Old Indo-Aryan word (marked * if reconstructed) which has been transmitted normally to modern Hindi: further details on these can usually be found in Turner (**763**). Arabic and Persian parent words are given in transliteration: a smaller proportion than in Platts's time of the potential users of such a dictionary will be able to read Arabic script. Platts's dictionary (**711**) remains a 'major source'.

715.

सत्यप्रकाश | बलभद्र प्रसाद मिश्र | मनक अंग्रेजी–हिन्दी कोश [Satyaprakāś, Balbhadra Prasād Miśra, *Manak Angrejī –Hindī koś*] = *Standard English–Hindi dictionary.* Prayag: Hindi Sahitya Sammelan, 1971. 1576 pp.

A large English–Hindi dictionary, intended for Hindi users, with variant meanings of English words explained in Hindi at length.

716.

Aryendra Sharma, Hans J. Vermeer, *Hindi–deutsches Wörterbuch.* Heidelberg: Groos, 1983– . 5 vols [1644 pp.].

[*Hindi–German dictionary.*] A fuller brief-entry bilingual dictionary than McGregor's (**714**). Pronunciation is given in the International Phonetic Alphabet. Taxonomic names are given for flora and fauna. The work is printed from typescript.

717.

श्यामसुंदरदास | हिंदी शब्दसागर अर्थात् हिंदी भाषा का एक बृहत् कोश [Śyāmsundardās, *Hindī śabdsāgar, arthāt Hindī bhāṣā kā ek bṛhat koś*]. Benares: Nagaripracarini Sabha, 1965–75. 11 vols. 2nd edn.
1st edn: Benares, 1916–28. See the criticisms of this by Hardev Bahri, 'Hindi lexicography since independence and its future' in Misra (**10**).

[*Ocean of Hindi words, or a big dictionary of the Hindi language.*] The largest monolingual dictionary of Hindi, with quotations from literature, particularly verse, but no precise references. Etymologies are given briefly – often simply सं 'Sanskrit loanword'.

718.

रामचंद्र वर्मा | संक्षिप्त हिंदी शब्दसागर [Ramcandra Varma, *Sanksipta Hindī śabdsāgar*]. Kaśī: Nāgarīpracāriṇī Sabhā [1971]. 1097 pp. 7th edn.

1st edn: 1933. 1097 pp. – 5th edn: 2008 [1951]. 1265 pp. with a supplement of 86 pp. – 6th edn: 2014 [1957]. 1067 pp.

Koś granthamālā, 2.

[*Abridged ocean of Hindi words.*] A brief-entry dictionary based on the *Hindī śabdsāgar* (above).

719.

H. W. Wagenaar, *Allied Chambers transliterated Hindi–Hindi–English dictionary*. New Delhi: Allied Chambers (India), 1993. 1149 pp. 81–86062–10–6.

An odd compilation in several sequences. The main dictionary has headwords in Hindi in Latin script and Latin alphabetical order, followed by the Devanagari spelling and an English gloss. Devanagari index, pp. 747–902; glossary of Hindu mythological names and Devanagari index to this; Anglo-Indian glossary, in English alone with etymologies, basically a modernisation of Hobson-Jobson (**382**) on a small scale, pp. 1099–1129; Mogul glossary of Persian and Turkish words used in India, pp. 1131–49.

Urdu

720.

Abdul Haq, *Standard English Urdu dictionary*. Delhi, 1937. 1513 pp.

721.

Bashir Ahmad Qureshi, *Standard twentieth century dictionary, Urdu into English*. Delhi: Educational Publishing House, 1984. 688 pp. 'Students edition' in nastaliq calligraphy.

Alternate title: *Kitabistan's twentieth century Urdu–English dictionary*.

A brief-entry bilingual dictionary, useful for the vocabulary of modern Urdu. I do not know the history of this work: it appears to be an Indian reprint of a Pakistani publication.

HITTITE

Hittite is the conventional name for a language recorded on clay tablets of the second millennium BC originating from Hattušas (Boğazköy) in central Anatolia. The Czech scholar Bedrich Hrozný showed in 1915 that these cuneiform tablets were a very ancient record of one of the INDO-EUROPEAN LANGUAGES, belonging to a branch hitherto unknown.

The language of the tablets is usually divided into three periods, Old Hittite (to about 1550 BC, coinciding with what historians call the Old Kingdom), Middle and Late Hittite.

After the destruction of Hattušas by invaders around 1200 BC, Hittites disappear completely from the historical and linguistic record.

LUWIAN and LYDIAN, known from a few tablets and inscriptions, were related to Hittite. With some other extinct languages of the Indo-European family they are grouped as 'Anatolian languages'.

722.

Johannes Friedrich, *Hethitisches Wörterbuch: Kurzgefaßte kritische Sammlung der Deutungen hethitischer Wörter*. Heidelberg: Winter, 1952–4. 4 parts [344 pp.].
Indogermanische Bibliothek. 2. Reihe, Wörterbücher.
Followed by: *Ergänzungsheft*, 1–3. 1957–66. [*Supplementary parts.*]

[*Hittite dictionary: a concise critical collection of the meanings of Hittite words.*] Now being replaced, very slowly, by Friedrich and Kammenhuber (**723**). The appendices have not yet been taken up in later dictionaries: Sumerian ideograms, pp. 264–301; numerals, pp. 301–4; Akkadian words and forms, 305–15; words from neighbouring languages recorded in Hittite texts, pp. 316–29 (including LUWIAN and Palaic). All these appendices were augmented in each of the three supplements.

723.

Johannes Friedrich, Annelies Kammenhuber, *Hethitisches Wörterbuch ... auf der Grundlage der edierten hethitischen Texte*. Heidelberg: Winter, 1975– .
Indogermanische Bibliothek. 2. Reihe, Wörterbücher.

[*Hittite dictionary on the basis of published Hittite texts.*] Fairly lengthy essays on some words, their historical development and their meanings. Note the use of abbreviations *aheth.* 'Early Hittite' and *jheth.* 'Late Hittite'.

Vol. 1, parts 1–8, covers **A** in 639 pages; vol. 2, parts 9–10, covers **E**; vol. 3, part 11 onwards, covering **H**, is in progress. This dictionary will eventually replace Friedrich's earlier one (**722**).

724.

Hans G. Güterbock, Harry A. Hoffner, *The Hittite dictionary of the Oriental Institute of the University of Chicago*. Chicago, 1980–.

A very full study of the vocabulary with citations and quotations and discussion of etymology and word forms. Controversial matter is in smaller font, with references to, and sometimes quotations of, scholarly literature. There is much reference to Akkadian as well as to Indo-European philology. Hoffner's lexicographical collections were first put to use in his *Alimenta Hethaeorum* [*Hittite foodstuffs*], New Haven: American Oriental Society, 1974.

With volume P, now in progress, the editors have adopted the new Hittite transliteration of Chr. Rüster and E. Neu's *Hethitisches Zeichenlexikon* (Wiesbaden, 1989: see the list of reviews of that work given at vol. P part 1 p. vii).

In order to avoid immediate overlap with Friedrich and Kammenhuber (**723**) publication began with vol. 3, which was to cover **L–N**. Parts 1 to 3 of this were published between 1980 and 1986. Volume numbering was then dropped, and vol. L–N part 4, completing **N** in 477 pages, appeared in 1989. Thus far the '*CHD*' ('Chicago Hittite dictionary') covers **L–Pattar**.

725.
Jaan Puhvel, *Hittite etymological dictionary*. Berlin: Mouton, 1984– .
Trends in linguistics. Documentation.
    Four volumes have now appeared: corrections and additions are at the end of successive volumes.
    'This volume marks a waystation at the approximate half-way point in the alphabetical inventory of Hittite. For better or worse it seems fated to be the one extensive **K**-lexicon for some time to come, until *HW²* [**723**] hopefully gets done first with **H** and **I** in the lamented wake of its (now second) posthumous author, and *CHD* [**724**] is completed with **K** sometime in the next millennium; thus its nonetymological use is likely to be above normal in the years ahead. Such a midpoint also impacts the sequel. With both the *CHD* and Tischler's markedly retooled and improved *Glossar* [**728**] as *piran huuiyatalles* from **L** forward, a second-half *HED* of the same complexity as heretofore may run some risk of supererogation. What changes there will be the future will determine' (preface to vol. 4).

726.
Edgar H. Sturtevant, *Hittite glossary: words of known or conjectured meaning, with Sumerian ideograms and Accadian words common in Hittite texts.*
Philadelphia: Linguistic Society of America, 1936. 192 pp. 2nd edn.
William Dwight Whitney linguistic series. Special publications of the Linguistic Society of America.
Followed by: *Supplement.* 1939.
1st edn of the main work: Baltimore, 1931.
    A brief dictionary, but with selective references to texts and to scholarly literature. Now largely superseded.

727.
Johann Tischler, *Hethitisch–deutsches Wörterverzeichnis, mit einem semasiologischen Index*. Innsbruck: Institut für Sprachwissenschaft der Universität Innsbruck, 1982. 153 pp. 3–85124–567–9.
Innsbrücker Beiträge zur Sprachwissenschaft, 39.
    [*Hittite–German word-list, with an index of meanings.*] The German–Hittite index, pp. 119–53, is arranged not alphabetically but by meanings.

728.
Johann Tischler, *Hethitisches etymologisches Glossar*. Innsbruck: Institut für Sprachwissenschaft der Universität Innsbruck, 1977– .
Innsbrücker Beiträge zur Sprachwissenschaft, 20.

[*Hittite etymological glossary.*] Concentrates, much more than Puhvel's dictionary (**725**) does, on historical and etymological discussion, citing relatively few original texts but much scholarly literature.

Vol. 1 was reproduced from typescript; things have now improved. Published sections now cover **A–Nuza** and **T–Tuzumazuwant**.

HO

An AUSTROASIATIC language of north-eastern India, with about 750,000 speakers.

729.
Braj Bihari Kumar, *Hindi–Ho dictionary* = हिन्दी–हो कोश. Kohima: Nagalaind Bhasha Parishad, 1982. 395 pp.

HUNGARIAN

Hungarian belongs to the URALIC language family, which is otherwise confined to northern Europe and northern Asia. Its closest relatives are KHANTY and MANSI, minority languages of the middle Ob valley in western Siberia.

There are over 15 million speakers of Hungarian. It is the national language of Hungary. There are several Hungarian-speaking minorities in neighbouring countries, the largest of them in Transylvania (Hungarian *Erdély*) in modern Romania. There are early records of the Hungarian speech of eastern Austria (see **747**).

There is a bibliography of older Hungarian dictionaries and grammars, compiled by Sági (**746**).

Hungarian alphabetical order

a/á b c cs d e/é f g gy h i/í j k l m n
o/ó ö/ő p q r s sz t ty u/ú ü/ű v w x y z zs

Q, W and *X* are used only in loanwords that retain their original foreign spelling.

Historical dictionaries

730.
Szarvas Gábor, Simonyi Zsigmond, editors, *Magyar nyelvtörténeti szótár a legrégibb nyelvemlékektol a nyelvújításig = Lexicon linguae hungaricae aevi antiquioris*. Budapest: Hornyánszky, 1890–93. 3 vols.
Magyar Tudományos Akadémia.

[*Dictionary of the Hungarian language from the oldest period to the language reform.*] A concise historical dictionary with quotations of Hungarian and some German and Latin sources. Medieval glossaries in all three languages are drawn on for glosses – which are kept to a bare minimum. The main feature is the quotations. Compounds are filed under base forms – thus, nearly always, not in their own alphabetical order.

A four-page introduction in German was tipped in vol. 1 of the copy I examined (at Cambridge University Library). Abbreviations for source texts, vol. 1 pp. xix–xxxiii.

The modern standard

731.
A magyar nyelv értelmező szótara. Budapest: Akadémiai Kiadó, 1959–62. 7 vols.
Edited by Bárczi Gésa, Országh László. Compiled by Balázs János and others. A Magyar Tudmányos Akadémia Nyelvtudományi Intézet.

[*Explanatory dictionary of the Hungarian language.*] The fullest dictionary of modern usage, with example phrases and also (separated off by ❏) sentences quoted from literary works. These are credited to authors, but without precise references.

Fold-out list of abbreviations and symbols at end of each volume.

732.
Grétsy László, Kovalovszky Miklós, *Nyelvmuvelő kézikönyv.* Budapest: Akadémiai Kiadó, 1980–85. 963–05–2350–7.
A Magyar Tudományos Akadémia Nyelvtudományi Intézet.

[*Concise dictionary of usage.*] A discursive dictionary most important for its citations, at the end of each entry, in a section headed *IRODALOM* 'bibliography', of previous writings on correct usage: references to these, vol. 1 pp. 35–73 with vol. 2 pp. 5–11. Note the frequent abbreviation *L.még* 'see also'.

733.
Juhász József [and other editors], *Magyar értelmező kéziszótár.* Budapest: Akadémiai Kiadó, 1972. 1550 pp.
A Magyar Tudományos Akadémia Nyelvtudományi Intézet.

[*Concise explanatory dictionary of Hungarian.*] A brief-entry dictionary with some illustrations. Abbreviations, pp. 1547–50.

734.
Országh László, *Angol–magyar nagyszótár = Comprehensive English–Hungarian dictionary.* Budapest: Akadémiai Kiadó, 1976. 2 vols. 5th edn. [963–05–6775–X.]
1st edn: *Angol–magyar szótár.* 1960. 2336 pp. – The 6th to 9th editions are reprints of the 5th.
Short version: *A concise dictionary of the English and Hungarian languages. Part 1: English–Hungarian.* Budapest: Franklin-Tarsulat, 1948. – 2nd edn: *Angol–Magyar kéziszótár.* 1950. – 3rd edn: 1957. – The latest edition of this was published: Budapest: Akadémiai Kiadó, 1981 (1053 pp.), and reprinted as: Laszló Országh, editor-in-chief, *A concise English–Hungarian dictionary.* Oxford: Oxford University Press, 1990. 0–19–864170–2.
On Országh's work, especially the 1948 *Concise dictionary*, see: Támás Magay, 'A chapter in the history of English lexicography in Hungary' in James (**8**) pp. 149–59.

[*English–Hungarian dictionary.*] A well-planned very large-scale brief-entry dictionary with numerous example phrases and much scientific and technical vocabulary. An early United States reviewer criticised Országh for 'a liberal, even feckless, sprinkling of words not admitted to drawing-rooms'.

735.

Országh László, *Magyar–angol szótár* = László Országh, *Hungarian–English dictionary*. Budapest: Akadémiai Kiadó, 1969. 2 vols [2159 pp.]. 3rd edn. [963–05–5799–1.]

1st edn: 1953. 1448 pp. 2nd edn: 1963. – The 4th to 6th editions are reprints of the 3rd.

Short version: T. Magay, L. Országh, *A concise Hungarian–English dictionary*. Oxford: Oxford University Press; Budapest: Akadémiai Kiadó, 1990. 1152 pp. 0–19–864169–9. Contributing editor, P. A. Sherwood. [The copyright date '1981' is incorrect.] – Earlier editions of this: 1959; 1973.

A comprehensive bilingual dictionary with room for numerous example phrases. Abbreviations and explanations, vol. 1 pp. x–xvi. The 3rd edition is a reprint of the 2nd with a supplement, pp. 2147–59.

Regional forms

736.

Balogh Éva Rózsa [and other editors], *Új magyar tájszótár*. Budapest: Akadémiai Kiadó, 1979– .

Chief editor, B. Lőrinczy Éva. A Magyar Tudományos Akadémia Nyelvtudományi Intézet.

[*New Hungarian dialect dictionary.*] Very concise entries under a normalised Hungarian form, followed by recorded dialect forms in italics, listing places of origin; then glosses in roman – in other words, following very closely the example of Szinnyéi (**737**). Taxonomic names are given for flora.

Covers all of Hungary and neighbouring countries, including Transylvania and other parts of Romania where there have been Hungarian-speaking communities: see the detailed maps in vol. 1 after p. 136, and full list of place names, giving modern standard names for places outside Hungary, vol. 1 pp. 61–133.

Numerical references to sources of information are keyed to the list in alphabetical order, vol. 1 pp. 23–60.

So far three volumes have been published, covering over half of the alphabet, **A–M**.

737.

Szinnyei József, *Magyar tájszótár*. Budapest: Hornyánszky, 1893–1901. 2 vols.

[*Hungarian dialect dictionary.*] Concise entries under normalised Hungarian form, which is followed by recorded dialect forms in italics (stating place and source of information) and by a brief gloss. There is no listing of place names. Based on earlier philological publications (abbreviations, p. xii): now gradually being superseded by Balogh (**736**).

Hungary

738.

Csury Bálint, *Szamosháti szótár*. Budapest: Magyar Nyelvtudományi Társaság, 1935–6. 2 vols.

[*Dictionary of the Szamos valley dialects.*] Includes numerous example sentences in a phonetic script. List of place names and informants, vol. 2 pp. 479–80.

Romania

739.

Szabó T. Attila, [Vámszer Márta and others,] *Erdélyi magyar szótörténeti tár = Dicţionarul istoric al lexicului maghiar din Transilvania = Wortgeschichtlicher Thesaurus der siebenbürgisch-ungarischen Sprache.* Bukarest: Kriterion; Budapest: Akadémiai Kiadó, 1975– . 963–05–6516–1; 973–26–0339–9.

Later versions of the Romanian and German titles: *Dicţionar istoric al lexicului maghiar din Transilvania = Historisches Wörterbuch der siebenbürgisch-ungarischen Wortschatzes.*

[*Historical dictionary of the Hungarian vocabulary of Transylvania.*] A complete dictionary of the older standard language of Transylvania, including words shared with standard Hungarian. Draws on both older and modern written and printed sources, covering the period from the mid-fifteenth century to the end of the nineteenth century.

Introductory matter and glosses in Hungarian, German and Romanian. The glosses are followed by datings and quotations (source references in square brackets).

Publication faltered after vol. 4, **Fem–Ha**, which appeared in 1984. It was renewed in 1993, this time with Akadémiai Kiadó taking the lead, and has reached vol. 8: the level of detail is increasing. Published volumes cover **A–Megszúpoztat**.

740.

Yrjö Wichmanns Wörterbuch des ungarischen moldauer Nordcsángó- und des Hetfalúer Csángódialektes, nebst grammatikalischen Aufzeichnungen und Texten aus dem Nordcsángódialekt. Helsinki: Suomalais-Ugrilainen Seura, 1936.

Lexica Societatis Fenno-Ugricae, 4. Edited by Bálint Csüry, Artturi Kannisto.

[*Yrjö Wichmann's dictionary of the Hungarian dialect of north Csangó and Hetfalú in Moldavia, with grammatical observations and texts from the north Csangó dialect.*] The dictionary is on pp. 3–173. Entries are under actual dialect forms in the Société Finno-Ougrienne's phonetic alphabet. In alphabetical filing, diacritics are ignored on vowels but counted as forming a separate letter on consonants.

Etymological dictionaries

741.

Bárczi Géza, *Magyar szófejtő szótár.* Budapest: Királyi Magyar Egyetemi Nyomda, 1941. 348 pp.

[*Hungarian etymological dictionary.*] Now outdated but occasionally handy. Each entry begins with earliest dating and source of information (usually a philological work); after this early word forms, a gloss and a linguistic origin (often credited to Gombocz and Melich, **743**). Fold-out key to abbreviations at end of volume.

742.

Benkő Loránd, chief editor, *A magyar nyelv történeti-etimológiai szótára.* Budapest: Akadémiai Kiadó, 1967–84. 4 vols.

A Magyar Tudomanyos Akadémia Nyelvtudományi Intézet; Az Eötvös Loránd Tudományegyetem I. sz. Magyar Nyelvészeti Tanszék.

[*Historical-etymological dictionary of the Hungarian language.*] A concise etymological dictionary in which each entry begins with a dating and usually with a quotation of the passage in which the word is first recorded. Full attention is given to changes of form and to compound words, again with datings. The second paragraph of each entry gives the linguistic origin of the word with cognates in other languages. The third paragraph gives references to scholarly literature, often on a generous scale.

Introductory matter is in Hungarian and German. Abbreviations for source references, vol. 1 pp. 43–83.

Vol. 4 consists of indexes by language: table of contents, pp. 5–8.

743.

Gombocz Zoltán, Melich János, *Magyar etimologiai szótár = Lexicon critico-etymologicum linguae Hungaricae*. Budapest: Magyar Tudományos Akadémia, 1914–44. Vols 1–2 [parts 1–18; no more published].

[*Hungarian etymological dictionary.*] A spacious and discursive etymological dictionary with generous citation of the scholarly literature and full discussion. The work covers only **A–Geburnus**, ceasing abruptly before any introduction, bibliography or abbreviations had been published; but its information is repeated, briefly, in Bárczi's one-volume dictionary (**741**).

744.

Lakó György, Rédei Károly, [K. Sal Éva,] editors, *A magyar szókészlet finnugor elemei: etimológiai szótár*. Budapest: Akadémiai Kiadó, 1967–78. 3 vols [727 pp.].
Accompanied by: A. Jászá Anna, K. Sal Éva, *Szómutató a magyar szókészlet finnugor elemei című etimológiai szótár*. 1981. 130 pp. [*Indexes.*]
A Magyar Tudományos Akadémia Nyelvtudományi Intézet.

[*The Finno-Ugric element of the Hungarian vocabulary: an etymological dictionary.*] Detailed etymological and comparative dictionary of major importance for Uralic studies. Cites sources both for Hungarian forms and for those in other Finno-Ugric languages, often with detailed discussion in small font. Bibliography, pp. 707–27.

The index volume contains separate indexes for each language from which forms are cited: table of contents, pp. 5–6. Many forms are in the phonetic script of the Société Finno-Ougrienne. This is very complex: it is useful that a table is provided of the alphabetical order that has been adopted.

Foreign words

745.

Bakos Ferenc, *A magyar szókészlet román elemeinek története*. Budapest: Akadémiai Kiadó, 1982. 560 pp. 963–05–2620–4.

[*Study of Romanian elements in the Hungarian vocabulary.*] Entries are arranged in categories, interspersed with discussion. Within each entry, paragraph *I* gives the dialect origins of the word, citing sources; paragraph *II* is the etymology, with references to scholarly literature. Bibliographical abbreviations, pp. 483–501; place name abbreviations, p. 502; Hungarian index, pp. 503–35; Romanian key to the Hungarian index, pp. 536–60.

Other works of interest

746.

Sági István, *A magyar szótárak és nyelvtanok könyvészete*. Budapest: Magyar Nyelvtudományi Társaság, 1922. 105 pp.

A Magyar Nyelvtudományi Társaság kiadványai, 18.

747.

Szamota István, *A Schlägli magyar szójegyzék: a XV. század első negyedéből*. Budapest: Magyar Tudományos Akadémia, 1894. 111 pp.

HURRIAN

This long-extinct language of eastern Anatolia is believed to be a North East CAUCASIAN language (for the evidence see Diakonoff and Starostin, **749**). The first Hurrian text to be discovered in modern times was a diplomatic letter from King Tushratta of Mitanni to the Egyptian Pharaoh Amenophis III, found at Tell el-Amarna.

748.

Emmanuel Laroche, *Glossaire de la langue hourrite*. Paris: Klincksieck, 1980. 322 pp. 2–252–01984–0.

Etudes et commentaires, 93.

[*Glossary of the Hurrian language.*] The only earlier glossary was that published by J. Friedrich as an appendix to his *Hethitisches Wörterbuch* (**722**). Laroche's dictionary is entirely in transliteration. Headwords are followed by a French gloss (if the meaning is known) with discussion and references to source texts (abbreviations, pp. 29–31). There are several appendices. Index of words cited from other ancient Near Eastern languages, pp. 314–18.

749.

I. M. Diakonoff, S. A. Starostin, *Hurro-Urartian as an Eastern Caucasian language*. Munich: Kitzinger, 1986. 103 pp. 3–920645–39–1.

Münchener Studien zur Sprachwissenschaft, Beiheft, N. F. 12.

IBAN

Iban or Sea Dayak is an AUSTRONESIAN language of Malaysia and Indonesia, spoken along the rivers of western Borneo. It has perhaps one and a quarter million speakers.

750.

Anthony Richards, *An Iban–English dictionary*. Oxford: Clarendon Press, 1981. 417 pp. 0–19–864325–X.

Very detailed dictionary begun in 1964 when the author retired from the Sarawak Civil Service; based both on oral work and on published literature. A proportion of the anthropological information embedded in entries is accessible through the very brief 'English–Iban guide to some of the longer entries', pp. xxvii–xxix.

751.
Kamus bahasa Iban–bahasa Malaysia. Kuala Lumpur: Dewan Bahasa dan Pustaka, 1989. 425 pp. 983–62–0740–6.
Edited by Hussain bin Jamil, Henry Gana Ngadi.

[*Iban–Malaysian dictionary.*] A useful modern dictionary, lacking the anthropological and botanical terminology of Richards (**750**).

ICELANDIC

Icelandic belongs to the GERMANIC branch of the Indo-European languages. It has only a quarter of a million speakers, and is Iceland's national language. Old Icelandic, the language of the sagas of the twelfth and thirteenth centuries, is scarcely distinguishable from the OLD NORSE of poetry, and is dealt with in this book under that heading. This entry covers modern Icelandic.

Icelandic alphabetical order

a á b d/ð e é f g h i í j k l m n o ó p r s t u ú v y ý þ æ ø

Historical dictionaries

752.
Jón Ólafsson, *Orðabók íslenzkrar tungu að fornu og nýju*. Reykjavík: Gutenberg, 1912. Parts 1–2 [no more published].

[*Dictionary of the Icelandic language, early and modern.*] The dictionary was to be in four volumes.

The modern standard

753.
A. Sigurdsson, *Íslenzk–ensk ordabók*. Reykjavík: Leiftur, 1983. 942 pp. 4th edn.

[*Icelandic–English dictionary.*] A brief-entry bilingual dictionary with many set phrases.

754.
Árni Böðvarsson, *Íslensk orðabók handa skólum og almenningi*. Reykjavík: Menningarsjóður, 1985. 1263 pp. 2nd edn reprinted with an expanded supplement.
1st edn: *Íslenzk orðabók handa skólum og almenningi*. 1963. 852 pp. 2nd edn: 1983. 1256 pp.

[*Icelandic dictionary for school and general use.*] A concise dictionary of modern usage.

755.

Sigfús Blöndal, *Islandsk–dansk ordbog* = *Íslensk–dönsk orðabók*. Reykjavík: Þórarin B. Þorláksson, 1920–24. 1052 pp.

Accompanied by: Halldór Halldórsson, Jakob Benediktsson, *Islandsk–dansk ordbog. Supplement = Íslensk–dönsk orðabók. Viðbætir*. Reykjavík: Islandsk–Dansk Ordbogsfond, 1963. 200 pp.

[*Icelandic–Danish dictionary*.] A very large-scale bilingual dictionary of the modern language with numerous examples and a considerable number of quotations from literature, attributed to authors but with no precise references.

The supplement adds many new words, and gives precise citations from literature or the press for nearly all of them.

756.

Sören Sörenson, *Ensk–íslensk orðabók*. Reykjavík: Örnog Örlygur, 1984. 1245 pp.

Based on E. L. Thorndike, Clarence L. Barnhart, *The Thorndike-Barnhart high school dictionary* (4th edn, 1965) in the version entitled *Scott Foresman advanced dictionary* (1979).

[*English–Icelandic dictionary*.] A fully illustrated encyclopaedic dictionary.

757.

Sverrir Hólmarsson, Christopher Sanders, John Tucker, *Íslensk–ensk orðabók* = *Concise Icelandic–English dictionary*. Reykjavík: Iðunn, 1989. 536 pp.

Orðabækur Iðunnar.

A brief-entry dictionary of the modern language. Glossary of common Icelandic abbreviations, pp. 521–36. Outline of morphology, pp. 33–49. Guide to the use of the dictionary (in English and Icelandic), pp. 11–31.

Etymological dictionaries

758.

Alexander Jóhannesson, *Isländisches etymologisches Wörterbuch*. Bern: Francke, 1951–6. 1406 pp.

[*Icelandic etymological dictionary*.] Strangely organised. The first section (pp. 1–933) is a dictionary of Indo-European roots that happen to have Icelandic descendants, with full information on cognates in other Indo-European languages, expecially Germanic. This is in Sanskrit alphabetical order, like some other old-fashioned works on Indo-European – but there is an index to it in Latin alphabetical order on pp. 1233–44.

The second section (pp. 935–1231), in normal alphabetical order, is an etymological dictionary of the origins of loanwords in Icelandic.

Icelandic index, pp. 1245–1402.

759.

Ásgeir Blöndal Magnússon, *Íslensk orðsifjabók*. Reykjavík: Orðabók Háskólans, 1989. 1231 pp. Corrected reprint.

1st edn: 1989.

[*Icelandic etymological dictionary.*] A full etymological dictionary with many Germanic cognates. A century dating is given for the first recorded use of words that are not already found in Old Norse. Abbreviations and bibliography, pp. xxiii–xxxix.

IGBO

Igbo or Ibo, with 12 million speakers, is one of the four major languages of Nigeria (alongside Hausa, Yoruba and English). It is a NIGER-CONGO language. The Official orthography, introduced in 1961, solved a long-running dispute among proponents of two older orthographies for Igbo.

760.
Michael J. C. Echeruo, *Dictionary of the Igbo language*. New Haven: Yale University Press, forthcoming. 0–300–07307–0.
Yale language series.

761.
Kay Williamson, editor, *Igbo–English dictionary based on the Onitsha dialect; based on the compilation by G. W. Pearman*. Benin City: Ethiope, 1972. 568 pp.
Revised and expanded by C. N. Madunagu, E. I. Madunagu, and others.
  Pearman's original work was not published.

ILOCANO

Ilocano is a regional language of La Union and Ilocos provinces in the Philippines. It is an AUSTRONESIAN language, with about five million speakers.

762.
Ernesto Constantino, *Ilokano dictionary*. Honolulu: University of Hawaii Press, 1971. 504 pp. 0–87022–152–3.
PALI language texts: Philippines.

INDO-ARYAN LANGUAGES

This large branch of the INDO-EUROPEAN LANGUAGES consists of languages of central and northern India and the Himalayas. The Indo-Aryan branch has a very long recorded history – back to the composition of the poems of the *Rgveda*, which are often dated to 1000 or even 1500 BC, though they were not written down for many centuries after that. They were composed somewhere in north-western India: a long migration had already separated prehistoric Indo-Aryan and Iranian speakers from the remainder of the Indo-European family, but the migration is completely unrecorded.

SANSKRIT is the language of the *Rgveda*, and the parent of the middle and modern Indo-Aryan languages, which are now spoken by over 600 million people in the Indian subcontinent and elsewhere.

Entries will be found in this book for PALI, PRAKRIT and ARDHAMAGADHI among middle Indo-Aryan languages, and for the following modern ones: ASSAMESE, BENGALI, DOGRI, GUJARATI, HINDI AND URDU, KASHMIRI, KONKANI, MARATHI, NEPALI, ORIYA, PANJABI, RAJASTHANI, ROMANI, SINDHI, SINHALA. Many others are excluded because no good dictionaries exist for them, notably Divehi, national language of the Maldives.

763.

Ralph L. Turner, *A comparative dictionary of the Indo-Aryan languages.*
London: Oxford University Press, 1962–6. 841 pp.
Accompanied by three supplementary volumes: *Indexes*, compiled by Dorothy Rivers Turner: 1969. – *Phonetic analysis*: 1971. – *Addenda et corrigenda*: 1985.

There are 14,189 numbered entries in the main sequence, arranged in alphabetical order under Sanskrit, or reconstructed proto-Indo-Aryan, forms (the latter marked * in accordance with custom). Entries (unnumbered) are also provided under the 'roots' familiar in Sanskrit and Indo-Aryan philology, with cross-references to the words that belong to them.

Additions and corrections are in several sequences, beginning in the main volume, pp. 821–36, 837–41. 'I regret that a further long list of corrigenda to the *Dictionary* must be added to [this] volume' (*Indexes*, pp. 355–7). '... Any further addenda assembled during the remainder of my life and unpublished at its end will be deposited in the Library of the School of Oriental and African Studies,' Turner continued. They were in fact gathered in the *Addenda et corrigenda* in 1985. 'A further volume of addenda to the *Comparative dictionary* is being prepared, with at present special reference to the older strata of the modern Indo-Aryan languages, and Apabhraṃśa, and Prakrit,' according to a note by Professor J. C. Wright in the 1989 printing of the main volume.

The *Comparative dictionary of the Indo-Aryan languages* represents a lifetime's development of the material that Turner began to work on in his *Nepali dictionary* (**1096**).

INDO-EUROPEAN LANGUAGES

The Indo-European (or Indo-Germanic or Aryan) family, recognised in outline before the end of the eighteenth century, includes nearly all the modern languages of Europe, many of those of central and southern Asia, and several early languages of great cultural significance, notably LATIN, GREEK, AVESTAN, SANSKRIT and PALI.

The concept of a language family, first elaborated in research on Indo-European, implies an ancestral language, a 'proto-language' from which all members of the family descend and which, if unrecorded (as is the case with proto-Indo-European) is theoretically reconstructable by comparing its descendents. But works such as Pokorny's dictionary of proto-Indo-European word roots (**771**) are really contributions to the historical study of the languages of the family. Pokorny can be seen as a kind of complement to the etymological dictionaries of individual languages and branches of the family. Two books that are more approachable, by Watkins (**772**) and Shipley (**781** –

not in alphabetical order), deal only with Indo-European roots that happen to have descendants in modern English.

Buck's comparative word-list (**765**) and Delamarre's lexicon (**766**) start from meanings rather than words: they stand to Pokorny rather as a thesaurus stands to a dictionary, and they help to provide the topic index which Pokorny does not have. Benveniste (**764**) goes further, rebuilding aspects of postulated proto-Indo-European thought patterns by way of the vocabulary; Gamkrelidze and Ivanov (**768**) carry out the same intention much more comprehensively, and try to show that the proto-language was spoken in eastern Anatolia. There are many attempts to link Indo-European with other language families, none of them totally consistent with one another (**773** to **780**).

Proto-Indo-European divided, several thousand years ago, into branches, each ancestral to one or several known languages. For the branches see ALBANIAN, ARMENIAN, BALTIC LANGUAGES, CELTIC LANGUAGES, GERMANIC LANGUAGES, GREEK, INDO-ARYAN LANGUAGES, IRANIAN LANGUAGES, ITALIC LANGUAGES, SLAVONIC LANGUAGES, TOCHARIAN. For the Anatolian branch, long extinct, see HITTITE.

Comparative dictionaries

764.

Emile Benveniste, *Le vocabulaire des institutions indo-européennes*. Paris: Editions de Minuit, 1969. 2 vols.

Edited by Jean Lallot.

Available in English translation by Elizabeth Palmer as: *Indo-European language and society*. Coral Gables: University of Miami Press (*Miami linguistics series*, 12); London: Faber, 1973.

[*The vocabulary of Indo-European society.*] A series of discussions of semantic areas, followed by a topic index, separate indexes by language, and a list of ancient texts cited.

765.

Carl Darling Buck, *A dictionary of selected synonyms in the principal Indo-European languages*. Chicago: University of Chicago Press, 1949. 1515 pp.

Reprints are in compact format.

Each easily read entry consists of a table of words in about thirty Indo-European languages (for the selection see p. xi: Albanian, Armenian, and modern Indian and Iranian languages are omitted), followed by an analysis of the semantic and etymological history. Entries are arranged by subject within 22 thematic chapters: English topic index, pp. 1505–15, but no index of foreign words.

766.

Xavier Delamarre, *Le vocabulaire indo-européen: lexique étymologique thématique*. Paris: Maisonneuve, 1984. 331 pp. 2–7200–1028–6.

[*The Indo-European vocabulary: an etymological thesaurus.*] Arranged by topics. Each entry, under reconstructed Indo-European form, is followed by a brief French gloss and selected derivatives. French–Indo-European glossary and index, pp. 313–30.

767.

August Fick, *Vergleichendes Wörterbuch der indogermanischen Sprachen.*
Göttingen: Vandenhoeck & Ruprecht, 1890–1909. 3 vols. 4th edn.

Contents of 4th edn: Vol. 1. A. Fick, *Wortschatz der Grundsprache, der arischen und der westeuropäischen Spracheinheit.* 1890. 580 pp. – Vol. 2: Whitley Stokes, *Urkeltischer Sprachschatz*, übersetzt, überarbeitet und herausgegeben von Adalbert Bezzenberger. 1894. 337 pp. Reprinted 1979. – Vol. 3: Alf Torp, *Wortschatz der germanischen Spracheinheit*, unter Mitwirkung von Hjalmar Falk. 1909. 573 pp. Reprinted 1979.

1st edn: *Wörterbuch der indogermanischen Grundsprache in ihrem Bestande vor der Völkertrennung.* 1868. 246 pp. – 2nd edn: 1870–71. 3 vols in 2 [1085 pp.]. – 3rd edn: 1874–6. 4 vols [844 + 802 + 372 + 503 pp.].

[*Comparative dictionary of the Indo-European languages.*] Vol. 1 contains a vocabulary of common Indo-European forms, pp. 1–154; of proto-Indo-Aryan, pp. 157–342; and of 'proto-West European' (not now usually recognised as a separate unit), pp. 345–580. Vol. 2 is a vocabulary of proto-Celtic, and vol. 3 of proto-Germanic, both with lengthy addenda.

The work is now very much outdated – but vols 2 and 3 have not truly been replaced.

768.

T. V. Gamkrelidze, V. V. Ivanov, *Indo-European and the Indo-Europeans: a reconstruction and historical analysis of a proto-language and a proto-culture.*
Berlin: Mouton De Gruyter, 1995. 2 vols. 3–11–009646–3.

English version 'compiled by Richard A. Rhodes; translated by Johanna Nichols'.

First published in Russian: Т. В. Гамкрелидзе, В. В. Иванов, *Индоэвропейский язык и индоэвропейцы* [*Indoevropeiskii yazyk i indoevropeitsy*].

Vol. 1: the structure of proto-Indo-European; semantic dictionary of the Proto-Indo-European language and reconstruction of the Indo-European proto-culture. Vol. 2: bibliography, pp. 1–107. Index of Indo-European roots, pp. 109–38; topic index in English of 'Proto-Indo-European semantemes', pp. 139–49; indexes of forms in individual languages, pp. 149–250; additional indexes of proper names, of taxonomic names for flora and fauna, and of ancient texts cited.

769.

Gerhard Köbler, *Indogermanisch–neuhochdeutsches und neuhochdeutsch–indogermanisches Wörterbuch.* Gießen, 1982. 388 pp. 2nd edn.

1st edn: 1980.

[*Indo-European–German and German–Indo-European dictionary.*] Not seen.

770.

Stuart E. Mann, *An Indo-European comparative dictionary.* Hamburg: Buske, 1984–7. 1682 pp.

See the review by Manfred Mayrhofer in *Kratylos* 34 (1989) pp. 41–5.

Entries are under reconstructed proto-Indo-European roots or forms, somewhat revised from those of Pokorny (**771**). Of little use because there is no index.

771.

Julius Pokorny, *Indogermanisches etymologisches Wörterbuch.* Bern: Francke, 1948–69. 2 vols [1183 + 495 pp.].

Vol. 2 contains the indexes, compiled by Harry B. Partridge. Both vols reprinted 1981.

Reviews: by Joshua Whatmough in *Language* vol. 25 (1949) pp. 285–90; by Gerhard Deeters in *Indogermanische Forschungen* vol. 60 (1952) pp. 317–20.
A reworking of: Alois Walde, Julius Pokorny, *Vergleichendes Wörterbuch der indogermanischen Sprachen*. Berlin: De Gruyter, 1927–32. 3 vols. This is still useful for its citations of older scholarly work, and was reprinted in 1973. It adopts the SANSKRIT alphabetical order. Vol. 3, the index, was compiled by Konstantin Reichardt. Reviews: by Antoine Meillet in *Litteris* vol. 6 (1929) pp. 1–6; by Friedrich Slotty in *Indogermanische Forschungen* vol. 51 (1933) pp. 143–8.

[*Indo-European etymological dictionary.*] Entries are under reconstructed proto-Indo-European root forms: but reconstructions vary. Thus Pokorny is to be approached, with patience, through the indexes. There are separate indexes for each language cited in the entries, and these indexes are arranged not alphabetically but in an order of precedence (see list of contents, vol. 2 pp. 493–5). Most likely to be cited in each case are ancient and medieval languages: etymological dictionaries for the separate branches of Indo-European may help to suggest which forms to search for here. Even the individual indexes are in a complicated alphabetical order and should be searched with care. The alphabetical order of the main work is, needless to say, not of the simplest.

772.

Calvert Watkins, *The American Heritage dictionary of Indo-European roots.* Boston: Houghton Mifflin, 1985. 113 pp. 0–395–37888–5.
Revised version of a section of the *American Heritage dictionary of the English language* (**364**).

A short glossary of reconstructed roots, with examples of derived forms (mainly from Greek, Latin and Germanic languages) followed by a full list of English derivatives, which are in small capitals. Index of these, pp. 81–110.

Proposed wider relationships

773.

Allan R. Bomhard, John C. Kerns, *The Nostratic macrofamily: a study in distant linguistic relationships.* Berlin: De Gruyter, 1994. 932 pp. 3–11–013900–6.
Trends in linguistics: studies and monographs, 74.
Earlier work: Allan R. Bomhard, *Toward proto-Nostratic: a new approach to the comparison of proto-Indo-European and proto-Afroasiatic.* Amsterdam: Benjamins, 1984. 356 pp. 90–272–3519–8. (*Current issues in linguistic theory*, 27.)

Consists partly of a lexicon of 601 reconstructed roots. There is no index by language, but there is an English–proto-Nostratic glossary and index of meanings, pp. 865–926. For Bomhard and Kerns, Nostratic includes Indo-European, Kartvelian, Afroasiatic, Uralic-Yukaghir, Elamo-Dravidian, Altaic, and with less confidence Sumerian, Chukchi-Kamchatkan, Gilyak, Eskimo-Aleut and Etruscan. They date the postulated parent language to 15,000 BC or earlier.

774.

Björn Collinder, *Indo-Uralisches Sprachgut: die Urverwandtschaft zwischen der indoeuropäischen und der uralischen (finnischugrischsamojedischen) Sprachfamilie.* Uppsala, 1934. 116 pp.

[*Indo-Uralic linguistic resources: the early relationship between the Indo-European and the Uralic (Finno-Ugro-Samoyedic) family.*]

775.

Владислав М. Иллич-Свитыч, *Опыт сравнения ностратических языков (семитохамитский, картвеьский, индоевропейский, уральский, дравидский, алтайский): сравнительный словарь* [Vladislav M. Illich-Svitych, *Opyt sravneniya nostraticheskikh yazykov*]. Moscow: Nauka, 1971–84. Vols 1–3 [no more published].

See also his preliminary work, 'Materialy k sravnitel'nomu slovaryu nostraticheskikh yazykov ...' in *Этимология* [*Etimologiya*] (1965) pp. 321–73.

[*Studies in the comparison of the Nostratic languages (Semito-Hamitic, Kartvelian, Indo-European, Uralic, Dravidian, Altaic): a comparative dictionary.*] The work remained incomplete.

776.

Aulis J. Joki, *Uralier und Indogermanen*. Helsinki: Suomalais-Ugrilainen Seura, 1973. 419 pp.

Suomalais-Ugrilaisen Seuran toimituksia, 151.

[*Uralians and Indo-Europeans.*] A list of reconstructed shared roots: 222 entries. Indexes by language, pp. 381–418, including Caucasian, Altaic, Palaeosiberian.

777.

Kalevi E. Koskinen, *Nilal: über die Urverwandtschaft des Hamito-Semitischen, Indogermanischen, Uralischen und Altaischen*. Helsinki, 1980. 155 pp. 951–99250–8–2.

[*Nilal: on the primitive unity of Hamito-Semitic, Indo-European, Uralic and Altaic.*]

778.

Hermann Möller, *Vergleichendes indogermanisch-semitisches Wörterbuch*. Göttingen: Vandenhoeck & Ruprecht, 1911. 316 pp.

Earlier version in Danish: Hermann Møller, *Indoeuropaeiskt-semitisk sammenlignende glossarium*. Copenhagen: Kjøbenhavns Universitet, 1909. (Festskrift udgivet af Kjøbenhavns Universitet i anledning af Universitets aarsfest.)

[*Indo-European and Semitic comparative dictionary.*] Entries are under reconstructed common roots. Addenda, pp. 273–4. Indexes by language: Indo-European languages, pp. 275–305; Semitic and Hamitic roots, pp. 305–16.

Other works of interest

779.

Saul Levin, *Semitic and Indo-European: the principal etymologies, with observations on Afro-Asiatic*. Amsterdam: Benjamins, 1995. 514 pp. 90–272–3632–1.

Current issues in linguistic theory, 129.

780.

Vitaly Shevoroshkin, editor, *Nostratic, Dene-Caucasian, Austric and Amerind*. Bochum: Brockmeyer, 1992. 552 pp. 3–8196–0032–9.

Materials from the First International Interdisciplinary Symposium on Language and Prehistory, Ann Arbor, 8–12 November, 1988. – Note Shevoroshkin's earlier work: *Dene-Sino-Caucasian languages*. 1991.

781.

Joseph T. Shipley, *The origins of English words: a discursive dictionary of Indo-European roots.* Baltimore: Johns Hopkins University Press, 1984. 636 pp.

INUIT

Inuit (often called Eskimo) is one of the Eskimo-Aleut languages, and the only language of the family that is in widespread everyday use, with about 65,000 speakers. Their habitat, when untrammelled by national frontiers, stretched from Greenland (where they are the dominant population) across the northern edge of Canada and Alaska to the Diomede Islands. The West Greenland dialect, under the name *Grønlandsk*, is one of the two official languages of Greenland (the other being Danish).

In Greenland Inuit is written in the Roman alphabet. In Siberia, it is written in Cyrillic (see Rubtsova, **783**). In Canada, since the mid-nineteenth century, a syllabary (based on the one that is used for CREE) has competed with the Roman alphabet.

782.

Aage Bugge [and others], *Dansk–grønlandsk ordbog.* [Nuuk]: Kalâtdlit-nunãne naKiterisitsissarfik, 1960. 739 pp.

    [*Danish–Inuit dictionary.*]

783.

Екатерина С. Рубцова, *Эскиммосско—русский словарь* [Ekaterina S. Rubtsova, *Eskimmossko–russkii slovar'*]. 1971. 644 pp.

    [*Inuit–Russian dictionary.*]

784.

Christian Wilhelm Schultz-Lorentzen, *Den grønlandske ordbog: grønlandsk-dansk.* København, Rosenberg, 1926. 360 pp.

Reprints include: Godthåb: Det Grønlandske Forlag, 1967.

    [*The Inuit dictionary: Inuit–Danish.*]

IRANIAN LANGUAGES

This branch of the INDO-EUROPEAN LANGUAGES is recorded over a very long period – at least 2500 years. Languages of the branch are now spoken from Dagestan to Pakistan, but with a concentration in Iran.

The two main Old Iranian languages, Old Persian and Avestan, are dealt with at AVESTAN. Middle Iranian includes BACTRIAN, KHOTANESE, KHWAREZMIAN, PEHLEVI and Sogdian. The best known of the modern Iranian languages is PERSIAN, but others with entries in this book are: BALUCHI, KURDISH, OSSETE, PASHTO, SHUGHNI.

Iranian studies are an exacting speciality, requiring the mastery of several scripts and the reading of difficult texts in several early languages. The business is not made easier by the absence of an up-to-date comparative dictionary of these languages: note, however, Bartholomae's *Altiranisches Wörterbuch* (**144**).

IRISH

Irish (with its offshoot, Scottish GAELIC) is the only surviving CELTIC language whose speakers remained outside the Roman Empire. It has the oldest literature in Europe after Greek and Latin. There are now only about 80,000 speakers of Irish as a mother tongue, though it is officially the first national language of Ireland.

The Irish alphabet

Modern Irish script is a local variant of the Latin alphabet, originating in medieval manuscripts. Irish can also be printed in Latin typefaces, and often is, but the script is seen on road signs and public notices throughout Ireland.

ᴀ b c ᴅ e ꝼ ᵹ h ı l m n o p ʀ s ꞇ u
ᴀ b c ᴅ e ꝼ ᵹ h ı l m n o p ꞃ ꞃ ꞇ u

Upper and lower case scarcely differ except for ʀ and s. An acute accent on a vowel marks length. Consonants may be written with a dot above to mark aspiration. When Irish is written in Latin script the dot is replaced by *h*, and there are other differences between the usual spellings in Irish and Latin scripts.

Historical dictionaries

785.

Carl Johan Sverdrup Marstrander, [Osborn Bergin, and other editors,] *Dictionary of the Irish language, based mainly on Old and Middle Irish materials*. Dublin: Royal Irish Academy, 1913–76.

Dictionary of the Irish language, based mainly on Old and Middle Irish materials. Compact edition. 1983. 632 pp. 0–901714–29–1.

Note also: Tomás de Bhaldraithe, *Innéacs nua-Ghaeilge don Dictionary of the Irish language.* Baile Atha Cliath: Acadamh Ríoga na hEireann, 1981. 78 pp. [*Modern Irish index to the Dictionary of the Irish language.*] See the review of the first part by Kuno Meyer in *Zeitschrift für celtische Philologie* vol. 10 (1915), alongside papers by Marstrander in *Norsk tidsskrift for sprogvidenskap* vol. 5 and in *Revue celtique* vol. 37 (1917/19).

Publication began with **D** and proceeded irregularly, with varying levels of completeness and revision. As a reminder of this, some parts were originally published under the title *Contributions to a dictionary of the Irish language*. The alphabetical order requires a sympathetic approach, naturally enough in view of the almost infinite number of spelling variations in earlier Irish texts.

The compact edition contains the whole original text, reprinted at small size. Additions and corrections for the letters **A**, **B**, **C**, **F** are gathered on pp. 631–2. The 'Historical note' on p. vi, by E. G. Quin, is new.

The modern standard

786.

Patrick S. Dinneen, ꝼoclóꞃ ʒaeꝺ'ilʒe aʒuꞃ béaꞃla = *An Irish–English dictionary, being a thesaurus of the words, phrases and idioms of the modern Irish language.* Dublin: Educational Company of Ireland, 1927. 1344 pp. New edn.

Published for the Irish Texts Society.

1st edn: ꝼoclóꞃ ʒaeꝺ'ilʒe aʒuꞃ béaꞃla. Dublin: Gill, 1904. 803 pp.

A concise dictionary with numerous example phrases. The Irish is in Irish script throughout. Paradigms of irregular verbs, pp. 1309–20; additions and corrections, pp. 1321–40 in two sequences. The second edition claims 'about 2½ times the amount of matter contained in the first edition'.

787.

Niall Ó Dónaill, *Foclóir Gaeilge–Béarla*. Baile Átha Cliath: Oifig an tSoláthair, 1977. 1309 pp. 1–85791–037–0.

Consulting editor, Tomás de Bhaldraithe.

[*Irish–English dictionary.*] Not well designed: the Irish, even lengthy phrases, is printed in a very bold broad face, and looks messy in later reprints. Still a copious up-to-date brief entry dictionary.

788.

Timothy O'Neil Lane, *Larger English–Irish dictionary*. Dublin: Educational Company of Ireland, 1916. 1748 pp.

789.

L. mc Cionnaiꞇ' [L. A. J. McKenna], ꝼoclóꞃ béaꞃla aʒuꞃ ʒaeꝺ'ilʒe = *English–Irish dictionary*. Baile Atha Cliath: Oifis Díolta Foillseachán Rialtais, 1935. 1546 pp.

An important concise dictionary of the modern language: 'We have decided to give what is actually said by native speakers.' Acknowledges local informants and sources, which are identified by county, in many entries: thus a useful source of information on dialect variation. Key to the abbreviations for source and dialect, pp. xv–xxii.

Older periods

790.

G. I. A. [G. I. Ascoli], 'Glossario dell'antica irlandese' in *Archivio glottologico italiano* vol. 6 (1879–1907) pp. v–cccclxxxvii.

Alternate title: 'Glossarium palaeohibernicum.'

[*Glossary of Old Irish.*] An etymological dictionary, arranged under base forms. The alphabetical order begins with the vowels and becomes more and more random, finally breaking off abruptly in the letter **C**, by which time a good deal of the alphabet has been covered. A collection of additions and corrections, pp. ccccvi–ccccxxxi.

791.

Séamus Caomhánach [and others], *Hessens Irisches Lexikon: kurzgefasstes Wörterbuch der alt- und mittelirischen Sprache mit deutscher und englischer Übersetzung = Hessen's Irish lexicon: a concise dictionary of early Irish with definitions in German and English.* Halle: Niemeyer, 1933–40. 2 vols.

A brief-entry dictionary that cites one textual or lexicographical source for most entries: abbreviations for sources, pp. xxi–xxvii. It was Dr Hans Hessen who planned this compilation of material from existing dictionaries and glossaries, but he 'fell on the field of battle' (Introduction).

792.

Kuno Meyer, *Contributions to Irish lexicography.* Halle: Niemeyer, 1906. Parts 1–2 [670 pp.].
Archiv für Celtische Lexikographie, Supplement.

'The following collection of words is the outcome of about twelve years desultory reading of Middle- and early Modern-Irish books and manuscripts.' Meyer usually quotes at least one text passage as context for each word, with precise references. The published collection covers **A–Dno**; additions and corrections, pp. i–xxxi.

Etymological dictionaries

793.

Joseph Vendryes, [E. Bachellery, P.-Y. Lambert,] *Lexique étymologique de l'irlandais ancien.* Dublin: Institute for Advanced Studies, 1959– .

[*Etymological dictionary of Old Irish.*] The dictionary is being published in parts and not in alphabetical order. So far six parts have appeared, covering **A–C** and **M–U**: the latest to date (**C**) appeared in 1987.

ITALIAN

Italian, one of the ROMANCE LANGUAGES that descend from Latin, has about 60 million speakers. It is the national language of Italy and one of the four national languages of Switzerland.

There is a long and honourable history of dictionary-making in Italy: historical and general dictionaries of the modern language are both good and plentiful. Dictionaries of older periods of Italian are not so easy to find. There is also a great number of dialect dictionaries. Some of the best-documented are listed at **802** onwards: note also the bibliography by Angelico Prati, *I vocabolari delle parlate italiane* (Rome, 1931. 68 pp.).

Etymological dictionaries are numerous (more than are listed below, **824** onwards). Foreign loanwords in Italian are dealt with to some extent by these: note also Hope (**502**), Serra (**827**), Pellegrini (**1257**) and Steiger (**1258**).

Historical dictionaries

794.

Salvatore Battaglia, *Grande dizionario della lingua italiana*. Turin: Unione Tipografico-Editrice Torinese, 1961– .

Chief editor, Giorgio Bárberi Squarotti.

Accompanied by: *Indice degli autori citati*. [1976.] 126 pp. [9th edn.] [*List of cited authors.*]

[*Big dictionary of the Italian language.*] A very large-scale but easily approachable historical dictionary, with numerous quotations from literature (in the narrow sense) both medieval and modern. As yet there is no bibliography of sources: these are cited precisely, but very laconically, in date order – but not explicitly dated – under each successive meaning. Etymologies are given briefly at the end of entries, preceded by =. Scientific and technical terms are included, but without quotations.

Sixteen volumes have appeared so far, covering **A–Sik**. A new cumulated edition of the list of cited authors appeared alongside each of vols 1–9 of the main work: I have not seen any later ones.

795.

Nicolò Tommaseo, Bernardo Bellini, *Dizionario della lingua italiana ... con oltre centomila giunte ai precedenti dizionari raccolte da Nicolò Tommaseo, Giuseppe Campi, Giuseppe Meini, Pietro Fanfani e da molti altri distinti filologi*. Turin, 1861–79. 4 vols.

Reissued: 1929. 6 vols.

On the work of Tommaseo, an important figure in Italian, Greek and Croatian culture, see Piero Tecchio, Ettore Poletti, *Bibliografia di Niccolò Tommaseo*. Milan: all'insegna del Pesce d'Oro, 1974. 125 pp.

[*Dictionary of the Italian language, with more than 100,000 additions to the earlier dictionaries by Tommaseo, Campi, Meini, Fanfani and other distinguished linguists.*] A large-scale dictionary of the Italian literary language illustrated with numerous well-chosen quotations from mainly older literature, with precise references. Tommaseo was the best-known of the lexicographers whose work went into this compilation. His own dictionary was *Nuovo dizionario de' sinonimi della lingua italiana* (5th edn: Milan, 1867. 1147 pp.).

In the 1929 edition, abbreviations for sources are in vol. 1 pp. lvi–cxxvii; additions and corrections, vol. 6 pp. 623–45.

796.

Vocabolario degli Accademici della Crusca. Florence: Tipografia Galileiana, 1863–1923. Vols 1–11. 5th edn.

Accompanied by a *Glossario* of uncommon and obsolete words, published in 1867 as a supplement to **A–B**.

1st edn: Venice: Giovanni Alberti, 1612. 960 pp. – 2nd edn: Venice: Jacopo Sarzini, 1623. – 'New edn': Venice: Combi e La Noù, 1686. – 3rd edn: Florence, 1691. – 4th edn: Florence: Manni, 1729–38. 6 vols. – 4th edn reprinted: Naples, 1746–8.

[*Dictionary of the Academicians of the Bran.*] A very large-scale dictionary with many quotations from Italian literature. The published volumes of the 5th edition, the only one likely to be much used now, cover **A–Ozioso**.

In the 4th edition, the latest that was completed, Italian glosses are often followed by translations in Latin, Greek and French and by discussion and quotations from literature. List of sources, vol. 8, first pagination, pp. 1–90; abbreviations, pp. 95–9; Latin index, vol. 8, second pagination, pp. 1–326; additions and corrections, vol. 8, third pagination, pp. 1–101.

The history of the dictionary, and the literary and linguistic academy that took responsibility for it, goes back to the end of the sixteenth century. A plan has been outlined for a new *Vocabolario storico della lingua italiana* ('VSLI') under the aegis of the Accademia della Crusca: it is to deal first with the early centuries of the language: see Avalle's paper (**828**).

The modern standard

797.

Vladimiro Macchi, general editor, *Sansoni-Harrap standard Italian and English dictionary*. London: Harrap, 1970–76. 2 parts in 4 vols [1472 + 1596 pp.].
Also published: Florence: Sansoni, 1970–75.

Considerably fuller than Reynolds (**799**) and, on a brief comparison, more reliable in its English. Gives taxonomic names for flora and fauna.

798.

Claudio Quarantotto, *Dizionario del nuovo italiano. 8000 neologismi della nostra lingua e del nostro parlare quotidiano dal dopoguerra ad oggi, con le citazioni dei personaggi che li hanno divulgati*. Rome: Newton Compton, 1987. 535 pp.
I manuali moderni, 24.

[*Dictionary of new Italian. 8000 new words of our language and our everyday speech, from the postwar period to today, with quotations of the writers and speakers who brought them into use.*] One to three quotations are given for each word, many of them from newspapers and magazines.

799.

Barbara Reynolds, general editor, *The Cambridge Italian dictionary*. Cambridge: Cambridge University Press, 1962–81. 2 vols [899 + 843 pp.].
Vol. 1 was reprinted with corrections in 1981.

A copious brief-entry dictionary which includes numerous technical terms: taxonomic names, as well as English popular ones, are given as glosses for Italian plant names.

As the introduction puts it, 'It is often assumed, quite wrongly, that the two parts of a bilingual dictionary should be the reverse of one another. Would that it were as easy as that! Or, to express it more concisely in Italian, *magari!*' Vol. 1, Italian–English, was designed to answer the question 'What does … mean?'; vol. 2, English–Italian, to answer 'How does one say …?'. Thus the dictionary is intended principally for English-speaking users, and perhaps especially for British ones, since 'Americanisms have been admitted sparingly'.

800.

Vocabolario della lingua italiana. Rome: Istituto della Enciclopedia Italiana, 1986–94. 4 vols in 5.

[*Dictionary of the Italian language.*] A very full dictionary of modern usage, with brief etymologies in square brackets and numerous brief example phrases (in italics), a few of which are attributed to literary authors, but without precise references. Many illustrations and diagrams. Explanation of entries, vol. 1 pp. xv–xxxviii; additions (including such new computer terminology as **backup**, **BBS** 'bulletin board' and **finestra** 'window'), vol. 4 pp. 1287–1305. Index of artists and other personal names in the illustration captions, vol. 4 pp. 1306–10.

Older periods

801.

Giorgio Colussi, *Glossario degli antichi volgari italiani.* Helsinki: Colussi; Foligno: Editoriale Umbra, 1983– .

Accompanied by: *Bibliografia dei volumi 1–4, 16/1, 16/2, 16/3.* Helsinki, 1994. 208 pp.

[*Glossary of the older Italian colloquials.*] A major historical dictionary of the non-Tuscan Italian dialects as recorded in documents and literary texts. Publication so far consists of vols 1 to 4 part 4 (**A–Duttore**) and vol. 16 parts 1–8 (**S–Svuotare**).

Regional forms

802.

Max Pfister, *Lessico etimologico italiano.* Wiesbaden: Reichert, 1979– .

Accompanied by: *Supplemento bibliografico.* 1991. 271 pp. 2nd edn. (1st edn: 1979. 119 pp.)

[*Italian etymological dictionary.*] This is most important for its coverage of Italian dialects (the same may be said of von Wartburg's *Französisches etymologisches Wörterbuch*, **501**, for French). The structure of the dictionary is in fact modelled on von Wartburg's, though the layout is more spacious and more approachable.

At each entry a dating of first recorded use is followed by a full list of dialect variants, then, often, by an etymological explanation of these. The coverage includes Corsican, Monégasque (the dialect of Monaco), and the Italian dialects of Switzerland and Slovenia. It naturally excludes SARDINIAN, OCCITAN and Franco-Provençal dialects spoken in Italy (for the last two see von Wartburg). FRIULIAN is also excluded, but LADIN is included.

Vol. 5 of this very ambitious dictionary has just been completed, taking the coverage so far from **A** to **Birotulare**. The *Supplemento bibliografico* contains the following aids: general abbreviations, pp. 1–2; order in which dialect forms are cited in the dictionary, pp. 3–22; alphabetical list of dialects and sources of infortmation for them, pp. 23–82, using abbreviations which are then explained in the main bibliography and list of abbreviations for sources, pp. 83–226; abbreviations for authors and collectors of oral records, pp. 227–71.

Corsica

803.

Mathieu Ceccaldi, *Dictionnaire corse–français Pieve d'Evisa*. Paris: Klincksieck, 1968. 25cm

Études linguistiques, 6.

[*Corsican–French dictionary of the Piève d'Evisa dialect.*] A brief-entry bilingual dictionary but with some longer entries of ethnographical interest and some short etymological notes. Words beginning with prefixes are listed under the base form (for example, **Sparte** 'share out' is filed under **P**), confusing the alphabetical order. I haven't discovered why some entries are marked with a cross.

Italy

804.

Angelo Biella [and others], *Vocabolario italiano–lecchese, lecchese–italiano, preceduto da una grammatica essenziale e da un saggio di toponomastica lecchese*. Oggiono: Cattaneo, 1992. 804 pp.

[*Italian–Leccese and Leccese–Italian dictionary, with a basic grammar and a study of Leccese place names.*] The Leccese–Italian dictionary, pp. 241–804, is the main feature. In this, entries conclude with historical-etymological notes, marked off by =.

805.

Guiseppe Boerio, *Dizionario del dialetto veneziano*. Venice: Santini, 1829. 802 pp.

[*Dictionary of the Venetian dialect.*] A very large-scale discursive dictionary, providing many example phrases. Additions, pp. 753–98; last-minute additions, p. 799; corrections, pp. 801–2.

806.

Manlio Cortelazzo, Carla Marcato, *Dizionario etimologico dei dialetti italiani*. Turin: UTET, 1992. 404 pp. 88–7750–039–5.

[*Etymological dictionary of the Italian dialects.*] Selective (about 2500 entries). Each entry gives geographical origin, standard Italian gloss, historical and etymological discussion, and sometimes a quotation from an ethnographical source. Includes LADIN, FRIULIAN, SARDINIAN and Sicilian. Bibliography: pp. xiii–xxx.

807.

Raffaele D'Ambra, *Vocabolario napoletano–toscano domestico di arti e mestieri*. Naples, 1873. 548 pp.

[*Neapolitan–Tuscan dictionary of the jargons of arts and crafts.*] A very full, well-documented dictionary, actually covering a wide spectrum of the local vocabulary of Naples. List of sources, pp. i–v.

808.

Francesco D'Ascoli, *Nuovo vocabolario dialettale napoletano: repertorio completo delle voci, approfondimenti etimologici, fonti letterarie, locuzioni tipiche*. Naples: Gallina, 1993. 866 pp.

[*New Neapolitan dialect dictionary: complete word-list, etymologies in depth, literary sources, typical expressions.*] Relatively brief entries, but with room for interesting etymological notes and for citations of printed sources. Abbreviations and bibliography, pp. xv–xx.

809.

Mario Doria, *Grande dizionario del dialetto triestino, storico, etimologico, fraseologico*. Trieste: Trieste Oggi, 1991. 1022 pp.
With the collaboration of Claudio Noliani.

[*Big dictionary of the Triestine dialect, historical, etymological and idiomatic.*] The standard Italian gloss is often followed by a quotation or a citation from a printed source. Most entries have a second paragraph, marked off by ||, with geographical, historical and etymological notes. There is a long supplement of additional entries, pp. 831–1022.

810.

Libero Ercolani, *Vocabolario romagnolo–italiano, italiano–romagnolo*. Ravenna: Edizioni del Girasole, 1994. 907 pp. New edn. 88–7567–237–7.
Spine title: *Nuovo vocabolario romagnolo–italiano, italiano–romagnolo*.
2nd edn: 1971. 915 pp.

[*Romagnol–Italian and Italian–Romagnol dictionary.*] The Romagna is the hinterland of Ravenna. This is a brief-entry dictionary, but with some quotations from printed sources, and some etymologies. Taxonomic names are provided for flora. The Italian–Romagnolo section, much briefer, is on pp. 701–915.

811.

Antonio Garrisi, *Dizionario leccese–italiano*. Cavallino di Lecce: Capone, 1990. 2 vols [845 pp.].

[*Leccese–Italian dictionary.*] There are illustrations (by Maria Teresa Tronci) for ethnographical realia and especially for flora and fauna, but no taxonomic names for these. Brief etymologies are given in square brackets.

812.

Angelico Prati, *Etimologie venete*. Venice: Istituto per la Collaborazione Culturale, 1968. 211 pp.
Edited by Gianfranco Folena, Giambattista Pellegrini.

[*Venetian etymologies.*]

813.

Emmanuele Rocco, *Vocabolario del dialetto napolitano*. Naples: Chiurazzi, 1890–91. Parts 1–17 [pp. 1–680; no more published]. Enlarged edn.
1st edn: 1882.

[*Dictionary of the Neapolitan dialect.*] An important work, fully documented with quotations. Published parts of the 1890–91 edition cover **A–Feletto**; publication apparently ceased abruptly, and there are no preliminaries or list of abbreviations for source texts. I have not seen the 1882 edition.

814.

Gerhard Rohlfs, *Dizionario dialettale delle Tre Calabrie, con note etimologiche e un'introduzione sulla storia dei dialetti calabresi*. Halle: Niemeyer, 1932–9. 2 parts in 3 vols.

Followed by: Gerhard Rohlfs, *Vocabolario supplementare dei dialetti delle Tre Calabrie (chi comprende il dialetto greco-calabro di Bova) con repertorio toponomastico*. Munich, 1965–7. 2 vols [621 pp.]. (Bayerische Akademie der Wissenschaften, Philosophisch-historische Klasse. *Abhandlungen*, N.F., 64, 66.) [*Supplementary dictionary of the dialects of the three provinces of Calabria, including the Greek-Calabrian dialect of Bova, with an index of place names.*]

[*Dialect dictionary of the three provinces of Calabria, with etymological notes and an introduction on the history of the Calabrian dialects.*] The main work consists of part 1 (2 vols): Calabro–Italiano; part 2: Italiano–Calabro. In the Calabrian–Italian part, the dialects of the three provinces are separately identified as *C* Cosenza, *M* Catanzaro, *R* Reggio Calabria, and subdivided, partly geographically (on the basis of original fieldwork by Rohlfs), partly according to written sources of information: for details see vol. 1 pp. 44–51 with vol. 2 pp. 427–8 and with pp. 8–13 and 419–20 of the *Vocabolario supplementare*. Rohlfs's alphabetical order wants some study: note that **B** is interfiled at **V**, and also that his invented letter **X χ** files between **K** and **L**.

The supplementary volume is arranged thus: main sequence, pp. 17–413; late additions, pp. 421–524; latest additions of all, pp. 525–6; standard Italian–Calabrian index, pp. 527–84; indexes of words cited in etymologies, by language, 585–612.

Place names are dealt with chiefly in the supplementary volume. There is an index of them, pp. 613–18, in which they are marked *A* if they are to be found among the 'late additions', *D* if they are in the original three-volume dictionary. Those not so marked are to be found in their alphabetical order on pp. 17–413.

815.

Gennaro Vaccaro, *Vocabolario romanesco belliano e italiano–romanesco*. Rome: Romana Libri Alfabeto, [1970]. 819 pp.

[*Roman–Italian and Italian–Roman dictionary of the vocabulary of Belli.*] The poet Giuseppe Gioachino Belli (1791–1863) wrote copiously and vigorously in the local dialect of Rome. Entries begin with an etymology in round brackets, then a gloss and comments, then one or more quotations from Belli's work, with precise references.

Sicily

816.

Salvatore Giarrizzo, *Dizionario etimologico siciliano*. [Palermo:] Herbita, [1989]. 388 pp.

[*Sicilian etymological dictionary.*] Relatively brief entries give a standard Italian gloss followed by a dash and an etymology (which is, naturally, sometimes conjectural).

Introduction, mainly on historical phonology, pp. 1–42. On the Arabic loanwords in Sicilian see also Steiger (**1258**).

817.

Giorgio Piccitto, [Giovanni Tropea,] *Vocabolario siciliano*. Catania, 1977– .
Centro di Studi Filologici e Linguistici Siciliani, Opera del Vocabolario Siciliano.

[*Sicilian dictionary.*] This is a major dictionary of the modern Sicilian dialects. Careful glosses are followed by a listing of dialect forms. No etymologies are given (see Giarrizzo, above, for these). Abbreviations for printed sources, vol. 3 pp. xii–xix; for place names, pp. xix–xxvi, with map. List of informants, vol. 1 pp. xvii–xxiii.

So far three volumes have appeared, covering **A–Q**.

Switzerland

818.

Silvio Sganzini, [Rosanna Zeli,] editors, *Vocabolario dei dialetti della Svizzera italiana*. Lugano: La Commerciale, 1952– .
Accompanied by a supplementary volume.

[*Dictionary of the dialects of Italian-speaking Switzerland.*] A very detailed dictionary mainly of the local spoken dialects. A list of towns and villages covered, a bibliography and a list of abbreviations are all to be found in the supplementary volume – but maps came as loose inserts with vol. 1 part 1. A table of sound correspondences among dialects is to be found in the supplementary volume, pp. 65–82.

So far 50 parts have appeared, covering **A–Capelada** and extending into vol. 4.

For the other big dictionaries of the local languages of Switzerland see **491**, **609**, **1293**.

Slang and special vocabularies

819.

Enrico Falqui, Angelico Prati, *Dizionario di marina, medievale e moderno*. Rome, 1937. 1366 pp.
With the assistance of Carlo Bardesono di Rigras and Augusto de Januari. *Dizionari di arti e mestieri*, 1.

[*Dictionary of seamanship, medieval and modern.*] Not seen.

820.

Ernesto Ferrero, *Dizionario storico dei gerghi italiani: dal Quattrocento a oggi*. Milan: Mondadori, 1991. 442 pp. 88–04–35174–8.

[*Historical dictionary of Italian argots, from the fifteenth century to today.*] A discursive dictionary with some attributed quotations (but no precise references) and with historical-etymological notes. Standard Italian–argot index, pp. 385–424; bibliography, pp. 427–42.

821.

Gianfranco Lotti, *Le parole della gente: dizionario dell' italiano gergale, dalle voci burlesche medievali ai linguaggi contemporanei dei giovani*. Milan: Mondadori, 1992. 88–04–35657–X.

Oscar dizionari.

[*The people's speech: dictionary of Italian argots, from the vocabulary of medieval farces to the youth language of today.*]

822.

Ugo Nanni, *Enciclopedia delle ingiurie*. Milan: Ceschina, 1953. 413 pp.

[*Encyclopaedia of insults.*] Consists partly (pp. 261–396) of an alphabetical dictionary with quotations from literature. Index of authors quoted and mentioned, pp. 399–411.

823.

Angelico Prati, *Voci di gerganti, vagabondi e malviventi, studiate nell'origine e nella storia*. Pisa: Giardini, 1978. 172 pp. New edn with a biographical note and revisions by Tristano Bolelli.

Orientamenti linguistici, 3.

1st edn: 1940. 227 pp.

[*The vocabulary of thieves, tramps and crooks: its origins and history* ('thieves' is not the *mot juste*, but Reynolds, **799**, didn't give me a translation for *gerganti*).] Highly important etymological dictionary of the jargons of the Italian underworld, with references to printed sources and to scholarly literature, and sometimes lengthy discussion. But all too brief – only 383 entries, with another 22 in the supplement (pp. 159–63). Word index, pp. 165–70. Notes and corrections by Bolelli, 171–2.

Etymological dictionaries

824.

Carlo Battisti, Giovanni Alessio, *Dizionario etimologico italiano*. Florence: Barbèra, 1950–57. 5 vols [4132 pp.].

Supplemented by: Giovanni Alessio, 'Nuove postille al *Dizionario etimologico italiano*' in *Biblioteca del Centro di Studi Filologici e Linguistici Siciliani* vol. 6 (1962) pp. 59–110.

[*Italian etymological dictionary.*] Entries are more concise and less readable than those of Cortelazzo and Zolli (**825**). The present dictionary is important for its greater range of vocabulary: note the inclusion of many more technical terms and, particularly, of dialect words.

825.

Manlio Cortelazzo, Paolo Zolli, *Dizionario etimologico della lingua italiana*. Bologna: Zanichelli, 1979–88. 5 vols [1470 pp.].

[*Etymological dictionary of the Italian language.*] A full and readable work. Entries generally include the date of first recorded use and a list of derived and compound forms, followed by a second paragraph (marked •) giving origins and history. Bibliography, vol. 5 pp. iii–xvii; abbreviations (including language names), vol. 5 pp. xviii–xx.

826.

K. Jaberg, J. Jud, *Index zum Sprach- und Sachatlas Italiens und der Südschweiz: ein propädeutisches etymologisches Wörterbuch der italienischen Mundarten.* Bern: Stämpfli, 1960. 744 pp.

[*Index to the Linguistic and ethnographical atlas of Italy and southern Switzerland: a preliminary etymological dictionary of the Italian dialects.*] A full listing of dialect words, including a separate list for ROMANSCH (pp. 631–91), but a long way from an etymological dictionary.

827.

Luigi Serra, *Sopravvivenze lessicali arabe e berbere in un'area dell'Italia meridionale: la Basilicata.* Naples: Istituto Universitario Orientale, 1983. 63pp.
Istituto Universitario Orientale. *Supplemento agli Annali,* 37.

[*Arabic and Berber linguistic survivals in a region of southern Italy: Basilicata.*] With detailed notes on local dialect variation and on the origin of the loanwords.

Other works of interest

828.

D'Arco Silvio Avalle, 'Le lexique italien des origines et l'informatique linguistique' in W. Pijnenburg, F. de Tollenaere, editors, *Proceedings of the Second International Round Table Conference on Historical Lexicography* (Dordrecht: Foris, 1980) pp. 175–97.

ITALIC LANGUAGES

A branch of the INDO-EUROPEAN LANGUAGES. The best known member was LATIN. Others were Oscan, Umbrian (see **830**) and Faliscan. These local languages of pre-Roman Italy became extinct as Latin spread to the whole of Italy – and beyond – in the last two centuries BC.

829.

Frederik Muller, Jzn, *Altitalisches Wörterbuch.* Göttingen: Vandenhoeck & Ruprecht, 1926. 583 pp.
Göttinger Sammlung indogermanischer Grammatiken und Wörterbücher.

[*Old Italic dictionary.*] Entries are under reconstructed proto-Italic forms, which are then followed by recorded forms in Latin, other Italic languages and selectively in other Indo-European languages. In the index, Latin forms predominate: those in Italic languages are picked out by abbreviations such as *osk. umbr. vo.*

830.

Alfred Ernout, *Le dialecte ombrien: lexique du vocabulaire des "Tables Eugubines" et des inscriptions*. Paris: Klincksieck, 1961.
Etudes et commentaires, 38.

[*The Umbrian dialect: dictionary of the vocabulary of the Iguvine Tables and the inscriptions.*] The texts, pp. 14–50; the vocabulary, classified, with comments, etymologies and conjectures, pp. 53–139. Alphabetical index, pp. 141–5.

JAPANESE

Japanese has no known relatives, though some have claimed to align Japanese with the Altaic languages (a postulated family including Turkic, Mongolian and Tungusic languages), while Benedict has now produced some evidence for a link with the AUSTRO-TAI family (**143**).

Japanese is the national language of Japan, with 120 million speakers. Throughout its history Japanese has been heavily influenced by Chinese, although the two languages are structurally utterly unalike. Japanese is written partly with Chinese characters, partly in a syllabic script.

This entry lists only a few dictionaries that are approachable by a user who is not fully familiar with Japanese script.

831.

F. Brinkley, *An unabridged Japanese–English dictionary, with copious illustrations*. Tokyo: Sanseido, 1896. 1687 pp.
Co-authors F. Nanjo, Y. Iwasaki, K. Mitsukuri for zoological terms, J. Matsumura for botanical terms.
Added title page in Japanese: *Wa–Ei daijiten*.
Reprinted with an introduction by E. B. Ceadel: Cambridge: Heffer, 1963. 2 vols.

Both headwords and example phrases are given in Latin transliteration and Japanese script: the transliteration is now outdated in a few respects. The alphabetical order is that of the Latin transliteration. A brief-entry dictionary, but 'its pages contain a surprising number of words, forms and meanings not found even in Japanese–Japanese dictionaries' (Ceadel). Taxonomic names and many illustrations of plants and animals.

832.

Jack Halpern, editor in chief, *New Japanese–English character dictionary*. Tokyo: Kenkyusha, 1990. 226a + 1992 pp. 4–7674–9040–5.

Arranged by character pattern, with various indexes (see charts in endpapers).

833.

Hisao Kakehi, Ikuhiro Tamori, Lawrence Schourup, *Dictionary of iconic expressions in Japanese*. Berlin: Mouton de Gruyter, 1996. 2 vols [1431 pp.].
With the assistance of Leslie James Emerson. *Trends in linguistics. Documentation*, 12.

Essentially these 'iconic expressions' are onomatopoeias, if the term is understood in the widest possible sense. This is a full dictionary of modern Japanese usage centred on this specialised field of vocabulary. It is arranged under the 'iconic expressions' as keywords (in alphabetical order of Latin transliteration), with long example sentences in Japanese (Japanese script) and in English translation. Most examples have a precise reference to a literary or journalistic source. The dictionary is much more generally useful than might appear at first glance, and is particularly approachable to users not yet wholly familiar with Japanese.

834.
Kenkyusha's New Japanese–English dictionary. Tokyo: Kenkyusha, 1974. 2110 pp. [0–317–59317–X.] Edited by K. Masuda.
1st edn: 1918. – 2nd edn: [reprinted] 1942. 2292 pp. – 3rd edn: 1954.

A very large brief-entry dictionary, with headwords in Japanese script and Latin transliteration, arranged in Latin alphabetical order. Compounds and phrases are given in Japanese script only.

835.
Shogakukan Random House English–Japanese dictionary. [Tokyo:] Shogakukan, 1973. 4 vols.

Intended for Japanese users, this large bilingual dictionary into Japanese is based on the *Random House dictionary of the English language*. Japanese glosses are in script only.

836.
Oreste Vaccari, E. E. Vaccari, *Vaccari's standard English–Japanese dictionary*. Tokyo: Vaccari's Language Institute, 1967. 2319 pp. 0–7101–0021–3.
Earlier work: O. Vaccari, E. E. Vaccari, *A. B. C. Japanese-English dictionary: an entirely new method of classification of the Chinese-Japanese characters*. Tokyo: O. Vaccari, 1950. 2 vols [1746 pp.].

A large-scale brief-entry dictionary. Glosses are in both script and Latin transliteration.

JAVANESE

Javanese has more speakers than any other AUSTRONESIAN language – about 75 million – and is a major language of Indonesia, but not the national language (see MALAY). Javanese literature, in its native script of Indic origin, dates back at least a thousand years. Arabic script was later used for Javanese; the Latin alphabet is most often used today, though the old script is still known.

The modern standard

837.
J. F. C. Gericke, T. Roorda, *Javaansch–Nederlandsch handwoordenboek*. Amsterdam: Muller, 1901. 2 vols.

[*Concise Javanese–Dutch dictionary.*] This substantial work has headwords and examples in kawi script, and is useful for providing scientific Latin glosses for botanical and zoological terms. Addenda, vol. 2 pp. 807–72.

838.

Elinor Clark Horne, *Javanese–English dictionary*. New Haven: Yale University Press, 1974. 728 pp. [0–300–01689–1.]

A substantial dictionary of the modern language, in roman script, with plenty of brief examples. Sadly, many botanical terms are glossed with vague phrases such as 'a certain kind of flower'. Phonology, spelling, morphology, pp. x–xxvii; social registers, pp. xxxi–xxxiii; alphabetical lists of initial and final 'disguising elements', pp. xxxv–xxxix.

839.

Th. Pigeaud, *Javaans–Nederlands handwoordenboek*. Groningen, 1938. 624 pp.
[*Concise Javanese–Dutch dictionary.*]

840.

Th. Pigeaud, *Nederlands–Javaans handwoordenboek*. Groningen, 1948. 663 pp.
[*Concise Dutch–Javaans dictionary.*] The largest bilingual dictionary into Javanese that I have come across.

841.

S. Prawiro Atmodjo, *Bausastra Jawa*. Surabaya: Djojo Bojo, 1987. 471 pp.
[*Javanese dictionary.*] A concise monolingual dictionary of modern Javanese. Supplement of modern loanwords, pp. 437–71.

842.

S. Prawiroatmodjo, *Bausastra Jawa–Indonesia*. Jakarta: Gunung Agung, 1981. 2 vols.
[*Javanese– Indonesian dictionary.*] About 40,000 brief entries.

Older periods

843.

P. J. Zoetmulder, S. O. Robson, *Old Javanese–English dictionary*. The Hague: Nijhoff, 1982. 2 vols [2368 pp.] 90–247–6178–6.

A splendid work: 25,500 entries (entirely in romanisation) with many sub-headings for compounds. Of these entries over half are for words of Sanskrit derivation: for these, where necessary, semantic changes are noted on the basis of the *Sanskrit–English dictionary* of Monier-Williams (**1357**). List of source texts, pp. xviii–xxii: precise references, and contexts, appear in the entries. A long-needed replacement for van der Tuuk (**163**).

JINGHPAW

Jinghpaw or Chingpho or Kachin, a SINO-TIBETAN language, has about 750,000 speakers in Burma and Yunnan. It has been described as the 'linguistic crossroads' of the Sino-Tibetan family, showing similarities with Tibetan to the north, with Burmese to the south and with Yi and its relatives to the east. The English influence on Jinghpaw results from the work of American Baptist missionaries: they also devised the Latin orthography in which Jinghpaw is normally written.

844.

O. Hanson, *A dictionary of the Kachin language*. Rangoon: American Baptist Mission Press, 1906. 752 pp.

Reprinted: Rangoon: Baptist Board of Publications, 1954.

A Jinghpaw–English dictionary, in the standard Latin alphabet, which does not mark tones: 'It would be useless to burden these pages with tonal marks in regard to which no two Europeans would ever agree.'

About 15,000 entries, including numerous example sentences, which are accompanied by English translations. There are also many verse quotations, apparently of proverbs etc., but these are not translated.

845.

Manam Hpang, *English Kachin Burmese dictionary = Inglik Jinghpaw Myen ga htai chyum*. Myitkyina, 1977. 644 pp.

This includes appendices of technical terms: fruit, vegetables, diseases, animals, insects, reptiles, fishes, birds, trees and flowers, colours.

JUDEZMO

In origin a variant of Spanish, Judezmo is the ROMANCE language spoken by the Sephardim, the Jewish communities that settled in the Balkans and western Turkey after their mass expulsion from Spain and Portugal in 1492. Perhaps 100,000 speakers still remain, now mainly in Israel. Judezmo differs most obviously from Spanish in its script: like other Jewish languages, it is customarily written in the Hebrew alphabet.

Judezmo is also called Spaniol and Judaeo-Spanish. Ladino is the term for a special form of Judezmo, scrupulously avoiding Hebrew loanwords, which is used in the explanation of Hebrew religious texts.

Apart from the dictionaries listed below, Judezmo is covered in the slowly growing Spanish historical dictionary, *Diccionario histórico de la lengua española* (**1432**).

846.

David M. Bunis, *A lexicon of the Hebrew and Arabic elements in modern Judezmo*. Jerusalem: Magnes Press, The Hebrew University, 1993. 512 pp. 965–223–803–1.

Studies in Jewish languages. The Language Traditions Project: Dictionary of Hebrew and Aramaic components in Jewish languages of the Mediterranean Basin. Institute of Jewish Studies, The Hebrew University of Jerusalem.

Added imprint: Misgav Yerushalayim, Institute for Research on the Sephardi and Oriental Jewish Heritage.

The 4233 entries are 'arranged alphabetically according to the traditional Jewish-letter spellings they receive in Modern Judezmo'. Headwords in Hebrew script; entries in romanised Judezmo with English explanations. Entries are numbered, a great help in cross-reference to those users who are unfamiliar with Hebrew script.

'Judezmo and its Hebrew and Aramaic component: an introduction', pp. 15–51. User's guide, pp. 53–63; important bibliography, including sources of quotations, pp. 65–82; romanised index of forms, pp. 463–508.

847.

Joseph Nehama, *Dictionnaire du judéo-espagnol*. Madrid, 1977. 609 pp. 84–00–03613–1.

Consejo Nacional de Investigaciones Científicas, Instituto "Benito Arias Montano".

[*Dictionary of Judaeo-Spanish.*] A dictionary of usage, with French glosses. There are no citations or quotations, but one-word etymologies are given for words of non-Spanish origin.

KALENJIN

Kalenjin, including Nandi and other dialects, is a NILO-SAHARAN language of north-western Kenya, with two and a half million speakers.

848.

A. C. Hollis, *The Nandi: their language and folk-lore*. Oxford: Clarendon Press, 1909. 328 pp.

Reprint 'edited with a new introduction by G. W. B. Huntingford' and some corrections in the vocabulary, 1969. 328 pp. 0–19–823132–6.

The original edition has an introduction by Sir Charles Eliot, and plates. These are omitted in the reprint.

Part 1: history and anthropology, pp. 1–151, including folk tales (in English translation only), p. 101ff.; proverbs and 'enigmas' [riddles], bilingual, p. 124ff.

Part 2: Nandi grammar, pp. 152–317, including English–Nandi vocabulary, pp. 232–312; list of Nandi trees, plants etc., p. 313.

The work is still cited by anthropologists, though in view of the hostility aroused by the recent British conquest, 1890–1906, Hollis had wisely 'collected his material outside the Nandi country from five informants, and the book is a tribute to the accuracy of those informants … His principal informant, Arap Chepsiet, sometimes introduced himself to visiting officials as "the man who wrote Bwana Hollis's book"' (according to G. W. B. Huntingford).

KANNADA

Kannada is one of the DRAVIDIAN LANGUAGES. With about 27 million speakers it is the state language of Karnataka state, India.

Kannada script: the consonant characters

ಕ ಖ ಗ ಘ ಜ ಚ ಛ ಜ ಥ ಇ ಟ ಠ ಡ ಢ ಣ ತ ಥ ದ ಧ ನ ಪ ಫ ಬ ಭ ಮ ಯ ರ ಲ ವ ಶ ಷ ಸ ಹ ಳ

k kh g gh ṅ c ch j jh ñ ṭ ṭh ḍ ḍh ṇ t th d dh n p ph b bh m y r ṛ l v ś ṣ s h ḷ

The Kannada alphabet is in all essential features identical with that of Telugu, though it has its own typical printed style. Consonants are combined with following vowels to form a single symbol.

BASED ON A FONT BY VIJAY K. PATEL

849.

М. С. Андронов, М. А. Дашко, В. А. Макаренко, *Каннада–русский словарь: около 35.000 слов* [M. S. Andronov, M. A. Dashko, V. A. Makarenko, *Kannada–russkii slovar': okolo 35.000 slov*]. Moscow: Russkii Yazyk, 1979. 762 pp.

Edited by Umapati Tumkura; with a Kannada grammar by M. S. Andronov.

[*Kannada–Russian dictionary: about 35,000 words.*]

850.

Kannada Sahitya Parisattina Kannada nighantu. Bengalore: Kannada Sahitya Parisattu, 1964– .

See N. Basavaradhya, 'Preparation of Kannada–Kannada dictionary on historical principles' in Misra (**10**).

[*Kannada dictionary of the Kannada Literary Academy.*] A historical dictionary covering Kannada literature from AD 850 to 1800, with quotations and precise references. Etymologies immediately follow the main entry: the principal categories are *sam.* 'Sanskrit' and *de.* '*desya*, native'; for the latter, cognates in other Dravidian languages are given. To be complete in seven volumes.

851.

Kittel's Kannada–English dictionary. Madras: University of Madras, 1968– 1971. 4 vols. New edn by M. Mariappa Bhatt.

1st edn: Ferdinand Kittel, *A Kannada–English dictionary*. Bangalore: Basel Mission Book & Tract Depository, 1894. 1752 pp. – 1st edn reprinted: New Delhi: Asian Educational Services, 1983.

A concise bilingual dictionary with citations and brief quotations from Kannada texts, giving precise references. Headwords are in Kannada script and in transliteration. Taxonomic names are given for fauna and flora.

The new edition adds nearly 8000 new entries, as well as new glosses and quotations, particularly for *desya* words. It also adds citations and quotations of a wide range of older Kannada literature, some of it unpublished and unknown in Kittel's time.

852.

Pi. Ke. Rajasekhara, Bi. Vi. Vasantakumar, *Pada vivarana kosa.* Mysore: Honnuru Janapada Gayakaru, 1993. 87 pp.

[*Dictionary of word history.*] A Kannada etymological dictionary.

KARACHAI-BALKAR

A TURKIC language of the northern Caucasus. The Karachai and Balkar see themselves as distinct peoples, but in language they scarcely differ. There are about a quarter of a million speakers.

853.

Е. Р. Тенишев, Х. И. Суйунчев, *Карачаево-балкарско–русский словарь: около 30.000 слов* [E. R. Tenishev, Kh. I. Suiunchev, editors, *Karachaevo-*

balkarsko–russkii slovar': okolo 30.000 slov]. Moscow: Russkii Yazyk, 1989.
830 pp.
Authors: S. A. Gochiyaeva, Kh. I. Suiunchev. Ordena Pocheta Karachaevo-Cherkesskii Nauchno-
Issledovatel'skii Institut Istorii, Filologii i Ekonomiki.
  [*Karachai-Balkar–Russian dictionary: about 30,000 words.*]

KAREN LANGUAGES

The Karen languages, differing quite fundamentally from the Tibeto-Burman languages
such as Burmese, are still evidently members of the SINO-TIBETAN family. There are
about four million speakers in total, in the mountains and valleys that separate southern
Burma from central Thailand.

854.
Geo. E. Blackwell, *The Anglo–Karen dictionary*. Rangoon: Baptist Board of
Publications, 1954. 543 pp.
Earlier version: J. Wade, Mrs J. P. Binney: *The Anglo–Karen dictionary*. Rangoon: American Baptist Mission
Press, 1883. 781 pp.
  A bilingual dictionary with English headwords and Karen glosses.

855.
Sau Kau-too, J. Wade, *Thesaurus of the Karen knowledge, comprising
traditions, legends or fables, poetry, customs, superstitions, demonology,
therapeutics etc., alphabetically arranged and forming a complete native Karen
dictionary, with definitions and examples illustrating the usages of every word.*
Tavoy, 1847–50. 4 vols.

856.
J. Wade, *A dictionary of the Sgau Karen language*. Rangoon: American Baptist
Mission Press, 1896. 1341 pp.
Assisted by Mrs S. K. Bennett; recompiled and revised by E. B. Cross.
Earlier version: J. Wade: *A vocabulary of the Sgau Karen language*. Tavoy: Karen Mission Press, 1849. 1024
pp.
  This is a Karen–English dictionary in the Karen script, which was adapted from
Burmese script under missionary influence.

KARTVELIAN LANGUAGES

Geographically this is one of the two families of CAUCASIAN LANGUAGES. The
Kartvelian and North Caucasian language families appear not to be linked. Some
propose a link between Kartvelian and Indo-European: see Illich-Svitych (**775**).
  Kartvelian is a small grouping whose best known member is GEORGIAN. It includes
three other languages. Svan has about 40,000 speakers in the central Caucasian valleys.
Mingrelian is the mother tongue of perhaps 500,000 people in the north-western districts

of Georgia. In north-eastern Turkey, in the valleys near the Black Sea coast, 50,000 people or more speak Laz , also known as Tsan.

857.

Arnold S. Čikobava, *Čanur–megrul–kartuli šedarebiti leksiḳoni = Dictionnaire comparé tchane–mégrélien–géorgien*. Tbilisi, 1938. 510 pp.

[*Comparative dictionary of Tsan, Mingrelian and Georgian.*] Not seen: cited from *Wörterbücher* (**12**).

858.

Heinz Fähnrich, Surab Sardshweladse, *Etymologisches Wörterbuch der Kartwel-Sprachen*. Leiden: Brill, 1995. 682 pp. 90–04–10444–5.

Handbuch der Orientalistik. Erste Abteilung, Der Nahe und der Mittlere Osten = Handbook of oriental studies. The Near and Middle East, 24.

Previously published in Georgian: Heinc Penrixi, Zurab Sarjvelaze, *Kartvelur enata eṭimologiuri leksiḳoni*. Tbilisi: Tbilisis Universiṭeṭis Gamomcemloba, 1990. 618 pp. 5–511–00330–1. See the review by G. A. Klimov in *Voprosy yazykoznaniya* 1993 no. 2 pp. 135–8.

Some material had previously appeared in a series of papers: Heinz Fähnrich, 'Kartwelischer Wortschatz' in *Georgica* vols 5–8 (1982–5).

Bibliography, pp. 578–97.

859.

Георгий А. Климов, *Этимологический словарь картвельских языков* [Georgii A. Klimov, *Etimologicheskii slovar' kartvel'skikh yazykov*]. Moscow: Nauka, 1964. 306 pp.

Additions in Georgii A. Klimov, 'Dopolneniya k *Etimologicheskomu slovaryu kartvel'skikh yazykov*' in *Этимология* [*Etimologiya*] (1971) pp. 356–67.

A revised edition in English has been announced: Georgij A. Klimov, *Etymological dictionary of the Kartvelian languages*. Berlin: Mouton de Gruyter, 1998. 3–11–015658–X.

[*Etymological dictionary of the Kartvelian languages.*]

KASHMIRI

Kashmiri, with about three million speakers, belongs to the INDO-ARYAN branch of the Indo-European family. Urdu is the language of administration, both in Pakistani Kashmir (where Urdu is also the national language) and in Indian Kashmir: Kashmiri is, however, growing in importance as a language of literature. It is normally written in a form of Arabic script.

860.

Sir George A. Grierson, *A dictionary of the Kāshmīrī language, compiled partly from materials left by the late Paṇḍit Īśvara Kaula*. Calcutta: Asiatic Society of Bengal, 1916–32. 1252 pp.

Assisted by Mukundarama Sastri.
Reprinted: Delhi: B.R., 1985. 4 vols.

Headwords are in a phonetic script (Grierson's own romanisation of Pandit Isvara Kaula's revised Kashmiri alphabet) filed in Latin alphabetical order – but beginning with all words that begin with a vowel (any vowel). Each headword is also given in Devanagari script, or in Arabic script if recorded only in that script. Taxonomic names are given for flora.

The Pandit's Kashmiri alphabet employed modifications of Nagari and Sharada symbols to denote vowel sounds. For a discussion see Georg Morgenstierne, 'The phonology of Kashmiri' in *Acta orientalia* vol. 19 (1943) pp. 79–99, reprinted in his *Irano-Dardica* (Wiesbaden: Reichert, 1973) pp. 277–97.

861.

Es. Ke. Toskha Khani [and other editors], *Kasir diksnari.* Srinagar: Jammu aind Kasmir Ikadami af Art, Kalcar aind Langvejiz, 1972–9. 9 vols.
See S. K. Toskhakhani, 'The Kashmiri dictionary' in Misra (**10**).

[*Kashmiri dictionary.*] In Kashmiri, in an adapted form of Urdu ('Perso-Arabic') script with added diacritics, the script now accepted as standard in Kashmir. Based on Grierson's dictionary (**860**) with numerous additions from later research. Dialect words are excluded.

KAZAKH

Kazakh is the TURKIC language of Kazakhstan, the largest state of formerly Soviet Central Asia. There are about eight million speakers, including significant minorities in Russia and in China.

Kazakh alphabetical order

а ә б в г ғ д е ё ж з и й к қ л м н ң о ө п р с т у ұ ү ф х һ ц ч ш щ ъ ы і э ю я

The modern standard

862.

А. Ы. Ысқақов, *Қазақ тілінің түсіндірме сөздігі* [A. Y. Ysqaqov, *Qazaq tilining tüsindirme sözdigi*]. Almaty, 1974–86. 10 vols.

[*Kazakh explanatory dictionary.*] Many quotations from literature, attributed to authors but with no precise references.

863.

Myrzabekova Q., Abdikarimova Q., Abdighaliev S., *Kasachisch–deutsches Wörterbuch*. Almaty: Rauan, 1992. 380 pp. 5–625–01848–0.

[*Kazakh–German dictionary.*] A brief-entry bilingual dictionary with about 31,000 entries.

864.

Н. Т. Сауранбаев, *Русско–казахский словарь* [N. T. Sauranbaev, *Russko–kazakhskii slovar'*]. Moscow, 1954. 935 pp.

[*Russian-Kazakh dictionary.*]

Regional forms

865.

Н. А. Баскаков, *Каракалпакско–русский словарь* = *Қарақалпақша-русша соɜлик* [N. A. Baskakov, editor, *Karakalpaksko–russkii slovar'*]. Moscow, 1967. 1124 pp.

Earlier edn: 1958. 892 pp.

Note also: N. A. Baskakov, editor, *Russko-karakalpakskii slovar'*. Moscow, 1947. 831 pp. [*Russian-Karakalpak dictionary.*]

[*Karakalpak–Russian dictionary.*] Dictionary of Karakalpak, a Kazakh dialect of Uzbekistan, which was given the status of a separate literary language under Soviet rule. About 30,000 entries, with a grammatical sketch. The alphabetical order is а ә б в г ғ д е ё ж з и й к қ л м н ң о ө п р с т у ұ ү ф х ҳ ц ч ш щ ъ ы ь э ю я.

866.

Qazaq tilining dialektologiialyq sozdigi. Almaty: Ghylym, 1996– . 5–628–01088–X.

Edited by Sh. Sarybaev, A. Nurmaghambetov. Qazaqstan Respublikasynyng Ghylym Ministrligi-Ghylym Akademiiasy. A. Baitursynov Atyndaghy Til Bilimi Instituty.

There was a much smaller earlier work under the same title: Zh. Dosqaraev, *Qazaq tilining dialektologiialyq sozdigi.* Alma-Ata, 1969. 426 pp. Akademiya Nauk Kazakhskoi SSR, Institut Yazykoznaniya.

[*Dialect dictionary of the Kazakh language.*] Vol. 1, the only one so far, covers **A–E**.

Etymological dictionaries

867.

Краткий этимологический словарь казахского языка [*Kratkii etimologicheskii slovar' kazakhskogo yazyka*]. Almaty: Ghylym, 1966. 240 pp.

Editors, A. Ysqaqov, R. Syzdyqova, Sh. Sarybaev.

At head of title: Qazaq SSR Ghylym Akademiyasy. Til Bilimi Instituty.

[*Little etymological dictionary of the Kazakh language.*] Bibliography, pp. 233–40.

868.

Л. З. Рустемов, *Казахско–русский толковый словарь арабско-иранских заимствованных слов* [L. Z. Rustemov, *Kazakhsko–russkii tolkovyi slovar' arabsko-iranskikh zaimstvovannykh slov*]. Almaty: Mektep, 1989. 320 pp. 5–625–00684–9.

[*Explanatory Kazakh–Russian dictionary of Arabic and Iranian loanwords.*]

KHANTY

A minority URALIC language of the middle Ob valley in western Siberia, and one of the closest relatives of Hungarian. There are about 12,000 speakers. The older name given by outsiders to the language was Ostyak.

869.

K. F. Karjalainens Ostjakisches Wörterbuch. Helsinki: Suomalais-Ugrilainen Seura, 1948. 2 vols [1199 pp.].

Edited by Y. H. Toivonen. *Lexica Societatis Fenno-Ugricae*, 10.

[*K. F. Karjalainen's Ostyak dictionary.*] Information collected in the course of ethnographical expeditions between 1898 and 1902. A copious Khanty–Finnish–German dictionary with indication of dialect variation (abbreviations for place names, p. xxxii). German index, pp. 1121–99. Corrections, pp. xxxiv–xxxv.

870.

H. Paasonens Ostjakisches Wörterbuch, nach den Dialekten an der Konda und am Jugan. Helsinki: Société Finno-Ougrienne, 1926. 334 pp.

Edited by Kai Donner. *Lexica Societatis Fenno-Ugricae*, 2.

[*H. Paasonen's Ostyak dictionary.*] A glossary from oral sources, based on information gathered in 1900–1901. In the transcription of the Société Finno-Ougrienne, with quotations of example sentences and with some etymological information.

German index, pp. 303–32, referring to the entry numbers, 1–3064, which appear in the left margin of the pages of the dictionary.

871.

Н. И. Терешкин, *Словарь восточно-хантыйских диалектов* [N. I. Tereshkin, *Slovar' vostochno-khantyiskikh dialektov*]. Leningrad: Nauka, 1981. 544 pp.

Akademiya Nauk SSSR, Institut Yazykoznaniya.

[*Dictionary of eastern Khanty dialects.*] In a phonetic script. Glosses in Russian.

KHASI

An AUSTROASIATIC language of the Indian state of Meghalaya, with about half a million speakers.

872.

E. Bars, *Khasi–English dictionary.* Shillong: Don Bosco, 1973. 1000 pp.

873.

Lili Rabel-Heymann, 'Analysis of loanwords in Khasi' in *Austroasiatic studies* ed. Philip N. Jenner and others (Honolulu: University Press of Hawaii, 1976) pp. 971–1034.

Includes (pp. 987–1033) a glossary of Indo-Aryan loanwords in Khasi.

KHAZAR AND KARAITE

Khazar was the language of the Khazar empire that flourished a thousand years ago in the Russian steppes. There are no long texts in Khazar, but the language can be partly reconstructed from words and phrases in non-Khazar records. It was apparently a TURKIC language. Karaite, a language of Jewish communities in Poland, Lithuania and the Crimea, with a few hundred speakers in total, may be regarded as a descendant of Khazar.

874.

N. A. Baskakov, A. Zaionchkovskii, S. M. Shapshal, editors, *Karaimsko-russko-pol'skii slovar'*. Moscow: Russkii Yazyk, 1974. 687 pp.

[*Karaite-Russian-Polish dictionary.*] Not seen: cited from the British Library catalogue.

875.

Peter B. Golden, *Khazar studies: an historico-philological inquiry into the origins of the Khazars*. Budapest: Akadémiai Kiadó, 1980. 2 vols.
Bibliotheca orientalis hungarica, 25.

Includes a listing and study of all recorded words and names in the Khazar language. Vol. 2 reproduces extracts from texts in Arabic, Greek, Armenian, Hebrew and Persian that contain Khazar vocabulary.

KHMER

Khmer or Cambodian belongs to the AUSTROASIATIC LANGUAGES. It is the national language of Cambodia, with about eight million speakers. The oldest dated Khmer inscription goes back to AD 611, and there are important literary texts from later periods.

876.

Dhanan Chantrupanth, Chartchai Phromjakgarin, *Photchananukrom Khamen (Surin)–Thai–'Angkrit = Khmer (Surin)–Thai–English dictionary*. Bangkok, 1978. 593 + 94 pp.
Khrongkan Wichai Phasa Thai læ Phasa Phunmuang Thin Tang Tang, Sathaban Phasa, Chulalongkon Mahawitthayalai.

A trilingual dictionary of the Khmer dialect spoken in Surin province, Thailand.

877.

Rüdiger Gaudes, *Wörterbuch Khmer–Deutsch*. Leipzig: VEB Verlag Enzyklopädie, 1985. 2 vols [1321 pp.]. 3–324–00291–5.

[*Khmer–German dictionary.*]

878.

Ю. А. Горгониев, *Кхмерско—русский словарь* [Yu. A. Gorgoniev, *Kkhmersko–russkii slovar'*]. Moscow: Russkii Yazyk, 1984. 983 pp.
Edited by Long Seama.
Earlier version: 1975. 952 pp.

[*Khmer–Russian dictionary.*] About 20,000 entries, followed by a brief grammatical sketch on pp. 904–52.

879.

J. Guesdon, *Dictionnaire cambodgien–français*. Paris: Plon, 1930. 2 vols (1982 pp.).

[*Khmer–French dictionary.*] The work was compiled in the late nineteenth century and long remained in manuscript. About 20,000 entries, many of considerable length, with cross-references and notes to explain etymology. Outdated but still useful. Tables of alphabet and numerals, pp. 7*–12*.

880.

Robert K. Headley [and others], *Cambodian–English dictionary*. Washington: Catholic University of America Press, 1977. 2 vols [1495 pp.]. 0–8132–0509–3.
Bureau of Special Research in Modern Languages. *Publications in the languages of Asia*, 3.

A very comprehensive work; about 30,000 entries with many sub-entries. Khmer script, phonetic transcription, gloss; includes indication of origin of loanwords. 'The text was prepared on a Varityper machine with a Khmer font which inexplicably lacked certain letters:' nonetheless clear printing. 13 plates (at end of vol. 2) giving terminology for agricultural implements, musical instruments, etc. Brief introduction includes notes on script and alphabetical order.

881.

Franklin E. Huffman, Im Proum, *English–Khmer dictionary*. New Haven: Yale University Press, 1978. 690 pp. 0–300–02261–1.
Yale linguistic series.

About 28,000 brief entries, very clearly printed in a letter-quality typewriter face. Short introduction.

882.

Judith M. Jacob, *A concise Cambodian–English dictionary*. London: Oxford University Press, 1974. 242 pp. 0–19–713574–9.
School of Oriental and African Studies.

About 8000 entries: spacious layout makes the work easy to read. Khmer script followed by phonetic transcription and English glosses. Extensive notes on orthography, transcription, alphabetical order etc., pp. xi–xxxii.

883.

Tep Yok, Thao Kun, *Dictionnaire français–khmer*. Phnom-Penh: Librairie Bouth-Neang, 1962–4. 2 vols.
Abridged edition: Tep Yok, Thao Kun, *Petit dictionnaire français–khmer*. Phnom-Penh: Librairie Phnom-Penh, 1967. 1377 pp. Another version of this, reprinted without attribution: *Petit dictionnaire français khmer*. Boulogne Billancourt: Alliance Christian et Missionaire [*sic*]; Groningen: Comite Hulpverlenning Z. O. Asie, n.d. [about 1977]. 808 pp.

[*French–Khmer dictionary.*] The largest bilingual dictionary into Khmer: about 50,000 entries with many phrases and specimen sentences. Addenda in preliminary pages.

884.

Vacananukrama Khmera = Dictionnaire cambodgien. Phnom-Penh: Buddhasasanapandity, 1967–8. 2 vols [1858 pp.]. 5th edn.

This was reprinted with a new introduction: N. p. [1981]. 1888 pp. 'Under the auspices of the Japan Committee for the Republication and Relief of Cambodian Buddhist Books.' – Another reprint: Tokyo: Japan Sotoshu Relief Committee, 1990. Added title in Japanese: *Kanbojia kokugo jiten.*

1st edn: Phnom Penh: Editions de la Bibliothèque Royale du Cambodge, 1938–43. – 2nd edn: 1951. – 4th edn: 1962.

[*Khmer dictionary.*] A medium-scale work (about 25,000 entries, many of some length), the first and still the only seriously useful dictionary that is entirely in Khmer.

In the first edition there was difficulty in the choice of spellings for many words whose initial consonant varies between aspirated and unaspirated. Sanskrit and Pali loanwords appear in an etymological spelling distant from modern pronunciation and from the usage of many earlier authors: see François Martini, 'De la réduction des mots sanskrits passés en cambodgien' in *Bulletin de la Société de Linguistique de Paris* vol. 50 (1954) pp. 244–61.

KHOISAN LANGUAGES

Like CAUCASIAN LANGUAGES, this heading covers not a single language family but a geographical grouping of them. They have in common that they are non-Bantu aboriginal languages of southern Africa; they also share a phonetic feature, the use of clicks, but this feature is also common to neighbouring Bantu languages including Xhosa and Zulu.

The Khwe languages are those of the people once called 'Hottentots': perhaps 150,000 speakers remain, most of them speakers of Nama. Namibia takes its name from them. The San or Bushman languages, of which there are apparently three families, have only a few thousand speakers in total.

885.

Dorothea F. Bleek, *A Bushman dictionary*. New Haven: American Oriental Society, 1956. 773 pp.

American Oriental series, 41.

Earlier work: Dorothea F. Bleek, *Comparative vocabularies of Bushman languages*. Cambridge, 1929. (University of Cape Town. *Publications of the School of African Life and Language.*)

A Bushman–English dictionary (686 pp.) followed by an English index. Reproduced from the author's typescript, this work compiles all then-available lexicographical material on the Bushman or San languages.

886.

Christopher Ehret, 'The first spread of food production to southern Africa' in *The archaeological and linguistic reconstruction of African prehistory* ed. C. Ehret, M. Posnansky (Berkeley: University of California Press, 1982) pp. 158–81.

Cited for tables 11–13, pp. 172–81, which are 'core vocabularies' of Khwe or Central Khoisan languages and short lists of early loanwords.

KHOTANESE

Khotanese was a Middle IRANIAN language, spoken in the Silk Route city of Khotan in modern Xinjiang (China), from about AD 300 to 1000, by a community far separated from its linguistic relatives. Khotanese was afterwards completely forgotten: texts in the language have been rediscovered and deciphered in modern times. It was written in an Indic script.

887.

H. W. Bailey, *Dictionary of Khotan Saka*. Cambridge: Cambridge University Press, 1979. 559 pp. 0–521–21737–7.

Additions, corrections and further discussion in: R. W. Emmerick, P. O. Skjærvø, *Studies in the vocabulary of Khotanese*. Vienna, 1982–7. 2 vols.

This is a concise dictionary mainly of the native Iranian element in the vocabulary, with source references, some brief quotations, English glosses, and parallel and cognate words from other Iranian languages and from additional languages of central Asia (e.g. Tibetan). Modestly described as 'no more than one contribution to the far vaster project of the etymological dictionary of all Iranian languages ... A strictly personal book; there has been no wish to list the different interpretations and etymological connexions proposed by others'.

Latin script in the usual Indological transliteration: no script table. Entries are in SANSKRIT alphabetical order, **A** to **H**. Indexes of words from Iranian languages, pp. 513–49; Tokharian, p. 549; 'Old Indian' (Sanskrit, Pali etc.) pp. 550–5; Greek, pp. 557–9. No indexes of other Indo-European or of any non-Indo-European forms.

Many source references are to the six volumes of Bailey's *Khotanese texts*, cited simply as *I–VI*; for further abbreviations see preface, p. ix, and bibliography, pp. xi–xvii.

KHWAREZMIAN

An extinct middle IRANIAN language of the lower Oxus valley.

888.

Johannes Benzing, *Chwaresmischer Wortindex*. Wiesbaden: Harrassowitz, 1983. 734 pp. 3–447–02362–7.

Edited by Zahra Taraf; introduction by Helmut Humbach.

[*Khwarezmian word index.*] In consonantal transcription. No transliteration table.

KIKUYU

A Bantu language of the NIGER-CONGO family, Kikuyu (or Gikuyu) is a major regional language of Kenya, with some four and a half million speakers.

889.

A. R. Barlow, *English–Kikuyu dictionary*. Oxford: Clarendon Press, 1975. 332 pp. 0–19–864407–8.
Edited by T. G. Benson.

890.

T. G. Benson, editor, *Kikuyu–English dictionary*. Oxford: Clarendon Press, 1964. 562 pp.

KLAMATH

A Penutian language, perhaps to be included in the wider AMERIND family. There are about a hundred remaining speakers of this North American Indian language, in north-western Oregon.

891.

M. A. R. Barker, *A Klamath dictionary*. Berkeley: University of California Press, 1963. 550 pp.
University of California publications in linguistics, 31.

KOMI

Komi or Zyrian is one of the URALIC LANGUAGES. It has about 350,000 speakers in the Arctic north-eastern extremity of European Russia.

892.

D. R. Fokos-Fuchs, *Syrjänisches Wörterbuch*. Budapest: Akadémiai Kiadó, 1959. 2 vols [1564 pp.].
[*Komi dictionary*.] A dialect dictionary in the transcription of the Société Finno-Ougrienne. Additions, pp. 1559–64. German–Komi index, pp. 1299–1554; index of (very few) Latin taxonomic names, p. 1555.

893.

Yrjö Wichmann, *Syrjänischer Wortschatz nebst Hauptzügen der Formenlehre*. Helsinki: Suomalais-Ugrilainen Seura, 1942. 486 pp.
Lexica Societatis Fenno-Ugricae, 7.
[*Komi vocabulary with outlines of the morphology*.] The Komi is in the transcription of the Société Finno-Ougrienne: the alphabetical order requires study. The Komi–German dictionary gives dialect variants (list of dialects, p. xiv) and a few quotations of example phrases. Brief etymological information at end of each entry. German index, pp. 412–86. Corrections, p. 487. Additional etymological notes, pp. 363–5. Grammar of word forms, based on the Vychegda dialect, pp. 368–411.

KONGO AND KITUBA

Kongo, a member of the Bantu branch of NIGER-CONGO LANGUAGES, has at least seven million speakers of its two main varieties. These are Kongo itself, direct descendant of the language of the kingdom of Kongo, with a long history of European interest; and Kituba, which grew up as the trade language of the routes that led to the inland kingdom from the Portuguese-dominated coast. Although the kingdom of Kongo and its overland trade have disappeared, Kituba remains – in two distinct regions to the south-east and to the north-west of the great city of Kinshasa.

894.

W. Holman Bentley, *Dictionary and grammar of the Kongo language as spoken at San Salvador, the ancient capital of the old Kongo Empire, West Africa.* London: Baptist Missionary Society, 1887. 718 pp.
Compiled and prepared for the Baptist Mission on the Kongo River, West Africa.
Reprinted: Farnborough: Gregg, 1967.

895.

J. van Wing, C. Penders, editors, *Vocabularium P. Georgii Gelensis: le plus ancien dictionnaire Bantou = het oudste Bantu-woordenboek.* Louvain: Imprimerie J. Kuyl-Otto, 1928. 365 pp.
Bibliothèque Congo, 27.

[*Father Georges de Gheel's glossary: the earliest Bantu dictionary.*] Publication, with French and Dutch glosses, of a manuscript Latin–Spanish–Kongo dictionary compiled in manuscript about 1652 by the Belgian Capuchin Georges de Gheel (Joris Willemsz. van Gheel), apparently on the basis of earlier work by a Spaniard, Roboredo.

896.

K. E. Laman, *Dictionnaire kikongo–français, avec une étude phonétique décrivant les dialectes les plus importants de la langue dite Kikongo.* Brussels, 1936. 1183 pp.
Reprinted: Ridgewood, New Jersey: Gregg Press, 1964. 2 vols.

[*Kongo–French dictionary, with a description of the major dialects of the so-called Kongo language.*] Dialect variation is noted in the body of the dictionary. The Kongo is in a Latin script that makes use of some extra characters (alphabetical order, p. xcii) and with diacritical marks for tones. Abbreviations, including names of major dialects, p. iii.

897.

François Lumwamu, *Lexique kikongo–français.* Brazzaville, 1976– .

[*Kongo–French dictionary.*] Each volume is devoted to a dialect or dialect group, vol. 1 to 'Munukutuba' (Kituba).

898.

Pierre Swartenbroeckx, *Dictionnaire kikongo– et kituba–français: vocabulaire comparé des langages kongo traditionnels et véhiculaires.* Bandundu, 1973. 815 pp.

CEEBA. *Publications*, 3rd series, 2.

[*Kongo–French and Kituba–French dictionary: a comparative vocabulary of the Kongo traditional and trade languages.*]

KONKANI

Konkani is the INDO-ARYAN (and thus Indo-European) language of the Indian coast southwards from Bombay to Goa. It shows more Portuguese influence than any other Indo-Aryan language, and is customarily written, since the sixteenth century, in the Latin alphabet – though Devanagari, Kannada and Malayalam scripts have also been used. The standard Latin spelling of Konkani is based on Portuguese orthography, and has no diacritical marks. Konkani has about one and a half million speakers.

899.

Sebastião Rodolpho Dalgado, *Diccionario Komkanî–Portuguez philologico-etymologico composto, no alphabeto Devanâgarî, com a translitteração segundo o systema Jonesiano = Konkani–Portuguese dictionary =* कोंकणी—पोरचीज़ शब्दकोष. Bombay: Indu-Prakash, 1893. 561 pp.

Reprinted: New Delhi: Asian Education Services, 1983.
Companion work: *Diccionario portuguez–komkanî.* Lisbon, 1905. 906 pp. [*Portuguese–Konkani dictionary.*]

[*Philological and etymological Konkani–Portuguese dictionary, arranged in the Devanagari alphabet, with transliteration according to the Jones system.*] The 'Jones system' is the International Phonetic Alphabet.

900.

श्रीपदरघुनाथदेसाय | कोंकणी शब्दकोश = Shripad Raghunath Desay, *Konkani shabdakosha.* Pedane, Goa: Srisitarama Prakasana; Pune: Saundayalahari Prakasana, 1980–90. 4 vols [1352 pp.].

[*Konkani dictionary.*] A bilingual Konkani–Marathi dictionary.

901.

L. Suneetha Bai, *Konkani–Hindi–Malayalam dictionary, with origin of words and meaning in English = Konkani–Hindi–Malayalama kosa.* Cochin: Cochin University of Science and Technology, 1987– .

A quadrilingual dictionary with etymologies.

902.

Angelus Francis Xavier Maffei, *An English–Konkani dictionary.* Mangalore, 1883. 545 pp.

His *A Konkani–English dictionary* (1883. 157 pp.) was published alongside this. The two have been reprinted in a single volume: New Delhi: Asian Educational Services, 1983. 545 + 157 pp.

The English–Konkani dictionary is entirely in Latin script.

KOREAN

Korean has no known linguistic relatives, unless, as some scholars now believe (see **908**), there is a distant link with Mongolian, Tungusic and other languages that have been grouped as 'Altaic'.

Korean is the national language of Korea. There are significant minorities in China, Japan, Kazakhstan and Uzbekistan, and perhaps 63 million speakers in total. This entry deals only with a small selection of Korean dictionaries, particularly some that are more approachable to users not wholly familiar with the script.

Hangul – Chosongul

ㄱ ㄲ ㄴ ㄷ ㄸ ㄹ ㅁ ㅂ ㅃ ㅅ ㅆ ㅇ ㅈ ㅉ ㅊ ㅋ ㅌ ㅍ ㅎ

k kk n t tt l m p pp s ss ng ch tch ch' k' t' p' h

ㅏ ㅐ ㅑ ㅒ ㅓ ㅔ ㅕ ㅖ ㅗ ㅘ ㅙ ㅚ ㅛ ㅜ ㅝ ㅞ ㅟ ㅠ ㅡ ㅢ ㅣ

a æ ya yæ ŏ e yŏ ye o wa wæ oe yo u wŏ we wi yu ŭ ŭi i

All writing in Korea was in the Chinese script, until 1443/4, when King Sejong, of the Chosŏn dynasty, invented the remarkable alphabet now known to southerners as *Hangŭl* 'Korean writing', to northerners as *Chosŏngŭl*. It has been rightly hailed as one of the most scientifically designed and efficient scripts in the world. Each sound is represented by a single, always indentifiable letter form, and each syllable by a block.

FONT: SORAWIN BY RHA SOOHYUN

903.

Ellit'u Han–Yong taesajon = Si-sa elite Korean–English dictionary. Seoul: Sisa Yongosa, 1995. 2520 pp. 89–17–00030–4.

Editor, Min Yong-bin. Sisa Yongosa, Sajon P'yonch'ansil.

Earlier title: *The new world comprehensive Korean–English dictionary*. Seoul: Si-sa-yong-o-sa, 1979. 2519 pp.

904.

James S. Gale, *Unabridged Korean–English dictionary*. Seoul: Christian Literature Society of Korea, 1931. 1781 pp. 3rd edn by Alexander A. Pieters.

1st edn: *A Korean–English dictionary*. Yokohama, 1897. – 2nd edn: Seoul, 1911.

Claims 75,000 entries. Gale aimed to highlight the native Korean vocabulary, as against Chinese and Japanese loanwords.

905.

S. E. Martin [and others], *A Korean–English dictionary*. New Haven: Yale University Press, 1967. 1902 pp. 0–300–00753–1.

A large-scale brief-entry bilingual dictionary with 'emphasis on the basic native Korean vocabulary. Limited entries for Chinese loanwords and very few for European loans ... Etymologies indicated where known' (annotation from *Walford's guide to reference material*).

906.

The new world comprehensive English–Korea dictionary. Seoul: Si-sa-yong-o-sa, 1979. 2959 pp.

907.

Л. Б. Никольский, Ch`oe Chon-hui, *Большой кореиско–русский словарь* [L. B. Nikol'skii, Ch`oe Chon-hui, *Bol'shoi koreisko–russkii slovar'*]. Moscow: Russkii Yazyk, 1976. 2 vols.

Akademiya Nauk SSSR. Institut Vostokovedeniya Cho-Ro Taesajo. Choson Minjujuui Inmin Konghwaguk Sahoe Kwahagwon, Unohak Yon'guso.

[*Big Korean–Russian dictionary.*] The Korean is in Korean script only, followed where needed by Chinese character spellings in brackets.

908.

G. J. Ramstedt, *Studies in Korean etymologies*. Helsinki: Suomalais-Ugrilainen Seura, 1949–53. 2 vols.

Mémoires de la Société Finno-Ougrienne, 95. Vol. 2 was edited after the author's death by Pentti Aalto. See also: G. J. Ramstedt, *Paralipomena of Korean etymologies*. 1982. 295 pp. Collected and edited by Songmoo Kho. (*Suomalais-Ugrilaisen Seuran toimituksia* = *Mémoires de la Société finno-ougrienne,* 182.)

KUKI-CHIN AND NAGA LANGUAGES

These SINO-TIBETAN LANGUAGES are spoken in the hills that mark the boundary between north-eastern India and western Burma. There are perhaps two million speakers.

909.

Ephraim W. Clark, *Ao-Naga dictionary*. Calcutta: Baptist Mission Press, 1911. 977 pp.

910.

J. Herbert Lorrain, *A dictionary of the Abor-Miri language*. Shillong: Assam Government, 1907. 572 pp.

911.

James Herbert Lorrain (Pu Buanga), *Dictionary of the Lushai language*. Calcutta: Royal Asiatic Society of Bengal, 1940. 576 pp.

An enlargement of the dictionary by Lorrain that appeared in: Fred. W. Savidge, J. Herbert Lorrain, *A grammar and dictionary of the Lushai language (Dulien dialect)*. Shillong: Assam Secretariat Printing Office, 1898.

A pleasantly discursive dictionary, highly informative on ethnobotany and cookery.

'With the suppression of headhunting and the establishment of law and order by the British Raj [1890] – followed almost immediately by the arrival of the late Rev. F. W. Savidge and myself as Christian missionaries [1892] – a new day dawned upon the Lushai Hills ... It fell to our lot to reduce the language to writing ... with a phonetic form of spelling still used throughout the tribe ...

'I used to keep the [Lushai word] slips in a number of long, narrow boxes in my office on a table of their own. One morning I found a few slips here and there protruding above their fellows. I found that other slips were scattered about in different parts of the room, and the nibbled edges of some of these revealed that *rats* were the culprits. A careful search followed but no more slips were discovered, and it was hoped that those already found represented the sum total of the thieves' booty, though why they had shown such an interest in the Lushai dictionary we did not know.

'Years later, when the office building was being reconstructed, I happened to look across at the men dismantling the roof. These, at that very moment, were throwing down to a group of happy Lushai children some pieces of screwed up paper which the latter were receiving with glee. Something in the size and shape of these playthings seemed familiar to me and I ran out to investigate. I found them to be a number of my precious Dictionary slips, which for years had evidently formed cosy nests for successive families of rats among the rafters. Ever since, when I have discovered an omission in my Dictionary, I have blamed "those rats"' (pp. vii, xv, abridged).

912.

Reginald Arthur Lorrain, *Grammar and dictionary of the Lakher or Mara language*. Gauhati: Department of Historical and Antiquarian Studies, Government of Assam, 1951. 372 pp.

913.

W. Pettigrew, *Tangkhul Naga grammar and dictionary (Ukhrul dialect)*. Shillong: Assam Secretariat Printing Office, 1918. 476 pp.

KURDISH

Kurdish in writing

Kurdish as a literary language can be found in three different scripts. The Latin alphabet now used for Kurmanji is similar to that of Turkish. An additional character x̄ is sometimes used.

A B C Ç D E Ê F G H İ Î J K L M N O P Q R S Ş T U Û V W X Y Z
a b c ç d e ê f g h i î j k l m n o p q r s ş t u û v w x y z

Until the twentieth century Kurdish was always written in the Arabic alphabet. Arabic script is still used for publications in Iran and Iraq. Arabic script is read from right to left, but the letters are given here from left to right, corresponding to the Latin script above:

ز ي خ و و وو و ت ش س ر ق پ و ن م ل ك ژ ي ى ه گ ف ي ه د چ ب ا

A form of the Cyrillic alphabet was assigned to Kurdish speakers in the Soviet Union in 1945. Here it is in Latin alphabetical order:

А Б Щ Ч Д Ә Е Ф Г Һ Ь И Ж К Л М Н О П Q Р С Ш Т Ö У В W Х Й З
а б щ ч д ә е ф г һ ь и ж к л м н о п q р с ш т ö у в w х й з

Kurdish is the best-known of the modern IRANIAN LANGUAGES after Persian. There are perhaps 14 million speakers, most of them in western Persia, northern Iraq and south-eastern Turkey, with smaller numbers in Syria and Armenia, and many migrant workers in western Europe (where they are classed vaguely as 'Turks'). Kurdish is nowhere a national language.

914.

Baran Rizgar, *Kurdish–English, English–Kurdish (Kurmancî) dictionary = Ferheng Kurdî–Îngîlîzî, Îngîlîzî–Kurdî*. London: Onen, 1993. 400 pp.

KYRGYZ

A TURKIC language, now the national language of independent Kyrgyzstan. There are one and a half million speakers.

Kyrgyz alphabetical order

а б в г д е ё ж з и й к л м н ң о ө п р с т у ү ф х ц ч ш щ ъ ы ь э ю я

915.

E. Abduldaev, D. Isaev, *Kyrgyz tilinin tushundurmo sözdügü*. Frunze, 1969. 775 pp.

Akademiya Nauk Kirgizskoi SSR. Institut Yazyka i Literatury.

[*Explanatory dictionary of the Kyrgyz language.*]

916.

Ж. Мукамбаев, *Кыргыз тилинин диалектологиалык сөздугу = Диалектологический словарь киргизского языка* [Zh. Mukambaev, *Kyrgyz tilinin dialektologiyalyk sözdügü*]. Frunze: Ilim Basmasi, 1972– .

[*Dialect dictionary of the Kyrgyz language.*] I have seen vol. 1, **А-Ж.**

917.

Русско–киргизский словарь [*Russko–kirgizskii slovar'*]. Moscow, 1957.

[*Russian-Kyrgyz dictionary.*] Not seen.

918.

К. К. Юдахин, *Кыргызча-орусча сөздук* [K. K. Yudakhin, *Kyrgyzcha–oruscha sözdük*]. Moscow: Sovetskaya Entisklopediya, 1965. 2 vols.

Earlier versions: K. K. Yudahin, Abdullah Taymas, *Kırgız sözlüğü*. Ankara: Millî Egitim Basimevi; Istanbul, 1945–8. 2 vols. – К. К. Юдахин, *Киргизско–русский словарь*. Moscow, 1940. 576 pp.

[*Kyrgyz dictionary.*] The 1945–8 version has glosses in Turkish.

LADIN

Ladin is a Rhaeto-ROMANCE language of the Alps. It has about 30,000 speakers in the Italian South Tyrol.

A Ladin alphabet

a b č d e f g ğ i k l m n ñ o p r s ś t u v ẑ

This is the alphabet used, with variants, in the dictionaries of the Istituto Bellunese di Ricerche Sociali e Culturali, two of which are listed below (**922, 923**).

919.

Reto R. Bezzola, Rudolf O. Tönjachen, *Dicziunari tudais-ch–rumantsch ladin.* Chur, 1944. 1194 pp.

The second and third (1982) printings contain a supplement, pp. 1175–1278.

[*German–Ladin dictionary.*]

920.

Johannes Kramer, *Etymologisches Wörterbuch des Dolomitenladinischen (EWD).* Hamburg: Buske, 1988– . 3–87118–999–5.

Note also: Johannes Kramer, *Etymologisches Wörterbuch des Gadertalischen.* Cologne, 1970–75. 8 parts.

[*Etymological dictionary of Ladin.*] This is a very spacious variorum dictionary of Ladin. Each entry begins with a summary of recorded forms, German gloss, and etymology. This is followed by a table of the glosses given by earlier dictionaries, sometimes with long lists of compounds and set phrases recorded by them; then comes an etymological and historical discussion.

Six volumes have been published, covering **A–S**; a seventh volume should complete the alphabet, and an eighth index volume is promised.

The table of concordance for the various spelling systems for Ladin, vol. 1 pp. 18–19, is repeated in each volume, as is the list of abbreviations.

921.

Archangelus Lardschneider-Ciampac, *Vocabulèr dl Ladin de Gherdëina: Gherdëina–Tudësch.* San Martin de Tor: Istitut Culturel Ladin 'Micurá de Rü', 1992. 211 pp. New edn, revised by Milva Mussner, Lois Craffonara.

Original edn: Archangelus Lardschneider-Ciampac, *Wörterbuch der Grödner Mundart.* Innsbruck: Universitäts-Verlag Wagner, 1933. 480 pp. (*Schlern-Schriften: Veröffentlichungen zur Landeskunde von Südtirol*, 23.)

[*Dictionary of the Ladin of Gardena: Ladin–German.*] The original edition is a brief-entry bilingual dictionary (6454 numbered entries) with etymological notes and some ethnographical information. Taxonomic names are given for flora and fauna. I have not seen the new edition.

922.

Vito Pallabazzer, *Lingua e cultura ladina: lessico e onomastica di Laste, Rocca Pietore, Colle S. Lucia, Selva di Cadore, Alleghe.* Belluno [1985?]. 711 pp.

Istituto Bellunese di Ricerche Sociali e Culturali. *Serie Dizionari*, 1.

[*Ladin language and culture: the vocabulary and names of Laste, Rocca Pietore, Colle S. Lucia, Selva di Cadore and Alleghe.*] A brief-entry Ladin–Italian dictionary with indication of local dialect variation (abbreviations for place names, p. 23) and occasional citation of sources (bibliography, pp. 19–22).

923.

Giovanni Battista Rossi, *Vocabolario dei dialetti ladini e ladino-veneti dell'Agordino: lessico di Cencenighe, San Tomaso, Vallada, Canale d'Agordo, Falcade, Taibon, Agordo, La Valle, Voltago, Frassenè, Rivamonte, Gosaldo, con note etnografico-demologiche.* Belluno, 1992. 1275 pp.
Istituto Bellunese di Ricerche Sociali e Culturali. *Serie Dizionari*, 5.

[*Dictionary of the Ladin and Ladin-Venetian dialects of the Agordino: the vocabulary of Cencenighe, San Tomaso, Vallada, Canale d'Agordo, Falcade, Taibon, Agordo, La Valle, Voltago, Frassenè, Rivamonte and Gosaldo, with ethnographical and local notes.*] Entries are under dialect forms, with careful indication of local variation: abbreviations of place names, p. 26. There are some lengthy entries with ethnographical information. Taxonomic names are given for flora. A few citations and quotations from printed sources: bibliography of these, pp. 19–25.

924.

Gilbert Taggart, *Dicziunari dal vocabulari fundamental = Dictionnaire du vocabulaire fondamental, romanche ladin vallader–français et français– romanche ladin vallader.* Cuoira: Ediziun Lia Rumantscha, 1990. 494 pp.

[*Dictionary of the basic vocabulary of the Romansch of Vallada: Ladin–French and French–Ladin.*]

LAHU

Lahu has half a million speakers in the hills of Yunnan and south east Asia. It belongs to the SINO-TIBETAN LANGUAGES.

925.

David Bradley [and others], *Thai hill tribes phrasebook: Lahu, Lisu, Karen and other hill tribes.* Melbourne: Lonely Planet, 1991. 181 pp. 0–86442–131–1.

926.

Paul Lewis, *Lahu–English–Thai dictionary = La hu li–Ka la hpu li–Htai li di sha na li* = Phon Luwit, *Phasa Lahu–phasa 'Angkrit–phasa Thai nangsu ditchanari.* Chiang Mai: Thailand Lahu Baptist Convention, 1986. 558 pp.

'In two sections: Lahu–English–Thai, English–Lahu.' Not seen; entry based on the Library of Congress catalogue.

927.

James A. Matisoff, *The dictionary of Lahu.* Berkeley: University of California Press, 1988. 1436 pp. 0–520–09711–4.
University of California publications in linguistics, 111.
An 8–page list of errata exists.

A Lahu–English dictionary with an introduction on the people and their culture; the whole amounts almost to a cultural encyclopaedia. The Lahu is in phonetic script (and not easy to read), filed in a phonetic alphabetical order in accordance with south Asian tradition; there is a key to the filing order at the foot of each page.

History of the project, p. 1; The Lahu people and language, p. 8; Transcription and alphabetical order, p. 14; Structure of entries, p. 28. Dictionary, pp. 65–1414, followed by a bibliography.

LANNA, KHÜN AND LÜ

These three TAI LANGUAGES are essentially one. Lanna or Tai Yuan or Northern Thai is the language of Chiangmai and its region, in north-western Thailand. Khün is the language of the most easterly of what the British called the 'Shan States', the state of Kengtung in eastern Burma. Lü or Dai is spoken in Xishuangbanna, in south-western Yunnan. There may be six and a half million speakers in total.

The script used (**932, 933**) resembles that of LAO. It is difficult to adapt to letterpress (though there used to be one printing shop that could handle it at Kengtung), but computer fonts work well. In Xishuangbanna a simplified script is now in use (**1385**).

928.

อุดมรุ่งเรืองศรี *พจนานุกรมล้านนา–ไทย* [Udom Rungruangsi, *Photchananukrom Lanna–Thai*]. Bangkok: Munnithi Mae Fa Luang, 2534 [1991]. 2 vols [1638 pp.].

[*Lanna–Thai dictionary.*] Headwords and sub-headings in Tai Yuan script, beautifully printed. Otherwise in Thai (but scientific Latin is added in glosses for flora and fauna).

The alphabet and numerals, preliminary pages ผ to ธ. Bibliography, pp. 1632–8.

929.

มธ รัตนประทธี *พจนานุกรมไทยยวน–ไทย–อังกฤษ* [Met Ratanaprasit, *Photchananukrom Thai Yuan–Thai–Angkrit*]. Bangkok, 1965. 378 pp.

[*Lanna–Thai–English dictionary.*] In three columns: the central column (Thai) is wider, with explanations and some examples. The Lanna is in central Thai script. Thai index, pp. 266–310: no English index. Supplementary glossary of botanical names, Tai Yuan–Thai–scientific Latin, pp. 311–60; there are Thai and Latin indexes to this.

930.

The Northern Thai dictionary of palm leaf manuscripts = *พจนานุกรมศัพท์ล้านนาเฉพาะคำที่ปรากฏในใบลาน.* Chiangmai: Silkworm Books, 2539 [1996]. 797 pp. 974–7047–77–2.

In central Thai script, with added Lanna script reproduced from handwriting. In Thai alphabetical order. A dictionary of the traditional literary language, with phonetic transcriptions, source references and brief English glosses. List of sources, pp. (17)–(25).

931.

Herbert C. Purnell: *A short Northern Thai–English dictionary (Tai Yuan)*. Chiangmai, 1963. 126 pp.

The Lanna forms are in phonetic script only.

Other works of interest

932.

S. Egerod, 'Essentials of Khün phonology and script' in *Acta Orientalia* vol. 24 no. 3/4 pp. 123–46.

933.

Harald Hundius, *Phonologie und Schrift des Nordthai.* Stuttgart: Franz Steiner, 1990. 265 pp.

Abhandlungen für die Kunde des Morgenlandes, vol. 48 part 3.

LAO

Lao, with fifteen million speakers, belongs to the TAI LANGUAGES. It is the national language of Laos, but the majority of speakers are in north-eastern Thailand.

The Lao alphabet

The thirty-three characters

ກຂຄງ ຈສຊຍ ດຕຖທນ ບປຜຝພຟມ ຍຣລວຫ ຫງຫຍຫນ ຫຼຫວຫ

g k k ng c s s ny d t t t n b p p f p f m y l l w h ng ny n m l w a h

Thirty-eight vowel-tone combinations, shown here with the character ອ a

ອະ ອ້າ ອາ ອິ ອີ ອຶ ອື ອຸ ອູ ເອະ ເອົາ ເອ ແອະ ແອ ໂອະ ໂອ ໂອ ເອາະ ອໍ ອໍ່ ອອອ ເອິ ເອີ ເອັຽ ເອຶອ ອົວະ ອົວ ເອີອ ເອືອ ຊໍອ ອໍອ ຊໍ ຊອອ ໃອ ໄອ ເອົາ ອໍາ

FONT: *ALICE_4.TTF* BY NGAKHAM SOUTHICHACK

934.

M.-J. Cuaz, *Lexique français–laotien.* Hong Kong: Société des Missions-Etrangères, 1904. 490 pp.

[*French–Lao dictionary.*] With an introductory ethnolinguistic survey of Laos and a brief grammatical outline of Lao. Not seen.

935.

Allen D. Kerr, *Lao–English dictionary.* Washington: Consortium Press, Catholic University of America Press, 1972. 2 vols [1223 pp.].

Publications in the languages of Asia, 2.

Lao in both script and phonetic transcription: about 24,000 entries. Claims to be 'the first reasonably comprehensive dictionary of the Lao language', temporarily forgetting Reinhorn (**938**) and Théodore Guignard's *Dictionnaire laotien–français* (Hong Kong: Imprimerie de Nazareth, 1912). 'Every [entry] has been discussed with at least three different [Lao] speakers.' Includes many botanical terms, based on local floras. Brief etymologies for Pali and Sanksrit loanwords.

936.

Russell Marcus, *English–Lao Lao–English dictionary* = ອັຈບານຸກົມ ອັຈກິດ-ລາວ ລາວ- ອັຈກິດ *[Vacananukram Anggrit–Law Law–Anggrit]*. Bangkok, 1968. 416 pp.

Reprinted: Rutland: Tuttle, 1970. 0–8048–0909–7. The 'revised edition' (1983. 416 pp.) has an identical main text, but with slight changes to the preliminary pages.

A pocket dictionary, but a good one. The English–Lao part includes both phonetic and Lao scripts. Brief guidance on pronunciation and filing order. Partly based on the larger dictionary by Kerr (**935**), which already existed in manuscript.

'Acknowledgements: … A Vietnamese man aided the project by locating 100 pages which accidentally blew into a rice paddy along the K-9 road.'

937.

ปรีชาพิณทอง *สารานุกรมภาษาอีสาน–ไทย–อังกฤษ [Saranukrom phasa Isan–Thai–Angkrit]* = Preecha Phinthong, *Isan–Thai–English dictionary*. Ubol: Sirithom Press, 1989. 1094 pp. 974–86948–9–5.

English glosses by Samuel A. Mattix.

16,000 entries: the only dictionary of Lao in the form in which it is spoken in north-eastern Thailand, where the name 'Isan' is preferred. Full glosses in Thai, with many examples in Isan and in Thai translation (in an 'italic' font); brief English glosses. Central Thai script is used for both Isan and Thai.

Description of the tone system in various dialects, pp. G–M; biographical photographs of the author, pp. N–R. The appendices, pp. 1049–94, are in Isan only: they include lists of idiomatic expressions, birds, fish, wild animals, small animals, plants, trees, weaving patterns.

938.

Marc Reinhorn, *Dictionnaire laotien–français*. Paris: Centre National de la Recherche Scientifique, 1970. 2 vols [2151 pp.]. 4th edn.

Centre de Documentation sur l'Asie du Sud-Est. *Atlas ethno-linguistique, 4e série: Dictionnaires*.
See the review by J. Filliozat in *Revue asiatique* vol. 259 pp. 387–90.
'1st' and '2nd' edns : Paris: CMISOM. 5 vols (634 pp.) I have not seen these; they are variously dated 1954, 1955, 1956 in references. – 3rd edn: Vientiane: Mission Militaire Française d'Instruction, 1968. 676 pp. Roneoed.

[Lao–French dictionary.] The fourth is much larger than the earlier editions, with about 40,000 entries, giving both Lao script and phonetic transcription. Annotations include etymology of loanwords and references to sources.

Introductory matter: language and script; alphabetical order, pp. xvii–xviii; weights and measures, pp. xxix–xxx; money; chronology, pp. xxxii–vi (with Lao calendar reproduced on xliii–xlviii); list of classifiers; administrative map; compass points, p. xlix. There is a long list of corrigenda, pp. 2143–50.

939.

ອັຈບານຸກົມ ພາສາ ລາວ *[Vacananukram phasa Law]*. Vientiane: Ministry of Education, 1962. 1145 pp. 2nd edn.

Edited by Maha Sila Viravong. Comité Littéraire.
1st edn: ອັຈບານຸກົມ ລາວ *[Vacananukram Law]*. 1957. 5 vols.

[*Dictionary of the Lao language.*] Small page size. A modest, 10,000–entry dictionary, but the only one entirely in Lao. No guidance on pronunciation. Innovative filing order based on initial and final consonants.

LATIN

Latin belongs to the ITALIC branch of the Indo-European languages. A major classical language of Europe, it originated as the local dialect of the city of Rome and became the ruling language of the Roman Empire, which reached its greatest extent 1900 years ago. It was the normal language of communication and education for the western half of the Empire (Greek was used in the eastern half). As the Christian Church spread within the Empire Latin also naturally became the normal language of communication within the western provinces of the Church. It has remained the first medium of communication for the Catholic Church till this century.

Although the Roman Empire crumbled in the fifth century, Latin retained its literary and educational position for at least a thousand years more. Throughout medieval times Latin was a language of government, literature and scholarship across most of Europe. In some specialised fields it remained pre-eminent for longer, even until the present day: Latin of a special kind, 'botanical Latin', is still required for the definitive publication of a new plant species (see **969**).

Classical Latin has never ceased to be a subject of study. There are many medium-sized dictionaries of some value for research: not all are listed here. The two major dictionaries are the *Thesaurus linguae Latinae* (**949**), a very ambitious project, and the relatively concise *Oxford Latin dictionary* (**945**).

There is a huge corpus of texts in medieval Latin, a corpus manageable only (it seems) by the superhuman efforts of an earlier generation of scholars (for example, **951**). In modern times, the result is a long series of historical dictionaries, supported by international and national academies, most of them unfinished and some of them far from completion (**955** onwards). For the medieval Latin of Spain see also Castro's dictionary based on the bilingual glossaries (**1442**).

In Latham and Howlett's *Dictionary of Medieval Latin from British sources* (**964**) there is an interesting 'Note on editorial method' (part 1 pp. xi-xiv). Latin words already known from classical texts are covered only briefly; 'post-classical' words are treated more fully, but naturally citing British sources only; fullest treatment is reserved for the distinctively British vocabulary. With variations, similar policies are followed by the editors of most of the other local dictionaries of medieval Latin, which are being compiled by national academies with international co-operation.

Latin is the language to which the Latin alphabet, now so widely used, was first applied – as an adaptation of the ETRUSCAN alphabet which itself derived from a version of the Greek alphabet. In Latin, **I** and **J** are variant forms of the same letter, as are **U** and **V**. Thus the usual Latin alphabet found in dictionaries is:

a b c d e f g h i k l m n o p q r s t u w x y z

X Y Z (and, with a few exceptions, **K**) are used only in loanwords. **W** does not occur at all in classical Latin, but is found in loanwords in medieval Latin.

Classical and Late Latin

940.

Albert Blaise, *Dictionnaire latin–français des auteurs chrétiens*. Turnhout: Brepols, 1962. 899 pp. Reprint of the 1st edn with a supplement (pp. 867–99).

The supplement was reprinted separately with an added sequence of corrections: Turnhout, 1967. Pp. 867–913. 1st edn of the main work: Strasbourg: 1954. 865 pp.

Later version: Albert Blaise, *Lexicon latinitatis Medii Aevi praesertim ad res ecclesiasticas investigandas pertinens = Dictionnaire latin-français des auteurs du Moyen Âge*. Turnhout, 1975. 970 pp. (*Corpus Christianorum. Continuatio mediaevalis.*) I have not seen this.

[*Latin–French dictionary of Christian authors.*] Meanings are carefully analysed and distinguished; they are supported by citations and brief quotations in Latin, for which – an unusual luxury in Latin dictionaries – French translations are often provided. The period covered is from Tertullian ('the beginning of Christian literature') to the end of the Merovingian period in France, that is, from about AD 200 to 750.

Blaise's work was revised for publication, with special attention to the theological vocabulary, by Henri Chirat.

941.

C. Cantueso [and others], *Diccionario latino*. Madrid, 1984– .

[*Latin dictionary.*] Not seen.

942.

J. Facciolati, Aeg. Forcellini, J. Furlanetti, *Totius latinitatis lexicon*. Padua: Seminarium Patavinum, 1864–1926. 6 vols. New edn by F. Corradini, J. Perin.

Reprinted, with a few additions in each volume compiled by J. Perin: 1940. – Reprinted: Padua: Gregoriana, 1965.

1st edn: Aegidius Forcellini, *Totius latinitatis lexicon*. Padua: Manfrè, 1771. 4 vols. Edited by Jacobus Facciolati.

'2nd edn': 1805. 3 vols. – Followed by: G. Cognolato, *Appendix ad Totius latinitatis lexicon Aegidii Forcellini*. 1816. Edited by J. Furlanetti.

English edition, with English glosses replacing the Italian, by J. Bailey and others: London, 1826. 2 vols.

3rd edn: 1827–31. 4 vols. Edited by J. Furlanetti. – English version of this: London: Baldwin and Cradock; Pickering, 1828. 2 vols.

German edition, further revised by A. Voigtländer, F. G. W. Hertel, C. Lehmann: Schneeberg, 1831–5. – Note also: E. F. Kaercher, *Nachträge zu Forcellini's Latein. Lexicon., mit einem grammatischen Excurse*. Karlsruhe, 1854. [*Supplement to Forcellini's Latin lexicon, with a grammatical excursus.*]

New Italian edn, with a first version of the dictionary of proper names, by V. de-Vit: Prati, 1858.

[*Dictionary of the whole of Latin.*] A lengthy gloss in Latin is followed by Italian, French, German, Spanish and English equivalents, then by quotations from Latin literature. Some texts as late as the eighth century are cited, but in general 'Forcellini' stops with the sixth century: it is a dictionary of classical and early Christian Latin, and for the later period it deals with the Latin writers of Italy much more fully than with others.

Vols 1–4 form the dictionary, **A–Z**. Vols 5–6 have a separate title: Joseph Perin, *Onomasticon totius Latinitatis*. 1913–26. This dictionary of Latin proper names is in essence encyclopaedic, but it contains numerous citations of classical texts.

943.

Wilhelm Freund, *Wörterbuch der lateinischen Sprache*. Leipzig, 1834–45. 4 vols.

[*Dictionary of the Latin language.*] Included here for its place in the tradition rather than its current reference use. Based on older works such as Scheller (see **944**) and Forcellini (**942**), Freund's dictionary served in turn – by way of an abridged English edition of 1850 by E. A. Andrews – as the basis of Lewis and Short (**947**).

944.

Karl Ernst Georges, *Ausführliches lateinisches–deutsches Handwörterbuch*. Leipzig: Hahn, 1912–18. 2 vols. 8th edn by Heinrich Georges.

'9th edn' (a reprint): Basle: Schwabe, 1951.

Earliest version: *I. J. G. Scheller's lateinisch-deutsches und deutsch-lateinisches Lexicon oder Wörterbuch.* Leipzig: Fritsch, 1783–4. 2 vols. – 3rd edn of this: *Imman. Joh. Gerhard Schellers ausführliches und möglichst vollständiges lateinisches–deutsches Lexicon oder Wörterbuch.* 1804. 5 vols [12,562 columns].

This was succeeded by: *Georg Heinrich Lünemanns lateinisches–deutsches und deutsch–lateinisches Handwörterbuch nach Imm. Joh. Gerh. Scheller's Anlage neu bearbeitet.* Leipzig, 1831. 4 vols. 7th edn. (1st edn: 1807.) The German–Latin section was by K. E. Georges. – The 1st edn entirely by Georges was in 1837–8.

[*Complete concise Latin–German dictionary.*] Titles have varied. The German–Latin sections were less frequently revised: the last to appear formed part of Georges' 7th edition in 1879–82.

945.

P. G. W. Glare, editor, *Oxford Latin dictionary*. Oxford: Clarendon Press, 1968–82. 2126 pp.

Note the reviews of successive fascicles by Hans Wieland in *Gnomon* vol. 41 pp. 746–52, vol. 49 pp. 136–41, vol. 52 pp. 53–4, vol. 55 pp. 586–9 (1969–83).

Based on a new reading of the texts, this historical dictionary covers literary and non-literary Latin down to AD 200, excluding all Christian authors. Work on it began in 1933. The corpus of surviving Latin from this period is luckily quite manageable: partly for this reason, the *Oxford Latin dictionary* was completed faster than many comparable works, once publication had got under way. It is modelled on the *OED* (**360**): the generously selected quotations illustrating each successive meaning are given in approximate chronological order, though precise dating is seldom possible. Brief etymologies are supplied.

List of works cited, pp. ix–xxi.

946.

Reinholdt Klotz, Alberto Grilli, *Dizionario della lingua latina*. Brescia: Paideia, 1974– .

Based on Reinhold Klotz: *Handwörterbuch der lateinischen Sprache*. 2 vols. Brunswick, 1862. 3rd edn. 2 vols.

[*Dictionary of the Latin language.*] Not seen; publication has ceased, apparently. Intended to cover the vocabulary down to the 7th century AD. The first of 24 planned parts was well reviewed (see J André in *Revue de philologie* vol. 49 (1975) pp. 141–2).

947.

Charlton T. Lewis, Charles Short, *A Latin dictionary*. Oxford: Clarendon Press, 1879. 2019 pp. [0–19–864201–9.]

A dictionary of literary Latin from the earlier texts to about AD 550, but patchy for the later period. 'Founded on Andrews' edition of Freund's Latin dictionary [**943**] ... revised, enlarged and in great part rewritten'. Among the closely packed citations and quotations it can be difficult to find one's way. Still, this practical one-volume dictionary has served generations of students and scholars.

948.

Alexander Souter, *A glossary of later Latin to 600 A.D.* Oxford: Clarendon Press, 1949. 454 pp. [0–19–864204–0.]

Intended to assist readers of Latin texts from AD 200 to 600 – since the *Oxford Latin dictionary* (**945**), already in preparation, was not to cover this period – this is a concise glossary of words and meanings not found in earlier Latin. Most entries are supported by at least one precise reference to a literary author, based on Souter's own notes and those of J. E. B. Mayor. List of texts cited, pp. vii–xxix.

949.

Thesaurus linguae Latinae. Leipzig: Teubner, 1900– . [3–322–00000–1.]

Accompanied by: [U. Keudel,] *Praemonenda de ratione et usu operis*. 1990. 72 pp. 3–322–00765–0. [*Foreword on the aim and use of the Thesaurus.*]

Index librorum scriptorum inscriptionum ex quibus exempla afferuntur. 1990. 228 pp. 3–322–00767–7. 2nd edn. [*List of books, writings and inscriptions excerpted for the Thesaurus.*] – 1st edn: 1904, followed by a supplement in 1958.

Onomasticon. 1909–23. Vols 2–3 [no other volumes were published]. [*Glossary of names.*]

Preceded by: Eduard Wölfflin, editor, *Archiv für lateinische Lexikographie und Grammatik ... als Vorarbeit zu einem Thesaurus linguae Latinae*. 1884–1908. [*Archive of Latin lexicography and grammar in preparation for a Thesaurus linguae Latinae.*] Preliminary work of this kind was later published in *Philologus*, from 1934, and in *Museum Helveticum*, from 1952 onwards, under the title 'Beiträge aus der Thesaurus-Arbeit' [Studies from the work on the *Thesaurus*].

A very large-scale dictionary of classical Latin. The aim, one displaying almost unexampled ambition, was to produce a complete index to a copious, though now partly lost, ancient literature. The dictionary covers all known texts before AD 150, and a large selection from then to 600 – but here the aim of completeness had to be abandoned, because, to take one example, 'a complete set of slips for [the works of Saint] Augustine would increase the present size of the archives by almost a half' (Keudel, *Praemonenda*). With such abatements as this, the original aim is actually being carried through for all but the commonest words. The symbol *x* preceding a headword means that some citations available in the *Thesaurus* office have been omitted.

The longer entries begin with information on pronunciation and spelling, with references to grammatical and lexical texts, followed by etymology. Then comes the mass of specialised meanings and supporting quotations. Finally there may be an *appendix grammatica et stilistica* with further discussion of usage.

Articles are signed. Those who dealt with the longest and most terrifying articles, such as **A, ab** 'from' (41 columns, by Lommatzsch), **Et** 'and' (47 columns, by Hofmann), **In** 'in, into' (73 columns), certainly deserve their credit.

The *Thesaurus* is now progressing through vol. 10. **A–M** and **O–P** are complete, or nearly, but **N** still has to be filled in. Entries for the letters **A–B** include proper names that occur in ancient texts. For **C–D** a separate *Onomasticon* or supplement of proper names was issued. After **D**, proper names are excluded.

Praemonenda means literally 'Things to be noted in advance'. It is a fine demonstration of the timelessness, not to say unreality, that is typical of such superhuman publishing projects that a booklet with such a title could appear a full ninety years after the first issues of the *Thesaurus* itself. It is in seven languages: the Latin on p. 5, the English beginning on p. 25; there is a list of signs and conventions on pp. 33–4.

The *Index* or list of works excerpted is arranged in five columns. These give the date; the abbreviation used, with a further column to clarify changes in practice over the century of publication; details of the works cited; and the editors of the texts that were used.

Medieval Latin

950.

Franz Blatt [and others], *Novum glossarium mediae latinitatis ab anno DCCC usque ad annum MCC*. Copenhagen: Munksgaard, 1957– .

Accompanied by: *Index scriptorum novus mediae Latinitatis*. 1973. 246 pp. 87–16–01390–5. 2nd edn. – With: *Supplementum*. 1989. 62 pp. (1st edn: *Index scriptorum mediae Latinitatis*. 1957. 194 pp.) [*New list of medieval Latin authors.*]

Note also: Lorenz Diefenbach, *Novum glossarium latino-germanicum mediae et infimae aetatis: Beiträge zur wissenschaftlichen Kunde der neulateinischen und der germanischen Sprachen*. Frankfurt am Main, 1867. 388 pp. [*A new Latin-German glossary of medieval and later times: contributions to the scientific study of the Roamnce and Germanic languages.*]

[*New glossary of medieval Latin from 800 to 1200.*] This glossary of the early medieval Latin vocabulary is a distillation from the various national Latin dictionaries that are now in progress (see next section). It provides French glosses, precise citations and brief quotations from medieval texts. No etymologies are given. Words known in classical Latin are excluded, unless their meaning has changed.

Progress is slow: the dictionary has so far covered **L–Pepticus**, about one sixth of the whole, the latest part having appeared in 1995. 'The "New Du Cange", planned since 1920, is still under way, and certainly nobody now past childhood will live to see its completion' (J. F. Niermeyer, **952**: for the 'old Du Cange' see **951**). In fact the plan can be traced back earlier, to Diefenbach's work of 1867 (see above).

951.

Carolus du Fresne dominus du Cange, *Glossarium mediae et infimae latinitatis*. Niort: Favre, 1883–7. 10 vols. Enlarged by Léopold Favre.

1st edn: 1678.

Note also: Lorenz Diefenbach, *Glossarium latino-germanicum mediae et infimae aetatis; supplementum lexici mediae et infimae latinitatis conditi a Carolo Dufresne Domino Du Cange*. Frankfurt am Main, 1857. 644 pp. [*Latin-German glossary of medieval and later times: a supplement to Du Cange ...*]

[*Glossary of middle and low Latin.*] A great work for its time, and still the largest dictionary of medieval Latin that goes all the way from **A** to **Z**. Its intended replacement is the *Novum glossarium* or 'New Du Cange' (**950**).

952.

J. F. Niermeyer, *Mediae latinitatis lexicon minus = Lexique latin médiéval–français/anglais = Latin–French/English dictionary.* Leiden: Brill, 1954–76. 1138 pp.

Completed by C. van de Kieft.

Accompanied by: C. van de Kieft, *Abbreviationes et index fontium.* 1976. 78 pp. [*Abbreviations and list of sources.*]

A very concise dictionary of Latin of the period AD 550–1150 (with a few words from later periods). Niermeyer excludes the strictly classical vocabulary but includes the new words of late classical (i.e. early Christian) Latin, from 200 to 550, in so far as they recur in medieval texts. Many words are illustrated by brief quotations, particularly those with complex variations of meaning. Other words are allowed only a brief gloss, or a gloss and a date.

953.

Otto Prinz [and other editors], *Mittellateinisches Wörterbuch bis zum ausgehenden 13. Jahrhundert.* Munich: Beck, 1959– .

Bayerische Akademie der Wissenschaften; Deutsche Akademie der Wissenschaften zu Berlin.

Accompanied by: *Abkürzungs- und Quellenverzeichnisse.* 1996. 153 pp. 3–406–41293–9. 2nd edn. (1st edn: 1959. 94 pp.) [*Lists of abbreviations and sources.*]

[*Middle Latin dictionary to the end of the thirteenth century.*] In intention, this large-scale (and gradually swelling) dictionary covers the whole geographical range of medieval Latin. In fact, the great weight of entries, citations and quotations relates to German, Austrian, Italian and French sources.

The first paragraph of major entries deals with spelling variants. Glosses are in Latin and German, but very litle space is given to them: the emphasis is on the quotations from Latin sources. These are brief, but sometimes eked out with explanatory supplements. Precise references are given.

So far vol. 1 (**A–B**) is complete; published parts of vol. 2 cover **C–Corregno**. The major feature of the supplementary volume is the list of source texts on pp. 15–153.

954.

Hans Walther, *Proverbia sententiaeque latinitatis medii aevi = Lateinische Sprichwörter und Sentenzen des Mittelalters in alphabetischer Anordnung.* Göttingen: Vandenhoeck & Ruprecht, 1963–9. 6 vols.

Carmina medii aevi posterioris latina, 2.

Followed by: Hans Walther, *Proverbia sententiaeque latinitatis medii ac recentioris aevi = Lateinische Sprichwörter und Sentenzen des Mittelalters und der frühen Neuzeit in alphabetischer Anordnung: neue Reihe.* 1982–6. Parts 7–9. 'Edited from Hans Walther's papers by Paul Gerhard Schmidt.'

[*Medieval Latin proverbs and sayings.*] Each Latin proverb is followed by citations of texts – but no quotations of contexts, and no translations or explanations. In spite of the title, some citations from the classical period are included. Vol. 6 is the index –

essential, because the listing itself is in simple alphabetical order by *first* word, not by keyword. The three-volume supplement adds the early modern period to the coverage.

Regional dictionaries of medieval Latin

955.

Franciscus Arnaldus [and others], 'Latinitatis Italicae medii aevi inde ab a. CDLXXVI usque ad a. MXXII lexicon imperfectum' in *Archivum latinitatis Medii Aevi (Bulletin Du Cange)* vols 10–34 (1936–64).

Reprinted: Turin: Bottega d'Erasmo, 1970. 3 parts [642 + 380 pp.].

Supplements were published in the same journal from 1967 onwards. They have been reprinted as: *Addenda I–III*. Turin, 1978. 143 pp. – *Addenda IV–V*. 1984. 118 pp.

[*An incomplete dictionary of Italian medieval Latin from 476 to 1022.*] A concise dictionary, though it expanded as it proceeded. Cites generously from a large range of sources and gives a few brief quotations. Notably strong in technical terms drawn from medical texts.

The *Addenda* have begun to make up a separate series in a new alphabetical order, which so far covers **A–Gyrus**.

956.

Antonius Bartel, *Glossarium mediae et infimae Latinitatis regni Hungariae.* Leipzig: Teubner, 1901. 723 pp.

Academia Litterarum Hungarica.

[*Glossary of middle and low Latin of the Kingdom of Hungary.*] With its wide range both geographically (Hungary was a big kingdom once) and chronologically (down to the nineteenth century) Bartel's excellent concise dictionary is not going to be replaced entirely by any of the large dictionaries now in progress.

Glosses in Latin and Hungarian are followed by at least one citation and usually by a quotation. Additions, pp. 710–22. Abbreviations for source texts, pp. xxi–xxviii; other abbreviations, p. 723.

957.

M. Bassols de Climent, J. Bastardas Parera [= Iohannes Bastarda] [and others], *Glossarium mediae latinitatis Cataloniae ab anno DCCC usque ad annum MC = Voces latinas y románicas documentadas en fuentes catalanas del año 800 al 1100.* Barcelona: Universidad de Barcelona, 1960– .

[*Glossary of the medieval Latin of Catalonia, 800–1100: Latin and Romance words documented in Catalonian texts.*] Vol. 1 covers **A–Dux** and was published between 1960 and 1985 in 1085 pages. List of source texts, pp. xxix–xxxiv.

958.

Franz Blatt, editor, *Lexicon mediae latinitatis Danicae = Ordbog over dansk middelalderlatin.* Aarhus: Aarhus Universitetsforlag, 1987– .

[*Dictionary of Danish medieval Latin.*] A relatively short work, with glosses in Danish only, followed by citations and relatively few quotations. Extends at present to 358 pages, covering **A–Increpito**; the last part so far appeared in 1992.

959.

W. Fuchs, Olga Weigers [and others], *Lexicon latinitatis Nederlandicae medii aevi*. Leiden: Brill, 1977– .

[*Dictionary of Netherlands medieval Latin.*] A full dictionary of the language of medieval texts from the Netherlands. Glosses are in Dutch and Latin. Some entries give brief quotations from source texts, some give citations only, some again rely only on a manuscript gloss or glossary. I know of parts 1–49, covering **A–Proportio.**

960.

Reino Hakamies, *Glossarium latinitatis medii aevi Finlandicae*. Helsinki, 1958. 188 pp.

Suomalaisen Tiedeakatemian julkaisemia pohjoismaiden historiaa valaisevia asiakirjoja, 10.

[*Glossary of Finnish medieval Latin.*] Published in the series of historical materials of the Finnish Academy of Sciences, this gives a brief gloss in Latin, with citations and quotations, for words and usages special to the medieval Latin of Finland. List of source texts, pp. vii–ix.

961.

János Harmatta, *Lexicon latinitatis medii aevi Hungariae* = Harmatta János, *A magyarországi középkori latinság szótára*. Budapest: Akadémiai Kiadó, 1987– .

Institutum Studiorum Antiquitatis Promovendorum Academiae Scientiarum Hungaricae.

[*Dictionary of the medieval Latin of Hungary.*] Glosses in Latin and Hungarian are followed by quotations from sources, of a generous length. This work covers a greater range of medieval sources than Bartel (**956**), but, unlike Bartel, it does not deal with Renaissance and later Latin. So far vols 1–4 have appeared, covering **A–Hyssopus.**

962.

Marko Kostrenčić [and others], *Lexicon latinitatis medii aevi Iugoslaviae*. Zagreb: Institutum Historicum Academiae Scientiarum et Artium Slavorum Meridionalium, 1969–78. 2 vols.

[*Dictionary of the medieval Latin of Yugoslavia.*]

963.

R. E. Latham, *Revised medieval Latin word-list from British and Irish sources*. London: Oxford Univeristy Press, 1965. 524 pp. New edn.

British Academy, Medieval Latin Dictionary Committee.

1st edn: J. H. Baxter, Charles Johnson, *Medieval Latin word-list from British and Irish sources*. 1934.

The 1934 edition very obviously represented work in progress towards the *Dictionary* (**964**): it was printed on the left side of each page only, to give plenty of room for contributors to add newly traced words. The 1965 edition has a more conventional layout: it still represents an abridgement of work so far done towards the *Dictionary*, giving known datings but no citations of sources.

964.

R. E. Latham, D. R. Howlett, *Dictionary of medieval Latin from British sources*. London: Oxford University Press, 1975– .

British Academy, Medieval Latin Dictionary Committee.

This is a full dictionary of the medieval Latin of British texts, literary and documentary, from the sixth to the sixteenth century. 'British' excludes Irish.

The layout resembles that of the *Oxford Latin dictionary* (**945**). Glosses are in English. Etymologies are very brief – often merely *[CL]* 'from classical Latin' – except for Arabic loanwords. There are relatively lengthy quotations from source texts, because the texts themselves tend to be less accessible than classical Latin ones. Many quotations are actually from manuscript glosses and glossaries. All quotations are dated, and precise references are given.

So far parts 1–4 have appeared, covering **A–H**.

965.

Marianus Plezia, *Lexicon mediae et infimae latinitatis Polonorum = Słownik łaciny średniowiecznej w Polsce.* Warsaw, Krakow, Wroclaw: Institutum Ossolinianum, 1953– .

Accompanied by: *Fasciculus extra ordinem. Index librorum laudatorum notarumque quibus significantur.* 1988. 50 pp. 83–04–00338–4. 2nd edn. [*Special issue: list of works cited and of the abbreviations for them.*]

[*Dictionary of the middle and low Latin of Poland.*] After initial references to other dictionaries, glosses are given in Polish and Latin, followed by copious citations and quotations from Latin texts from Poland. Volumes 1–6 have appeared, covering **A–Oxymel**. There are irritatingly scattered collections of addenda to each volume at the end of every later one.

966.

Bohumil Ryba [and others], *Latinitatis medii aevi lexicon Bohemorum = Slovník středověké Latiny v českých zemích.* Prague: Academia, 1977– .

Academia Scientiarum Bohemoslovaca.

[*Dictionary of the medieval Latin of Bohemia.*] Glosses are in Latin and Czech, and are followed by citations and brief quotations. Explanatory matter is also in Latin and Czech. General abbreviations, vol. 1 pp. xv–xviii; list of source texts, pp. xix–lx. The published volumes 1–2 cover **A–H**.

967.

Ulla Westerbergh, [Eva Odelman,] *Glossarium mediae latinitatis Sueciae = Glossarium till medeltidslatinet i Sverige.* Stockholm, 1968– .

Kungl. Vitterhets Historie och Antikvitets Akademien; Riksarkivet.

[*Glossary of the middle Latin of Sweden.*] Glosses are in Swedish and German (and not in Latin), followed by sometimes lengthy quotations. The entry tends to be under the 'standard' form of the Latin word as preferred by modern scholars, e.g. **Caryophyllum** in place of classical and medieval **Gariofilum** 'cloves'.

Published parts, up to vol. 2 part 5, cover **A–Rytenus**. A series of lists of abbreviations for source texts is building up anarchically on grey pages that come loosely inserted in successive parts.

Renaissance Latin

968.

René Hoven, *Lexique de la prose latine de la Renaissance.* Leiden: Brill, 1994. 427 pp. 90–04–09656–6.

[*Dictionary of Renaissance Latin prose.*] A brief-entry dictionary with a few citations of texts but no quotations. Glosses are in French. The source of loanwords is indicated. Note the use of asterisks at the beginning of entries for words that are also recorded in Latin texts at earlier periods: *** 'first found in classical texts', ** 'first found in late classical texts', * 'first found in medieval texts' (see discussion, pp. ix–xi).

Special vocabularies

969.

William T. Stearn, *Botanical Latin: history, grammar, syntax, terminology and vocabulary.* London: Nelson, 1966. 566 pp.

'2nd edn': Newton Abbot: David & Charles, 1973. 566 pp. 0–7153–5645–3.

Vocabulary (Latin–English and English–Latin in one alphabet), pp. 377–548. Glossary of usual symbols and abbreviations, pp. 364–73. Chapters xvi–xxiii, pp. 202–363, consist largely of specialised word-lists with indexes and examples of usage.

Etymological dictionaries

970.

Giovanni Alessio, *Lexicon etymologicum = Supplemento ai dizionari etimologici latini e romanzi.* Naples: Arte Tipografica, 1976. 691 pp.

[*Supplement to Latin and Romance etymological dictionaries.*] A series of etymological notes and comments, alphabetically arranged.

971.

A. Ernout, A. Meillet, *Dictionnaire étymologique de la langue latine: histoire des mots.* Paris: Klincksieck, 1959–60. 2 vols [820 pp.] 4th edn.

1st edn: 1932. 1108 pp. – 2nd edn: 1939. 1184 pp. – 3rd edn: 1951. 2 vols [1385 pp.]. The 3rd edn was reproduced from typescript, and printed on very poor paper.

[*Etymological dictionary of the Latin language: history of words.*] The result of a partnership in which Meillet deals with word origins, in proto-Indo-European or elsewhere, while Ernout deals with the history of word families from archaic to medieval Latin and with their survival in Romance, Celtic, Germanic and Slavonic languages. Derived words are grouped under base forms, with something of a shortage of cross-references. This is the best and most useful etymological dictionary of Latin.

Indexes, by language, pp. 761–812, with a guide on p. 813. Additions and corrections, pp. 815–20.

972.

Alois Walde, *Lateinisches etymologisches Wörterbuch.* Heidelberg, 1930–56. 3 vols. '3rd edn' by Johann Baptist Hofmann.

Indogermanische Bibliothek, 1. Abteilung, 2. Reihe: Wörterbücher, 1.
1st edn: Heidelberg, 1905–6. 870 pp. (*Sammlung indogermanischer Lehrbücher, 2. Reihe, 1.*) – 2nd edn: 1910.
1044 pp.

[*Latin etymological dictionary.*] Generally briefer and denser than Ernout and Meillet
(**971**), with a greater number of references to scholarly literature and to other
dictionaries. Addenda to vol. 1 are on pp. 842–72 of that volume.

Vol. 3, by Elspeth Berger, is a series of indexes by language: detailed table of
contents, vol. 3 pp. v–viii.

Foreign words

973.

Alfred Ernout, *Les éléments dialectaux du vocabulaire latin.* Paris: Société de
Linguistique, 1909. 253 pp.
Collection linguistique, 3.

[*The dialect elements in the Latin vocabulary.*] Ernout's doctoral dissertation is
arranged largely as a dictionary, pp. 89–244, preceded by a phonetic study (pp. 36–86)
and followed by an index of Latin words, excluding the headwords of the dictionary (pp.
245–50). Errata, pp. 251–3.

974.

Günther Alexander E. A. Saalfeld, *Tensaurus italograecus = Ausführliches
historisch-kritisches Wörterbuch der griechischen Lehn- und Fremdwörter im
Lateinischen.* Vienna, 1884. 1184 columns.

[*Comprehensive historical and critical dictionary of the Greek loanwords and
foreign words in Latin.*] Headwords are in Latin. Information includes: the Greek
original, the first Latin author known to have used the word, a German gloss, further
source texts and quotations. A second paragraph in small font gives citations of ancient
grammatical works and of modern scholarly literature, sometimes with a summary of
their comments.

LATVIAN

One of the small group of BALTIC LANGUAGES of the Indo-European family. Latvian is
the national language of Latvia, now an independent state, and has about one and a half
million speakers.

Latvian alphabetical order

a/ā b c č d e/ē f g ġ h i/ī j k ķ l ļ m n ņ o p r s š t u/ū v z ž

975.

E. Kagaine, S. Raġe, *Ērġemes izloksnes vārdnīca.* Riga, 1977–83. 3 vols.
Latvijas PSR Zinātņu Akademija, Valodas un Literaturas Instituts.

[*Dictionary of the Ērġeme dialect.*]

976.

Latvie šu literārās valodas vārdnīca. Riga: Zinatne, 1972– .

Chief editors: R. Grabis, [H. Bendiks, R. Bāliṇa and others.] Latvijas Zinātṇu Akademija, Valodas un Literaturas Instituts.

[*Dictionary of the Latvian literary language.*] A well-planned dictionary of Latvian with quotations from published texts (list of sources, vol. 1 pp. 19–28). Intended to be in eight volumes: but the sixth, the latest so far, has had to be split in two. With vol. 6 part 2 published, the whole dictionary now covers **A–R**.

977.

Latvie šu valodas vārdnīca: A–Z. Riga: Avots, 1987. 883 pp.

Editor: Dainuvīte Gulevska. Authors: Rita Bāliṇa and others.

[*Dictionary of the Latvian language, A to Z.*] A concise dictionary of modern usage, with numerous phrases and examples. An abridgement of the material being used in *Latvie šu literārās valodas vārdnīca* (**976**), omitting rarer words, technical terms and quotations from named authors.

978.

E. Turkina, *Latvie šu–angḷu vārdnīca: ap 30000 vardu = Latvian–English dictionary: approx. 30000 entries*. Riga: Avots, 1982. 638 pp. 4th edn.

A brief-entry dictionary.

LEPCHA

A SINO-TIBETAN language of Sikkim, on the northern edge of India.

979.

I. S. Chemjong, *Lepcha–Nepali–English dictionary*. Kathmandu: Royal Nepal Academy, 2026 [1970]. 340 pp.

Not seen.

980.

George Byres Mainwaring, *Dictionary of the Lepcha language*. Berlin, 1898. 552 pp.

Revised and completed by Albert Grünwedel.

A very full dictionary, in Latin transcription (table of Lepcha script, p. x). English–Lepcha glossary, pp. 457–549.

LITHUANIAN

One of the small group of BALTIC LANGUAGES of the Indo-European family, Lithuanian is the national language of Lithuania, now an independent state, and has about three and a half million speakers.

Lithuanian alphabetical order

a/ą b c č d e/ę/ė f g h i/į/y j k l m n o p r s š t u/ų/ū v z ž

Historical dictionaries

981.

Alexander Kurschat, *Litauisch–deutsches Wörterbuch* = *Thesaurus linguae Lituanicae* = Aleksandras Kuršaitis, *Lietuviškai–vokiškas žodynas*. Göttingen: Vandenhoeck & Ruprecht, 1968–73. 4 vols [2773 pp.].

Edited by Wilhelm Wissmann, Erich Hofmann, Armin Kurschat and others.

[*Lithuanian–German dictionary.*] A concise bilingual dictionary with some precise citations of literary texts (abbreviations for source texts, vol. 1 pp. xxiii–xxxiii) and with brief etymological indications in brackets (abbreviations for these, pp. xxxiv–xxxix). Note that * means 'loanword from …' (preface, p. ix).

982.

Lietuvių kalbos žodynas. Vilnius, 1956– .

Chief editor: J. Kruopas. Lietuvos TSR Mokslų Akademija. Lietuvių Kalbos ir Literaturos Institutas.

[*Dictionary of the Lithuanian language.*] A very large-scale dictionary, historical in intention. Words are attributed to authors, and some quotations are given, but there are no precise references (so the attributions cannot easily be verified or evaluated by the user). Now nearing completion: vols 1–15, so far published, cover **A–Telžti**.

The modern standard

983.

Dabartinės lietuvių kalbos žodynas: DZ: apie 50 000 žodžių lizdų. Vilnius: Mokslo ir Enciklopedijų Leidykla, 1990. 967 pp. 3rd edn. 5–420–01242–1.

Editorial board: St. Keinys and others. Lietuvių Kalbos Institutas.

Corrected reprint: 1993.

1st edn: 1954. – 2nd edn: *Dabartinės lietuvių kalbos žodynas: apie 60 000 žodžių*. Vilnius: Mintis, 1972. 974 pp. Chief editor: J. Kruopas. Lietuvos Mokslų Akademija. Lietuvių Kalbos ir Literaturos Institutas.

[*Dictionary of the modern Lithuanian language: about 50,000 words.*] A concise dictionary of modern usage. Detailed indication of morphological classes for nouns and verbs: see tables, pp. xiv–xx.

984.

A. Laučka, B. Piesarskas, E. Stasiulevičiūte, *Anglų–lietuvių kalbų žodynas* = *English–Lithuanian dictionary*. Vilnius: Mintis, 1975. 1096 pp.

Reprinted: Vilnius: Mokslas, 1986.

A brief-entry bilingual dictionary.

985.

Max Niedermann, Alfred Senn, Franz Brender, [A. Salys,] *Wörterbuch der litauischen Schriftsprache, Litauisch–Deutsch = Lietuvių rašomosios kalbos žodynas, lietuviškai–vokiška dalis.* Heidelberg: Winter, 1926–68. 5 vols.
Indogermanische Bibliothek. 5. Abteilung, Baltische Bibliothek, 3–. Later volumes are in the series *Indogermanische Bibliothek. 2 Reihe, Wörterbücher.*

[*Dictionary of the Lithuanian written language, Lithuanian–German.*] A large-scale dictionary with plenty of examples of usage, all of which are in both Lithuanian and German, and with grammatical information. The work grew as it proceeded: vol. 1 alone covers **A–K**. Supplement, vol. 5 pp. 481–560.

986.

Bronius Piesarskas, Bronius Svecevičius, *Lietuvių–anglų kalbų žodynas = Lithuanian–English dictionary.* Vilnius: Mokslas, 1991. 832 pp. 5–420–00855–6.
1st edn: B. Piesarskas, B. Svecevičius, *Lietuvių–anglų kalbų žodynas.* Vilnius: Mokslas, 1979. 911 pp.

987.

Bronius Piesarskas, Bronius Svecevičius, *Lithuanian dictionary: English–Lithuanian, Lithuanian–English.* London: Routledge, 1995. 799 pp. 2nd edn, with a supplement by Ian Press. 0–415–12856–0.
1st edn: Vilnius: Zodynas, 1994.

An abridgment of material published in the larger one-way dictionaries (**984, 986**).

Etymological dictionaries

988.

Ernst Fraenkel, *Litauisches etymologisches Wörterbuch.* Heidelberg: Winter, 1955–65. 2 vols [1560 pp.].
Indogermanische Bibliothek. 2. Reihe, Wörterbücher.

[*Lithuanian etymological dictionary.*] The first paragraph of each entry gives Lithuanian information, including glosses (these are in German) and internal word history. A second paragraph deals with wider relationships and history. Corrections, pp. 1546–56; indexes by language (see table of contents for details), pp. 1331–1545.

Supersedes Bender's preliminary work (**991**).

Loanwords

989.

Kazimieras Alminauskis, *Die Germanismen des Litauischen. 1. Die deutschen Lehnwörter im Litauischen.* Leipzig, 1934–5.

[*The Germanisms of Lithuanian, 1: German loanwords in Lithuanian.*] Not seen: cited from Malkiel (**9**).

990.

Alexander Brückner, *Die slawischen Fremdwörter im Litauischen*. Weimar: Böhlau, 1877.

Litauisch-slawische Studien, 1.

  [*The Slavonic loanwords in Lithuanian.*] Not seen: cited from Malkiel (**9**).

Other works of interest

991.

Harold H. Bender, *A Lithuanian etymological index, based upon Brugmann's Grundriss and etymological dictionaries of Uhlenbeck (Sanskrit), Kluge (German), Feist (Gothic), Berneker (Slavic), Walde (Latin), and Boisacq (Greek)*. Princeton: Princeton University Press, 1921. 307 pp.

LIVONIAN

An almost extinct URALIC language, most closely related to Estonian, spoken by fewer than 400 people on the coast of north-western Latvia.

992.

Lauri Kettunen, *Livisches Wörterbuch, mit grammatischer Einleitung*. Helsinki: Suomalais-Ugrilainen Seura, 1938. 648 pp.

Lexica Societatis Fenno-Ugricae, 5.

Johanna Laakso, editor, *Rückläufiges Wörterbuch des Livischen, anhand des Livischen Wörterbuches von Lauri Kettunen*. Helsinki: Suomalais-Ugrilainen Seura, 1988. 180 pp. 951–9403–20–5. [*Reverse dictionary of Livonian, based on the Livonian dictionary of Lauri Kettunen.*]

  [*Livonian dictionary, with grammatical introduction.*] Dictionary of an almost-extinct language spoken in some villages of north-western Latvia (map, p. iii). Its speakers bore the brunt of German settlement and conquest from the eleventh century; the Latvians were settled further inland. The Livonian is in the Société Finno-Ougrienne's transcription (alphabetical order, p. lxxii). Abbreviations, pp. xvi–xvii; grammatical introduction, pp. xviii–lxxi; German index, pp. 518–600. Entries quote example phrases and sentences from earlier records and from oral sources: etymological notes give cognates in Lithuanian and Latvian and the sources of loanwords. Index of forms cited in the etymologies, pp. 601–48: Latvian, German ('mostly Middle Low German'), Russian, Estonian, Finnish.

LOW GERMAN

One of the GERMANIC LANGUAGES of the Indo-European family, Low German (in the form of Old Saxon) was used for written literature earlier than 'High' German to the south. In medieval times Low German was a language of north German courts and documents, as well as of literature. DUTCH is in origin the westernmost variant of Low German.

Low German is nowadays generally regarded as nothing more than a series of dialects of German, spoken across the northern haif of Germany. There is no overall literary standard and very little modern literature in any Low German dialect. Dialect studies, however, attract plenty of official support, and the range of large-scale dictionaries is impressive.

Wander's big dictionary of German proverbs (**566**) covers Low German.

Modern regional forms

993.

Anneliese Bretschneider, editor, *Brandenburg-Berlinisches Wörterbuch*. Berlin: Akademie-Verlag, 1968– .

Includes materials collected by Hermann Teuchert. Deutsche Akademie der Wissenschaften zu Berlin, Institut für Deutsche Sprache und Literatur; Sächsische Akademie der Wissenschaften zu Leipzig, Sprachwissenschaftliche Kommission.

[*Brandenburg-Berlin dialect dictionary.*] Entries are usually under normalised German forms, which are in upper case if they do not correspond to anything in the local dialect. Actual local forms, as headwords or sub-headings, are given in bold lower case. Entries include quotations from oral collections and from printed texts: list of sources, vol. 1 pp. xxii–xxx. Abbreviations for place names, vol. 1 pp. xii–xxi. There are many small word maps.

The dictionary is now in its fourth volume, and covers **A–Tun** (but this is not very far, because **T** is interfiled with **D**).

994.

H. Frischbier, *Preussisches Wörterbuch: ost- und westpreussische Provinzialismen in alphabetischer Folge*. Berlin: Enslin, 1882–3. 2 vols.

[*Prussian dialect dictionary: East and West Prussian provincialisms in alphabetical order.*] Brief, but with references to literature. Supplement, vol. 2 pp. 504–52; sources and other abbreviations, vol. 1 pp. vii–xv with vol. 2 p. 552.

Now largely replaced by Riemann (**1000**).

995.

Wolfgang Jungandreas [and others], *Niedersächsisches Wörterbuch*. Neumünster: Wachholtz, 1953– .

See: Ulrich Scheuermann, *Linguistische Datenverarbeitung und Dialektwörterbuch, dargestellt am Beispiel des Niedersächischen Wörterbuches*. Wiesbaden: Steiner, 1974. 122 pp. 3–515–01931–6. (*Zeitschrift für Dialektologie und Linguistik. Beiheft*, 11.) [*Linguistic computing and the dialect dictionary: a study of the Niedersächsisches Wörterbuch.*]

[*Lower Saxon dialect dictionary.*] Quotations and citations are mainly of dialect collections. There are illustrations, including some word maps, and numerous quotations from folk poetry. The dictionary has reached volume 5 part 3 and covers **A–Gest**. Abbreviations, vol. 1 pp. xi–xiii; abbreviations of district names, p. xiv; sources, pp. xv–xxiii.

996.

Eduard Kück [and others], *Lüneburger Wörterbuch: Wortschatz der Lüneburger Heide und ihrer Randgebiete*. Neumunster: Wachholtz, 1942–67. 3 vols.

There is an undated (1960s) reprint of vol. 1.

[*Lüneburg dialect dictionary: vocabulary of the Lüneburg Heath and its environs.*] Entries are filed under imitative spellings of local forms, with discussion of history, usage, pronunciation and local peculiarities. Relatively modest in scale, but with citations and some quotations from sources. Vol. 1 is in Fraktur type.

997.

Hans Kuhn, Ulrich Pretzel, [Jürgen Meier, Dieter Mohn,] editors, *Hamburgisches Wörterbuch*. Neumünster: Wachholtz, 1956– . 3–529–030140–7.

[*Hamburg dialect dictionary.*] One of the livelier of the modern German dialects dictionaries, with quotations of folk poetry and of much early printed material (from about 1600 onwards) alongside some well-chosen illustrations. Bibliography of source texts, vol. 1 pp. xvi–xxxix.

Fourteen parts have been published. Vol. 2 is in progress, and the dictionary now covers **A–huusdörslötel**.

998.

Otto Mensing, editor, *Schleswig-Holsteinische Wörterbuch (Volksausgabe)*. Neumünster: Wachholtz, 1927–35. 5 vols.

[*Schleswig-Holstein dialect dictionary: popular edition.*] Slightly unusual layout for a German dictionary, with glosses between inverted commas and quotations (which are numerous) in italic. List of informants, vol. 1 pp. xvii–xix; printed sources, pp. xix–xxi; place names, pp. xxii–xxiv.

999.

Elisabeth Piirainen, Wilhelm Elling, *Wörterbuch der westmünsterländischen Mundart*. Vreden: Heimatverein Vreden, 1992. 1066 pp. 3–926627–09–3.

Beiträge des Heimatvereins Vreden zur Landes- und Volkskunde, 40.

[*Dictionary of the Westmünster dialect.*] A concise dictionary based on both oral and written sources. Introduction, by Piirainen, including: phonetics and spelling, pp. 23–31; arrangement of entries, pp. 32–44; sources and compilation, pp. 45–8. Details of oral informants, by Elling, pp. 54–64.

1000.

Erhard Riemann, [Ulrich Tolksdorf,] editors, *Preussisches Wörterbuch: deutsche Mundarten Ost- und Westpreußen*. Neumünster: Wachholtz, 1974– . 3–529–04611–6.

Akademie der Wissenschaften und der Literatur, Mainz.

[*Prussian dialect dictionary: German dialects of East and West Prussia.*] Covers the dialects of East Prussia, Danzig (Gdansk) and its hinterland as they were up to the Second World War, after which this German-speaking population was expelled. A concise dictionary, with many quotations of examples from oral collections. Printed literature is cited rather than quoted. There are numerous maps and illustrations.

The *Preussisches Wörterbuch* began publication with vol. 2, continuing where an older incomplete work, by Walther Ziesemer (*Preussisches Wörterbuch*. Königsberg, 1935–44), left off. Vol. 4 of the new dictionary is now complete, and **Fi–R** is covered.

1001.

Richard Wossidlo, Hermann Teuchert [and other editors], *Wossidlo-Teuchert Mecklenbürgisches Wörterbuch*. Neumünster: Wachholtz, 1942–92. 7 vols.

[*Mecklenburg dialect dictionary.*] Much fuller than the Lower Saxon dictionary (**995**), with many more quotations from written and printed sources, early and modern. Abbreviations, including list of sources, vol. 1 pp. xvii–xxxi.

Older periods

Old Saxon

1002.

Ferdinand Holthausen, *Altsächsisches Wörterbuch*. Münster: Böhlau, 1954.
Niederdeutsche Studien, 1.

[*Old Saxon dictionary.*]

1003.

Edward H. Sehrt, *Vollständiges Wörterbuch zum Heliand und zur altsächsischen Genesis*. Göttingen: Vandenhoeck & Ruprecht, 1966. 738 pp. 2nd edn.
1st edn: 1925.

[*Complete dictionary to the Heliand and the Old Saxon Genesis.*] These two texts are the oldest literary works in any German dialect.

Middle Low German

1004.

Mittelniederdeutsches Handwörterbuch. Neumünster: Wachholtz, 1928– .
Begun by A. Lasch, C. Borchling; continued by Gerhard Cordes. *Wörterbücher herausgegeben vom Verein für Niederdeutsche Sprachforschung*, 2.
Vol. 1 (**A–Heger**) is complete; vols 2 (**H–**) and 3 (**S–**) are both in progress.

[*Concise Middle Low German dictionary.*] Brief entries, but with selective short quotations and citations of texts.

1005.

Karl Schiller, August Lübben, *Mittelniederdeutsches Wörterbuch*. Bremen: Kühtmann, Fischer, 1875–81. 6 vols.
Abridged version: August Lübben, *Mittelniederdeutsches Handwörterbuch*, vollendet von Christoph Walther. Norden, 1888. Reprinted: Darmstadt, 1979.

[*Middle Low German dictionary.*] Vol. 6 is a supplement.

LUBA

A Bantu language, and thus a member of the NIGER-CONGO family, Luba or Kiluba has about 8,000,000 speakers in Congo (Kinshasa) and Zambia.

1006.
E. van Avermaet, *Dictionnaire kiluba–français*. Tervuren, 1954. 838 pp.
Annales du Musée Royale du Congo Belge, linguistique, 7.

LUWIAN

An extinct member of the Anatolian branch (cf. HITTITE) of the INDO-EUROPEAN language family.

1007.
Emmanuel Laroche, *Dictionnaire de la langue louvite*. Paris: Adrien-Maisonneuve, 1959. 179 pp.
Bibliothèque archéologique et historique de l'Institut Français d'Archéologie d'Istanbul, 6.
See also: J. D. Hawkins, Anna Morpurgo-Davies, Günter Neumann, *Hittite hieroglyphs and Luwian: new evidence for the connection.* Göttingen: Vandenhoeck & Ruprecht, 1974. 55 pp. (*Nachrichten der Akademie der Wissenschaften in Göttingen, 1. Philosophisch-historische Klasse,* 1973, no. 6 [pp. 143–97].)

[*Dictionary of the Luwian language.*] The main alphabetical sequence, of Luwian forms with Lycian and Hittite cognates, is followed by separate lists of fragmentary words (pp. 116–18), ideograms of unknown pronunciation (pp. 119–25), and proper names (pp. 125–30). Many words in Luwian texts remain unexplained and are listed here without glosses.

There are some updates to Laroche in the work by Hawkins and others that is cited in the note above.

LUXEMBURGISH

A GERMANIC language, and indeed a German dialect, Luxemburgish (or Letzeburgisch) is the local spoken language of Luxembourg, though outsiders are more aware of French and German, which are used there for most literary and official purposes. There are about 300,000 speakers of Luxemburgish.

1008.
Luxemburger Wörterbuch. Luxemburg: P. Linden, 1950–77. 5 vols.
Under the aegis of the Grand Ducal Government of Luxembourg. Edited by the Wörterbuchkommission on the basis of collections made since 1925 by the Luxemburgische Sprachgesellschaft, and since 1935 by the Linguistic Section of the Großherzogliches Institut.

[*Luxemburgish dictionary.*] A large-scale dictionary of modern, mainly spoken, usage. The language, vol. 1 pp. ix–lxi; dialect map and charts, after p. lxiv. Vol. 5 consists mainly of additions and corrections (pp. 1–203), followed by sources of information, pp. 209–12; abbreviations, pp. 213–15; place names, pp. 216–27, with map following p. 228. Coverage includes the Germanic dialects spoken in parts of the Belgian province of Luxembourg.

LYDIAN

An extinct member of the Anatolian branch (see HITTITE) of the INDO-EUROPEAN language family.

1009.
Roberto Gusmani, *Lydisches Wörterbuch: mit grammatischer Skizze und Inschriftensammlung*. Heidelberg: Winter, 1964. 280 pp.
Supplemented by: Roberto Gusmani, *Lydisches Wörterbuch*. Ergänzungsband, parts 1–3. Heidelberg: Winter, 1980–86.

[*Lydian dictionary, with grammatical sketch and a collection of inscriptions.*] An extinct language of Anatolia, related to Hittite.

MACEDONIAN

One of the SLAVONIC LANGUAGES, Macedonian is the national language of one of the new states of former Yugoslavia. Until early this century it was almost universally regarded as a dialect of Bulgarian. There are over two million speakers.

The Macedonian alphabet

АБВГДЃЕЖЗSИЈКЛЉМНЊОПРСТЌУФХЦЧЏШ

а б в г д ѓ е ж з ѕ и ј к л љ м н њ о п р с т ќ у ф х ц ч џ ш

a b v g d gy e zh dz i y k l ly m n ny o p r s t ky u f kh ts j sh

1010.
Тодор Димитровски, *Речник на македонската народна поезија* [Todor Dimitrovski, editor, *Rechnik na makedonskata narodna poeziya*].
Skopje, 1983– .

[*Dictionary of Macedonian oral poetry.*] I know only of the first volume, covering the first four letters of the alphabet.

1011.
Блаже Конески, Тодор Димитровски, *Речник на македонскиот јазик со српскохрватски толковања* [Blazhe Koneski, editor, Todor Dimitrovski and others, *Rechnik na makedonskiot yazik so srpskokhrvatski tolkovanya*]. Skopje: Universityeska Pechatniska, 1961–6. 3 vols.

[*Dictionary of the Macedonian language with glosses in Serbo-Croat.*] A brief-entry bilingual dictionary, with numerous cross-references for noun and verb forms. The

'Serbo-Croat' is in Latin script, normally the mark of Croatian. Latin taxonomic names are given for fauna and flora.

MADURESE

One of the AUSTRONESIAN LANGUAGES, spoken in the island of Madura off the north-eastern coast of Java. Madurese was traditionally written in Javanese script. There are nine million speakers.

1012.
H. N. Kiliaan, *Madoereesch–Nederlandsch woordenboek*. Leiden: Brill, 1904–5. 2 vols.

[*Madurese–Dutch dictionary.*] In this extensive work the headwords are in the traditional Madurese (Javanese) script followed by romanisation. Etymologies are given, as well as Dutch glosses.

MAGINDANAON

An AUSTRONESIAN language of the Philippines, with nearly a million speakers.

1013.
Robert E. Sullivan, *A Maguindanaon dictionary, Maguindanaon–English English–Maguindanaon*. Cotobato City: Notre Dame University, Institute of Cotobato Cultures, 1986. 545 pp. 971–129–000–6.

A southern Philippine language. Includes lists of numerals, weights and measures, months, colours; male and female personal names, pp. 18–25; verbal inflection, pp. 26–53. English–Maguindanaon section, pp. 360–545.

MAKASAR

An AUSTRONESIAN language of southern Sulawesi, in Indonesia, with 1,600,000 speakers. As the language of the old Sultanate of Gowa, and of the trading city now known as Ujungpandang, Makasar was the first traceable external source of loanwords in Australian languages – evidence of contacts that were established before Europeans began to explore Australia.

Makasar script: the 19 characters

ka ga nga nka pa ba ma mpa ta da na nra ya ra la wa sa a ha

Makasar was traditionally written in Lontara script, unusual in its appearance but a true descendant of ancient Indic scripts. This is used in Matthes' dictionary (**1015**).

1014.

A. A. Cense, Abdoerrahim, *Makassaars–Nederlands woordenboek, met Nederlands–Makassaars register*. The Hague: Nijhoff, 1979. 989 pp. 90–247–2320–5.
Koninklijk Instituut voor Taal-, Land- en Volkenkunde.

[*Makasar–Dutch dictionary with Dutch–Makasar index.*] A historical and general dictionary, in the Latin alphabet, with some notes on word origins. The Dutch–Makasar section, pp. 917–89, is by J. Noorduyn.

1015.

B. F. Matthes, *Makassaarsch–Hollandsch woordenboek met Hollandsch–Makassaarsche woordenlijst*. The Hague: Nijhoff, 1885. 1170 pp. New edn.
1st edn: Amsterdam: Muller, 1859. 943 pp. Separate indexes to plant names, pp. 855–77.

[*Makasar–Dutch dictionary with Dutch–Makasar glossary.*] Makasarese terms are given both in Lontara script and Latin transliteration. Additional notes on plant names, pp. 1108–21. List of boat terms, pp. 1156–8.

MALAGASY

An AUSTRONESIAN language, established on this great island off south-eastern Africa as a result of a long distance colonisation that took place perhaps two millennia ago. There are ten million speakers.

1016.

J. Richardson, *A new Malagasy–English dictionary*. Tananarive: London Missionary Society, 1885. 832 pp.

Not seen.

MALAY

Malay has about 35 million first-language speakers; many millions more use it as their second or third language.

It has the greatest international importance of any AUSTRONESIAN language, having grown from the status of a lingua franca of the Indonesian archipelago to that of the national language of four states, Malaysia, Indonesia, Brunei and Singapore. In its slightly different official standards it is known variously as Indonesian, Malaysian and Malay (*bahasa Indonesia, bahasa Malaysia, bahasa Melayu*).

The language of a mainly Islamic culture, Malay was once written in Arabic script (Jawi). This is now obsolete except for religious purposes, and the standard alphabet is Latin.

The modern standards

1017.

John M. Echols, Hassan Shadily, *Kamus Indonesia–Inggris = An Indonesian–English dictionary*. Jakarta: Gramedia, 1989. 618 pp. New edn.

Revised by John U. Wolff, James T. Collins.
Also published as: *An Indonesian–English dictionary*. Ithaca: Cornell University Press, 1989. 0–8014–2127–6.
1st edn: 1961. 384 pp. – 2nd edn: 1963. 431 pp. 0–8014–0112–7.

The standard Indonesian–English dictionary, an important feature of which is that it resolves an ambiguity in the orthography of Malay by distinguishing the open 'e' vowel as *é*.

1018.

John M. Echols, Hassan Shadily, *Kamus Inggris–Indonesia*. Jakarta: Gramedia, 1975. 660 pp.

Also published as: *An English–Indonesian dictionary*. Ithaca: Cornell University Press, 1975. 0–8014–0728–1.

About 33,000 concise entries: a very practical work, well printed and compact, 'primarily for the use of Indonesians.'

1019.

Kamus besar bahasa Indonesia. Jakarta: Balai Pustaka, 1991. 1278 pp. 979–407–182–X.

Pusat Pembinaan dan Pengembangan Bahasa, Tim Penyusun Kamus. *BP*, 3658.
1st edn: 1988. 1090 pp.

[*Big dictionary of Indonesian.*] A large-scale monolingual dictionary of Indonesian: about 50,000 entries. Appendices: grammar and stylistics, pp. 1147–81; foreign words and elements, pp. 1183–1219; abbreviations, pp. 1221–36; scripts used in Indonesia, pp. 1237–8; gazetteer of administrative subdivisions of Indonesia, pp. 1243–60; names of foreign countries, pp. 1261–5; and more.

1020.

Kamus Dewan. Kuala Lumpur: Dewan Bahasa dan Pustaka, 1994. 1566 pp. 3rd edn. 983–62–4456–5.

Chief editor: Sheikh Othman bin Sheikh Salim.
1st edn: 1970. 1352 pp. Edited by Teuku Iskandar. – 2nd edn: 1989. 1480 pp. 983–62–0979–4.

[*Council dictionary.*] A big monolingual dictionary of Malaysian, beautifully printed. About 45,000 entries, with many sub-headings and examples.

1021.

Kamus dwibahasa: bahasa inggeris–bahasa Malaysia. Kuala Lumpur: Dewan Bahasa dan Pustaka, Kementerian Pelajaran Malaysia, 1979. 1457 pp.

[*Bilingual dictionary, English–Malaysian.*] Intended for Malay speakers: about 28,000 entries, often with explanation rather than translation in Malay.

1022.

Kamus inggeris–melayu Dewan = An English–Malay dictionary. Kuala Lumpur: Dewan Bahasa dan Pustaka, 1992. 1945 pp. 983–62–2282–0.

[*Council English-Malay dictionary.*] Begun by the Australian National University and taken over by the Malaysian Language and Literature Council in 1977. A large-scale work with over 40,000 entries. 'What distinguishes it from other English–Malay dictionaries published to date is that it does not give definitions, but instead provides Malay equivalents based on context and usage.' Intended for people who speak English as their first or second language. A highly professional, well-planned and well-produced dictionary.

1023.

Pierre Labrousse, *Dictionnaire général indonésien–français.* Paris: Association Archipel, 1984. 934 pp.

Cahier d'Archipel, 14.

[*General Indonesian–French dictionary.*] About 27,000 entries, with generous exemplification; many sub-entries. Very well laid out.

1024.

Peter Salim, *The contemporary English–Indonesian dictionary.* Jakarta: Modern English Press, 1989. 2358 pp. 4th edn.

1st edn: 1985.

'A colossal work of art', according to the author's preface. Over 60,000 entries, some of them very lengthy with useful phrases and sentences, but also some rather odd English. Reproduced from neat typescript, illustrated with line drawings.

1025.

Farida Soemargono, Winarsih Arifin, *Dictionnaire français–indonésien.* Paris: Association Archipel, 1991. 1115 pp. 979–511–388–7.

Cahier d'Archipel, 18.

[*French–Indonesian dictionary.*] About 25,000 detailed entries: an impressive work, with generous exemplification, on the basis of the French *Micro Robert.*

1026.

A. Teeuw, *Indonesisch–Nederlands woordenboek.* Leiden: KITLV, 1990. 764 pp. 90–6718–021–1. New edn.

Koninklijke Instituut voor Taal-, Land- en Volkenkunde.

1st edn: 1950. 369 pp. – 2nd edn: W. J. S. Poerwadarminta, A. Teeuw, *Indonesisch–Nederlands woordenboek.* Groningen: Wolters, 1952. 383 pp.

[*Indonesian–Dutch dictionary.*] The current representative of a long tradition of Malay–Dutch lexicography. The 1st and 2nd editions were strong in the traditional literary vocabulary of Malay.

The older period

1027.

P. Favre, *Dictionnaire malais–français*. Vienna: Imprimerie Impériale et Royale; Paris: Maisonneuve, 1875. 2 vols.

Companion work: P. Favre, *Dictionnaire français–malais*. Vienna, Paris, 1880. 2 vols.

[*Malay–French dictionary.*] A large-scale work in Jawi (Arabic script, at that time the standard for Malay) with Latin transliteration; includes etymological notes. 'Rich in passages from Malay literature', according to Wilkinson (**1028**).

1028.

R. J. Wilkinson, *A Malay–English dictionary (romanised)*. Mytilene, 1932. 2 vols.

This has never been superseded as a large-scale dictionary of older literary Malay. The eventful history of the work, its loss in the sack of Smyrna in 1922 and obstinate recompilation, can be read in the preface (pp. i–iv). 'Mytilene [on the Greek island of Lesbos] is a poor centre for Malay studies. My only local helper has been my wife. Printing also was hard in a place where no compositor knows English, much less Malay,' but the printers, Salavopoulos & Kinderlis, did well. Malay manuscripts had provided the initial vocabulary (precise references to sources are given) but 'many Malay terms lie quite outside literature'. The origin of loanwords is indicated: there are no other etymologies.

Scientific Latin names are given for plants and animals: 'in most cases that meant catching the fish and having it identified by a zoologist.' Two zoologists 'did me the honour of naming a shrew after me … though this (I am told) was only a tribute to my mischievous activities as a Secretariat officer.'

1029.

R. J. Wilkinson, *A Malay–English dictionary*. Singapore: Kelly & Walsh, 1901–3. 776 pp.

A lavishly printed dictionary of Malay in the now old-fashioned jawi script: a Latin transliteration is also given. The dictionary is in Arabic alphabetical order: note the index in roman script, 54 pp. at end, followed by 'Malay names of snakes', 1 page.

Other works of interest

1030.

A. Teeuw, H. W. Emanuels, *A critical survey of studies on Malay and Bahasa Indonesia*. The Hague: Nijhoff, 1961. 176 pp.

Koninklijk Instituut voor Taal-, Land- en Volkenkunde. (*Bibliographical series*, 5.)

For some additions see E. M. Uhlenbeck, 'Indonesia and Malaysia' in Thomas A. Sebeok, editor, *Linguistics in east Asia and south east Asia* (The Hague: Mouton, 1967. *Current trends in linguistics*, 2).

MALAYALAM

One of the DRAVIDIAN LANGUAGES of southern India, Malayalam is the state language of Karnataka and an official language of India. There are 22 million speakers.

It is normally written in its own script, which is related to that of Tamil but, as normally printed, looks very different, as can be seen from the consonant characters in the table. Jawi (Arabic) script is still used by the large Malayalam-speaking communities in Singapore and Malaysia.

Malayalam script: the consonant characters

കഖഗഘങ ചഛജ്ജ്ഝഞ ടഠഡഢണ തഥദധന

k kh g gh ṅ   c ch j jh ñ   ṭ ṭh ḍ ḍh ṇ   t th d dh n

പഫബഭമ   യരറലവ ളഴ ശഷസഹ

p ph b bh m   y r ṟ l v   ḷ ḻ   ś ṣ s h

The fourteen vowels shown with പ *p*

പ പാ പി പീ പ പ പൃ പെ പ പൈ പൊ   പാ പൗ പ്

pa pā pi pī pu pū pṛ pe   pē   pai   po   pō pau pĕ

BASED ON A FONT BY VIJAY K. PATEL

1031.

A comprehensive Malayalam–Malayalam–English dictionary. Trivandrum: University of Kerala, 1965– .

Edited by Suranad Kunjan Pillai, K. V. Namboodiripad and others.

A major historical dictionary with quotations from Malayalam literature. Glosses are given both in Malayalam and in English, as indicated by the title. To be complete in seven volumes.

1032.

C. Madhavanpillai, *NBS concise English–Malayalam dictionary*. Kottayam: Sahitya Pravarthaka, 1972. 915 pp. Revised by S. Guptan Nair.

1st edn: 1971.

MALTESE

Maltese belongs to the SEMITIC LANGUAGES: it is in origin a variant of Arabic. From its long use in a Christian country under Italian and British influence it has become very different from the parent language. It is written in a special form of the Latin alphabet. There are about 350,000 speakers of Maltese.

Maltese alphabetical order

a b ċ d e f ġ g h ħ i j k l m n għ o p q r s t u v w x ż z

1033.

Joseph Aquilina, *Maltese–English dictionary*. Valletta: Midsea Books, 1987–90. 2 vols [1673 pp.].

Obituary of the author: *Daily Telegraph* (6 October 1997).

A bilingual dictionary with numerous set phrases, etymological notes and philological discussion. Taxonomic names are given for flora and fauna. Main entries are in upper case, cross-references in lower case. There are frequent references to earlier sources, notably earlier dictionaries (bibliography of these, vol. 1 pp. xxv–xxvi). Aquilina's dictionary is somewhat taxing to the eye – too many square brackets – but is full of information. Additions, pp. 1639–50, followed by various appendices.

1034.

G. Barbera, *Dizionario maltese–arabo–italiano, con una grammatica comparata arabo–maltese*. Beirut: Imprimerie Catholique, 1939–40. 2 vols.

[*Maltese–Arabic–Italian dictionary, with an Arabic–Maltese comparative grammar.*]

1035.

Pawlu Bugeja, *Kelmet il-Malti: dizzjunarju Malti–Ingliz, Ingliz–Malti = Dictionary Maltese–English, English–Maltese*. Malta: Gulf, 1984. 536 pp. New edn.

1st edn: 1982.

The English–Maltese section is by far the larger (pp. 167–536).

1036.

Vincenzo Busuttil, *Diziunariu mill Inglis ghall Malti*. [Valletta:] Stamperia tal Malta, 1900. 1399 pp.

[*English–Maltese dictionary.*] The largest dictionary into Maltese, with 90,000 entries: vitiated by the exclusion of loanwords in favour of compounds and phrases invented by the author. Largely superseded by Bugeja (**1035**).

The same author's *Diziunariu mill Malti ghall Inglis* (1900. 583 pp.) claimed 30,000 entries. It has been superseded by more recent works such as that of Aquilina (**1033**).

MANCHU

Manchu speakers have the status of an 'official nationality of China', though there are fewer than 1000 of them; a linguistic offshoot, 'colloquial Manchu' or Xibo, has about 27,000 speakers in an isolated corner of Xinjiang. Manchu has its own traditional script, written vertically on the page like Mongolian.

It belongs to the small and obscure family of Tungusic languages of north-eastern Asia. EVEN is another member of the family. Many scholars now make Tungusic a member of the wider Altaic family, like Mongolian and Turkic.

1037.

H. C. von der Gabelentz, *Sse-schu, Schu-king, Schi-king in mandschuischer Uebersetzung, mit einem mandschu–deutsches Wörterbuch*. Leipzig: Brockhaus, 1864. 2 parts.

Abhandlungen für die Kunde des Morgenlandes, vol. 3 parts 1–2.

Note also: Hartmut Walravens, Martin Gimm, *Deutsch–mandjurisches Wörterverzeichnis (nach H. C. von der Gabelentz' Mandschu–deutschen Wörterbuch)*. Wiesbaden: Steiner, 1978. 612 pp. (*Sinologica Coloniensia*, 4.) [*German–Manchu word-list on the basis of von der Gabelentz.*]

[*Manchu–German dictionary.*] The dictionary, in Latin script, forms part 2 (232 pp.).

1038.

Erich Hauer, *Handwörterbuch der Mandschusprache*. Wiesbaden: Harrassowitz, 1952–5. 3 parts [1032 pp.].

[*Concise dictionary of the Manchu language.*] In Latin script.

1039.

Jerry Norman, *A concise Manchu–English lexicon*. Seattle: University of Washington Press, 1978. 320 pp. 0–295–95574–0.

Publications on Asia of the School of International Studies, 32.

A brief-entry dictionary in Latin transcription, also supplying Chinese script equivalents for official administrative terms.

1040.

William Rozycki, *Mongol elements in Manchu*. Bloomington: Research Center for Inner Asian Studies, 1994. 255 pp. 0–933070–31–4.

Indiana University Uralic and Altaic series, 157.

In alphabetical order under Manchu words, which are given in Latin script. Index of Mongol words, pp. 232–48.

MANGGARAI

An AUSTRONESIAN language of Flores in Indonesia, with half a million speakers.

1041.

Jilis A. J. Verheijen, *Kamus Manggarai*. The Hague: Nijhoff, 1967–70. 2 vols.

Koninklijk Instituut voor Taal-, Land- en Volkenkunde.

[*Manggarai dictionary.*] A dictionary which is particularly informative on dialect variation and includes some etymological notes. Vol. 1 (772 pp.): Manggarai–Indonesian dictionary. Vol. 2 (269 pp.): Indonesian–Manggarai dictionary.

MANIPURI

Language of the small state of Manipur in north-eastern India, Manipuri (or Meithei, Meithlei) belongs to the Tibeto-Burman group of SINO-TIBETAN LANGUAGES. It has just over a million speakers.

1042.

Ningthaukhongjam Khelchandra Singh, *Manipuri to Manipuri and English dictionary*. Imphal, 1964. 656 pp.

Not seen.

MANSI

One of the URALIC LANGUAGES, also known as Vogul. Mansi has about 5000 speakers in the middle Ob valley in western Siberia.

1043.

Béla Kálmán, editor, *Wogulisches Wörterbuch, gesammelt von Bernát Munkácsi*. Budapest: Akadémiai Kiadó, 1986. 950 pp. 963–05–3867–9.

[*Mansi dictionary, collected by Bernát Munkácsi.*] A Mansi–Hungarian–German dictionary, with German index, pp. 747–835, and Hungarian index, pp. 841–950. The materials were collected in 1888–9. The Mansi is in the phonetic script of the Société Finno-Ougrienne: the alphabetical order demands some study. There is full indication of dialect variation (abbreviations for place names, p. 14). Plenty of example phrases are quoted, in Mansi and German (not Hungarian).

MANX

The extinct CELTIC language of the Isle of Man. Always the poor relation among Celtic languages of modern times, Manx has very little literature and no large-scale dictionary.

1044.

George C. Broderick, *A handbook of late spoken Manx*. Tübingen, 1984. 2 vols.

Vol. 2 (523 pp.) is a Manx–English dictionary based on material collected from the last remaining speakers.

1045.

Douglas C. Fargher, *Fargher's English–Manx dictionary*. Douglas: Shearwater Press, 1979. 894 pp. 0–904980–23–5.

Edited by Brian Stowell, Ian Faulds.

A brief-entry dictionary with plenty of example phrases.

1046.

Robert Leith Thomson, 'A glossary of early Manx' in *Zeitschrift für keltische Philologie* vols 24–27 (1954–9).

Deals with the language of seventeenth century Manx texts.

MAORI

The AUSTRONESIAN language of New Zealand, Maori may have as many as 100,000 speakers.

1047.

Bruce Biggs, *The complete English–Maori dictionary*. Auckland: Auckland University Press, 1981. 227 pp. 0–19–647989–4.

Very brief for a dictionary that claims to be 'complete'. It will be useful to some that Latin taxonomic names for plants and animals are to be found interfiled with the English headwords, making it easy to trace Maori names for flora and fauna.

Biggs's first Maori glossary was published in 1960.

1048.

Te Matatiki: contemporary Māori words. Auckland: Oxford University Press, 1996. 289 pp. Revised edn. 0–19–558341–8.

Māori Language Commission.

Earlier edn: Wellington: Te Taura Whiri i te Reo Māori, 1992.

A two-way brief-entry dictionary of neologisms for modern developments and concepts. The revised edition indicates the Maori derivations of new compound words (many of which are calques on English words).

1049.

Edward Tregear, *The Maori–Polynesian comparative dictionary*. Wellington: Lyon & Blair, 1891. 675 pp.

Note also: A. S. Atkinson, *Notes on the Maori–Polynesian comparative dictionary of Mr. E. Tregear*. Nelson, New Zealand: Bond, 1893. 69 pp.

1050.

Herbert William Williams, *A dictionary of the Maori language*. Wellington: Government Printer, 1957. 499 pp. 6th edn, 'revised and augmented by the Advisory Committee on the Teaching of the Maori Language, Department of Education.'

Reprints ('7th edn', '8th edn'): 1971, 1985.

1st edn: William Williams, *A dictionary of the New Zealand language*. Paihia, 1844. – 2nd edn: London, 1852. – 3rd edn: 1871. – 4th edn: Auckland: Upton, 1892. 325 pp. – 5th edn, revised by Herbert William Williams: Wellington: Marks, 1917. 590 pp.

A Maori–English dictionary with example sentences. Loanwords are listed separately in an appendix. The 4th edition included an English–Maori section by W. L. Williams.

MARATHI

Marathi is the language of Maharashtra state, and one of the official languages of India. It belongs to the INDO-ARYAN group of Indo-European languages, and has 50 million speakers.

The Devanagari alphabet for Marathi

अआइईउऊऋ एऐओऔ

a ā i ī u ū ṛ   e ai o au

कखगघङ चछजझञ टठडढण तथदधन पफबभम यरलव शषसह

k kh g gh ṅ   c ch j jh ñ   ṭ ṭh ḍ ḍh ṇ   t th d dh n   p ph b bh m   y r l v   ś ṣ s h

The cursive मोडी *Modi* script was invented for Marathi in the seventeenth century, but it is now less commonly found even in handwriting: since 1800 it has been officially replaced by a Devanagari alphabet, almost as used for Hindi but with a few different character shapes. It is usually called बालबोध *Balbodh* 'that can be understood by a child'. Consonants are combined with a following vowel to make a single character. For a table of the secondary vowel signs see SANSKRIT.

1051.

T. R. Date [and others], *Maharastra sabdakos*. Poona, 1932–8. 7 vols.
Followed by a supplement: 1950. 254 pp.

[*Maharashtra dictionary.*] A large-scale monolingual dictionary covering older forms of the language, dialects and colloquialisms as well as the modern standard. Brief etymologies.

1052.

K. P. Kulkarni, *Marathi vyutpatti kos*. Poona, 1964. 829 pp. 2nd edn.
1st edn: Bombay, 1947.

[*Marathi etymological dictionary.*]

1053.

J. T. Molesworth, *A dictionary, Maráthí and English*. Bombay, 1857. 921 pp. 2nd edn.
'Printed for Government.'
1st edn: *A dictionary, Murathee and English*. 1831. 1162 pp. 'Assisted by Lieutenants T. and G. Candy.'

A very copious dictionary of nineteenth century Marathi with glosses in English. The Marathi is given in Devanagari script only. The story of how the work was done, drawing from both oral and written material, is well worth reading (p. xxi).

1054.

J. T. Molesworth, T. Candy, *A dictionary, English and Maráthí*. Bombay: Kanoba, 1873. 974 pp. '2nd edn revised and enlarged.'
1st edn: 1847. – 2nd edn: 1857.

A full dictionary into Marathi, with numerous equivalents for English proverbs and sayings, and with some ethnographical notes on Marathi topics (see for example the entry **Charms**).

1055.

N. B. Ranade, *The twentieth century English–Marathi dictionary, pronouncing, etymological, literary, scientific, and technical*. Irani's Wadi: Ranade [1916]. 2 vols [2012 pp.]. New edn or reprint.
1st edn: Bombay, 1903.

By far the largest dictionary into Marathi, this early twentieth century publication was intended for Marathi-speaking users.

Other works of interest

1056.

Ashok R. Kelkar, 'The anatomy of a dictionary entry with samples proposed for a Marathi–English dictionary' in B. G. Misra, editor, *Lexicography in India: proceedings of the First National Conference on Dictionary Making in Indian Languages, Mysore, 1970* (Manasagangotri, Mysore: Central Institute of Indian Languages, 1980) pp. 199–227.

MARI

Mari or Cheremis is a URALIC language of European Russia. It has 600,000 speakers. Like Russian, it is written in the Cyrillic alphabet.

1057.

H. Paasonens Ost-Tscheremissisches Wörterbuch. Helsinki: Suomalais-Ugrilainen Seura, 1948. 210 pp.

Edited by Paavo Siro. *Lexica Societatis Fenno-Ugricae*, 11.

[*H. Paasonen's Eastern Mari dictionary.*] The Mari is in the transcription of the Société Finno-Ougrienne. A short dictionary with glosses variably in Finnish, German and Russian (usually in at least two of these) and etymological notes. German index, pp. 178–210. Additions, pp. 171–7; corrections, p. xii.

1058.

Марий мутер = Словарь марийского языка [*Marii muter = Slovar' mariiskogo yazyka*]. Yoshkar-Ola: Mariiskoe Knizhnoe Izdatel'stvo, 1990– .

By A. A. Abramova and others; chief editor, I. S. Galkin. Iylmym, Literaturym da Istoriiym Nauchno Shymlyshe 'Znak Pocheta' Ordenan V. M. Vasil'ev Lümesh Marii Institut.

[*Mari dictionary.*] I have seen only vol. 1, which covers **A–З**. Glosses are in Russian. A concise historical dictionary in which quotations are given from named authors, but without precise references. They are accompanied by Russian translations. Within each entry a white square □ marks the beginning of the section of quotations.

1059.

The first Cheremis grammar (1775). Chicago: Newberry Library, 1956. 64 + 136 pp. Facsimile with introduction and analysis by Thomas A. Sebeok and Alo Raun.

Original edn: *Sochineniya prinadlezhashchiya k grammatike Cheremiskago yazyka.* Kazan', 1775. 136 pp.

[*Writings on the grammar of the Mari language.*] Probably compiled under the supervision of Venyamin Putsek-Grigorovich, Archbishop of Kazan' and an accomplished linguist. The Chicago reprint includes an etymological word-list (pp. 19–

48), a morpheme index (pp. 49–61) and a two-page list of misprints, all keyed to the original grammar.

1060.

Васильев В. М., Саваткова А. А., Учаев З. В., *Марийско–русский словарь = Марла рушла мутер* [Vasil'ev V. M., Savatkova A. A., Uchaev Z. V., *Mariisko–russkii slovar'*]. Yoshkar-Ola: Mariiskoe Knizhnoe Izdatel'stvo, 1991 508 pp. 2nd edn.

[*Mari–Russian dictionary.*] About 20,000 entries, followed by a short grammatical sketch.

MASAI

A NILO-SAHARAN language of Tanzania and Kenya, with 750,000 speakers.

1061.

Johannes Hohenberger, *Semitisches und hamitisches Sprachgut im Masai, mit vergleichendem Wörterbuch*. Sachsenmühle, 1958. 508 pp.

[*Semitic and Hamitic vocabulary in Masai, with a comparative dictionary.*] The dictionary, pp. 295–450. German–Masai annotated index, pp. 451–92. Semitic word index, pp. 493–508.

MAYAN LANGUAGES

The family relationship of the Mayan languages of Mexico and Central America was already noted by Lorenzo Hervás y Panduro in *Catalogo delle lingue conosciute e notizia della loro affinità e diversità* (Italy, 1784). Languages of the group include Cakchiquel, Chol, Kekchí, Mam dialects, Quiche, Tzotzil dialects and – the best known – Yucatec. Mayan languages are included by Joseph Greenberg in his controversial family of AMERIND LANGUAGES. There are more than two million speakers. Mayan languages have no national status. In pre-Columbian times they were written in hieroglyphic scripts, which are gradually being deciphered; the Latin alphabet was introduced by the Spanish invaders and is now currently used when Mayan languages are written.

1062.

John M. Dienhart, *The Mayan languages: a comparative vocabulary*. Odense: Odense University Press, 1989. 3 vols. 87–7492–722–1.

A useful compilation from earlier sources. The dictionary, vols 2–3, arranged under English meanings. Spanish–English index, vol. 1 pp. 60–78. Much wasted blank paper.

1063.

Munro S. Edmonson, *Quiche–English dictionary*. New Orleans: Tulane University, Middle American Research Institute, 1965.

Not seen.

1064.

Jo Ann Munson L., *Diccionario cakchiquel central y español*. Guatemala: Instituto Lingüístico de Verano de Centroamérica, 1991. 383 pp.
Research by Déborah Ruyán Canú, Rafael Coyote Tum.

[*Central Cakchiquel and Spanish dictionary.*]

1065.

Ortwin Smailus, *Vocabulario en lengua castellana y guatemalteca que se llama Cakchiquel Chi: análisis gramatical y lexicológico del Cakchiquel colonial según un antiguo diccionario anónimo*. Hamburg: Wayasbah, 1989. 3 vols. 3–925682–14–7.
Wayasbah publication, 14.

[*Vocabulary in Spanish and the Guatemaltec language called Cakchiquel Chi: a grammatical and lexical analysis of colonial Cakchiquel on the basis of an early anonymous dictionary.*] Vol. 1, grammar; vols 2–3, vocabulary.

1066.

Francisco Ximénez, *Tesoro de las tres lenguas. Primera parte del Tesoro de las lenguas cakchiquel, quiché y zutuhil, en que las dichas lenguas se traducen a la nuestra española: de acuerdo con los manuscritos redactados en la Antigua Guatemala a principios del siglo XVIII, y conservados en Córdoba (España) y Berkeley (California)*. Guatemala: Academia de Geografía e Historia de Guatemala, 1985. 659 pp.
Edición crítica por Carmelo Sáenz de Santa María. *Publicación especial*, 30.

[*Treasury of the three languages: part one of the Treasury of the Cakchiquel, Quiche and Zutuhil languages, giving Spanish equivalents for all three, on the basis of manuscripts compiled in early Guatemala at the beginning of the eighteenth century and preserved at Cordoba and Berkeley.*]

MIAO

Miao and YAO, minority languages of mountain dwellers in southern China and northern south east Asia, together make up the small Miao-Yao language family. Following the work of Paul Benedict, the Miao-Yao languages are now generally agreed to belong to the wider family of AUSTRO-TAI LANGUAGES.

Miao itself is a group of fairly divergent dialects, with about five million speakers in total.

There is no tradition of indigenous literacy. The Smalley-Heimbach Latin orthography, devised for missionary purposes, has become the de facto standard. It is used in all the dictionaries listed here except that by Lyman, which is in a phonetic transcription.

Miao alphabetical order

Dictionary alphabetical order in the standard Smalley-Heimbach orthography for Miao is more complicated than in any other language that uses the Latin alphabet. The same system is used in **1067, 1068, 1070**. The following are treated as single characters in filing:

a aa ai au aw b c ch d dl dlh e ee f g h hl i ia j k kh l m ml n nc ndl ndlh
ng nk nkh np nph npl nplh nq nqh nr nrh nt nth nts ntsh ntx ntxh ny o
oo p ph pl plh q qh r rh s t th ts tsh tx txh u ua v w x xy y z

B, D, G, J are found only at the end of syllables, where they function not as consonants but as tone markers. M, S, V function as consonants initially, as tone markers when placed at the end of syllables. W is a vowel.

1067.

Yves Bertrais, R. P. Charrier, *Dictionnaire hmong (mèo blanc)–français*.
Vientiane: Mission Catholique, 1964. About 500 unnumbered pages.
Reprinted: Bangkok: Assumption Press, 1979.

[*White Miao-French dictionary.*] Roneoed. A large-scale work perhaps rather hastily reconstituted after the original data were lost. This remains the largest dictionary of a Miao language: about 7500 entries, with many sub-entries and examples.

1068.

Ernest E. Heimbach, *White Meo–English dictionary*. Ithaca: Cornell University,
Department of Asian Studies, 1969. 497 pp.
Southeast Asia Program. *Data paper*, 75. *Linguistics series*, 4.

Material gathered between 1954 and 1963 in missionary work in northern Thailand, with visits to Laos. Appendices: patterns of tone change; classifiers; useful phrases; proverbs, pp. 461–6; farming calendar, p. 467; post-verbal intensifiers; classified vocabulary (a partial index) pp. 480–492; kinship charts, pp. 492–7.

1069.

Thomas Amis Lyman, *Dictionary of Mong Njua, a Miao (Meo) language of Southeast Asia*. The Hague: Mouton, 1974. 403 pp.

The language is also known as Green Miao. Lyman worked with speakers in Nan province of Thailand. His work is a Hmong Neua–English dictionary employing a phonetic script. Explanations, pp. 15–40; correspondences with the Smalley-Heimbach orthography for White Miao (see Heimbach, **1068**), pp. 65–6. Appendices (forming a partial English index) include: body terms; colours; compass; kinship terms; minerals; numerals; opium etc.; rice; seasons; sickness and medicine; day, month and year names; tools, instruments and weapons; weaving. List of clans, p. 383.

1070.

Lang Xiong, William J. Xiong, Nao Leng Xiong, *English–Mong–English dictionary = Phoo txais lug Aakiv–Moob–Aakiv*. Milwaukee: Xiong, 1983. 570 pp.

A brief-entry dictionary intended for migrants from Vietnam settled in the United States. English–Miao section, pp. 1–460; Miao–English, pp. 462–547.

MINANGKABAU

The most widespread of the regional languages of Sumatra, Minangkabau is one of the AUSTRONESIAN LANGUAGES. Until recently there was no indigenous written literature, but there is a rich tradition of Minangkabau oral poetry. There are over six million speakers.

1071.

Gérard Moussay, *Dictionnaire minangkabau indonésien français*. Paris: L'Harmattan, 1995. 2 vols [1328 pp.]. 2–7384–3126–7.
Cahier d'Archipel, 27. Collection "Recherches asiatiques".

   [*Minangkabau–Indonesian–French dictionary.*] A large-scale, illustrated, encyclopaedic dictionary. Headwords are immediately followed by a brief Indonesian gloss, then French; then phrases and example sentences, with French translations. Taxonomic names are given for flora and fauna. A white square □ marks the beginning of each section of examples; the abbreviations *exp.* 'popular saying' and *kb.* '*kaba*, tale' identify the origins of many examples. Brief etymologies are given in square brackets.

   The work is based on a written corpus, mainly journalism, published between 1965 and 1990. It is a highly important source for colloquialisms, dialects, traditions and popular beliefs.

1072.

J. L. van der Toorn, *Minangkabausch–Maleisch–Nederlandsch woordenboek*. The Hague: Nijhoff, 1891. 392 pp.

   [*Minangkabau–Malay–Dutch dictionary.*] Headwords in Arabic script followed by Latin transliteration.

MON

Mon is an AUSTROASIATIC language of southern Burma and central Thailand, with about 200,000 speakers. It is normally written in a script similar to – and indeed ancestral to – that of Burmese. The dictionaries by Shorto, **1073** and **1075**, are in romanisation; Stevens's, **1074**, uses Mon script.

1073.

H. L. Shorto, *A dictionary of modern spoken Mon*. London: Oxford University Press, 1962. 280 pp. 0–19–713524–2.
School of Oriental and African Studies.

   An extensive Mon–English dictionary by an academic linguist (Professor at the School of Oriental and African Studies, London). The main dictionary is in Latin transliteration, followed by an index in Mon script, not complete but covering words encountered in literature.

1074.

Edward O. Stevens, *A vocabulary English and Peguan to which are added a few pages of geographical names*. Rangoon: American Baptist Mission Press, 1896. 139 pp.

The only bilingual dictionary into Mon that I have come across.

1075.

H. L. Shorto, *A dictionary of the Mon inscriptions from the sixth to the sixteenth centuries*. London: Oxford University Press, 1971. 406 pp. 0–19–713565–X.

London Oriental series, 24. Incorporating materials collected by C. O. Blagden.

In Latin transliteration throughout.

MONGOLIAN LANGUAGES

A family which some have linked with TURKIC, Tungusic (see MANCHU) and sometimes Korean and Japanese under the general name of 'Altaic languages'.

The Mongolian family includes Mongolian in the narrow sense (Khalkha), Buryat, Kalmyk-Oirat. Khalkha is spoken in Inner Mongolia (in China) and is also the national language of Mongolia (sometimes called 'Outer Mongolia'). Oirat, with Monguor, Ordos and other minority languages, is also spoken in China; Buryat and Kalmyk are languages of Russia, Kalmyk being spoken far away from all its relatives on the north-western shore of the Caspian Sea. These languages separated from one another relatively recently, in the course of migrations and conquests which mostly took place less than a thousand years ago, and remain similar. There are perhaps five million speakers of Mongolian languages today.

Cyrillic script is used in Mongolia and in Russia, Uigur script in China. The traditional Mongolian script, written vertically on the page, is by no means forgotten.

Mongolian (Cyrillic) alphabetical order

А Б В Г Д Е Ё Ж З И Й К Л М Н О Ѳ П Р С Т У У Ф Х Ц Ч Ш Щ Ъ Ы Ь Э Ю Я

а б в г д е ё ж з и й к л м н о ѳ п р с т у у ф х ц ч ш щ ъ ы ь э ю я

The modern standards and dialects

Buryat

1076.

К. М. Черемисов, *Бурятско–русский словарь = Буряад–ород словарь* [K. M. Cheremisov, *Buryatsko–russkii slovar'*]. Moscow: Sovetskaya Entsiklopediya, 1973. 803 pp.

[*Buryat–Russian dictionary*.] 44,000 entries.

1077.

Ц. Б. Цыдендамбаев, *Русско–бурят-монгольский словарь = Ород–бурят-монгол словарь* [Ts. B. Tsydendambaev, *Russko–buryat-mongol'skii slovar'*]. Moscow, 1954. 750 pp.

[*Russian–Buryat dictionary.*]

Kalmyk

1078.

G. J. Ramstedt, *Kalmückisches Wörterbuch*. Helsinki: Suomalais-Ugrilainen Seura, 1935. 560 pp.

Lexica Societatis Fenno-Ugricae, 3.

[*Kalmyk dictionary.*] A copious short-entry Kalmyk–German dictionary with some etymological information. The Kalmyk is in the Société Finno-Ougrienne's transcription: alphabetical order, p. xxx. 'Only a part of the linguistic material comes from the people who call themselves Kalmyks. We are concerned with the language of the Western Mongols, a linguistically and ethnically homogeneous group of Mongol nomadic clans, who call themselves, in distinction from other Mongols, Oirats.'

Grammatical introduction, pp. viii–xxv; abbreviations, pp. xxvi–xxx. Corrections, pp. 485–8 ('the early pages were printed off more than twenty years ago,' wrote Ramstedt); very full German index, pp. 489–560.

Khalkha

1079.

Charles Bawden, *Mongolian–English dictionary*. London: Kegan Paul International, 1997. 595 pp. 0–7103–0439–0.

A brief-entry bilingual dictionary in which the Mongolian is in Cyrillic script only. 'I have avoided using earlier dictionaries as a source for keywords. My procedure has been to read contemporary publications and to extract words and phrases from them, with the joint aims of avoiding the strait-jacket of a pre-set pattern of entries, of including only living vocabulary, and of trying to record current meanings ... I have done my best to follow the wise precept enunciated by Father Antoine Mostaert in respect of his *Dictionnaire Ordos* [**1084**] of excluding everything which appeared uncertain.'

About 26,000 entries. Taxonomic names are given where these were provided in the sources used. Chinese and Tibetan origin is indicated for loanwords.

1080.

Ц. Дамдинсүрэн, А. Лувсандэндэв, *Орос–монгол толь = Русско–монгольский словарь* [Ts. Damdinsüren, A. Luvsandendev, *Oros–Mongol tol'*]. Ulan Bator: Ulsyn Khevleliin Gazar, 1982. 840 pp.

BNMAU-yn Shinzhlekh Ukhaany Akad., Khel Zokhilyn Khureelen.

[*Russian–Mongolian dictionary.*] A big dictionary in Cyrillic script. 55,000 entries.

1081.

Ferdinand G. Lessing, general editor, Mattai Haltod [and others], *Mongolian–English dictionary*. Berkeley: University of California Press, 1960. 1217 pp.

A brief-entry dictionary, necessarily spacious in layout because headwords are in the traditional Mongolian script, written vertically, as well as in Cyrillic and in a Latin transcription (details, p. xii). Arranged in Latin alphabetical order, but there is also an index in Cyrillic (pp. 1089–1133) and a partial 'index of variant readings' which helps, up to a point, the reader of Mongolian script (pp. 1137–55).

Supplement of Buddhist terms and phrases that are not fully integrated in everyday speech, pp. 1159–93: Tibetan and Sanskrit equivalents are given for these. Additions and corrections, pp. 1197–1217.

Monguor

1082.

A. de Smedt, Antoine Mostaert, *Dictionnaire monguor–français*. Beijing: Catholic University, 1933.

[*Monguor–French dictionary.*] Monguor is the Mongolian language spoken in the Chinese province of Gansu. A grammar by the same authors appeared in 1944.

Oirat

1083.

John R. Krueger, *Materials for an Oirat-Mongolian to English citation dictionary*. Bloomington: Mongolia Society, 1978–84. 3 vols [816 pp.].
Publications of the Mongolia Society.

Ordos

1084.

Antoine Mostaert, *Dictionnaire ordos*. Beijing, 1941–4. 3 vols.

[*Ordos dictionary.*]

Older periods

1085.

Folke Boberg, *Mongolian–English dictionary in three volumes*. Stockholm: Forlaget Filadelfia, 1954–5. 3 vols.

A brief-entry dictionary: the Mongolian is in traditional Mongolian script only. Vol. 3 (600 pp.) is an English–Mongolian index. Boberg includes some obsolete and dialect words excluded by later dictionaries.

1086.

О. Ковалевскій, *Монгольско-русско-французскій словарь* = J. E. Kowalewski, *Dictionnaire mongol-russe-français*. Kazan', 1844–9. 3 vols [2690 pp.].

[*Mongol–Russian–French dictionary.*] 'A dictionary can be eminently good only to the extent that it is complete and exact' (Kowalewski, quoted by Bawden, **1079**). Kowalewski, best known for the wild horse of the steppes which is named after him, included in his dictionary 'a substantial part of the difficult Buddhist terminology, with Tibetan and even some Sanskrit equivalents' (Lessing, **1081**).

Other works of interest

1087.

Диалектная лексика в монгольских языках [*Dialektnaya leksika v mongol'skikh yazykakh*]. Ulan-Ude, 1987. 167 pp.

Edited by L. D. Shagdarov.

MORDVIN

Erzya and Moksha are two URALIC LANGUAGES traditionally grouped together under the name Mordvin. These two languages of European Russia, with 850,000 speakers, are written in the Cyrillic alphabet.

1088.

Б. А. Серебренников, *Эрзянь–рузонь валкс = Эрзянско–русский словарь* [B. A. Serebrennikov and other editors, *Erzyan'–ruzon' valks = Erzyansko–russkii slovar'*]. Moscow: Russkii Yazyk, 1993. 803 + 48 pp. 5–200–01585–5.

Mordovskoi SSR-n' Pravitel'stvaso Znak Pocheta Ordenen' Kelen', Literaturan', Istoriian' dy Ekonomikan' Nauchno-issledovatel'skoi Institutos.

[*Erzya–Russian dictionary.*] A brief-entry dictionary with indication of dialect variation (list of place names, pp. 23–5). About 27,000 entries.

1089.

В. И. Щанкина, *Мокшень–рузонь валкс; русско–мокшанский словарь* [V. I. Shchankina, *Mokshen'–ruzon' valks; russko–mokshanskii slovar'*]. Saransk: Mordovskiai Knizhnai Izdavatel'stvas', 1993. 445 pp.

[*Moksha–Russian and Russian–Moksha dictionary.*] Brief-entry two-way dictionary.

MUNDARI

The best known of the AUSTROASIATIC LANGUAGES of central India, with about 850,000 speakers.

1090.

Johann Hoffmann, A. van Emmelen [and others], *Encyclopaedia Mundarica*. Patna, 1930–79. 15 vols [4889 pp.].

Vols 1–13 were published between 1930 and 1950. The last two volumes took nearly thirty years to appear.

Includes dialect forms, and words drawn from songs and other oral literature. Full of ethnographical and historical information. Loanwords, mostly from the Sadani dialect of Hindi, are identified.

See P. Ponette, 'Hoffmann's two important collaborators … van Emmelen and Menas Orea' in *The Munda world: Hoffmann commemoration volume* ed. P. Ponette (Ranchi, 1978) pp. 42–6.

NAHUATL

Nahuatl is a member of the Uto-Aztecan family of AMERIND LANGUAGES, of which it is the most southerly representative except for the closely related Pipil, a dying language of Guatemala. Nahuatl was the language of the powerful Aztecs. Their pictographic writing system was replaced, under Spanish rule and missionary influence, by Latin script. Nahuatl and related dialects now have perhaps 1,250,000 speakers.

1091.

John Bierhorst, *A Nahuatl–English dictionary and concordance to the Cantares mexicanos, with an analytic transcription and grammatical notes*. Stanford: Stanford University Press, 1985. 751 pp.

A glossary to the most important collection of early Nahuatl poetry, forming a partial dictionary of the 'classical' and late pre-Columbian language.

1092.

Frances Karttunen, *An analytical dictionary of Nahuatl*. Austin: University of Texas Press, 1983. 349 pp. 0–292–70365–1.
Texas linguistics series.

The main section is Nahuatl–English; there is also a briefer English–Nahuatl section.

NAVAHO

Navaho is one of the small family of Na-Dené languages of North America, and is closely related to the various Apache dialects. It has about 120,000 speakers in the south-western United States.

1093.

Robert W. Young, William Morgan, *The Navajo language: a grammar and colloquial dictionary*. Albuquerque: University of New Mexico Press, 1987. 2nd edn.
1st edn: 1980. 472 + 1069 pp. 0–8263–0536–9.

NAXI

Naxi is a SINO-TIBETAN language, also known as Moso and Na-Khi, with a pictographic writing system of its own. This is used for religious and literary texts. There are 250,000 speakers in Yunnan, in south-western China.

1094.
J. F. Rock, *A ¹Na-²khi–English encyclopedic dictionary*. Rome: Istituto Italiano per il Medio ed Estremo Oriente, 1963–72. 2 vols.
Serie orientale Roma, 28.
Reviews of vol. 1: R. A. Stein in *T'oung Pao* vol. 51 (1964) pp. 114–16; J. W. de Jong in *Indo-Iranian journal* vol. 7 (1963/4) pp. 236–8.
On the author see: Stephanne Barry Sutton, *In China's border provinces: the turbulent career of Joseph Rock, botanist-explorer*. New York: Hastings House, 1974. 334 pp.
    Originally a botanist, Rock made the study of Naxi manuscripts his life's work.

NENETS

Nenets or Yurak is a SAMOYEDIC language of the far north of Siberia. It has about 25,000 speakers, widely scattered.

1095.
T. Lehtisalo, *Juraksamojedisches Wörterbuch*. Helsinki: Suomalais-Ugrilainen Seura, 1965. 601 pp.
Lexica Societatis Fenno-Ugricae, 13.
    [*Yurak dictionary.*] A Nenets–German dictionary with many examples quoted from oral sources and with brief etymological notes. Covers dialects of both Tundra and Forest Nenets. German index, pp. 523–600; index of taxonomic names, p. 600; Russian index, p. 601. Record of research journeys, pp. vii–cii. Abbreviations for place names and informants, pp. cii–cv.

NEPALI

Nepali, one of the INDO-ARYAN LANGUAGES of the Indo-European family, is the national language of Nepal, with at least eight million speakers. Older names are Khas Kurā and Parbatiya. The lingua franca of 'Gurkha' mercenary regiments is called Gurkhali in the British army and Gorkhali in the Indian army.
    The monument of Nepali lexicography is Turner's dictionary (**1096**), but there have been many changes in the language since the 1920s.

Nepali and Gurkhali in writing:

Devanagari script and the British Army's standard romanisation

प्रप्राइईउऊ एऐप्रोप्रौ

a ā i i u u e ai o au

कखगघङ चछजझञ टठडढण तथदधन पफबभम यरलव शषसह

k kh g gh ng ch chh j jh ñ ṭ ṭh ḍ ḍh ṇ t th d dh n p ph b bh m y r l v sh sh s h

Consonants are combined with a following vowel to make a single character. For a table of the secondary vowel signs see SANSKRIT.

1096.

Ralph Lilley Turner, *A comparative and etymological dictionary of the Nepali language*. London: Routledge, 1961.

Corrected reprint, with new indexes (by Dorothy Rivers Turner) of forms cited from other Indo-European languages.

First published: London: Kegan Paul, 1931. 935 pp.

'Four years of active service in the Indian Army provided me with much first-hand material from ... Nepali'. The dictionary was compiled in the 1920s with the active support of the Maharaja of Nepal. Headwords appear in Devanagari and romanisation; many examples of colloquial usage are given. Brief etymological information is provided: each entry includes a list of related words in other Indo-Aryan languages. The index consists of a series of lists in which Nepali words are set beside related forms in over fifty languages. The Nepali dictionary thus prefigures Turner's *Comparative dictionary of the Indo-Aryan languages* (**763**).

Turner's Devanagari spellings include two 'reforms' which have not caught on, though they cause no difficulty in consultation. The distinctions between इ *i* and ई *ī* and between उ *u* and ऊ *ū*, which have no relevance to Nepali pronunciation, are dropped, just as they are in the Army romanisation; and all syllable-final consonants are marked with the *halanta* stroke .

1097.

पुष्कर शम्शेर | अंग्रेजी–नेपाली कोष [Puṣkar Śaṁśer, *Aṅgrejī–Nepālī koṣ*]. Kathmandu: Nepālī Bhāṣā Prakāśinī Samiti, 1936. 2 vols.

[*English–Nepali dictionary.*] Compiled by translating the *Concise Oxford dictionary* into Nepali word by word. Both glosses and quotations are translated in full, and English pronunciation is indicated in Devanagari script.

1098.

बालचन्द्र शर्मा | नेपाली शब्दकोष [Bālcandra Śarmā, *Nepālī śabdakoṣ*]. Kathmandu: Royal Nepal Academy, 1962. 1146 pp.

[*Nepali dictionary.*] A single-language dictionary of Nepali, including brief etymological and grammatical information. Fairly strong on modern vocabulary, though technical, legal and administrative terms are included only when they form part of the everyday language.

Spelling variants, which are numerous in Nepali, are included generously, with cross-references. The frequent variation in nouns between final ा *a* and ो *o* is not fully dealt with, but this gives the user little difficulty.

NEWARI

Newari is the local language of the Kathmandu valley, and thus of most inhabitants of Kathmandu itself, though it is now surrounded by speakers of Nepal's national language, Nepali. It is a SINO-TIBETAN language, but is normally written in the Devanagari script that is standard for Nepali and for Hindi. There are about half a million speakers.

1099.
Hans Jørgensen, *A dictionary of the classical Newari*. Copenhagen: Levin & Munksgaard, 1936. 178 pp.
Det Kgl. Danske Videnskabernes Selskab. *Historisk-filologiske meddelelser*, vol. 23 part 1.

1100.
वैद्य पन्नप्रसाद जोशी | संक्षिप्त नेपाल भाषा शब्दकोष नेपाल भाषा नेपाली अर्थ [Vaidya Pannaprasād Josī, *Saṅkṣipta Nepāl bhāṣā śabdakoṣ, Nepāl bhāṣā Nepālī artha*]. Kathmandu: Nepal Press, 1076 [1955/6]. 283 pp.
Accompanied by a supplement, a Nepali–Newari index.
[*Concise dictionary of Newari, from Newari to Nepali.*]

1101.
Ulrike Kölver, Iswarananda Shresthacarya, *A dictionary of contemporary Newari: Newari–English*. Bonn: VGH Wissenschaftsverlag, 1994. 341 pp. 3–88280–049–6.
Nepalica, **8.**
A concise dictionary of the spoken language with interesting ethnographical notes. Headwords are in Devanagari accompanied by Latin transliteration.

NIGER-CONGO LANGUAGES

The very large and old Niger-Congo language family has hundreds of members in western, central and southern Africa. Niger-Congo languages with separate entries here include: EDO, FULANI, GBE, IGBO, SANGO, TIV, YORUBA. There are small dictionaries for many other languages of this family, but scarcely any major dictionaries exist: much lexicographical and etymological work remains to be done.

An offshoot of the Benue-Congo group of Niger-Congo, the Bantu language group has spread in the last two millennia across almost all the southern third of the African continent. The Bantu languages with separate entries in this book are BEMBA, CHOKWE, GANDA, KIKUYU, KONGO AND KITUBA, LUBA, NYANJA, RUNDI, SHONA, SOTHO, SWAHILI (internationally the most important of all), TSWANA, XHOSA and ZULU. Its shorter history makes the internal relationships of the Bantu group easier to explore, hence the relatively solid comparative Bantu works listed below.

Comparative dictionaries

1102.

Philip Elias, Jacqueline Leroy, Jan Voorhoeve, 'Mbam-Nkam or Eastern Grassfields' in *Afrika und Übersee* vol. 67 (1984) pp. 31–107.

1103.

Ludwig Gerhardt, *Beiträge zur Kenntnis der Sprachen des nigerianischen Plateaus.* Glückstadt: J. J. Augustin, 1983. 246 pp.

[*Studies on the languages of the Nigerian Plateau.*] Includes a listing of cognate forms.

1104.

Malcolm Guthrie, *Comparative Bantu.* Farnborough: Gregg, 1967–71. 4 vols.

Consists partly of a dictionary of proto-Bantu. Entries in this 'comparative series' are numbered, and other authors refer to them as 'CS'. Reconstructions whose descent from proto-Bantu cannot be proved, because their reflexes occur in only a single branch of Bantu, are placed by Guthrie in his 'partial series'.

1105.

Bernd Heine, *Die Verbreitung und Gliederung der Togorestsprachen.* Berlin: Reimer, 1968. 311 pp.
Kölner Beiträge zur Afrikanistik, 1.

[*The spread and differentiation of the Togo Remnant languages.*] Includes a listing of cognate forms.

1106.

Gabriel Manessy, *Les langues oti-volta:classification généalogique d'un groupe de langues voltaïques.* Paris: SELAF, 1975. 314 pp.
Followed by: Gabriel Manessy, *Contribution à la classification généalogique des langues voltaïques.* Paris, 1979. 107 pp. [*Contribution to the genetic classification of the Volta languages.*]

[*The Oti-Volta languages: genetic classification of a group of Volta languages.*] Includes a listing of cognate forms. This subgroup of Niger-Congo is now better known as the Gur languages.

1107.

Achiel E. Meeussen, *Bantu lexical reconstructions.* Tervuren: MRAC, 1980. 55 pp.
Archief voor anthropologie, 27.
Followed by: A. E. Meeussen, 'Bantu grammatical reconstructions' in *Africana linguistica* vol. 3 (1967).

1108.

Carl Meinhof, *Grundriss einer Lautlehre der Bantusprachen*. Berlin, 1910. 340 pp. 2nd edn.

1st edn: 1899. 245 pp.

English translation by N. J. van Warmelo: *Introduction to the phonology of the Bantu languages*. Berlin: Reimer, 1932. 248 pp.

[*Outlines of a phonology of the Bantu languages.*] The first attempted reconstruction of 'Ur-Bantu' or proto-Bantu, with a vocabulary of reconstructed roots. Includes detailed phonological studies of six languages, Pedi (Northern Sotho), Swahili, Makonde, Herero, Duala, Sango; a study of Zulu was added in the 2nd edition and the studies of Herero and Duala were dropped.

The vocabulary of proto-Bantu was extended by O. Dempwolff and W. Planert, and especially by W. Bourquin, *Neue Ur-Bantu-Wortstämme* (1923).

1109.

Hans Mukarovsky, *A study of western Nigritic*. Vienna: Afro-Pub, 1976–7. 2 vols.

Vol. 2, published first, contains a numbered list of 653 reconstructed roots. Mukarovsky's 'Western Nigritic' is a subdivision of Niger-Congo defined by himself: it excludes Mande, includes the Kwa, Gur, Togo Remnant and Atlantic groups but treats Benue-Congo (including Bantu) with suspicion.

1110.

Kiyoshi Shimizu, *Comparative Jukunoid*. Vienna: Afro-Pub, 1980. 2 vols [255 + 324 pp.].

1111.

Diedrich Westermann, *Die westlichen Sudansprachen und ihre Beziehungen zum Bantu*. Berlin, 1927. 313 pp.

Diedrich Westermann, *Die Sudansprachen: eine sprachvergleichende Studie*. Hamburg, 1911. 222 pp. [*The Sudan languages: a study in comparative linguistics.*]

[*The West Sudanic languages and their relationship with Bantu.*] Includes an early listing of cognate forms.

1112.

Kay Williamson, Kiyoshi Shimizu, editors, *Benue-Congo comparative wordlist*. Ibadan: West African Linguistic Society, University of Ibadan, 1968–73. 2 vols [473 pp.].

From contributions by members of the Benue-Congo Working Group.

Multilingual dictionaries

1113.

Heinrich Barth, *Sammlung und Bearbeitung Central-Afrikanischer Vokabularien* = Henry Barth, *Collection of vocabularies of Central-African languages*. Gotha: Justus Perthes, 1862–6. 3 parts.

Note also: P. A. Benton, *Notes on some Languages of the Western Sudan, including 24 unpublished vocabularies of Barth, extracts from correspondence regarding Richardson's and Barth's expeditions, and a few Hausa riddles and proverbs.* London: Oxford University Press, 1912.

The main work has glosses in German and English.

1114.

Maurice Delafosse, *Vocabulaires comparatifs de plus de 60 langues ou dialectes parlés à la Côte d'Ivoire et dans les régions limitrophes, avec des notes linguistiques et ethnologiques.* Paris: E. Leroux, 1904.

[*Comparative vocabularies of more than sixty languages or dialects spoken in Ivory Coast and neighbouring regions, with linguistic and ethnographical notes.*]

1115.

Sir Harry H. Johnston, *A comparative study of the Bantu and Semi-Bantu languages.* Oxford, 1919–22. 2 vols [819 + 544 pp.].

Most of this work consists of 'illustrative vocabularies of 276 Bantu and 24 Semi-Bantu languages' based on published sources, on Johnston's fieldwork, and on replies to questionnaires. Vol. 2 includes an English index to the vocabularies. For Johnson's 'Semi-Bantu' linguists would now say 'other Niger-Congo languages'.

NILO-SAHARAN LANGUAGES

The widespread Nilo-Saharan language family of central Africa incudes no languages that are well known on a world scale. There are many obscure members of the family on which all too little lexicographical work has been done. Only four have entries in this book: DINKA, KALENJIN, MASAI, NUBIAN.

1116.

Franz Rottland, *Die südnilotischen Sprachen: Beschreibung, Vergleichung und Rekonstruktion.* Berlin: Reimer, 1982. 563 pp.

[*The South Nilotic languages: description, comparison and reconstruction.*] The grouping includes Kalenjin and some of its neighbours. Rottland's study includes a comparative vocabulary.

1117.

M. Lionel Bender, 'Proto-Koman phonology and lexicon' in *Afrika und Übersee* vol. 66 (1983) pp. 259–97.

This linguistic grouping includes Gumuz and other minority languages of Ethiopia.

NORN

This descendant of OLD NORSE was once the language of the Shetland Islands. Now extinct, it has left its mark in the English dialect spoken in the Shetlands.

1118.

Jakob Jakobsen, *An etymological dictionary of the Norn language in Shetland.*
London: Nutt, 1928–32. 2 vols.

Preface by Anna Horsböl, née Jakobsen.
First published in Danish: *Etymologisk ordbog over det norrøne sprog på Shetland.* Copenhagen: Prior, 1921.
Edited by Marie Mikkelsen.

Jakobsen's notes were in English: the English edition was revised directly from his manuscript. 'At the time of his death the work was practically complete … with the exception of about two pages of the letter Ø … In the introduction to this English edition appears some hitherto unprinted matter from Dr Jakobsen's manuscript, such as the Norn fragments to which reference is made in the dictionary' (Horsböl, 'Preface').

In Scandinavian alphabetical order, ending with Æ and Ø. The letters **W** and **V** are interfiled. Abbreviations of place names, p. x.

NORTH HALMAHERA LANGUAGES

Classed geographically among PAPUAN LANGUAGES, the North Halmahera or West Papuan family includes Galela, Ternate, Tidore and other local languages of eastern Indonesia. Speakers are numbered in the tens of thousands.

1119.

J. Fortgens, *Woordenlijst van het Ternatesch.* Semarang: Van Dorp, 1917.

[*Glossary of Ternate.*] Not seen.

1120.

A. Hueting, 'Iets over de "Ternataansch-Halmaherasche" taalgroep' in *Bijdragen tot de taal-, land- en volkenkunde* vol. 60 (1908) pp. 370–411.

[*More on the Ternate-Halmahera family.*] A survey of languages of the family with a comparative word-list.

1121.

A. Hueting, *Tobèloreesch–Hollandsch woordenboek met Hollandsch–Tobèloreesch inhoudsopgave.* The Hague: Nijhoff, 1908. 516 pp.

[*Tobelo–Dutch dictionary with Dutch–Tobelo contents guide.*]

1122.

M. J. van Baarda, *Woordenlijst Galelareesch–Hollandsch, met ethnologische aantekeningen op de woorden die daartoe aanleiding gaven.* The Hague: Nijhoff, 1895. 536 pp.

[*Galela–Dutch dictionary with ethnographical notes to relevant entries.*] Galela is a language of the North Halmaheran family. No Dutch index. Not seen.

Other works of interest

1123.

Paul Michael Taylor, *The folk biology of the Tobelo people: a study in folk classification*. Washington: Smithsonian Institution Press, 1990. 187 pp.

Appendixes 1–3, 'The Tobelo classification' (alphabetical order, with commentary) pp. 84–141; appendixes 4–5, taxonomic lists with indexes to the Tobelo classification, pp. 142–82.

NORWEGIAN

Norwegian belongs to the Scandinavian sub-group of GERMANIC LANGUAGES. It is the national language of Norway, with about five million speakers.

There has been a long-standing debate in Norway on the relative merits of the traditional literary language (Bokmål, Riksmål), heavily influenced by Danish from the long centuries of Danish rule over Norway, and the 'New Norwegian' (Nynorsk, Landsmål) that was tailor-made in the nineteenth century out of regional Norwegian dialects. Of the dictionaries listed below, only Haugen's (**1124**) deals openly and clearly with both standards.

Norwegian alphabetical order

a b c d e f g h i j k l m n o p q r s t u v w x y z æ å

The modern standards

1124.

Einar Haugen, editor-in-chief, *Norwegian English dictionary: a pronouncing and translating dictionary of modern Norwegian (Bokmål and Nynorsk) with a historical and grammatical introduction = Norsk engelsk ordbok: norsk (bokmål og nynorsk) rettskrivnings- og uttaleordbok med oversettelser til amerikansk engelsk*. Oslo: Universitetsforlaget; Madison: University of Wisconsin Press, 1965. 500 pp.

Kenneth G. Chapman, Dag Gundersen, Jørgen Rischel, associate editors.
Reprinted: Madison: University of Wisconsin Press, 1974. 504 pp. 0–299–03870–X.

'It is the first dictionary in any language to include both forms of Norwegian, Bokmål (Riksmål, Dano-Norwegian) and Nynorsk (Landsmål, New Norwegian) in one alphabet.' Pronunciation guidance is also given, on word stress, vowel length, and silent letters. This is a particularly informative, though compressed, brief-entry dictionary, with a useful introduction on the varieties of Norwegian and on its grammatical forms.

Each entry is marked + Bokmål, * Nynorsk, ° dialect word. There are numerous cross-references between varieties.

The 'new and enlarged American printing' of 1974 includes a five-page supplement of additions and corrections, pp. 500–504.

Bokmål and Riksmål

1125.

Tor Guttu, editor, *Aschehoug og Gyldendals store norske ordbok: moderat bokmål og riksmål*. Oslo: Kunnskapsforlaget, 1991. 692 pp. 82–573–0312–7.

[*Aschehoug and Gyldendal's big Norwegian dictionary of moderate Bokmål and Riksmål.*] Aschehoug and Gyldendal are two venerable publishing houses, now combined as Kunnskapsforlaget but not yet forgotten. This is a short dictionary of modern Norwegian with some illustrations. Taxonomic names are given for flora and fauna. Nynorsk forms are not supplied.

1126.

W. A. Kirkeby, *Engelsk–norsk ordbok*. Oslo: Kunnskapsforlaget, 1991. 1262 pp. 82–573–0417–4.

[*Norwegian–English dictionary.*] A bilingual dictionary into Bokmål based on a shorter *English–Norwegian dictionary* published in 1989, and including material from Kirkeby's *Supplementsordbok* of 1983 (see **1127**).

1127.

W. A. Kirkeby, *Norsk–engelsk ordbok*. Oslo: Kunnskapsforlaget, 1986. 1373 pp. 2nd edn.

1st edn: 1979. 1276 pp. 82–573–0135–3. – This was followed by: W. A. Kirkeby, *Norsk–engelsk supplementsordbok = Norwegian–English supplementary dictionary*. Bergen: Universitetsforlaget, 1983. 198 pp. 82–00–06647–9.

[*Norwegian–English dictionary.*] This large bilingual dictionary of Bokmål is 'based on my smaller Norwegian–English dictionary ... first published in 1970' (Preface). There is a generous supply of example phrases. Note the frequently used abbreviations *el.* 'or', *jvf.* 'compare', *fx* 'for example'.

The supplement is described as 'a kind of "odds-and-ends" volume for updatings, words and expressions left out previously, and new shades of meaning of well-known headwords'.

1128.

Trygve Knudsen, Alf Sommerfelt, [Harald Noreng,] *Norsk riksmålsordbok*. Oslo: Aschehoug, 1930–57. 2 vols in 4.

Published by Riksmålsvernet.

[*Dictionary of Norwegian Riksmål.*] A large-scale dictionary of the modern language, with brief etymologies. Quotations are supplied for most but not all entries, particularly not for scientific and technical terms. Precise references are given: list of cited authors, vol. 1 part 1 pp. xvi–xix, with additions in vol. 1, final preliminaries, pp. i–vi.

1129.

Marit Ingebjørg Landrø, Boye Wangensteen, editors, *Bokmålsordboka: definisjons- og rettskrivningsordbok*. Bergen: Universitetetsforlaget, 1986. 697 pp. 82–00–07667–9.

Edited by Avdeling for Bokmål ved Norsk Leksikografisk Institutt, Universitetet i Oslo, in collaboration with Norsk Språkråd.

[*Dictionary of Bokmål: an explanatory and orthographical dictionary.*] Designed in tandem with the *Nynorskordboka* (**1131**), this is a concise dictionary of Bokmål which includes some alternative forms that are in fact Nynorsk, for example, **Veg** as an alternative to **Vei** 'road, way'. Brief etymologies.

Regional forms and Nynorsk

1130.

Alf Hellevik, chief editor, *Norsk ordbok: ordbok over det norske folkemålet og det nynorske skriftmålet*. Oslo: Det Norske Samlaget, 1950– .

[*Norwegian dictionary: a dictionary of the Norwegian popular language and of written Nynorsk.*] A historical dictionary of Nynorsk with generous quotations – in italic – from printed sources. Spoken dialect forms are provided, in square brackets, at the beginning of each entry. Abbreviations for source texts, vol. 1 pp. xviii–xlvii; other abbreviations, including those for local dialects, pp. xlviii–lii.

The dictionary is expanding as work proceeds. Three volumes have been published: with vol. 3, which appeared in 1994, entries **A**–**Gigla** are now covered.

1131.

Marit Hovdenak [and other editors], *Nynorskordboka: definisjons- og rettskrivningsordbok*. Oslo: Det Norske Samlaget, 1986. 870 pp. 82–521–2165–9.

Edited by Avdeling for Nynorsk ved Norsk Leksikografisk Institutt, Universitetet i Oslo, in collaboration with Norsk Språkråd.

[*Dictionary of Nynorsk: an explanatory and orthographical dictionary.*] Designed in tandem with the *Bokmålsordboka* (**1129**), though the two have different publishers and editors. In keeping with the philosophy of Nynorsk, this dictionary, unlike its companion, has no truck at all with Bokmål: Nynorsk words are defined strictly in Nynorsk, without cross-reference.

Etymological dictionaries

1132.

Hjalmar Falk, Alf Torp, *Norwegisch-dänisches etymologisches Wörterbuch, mit Literaturnachweisen strittiger Etymologien sowie deutschem und altnordischem Wörterverzeichnis*. Oslo: Universitetsforlaget, 1960. 2 vols [1722 pp.]. New edn.

First published in Norwegian: *Etymologisk ordbog over det norske og det danske sprog*. Kristiania: Aschehoug, 1900–1906. 2 vols. This was reprinted: Oslo: Bjørn Ringstrøms Antikvariat, 1991.

First German edn, translated by H. Davidsen: Heidelberg: Winter, 1910–11. 2 vols. (*Germanische Bibliothek, 1: Sammlung germanischer Elementar- und Handbücher, 4. Reihe, Wörterbücher,* 1.) This was a revised version of the first Norwegian edition, with an additional German index.

[*Norwegian and Danish etymological dictionary, with bibliographical references on disputed etymologies and with German and Old Norse indexes.*] Headwords are Norwegian forms (Bokmål) where available, with cross-references from Danish forms where necessary. Supplement, pp. 1428–1582. Old Norse and German indexes, pp. 1583–1722. Abbreviations for sources, pp. 1425–7; other abbreviations, vol. 1 p. vii.

The Norwegian edition has, in addition, an index of Norwegian dialect words, vol. 2 pp. 521–551.

1133.

Alf Torp, *Nynorsk etymologisk ordbok.* Kristiania: Aschehoug, 1915–19. 886 pp.
Edited by M. Haegstad, H. Falk.

[*Etymological dictionary of Nynorsk.*] Deals with the origins and history of the Norwegian dialect words that formed the basis, in a normalised or standardised form, of Nynorsk, the purified, un-Danish form of Norwegian promulgated in the late nineteenth century.

NUBIAN

One of the NILO-SAHARAN LANGUAGES. There are perhaps a million speakers in Sudan and the southern edge of Egypt.

1134.

Charles H. Armbruster, *Dongolese Nubian: a lexicon, Nubian–English, English–Nubian.* Cambridge: Cambridge University Press, 1965. 269 pp.

Based on fieldwork gathered over a long period: the author was an officer of the Sudan Service, stationed in Dongola. Very generous quotation of example phrases; frequent references to Armbruster's *Dongolese Nubian: a grammar* (Cambridge, 1960. 460 pp.), in which the phonetic script he uses is explained. Some Arabic and Amharic equivalents are supplied.

English–Nubian section, pp. 223–69.

1135.

Inge Hofmann, editor, *Das nubische Wörterverzeichnis des Arcangelo Carradori (O.F.M.) aus dem frühen 17. Jahrhundert.* Wien: Afro-Pub, 1983. 381 pp.
Veröffentlichungen der Institute für Afrikanistik und Ägyptologie der Universität Wien, 26. *Beiträge zur Afrikanistik,* 19.

[*The early seventeenth century Nubian glossary of Arcangelo Carradori, O.F.M.*] Carradori's dictionary was first printed in the nineteenth century. Hofmann's edition includes German glosses.

NYANJA

A Bantu language, and thus a member of the NIGER-CONGO family, Nyanja is a major language of Malawi, Zambia and Mozambique.

1136.

David Clement Scott, *Dictionary of the Nyanja language*. London: RTS, 1929. 612 pp. New edn by Alexander Hetherwick.

1st edn: *A Cyclopaedic Dictionary of the Mang'anja Language spoken in British Central Africa.* Edinburgh: Foreign Mission Committee of the Church of Scotland, 1892. 737 pp.

OCCITAN

One of the ROMANCE LANGUAGES, Occitan or Provençal still has several million speakers in southern France. Generally regarded nowadays as a *patois* or regional dialect of French, this language of a great medieval literature is now in steep decline.

Modern regional forms

1137.

Louis Boucoiran, *Dictionnaire analogique et étymologique des idiomes méridionaux qui sont parlés depuis Nice jusqu'à Bayonne et depuis les Pyrénées jusqu'au centre de la France, comprenant tous les termes vulgaires de la flore et de la faune méridionale, un grand nombre de citations prises dans les meilleurs auteurs, ainsi qu'une collection de proverbes locaux tirés de nos moralistes populaires*. Nimes: Imprimerie Roumieux, 1875. 1344 pp.

[*Explanatory and etymological dictionary of the southern dialects, spoken from Nice to Bayonne and from the Pyrenees to the centre of France, including all the vernacular names for the southern flora and fauna, a great number of quotations taken from the best authors, and a collection of regional proverbs drawn from our popular moralists.*] Brief glosses followed by a fine collection of quotations, mainly from post-medieval Occitan poetry. Boucoiran's dictionary is less inclusive than Mistral's (**1139**) but far from negligible.

1138.

Jules Coupier, *Dictionnaire français–provençal = Diciounàri francés– prouvençau*. Aix-en-Provence: Edisud, 1995. 1511 pp. 2–85744–824–4.

Association Dictionnaire Français–Provençal.

[*French–Provençal dictionary.*] An excellent bilingual dictionary into Occitan, based on the Rhone Valley dialects which were favoured by Mistral and many later authors. Other dialects are also drawn on.

1139.

Frédéric Mistral, *Lou tresor dou Felibrige ou dictionnaire provençal–français.*
Aix-en-Provence: Remondet-Aubin, 1879–86. 2 vols.
'Centenary edition': a reprint with added biographical material on Mistral. Paris: Delagrave, 1932. 2 vols.
Reprint with introduction by Jean-Claude Bouvier. Aix-en-Provence, 1979. 2360 pp.

[*Thesaurus of the Felibrige, or Provençal–French dictionary.*] A modern Occitan to French dictionary, with fairly brief entries, including in one alphabet forms drawn from many different dialects. Short etymologies, French glosses and one or two example phrases are provided, drawing on named authors but without precise references. Numerous proverbs and sayings are among the examples. Taxonomic names are given for flora and fauna.

France

1140.

Louis Alibert, *Dictionnaire occitan–français d'après les parlers languedociens.*
1966. 701 pp.
2nd edn: 1977. – '5th edn': Toulouse: Institut d'Études Occitanes, 1993. 710 pp. 2–85910–069–5.

[*Occitan–French dictionary based on the dialects of Languedoc.*] The 5th edition contains a few additions, pp. 9–10, that first appeared in the second edition, together with a further supplement, pp. 703–10, which is dated 1987 (apparently the date of the 4th edition). Its only novelty, therefore, is a preface dated 1993.

1141.

Dictionnaire occitan–français: dialecte gévaudanais. [Mende]: L'Escolo
Gabalo, 1992. 514 pp. 2–9506729–0–6.

[*Occitan–French dictionary of the Gévaudan dialect.*] A bilingual dictionary of the dialects of the Lozère. Entries are relatively brief but there are some ethnographical notes as well as quotations from named authors (list, pp. xxiii–xxiv) and from folk poetry. A local spelling is used: concordance with older Occitan orthography, pp. xxviii–xxxii.

Italy

1142.

Teofilo G. Pons, *Dizionario del dialetto valdese della Val Germanasca (Torino).*
Torre Pellice, 1973. 282 pp.
Note fonetiche e morfologiche di A. Genre; 15 tavole fuori testo dell'ing. G. Grill.
Collana della Società di studi valdesi, 6.

[*Dictionary of the Waldensian dialect of the Val Germanasca.*] With Italian glosses. This has relatively brief entries, but has etymological notes in square brackets, and quotations, particularly of local proverbs. Corrections, pp. 279–82.

Older periods

1143.

Kurt Baldinger, *Dictionnaire onomasiologique de l'ancien occitan: DAO*.
Tübingen: Niemeyer, 1975– .

Accompanied by: *Supplément: DAOSuppl*. 1980– .
See: Max Pfister, 'L'avenir de la recherche lexicographique en ancien occitan' in Stewart Gregory, D. A.
Trotter, editors, *De mot en mot: essays in honour of William Rothwell* (Cardiff: University of Wales Press,
1997) pp. 161-71.

[*Thesaurus of old Occitan.*] A rearrangement in conceptual order of material from
existing lexicographical sources, notably Walther von Wartburg's *Französisches
etymologisches Wörterbuch* (**501**) and the dictionaries of Raynouard (**1145**) and Levy
(**1144**), repeating the glosses that are given in these sources.

The *DAO* itself does not give quotations or citations from primary sources. The
Supplement, however, does exactly this, drawing on Baldinger's 'unsystematic' but
copious collection to provide an important supporting fund of quotations, particularly
from prose literature and documents. The work will gain in usefulness as it grows: seven
parts have been published (with six of the supplement), containing a total of 1233
entries, and the *DAO* has already covered the important subject area of flora among
others.

A similar work dealing with Gascon is also in progress (**546**).

1144.

Emil Levy, *Provenzalisches Supplement-Wörterbuch: Berichtigungen und
Ergänzungen zu Raynouards Lexique roman*. Leipzig: Reisland, 1892–1924. 8
vols.

Reprinted: Hildesheim, 1973.
Accompanied by: Kurt Baldinger, *Complément bibliographique au Provenzalisches Supplement-Wörterbuch
d'Emil Levy: sources, datations*. Geneva: Slatkine, 1983.
See Carl Appel, 'Die Fortführung des provenzalischen Supplement-Wörterbuchs von Emil Levy' in *Behrens-
Festschrift zum 70. Geburtstag* (Jena, 1929).

[*Supplementary dictionary of Provençal: corrections and additions to Raynouard's
Lexique Roman.*] Only brief glosses are given: the main point is the copious collection of
well-chosen quotations. Where an entry supplements one already to be found in
Raynouard (below), a page reference is given: but very many entries are new.

Levy's great work was completed and the last volume published by Carl Appel. Vol.
8 contains photographs and a biography of Levy.

Baldinger's recent *Complément* is indispensable, for neither Levy nor Appel issued a
list of the sources they had drawn on, the editions used, and the abbreviations employed
in the dictionary. The *Complément* is based on elaborate manuscript notes gathered by
Baldinger and others who worked on Walther von Wartburg's *Französisches
etymologisches Wörterbuch* (**501**), for which Levy's material could only be used after it
had been identified and checked.

1145.

[François] Raynouard, *Lexique roman ou dictionnaire de la langue des troubadours comparée avec les autres langues de l'Europe latine*. Paris: Silvestre, 1838–44. 6 vols.

Reprinted: Heidelberg, 1928–9.

[*Romance lexicon: dictionary of the language of the troubadours, compared with the other languages of Romance Europe.*] A comparative dictionary centring on the Occitan (*langue romane*) of twelfth to fourteenth century lyric poetry. The title signals Raynouard's belief, no longer tenable now, that the language of Provençal lyric was the direct ancestor of the other Romance languages.

Entries give quotations from these texts and from other medieval Romance literatures, especially French. Compounds and derived words are filed under base forms (e.g. **abelivol** and **embellezir** under **bel**): the index-glossary, vol. 6 pp. 41–555, is essential in locating them.

The dictionary, vol. 2 p. 1 to vol. 5 p. 581. Abbreviations, vol. 5 pp. 583–7; authors and source texts, pp. 589–611. *Supplément* (addenda) vol. 6 pp. 1–40.

Occitan grammar, vol. 1 pp. xliii–lxxxviii; selected texts, pp. 1–580. Observations on comparative Romance philology, vol. 2 pp. i–xcii.

1146.

Helmut Stimm, Wolf-Dieter Stempel, *Dictionnaire de l'occitan médiéval: DOM*. Tübingen: Niemeyer, 1996– . 3–484–50509–5.

Accompanied by: *Supplément 1*. 1997. 157 pp.

Stimm died in 1987 but still gets first place on the title page. See H. H. Christmann, 'Helmut Stimm (1917–1987)' in *Zeitschrift für romanische Philologie* vol. 104 (1988) pp. 600–609.

Note also: H. Stimm, 'Dictionnaire étymologique de l'ancien provençal' in Stimm and Briegel (**1261**).

[*Dictionary of medieval Occitan.*] I have only seen one part so far, covering **A–Acceptar** in 80 pages. Each entry gives gloss, citations of sources (but no quotations), historical and etymological discussion, references to other dictionaries and cross-references. GASCON and Franco-Provençal are included: on the 'linguistic identity' of Occitan see part 1 pp. vii–viii.

The supplement includes an explanation of the layout, a list of abbreviations (pp. 13–16) and a bibliography (pp. 17–154) with a separate list of *chansonniers*, medieval song books, the major source for Provençal lyric poetry (pp. 155–7).

Max Pfister, 'Beiträge zur altprovenzalischen Lexikologie I: abbatem – avunculus' in *Vox romanica* vol. 18 (1960) pp. 220–96, consists of a series of entries for a projected dictionary, afterwards abandoned.

OLD NORSE

Old Norse is the GERMANIC language of early Scandinavia. It is the language of early Norse poetry, and is practically identical with the Old Icelandic of the prose sagas. Both forms, Old Norse and Old Icelandic, are dealt with together in this article.

Old Norse may be regarded as the ancestor of ICELANDIC, FAROESE, NORN, DANISH, NORWEGIAN and SWEDISH. Early medieval inscriptions use a special alphabet, derived from Latin: the letters are called 'runes' and the alphabet is known as Futhark from its first six letters.

Futhark

ᚠᚢᚦᚨᚱᚲᚷᚹᚺᚾᛁᛃᛂᛇᚲᛉᛋᛏᛒᛗᛘᛚᛜᛞᛟ

f u th a r k g w h n i j ê p z s t b e m l ng d o

FONT: *RUNIC.TTF* OF DIGITAL TYPE FOUNDRY

1147.

Richard Cleasby, *An Icelandic–English dictionary*. Oxford: Clarendon Press, 1957. 833 pp. 2nd edn, with a supplement by William A. Craigie.

1st edn: 1869–74. Revised, enlarged and completed by Guðbrand Vigfússon.

'Many years ago, Richard Cleasby projected a general dictionary of the Old Scandinavian language … He reserved for himself the old prose literature; while Dr Egilsson was engaged on the poetical vocabulary … In [1847] Mr Cleasby caused five words – **bragð**, **búa**, **at**, **af**, and **ok** – to be set up in type as specimens of the projected Prose Dictionary. These he sent to several foreign friends, and among others to Jacob Grimm, who returned a most kind and friendly answer, warmly approving of the plan … and adding many good wishes that Mr Cleasby might have health and life to complete the work. Unhappily these wishes were not to be realised. In the autumn of the same year he was taken ill, but was in a fair way to recovery, when, by resuming the work too soon, he suffered a relapse. His illness took the form of typhus fever, and he died insensible, without being able to make arrangements respecting his papers and collections' (H. G. Liddell, Preface to the 1st edition).

Entries are highly compressed and full of information. They usually begin with etymological remarks, then citations and quotations from the literature. Glosses are in italics. There are numerous brief quotations, some of which are accompanied by English translations.

Errata, p. 770; additions, pp. 771–9; list of British river names and Gaelic personal names occurring in Old Norse sources, p. 780; Craigie's supplement, pp. 781–833. Abbreviations for source texts, pp. xiii–xiv and 783–4; classification of source literature, pp. ix–xi with 770. Short grammar, pp. xv–xlv.

1148.

Johan Fritzner, *Ordbog over det gamle norske sprog*. Christiania: Den Norske Forlagsforening, 1883–96. 3 vols [30 parts]. New edn.

Supplemented by: Finn Hødnebø, *Ordbog over det gamle norske sprog*, vol. 4: *rettelser og tillæg*. Oslo: Universitetsforlaget, 1972. 453 pp. 82–00–08830–8. [*Corrections and additions.*] – An earlier *Supplement*, by Didrik Arup Seip and Trygve Knudsen, appeared in 1955 (I have not seen it).

1st edn of the main work: 1862–7. 874 pp.

[*Dictionary of the Old Norse language.*] This is the fullest complete dictionary as yet, with more generous quotations than Cleasby (**1147**) or Sveinbjörn Egilsson (**1153**). Glosses are in Fraktur type. Abbreviations, vol. 1 pp. v–xii.

Hødnebø's presumptuously labelled 'vol. 4' contains a large number of brief entries. Those marked ° are new; others provide addenda to Fritzner's existing entries.

1149.

Leiv Heggstad, Finn Hødnebø, Erik Simensen, *Norrøn ordbok*. Oslo: Samlaget, 1975. 518 pp. 3rd edn. 82–521–0419–3.

1st edn: Marius Hægstad, Alf Torp, *Gamalnorsk ordbok*. 1909.
2nd edn: Leiv Heggstad, *Gamalnorsk ordbok*. 1930.

[*Norse dictionary*.] A brief-entry dictionary, but with a few citations of source texts. Note the abbreviation *sk.* 'poetic language'. The alphabetical order ends with þ æ ø œ ǫ; note that accented vowels are interfiled with unaccented ones.

1150.

Ferdinand Holthausen, *Vergleichendes und etymologisches Wörterbuch des Altwestnordischen, Altnorwegisch-Isländischen, einschließlich der Lehn- und Fremdwörter sowie der Eigennamen*. Göttingen: Vandenhoeck & Ruprecht, 1948.

[*Comparative and etymological dictionary of Old West Nordic, Old Norse/Icelandic, including loanwords, foreign words and proper names*.]

1151.

Jón Þorkelsson, *Supplement til islandske ordbøger*. Reykjavík: Einar Þórdarson, Isafold, Foreningstrykkeriet; Copenhagen: Høst, 1876–99. 4 series [96 + 639 + 1392 + 195 pp.].

[*Supplement to Icelandic dictionaries*.] Each successive series is in a new alphabetical order, **A–Z**. Glosses are in Norwegian (which is printed in Fraktur in the first series). Each entry includes a supporting quotation, with precise reference, from Old Norse/Icelandic literature.

1152.

Ordbog over det norrøne prosasprog = A dictionary of Old Norse prose. Copenhagen: Det Arnamagnæanske Kommission, 1989– .

Edited by Helle Degnbol and others.
Accompanied by: *Indices*. 1989. – *ONP 1 Nøgle = ONP 1 Key*, 1995. 122 pp.

Spelling is normalised in a slightly unfamiliar style, using ǽ for the traditional æ and ǿ for œ. 'A full description of ONP's normalisation practice can be obtained on request.' Glosses are given in Danish and English. There is very full quotation of examples from the corpus of Old Norse prose, with exact references to printed editions or manuscripts. The examples are not translated.

Vol. 1, published in 1995, covers **A–Bon** in 906 columns. 'This is the first of eleven volumes containing dictionary entries.'

The 1989 volume of *Indices* contains an introduction to the project. The pamphlet with the arcane title *ONP 1 Nøgle* is a spiral-bound supplement containing a user's guide, corrections to the *Indices*, a bibliography and corrigenda to vol. 1, and an updated list of abbreviations and symbols.

1153.

Sveinbjörn Egilsson, *Lexicon poeticum antiquæ linguæ septentrionalis = Ordbog over det norsk-islandske skjaldesprog*. 1931. Revised by Finnur Jónsson. 2nd edn.

Reprinted: Copenhagen: Lynge, 1966. 667 pp. Kongelige Nordiske Oldskriftselskab.
1st edn of Jónsson's revision: 1916.

[*Dictionary of the Norse-Icelandic poetic language.*] A careful listing of word forms found in the sources, with copious and precise references but only few and brief quotations. Glosses are in Danish. List of abbreviations for sources, pp. xiii–xvi. The alphabetical order ends with þ æ œ ǫ ǿ ø.

1154.

Jan de Vries, *Altnordisches etymologisches wörterbuch*. Leiden: Brill, 1957–61. 689 pp.

Reissued 1962.

[*Old Norse etymological dictionary.*] Like Ernout and Meillet's etymological dictionary of Latin (**971**), this work is especially innovative because it looks forward as well as back: note the index, incorporated in the introduction (pp. xiii–xli), of Old Norse words that were afterwards borrowed into the Shetland and Orkney dialects, the Celtic languages, English, Frisian, Low German, Norman French, Estonian, Finnish, Sami and various other languages. Main entries are relatively concise but are often followed by long, more discursive, controversial passages (indented). Corrections, pp. xlii–xlv. Abbreviations, pp. xlvi–l.

OLD PRUSSIAN

The extinct BALTIC language of the territory known until the Second World War as East Prussia. East Prussia was then divided between Poland and Russia. Old Prussian had been supplanted by German in the seventeenth century (for the Prussian dialect see LOW GERMAN). Polish and Russian are the languages now spoken here.

1155.

Erich Berneker, *Die preussische Sprache: Texte, Grammatik, etymologisches Wörterbuch*. Strasbourg, 1896. 333 pp.

[*The Prussian language: texts, grammar and etymological dictionary.*]

1156.

Vytautas Mažiulis, *Prūsų kalbos etimologijos žodynas*. Vilnius: Mokslas, 1988– .

Alternate titles: *Etimologicheskii slovar' prusskogo yazyka = Altpreussisches Wörterbuch*.

[*Etymological dictionary of the Prussian language.*] Source texts are cited selectively. Glosses in German and Lithuanian. The two volumes I have seen cover **A–K**.

1157.

В. И. Топоров, *Прусский язык (словарь)* [*Prusskii yazyk (slovar')*]. Moscow: Akademiya Nauk, 1975– .

[*The Prussian language: a dictionary*.] The four volumes I have seen cover **A–D**, **I– L**. A historical rather than an etymological dictionary, with full citations and many quotations of the source texts (most of which are glossaries and texts in German) and references to scholarly literature. Glosses in Russian.

OLD SLAVONIC

The SLAVONIC language of the early Bible translations and Christian theological works of eastern Europe in the first millennium AD is known as Old Church Slavonic or Old Bulgarian. It remained in use as a literary and religious language until relatively recently, and indeed is still used liturgically: later forms, influenced by the various national languages, are called Church Slavonic. It has influenced practically all the modern languages of eastern Europe.

According to tradition, both alphabets shown here were devised by Cyril, missionary to the Slavs. The Cyrillic alphabet (top line) is the direct ancestor of that used for RUSSIAN, SERBIAN and many other languages today; the Glagolitic alphabet (middle line) never spread widely, and has finally fallen out of current use.

The Cyrillic and Glagolitic alphabets in Church Slavonic

АБВГДЕЖЅЗНІ ҺКЛМНОПРСТОУ ФХѠЦЧШЩЪЫЬѢЮꙖѤѦѨѪѬѮѰѲѴ

ⰀⰁⰂⰃⰄⰅⰆⰇⰈⰉⰊⰋⰌⰍⰎⰏⰐⰑⰒⰓⰔⰕⰖⰗⰘⰙⰚⰛⰜⰝⰞⰟⰠⰡⰢⰣⰤⰥⰦⰧⰨⰩ __ ⰮⰯⰰⰱ __ ⰲ _

a b v g d e zh dz z i i gy k l m n o p r s t u f kh o ts ch sh sht ə y ' yɛ yu ya ye ē õ yẽ yõ x ps f i

Historical dictionaries

1158.

Григорій Дьяченко, *Полный церковно-славянскій словарь (со внесеніем въ него важнѣйшихъ древне-русскихъ словъ и выраженій)* [Grigorii D'yachenko, *Polnyi tserkovno-slavyanskii slovar' (so vneseniem v nego vazhnyeishikh drevne-russkikh slov i vyrazhenii)*]. Moscow: Vil'de, 1899. 1120 pp.
Reprinted: Rome: JUH, 1976. 2 vols [1120 pp.].

[*Complete Church Slavonic dictionary, including the most important Old Russian words and phrases.*] A concise dictionary of Church Slavonic emphasising etymology and history, but with room for some quotations from texts.

1159.

Slovník jazyka staroslověnského = Lexicon linguae palaeoslovenicae. Prague: Nakladatelství Československé Akademie Věd, Academia, 1958– .
Chief editor: J. Kurz.

[*Dictionary of the Old Slavonic language.*] This is the major historical dictionary of Old Slavonic. It uses Old Church Slavonic script for headwords and quotations, and supplies glosses and equivalents in Czech, Russian, German, Greek and Latin. The introduction and preliminaries appear in all these languages in turn, except Greek.

Entries are sometimes very long, with generous citation of sources. The dictionary is well advanced, having reached part 44 and already covering A–OУ.

1160.

Старославянский словарь (по рукописям X–XI веков) [*Staroslavyanskii slovar' (po rukopisyam X–XI vekov)*]. Moscow: Russkii Yazyk, 1994.

V. B. Krys'ko, 'Marginalii k Staroslavyanskomu slovaryu' in *Voprosy yazykoznaniya* 1996 no. 5 pp. 20–39.

[*Old Slavonic dictionary, from 10th and 11th century records.*] Not seen.

Limited periods and regions

1161.

Петр Андреевич Гильтебрандт, *Справочный и объяснительный словарь къ Новому Завету* [Petr Andreevich Gil'tebrandt, *Spravochnyi i ob"yasnitel'nyi slovar' k Novomu Zavetu*]. Petrograd: Kotomin, 1882–5. 2 vols [2448 pp.].

Reprinted: Munich: Sagner, 1988–9. 6 vols in 5. Edited by Helmut Keipert, Frantisek Václav Mares. *Sagners slavistische Sammlung*, 14.

[*Dictionary and concordance of the New Testament.*] A full vocabulary of the Church Slavonic translation of the New Testament. Vol. 1 of the reprint edition is a newly written history of Slavonic Bible concordances; vol. 2 is a study of Russian Late Church Slavonic and its writing system.

1162.

T. A. Lysaght, *Old Church Slavonic (Old Bulgarian)–middle Greek–modern English dictionary*. Vienna: Brüder Hollinek, 1983. 471 pp. 3–85119–198–6.

A revision of: T. A. Lysaght, *Material towards the compilation of a concise Old Church Slavonic–English dictionary*. Wellington, New Zealand: Victoria University Press, 1978. 472 pp. 0–7055–0668–1.

Russian version: T. A. Lysaght, *Altslavisches–Russisches Handwörterbuch* = Ф. Ф. Лайсарт, *Старославянско–современнорусский словарь*. Vienna: Lysaght, 1986. 3–900753–01–6. Alternate titles: *Old Slavonic–Russian dictionary* = *Старославянско–русский словарь* = *Altkirchenslavisches–Russisches Handwörterbuch*.

Reproduced from unlovely typescript. 'Our principal sources have been the language of the Gospels in the Codices Marianus and Zographensis, the language of the Psalms in Psalterium Sinaiticum, and finally the rich and wide ranging vocabulary of Codex Suprasliensis ... based largely on Greek sources ...' The work also draws on early Bulgarian inscriptions; but precise references are given only to the Gospels and Psalms.

In the 1983 edition, additional references and the Greek equivalents have been added to the typescript.

1163.

Fran Miklošič, *Lexicon palaeoslovenico–graeco–latinum emendatum, auctum*. Vienna, 1862–5. 2 vols [1171 pp.].

Reprinted: Aalen: Scientia, 1963. 1171 pp.

Earlier version: Franz von Miklosich, *Lexicon linguae Slovenicae veteris dialecti*. Vienna, 1850.

[*Old Slovene–Greek–Latin dictionary, revised and enlarged.*] Deals with Slavonic texts linked with Slovenia, from the Old Slavonic period to the seventeenth century. Useful, particularly for the later period, in reflecting what is in effect early Slovene.

1164.

Johan Gabriel Sparwenfeld, *Lexicon Slavonicum*. Uppsala: Uppsala Universitetsbibliotek, 1987–92. 5 vols.

Edited by Ulla Birgegård; compiled by Boris Ivanov. *Acta Bibliothecae R. Universitatis Upsaliensis*, 24.

See Ulla Birgegård, *Johan Gabriel Sparwenfeld and the Lexicon Slavonicum: his contribution to 17th century Slavonic lexicography*. Uppsala, 1985.

[*Slavonic dictionary.*] This is a Church Slavonic–Latin dictionary largely of seventeenth century Church Slavonic, though also based on earlier dictionaries. It was compiled between 1684 and 1705. History of the work, vol. i pp. viii–ix. Birgegård's annotations help to distinguish the different layers of vocabulary involved – and to identify Sparwenfeld's errors.

Etymological dictionaries

1165.

Etymologický slovník jazyka staroslověnského. Prague: Academia, 1989– .

Chief editor, Eva Havlová. Československá Akademie Věd, Ústav Slavistiký.

[*Etymological dictionary of the Old Slavonic language.*] A full etymological dictionary, in course of publication in loose sheets. Latin script is used in place of Cyrillic – but Greek still appears in the Greek alphabet. Bibliography: part 1 pp. 5–34. The work has reached p. 380, in six published parts, and covers **A–Kuditi**.

ORIYA

Oriya, an INDO-ARYAN language of the Indo-European family, is the least known abroad of the major languages of India. It is the language of Orissa state, and has about 22 million speakers.

Oriya script: the consonant characters

କ ଖ ଗ ଘ ଙ ଚ ଛ ଜ ଝ ଞ ଟ ଠ ଡ ଢ ଣ ତ ଥ ଦ ଧ ନ ପ ଫ ବ ଭ ମ ଯ ର ଲ ଳ ଶ ଷ ସ ହ

k kh g gh ṅ c ch j jh ñ ṭ ṭh ḍ ḍh ṇ t th d dh n p ph b bh m y r l ḷ ś ṣ s h

Eleven vowels shown with the consonant କ *k*

କ କା କି କୀ କୁ କୂ କୃ କେ କୈ କୋ କୌ

ka kā ki kī ku kū kṛ ke kai ko kau

The alphabet is historically related to Bengali, but it looks wholly different: whereas Bengali script is suited to writing with a pen, Oriya is perfectly adapted to writing with a stylus on palm leaves, the traditional material for manuscript texts. There must be no long horizontal strokes – like the 'washing-line' on which Devanagari and Bengali scripts appear to depend – because these would split the leaf. Oriya substitutes the half-circles built into almost every character.

BASED ON A FONT BY VIJAY K. PATEL

1166.

Jagan Mohan Patnaik, *English–Oriya dictionary*. 1964. 2 vols.

1167.

G. C. Praharaj, *Pūrṇṇachandra Orḍiā bhāshākosha = A lexicon of the Oriya language*. 1931–40. 7 vols.

In about 9000 pages this is by far the largest Oriya dictionary in existence. English glosses are given.

1168.

Amos Sutton, *An Oriya dictionary in three volumes*. Cuttack, 1841–3. 3 vols.

'Vol. 1 embracing an introductory grammar, an English and Oriya dictionary, and a list of official terms ... Vol. 2 an Oriya dictionary, with Oriya synonyms ... by Rev. A. S. and Bhobananund Niaya Alaukar ... Vol. 3 embracing an Oriya and English dictionary, official terms, and a list of materia medica, etc.' Not seen: entry based on the British Library catalogue.

OROMO

Oromo or Galla is a CUSHITIC language and thus belongs to the Afroasiatic family. There are over seven million speakers in Ethiopia, Kenya and Somalia.

1169.

Gene B. Gragg, editor, *Oromo dictionary*. East Lansing: African Studies Center, Michigan State University, 1982. 462 pp.

Committee on Northeast African Studies. *Monograph*, 12. In cooperation with Oriental Institute, University of Chicago.

Entries give information on derivation and compounding, and are accompanied by example sentences. They are keyed to the English–Oromo thesaurus on pp. 409–62.

A grammatical outline of Oromo can be found in Gene Gragg, 'Oromo of Wellegga' in M. L. Bender, editor, *The non-Semitic languages of Ethiopia* (East Lansing: African Studies Center, Michigan State University, 1976) pp. 166–95.

OSSETE

One of the IRANIAN LANGUAGES, Ossete is spoken in the northern Caucasus – partly in Georgia, partly in Russia. It has about half a million speakers and is written in a form of Cyrillic script.

Ossete alphabetical order

а æ б в г ҕ q д дж дз з i j к ќ л м н о п ṕ р с т т́ ў/у v ф х ц ц́ ч ч́ ҳ

1170.

В. И. Абаев, *Историко-этимологическийсловарьосетинскогоязыка* [V. I. Abaev, *Istoriko-etimologicheskii slovar' osetinskogo yazyka*]. Moscow, Leningrad, 1958– .

See Abaev's 'Corrections and additions to the Ossetic etymological dictionary' in: Hans Henrich Hock, editor, *Historical, Indo-European and lexicographical studies: a Festschrift for Ladislav Zgusta on the occasion of his 70th birthday* (Berlin: Mouton De Gruyter, 1997. *Trends in linguistics, studies and monographs,* 90) pp. 197–219.

[*Historical and etymological dictionary of the Ossete language.*] Ossete is given in a Latin phonetic script. Glosses and discussion in Russian. I have seen vols 1–3, **A–T**.

1171.

Wsewolod Miller, *Ossetisch–russisch–deutsches Wörterbuch* = Всеволод Федорович Миллер, *Осетинско–русско–немецкий словарь*. Leningrad: Akademii Nauk, 1927–34. 3 vols [1730 pp.].

Edited and enlarged by A. Freiman.

[*Ossete–Russian–German dictionary.*] A brief entry dictionary with some quotations from folk poetry and other example sentences. Corrections, vol. 1 pp. 575–618, vol. 2 pp. 1173–6, vol. 3 p. 1730.

PALAUNG

Palaung is a language, or perhaps rather a language group, also known in China as De'ang and Benglong. There are at least half a million speakers in China and Burma.

1172.

Mrs Leslie Milne, *A dictionary of English–Palaung and Palaung–English*. Rangoon: Superintendent, Government Printing, 1931. 383 + 290 pp.

Based on the dialect of the Palaung speakers at Namhsan, capital of Tawngpeng (northern Shan State). Appendices at end of first pagination: kinship terms; weights and measures; glossaries of other dialects, pp. 355–83.

1173.

V. Mitani, 'Palaung dialects: a preliminary comparison' in *Tōnan Ajia kenkyū* vol. 15 no. 2 (1977) pp. 193–212.

PALI

Pali, a middle INDO-ARYAN language, developed around 200 BC (rather later according to some) as the language in which the dialogues of the Buddha and other Buddhist scriptures of the Theravada tradition were recorded and recited. It is a mixed dialect, not identical with the speech of any district of northern India, but would have been easily comprehensible to speakers of the Middle Indo-Aryan dialects of that time.

Once fixed in writing, Pali became the almost unchanging medium in which all southern Buddhists studied and wrote. The religion, and with it the Pali canon, spread successively to speakers of Sinhalese, Mon, Burmese, Thai and various languages of inland south east Asia. Buddhism eventually disappeared from India proper, but Buddhists from Sri Lanka, Burma and Thailand have continued to learn and use this now-classical language of northern India.

There is no single typical script for Pali: it can be written in most of the Indic scripts of India and south east Asia, and is in fact written and printed in many of them. Most Western scholars use the Latin alphabet.

1174.

Robert Caesar Childers, *A dictionary of the Pali language*. London: Trübner, 1872–5. 624 pp.

Several reprints, including: Rangoon: U Hla Maung, 1974.
Note also: Prince Kitiyakara Krommaphra Chandaburinarünath: *Pali–Thai–English–Sanskrit dictionary*. Bangkok, 1970. 906 pp.

Childers' dictionary is largely superseded, but occasionally useful for its citations from the literature. In Latin script and – unlike other Pali dictionaries – in Latin alphabetical order.

The 1970 Bangkok edition is based on the Prince's manuscript notes, made in the early twentieth century, in a 1909 reprint of Childers. It is useful as a guide to Thai Buddhist terminology. Pali headwords in both roman and Thai script: the Sanskrit terms offered are not necessarily translations but etymologies. Transliteration table of Thai script as used in Pali and Sanskrit, p. 893.

1175.

A critical Pali dictionary. Copenhagen: Munksgaard, 1924– .

Begun by V. Trenckner; revised, continued and edited by Dines Andersen, Helmer Smith, Hans Hendriksen, [F. Møller-Kristensen, L. Alsdorf, K. R. Norman, Oskar v. Hinüber, Ole Holten Pind.] 'Published by the Royal Danish Academy of Sciences and Letters.'
Accompanied by: Helmer Smith, *Epilegomena to vol. 1*. 1948. 97* pp.

A massive historical dictionary of Pali, including all recorded compound words in a language which is infinitely fertile in compounds. The dictionary is entirely in Latin script, in Indic alphabetical order. It covers a wide historical range of Pali literature, and is generous in citations, though with relatively few quotations.

The preliminary pages to vol. 1 were originally issued in instalments with successive parts of vol. 1. They include a memoir of Trenckner, by Andersen, pp. i–viii; preface, pp. ix–xi; 'On critics and new texts', pp. xxvii–xxix, with references to early reviews; and an obituary of Andersen. There is more in the preliminaries to vol. 2.

The volume of *Epilegomena* includes abbreviations for texts, p. 5, and for other works and authors, p. 15; general abbreviations and symbols, p. 19; a classified bibliography of Pali literature, p. 37, and an index to this, p. 70; concordances of reference systems to texts, p. 92; transliterations, p. 98. Addenda to these various aids appear in some parts of vol. 2.

Publication lapsed in 1940 and was revived in 1958. The *Critical Pali dictionary* will take nearly three centuries to complete at the average rate of progress achieved so far. With the recent publication of vol. 3 part 4/5 it now covers **A–Kayavikkayasikkhapada** 'the rule about bartering' (*K* is the first consonant of Indic alphabets).

1176.

T. W. Rhys Davids, William Stede, editors, *The Pali Text Society's Pali–English dictionary*. Chipstead: Pali Text Society, 1921–5. 8 parts [738 pp.].
Reprints include: London: Luzac, 1966.

A concise one-volume dictionary which finds room for about 160,000 citations from the Buddhist scriptures and other early works, and gives brief etymologies. Entirely in Latin script.

1177.

U Hoke Sein, *The universal Burmese–English–Pali dictionary*. Rangoon, 1981. 1066 pp.

A unique work offering Pali translations for many modern and scientific terms. The biggest dictionary into Pali, and large enough (about 60,000 entries) to be of some use also as a Burmese–English dictionary in spite of the brevity of individual entries. Includes taxonomic names for flora and fauna. The Pali is in Burmese script.

1178.

တိပိဋက ပါဠိ–မြန်မာ အဘိဓာန် [*Tipitaka Pali–Myanma abidan*]. Rangoon, 1964– .

[*Pali–Burmese dictionary of the Tipitaka.*] A very extensive work dealing exhaustively with the vocabulary of the Pali Buddhist scriptures. The work was nearing completion with vol. 15, published in 1982. Entirely in Burmese script.

PANGASINAN

An AUSTRONESIAN language with about 1,650,000 speakers in the Philippines.

1179.

Richard A. Benton, *Pangasinan dictionary*. Honolulu: University of Hawaii Press, 1971. 313 pp. 0–87022–071–3.
Pacific & Asian Linguistics Institute. *PALI language texts: Philippines*.

English–Pangasinan index, pp. 187–313. This work forms a companion to the same author's *Pangasinan reference grammar* (Honolulu: University of Hawaii Press, 1971).

PANJABI

Panjabi is an INDO-ARYAN language of India and Pakistan, with perhaps as many as 60 million speakers. It is an official language of India, but in Pakistan, where the majority of speakers are to be found, Urdu is regarded as the standard language and Panjabi has no official status.

The spelling 'Punjabi', based on early nineteenth century English spelling conventions for Indian names, is still preferred by some writers and is usual in Pakistan.

The Gurmukhi alphabet

ਅ ਆ ਇ ਈ ਉ ਊ ਏ ਐ ਓ ਔ

a ā i ī u ū e ai o au

ਕਖਗਘਙ ਚਛਜਝਞ ਟਠਡਢਣ ਤਥਦਧਨ ਪਫਬਭਮ ਯਰਲਵ ਸ਼ਸਹ

k kh g gh ṅ c ch j jh ñ ṭ ṭh ḍ ḍh ṇ t th d dh n p ph b bh m y r l v ś s h

Panjabi is most often written and printed in Gurmukhi script, 'from the mouth of the Guru'. This was devised by Angad, the second Sikh guru, in the sixteenth century. It is a formalised and extended version of the Landa script that was and still is used by tradespeople in Panjab and Sind. The usual Roman transliteration, given here, follows the normal style for South Asian romanisation and does not attempt to mark tones.

In Pakistan, Panjabi is written in the Perso-Arabic script that is also used for Urdu.

1180.

Edward O'Brien, *Glossary of the Multani language, or (South-Western Panjabi)*. Lahore: Punjab Government Press, 1903. Various paginations. Revised by J. Wilson, Hari Kishen Kaul.

1st edn: *Glossary of the Multani language compared with Panjábi and Sindhí*. Lahore: Civil Secretariat Press,1881.

A series of thematic glossaries followed by a Panjabi–English glossary (103 pp.) in Latin script. This form of Panjabi is now regarded as a separate language, Siraiki.

1181.

Balbhir Singh Sandhu, Attar Singh, chief editors, *PSUTB English–Punjabi dictionary*. Chandigarh: Punjab State University Text-Book Board, 1982. 1407 pp.

A large-scale brief-entry dictionary. The pronunciation of English words is indicated in Panjabi script, in bold face aligned to the right of each column.

1182.

Bhai Maya Singh, *The Panjabi dictionary*. Lahore, 1895. 1221 pp.

A brief-entry Panjabi–English dictionary. Panjabi headwords are in both Gurmukhi and Latin script.

1183.

ਕਾਨ੍ ਸਿੰਘ, *ਗੁਰੁਸ਼ਬਦ ਰਤਨਾਕਰ ਮਹਾਨ ਕੋਸ਼* [*Guruśabd ratnakar mahan koś*] = Kahan Singh, *Encyclopaedia of Sikh literature*. Patiala: Bhasa Vibhaga, 1981. 1247 pp.

Encyclopaedic dictionary of the language of classical literature, entirely in Panjabi.

1184.

ਵੀਰ ਸਿੰਘ, *ਸ੍ਰੀ ਗੁਰ ਗ੍ਰੰਥ ਕੋਸ਼* [Vir Singh, *Sri Guru Granth koś*]. Amritsar: Khalsa Tract Society, 1983. 900 pp.

[*Dictionary of the holy book.*] A dictionary of the classical Panjabi language of the Adi-Granth, the collection of scriptures of the Sikh religion.

PAPUAN LANGUAGES AND THEIR NEIGHBOURS

'Papuan' is a catch-all designation for those languages of New Guinea and neighbouring islands that are not Austronesian. Listed below are two Papuan word-lists. Voorhoeve (**1186**) simply brings together short glossaries for nearly two hundred Papuan and Austronesian languages of New Guinea. Greenberg (**1185**), linguistically more ambitious, attempts to find a relationship among various Papuan and other language families.

There are as yet no large-scale dictionaries for any Papuan languages. The series *Pacific linguistics* contains many dictionaries and glossaries of Papuan languages, in most cases forming the best available sources for the languages concerned. Full lists of the series appear at the end of each published volume: see **1254** for an example. See also NORTH HALMAHERA LANGUAGES for a Papuan family on which some lexicographical work has been done.

1185.

Joseph H. Greenberg, 'The Indo-Pacific hypothesis' in *Current trends in linguistics* vol. 8 part 1 ed. Thomas A. Sebeok (The Hague: Mouton, 1971) pp. 807–71.

Includes a list of 84 'etymologies' in Andamanese, Timor-Alor, North Halmaheran, New Britain, New Ireland, Bougainville, Santa Cruz and Tasmanian languages and in several language families of New Guinea, intended to demonstrate their family relationship.

1186.

C. L. Voorhoeve, *Languages of Irian Jaya: checklist, preliminary classification, language maps, wordlists*. Canberra: Australian National University, Research School of Pacific Studies, 1975. 129 pp. 0–85883–128–7.

Pacific linguistics, series B, 31.

A list of 199 languages, with bibliographical references, pp. 21–60; then a glossary of forty words in 191 of these languages.

PASHTO

One of the IRANIAN LANGUAGES, Pashto or Pushtu or Pukhtu is one of the two major languages of Afghanistan and is also a regional language of north-western Pakistan. There are about 14,000,000 speakers in total.

1187.

М. Г. Асланов, *Пушту–русский словарь* [M. G. Aslanov, *Pushtu–russkii slovar'*]. Moscow: Russkii Yazyk, 1985. 1007 pp. 2nd edn by N. A. Dvoryakova.

1st edn: *Afghansko–russkii slovar' (pushtu)*. 1966. 994 pp.

[*Pashto–Russian dictionary.*] 50,000 entries, in Pashto script followed by a Cyrillic phonetic transcription, which helps with the vowels. Supplement, pp. 995–1007.

1188.

К. А. Лебедев, Л. С. Яцевич, Э. М. Калинина, *Русско–пушту словарь* [K. A. Lebedev, L. S. Yatsevich, E. M. Kalinina, *Russko–Pushtu slovar'*]. Moscow: Russkii Yazyk, 1983. 880 pp. 2nd edn with supplement.

1st edn: *Russko-afganskii slovar' (pushtu)*. Moscow: Sovetskaya Entsiklopediya, 1973.

[*Russian–Pashto dictionary.*] 32,000 entries. Supplement, pp. 875-80.

1189.

Georg Morgenstierne, *An etymological vocabulary of Pashto*. Oslo, 1927. 120 pp.

Skrifter utgitt av Det Norske Videnskaps-Akademi i Oslo, II: Hist.-filos. klasse, 1927 part 3.

A manuscript revision of this is to be found 'in Morgenstierne's Nachlaß at the Indo-Iranian Institute, University of Oslo' (P. O. Skjærvø in *Compendium linguarum iranicarum* ed. Rüdiger Schmitt, Wiesbaden: Reichert, 1989, p. 409).

PEHLEVI

Pehlevi is a middle IRANIAN language, vehicle of an abundant literature including the later sections of the Avesta. It thus remains important to Zoroastrians, for many of whom Gujarati is the everyday language – hence the trilingual dictionary listed here. Pehlevi was normally written in a script derived from Aramaic.

1190.

જામાસ્પજી દસ્તુર મીનોચેહેરજી જામાસ્પ આસાના, *પેહેલવી–ગુજરાતી અને ઈંગ્રેજી શબ્દકોષ* = Jamaspji Dastur Minocheherji Jamasp Asana, *Pahlavi, Gujarâti and English dictionary*. [Bombay] 1877–86. 4 vols [1090 pp.].

A brief-entry dictionary: the Pehlevi is in its own script, Gujarati in Gujarati script. Apart from the Gujarati and English glosses, Sanskrit and Avestan equivalents are sometimes supplied.

PERSIAN, DARI AND TAJIK

With over 30 million speakers, Persian is the most important of the modern IRANIAN LANGUAGES – and is thus a member of the Indo-European family. There are three modern standards, those of Iran (Persian), Afghanistan (most often called Dari) and Tajikistan (Tajik). Tajik is written in Cyrillic script; otherwise, Persian uses a variant of Arabic script, introduced with the Islamic expansion in the seventh century AD.

Persian was a language of administration in India for hundreds of years, and has influenced all the languages of northern India.

Old Persian is dealt with in this book at AVESTAN; for middle Persian see PEHLEVI.

The Persian alphabet

ا ب پ ت ث ج چ ح خ د ذ ر ز ژ س ش ص ض ط ظ ع غ ف ق ک گ ل م ن و ه ي

a b p t ṣ j č ḥ k h d ẕ r z ž s š ṣ ẓ ṭ ẓ ' g h f q k g l m n v h y

The letters ث ص sound like Persian س; ط sounds like Persian ت. The three letters ث ص ط, along with

ح ذ ظ ض ع, are hardly ever used except in Arabic loanwords.

In Soviet Tajikistan Latin script was adopted in the 1920s, to be replaced by Cyrillic script around 1940.

The modern standards

1191.

Abbas Aryanpur (Kashani), *The new unabridged English–Persian dictionary.*
Tehran: Amir Kabir, 1963–5. 5 vols.

Abridged edn: Abbas Aryanpur Kashani, Manuchihr Aryanpur Kashani, *The concise English–Persian dictionary.* 1978. 1269 + 46 pp. 2nd edition. – 1st edn: 1975.

A very copious brief-entry dictionary on the basis of Webster's *International* (**363**) and the *Shorter Oxford* (see **360**).

1192.

Abbas Aryanpur-Kashani, Manoochehr Aryanpur-Kashani, *The concise Persian–English dictionary.* Tehran: Amir Kabir, 1976. 1440 pp.

1193.

علی اکبر دهخدا هذا الغتنامه = Alî Akbar Dehkhodâ, [Mohammad Moîn, Dj. Shahîdy,]
Loghat-nama = Dictionnaire encyclopédique. Tehran: Danishgah-i Tihran,
Danishkadah-i Adabiyat, Sazman-i Lughat-namah, 1946–[1975?]. 52 vols [about 220 parts?].

Reprinted: 1372–3 [1993–4]. 15 vols.

[*Encyclopaedic dictionary.*] A vast work, entirely in Persian (but with many scientific terms, proper names, etc., inserted in Latin script), with illustrations. The set was not published in alphabetical sequence and copies available to me are not easy to catalogue: libraries have discarded later title pages in binding, concealing the date and number of the most recent parts.

1194.

Wilhelm Eilers, *Deutsch–Persisches Wörterbuch.* Wiesbaden: Harrassowitz, 1959– .

[*German–Persian dictionary.*] A very copious dictionary into modern Persian. I have seen two volumes, covering **A–Feucht**.

1195.

Sulaiman Haïm, *New Persian–English dictionary.* Tehran, 1962. 2 vols [1246 pp.].

A brief-entry dictionary with a good selection of example phrases, all of which are given both in Persian and in English.

Older periods

1196.

Moḥammad Ḥosayn ebn-e Khalaf de Tabriz [Burhān], *Borhān-e qate`* = *Dictionnaire de la langue persane*. Tehran: Librairie Zowwār, 1951–6. 4 vols. Revised edn with additions by Moh. Mo'in.

[*Dictionary of the Persian language.*] A seventeenth century classic of lexicography, supplemented (indeed, occasionally overwhelmed) by very copious etymological and historical footnotes.

1197.

J. J. P. Desmaisons, *Dictionaire persan–français*. Rome: Typographie Polyglotte, 1908–14. 4 vols.
'Publié par ses neveux.'

[*Persian–French dictionary.*] Similar in scale to Steingass (**1198**), though more generously laid out and more finely printed.

1198.

F. Steingass, *A comprehensive Persian–English dictionary, including the Arabic words and phrases to be met with in Persian literature*. London: Allen [1892].
'Being Johnson and Richardson's Persian, Arabic and English dictionary [i. e. Johnson's enlargement of Wilkins-Richardson's *A dictionary, Persian, Arabic and English*] revised, enlarged and entirely reconstructed.' Another issue, with cancel title page: London: Sampson Low, Marston. Reprinted: London: Kegan Paul, Trench, Trubner, 1930, 1947, 1957.

Strong in the vocabulary of classical Persian literature. No quotations but numerous citations.

Regional languages

1199.

Giti Shukri, *Guyish-i Sari (Mazandarani)* = *Sari dialect (Mazandarani)*. Tehran, 1374 [1995]. 481 pp.

Mazandarani is an Iranian language of the southern coast of the Caspian. The Mazandarani forms are given in Arabic and Latin scripts, with glosses in Persian.

Etymological dictionaries

1200.

Paul Horn, *Grundriß der neupersischen Etymologie*. Strasbourg: Trübner, 1893.
See also: Heinrich Hübschmann, *Persische Studien*. Strasbourg: Trübner, 1895.

[*Foundations of modern Persian etymology.*]

1201.

M. J. Mashkour, = *A comparative dictionary of Arabic, Persian and the Semitic languages.* Tehran: Bunyad-i Farhang-i Iran, 1357 [1978]. 2 vols.

Zaban-shinasi-i Irani, 12–13. *Intisharat-i Bunyad-i Farhang-i Iran,* 276–7.

1202.

Ioannis Augusti Vullers, *Lexicon persico–latinum etymologicum.* Bonn: A. Marcus, 1855–64. 2 vols.

Accompanied by: *Verborum linguae persicae radices e dialectis antiquioribus persicis et lingua sanscrita et aliis linguis maxime cognatis erutae atque illustratae: supplementum lexici sui persico–latini.* 1867. 136 pp. [*Persian word roots extracted and explained from early Iranian languages, Sanskrit and other closely related languages: a supplement to his Persian–Latin dictionary.*]

[*Persian–Latin etymological dictionary.*] Naturally outdated in many areas now. The supplement includes an index of roots, in Latin script, with Avestan and Sanskrit cognates, pp. 117–36.

PHOENICIAN

The early SEMITIC language of the Syrian and Palestinian coast, known from inscriptions. The Phoenician colony of Carthage, in modern Tunisia, developed a distinct dialect known as Punic. Apart from the Phoenician dictionaries below, note Hoftijzer and Jongeling (**1370**).

1203.

Maria-José Fuentes Estañol, *Vocabulario fenicio.* Barcelona: CSIC, 1980. 391 pp. 84–00–04757–5.

Biblioteca fenicia, 1.

[*Phoenician dictionary.*] Forms are listed in consonantal transcription, followed by a gloss, possible pronunciation, and citations of texts.

1204.

Richard S. Tomback, *A comparative Semitic lexicon of the Phoenician and Punic languages.* Missoula: Scholars Press, 1978. 361 pp. 0–89130–126–7.

Society of Biblical Literature. *Dissertation series,* 32.

Forms are listed in consonantal transcription. Entries give Semitic cognates, then a series of brief quotations from Phoenician and Punic texts, with precise references; then a bibliography of modern scholarly literature.

POLABIAN

Polabian is an extinct West SLAVONIC language once spoken in eastern Germany.

1205.

Tadeusz Lehr-Spławiński, Kazimierz Polański, *Słownik etymologiczny języka drzewian połabskich.* Wroclaw: Ossolineum, 1962–71. Parts 1–2 [346 pp.].

[*Etymological dictionary of the old Polabian language.*] Covers **A–L'**.

1206.

Kazimierz Polański, James A. Sehnert, *Polabian-English dictionary*. The Hague: Mouton, 1967. 239 pp.

Slavistic printings and reprintings, 61.

A brief-entry dictionary with single-letter abbreviations to identify source texts; no precise references. 'Backwards dictionary', pp. 221–39.

POLISH

One of the SLAVONIC LANGUAGES of the Indo-European family, Polish is most closely related to Czech, Slovak and Sorbian. It is the national language of Poland, and has about 40 million speakers.

There is a bibliography of Polish dictionaries by Grzegorczyk (**1228**).

Polish alphabetical order

a ą b c ć d e ę f g h i j k l ł m n ń o ó p q r s ś t u v w x y z ź ż

The letters **Q** and **X** occur only in foreign words.

Historical dictionaries

1207.

W. Doroszewski, chief editor, *Słownik języka polskiego*. Warsaw, 1958–69. 11 vols.

With the assistance of S. Skorupka, Halina Auderska.

[*Dictionary of the Polish language.*] A well-planned historical dictionary with generous quotations from the texts.

Vol. 11 is the supplement, **A–Ż** (566 pp.). It includes new entries, many of them for technical words and other neologisms; an important list of cited authors that gives their dates (pp. 553–5); and also a list of errata to vols 1–10 (pp. 557–66). As to the errata for vol. 11, these appear on a loose inserted page.

1208.

Samuel Bogumil Linde, *Słownik języka polskiego*. Warsaw, 1807–14. 6 vols.

Note also: Witold Doroszewski, *Indeks a tergo do Słownika języka polskiego S. B. Lindego*. Warsaw: Wydawnictwa Uniwersytetu Warszawskiego, 1965. 392 pp. [*Reverse index to Linde's Dictionary of the Polish language.*]

[*Dictionary of the Polish language.*] Glosses are supplied in Polish (roman font) and German (Fraktur). Practically all entries are supported by citations, and usually quotations, from Polish literature. Abbreviations for these: vol. 1, preliminary pages.

Informative on usage as well as on etymology: 'parallels with other Slavic languages and with German were often cited … a great storehouse of the Polish language and its usage up to the end of the eighteenth century' (Collison, **7**). 'Of lasting significance for the codification of the literary language' (*The Slavic literary languages: formation and* *development* ed. Alexander M. Schenker, Edward Stankiewicz, New Haven, 1980, p. 209).

The modern standard

1209.

Bogusław Dunaj, editor, *Słownik współczesnego języka polskiego*. Warsaw: Wilga, 1996. 1393 pp. 83–7156–068–0.

[*Dictionary of the contemporary Polish language.*] A very full brief-entry dictionary of the modern language. Word forms are keyed to the morphological tables on pp. xxi–xxxv.

1210.

Jan Karłowicz, Adam Kryński, Władysław Niedźwiedzki, editors, *Słownik języka polskiego*. Warsaw, 1900–19. 8 vols.

Reprinted: Poznan, 1952.

[*Dictionary of the Polish language.*] I have found this dictionary far richer than any of its competitors in regional and traditional names for flora and fauna. Taxonomic Latin names are given as glosses.

1211.

Słownik języka polskiego. Warsaw: Państwowe Wydawnictwo Naukowe, 1978–81. 3 vols. 83–01–10902–5.

Edited by Mieczysław Szymczak.

Followed by: *Suplement*. 1992. 124 pp. 83–01–10906–8.

[*Dictionary of the Polish language.*] A concise dictionary of modern usage. Information on word forms is keyed to the morphological tables, vol. 1 pp. xiv–xxviii.

1212.

Jan Stanisławski, *The great English–Polish dictionary = Wielki słownik angielsko–polski*. Warsaw: Wiedza Powszechna, 1964. 1175 pp.

'Scientific supervision: Wiktor Jassem.'

A brief-entry dictionary. Appendices of geographical names, of Christian names, of abbreviations (pp. 1128–75) etc. There is a loose sheet of errata.

1213.

Jan Stanisławski, *Wielki słownik polsko–angielski = The great Polish–English dictionary*. Warsaw: Wiedza Powszechna, 1969. 1583 pp.

Edited by Wiktor Jassem.

Followed by: Jan Stanisławski, Małgorzata Szercha, *Supplement = Suplement*. 1977. 144 pp.

A brief-entry dictionary with plenty of set phrases and examples. Appendices of geographical names and of abbreviations.

In the supplement, an upward arrow is used to mark an entry that adds further information to an entry in the main volume.

1214.

Halina Zgółkowa, *Praktyczny słownik współczesnej polszczyzny*. Poznan: Kurpisz, 1994– . 83–900203–3–5.

[*Practical dictionary of contemporary Polish.*] A large-scale dictionary of modern usage, with full definitions and historical explanations of meaning, but no attributed quotations. Designed, impractically, in a large and broad typeface and in small volumes, of which 11 (**A–Framuzka**) have so far appeared.

Older periods

1215.

Никита Горбачевский, *Словарь древняго актоваго языка Сѣверо-западнаго Края и Царства Полскаго* [Nikita Gorbachevskii, *Slovar' drevnago aktovago yazyka Severo-zapadnago Kraya i Tsarstva Polskago*]. Vilnius: Zaka, 1874. 397 pp.

Reprint: Nikita Ivanovič Gorbačevskij, *Wörterbuch der alten Urkundensprache des Grossfürstentums Litauen und des Königreichs Polen*. Munich: Sagner, 1992. Edited by O. Horbatsch. (*Specimina philologiae Slavicae*, 95.)

[*Dictionary of the old chancery language of Lithuania and the Kingdom of Poland.*] In Russian. Citations and some quotations of source documents.

1216.

Stefan Reczek, *Podręczny słownik dawnej polszczyzny: staropolsko–nowopolskam, nowopolsko–staropolska*. Wrocław: Ossolineum, 1968. 934 pp.

[*Concise dictionary of early Polish: old Polish–modern Polish, modern Polish–old Polish.*] In the main sequence of entries headwords are in old Polish with glosses in the modern language. Authors are cited and some quotations are given, but there are no precise references. The index in modern Polish is on pp. 681–933.

1217.

Słownik polszczyzny XVI wieku. Wrocław: Ossolineum, 1966– .
Editorial Committee: Stanisław Bak, Maria Renata Mayenowa and others.

[*Dictionary of sixteenth-century Polish.*] An extremely full and detailed historical dictionary of the sixteenth-century language. Meanings are very carefully analysed and each is supported with quotations.

Prefatory matter includes a full bibliography of sources, vol. 1 pp. xliv–cxi, followed by lists of printers and biographies of authors, editors and printers. Each volume contains loose lists of abbreviations and of errata.

The last volume I have seen is vol. 21, published in 1992: the dictionary now covers **A–opoślad**.

1218.

Stanisław Urbanczyk, K. Nitzsch [and other editors], *Słownik staropolski*. Warsaw: Polska Akademia Nauk, 1953– .

[*Dictionary of old Polish.*] This is an important full historical dictionary of fourteenth and fifteenth century Polish. Each entry begins with a paragraph listing recorded word forms, followed by numerous quotations from sources, both Polish and Latin. Glosses are given in Polish and Latin (in the case of flora and fauna, this means scientific Latin).

The last issue I have seen is part 63, belonging to vol. 10 and published in 1990. At that time the dictionary covered **A–Wjechac**.

Regional forms

1219.

Mieczysław Karas, [Jerzy Reichan,] *Słownik gwar polskich*. Wrocław: Ossolineum, 1979– . 83–04–00468–2.

Accompanied by: *Zródła*. 1977. 151 pp. [*Lists of abbreviations and of informants*.]

[*Dictionary of Polish dialects*.] Based on both printed sources and oral information. Numerous cross-references from variant forms of words. The variety of sources used results in a complex range of references to villages, districts, regions, etc.: for geographical guidance see vol. 1 pp. lii–lxxii, with six maps.

The most recent part I have seen, vol. 4 part 11, appeared in 1993: with it the dictionary covers **A–Ciupaga**.

1220.

Jan Karłowicz, *Słownik gwar polskich*. Kraków: Nakładem Akademii Umiejętności, 1900–1911. 6 vols.

Vols. 4–6 edited by J. Łos.

Reprinted: Warsaw: Wydawnictwa Artystyczne i Filmowe, 1974.

[*Dictionary of Polish dialects*.] A concise dictionary in which each word is supported by at least one citation from a textual source but relatively few quotations are given. It may be regarded as a dialect supplement to the big Polish dictionaries, based on printed sources. Entries do not always make it easy to see in which particular regional dialects a word is known. List of abbreviations, vol. 6 pp. 457–70.

Kashubian

1221.

Wiesław Bory, Hanna Popowska-Taborska, *Słownik etymologiczny Kaszubszczyzny*. Warsaw: Slawistyczny Ośrodek Wydawniczy, 1994– .

Polska Akademia Nauk, Instytut Slawistyki.

Vol. 1 covers **A–C**. Introduction on earlier research and publications, pp. 7–36: survey of dictionaries and glossaries of Kashubian, pp. 15–25. Bibliography, pp. 37–62.

1222.

Stefan Ramułt, *Słownik języka pomorskiego czyli kaszubskiego*. Kraków: Nakładem Akademii Umiejętności, 1893. 298 pp.

[*Dictionary of the Kashubian language*.] A Kashubian–Polish dictionary of the spoken language, based on oral collections, with plenty of example phrases. Selection of folklore texts, pp. 281–98.

1223.

Bernard Sychta, *Słownik gwar kaszubskich*. Wrocław: Ossolineum, 1967–76. 7 vols.

[*Dictionary of Kashubian dialects.*] Glosses are in Polish. Entries are of varying length, most of them indicating the geographical range of the word concerned (list of place names, vol. 1 pp. xxiv–xxvi). Many example sentences, with explanations in Polish. The main alphabetical sequence is in vols 1–6; vol. 7 is a supplement of added entries.

Slang and special vocabularies

1224.

Stanisław Kania, *Słownik argotyzmów*. Warsaw: Wiedza Powszechna, 1995. 275 pp. 83–214–0993–8.

[*Dictionary of argot.*] Many examples of usage are given. Literary sources, where used, are cited precisely. About 7000 entries. Bibliography of sources, pp. 21–34; of books on Polish slang and special vocabularies, pp. 266–74.

Etymological dictionaries

1225.

Aleksander Brückner, *Słownik etymologiczny języka polskiego*. Warsaw: Wiedza Powszechna, 1957.

1st edn: Kraków: Krakowska Spółka Wydawnicza [1926–7]. 2 vols in 1 [806 pp.].

[*Etymological dictionary of the Polish language.*] A concise dictionary concentrating on native words and the better-established loanwords. Among frequently-used abbreviations for language names note *łac.* 'Latin', *niem.* 'German'. I do not know whether the 1957 publication is a new edition or a reprint.

1226.

Franciszek Sławski, *Słownik etymologiczny języka polskiego*. Kraków: Nakładem Towarzystwa Miłosników Języka Polskiego, 1952– .

[*Etymological dictionary of the Polish language.*] Considerably fuller than Brückner (**1225**), with discussion of Old Slavonic sources and modern cognates and with references to the scholarly literature.

Publication is very slow. I have seen parts 1–25, completing five volumes and covering **A–Łżywy**.

Foreign words

1227.

Słownik wyrazów obcych PWN. Warsaw: Państwowe Wydawnictwo Naukowe, 1971. 828 pp.

Edited by Jan Tokarski, Hipolit Szkiladz.

[*PWN dictionary of foreign words.*] Copious, fairly brief entries supplying the original foreign form between angle brackets <>, followed by a gloss.

Other works of interest

1228.

S. Grzegorczyk, *Index lexicorum Poloniae = Bibliografia słowników polskich.* Warsaw: Państwowe Wydawnictwo Naukowe, 1967. 286 pp.

PORTUGUESE

Portuguese is a ROMANCE language, in origin the southern dialect of GALICIAN, but it has grown to far greater world-wide importance than its twin. Although the former Portuguese colonial empire has melted away, Portuguese is now the national language of Brazil as well as Portugal, and has perhaps 155 million speakers as a first language.

Much spelling variation is seen in Portuguese texts before 1945, when Portugal and Brazil agreed on a new orthography (see **1230**). For a bibliography of Portuguese dictionaries see **1247**.

Historical dictionaries

1229.

Dicionário da lingua portuguesa. Lisbon, 1976. Vol. 1 [678 pp.; no more published].

Academia das Ciências de Lisboa.

1st edn: *Diccionario da lingoa portugueza.* Lisbon, 1793. Vol. 1 [543 pp.; no more published].

[*Dictionary of the Portuguese language.*] The Lisbon Academy's 1793 dictionary got only as far as the letter **A**, and the 1976 edition seems to have had the same fate. It covers **A–Azuverte.**

1230.

António de Morais Silva, *Grande dicionário da lingua portuguesa.* Lisbon: Confluencia, 1948–60. 12 vols. 10th edn by Augusto Moreno, Cardoso Júnior and José Pedro Machado.

Cover title: *Dicionário de Morais.*

1st edn: 1789. – This was successor to: Raphael Bluteau, *Vocabulario portuguez e latino.* Coimbra, Lisbon, 1712–28. 10 vols.

2nd edn: 1813. This was the first to credit Morais as author. – Reprint of the 2nd edn, with an introduction by Laudelino Freire: Rio de Janeiro, 1922.

3rd edn: 1823. – 4th edn: 1831, with additions by Theotonio José de Oliveira Velho. – 5th edn: 1844. – 6th edn: 1858, edited by Agostinho de Mendonça Falcão. – 7th edn: 1877–8. – 8th edn: 1891.

Abridged Brazilian edition: *Novo dicionário compacto da lingua portuguesa.* Rio de Janeiro, 1980. 5 vols.

[*Big dictionary of the Portuguese language.*] Concise entries include numerous brief quotations from literary sources, with precise references. There is no list of authors and works cited, and the user has to be familiar with the catch-names for major Portuguese authors, e.g. *Camilo* for Camilo Castelo Branco. The 1948–60 edition follows 'the rules of the Acordo Ortográfico Luso-Brasileiro of 10 August 1945'.

Vol. 12 is a supplement including the original grammar of Portuguese ('Epítome') by Morais, a statement of the new 1945 spelling rules, a list of foreign words and phrases, and finally on pp. 857–1098 a sequence of additions, corrections and cross-references.

Among earlier editions, the 7th was notable for its inclusion of new vocabulary from Brazil and from the Portuguese possessions in the East.

The modern standard

1231.

Aurélio Buarque de Holanda Ferreira, *Novo dicionário da lingua portuguesa.* Rio de Janeiro: Nova Fronteira, 1986. 1838 pp. 2nd edn, revised and enlarged.
1st edn: 1975.

[*New dictionary of the Portuguese language.*]

1232.

Cândido de Figueiredo, *Dicionário da língua portuguesa.* Lisbon: Bertrand, 1975–8. 2 vols.
Cover title: *Grande dicionário de Cândido de Figueiredo.*
Earlier title: *Novo dicionário de língua portuguesa.* 5th edn: 1936. – 14th edn: 1949.

[*Dictionary of the Portuguese language.*] A large-scale brief-entry dictionary.

1233.

Laudelino Freire, *Grande e novíssimo dicionário da lingua portuguesa.* Rio de Janeiro, 1954. 5 vols [5372 pp.]. 2nd edn.
1st edn: 1939–44. – The '3rd edn', 1957, is a reprint of the 2nd.

[*Big new dictionary of the Portuguese language.*]

1234.

José Pedro Machado, *Dicionário da lingua portuguesa.* Lisbon, 1958–71. 7 vols.
Published as a series of supplements to *Boletim mensal da Sociedade de língua portuguesa.*
Reprinted as: *Grande dicionário da lingua portuguesa.* Lisbon: Sociedade da Lingua Portuguesa, 1981. 12 vols.

[*Dictionary of the Portuguese language.*]

1235.

Nôvo Michaelis dicionário ilustrado = The new Michaelis illustrated dictionary. São Paulo: Melhoramentos. 4 vols.
Earlier version: São Paulo: Melhoramentos; Wiesbaden: Brockhaus, 1958–61. 2 vols [1151 + 1328 pp.]. New edn by Fritz Pietzschke and others.

The largest available bilingual dictionary of Portuguese. Vols 1–2: English–Portuguese; vols 3–4: Portuguese–English.

1236.

Antenor Nascentes, editor, *Dicionário ilustrado da lingua portuguesa da Academia Brasileira de Letras.* Rio de Janeiro, 1971– .
Preliminary edn: 1961–7. 4 vols.

[*Illustrated dictionary of the Portuguese language of the Brazilian Academy of Letters.*]

1237.

James L. Taylor, *A Portuguese–English dictionary.* Stanford: Stanford University Press, 1958. 662 pp.

Corrected reprint: 1963. Also published: London: Harrap.

Strong in Brazilian terminology, notably for flora and fauna, for which taxonomic names as well as English glosses are provided.

Older periods

1238.

Antônio Geraldo da Cunha, *Indice do vocabulário português medieval.* Rio de Janeiro: Casa Barbosa, 1986–8. Parts 1–2 [no more published]. 85–7004–097–0.

[*Index of the medieval Portuguese lexicon.*] Citations with brief glosses. Covers **A–C**.

1239.

Joaquím de Santa Rosa de Viterbo, *Elucidário das palavras, termos e frases que em Portugal antigamente se usaram e que hoje regularmente se ignoram: obra indispensável para entender sem erro os documentos mais raros e preciosos que entre nós se conservam.* Oporto: Civilização, 1962–6. 2 vols. Critical edition by Mário Fiúza, based on Viterbo's original manuscripts.

Original edn: Lisbon, 1798–9. 2 vols. – 2nd edn, 1865. 649 pp.

[*Glossary of the words, expressions and phrases formerly used in Portugal and now generally unknown, an indispensable guide to the correct interpretation of the rarest and most precious of our early records.*] This translated title does scant justice to the poetic prose of the original Portuguese. Viterbo's work is an important dictionary of early Portuguese, giving long quotations from the texts (list of cited texts, vol. 1 pp. 71–86). The letter A is covered at length, occupying half of Fiúza's edition. Index of proper names in quotations and glosses, vol. 2 pp. 669–739, followed by a word index, useful because it provides cross-references among entries, pp. 740–78.

Regional forms

Brazil

1240.

Tomé Cabral, *Novo dicionário de termos e expressões populares.* Fortaleza Ceará: Universidade Federal do Ceará, 1982. 786 pp. New edn.

1st edn: *Dicionário de termos e expressões populares.* 1973.

[*New dictionary of popular words and phrases.*] A glossary of Brazilian regional and popular usage. Most entries give a quotation from a literary source (list of these, pp. 769–83) with a precise reference. List of reviews of 1st edn, p. 784.

1241.

Antônio Joaquim de Macedo Soares, *Dicionário brasileiro da lingua portuguêsa: elucidário etimológico crítico das palavras e frases que, originárias do Brasil, ou aqui populares, se nao encontram nos dicionários da lingua portuguêsa, ou neles vêm com forma ou significação diferente.* Rio de Janeiro, 1954–5. 2 vols [275 + 207 pp.].

Incomplete 1st edn: *Dicionario brasileiro da lingua portugueza.* Rio de Janeiro, 1889. (*Anais da Biblioteca Nacional,* vol. 13, 1888, supplement.)

[*Brazilian dictionary of the Portuguese language: a critical etymological glossary of words and phrases originating in Brazil or commonly used there, and either not listed at all in Portuguese dictionaries, or listed with a different form or meaning.*] Compiled between 1875 and 1888, the work was finally revised for publication by the author's son. The 1889 publication covers **A–Candeieiro** only.

Etymological dictionaries

1242.

José Pedro Machado, *Dicionário etimológico da língua portuguesa.* Lisbon: Confluência, 1978. 5 vols.

The British Library catalogue gives the imprint as Lisbon: Horizonte, 1977.

1st edn: *Dicionário etimológico da língua portuguesa, com a mais antiga documentação escrita e conhecida de muitos dos vocábulos estudados.* Oporto:, 1952–9. 2 vols [2379 pp.]. – See: José Pedro Machado, *À margem do meu Dicionario etimológico da língua portuguesa.* N.p.: Confluência [1965?]. [*In the margin of my Etymological dictionary of the Portuguese language.*]

2nd edn: Lisbon: Confluência, 1967-73. 3 vols [2351 pp.].

Note also: Ramón Lorenzo, *Sobre cronologia do vocabulário Galego-Portugués: anotações ao "Dicionário etimológico" de José Pedro Machado.* Vigo: Galaxia, 1968. 382 pp. (Fundación Penzol. *Colección filolóxica.*)

[*Etymological dictionary of the Portuguese language.*] Entries are sometimes quite lengthy, and often – as promised in the title of the first edition – quote the text that includes the oldest recorded occurrence of the word in question. Abbreviations, vol. 1 pp. 9–11.

An earlier version of Machado's notes, *À margem* ..., appeared in the *Boletim da Sociedade de Língua Portuguesa.*

1243.

Anténor Nascentes, *Dicionário etimológico da lingua portuguesa.* Rio de Janeiro, 1932. 829 pp.

Abridged edn: Anténor Nascentes, *Dicionário etimológico resumido.* Rio de Janeiro: Instituto Nacional do Livro, 1966. 791 pp. This includes some corrections, but lacks the bibliographical references.

A polemical review was published: Eduardo de Lisboa, *O dicionário do Sr. Nascentes e o "REW": rectificações.* Rio de Janeiro: Pimenta de Mello, 1937. The *REW* in the title is Meyer-Lübke (**1256**). I owe the reference to Malkiel (**9**).

[*Etymological dictionary of the Portuguese language.*]

Foreign words

1244.

Sebastião Rodolfo Dalgado, *Glossário luso-asiático*. Coimbra: Imprensa da Universidade, 1919–21. 2 vols.

Note also: S. R. Dalgado, *Contribuições para a lexiologia luso-oriental*. Coimbra, 1916. 192 pp. [*Contributions to Portuguese–Oriental lexicography*.] – José Pedro Machado, *Coisas Luso-Orientais*. 1943. [*Portuguese–Oriental matters*.]

[*Portuguese Asiatic glossary*.] Handbook of Asian words in early Portuguese sources.

1245.

José Pedro Machado, *Estrangeirismos na língua portuguesa*. Lisbon: Notícias, 1994.

[*Foreign words and expressions in Portuguese*.]

1246.

José Pedro Machado, *Vocabulário português de origem árabe*. Lisbon: Notícias, 1991.

Earlier work: José Pedro Machado, *Influência arábica no vocabulário português*. Lisbon, 1953–61. 285 pp. (*Revista de Portugal, s uplemento*.)

[*Portuguese vocabulary of Arabic origin*.]

Other works of interest

1247.

Átila Almeida, *Dicionários parentes & aderentes: uma bibliografia de dicionários, enciclopédias, glossários, vocabulários e livros afins em que entra a língua portuguesa*. João Pessoa: FUNAPE, 1988. 349 pp.

PRAKRIT

A middle INDO-ARYAN language of northern India, known from Jaina texts and others.

1248.

आनदंसागरसूरि | अल्पपरिचितसैद्धान्तिकशब्दकोष: =Anandsagarsurishwarji, *Shree alpaparicit saidhantik shabda-kosh*. Surat: Choksi, 1954–74. Vols 1–4.

Sresthi-Devacandalalabhai-Jainapustakoddhare, 101, 115–116, 125.

[*Detailed dictionary of the scriptures*.] Introduction in Gujarati; glosses in Sanskrit.

QUECHUA

Quechua may be a language isolate, or a member of 'Quechumaran' (see **68**), a postulated small language family linking it with AYMARA. It may also be counted a member of the controversial family of AMERIND LANGUAGES. However this may be, it was the ruling language of the powerful Inca empire destroyed by Spanish conquerors in the sixteenth century. Quechua is still a major language of Peru and Bolivia, and has nine million speakers in these and other South American countries.

There are many modern Quechua dictionaries, but practically all of them are brief-entry works which do not meet the criteria for inclusion here.

1249.

Gerald Taylor, *Diccionario normalizado y comparativo quechua: Chachapoyas-Lamas*. Paris: L'Harmattan, 1979.

[*Standard and comparative Quechua dictionary of Chachapoyas-Lamas.*]

1250.

Vocabulario políglota incaico: comprende más de 12,000 voces castellanas y 100,000 de keshua del Cuzco, Ayacucho, Junín. Lima: Colegio De Propaganda Fide del Perú, 1905. Various paginations.

Accompanied by: *Vocabulario castellano–aymará; forma parte del Políglota incaico.* 1905. 512 pp.

[*Multilingual Inca dictionary, comprising more than 12,000 Spanish words and 100,000 in Quechua of Cuzco, Ayacucho, Junín.*]

RAJASTHANI

One of the INDO-ARYAN LANGUAGES, Rajasthani has about 20 million speakers in the Indian state of Rajasthan. There is relatively little modern literature in the language – modern writers choose Hindi – but some important historical poetry from earlier centuries. Rajasthani is written in the Devanagari alphabet, as used for Hindi.

1251.

सीतारांम लाळस | *राजस्थानी सबद कोस = राजस्थानी हिन्दी बृहत् कोश* [Sitaramm Lalas, *Rajasthanni sabad kos*]. Jaipur, 1962–78. 8 vols.

[*Rajasthani dictionary.*] Glosses in Hindi; numerous quotations from literature. Vol. 1 includes a short history of the Rajasthani language and literature in Hindi. The biggest dictionary to date of any of the Hindi-related regional languages.

1252.

बदरी प्रसाद साकरिया | भूपतिराम साकरिया | *राजस्थानी हिन्दी शब्द कोश* [Badrī Prasād Sākriyā, Bhūpatirām Sākriyā, *Rājasthānī Hindī śabda kos*]. Jaipur: Pancasila Prakasan, 1977–82. 2 vols [1237 pp.].

[*Rajasthani–Hindi dictionary.*] A brief-entry dictionary.

RHADÉ

A minority AUSTRONESIAN language of inland southern Vietnam.

1253.

J. Davias-Baudrit, *Dictionnaire rhadé–français*. Dalat: Mission Catholique de Banmêthuôt, 1966.

[*Rhadé–French dictionary.*] Not seen. 'Substantial: extensive coverage of compounds and generous inclusion of sample sentences', according to J. A. Tharp (**1254**).

1254.

James A. Tharp, Y-Bham Duôn-ya, *A Rhade–English dictionary with English–Rhade finderlist*. Canberra: Australian National University, Research School of Pacific Studies, Department of Linguistics, 1980. 271 pp.
Pacific linguistics, series C, 58.

Independent of Davias-Baudrit, and apparently based on a different dialect. In spite of the title, the two halves of the work are of similar size.

ROMANCE LANGUAGES

The Romance languages are the direct descendants of LATIN, the ruling language of the Roman Empire. Latin began to split into dialects, and eventually into separate languages, as the Empire crumbled.

Latin was an Italic language, and thus a member of the Indo-European family. The following modern descendants have entries in this book: AROMUNIAN, CATALAN, FRENCH, FRIULIAN, GALICIAN, GASCON, ITALIAN, JUDEZMO, LADIN, OCCITAN, PORTUGUESE, ROMANIAN, ROMANSCH, SARDINIAN, SPANISH, VEGLIOTE.

There is a long history of scholarly work on the Romance languages, a field in which German scholars have been eminent: see the survey by Stimm and Briegel (**1261**).

For Romance loanwords in other languages see **200** in addition to **1257** and **1258**.

Comparative dictionaries

1255.

Friedrich Diez, *Etymologisches Wörterbuch der romanischen Sprachen*. Bonn: Marcus, 1887. 864 pp. 5th edn.
1st edn: 1853. – 2nd edn: 1861. – 3rd edn: 1869–70. 2 vols. – 4th edn (reprint of the third, with corrections by A. Scheler): 1878.
Jan Urban Jarník, *Neuer vollständiger Index zu Diez' "EWRS"*. Heilbronn: Henninger, 1889. First published 1878. [*New complete index to Diez's EWRS.*]
See also: Rudolf Thurneysen, *Keltoromanisches: die keltischen Etymologien im Etymologischen Wörterbuch der romanischen Sprachen von F. Diez*. Halle: Niemeyer, 1884. [*Celto-Romance studies: the Celtic etymologies in Diez's dictionary.*]

[*Etymological dictionary of the Romance languages.*] In four main sections, each alphabetical: 'Common Romance', pp. 1–347 (arranged under Italian form if any); 'Italian area', pp. 351–412; 'Spanish area', pp. 413–501; 'French area', pp. 502–701. These sections are essentially unchanged from the third edition onwards: the fifth adds a supplement to each section in the form of the *Anhang* [*Appendix*] by August Scheler, pp.

705–818. Diez's own index is patchy and does not include headwords, but Jarník's separately published index made up the deficiency.

Superseded by Meyer-Lübke (**1256**) except to the extent that the geographical arrangement may occasionally be useful.

1256.

Wilhelm Meyer-Lübke, *Romanisches etymologisches Wörterbuch.* Heidelberg: Winter, 1930–35. 1204 pp. 3rd edn.

Sammlung romanischer Elementar- und Handbücher, 3rd series, 3.

1st edn: 1911–20. 1092 pp. The '2nd edn' was a reprint of this.

A reverse or 'rhyming' index [*Rückläufiges Stichwortindex*], by Annegret Alsdorf-Bollée and Isolde Burr, was published in 1969. 124 pp.

[*Romance etymological dictionary.*] An extremely well-organised and concise dictionary, arranged in a single alphabetical order of Latin, reconstructed proto-Romance or other parent words ('Meyer-Lübke' is as essential to Latin as to Romance scholars). Reconstructed proto-forms, not recorded in surviving Latin texts, are marked with an asterisk. Under these headings, all major Romance language forms are listed as well as many from dialects. There are numerous very brief references to scholarly articles, but, apart from this, sources are not usually cited: thus some dialect forms turn out to be ghosts because they are drawn from unreliable dialect dictionaries.

The dictionary, pp. 1–803; addenda, pp. 804–14. Complete index of forms cited: Romance languages, pp. 815–1153 (most searches start here), followed by separate indexes for Albanian, Amerindian languages, Arabic–Persian–Hebrew, south and east Asian, Basque–Iberian (note the study by Hubschmid, **1259**), Berber, Personal names, Germanic, Greek, Celtic–Ligurian, Hungarian, onomatopoeias, Slavic–Baltic, Turkish.

German-to-Romance index, a new feature of the 3rd edition, pp. 1187–1200. Errata, pp. 1201–4.

Note Moll's Catalan supplement to Meyer-Lübke (**242**).

Foreign words

1257.

Giovanni Battista Pellegrini, *Gli arabismi nelle lingue neolatine, con speciale riguardo all'Italia.* Brescia: Paideia, 1972. 2 vols.

See also: Giovan Battista Pellegrini, *Ricerche sugli arabismi italiani con particolare riguardo alla Sicilia.* Palermo: Centro di Studi Filologici e Linguistici Siciliani, 1989. 279 pp. (*Bollettino del Centro di studi filologici e linguistici siciliani, Supplementi*, 10.) [*Studies on Italian Arabisms with special attention to Sicily.*]

[*Arabic loans in the Romance languages, with special attention to Italy.*]

1258.

Arnald Steiger, *Contribución a la fonética del hispano-árabe y de los arabismos en el ibero-románico y el siciliano.* Madrid, 1932. 519 pp.

Revista de filología española, supplement 17.

[*Contribution to the phonetics of Hispano-Arabic and of the Arabic elements in Ibero-Romance and Sicilian.*] Headwords are Arabic words, which are grouped under phonetic categories. Alphabetical index of Arabic words, pp. 391–437, followed by indexes of Hispano-Arabic, Maghrebi dialects, Berber, Catalan, Spanish, Portuguese, etc.

Other works of interest

1259.

Johannes Hubschmid, *Thesaurus praeromanicus*. Bern: Francke, 1963–5. 2 parts.

Part 1: *Grundlagen für ein weitverbreitetes mediterranes Substrat*; part 2: *Probleme der baskischen Lautlehre und baskisch-vorromanische Etymologien.*

Long reviews by Y. Malkiel in *Language* vol. 47 (1971) pp. 465–87; O. Szemerényi in *Romance philology* vol. 20 (1966/7) pp. 530–42.

1260.

Yakov Malkiel, *Theory and practice of Romance etymology: studies in language, culture and history*. London: Variorum Reprints, 1989. 368 pp.

Variorum reprints. Collected studies series, CS288.

1261.

H. Stimm, M. Briegel, editors, *Wörterbücher der deutschen Romanistik*. Weinheim: Acta Humaniora, 1984. 131 pp. 3–527–17013–8.

ROMANI

There seem to have been three separate westward emigrations of nomadic peoples from India in medieval times. From one of these descend the Lomavren, nomadic groups of Azerbaijan and Armenia, who once spoke a quite distinct language. From another came the Domari (Nawari or Nuri), the still numerous gypsies of Syria, Lebanon, Israel, Egypt and other Middle Eastern countries. The third migration is that of the Roma, with whose language, Romani, this article is concerned. It is an INDO-ARYAN and thus an Indo-European language, with possibly three million or more speakers. Important Roma minorities are to be found in Macedonia, Romania, Slovakia, Russia and the Czech Republic, but Romani dialects are spoken in many other countries.

Grant (**1272**) demonstrates the false and unverified information to be found in many Romani dictionaries, whose authors allowed their enthusiasm for Indo-Aryan derivations and for full lexica to overcome their scientific scruples. Bischoff (**1271**) and Wolf (**1270**) are unreliable because their work was partly based on such untrustworthy sources.

Modern regional forms

1262.

Р. С. Деметер, П. С. Деметер, *Цыганско-русский и русско-цыганский словаь: келдерарский диалект* [*Tsygansko–russkii i russko–tsyganskii slovar': kelderarskii dialekt*] = R. S. Demeter, P. S. Demeter, *Gypsy–Russian and*

Russian–Gypsy dictionary (Kalderash dialect). Moscow: Russkii Yazyk, 1990.
336 pp.

The main dictionary is entirely in Cyrillic script. Russian index, pp. 183–229.
Kalderash–English dictionary, by L. N. Cherenkov, pp. 233–81.

1263.

Norbert Boretzky, Birgit Igla, *Wörterbuch Romani–Deutsch–Englisch für den
südosteuropäischen Raum*. Wiesbaden: Harrassowitz, 1994.

[*Romani–German–English dictionary of the south-eastern Europe region.*]

1264.

Georges Calvet, Bernard Formoso, *Lexique tsigane 2: le sinto piémontais*. Paris:
PoF, 1987.

[*Gypsy dictionary 2: Piedmontese Sinto.*]

1265.

Milena Hübschmannová, Hana Sebková, Anna Zigová, *Romsko–český a česko–
romský slovník*. Praha: Státní Pedagogické Nakladatelství, 1991.

[*Romani–Czech and Czech–Romani dictionary.*] Dictionary of the eastern variety of
Slovak Romani, a Carpathian dialect.

1266.

Viljo Koivisto, *Romano–finitiko–angliko laavesko liin = Romani–suomi–
englanti sanakirja = Romany–Finnish–English dictionary*. Helsinki:
Painatuskeskus, 1994. 366 pp. 951–371–363–6.

Kotimaisten kielten tutkimuskeskuksen julkaisuja, 74.

1267.

Яшар Маликов, *Циганско-български речник* [Yashar Malikov, *Tsigansko-
bălgarski rechnik*]. Sofiya: Fondatsiya Otvoreno Obshtestvo, 1992.

[*Gypsy–Bulgarian dictionary.*]

1268.

Rajendra Weer Rishi, *Multilingual Romani dictionary*. Chandigarh: Roma
Publications, 1974. 65 pp.

See the review by Terrence Kaufman in: Ian F. Hancock, editor, *Romani sociolinguistics* (*International journal
of the sociology of language*, 19. The Hague: Mouton, 1979) pp. 131–44.

In tabular format: glosses in Hindi, English, French, Russian. Brief etymologies.

1269.

Rudolf von Sowa, *Wörterbuch des Dialekts der deutschen Zigeuner*. Leipzig:
Brockhaus, 1898. 128 pp.

Abhandlungen für die Kunde des Morgenlandes, vol. 11 part 1.

[*Dictionary of the dialect of the German Gypsies.*] A dictionary of German Sinto
based on fieldwork in Westphalia and East Prussia. Words of which the compiler felt
certain are in italics: those noted from a single dialect, or otherwise dubious, in roman.

1270.

Siegmund A. Wolf, *Großes Wörterbuch der Zigeunersprache (romani tsiw): Wortschatz deutscher und anderer europäischer Zigeunerdialekte*. Mannheim, 1960. 287 pp.

Reprinted Hamburg: Buske, 1987.

[*Big dictionary of the Gypsy language: the vocabulary of German and other European Gypsy dialects.*] Usefully cites earlier sources (list, pp. 36–43). Some of these are highly unreliable (see Grant, **1272**).

Early dictionaries

1271.

Ferdinand Bischoff, *Deutsch–Zigeunerisches Wörterbuch*. Ilmenau, 1827.

[*German-Gypsy dictionary.*] Not seen. Based on fieldwork and on earlier printed sources, some unreliable, drawn from a mixture of dialects, according to Grant (**1272**): see further comments there.

Other works of interest

1272.

Anthony P. Grant, 'Plagiarism and lexical orphans in the European Romani lexicon' in *Romani in contact: the history, structure and sociology of a language* ed. Y. Matras (Amsterdam: Benjamins, 1995) pp. 53–68.

ROMANIAN

Romanian is the easternmost of the ROMANCE LANGUAGES, with about 24 million speakers in Romania and Moldova. Until the mid-nineteenth century it was written in a form of the Cyrillic alphabet close to that used for Old Slavonic. The modern Cyrillic alphabet was imposed on Moldavia on the Russian takeover in 1944, and the language was there called 'Moldavian'. In independent Moldova the Latin alphabet is once more standard, as is the name Romanian.

Romanian dictionaries are good at dealing with regional dialects, but tend to leave urban slang and jargon alone. A paper by Vasiliu (**1290**) helps to fill the gap.

There are no texts in Romanian earlier than the sixteenth century. The medieval language emerges fitfully from Church Slavonic documents written in what is now Romania (**1281**).

The Romanian alphabet and the Moldavian equivalents

a ă â b c d e f g h i î j k l m n o p r s ş t ţ u v w x z

а э ы б к/ч д е ф г/дж х и ы ж к л м н о п р с ш т ц у в в кс з

Moldavian ю represented Romanian iu; Moldavian я represented Romanian ea and ia.

This table is in Romanian alphabetical order: Moldavian alphabetical order was the same as that of Russian.

Historical dictionaries

1273.

Dicţionarul limbii române întocmit şi publicat după îndemnul şi cu cheltuiala Maiestăţii Sale Regelui Carol I. Bucharest: Socec, Academia Română, [1907]– .
Edited by Sextil Puşcariu, Iorgu Iordan and others.

[*Dictionary of the Romanian language, prepared and published with the support of His Majesty King Carol I.*] A highly important historical dictionary, very hospitable to regional and dialect forms. The project was planned by the Societate Academica, precursor to the Romanian Academy, as early as 1869, and it is now continuing with renewed vigour.

Early bibliography, vol. 1 pp. xliii–xlix with liii–lv; list of local informants, vol. 1 pp. lv–lxvi. Latest bibliography in vol. 6 p. xxiii ff., supplemented at vol. 8 part 1 p. v, vol. 10 part 1 p. v, vol. 12 part 1 p. vols. Full list of places covered by oral information, with abbreviations and reference numbers used, vol. 12 part 1 pp. xvii–xlii.

Published volumes and parts so far cover **A–Cojoaică**, **F–Izvrăti**, **J–Lojniţă**, **M–Ţvişgold**.

1274.

Dicţionarul limbii romîne literare contemporane. Bucharest: Editura Academiei, 1955–7. 4 vols [3025 pp.].

[*Dictionary of the contemporary Romanian literary language.*] A concise dictionary. For the general vocabulary (but not for technical words) there is a selection of quotations, attributed to named authors, and with precise references: these draw on the files of the *Dicţionarul limbii române* (**1273**). No etymologies.

1275.

B. Petriceïcu-Hasdeu, *Etymologicum magnum Romaniae = Dicţionarul limbei istorice şi poporane a românilor.* Bucharest: Socecŭ, 1885–98. Vols 1–4 [3253 columns + cclxxxvi pp.; no more published].
New edition by G. Brâncuş: Bucharest, 1972–6. 429 + 1627 pp.

[*Dictionary of the early and colloquial language of the Romanians.*] An extremely leisurely and discursive work, interesting for its quotations from folk poetry. There are many encyclopaedic articles, e.g. **Ban** 'coin' with plates and descriptions of early coinage from Romanian lands, columns 2415–51.

The published volumes 1–3 cover **A–Bărbat** 'man'. Of vol. 4 only a very long 'introduction' was published: this goes off at a tangent from the main work, being a 286–page excursus on the early history of the principality of Wallachia.

1276.

Hariton Tiktin, *Rumänisch–deutsches Wörterbuch*. Wiesbaden: Harrassowitz, 1985–9. 3 vols [18 parts]. 2nd edn by Paul Miron.

1st edn: Bucharest: Staatsdruckerei, 1903–24. 3 vols [1834 pp.].

[*Romanian–German dictionary.*] An unusually scholarly bilingual dictionary, with selective quotations from literature (list of sources, vol. 1 pp. 17–79; chronology, pp. 81–5), with datings, and with etymologies (marked *ET.*) and grammatical notes (*GR.*). Its only fault is its printed appearance, reproduced from typescript.

The 1st edition was described as 'a remarkable work of Romanian lexicography, as much for the precision with which the meanings of words are defined and richly exemplified with quotations, as from the etymological point of view' (**1274**, Preface).

The modern standard

1277.

Ion Coteanu [and others], *Dicţionarul explicativ al limbii române: DEX*. Bucharest: Editura Academiei, 1975. 1049 pp.

Followed by: *Supliment la Dicţionarul explicativ al limbii române: DEX-S*: 1988. 198 pp.

Older version: *Dicţionarul limbii romîne moderne*. 1958. 961 pp. Edited by Iorgu Iordan, Alexandru Rosetti and others.

[*Explanatory dictionary of the Romanian language.*] Concise entries with brief etymologies, and some illustrations.

1278.

Dicţionar englez–român. Bucharest: Editura Academiei, 1974. 825 pp.

Academia Republicii Socialiste Română, Institutul de Lingvistică. Redactor responsabil: Leon Leviţschi.

[*English–Romanian dictionary.*] The largest current dictionary into Romanian.

1279.

Florin Marcu, Constant Maneca, *Dicţionar de neologisme*. Bucharest: Editura Academiei, 1986. 1168 pp.

[*Dictionary of new words.*]

Older periods

1280.

Mariana Costinescu, Magdalena Georgescu, Florentina Zgraon, *Dicţionarul limbii române literare vechi, 1640–1780: termeni regionali*. Bucharest: Editura Ştiinţifică şi Enciclopedică, 1987. 330 pp.

Institutul de Lingvistica din Bucureşti.

[*Dictionary of the old Romanian literary language, 1640–1780: regional terms.*]

1281.

Dicţionarul elementelor româneşti din documentele slavo-române, 1374–1600. Bucharest: Editura Academiei, 1981. 369 pp.

Institutul de Lingvistica din Bucureşti.

[*Dictionary of Romanian elements in the Slavonic documents from Romania, 1374–1600.*] Romanian at this time was seldom or never recorded as a language, hence the interest attaching to Romanian words that occur in Slavonic manuscripts. Full, precise citations and many quotations are given, in Church Slavonic script.

Headwords are modern Romanian forms, and are marked * where the early word is recorded only in the form of compounds, proper names, etc. List of Romanian morphological forms, pp. 270–94; list of source documents (*A*: Moldavia; *B*: Wallachia), pp. 295–366.

1282.

G. Mihăilă, *Dicţionar al limbii române vechi*. Bucharest, 1974.

[*Dictionary of the old Romanian language.*] Not seen.

Regional forms

Greece, Macedonia, Albania

1283.

T. Papahagi, *Dicţionarul dialectului aromîn, general şi etimologic = Dictionnaire aroumain (macédo-roumain) général et étymologique*. Bucharest: Editura Academiei, 1963. 1264 pp.

Reprinted as: *Dicţionarul dialectului aromân, general şi etimologic*. 1974.

[*General and etymological dictionary of the Aromunian dialect.*] An important concise dictionary dealing with the Aromunian (Vlach) dialects of Greece, Macedonia and Albania: see map at end. Headwords are followed by variant word forms, Romanian gloss, French gloss in guillemets «», and references to sources of information. Then the symbol –< introduces an etymological note, sometimes a commendably brief –<?.

Indexes of words cited in entries, pp. 1153–1234; list of words of 'uncertain Balkan' and otherwise uncertain origin, pp. 1235–40; of unknown origin, pp. 1241–8; list of abbreviations, pp. 1250–64.

Moldova

1284.

Силвиу Бережан, *Дикционар експликатив ал лимбий молдовенешты* [Silviu Berejan, *Dicţionar explicativ al limbii moldoveneşti*]. Kishinev: Cartea Moldovenească, 1977–85. 2 vols.

Academia de Stiinţe a RSS Moldoveneşti, Institutul de Limbă şi Literatură.

[*Explanatory dictionary of the Moldavian language.*] A concise dictionary of modern usage, in Cyrillic script.

Slovenia

1285.

A. Byhan, 'Istrorumänisches Glossar' in *Jahrbuch des Instituts für rumänische Sprache in Leipzig* vol. 67 (1899) pp. 174–398.

    [*Istroromanian glossary.*]

Etymological dictionaries

1286.

A. de Cihac, *Dictionnaire d'étymologie daco-romane*. Frankfurt am Main: St. Goar, 1870–79. 331 + 816 pp.

See N. Timiras in *Romance philology* vol. 17 (1963) pp. 471–5.

    [*Dictionary of Daco-Romanian etymology.*] Part 1: words of Latin origin, with cognates in other Romance languages. Part 2: words of Slavonic, Hungarian, Turkish, modern Greek and Albanian origin. May occasionally be of use because of this classified arrangement.

1287.

Alejandro Cioranescu, *Diccionario etimológico rumano*. Tenerife: Biblioteca Filológica, Universidad de La Laguna, 1958–66. 1184 pp.

See the review by Robert Austerlitz in *Romance philology* vol. 20 (1967) pp. 551–7, to which I am indebted.

    [*Romanian etymological dictionary.*] A concise etymological dictionary with 9532 numbered entries. Glosses are in Spanish. Cognates from Aromunian and Megleno-Romanian are included. The more puzzling abbreviations include *saj.* 'Saxon, i.e. Transylvanian German', *germ.* 'thieves' argot', *rut.* 'Carpatho-Ruthenian'.

    There are indexes of forms cited from other languages (list, p. 1184) including separate indexes of Romanian (excluding headwords), Aromunian, Megleno-Romanian and Istroromanian.

1288.

Н. Раевский, М. Габинский, *Скурт дикционар етимоложик ал лимбий молдовенешть* [N. Raevschi, M. Gabinschi, *Scurt dicţionar etimolojic al limbii moldoveneşti*]. Kishinev: Redacţia Principală a Enciclopediei Sovietice Moldoveneşti, 1978. 676 pp.

Academia de Stiinţe a RSS Moldoveneşti, Institutul de Limbă şi Literatură.

    [*Short etymological dictionary of the Moldavian language.*] A very compressed etymological dictionary of Romanian in Cyrillic script. Cross-references for derived forms that are not listed in alphabetical order, pp. 517–676.

Foreign words

1289.

L. Tamás, *Etymologisch-historisches Wörterbuch der ungarischen Elemente im Rumänischen, unter Berücksichtigung der Mundartwörter*. The Hague: Mouton, 1967. 937 pp.

Indiana University publications, Uralic and Altaic series, 83.

[*Etymological and historical dictionary of the Hungarian elements in Romanian, with attention to dialect words.*] Headwords are in Romanian. Indexes by language, pp. 873–936.

Other works of interest

1290.

Alexandru Vasiliu, 'Din argoul nostru' in *Grai și suflet* vol. 6/7 (1933/4) pp. 95–131, 309–12.

ROMANSCH

Romansch is one of the ROMANCE LANGUAGES, and one of the four languages of Switzerland. It has about 65,000 speakers.

1291.

Theodor Ebneter, *Wörterbuch des Romanischen von Obervaz, Lenzerheide, Valbella, Romanisch–Deutsch, Deutsch–Romanisch.* Tübingen, 1981. 686 pp. 3–484–52187–2.

Beihefte zur Zeitschrift für romanische Philologie, 187.

[*Dictionary of the Romansch of Obervaz, Lenzerheide, Valbella: German–Romansch, Romansch–German.*]

1292.

Zaccaria Pallioppi, Emil Pallioppi, *Dizionari dels idioms romauntschs d'Engiadin'ota e bassa, delle Val Müstair, da Bravuogn e Filisur con particulera consideraziun del idiom d'Engiadin'ota.* Samedan, 1895. 824 pp.

Later version: Emil Pallioppi, *Wörterbuch der romanischen Mundarten des Ober- und Unterengadins, des Münsterthales, von Bergün und Filisur mit besonderer Berücksichtigung der oberengadinischen Mundart.* Samedan, 1902. 986 pp.

[*Dictionary of the Romansch dialects of the Upper and Lower Engadine, the Münstertal, Bergün and Filisur, with special attention to the Upper Engadine dialect.*] The 1902 publication has a German title with the same meaning: I have not seen it.

1293.

Chasper Pult [and other editors], *Dicziunari rumantsch grischun.* Chur: Bischofberger, 1939– .

Fundà da Robert de Planta, Florian Melcher. Publichà da la Società Retorumantscha.

[*Dictionary of Romansch of the Grisons.*] A very large-scale dictionary, quite on a par with those of the other three local languages of Switzerland (**491**, **609**, **818**), based on both printed and oral sources. Plenty of illustrations and a good many word maps. Entries generally end with a paragraph in small type with etymological and historical discussion. Although the title is in Romansch, preliminary matter, glosses and discussion are in German.

Each volume contains elaborate indexes of linguistic changes that are exemplified ('*Sprachgeschichtlicher Abriß*'), and of etymological origins; these are followed by a German–Romansch topic index ('*Sachindex*').

Each part has a map of place names inside the front cover. List and guide to place names, vol. 1 pp. 23–9; bibliography, vol. 1 pp. 30–44; list of local sources of information, vol. 1 pp. 46–51.

Part 129, just published in 1997, completes vol. 9. The dictionary now covers **A–Ipsometric**.

1294.

Ramun Vieli, *Vocabulari tudestg–romontsch sursilvan = Deutsch–romanisches Wörterbuch Surselvisch*. Chur: Ligia Romontscha, 1944. 916 pp.
Vocabularis retoromontschs = Rätoromanische Wörterbücher.

[*German–Sursilvan dictionary.*] A brief-entry dictionary.

1295.

Ramun Vieli, Alexi Decurtins, *Vocabulari romontsch sursilvan–tudestg*. Chur: Ligia Romontscha, 1962. 831 pp.

[*Sursilvan–German dictionary.*] A brief-entry dictionary but with many example phrases. Supplement of geographical and historical names, pp. 821–31 (coloured pages).

ROTI

The AUSTRONESIAN language of the island of Roti, south-west of Timor.

1296.

J. C. G. Jonker, *Rottineesch–Hollandsch woordenboek*. Leiden: Brill, 1908. 806 pp.

[*Roti–Dutch dictionary.*] In Latin script.

RUNDI

A Bantu language, and thus a member of the NIGER-CONGO family, this is the national language of Burundi, with about six million speakers.

1297.

F. M. Rodegem, *Dictionnaire rundi–français*. Tervuren, 1970. 644 pp.
Annales du Musée Royale d'Afrique Centrale, sciences humaines, 69.

[*Rundi–French dictionary.*]

RUSSIAN

Russian is the best known and most widely spoken of the SLAVONIC LANGUAGES. It was already spreading across eastern Russia (as we now call it) and Siberia in the sixteenth century with Russian trade and government. It was the ruling language of the Russian Empire and then of the Soviet Union (though many other languages of the USSR had official status locally). Russian is therefore an important second language in the countries of the former Soviet Union and in eastern Europe, though its position is now weakening in face of the national languages and of English, German and Turkish. It has about 175 million speakers as a first language.

Note the bibliographical sources cited at the end of this article (**1332** to **1334**). Particularly interesting is **1333**: this work, in dictionary format, is actually an index to words that are covered in the major twentieth century Russian dictionaries.

The Russian alphabet

АБВГДЕЁЖЗИЙКЛМНОПРСТУФХЦЧШЩЪЫЬЭЮЯ

абвгдеёжзийклмнопрстуфхцчшщъыьэюя

АБВГДЕЁЖЗИЙКЛМНОПРСТУФХЦЧШЩЪЫЬЭЮЯ

абвгдеёжзийклмнопрстуфхцчшщъыьэюя

a b v g d e yo zh z i ĭ k l m n o p r s t u f kh ts ch sh shch ” y ’ e yu ya

This *grazhdanka* or secular alphabet was introduced by Peter the Great in 1708 to take the place of the Church Slavonic form of the Cyrillic script.

Four more letters, carried over from Old Church Slavonic, were eliminated in a spelling reform in 1917/18:

IVѢѲ – ivѣѳ – i i ye f

Some lower-case letter forms differ in the usual 'italic' Cyrillic font, given in the third and fourth lines of the table. The font group used for modern Russian in this book has a correct 'italic' version, seen in most of the titles below; that used for some other Cyrillic scripts, including Serbian, has not.

Several variations will be found in transliteration. Often, as in this book, Russian E is transliterated *ye* when it occurs at the beginning of a word. Following German practice, some authors substitute *je, jo, ju, ja* for the transliterations *ye, yo, yu, ya* given here. Russian X may be transliterated *h* or *x* instead of *kh*.

Historical dictionaries

1298.

Словарь русскаго языка [*Slovar' russkago yazyka*]. 1891–1920. Vols 1–2; parts of vols 3, 4, 5, 6 and 8.

Compiled by the Second Section of the Imperial Academy of Sciences.

2nd edn: *Slovar' russkogo yazyka, sostavlennyi Komissei po Russkomu Yazyku Akademii Nauk SSSR*. 1930–37. Parts of vols 1, 5, 9, 5 [*bis*], 6/12, 8/13 and 9/14.

1st and 2nd edns reprinted in full: London: Flegon Press [1985?] 16 vols.

An older dictionary under the aegis of the Imperial Academy had appeared in 1806–22, and has been reprinted: *Slovar' Akademii Rossiiskoi: 1–6 tom reproduktirovany fotomekhanicheskim sposobom so vtorogo izdaniya, 1806–1822 g.g.* [Odense]: Izdatel'stvo pri Universitete Odense, 1971. 7 vols. Edited by M. G. Oesterby.

[*Dictionary of the Russian language.*] A historical dictionary of the modern Russian language, with citations and quotations from literary texts, for which precise references are given. Verse quotations are set line for line. Each entry begins with a brief etymology in round brackets. Latin taxonomic names are given for flora and fauna.

The first edition, which is in the older Russian orthography throughout, covers the following sections of the alphabet: **А–Издёргивать, К–Крошечный, Л–Лисичнiй, М–Маститый, Не–Недорубщикъ**. Vol. 1, the first to be completed, is much briefer than the rest; for many words there are no quotations or citations.

The second edition is in modern orthography. No single letter of the alphabet was completed in this edition, which covers half of **А** and small parts of **Д, И, Л, М, Н, О**. The second edition began by retaining the volume numbering of the first, though the planned length was much greater. Around 1934 a new volume numbering was introduced: hence, in the letter **М** for example, vol. 6 part 1 is followed by vol. 12 part 2. Hence also there is an older vol. 5, beginning the letter **Л**, and a newer one beginning the letter **Д**. Publication ceased entirely in 1937.

There are several minor variations in title.

A new historical dictionary of modern Russian has been projected: see the paper by E. E. Babaeva in *Voprosy yazykoznaniya*, 1997 no. 2.

The modern standard

1299.

Н. З. Котеловой, *Словарь новых слов русского языка (середина 50-х–середина 80-х годов)* [N. Z. Kotelovoi, *Slovar' novykh slov russkogo yazyka*]. St Petersburg: Bulanin, 1995. 877 pp. 5–86007–016–0.

[*Dictionary of new words in the Russian language, from the mid-1950s to the mid-1980s.*] A large-scale listing, both of scientific-technical words and of modern jargon and slang. Entries are supported by quotations from newspapers and magazines (abbreviations, p. 20). References to other lexicographical sources (list of these, pp. 17–18), with a brief etymological note, are given in a smaller font.

1300.

Sophia Lubensky, *Random House Russian–English dictionary of idioms*. New York: Random House, 1995. 1017 pp. 0–679–40580–1.

Review in *Voprosy yazykoznaniya*, 1996 no. 3.

An extensive dictionary in which idiomatic phrases and sentences are filed under keywords (index of other significant words, pp. 849–1017). All words and examples are given in Russian and English. The examples are taken from a corpus of Russian literature of the nineteenth and twentieth centuries, with references in brackets: these give author's surname and the number of the work, keyed to the bibliography on pp. 837–48. A very approachable dictionary.

1301.

Э. М. Медникова, Ю. Д. Апресян, *Новий большой англо–русский словарь* [E. M. Mednikova, Yu. D. Apresyan, editors, *Novyi bolshoi anglo–russkii slovar'*] = *New English–Russian dictionary*. Moscow: Russkii Yazyk, 1993– .

Earlier version: I. R. Gal'perin, E. M. Mednikova, *Bolshoi anglo–russkii slovar' = New English–Russian dictionary*. 1987–8. 2 vols. '4th edn, with a supplement' – but the supplement (vol. 2 pp. 925–1072) is dated 1980.

This has grown into a very large-scale brief-entry dictionary, planned in three volumes, of which I have seen only the first two.

1302.

The Oxford Russian dictionary. Oxford: Oxford University Press, 1993. 1340 pp. Revised by Colin Howlett. 0–19–860153–0.

English–Russian section edited by Paul Falla; Russian–English section edited by Marcus Wheeler and Boris Unbegaun. 'An amalgamation, harmonization and updating of *The Oxford Russian–English dictionary* (2nd edn, 1984) and *The Oxford English–Russian dictionary* (1984).'

1st edn of part 1: Marcus Wheeler, *The Oxford Russian–English dictionary.* Oxford: Clarendon Press, 1972. 918 pp. 'General editor, B. O. Unbegaun.'

1303.

Словарь русского языка в четырех томах [*Slovar' russkogo yazyka v chetyrekh tomakh*]. Moscow: Russkii Yazyk, 1981–4. 4 vols. 2nd ed. by A. P. Yevgen'eva.

Akademiya Nauk SSSR, Institut Russkogo Yazyka.

1st edn: 1957–61.

[*Dictionary of the Russian language in four volumes.*] A large-scale dictionary of modern usage with selective quotations from named literary authors of the nineteenth and twentieth centuries. No precise references.

1304.

Словарь современного русского литературного языка в 20 томах [*Slovar' sovremennogo russkogo literaturnogo yazyka v 20 tomakh*]. Moscow: Russkii Yazyk, 1991– . 2nd edn.

Edited by K. S. Gorbachevich. – Review of vol. 1 in *Izvestiya Akademii Nauk, ser. lit. i yaz.*, 1992 no. 3.

1st edn: Moscow: Nauka, 1948–65. 17 vols.

[*Dictionary of the contemporary Russian literary language in 20 volumes.*] A very large-scale dictionary of the modern language. Brief glosses are followed by long quotations from named literary authors: these quotations constitute the main purpose of the dictionary. There is no list or bibliography of authors and works quoted, and there are no precise references. At the end of each entry, in small type, are references to other dictionaries that cite the word.

Most, but not all, of the quotations in the first edition are used again in the second. The second edition has so far reached **А–Зятюшка** in five volumes.

Older periods

Eleventh to fourteenth centuries

1305.

Р. И. Аванесов, *Словарь древнерусского языка (XI–XIV вв.)* [R. I. Avanesov, editor, *Slovar' drevnerusskogo yazyka (XI–XIV vv.)*]. Moscow: Russkii Yazyk, 1988– .

Review of vols 1–2 in *Izvestiya Akademii Nauk SSSR, seriya literatury i yazyka*, 1990 no. 6.

[*Dictionary of the Old Russian language, eleventh to fourteenth centuries.*] A dictionary of the oldest recorded vocabulary of Russian, naturally not fully separable at this point from Old Church Slavonic. Very generous citations and long quotations from the texts, often accompanied by the Greek words and phrases of which the Russian is the translation.

So far I have seen four volumes, covering **A–M**, the last of which (so far as I know) appeared in 1991. Abbreviations and list of source texts, vol. 1 pp. 28–68.

1306.

Karla Günther-Hielscher, Victor Glötzner, Helmut Wilhelm Schaller, *Real- und Sachwörterbuch zum Altrussischen.* Neuried: Hieronymus Verlag, 1985. 381 pp.
Selecta Slavica, 7.

[*Thesaurus of Old Russian.*]

1307.

И. И. Срезневскій, *Материалы для словаря древне-русскаго языка* [I. I. Sreznevskii, *Materialy dlya slovarya drevne-russkago yazyka*]. St Petersburg: Tip. Imp. Akademii Nauk, 1890–1903. 3 vols.

Followed by: *Dopolneniya.* 1912. 272 columns + 13 pp. [*Supplement.*]
Reprinted with modernised title: 1958. – Reprinted as: *Slovar' drevnerusskogo yazyka.* Moscow: Kniga, 1989. 3 vols in 6. Both reprints include the supplement.
Note also: Irena Dulewicz, Iryda Grek-Pabisowa, Irena Maryniak, *Indeks a tergo do Materiałów do słownika języka staroruskiego I. I. Srezniewskiego.* Warsaw: Państwowe Wydawnictwo Naukowe, 1968. 386 pp.
[*Reverse index to Sreznevskii's Materials for a dictionary of the Old Russian language.*]

[*Materials for a dictionary of the Old Russian language.*] Entries are supported by quotations, often with Greek or Latin originals alongside if they are translations.

List of sources with abbreviations, vol. 1, final pages 1'–49', with final pages 1–13 of the supplement.

Fifteenth to seventeenth centuries

1308.

Словарь русского языка XI–XVII вв. [*Slovar' russkogo yazyka XI–XVII vv.*]. Moscow: Nauka, 1975– .

Chief editor, S. G. Barkhudarov. Akademiya Nauk SSSR, Institut Russkogo Yazyka.
See A. N. Shalamova, 'The dictionary of the Russian language from the 11th to the 17th century: problems and achievements', a paper in Russian in *Voprosy yazykoznaniya*, 1997 no. 5.

[*Dictionary of the Russian language from the eleventh to the seventeenth century.*] This is the major historical dictionary of Old Russian. Avanesov (**1305**) takes the Old Russian vocabulary on its own and in greater depth, and the greatest contribution of the present work is to the Russian vocabulary of the fifteenth to seventeenth centuries. Headwords, in nineteenth-century orthography, are followed by brief glosses and quotations from source texts, with explicit dates – but there is no bibliography of sources as yet.

The set now runs to 23 slim volumes, and covers **A–Сдымка**.

Eighteenth century

1309.

Словарь русского языка XVIII века [*Slovar' russkogo yazyka XVIII veka*].
Leningrad: Nauka, 1984– .

Chief editor, Yu. S. Sorokin. Akademiya Nauk SSSR, Institut Russkogo Yazyka.

Accompanied by: L. L. Kutina and others, *Slovar' russkogo yazyka XVIII veka: pravila pol'zovaniya slovarem, ukazatel' istochnikov.* 1984. 141 pp. [*Explanation of entries; list of abbreviations.*]

[*Dictionary of the Russian language in the eighteenth century.*] Entries begin with a list of variant forms, followed by quotations from literature. Words newly recorded in the eighteenth century are marked with a black triangle.

For other geometrical symbols see the *Pravila* 'Explanations', p. 48. Bibliography, pp. 58–139.

Nine volumes have appeared so far, covering **A–K**.

1310.

М. Ф. Палевская, *Материалы для фразеологического словаря русского языка XVIII века* [M. F. Palevskaya, *Materialy dlya frazeologicheskogo slovarya russkogo yazyka XVIII veka*]. Kishinev: Ştiinţa, 1980. 365 pp.

[*Materials for a dictionary of idioms of the eighteenth century Russian language.*] Alphabetical under keywords. Quotations from named authors, but no precise references.

Nineteenth century

1311.

Толковый словарь живого великорусскаго языка Владимира Даля [*Tolkovyi slovar' zhivogo velikorusskago yazyka Vladimira Dalya*]. St Petersburg: Vol'f, 1903–9. 4 vols. 3rd edn by [I. A. Baudouin de Courtenay].

1st edn: Moscow, 1863–6. 2nd edn: St Petersburg, 1880–82.

[*Vladimir Dal's big dictionary of the living Great Russian language.*] A very capacious dictionary of nineteenth-century Russian, particularly strong on dialect variation. Glosses are in Russian only except that taxonomic names are given for flora – the vocabulary for which in Russian dialects is varied and copious. Naturally headwords and text are in the older Russian orthography.

Corrections, vol. 4 pp. 1593–1619. Abbreviations (including numerous philological works cited in the entries) vol. 4 final pages i–xiv.

'Great Russian' was so called to distinguish it from Ukrainian ('Little Russian') and Belorussian ('White Russian').

Regional forms

1312.

Ф. П. Филин, *Словарь русских народных говоров* [F. P. Filin, editor, *Slovar' russkikh narodnykh govorov*]. Moscow: Nauka, 1965– .

[*Dictionary of Russian popular dialects.*] A large-scale dictionary of Russian dialects – a rich compilation from a wide geographical area. Vol. 1 consists largely of a bibliography and list of local sources of information (pp. 21–160) followed by a list of place names. In the body of the dictionary, place names are conveniently picked out in a bold sloping Cyrillic font and are followed by a reference to the source (see bibliography) and a date. There are many local names for flora, for which taxonomic names are supplied.

So far 29 slim volumes have appeared, covering **А–Попричиться**.

1313.

Опытъ областнаго великорусскаго словаря [*Opyt" oblastnago velikorusskago slovarya*]. St Petersburg: Tip. Imperatorskoi Akademii Nauk, 1852–58. 2 vols.
Edited by the Second Section of the Imperial Academy of Sciences.
Reprinted: Leipzig: Zentralantiquariat der Deutschen Demokratischen Republik, 1970.

[*Preliminary regional Great Russian dictionary.*] A brief-entry dictionary with geographical indications: list of local soiurces, vol. 1 pp. v–xii. Vol. 2 was a supplement; latest additions, vol. 2 pp. 315–28. 'Great Russian' was so called to distinguish it from Ukrainian ('Little Russian') and Belorussian ('White Russian').

Belarus

1314.

А. Ф. Манаенкова, *Словарь русских говоров Белоруссий* [A. F. Manaenkova, *Slovar' russkikh govorov Belorussii*]. Minsk: Universitetskoe, 1989. 231 pp. 5–7855–0220–8.
Review in *Voprosy yazykoznaniya*, July 1992.

[*Dictionary of the Russian dialects of Belarus.*]

Russia in Asia

1315.

Л. Е. Элиасов, *Словарь русских говоров Забаикалья* [L. E. Eliasov, *Slovar' russkikh govorov Zabaikal'ya*]. Moscow: Nauka, 1980. 470 pp.

[*Dictionary of the Russian dialects of Transbaikalia.*] Quotations from named authors, but no precise references.

1316.

А. И. Федоров, *Фразеологический словарь русских говоров Сибири* [A. I. Fedorov, *Frazeologicheskii slovar' russkikh govorov Sibiri*. Novosibirsk: Nauka, 1983. 232 pp.

[*Dictionary of idioms of the Russian dialects of Siberia.*] Alphabetical under keywords. Dates and locations are given, but source texts are not individually credited.

1317.

Мотивационный диалектный словарь (говоры Среднего Приобья)
[*Motivatsionnyi dialektnyi slovar' (govory Srednego Priob'ya)*]. Tomsk:
Izdatel'stvo Tomskogo Universiteta, 1982–3. 2 vols.

By L. A. Araeva and others; edited by O. I. Blinova.

    [*Dialect dictionary of the middle Ob valley.*]

1318.

Л. Г. Панин, *Словарь русской народно-диалектной речи в Сибири XVII–*
первой половины XVIII в. [*L. G. Panin, Slovar' russkoi narodno-dialektnoi rechi*
v Sibiri XVII–pervoi poloviny XVIII v.]. Novosibirsk: Nauka, 1991. 179 pp. 5–
02–029632–5.

Edited by V. V. Palagina, K. A. Timofeev.

    [*Dictionary of the Russian colloquial and dialect speech of Siberia in the seventeenth*
and early eighteenth centuries.]

1319.

Полный словарь Сибирского говора [*Polnyi slovar' Sibirskogo govora*].
Tomsk: Izdatel'stvo Tomskogo Universiteta, 1992– .

By L. A. Araeva and others. Chief editor: O. I. Blinova. – Review in *Voprosy yazykoznaniya*, February 1996.

    [*Full dictionary of the Siberian dialect.*] Vols 1–3, which I have seen, cover **A–R**.

1320.

Словарь русских говоров Прыамурья [*Slovar' russkikh govorov Pryamur'ya*].
Moscow: Nauka, 1983. 341 pp.

By F. P. Ivanova and others; edited by F. P. Filin.

    [*Dictionary of the Russian dialects of the Amur valley.*]

Russia in Europe

1321.

Словарь русских донских говоров [*Slovar' russkikh donskikh govorov*]. Rostov-
na-Donu: Izdatel'stvo Rostovskogo Universiteta, 1975–6. 3 vols.

Edited by V. S. Ovchinnikova.

2nd edn: 1991– . Edited by Z. V. Valyusinskaya, V. S. Ovchinnikova and others. 5–7507–0227–8.

    [*Dictionary of the Russian dialects of the Don valley.*]

Slang and special vocabularies

1322.

В. С. Елистратов, *Словарь московского арго: материалы 1980–1994 г.г.*
[*V. S. Elistratov, Slovar' moskovskogo argo: materialy 1980–1994 g.g.*].
Moscow: Russkie Slovary, 1994. 699 pp.

    [*Dictionary of Moscow argot, collected 1980–1994.*] Claims 8000 words and 3000
idiomatic phrases. An essay 'Argot and culture' occupies pp. 592–674.

1323.

А. Флегон, *За пределами русских словарей* [A. Flegon, *Za predelami russkikh slovarei*]. London: Flegon Press, 1973. 413 pp.

[*Beyond the bounds of Russian dictionaries.*] The subtitle offers 'additional words and meanings with citations from Lenin, Khrushchev, Stalin, Barkov, Pushkin, Lermontov, Yesenin, Mayakovskii, Solzhenitsyn, Vosnesenskii and others'. Each entry for an obscene or otherwise unmentionable word is followed by one or two quotations, more or less discreditable, from these honoured authors (greying portraits are also supplied). No precise references. Bibliography, pp. 405–13.

1324.

Meyer Galler, *Soviet camp speech*. Jerusalem: Magnes Press, The Hebrew University, 1994. 253 pp. 965–223–865–1.

A brief-entry dictionary of the jargon of Russian labour camps and prisons. English-Russian section, pp. 137–253.

1325.

Henry K. Zalucky, *Compressed Russian: Russian–English dictionary of acronyms, semiacronyms and other abbreviations used in contemporary standard Russian, with their pronunciation and explicit correlates in Russian, and equivalents in English* = X. K. Залуцкий, *Русские аббревиатуры*. Amsterdam: Elsevier, 1991. 890 pp. 0–444–98728–2.

A brief-entry dictionary, unexpectedly large in size because of the importance of abbreviations in the everyday and administrative jargon of Soviet Russia.

Etymological dictionaries

1326.

П. Я. Черных, *Историко-этимологический словарь современного русского языка* [P. Ya. Chernykh, *Istoriko-etimologicheskii slovar' sovremennogo russkogo yazyka*]. Moscow: Russkii Yazyk, 1993. 2 vols. 5–200–01259–9.

[*Historical-etymological dictionary of the contemporary Russian language.*] A compressed, very informative etymological dictionary which always tries to date the first record of a word, often supplying a quotation. There are some references to scholarly literature.

1327.

Антонин Преображенскій, *Этимологическій словарь русскаго языка* [Antonin Preobrazhenskii, *Etimologicheskii slovar' russkago yazyka*]. Moscow, 1910–49. 3 vols.

Imp. Akademiya Nauk. Vol. 3 was published in a series: Akademiya Nauk SSSR. *Trudy Instituta Russkogo Yazyka*, 1.

Reprinted with a new title page and English preface: A. G. Preobrazhensky, *Etymological dictionary of the Russian language*. New York: Columbia University Press, 1951. 3 vols in 1.

See Roman Jakobson in *Word* vol. 7 (1951) pp. 187–8.

A concise etymological dictionary in which Old Church Slavonic, Greek and Latin forms are given in their own scripts. Compound words are dealt with under base forms, with no cross-references. There are brief references to scholarly literature.

The section **Сулея–Туг** is omitted, as this part of the manuscript disappeared following the author's death.

Corrections and additions, vol. 1 pp. xxv–xxx and vol. 2 pp. i–v.

1328.

Николай М. Шанский, *Этимологический словарь русского языка* [Nikolai M. Shanskii, *Etimologicheskii slovar' russkogo yazyka*]. Moscow: Izdatel'stvo Moskovskogo Universiteta, 1963–82. Vols 1–2 in 8 vols.

Abridged edn: Николай М. Шанский, *Краткий этимологический словарь русского языка* [Nikolai M. Shanskii, *Kratkii etimologicheskii slovar' russkogo yazyka*]. Moscow: Prosveshchenie, 1971. 2nd edition. – 1st edn: Moscow: Gosudarstvenno-Pedagogicheskoe Izdatel'stvo, 1961.

[*Etymological dictionary of the Russian language.*] The main work ceased publication after reaching **K**. It is a detailed etymological dictionary with references to other scholarly literature. The abridged edition covers the whole alphabet, but is now largely superseded.

1329.

Max Vasmer, *Russisches etymologisches Wörterbuch*. Heidelberg: Winter, 1953–8. 3 vols.

Indogermanische Bibliothek. 2. Reihe, Wörterbücher.

Also available in a Russian version, translated and edited by O. N. Trubachev, B. A. Larin: *Этимологический словарь русского языка*. Moscow: Progress, 1964–71. 3 vols.

[*Russian etymological dictionary.*] A brief etymological dictionary which may be more approachable than its rivals to some users because the body of entries is mainly in German, and thus in the Latin alphabet. Glosses are given in German. There are numerous references to other etymological dictionaries.

Foreign words

1330.

А. М. Бабкин, В. В. Шендецов, *Словарь иноязычных выражений и слов* [A. M. Babkin, V. V. Shendetsov, *Slovar' inoyazychnykh vyrazhenii i slov*]. Leningrad: Nauka, 1981–7. 2 vols.

1st edn: Moscow: Nauka, 1966. 2 vols [1344 pp.].

[*Dictionary of foreign language expressions and words.*] A dictionary of foreign sayings and catchphrases that typically appear in Latin script when used in written Russian: examples include **Fête champêtre, In-folio.** Headwords are in the Latin alphabet, etymological origins are given and quotations are supplied (with precise references).

1331.

Современный словарь иностранных слов [*Sovremennyi slovar' inostrannykh slov*]. Moscow: Russkii Yazyk, 1992. 740 pp. 5–200–01104–3.

Edited by E. A. Grishina, L. N. Komarova.

[*Contemporary dictionary of foreign words.*] 20,000 entries; many scientific terms.

Other works of interest

1332.
Yrjö Aav, *Russian dictionaries: dictionaries and glossaries printed in Russia, 1627–1917*. Zug: Inter Documentation, 1977. 196 pp. 3–85750–019–0.
Bibliotheca slavica, 10.

1333.
Сводный словарь современной русской лексики [*Svodnyi slovar' sovremennoi russkoi leksiki*. Moscow: Russkii Yazyk, 1991. 2 vols. 5–200–01536–7.
Edited by R. P. Rogozhnikova. Akademiya Nauk SSSR, Institut Russkogo Yazyka.

1334.
W. Zalewski, *Russian–English dictionaries with aids for translators: a selected bibliography*. New York: Russica, 1981. 101 pp. 0–89830–041–X.

SABAEAN

Epigraphic South Arabian, a SEMITIC language, is recorded on inscriptions of the early city states of south-west Arabia, possibly beginning as early as the eighth century BC and continuing to the sixth century AD.

The scripts used in early South Arabian inscriptions are closely related to early Arabic scripts and to the writing system used for Ethiopic.

1335.
A. F. L. Beeston [and others], *Sabaic dictionary, English–French–Arabic = Dictionnaire sabéen–anglais–français–arabe*. Louvain-la-Neuve, Beirut, 1982. 173 pp.

1336.
Joan Copeland Biella, *Dictionary of old South Arabic: Sabaean dialect*. Chico: Scholars Press, 1982. 561 pp.
Harvard Semitic studies, 25.

SAMI

Sami or Lapp is a URALIC language, though quite distinct from Finnish, its nearest neighbour. It has about 30,000 speakers in northern Norway, Sweden, Finland and Russia. Dialects vary considerably and there is no full agreement on a literary standard.

Modern regional forms

1337.

Eliel Lagercrantz, *Lappischer Wortschatz*. Helsinki: Suomalais-Ugrilainen Seura, 1939. 2 vols [1250 pp.].

Lexica Societatis Fenno-Ugricae, 6.

[*Lapp vocabulary.*] The material was collected between 1919 and 1926 in Norway, Sweden and Finland and represents 30 Sami dialects. Dialects and informants are separately credited in the dictionary: list of dialects and informants, pp. 1195–1208. The main Sami–German dictionary has 8859 entries. Under each headword there tends to be a long list of all the word variants that were collected from different dialects, whether or not these are predictable by regular rule, with some example phrases. Original forms of loanwords are given when known: these, as well as taxonomic names for flora and fauna, are picked out in bold face. The Sami is in the Société Finno-Ougrienne's transcription in a very narrow version to clarify dialect differences: see table of alphabetical order and variant forms, pp. 1237–8. There is no alphabetical index but a German thesaurus-index keyed to entry numbers, pp. 1037–1179, and a brief alphabetical guide to this, pp. 1180–82.

Norway

1338.

J. A. Friis, *Lexicon lapponicum, cum interpretatione Latina et Norvegica adjuncta brevi grammaticae adumbratione = Ordbog over det lappiske sprog med latinsk og norsk forklaring, samt en oversigt over sprogets grammatik.* Christiania: Dybwad, 1887. 6 parts [868 pp.].

[*Lapp dictionary, with Latin and Norwegian glosses and a brief grammatical sketch of the language.*] A large-scale brief-entry dictionary. The Norwegian glosses are in Fraktur type. Additions, pp. 862–8; bibliography, six pages at end. The grammar, pp. xiv–lix.

On the alphabetical order, note that Æ files at the end of the alphabet and that **C** files after **T**.

1339.

Konrad Nielsen, [Asbiørn Nesheim,] *Lappisk ordbok, grunnet på dialektene i Polmak, Karasjok og Kautokeino*. Oslo: Aschehoug, Universitetsforlaget, 1932–62. 5 vols.

Instituttet for Sammenlignende Kulturforskning. *Serie B, Skrifter*, 17.

[*Lapp dictionary, based on the dialects of Polmak, Karasjok and Kautokeino.*] Prefatory matter and glosses in Norwegian and English. The fifth volume is a supplement.

Russia

1340.

T. I. Itkonen, *Wörterbuch des Kolta- und Kolalappischen = Koltan- ja Kuolanlapin sanakirja*. Helsinki: Suomalais-Ugrilainen Seura, 1958. 2 vols [1236 pp.].
Lexica Societatis Fenno-Ugricae, 15.

[*Dictionary of Kolta and Kola Lapp.*] A Sami–Finnish–German dictionary with attention to dialect variants: abbreviations, including place names, pp. xl–xliv. Map, p. xxxix. The Sami is in a narrow version of the Société Finno-Ougrienne's transcription. There are brief etymological notes.

Vol. 2 consists of a Supplement, pp. 805–963 and 1057–72, a dictionary of place names, pp. 965–1038, personal names, pp. 1039–54, family names, pp. 1054–56. Then there is an index in Norwegian Sami, pp. 1073–1175, and a German index, pp. 1176–1236.

1341.

Р. Д. Куруч, *Саамско—русский словарь: 8000 слов* [R. D. Kuruch, editor, *Saamsko–russkii slovar': 8000 slov*] = *Са́мь-ру́сс соагкнэ҄кь: 8000 са́ннӭ*. Moscow: Russkii Yazyk, 1985. 566 pp.

[*Sami–Russian dictionary: 8000 words.*] In the Cyrillic script as adapted for Sami in Russia.

Sweden

1342.

Gustav Hasselbrink, *Südlappisches Wörterbuch = Oårj'elsaamien baaguog'ärjaa*. Uppsala: Lundequistska Bokhandeln, 1981–5. 3 vols [1488 pp.].
Vols 2–3 edited by Sven Söderström.
Schriften des Instituts für Dialektforschung und Volkskunde in Uppsala. Ser. C, Sprache und Kultur der Lappen = Skrifter utgivna genom Dialekt- och Folkminnesarkivet i Uppsala. Ser. C, Lapskt språk och lapsk kultur, 4.

[*South Lapp dictionary.*] A dictionary of Swedish Sami dialects, with glosses in German, with generous quotation of example sentences in Sami with German translation, and with very full attention to local dialect variation. Abbreviations for place names, pp. 11–12; other abbreviations, pp. 12–18. The alphabetical order, vol. 1 p. 23.

Grammar, vol. 1 pp. 25–186, including lists of noun and verb prefixes, pp. 166–86.

1343.

Wolfgang Schlachter, *Wörterbuch des Waldlappendialektes von Malå und Texte zur Ethnographie*. Helsinki: Suomalais-Ugrilainen Seura, 1958. 294 pp.
Lexica Societatis Fenno-Ugricae, 14.

[*Dictionary of the Forest Lapp dialect of Malå with ethnographic texts.*] The Sami-German dictionary, pp. 1–162, has some brief etymological notes. It is in Roman script followed by transcription in the Société Finno-Ougrienne's alphabet. German index, pp. 266–94.

Etymological dictionaries

1344.

Juhani Lehtiranta, *Yhteissaamelainen sanasto*. Helsinki: Suomalais-Ugrilainen Seura, 1989. 180 pp. 951–9403–23–X.

Suomalais-Ugrilaisen Seuran toimituksia = Mémoires de la Société Finno-Ougrienne, 200.

[*Comparative Sami dictionary.*] Consists of a tabular list of equivalents in nine modern Sami dialects for the starred forms – proto-Sami reconstructions – which are given with Finnish glosses. There is a total of 1479 entries. Classified index in Finnish, pp. 158–77.

Foreign words

1345.

Just Knud Qvigstad, *Nordische Lehnwörter im Lappischen*. Oslo: Norske Videnskaps Akademie, 1893.

Forhandlinger i Videnskabs-Selskabet i Kristiania.

[*Norwegian loanwords in Lapp.*] Not seen.

SAMOAN

The AUSTRONESIAN language of Samoa, with about 325,000 speakers.

1346.

George B. Milner, *A Samoan–English dictionary*. London, 1966. 464 pp.

SAMOYEDIC LANGUAGES

This is a distinct group of URALIC LANGUAGES spoken by small minorities in north-western Siberia. It includes NENETS, Selkup, Enets, Nganasan and the extinct Kamas, Koybal and Karagas.

1347.

Juha Janhunen, *Samojedischer Wortschatz: gemeinsamojedische Etymologien*. Helsinki: Helsingin Yliopisto, 1977. 185 pp.

[*Samoyed vocabulary: Common Samoyed etymologies.*]

1348.

Nordische Reisen und Forschungen von M. A. Castrén. 1853–62. 12 vols.

[*Northern travels and researches of M. A. Castrén.*] The result of two epic journeys in Arctic Russia and Siberia in 1842–4 and 1845–9. 'We can follow his activities in his "Reiseberichte" and "Reiseerinnerungen", which not only make very interesting reading, but at the same time are very valuable from ethnographical, geographical, historical and linguistic points of view. From these works we can see what superhuman will power and what self-sacrificing, heroic devotion to learning went into the preparation of the Samoyed grammar and dictionary. A Samoyed from Kanin, who happened to be in Finland, was a great help to him in this work. In 1851 he won the newly constituted chair of the Finnish language at Helsinki University. At this point Castrén was again stricken by his lung ailment in 1852, and ended his earthly career after a few weeks of suffering. He was unable to complete the major fruit of his journey of several years, the Samoyed grammar. Castrén's family sent the manuscripts he left behind to the St. Petersburg Academy of Sciences, which entrusted his good friend Anton Schiefner with their publication' (Péter Hajdú, *The Samoyed peoples and languages*, Bloomington: Indiana University, 1963, pp. 84–5, abridged). The collection includes:

Grammatik der samojedischen Sprachen [*Grammar of the Samoyed languages*], 1854, in which the phonology of Nganasan, Enets, Selkup and Kamassian were completed by Schiefner. Verb morphology and syntax were never completed.

Wörterverzeichnisse aus den samojedischen Sprachen [*Word-lists from the Samoyed languages*], 1855.

1349.

T. Lehtisalo, editor, *Samojedische Sprachmaterialien gesammelt von M. A. Castrén und T. Lehtisalo*. Helsinki: Suomalais-Ugrilainen Seura, 1960. 463 pp.
(*Mémoires de la Société Finno-Ougrienne*, 122.)

[*Samoyed linguistic materials collected by M. A. Castrén and T. Lehtisalo.*] Castrén's comparative word-list of about eight Samoyedic dialects, pp. 8–116, and grammar, pp. 117–257. No explanations are given of the dialect abbreviations.

Castrén's notes on Forest Nenets (compiled 1845), pp. 262–316, and Lehtisalo's notes on the Turuhan dialect of Selkup (compiled 1957), pp. 317–38. These sections both contain brief word-lists and grammars.

SANGIR

An AUSTRONESIAN language of the islands north of Sulawesi.

1350.

K. G. F. Steller, W. E. Aebersold, *Sangirees–Nederlands woordenboek met Nederlands–Sangirees register*. The Hague: Nijhoff, 1959. 622 pp.

[*Sangir Dutch dictionary with Dutch Sangir index.*] Based on the dialect of Manganitu (Pulau Sangihe) with additional information on others. The culmination of almost sixty years of research. Roman script.

SANGO

A modern creole based on a dialect of Ngbandi, which is one of the Ubangi group of NIGER-CONGO LANGUAGES. Originally a trade language of the Ubangi river, Sango has become the national language of the Central African Republic (though French is used for many official purposes). There are not yet very many speakers of Sango as a mother tongue, but probably as many as five million speak it as a second or third language.

1351.

Luc Bouquiaux, *Dictionnaire sango–français et lexique français–sango*. Paris: SELAF, 1978. 668 pp.
Langues et civilisations à tradition orale, 29.
[*Sango–French dictionary and French–Sango index.*]

SANSKRIT

Sanskrit is the great classical language of India. Its oldest recorded form is Vedic, language of the four Vedas, the classic texts of Hinduism, which are to be dated – without any certainty – somewhere around 1000 BC, though they were first written down much later. The language was codified in a somewhat later form by the grammarian Panini, around 400 BC. This 'classical Sanskrit' has continued to be used for literature throughout later times, and is still used for philosophical and scholarly writing today.

Sanskrit is the oldest known INDO-ARYAN language: it is the direct ancestor of the middle and modern Indo-Aryan languages of south Asia. Until the decipherment of Hittite, Sanskrit was also the oldest recorded form of any Indo-European language – indeed, some Western scholars of the late eighteenth and early nineteenth centuries regarded Sanskrit as more or less identical with proto-Indo-European, the parent of all the Indo-European languages.

Sanskrit can be written in most of the Indic scripts of south and south east Asia, and it still is written and printed in many of them. Most frequently seen in modern printed texts are Devanagari (also used for Hindi, Marathi and Nepali) and the Latin alphabet, which is sometimes favoured by Western scholars or their publishers.

Sanskrit in Devanagari and Roman: the alphabet

अ आ इ ई उ ऊ ऋ ऌ ए ऐ ओ औ

a ā i ī u ū r̥ l̥ e ai o au

कखगघङ चछजझञ टठडढण तथदधन पफबभम यरलव शषसह

k kh g gh ṅ c ch j jh ñ ṭ ṭh ḍ ḍh ṇ t th d dh n p ph b bh m y r l v ś ṣ s h

The secondary vowel signs: twelve vowels shown with क k

क का कि की कु कू कृ कॢ के कै को कौ

ka kā ki kī ku kū kr̥ kl̥ ke kai ko kau

Secondary vowels signs are used because consonants are combined with a following vowel to make a single character. The standard romanisation given here was adopted by a congress of Orientalists a century ago and, with a few minor variations, is universally accepted among modern scholars. The long vowels corresponding to r̥ and l̥ do not occur in real Sanskrit and are not shown in the table.

Vedic

1352.

Suryakanta, *A practical Vedic dictionary*. Delhi: Oxford University Press, 1981. 750 pp.

A concise dictionary of the language of the oldest Sanskrit literature: coverage extends forward in time to the Brahmanas and Upanishads. The Sanskrit is in Devanagari script throughout.

Classical and post-classical Sanskrit

1353.

Revised and enlarged edition of Prin. V. S. Apte's The practical Sanskrit–English dictionary. Poona: Prasad Prakashan, 1957–59. 3 vols. P. K. Gode, C. G. Karve, editors in chief.

1st edn: V. S. Apte, *The practical Sanskrit–English dictionary.*

The Sanskrit is in Devanagari script throughout. Major words are given citations and brief quotations from Sanskrit literature: quotations are in Sanskrit only. English glosses are based more firmly on literature, with fewer direct borrowings from traditional lexicography, than is the case with Monier-Williams's dictionary (**1357**).

Appendices, in vol. 3, include: names of metres, final pages 12–32; biographies and dates of cited authors, final pages 33–8 (see list of abbreviations for authors, vol. 1 pp. 5–7); maxims and proverbs, final pages 52–76; grammatical terms, final pages 77–112. Biography and portrait of Apte, vol. 1 pp. 5–6.

1354.

Otto Böhtlingk, Rudolph Roth, *Sanskrit-Wörterbuch*. St Petersburg: Kaiserliche Akademie der Wissenschaften, 1852–75. 7 vols.

Abridged version: Otto Böhtlingk, *Sanskrit-Wörterbuch in kürzerer Fassung.* 1879–89. 7 vols in 8 parts. Reissued: 1923–5.

This was supplemented by: Richard Schmidt, *Nachträge zum Sanskrit-Wörterbuch in kürzerer Fassung von Otto Böhtlingk.* Hanover: Lafaire; Leipzig: Harrassowitz, 1924–8. 397 pp.

[*Sanskrit dictionary.*] The fullest complete dictionary of Sanskrit, with German glosses and numerous quotations, mainly from the older literature. Additions in each volume; the last section of additions, with a cumulative index to all seven, is in vol. 7 pp. 289–390.

The abridged version retains some of the citations (not for every word, however) but none of the quotations. Sanskrit is in Devanagari script throughout.

In Schmidt's supplement the Sanskrit is in Latin transliteration. Addenda, pp. 381–96.

1355.

A. M. Ghatage, [S. D. Joshi,] editors, *An encyclopaedic dictionary of Sanskrit on historical principles*. Poona: Deccan College Postgraduate and Research Institute, 1976– .

See: A. Kelkar, 'The scope of a historical dictionary' in *Studies in historical Sanskrit lexicography* (Poona: Deccan College, 1953) pp. 57–69.

This enormous undertaking is based on a new reading of Sanskrit literature, a vast corpus, demanding a 'scriptorium' (the term is borrowed from the *Oxford English dictionary*'s arrangements) of a very large size. The whole literature is dealt with, from Vedic to modern times, which poses a major dating problem for a historical dictionary since many works are entirely undated and it can be difficult or impossible even to place them in the correct century. The interrelationship of texts and commentaries is also difficult to disentangle in Sanskrit. 'Some of the important articles extend over a thousand lines and include seven to eight hundred quotations from as many books.' Sanskrit is infinitely fertile in compounds, all of which are in theory to be covered: the advance estimate is two million entries.

Vol. 1 part 1 includes preliminary material: general introduction, pp. i–xxviii; abbreviations for source texts, pp. xxix–lxx (there are additional texts cited without abbreviation); an important classification and chronology of source texts, pp. lxxiii–lxxxi; user's guide, pp. lxxxii–lxxxvi; general abbreviations, pp. lxxi–lxxii and lxxxvii–lxxxviii.

The last published part is vol. 5 part 2, dated 1994/5. The 2686 pages completed in the first twenty years of publication cover **A–Anugatākārāvagāhitva** (glossed 'the state of being that which comprises of a common form'). One hardly likes to point out that this section of the alphabet occupies 30 pages in Monier-Williams's dictionary (**1357**), less than a fortieth of the total.

1356.

Monier Williams, *A dictionary, English and Sanskrit*. London: W. H. Allen, 1851. 861 pp.
'Published under the patronage of the Honourable East-India Company.'

An English–Sanskrit dictionary in which the Sanskrit is in Devanagari script throughout. Rich in synonyms; there is guidance on shades of meaning, sometimes, but not on literary style.

1357.

Sir Monier Monier-Williams, *A Sanskrit–English dictionary, etymologically and philologically arranged with special reference to cognate Indo-European languages*. Oxford: Clarendon Press, 1899. 1333 pp. New edn. [0–19–864308–X.]
1st edn: *A Sanskrit-English dictionary etymologically and philologically arranged with special reference to Greek, Latin, Gothic, German, Anglo-Saxon, and other cognate Indo-European languages*. 1872. 1186 pp.
'The extent of its indebtedness to the great seven-volumed Sanskrit–German thesaurus [**1354**] ... then only completed as far as the letter व **v**, was fully acknowledged by me in the Preface.'

A highly concise dictionary, but with selective references to written sources (note that many citations are simply *L*. 'lexicographers', words or meanings not then traced in literary texts). Includes many proper names.

The text of the dictionary is in Latin transliteration, in the now old-fashioned variant in which the vowel ऋ is represented by *ṛi* (not *ṛ*) and the consonants च छ by *ch, chh* (not *c, ch*).

Devanagari script is however used for certain headwords. These are arranged to show etymological relationships. Entries for roots are in large Devanagari type, and for derived and prefixed forms (when filed separately) in small Devanagari type. Sub-entries for derivatives and compounds are in a bold roman font, sub-sub-entries in italic. In these, the symbol ° saves repetition of the headword. Although there are some cross-references, the fact that derived words are partly filed independently, partly listed as sub-entries under roots, does slow down the user of this dictionary. However, with some knowledge of the language, it soon becomes clear within which group of entries any unknown form has to be hunted for.

Buddhist Sanskrit

1358.

Heinz Bechert, editor, *Sanskrit-Wörterbuch der buddhistischen Texte aus den Turfan-Funden und der kanonischen Literatur der Sarvāstivāda-Schule = Sanskrit dictionary of the Buddhist texts from the Turfan finds and of the canonical literature of the Sarvāstivāda school*. Göttingen: Vandenhoeck & Ruprecht, 1973– .

Begun by Ernst Waldschmidt. Edited by the Akademie der Wissenschaften in Göttingen.

A full historical dictionary with German glosses, careful discussion of meaning, and lengthy quotations from the Buddhist texts. Sanskrit is in Latin transliteration. List of source texts, vol. 1 pp. lx–lxvii, followed by general abbreviations.

The dictionary is into its second volume with the publication of part 9. So far it covers **A—Kukkuṭyāṇḍavat** ('like a hen's egg'), about a fifth of the Sanskrit alphabet.

1359.

Edward Conze, *Materials for a dictionary of the Prajñāpāramitā literature*. Tokyo: Suzuki Research Foundation, 1967. 447 pp.

A short dictionary but with citations from this Buddhist literature. Sanskrit is in Latin transliteration. Abbreviations, pp. v–vi: for full references see Conze's *The Prajñāpāramitā literature* (1960).

1360.

Franklin Edgerton, *Buddhist hybrid Sanskrit grammar and dictionary*. New Haven: Yale University Press, 1953. 2 vols.

Vol. 1 is the grammar. Vol. 2 (627 pp.) is the dictionary, with English glossses and with generous quotations from Buddhist literature in Sanskrit, dating from the first century BC onwards. Entries begin with an etymological note which often serves to demonstrate how the word was invented, by back-formation or false etymology, from Pali or the current Prakrits of the period. Sanskrit is in Latin transliteration.

Bibliography and abbreviations, vol. 1 pp. xxv–xxx. Historical introduction, vol. 1 pp. 1–14.

Etymological dictionaries

1361.

Manfred Mayrhofer, *Etymologisches Wörterbuch des Altindoarischen.* Heidelberg: Winter, 1986– .

Indogermanische Bibliothek. 2. Reihe, Wörterbücher.

[*Etymological dictionary of Old Indo-Aryan.*] A detailed etymological dictionary with many references to scholarly literature. With part 22, published 1997, vol. 3 is in progress and the dictionary covers **A–guna**, over a third of the whole.

1362.

Manfred Mayrhofer, *Kurzgefaßtes etymologisches Wörterbuch des Altindischen = A concise etymological Sanskrit dictionary.* Heidelberg: Winter, 1953–80. 4 vols.

Indogermanische Bibliothek. 2. Reihe, Wörterbücher.

See also: Manfred Mayrhofer, Vasilij Ivanovic Abaev and others, *Zur Gestaltung des etymologischen Wörterbuches einer 'Grosscorpus-Sprache'.* Vienna: Österreichische Akademie der Wissenschaften, 1980. 58 pp. (*Sitzungsberichte, philosophisch-historische Klasse*, 368. *Veröffentlichungen der Kommission für Linguistik und Kommunikationsforschung*, 11.)

This etymological dictionary is entirely in Latin transliteration, but in Sanskrit alphabetical order.

1363.

Walther Wüst, *Vergleichendes und etymologisches Wörterbuch des Alt-Indoarischen (Altindischen).* Heidelberg: Winter, 1933–5. Part 1/3 [208 pp.; no more published].

Indogermanische Bibliothek, 1. Abteilung: Sammlung indogermanischer Lehr- und Handbücher, 2. Reihe: Wörterbücher, 4.

[*Comparative and etymological dictionary of Old Indo-Aryan.*] The single published part contained a long introduction, a bibliography and a mere 12 pages of dictionary. In these twelve pages Wüst was still working through the entry for the prefix **A-**.

SANTALI

One of the AUSTROASIATIC LANGUAGES of India, Santali has as many as four million speakers, most of them in the state of West Bengal.

1364.

P. O. Bodding, *A Santal dictionary.* Oslo, 1929–36. 5 vols.

Includes dialect forms, and words drawn from oral literature. Full of ethnographical and historical information. Loanwords, mostly from Bengali, are identified.

Bodding was a Christian missionary. He published an elementary grammar (*A Santali grammar for beginners*, Benegaria, 1929) and two volumes of a fuller grammatical study (*Materials for a Santali grammar*, Dumka, 1922–9) which remained unfinished at his death.

1365.

Andrew Campbell, , *A Santali–English and English–Santali dictionary*.
Pokhuria: Santal Mission Press, 1933. 2 parts. 2nd edn by R. W. Macphail.
1st edn: *A Santali-English dictionary*. Pokhuria, 1899–1905. 2 parts [888 pp.].

Useful for its English–Santali section, which was already present, though not signalled in the title.

1366.

Svarnalat Prasad, *Hindi Santali sabdakos*. Rañci: Bihara Janajatiya Kalyana
Sodha Samsthana, 1989. 765 pp.

[*Hindi–Santali dictionary.*]

SARDINIAN

Sardinian is one of the less-known ROMANCE LANGUAGES, with perhaps one and a half million speakers, but no literary status, as Italian is used for official purposes. Its phonetics and vocabulary are in some ways closer to classical Latin than those of any other language of the group.

1367.

Maria Teresa Atzori, *Glossario di sardo antico*. Modena, 1975. 463 pp. 2nd edn.
1st edn: Parma, 1953. 354 pp.

[*Glossary of Old Sardinian.*]

1368.

Vincenzo Porru, *Dizionariu Sardu-Italianu*. Casteddu, 1866. 2nd edn.
1st edn: *Nou dizionariu universali Sardu–Italianu*. 1832. 1427 pp. [*New universal Sardinian–Italian dictionary.*]

[*Sardinian–Italian dictionary.*]

1369.

Max Leopold Wagner, *Dizionario etimologico sardo*. Heidelberg, 1957–64. 3 vols.

[*Sardinian etymological dictionary.*] Indexes, compiled by Raffaele G. Urciolo, vol. 3.

SEMITIC LANGUAGES

This is the best-known group of AFROASIATIC LANGUAGES. Its recorded history goes back to the second millennium BC, with clay tablets in Akkadian and then in other early languages of the Near East.

In earliest written records, speakers of Semitic languages – AKKADIAN, ARAMAIC, HEBREW, PHOENICIAN, SABAEAN, SYRIAC, UGARITIC and others – lived in what are now Arabia, Iraq, Syria, Lebanon, Jordan and Israel. Historical population movements took early ARABIC and ETHIOPIC far beyond this region. Modern members of the family include AMHARIC, ARABIC, ARAMAIC, GURAGE, HEBREW, SOUTH ARABIAN DIALECTS, TIGRE and TIGRINYA.

1370.

Jacob Hoftijzer, K. Jongeling, *Dictionary of the North-West Semitic inscriptions.* Leiden: Brill, 1995. 2 vols [lxxi, 1266 pp.].

With appendices by R. C. Steiner, A. Mosak Moshavi, B. Porten.

Handbuch der Orientalistik = Handbook of Oriental studies. 1. Abteilung, Der Nahe und Mittlere Osten = The Near and Middle East, 21.

Older version: C. F. Jean, Jacob Hoftijzer, *Dictionnaire des inscriptions sémitiques de l'Ouest*. Leiden, 1965. 342 pp.

A very compressed dictionary of the language of a corpus that spreads into several dialects. There are numerous citations (and many quotations, for which English translations are supplied).

The dictionary covers Phoenician, Punic, Moabite, Ammonite, Hebrew (inscriptions, of course, not Biblical texts), the dialect of Deir Alla, Samalian, Old Aramaic (down to 700 BC), Official Aramaic, Nabataean, Palmyrene, the dialects of Hatra and Waw, and Jewish Aramaic. Coverage closes around AD 300. Syriac, being mostly later than that date, is excluded; so is Ugaritic 'because of the difference in approach between the study of Ugaritic and that of Northwestsemitic epigraphics'. Abbreviations for source texts etc., vol. 1 pp. xix–lxxi.

1371.

David Cohen, *Dictionnaire des racines sémitiques ou attestées dans les langues sémitiques*. Paris: Mouton; n.p.: Peeters, 1970– .

[*Dictionary of Semitic roots and roots attested in Semitic languages.*] A concise etymological dictionary arranged under consonantal roots in Latin alphabetical order. With part 5 (1995) coverage has reached **H** in a total of 467 pages.

SERBIAN, CROATIAN, BOSNIAN

Speakers of this divided language use two scripts and adhere to three religions: they are now citizens of three countries carved out of the old Yugoslavia. These three countries are Yugoslavia (Serbia and Montenegro), Bosnia and Croatia. Serbo-Croat (as it is still sometimes called) belongs to the SLAVONIC group of Indo-European languages. There are nearly 19 million speakers. The two alphabets are shown on page 381.

Historical dictionaries

1372.

Đ. Daničić [and other editors], *Rječnik hrvatskoga ili srpskoga jezika*. Zagreb, 1880–1976. 23 vols.

Jugoslavenska Akademija Znanosti i Umjetnosti.

[*Dictionary of the Croatian or Serbian language.*] A triumphantly completed large-scale historical dictionary of Serbo-Croat. Includes entries for place names. All but very minor entries are supported by quotations, often beginning as far back as early glossaries and dictionaries that give Latin glosses. Otherwise entirely in Serbo-Croat, in Latin (i.e. Croatian) script.

Bibliography of source texts, vol. 3 pp. 541–64. In vol. 23, separately paginated, is an appendix (144 pp.) setting out the history of the dictionary, with biographies of editors.

1373.

Речник српскохрватског књижевног и народног језика [*Rečnik srpskohrvatskog književnog i narodnog jezika*]. Belgrade: Institut za Srpskohrvatski Jezik, 1959– .
Edited by Aleksandar Belić and others. Srpska Akademija Nauka i Umetnosti.

[*Dictionary of the Serbo-Croat literary and national language.*] A historical dictionary of Serbo-Croat in Cyrillic (i.e. Serbian) script. Largely parallels Daničić (**1372**) and is on a similar scale, but gives additional citations and many new words. So far 15 volumes have appeared, covering **A–Nokavac**.

The Serbian alphabet and the Latin equivalents

А Б В Г Д Ђ Е Ж З И Ј К Л Љ М Н Њ О П Р С Т Ћ У Ф Х Ц Ч Џ Ш

а б в г д ђ е ж з и ј к л љ м н њ о п р с т ћ у ф х ц ч џ ш

a b v g d đ e ž z i j k l lj m n nj o p r s t ć u f h c č dž š

Croatian/Bosnian alphabetical order

a b c č ć d dž đ e f g h i j k l lj m n nj o p r s š t u v z ž

The modern standard

1374.

Milan Drvodelić, *Engelsko–hrvatski ili srpski rječnik = English–Croatian or Serbian dictionary*. Zagreb: Skolska Knjiga, 1981. 880 pp. '6th edn' revised by Zeljko Bujas.
1st edn: 1954. Changes between editions are relatively minor.

A brief-entry dictionary.

1375.

Milan Drvodelić, *Hrvatsko ili srpsko–engelski rječnik = Croatian or Serbian–English dictionary*. Zagreb: Skolska Knjiga, 1978. 847 pp. '4th edn' revised by Zeljko Bujas.
1st edn: 1953.

A brief-entry dictionary.

Regional forms

1376.

Alija Isaković, *Rječnik karakteristične leksike u bosanskome jeziku*. Sarajevo: Svjetlost, 1992. 502 pp.

Reprinted: Wuppertal: Bambi, 1993. 3–929678–03–8. Alternate title: *Dictionary of characteristic words of the Bosnian language.*

A brief-entry Bosnian-to-Croatian glossary of regionalisms. Gives precise references to literary sources (bibliography, pp. 29–37).

Etymological dictionaries

1377.

Petar Skok, *Etimologijski rječnik hrvatskoga ili srpskoga jezika = Dictionnaire étymologique de la langue croate ou serbe*. Zagreb: Académie Yougoslave des Sciences et des Beaux Arts, 1971–4. 4 vols.

Edited by Mirko Deanović, Liudevit Jonke.

[*Etymological dictionary of the Croatian or Serbian language.*] Highly informative, but compact, etymological entries packed with cognates from Slavonic and other Indo-European languages. A final paragraph gives copious but highly abridged references to the scholarly literature; the dictionary makes excellent use of space. Latin script throughout.

Vol. 4 contains the indexes, which run to 820 pages: there is an alphabetical index to the indexes on four preliminary pages. Errata to all four volumes are also in vol. 4.

Foreign words

1378.

Милан Вујаклија, *Лексикон страних речи и израза* [Milan Vujaklija, *Leksikon stranih reči i izraza*]. Belgrade: Prosveta, 1970. New edn by Svetomir Ristić, Radomir Aleksić.

1st edn: 1954. 1103 pp.

[*Dictionary of foreign words and expressions.*] A remarkably copious brief-entry dictionary which indicates the origins of loanwords and foreign words. Note the abbreviations *тал.* 'Italian', *арб.* 'Albanian'.

Other works of interest

1379.

B. Franolić, *A bibliography of Croatian dictionaries*. Paris: Nouvelles Editions Latines, 1985. 139 pp. 2–7233–0302–0.

SHAN

Shan belongs to the TAI LANGUAGES. It is the most widely spoken language of the Shan State in eastern Burma and the Dehong Dai autonomous region of Yunnan, China. There are perhaps three million speakers.

The traditional alphabet (see **1384**) has not enough symbols to express the sounds of Shan fully. There are two standard styles of writing, known traditionally as Burmese Shan (with rounded characters) and Chinese Shan (a cursive script). Based on these, new extended alphabets, with symbols indicating the tones, have now been adopted in printing in China (see **1385**) and, after much delay, in Burma.

The older dictionaries by the Baptist missionaries, Cushing and Mix (**1380**, **1382**), are based on the Burmese Shan standard of Möngnai in the southern Shan State. The Burmese standard is also adopted in Sao Tern Moeng's excellent reworking of Cushing's dictionary (**1383**). For the Chinese Shan or Tai Nüa of Hsenwi and Yunnan – a rather different dialect, with six tones instead of five – a short glossary by a linguist (**1381**) supplements them.

1380.

J. N. Cushing, *A Shan and English dictionary*. Rangoon: American Baptist Mission Press, 1914. 708 pp. 2nd edn, with preface by H. W. Mix.
1st edn: Rangoon: American Mission Press, 1881. 600 pp.
On the author see: Wallace Saint John, *Josiah Nelson Cushing, missionary and scholar, Burma*. Rangoon, 1912. 208 pp.

Shan–English only: about 21,000 entries. 'The pronunciation common in the principalities of Laihka and Möngnai has been taken as standard,' but the dictionary also includes Hkamti Shan and Chinese Shan words. In traditional Shan script, with no indication of tones. Now superseded for modern use by Sao Tern Moeng's dictionary (**1383**).

1381.

Jimmy G. Harris, 'A comparative word list of three Tai Nüa dialects' in *Studies in Tai linguistics in honor of William J. Gedney* (Bangkok, 1975) pp. 202–30.
In Latin script.

1382.

Mrs H. W. Mix, editor, *An English and Shan dictionary*. Rangoon: American Baptist Mission Press, 1920. 968 pp.

This English–Shan dictionary is based on materials collected by J. N. Cushing, Maung Kham Mun, and Mrs Cushing. About 20,000 entries, including numerous phrases.

1383.

Sao Tern Moeng, *Shan–English dictionary*. Kensington, Maryland: Dunwoody Press, 1995. 367 pp. 0–931745–92–6.

Using Cushing's dictionary (**1380**) as a basis, this short-entry dictionary gives the new script which was promulgated in Shan State in 1958 but long remained under-used. A careful explanation of the new script and comparison with the old is to be found on pp. iii–x. Dialects, pp. xi–xiii; Shan personal names, titles and terms of address, pp. xiv–xxiii.

Other works of interest

1384.
S. Egerød, 'Essentials of Shan phonology and script' in *Bulletin of the Institute of History and Philology, Academia Sinica* vol. 29 (1957) pp. 121–9.

1385.
A. Dalby, 'Suggested transliterations for two Tai languages of China' in *South-East Asia Library Group newsletter* no. 27/8 (July 1984) pp. 12–13.

SHONA

One of the Bantu languages of the NIGER-CONGO family, Shona is one of the two national languages of Zimbabwe (the other being Ndebele). There are about eight million speakers, including some in Mozambique.

1386.
M. Hannan, *Standard Shona dictionary*. Salisbury: Rhodesia Literature Bureau, 1974. 996 pp. 2nd edn.
1st edn: 1959.
   A concise Shona–English dictionary followed by an English–Shona index (pp. 759–996). In the Shona–English section, tone patterns are given (*[L]* 'low', *[H]* 'high') following headwords: for the way that these patterns apply to verbs see p. viii. After these tone marks, additional upper-case letters indicate dialect variation (abbreviations, p. viii), a significant matter in Shona, for the establishment of a 'Standard Shona' has been difficult and controversial.

SHUGHNI

A minority IRANIAN language of the Pamir mountains, in north-eastern Afghanistan.

1387.
Д. Карамшоев, *Шугнанско–русский словарь* [D. Karamshoev, *Shugnansko-russkii slovar'*]. Moscow: Nauka, 1988– .
Edited by A. L. Griunberg. Akademiya Nauk SSSR, Ordena Trudovogo Krasnogo Znameni Institut Vostokovedeniya; Akademiya Nauk Tadzhikskoi SSR, Institut Yazyka i Literatury im. Rudaki.
   [*Shughni–Russian dictionary.*] Planned to contain about 30,000 entries in three volumes, of which the first two have appeared.

1388.

G. Morgenstierne, *Etymological vocabulary of the Shughni group*. Wiesbaden: Reichert, 1974.

Beiträge zur Iranistik.

SINDHI

Sindhi is the INDO-ARYAN language of the lower Indus valley, in southern Pakistan; there are also some speakers across the border in India. It has about nine million speakers in total.

1389.

Lachman M. Khubchandani, editor, *A Comprehensive Sindhi–English Dictionary*. Pune: Centre for Communication Studies, 1981– .

Deccan College. *Studies in linguistics mimeograph series*, 13.

1390.

G. Shirt, Udharam Thavurdas, S. F. Mirza, *A Sindhi–English dictionary*. Karachi: Commissioners Printing Press, 1879. 919 pp.

Father Shirt's dictionary remains a local classic. On the title page the place of publication is spelt 'Kurrachee'.

SINHALA

Sinhala is the majority language of Sri Lanka, with about 12 million speakers. It is an INDO-ARYAN language, separated by some hundreds of miles from its linguistic relatives.

1391.

C. Carter, *A Sinhalese–English dictionary*. Colombo: Baptist Missionary Society, 1924. 806 pp.

Companion work: C. Carter, *An English–Sinhalese dictionary*. Colombo: Ceylon Observer Press, 1936. 535 pp. 2nd edn – 1st edn: Colombo: Skeen, 1891.

1392.

B. Clough, *A Sinhalese–English dictionary*. Colombo: Wesleyan Mission Press, 1887–92. 824 pp. New edn by George Baugh, Robert Tebb, Bartholomew Gunasekara.

'Under the patronage of the Government of Ceylon.'

Reprinted: *Clough's Sinhala English dictionary*. New Delhi: Asian Educational Services, 1982. 824 pp. 1st edn: 1830.

Headwords are in Sinhala script followed by Latin transliteration. The new edition of 1887–92 is important for the inclusion of many names of plants and animals, with taxonomic names.

1393.

D. B. Jayatilaka, editor-in-chief, *Dictionary of the Sinhalese language*.
Colombo: Ceylon Branch, Royal Asiatic Society; University of Ceylon; Ministry
of Cultural Affairs, 1935– .
Compiled by A. M. Gunasekara, W. F. Gunawardhana, Julius de Lanerolle [and others].

Work on this large-scale historical dictionary began in 1926, under the direction of
Wilhelm Geiger and with government support; it was taken over by the University of
Ceylon in 1941. According to the Geiger, it 'can be justly regarded as the most important
literary work undertaken in Ceylon in recent times'. I have not seen recent parts:
Walford's guide to reference material vol. 3 (6th edn: London: Library Association
Publishing, 1995) reports vol. 1 part 15 in 1988.

1394.

Wilhelm Geiger, *An etymological glossary of the Sinhalese language*. Colombo:
Royal Asiatic Society, 1941.
Earlier version: *Etymologie des Singhalesischen*. Munich: Franz, 1897. 99 pp.

SINO-TIBETAN LANGUAGES

The two main branches of the Sino-Tibetan language family must have separated many
thousands of years ago. One branch is represented by CHINESE and the Chinese regional
languages. The other is that of the Tibeto-Burman languages. Some linguists consider
KAREN LANGUAGES to belong to these; others make them a third main branch.

The following Tibeto-Burman languages have entries in this book: AKHA, BAI, BODO,
BURMESE, KUKI-CHIN AND NAGA LANGUAGES, LAHU, LEPCHA, MANIPURI, NAXI, NEWARI,
TANGUT, TIBETAN.

1395.

Paul K. Benedict, *Sino-Tibetan: a conspectus*. Cambridge: Cambridge
University Press, 1972. 230 pp.
Contributing editor: James A. Matisoff. *Princeton-Cambridge studies in Chinese linguistics*, 2.

'The manuscript of this book was originally drafted [c. 1942–3]. It was a distillation
of a far more extensive compilation, *Sino-Tibetan linguistics*, on which Paul Benedict
and Robert Shafer had been working for many years and which still exists as an
unpublished manuscript in the files of the University of California and of the authors'
(Frank A. Kiernan, Foreword).

1396.

Weldon South Coblin, *A sinologist's handlist of Sino-Tibetan lexical
comparisons*. Nettetal: Steyler Verlag, 1986. 186 pp. 3–87787–208–5.
Monumenta serica monograph series, 18.

Based on the reconstructions of Karlgren and Li for Middle Chinese, and of Benedict
for Tibeto-Burman. The comparative vocabulary is arranged in alphabetical order of

English meanings, pp. 35–163, with addenda (not indexed) on p. 164. Indexes of Tibetan and Chinese forms (no others), pp. 165–84. Bibliography, pp. 184–6.

1397.

G. H. Luce, *Phases of pre-Pagan Burma: languages and history*. Oxford: Oxford University Press, 1985. 2 vols.

Note also: Gordon H. Luce, *A comparative word-list of Old Burmese, Chinese and Tibetan*. London, 1981. **88 pp.**

I have seen better-organised publications than this, but it was far better published thus than not at all, and there was certainly no third alternative. No blame to Luce, who had died in 1972, or to E. J. A. Henderson, who saw his work through the press. Vol. 1 is the revised text of historical lectures given in Paris in 1966; vol. 2, at twice the page size, contains word-lists (list of these, vol. 1 p. xii) in numerous Sino-Tibetan languages, in various formats.

Index of English meanings to the word-lists, vol. 1 pp. 109–24. These are keyed to the lettered word-lists A to Z and to line numbers within them. The user has to letter each page of the word-lists in order to make the index usable.

1398.

Walter Simon, 'Tibetisch–chinesische Wortgleichungen', in *Mitteilungen des Seminars für Orientalische Sprachen* vol. 32 (1929) pp. 157–228.

[*Tibetan–Chinese lexical comparisons.*]

SLAVONIC LANGUAGES

The Slavonic or Slavic branch of the INDO-EUROPEAN LANGUAGES was probably less affected by migration in prehistoric times than any other. It was only in the fifth and sixth centuries of the present era that early Slavonic speakers spread westwards into central and south-eastern Europe from their earliest traceable locations in Russia and Ukraine.

The Old Church Slavonic language (see OLD SLAVONIC) was used for early Bible translations and religious works. Modern Slavonic languages became gradually more distinctive from about a thousand years ago. See BULGARIAN, CZECH, MACEDONIAN, POLABIAN, POLISH, RUSSIAN, SERBIAN AND CROATIAN, SLOVAK, SLOVENE, SORBIAN, UKRAINIAN. Kashubian is dealt with in this book under the heading POLISH.

Apart from the truly etymological works there are several multilingual dictionaries and grammars of the Slavonic languages, because, perhaps more than the other Indo-European branches, they can conveniently be studied as a group and often are.

Lewanski's bibliography (**1407**) is useful for its inclusion, in the Russian section, of many bilingual dictionaries of obscure languages, both within the former Soviet Union and beyond.

Comparative dictionaries

1399.

Erich Berneker, *Slavisches etymologisches Wörterbuch*. Heidelberg, 1908–14.
Vols 1–2 part 1 [760 + 80 pp.; no more published].

Indogermanische Bibliothek, 1. Abteilung, 2. Reihe, 2. Sammlung slavischer Lehr- und Handbücher, 2. Reihe, 2.

[*Slavic etymological dictionary.*] Covers **A–Mor**. The arrangement is alphabetical under reconstructed forms, which are followed first by descendant forms in Slavonic languages, then by Indo-European cognates. An interesting discussion of Berneker's work and its layout can be found in Malkiel (**9**) p. 22.

1400.

František Kopečný and others, *Etymologický slovník slovanských jazyků*. Prague, 1973– .

[*Etymological dictionary of the Slavonic languages.*]

1401.

Franz von Miklosich, *Etymologisches Wörterbuch der slavischen Sprachen*. Vienna: Braumüller, 1886. 547 pp.

Reprinted 1922. Reprinted: Amsterdam: Philo Press, 1970. 90–6022–039–0.

[*Etymological dictionary of the Slavic languages.*] This concise etymological dictionary of the inherited vocabulary remains important because none of its intended replacements is yet complete. Entries are under Old Church Slavonic forms and roots, with brief glosses in German or Latin followed by a list of forms in modern Slavonic languages. Supplement, pp. 414–32. Multilingual index of Slavonic forms cited, pp. 433–545. Abbreviations of language names, pp. 546–7.

1402.

Linda Sadnik, Rudolf Aitzetmüller, *Vergleichendes Wörterbuch der slavischen Sprachen*. Wiesbaden: Harrassowitz, 1963–75. Vol. 1 [643 pp.: no more published].

[*Comparative dictionary of the Slavic languages.*] The completed section, letters **A–B**, has 381 numbered entries in approximate Old Church Slavonic alphabetical order. Headwords are transliterated Old Church Slavonic forms, accompanied by original script. On pp. 495–643 there are no fewer than 124 separate indexes to cited forms in Slavonic and other languages – but no index to the indexes. The prefatory notes on p. vii betray a disagreement between authors, funding institution and publisher.

1403.

Słownik prasłowiański. Wrocław: Ossolineum, 1974– .

Edited by Franciszek Sławski.

[*Proto-Slavonic dictionary.*] A concise historical dictionary of the forms of proto-Slavonic and its offspring, with citations and a few quotations from the texts. Articles are signed. The proto-Slavonic is in Latin script but Cyrillic is used for Bulgarian, Russian and other modern languages customarily written in Cyrillic.

So far six thin volumes have appeared, covering **A–ĕždžь**.

1404.

О.Н.Трубачев, *Этимологический словарь славянских языков: праславянский лексический фонд* [O. N. Trubachev, *Etimologicheskii slovar' slavyanskikh yazykov: praslavyanskii leksicheskii fond*]. Moscow: Nauka, 1974–

Preceded by: *Etimologicheskii slovar' slavyanskikh yazykov: probniye stat'i.* 1963.

[*Etymological dictionary of the Slavonic languages: the proto-Slavonic lexicon.*] Headwords are reconstructed proto-Slavonic forms and these are followed by the recorded Old Church Slavonic ones, in Church Slavonic script. This work forms a full comparative dictionary of developments in the later Slavonic languages, but only for the native Slavonic vocabulary, as loanwords are excluded.

Publication is rapid: 22 small volumes have appeared, covering А—*народъ.

Multilingual dictionaries

1405.

Louis Jay Herman, *A dictionary of Slavic word families*. New York: Columbia University Press, 1975. 667 pp. 0–231–03927–1.

A parallel dictionary, focusing on compounds and derivatives from roots, of four Slavonic languages. Russian, Polish, Czech, and Serbo-Croat entries are in four parallel columns. 'The roots are arranged in Latin alphabetical order, although the vagaries of phonetic development in the four languages make a completely consistent scheme impossible' but the running-heads are in Cyrillic! There is an index of root-forms in each language and a partial index of forms with unrecognisable roots, pp. 659–67.

1406.

F. Miklosich, *Dictionnaire abrégé de six langues slaves: russe, vieux-slave, bulgare, serbe, tchèque et polonais, ainsi que langues français et allemand* = Ф. Миклошич, *Краткій словарь шести славянскихъ языковъ*. St Petersburg: Wolff, 1885. 955 pp.

[*Short dictionary of six Slavonic languages: Russian, Old Slavonic, Bulgarian, Serbian, Czech and Polish, and of French and German.*] An extremely full and informative dictionary in spite of its columnar arrangement. The Russian and Old Slavonic are in column 1, distinguished by typeface.

Other works of interest

1407.

Richard C. Lewanski, *A bibliography of Slavic dictionaries*. Bologna: Editrice Compositori, 1972–3. 4 vols. 2nd edn.

World bibliography of dictionaries. Johns Hopkins University, *Bologna Center Library publications*. Vol. 4 is a supplement.

1408.

F. Scholz, *Slavische Etymologie: eine Anleitung zur Benutzung etymologischer Wörterbücher*. Wiesbaden: Harrassowitz, 1966.
Slavistische Studienbücher, 3.

1409.

Edward Stankiewicz, *Grammars and dictionaries of the Slavic languages from the Middle Ages up to 1850: an annotated bibliography*. Berlin: Mouton, 1984. 190 pp. 3–11–009778–8.

SLOVAK

Slovak, the SLAVONIC language of Slovakia, was one of the two national languages of Czechoslovakia. When that state disintegrated, Slovakia became an independent state as one of its two successors. Slovak is said to be mutually intelligible with Czech. It has about five and a half million speakers.

There is no recent etymological dictionary of Slovak, but one may point to Machek (**310**), whose first edition professedly covered Slovak as well as Czech.

Slovak alphabetical order

a/á ä b c č d dz dž e/é f g h ch i/í j k l/ĺ m n/ň

o/ó ô p q r s š t/ť u/ú v w x y/ý z ž

Q occurs only in foreign loanwords.

1410.

Historický slovník slovenského jazyka. Bratislava: Veda, 1991– .
Chief editor, Milan Majtán. Authors, V. Blanár and others. Slovenská Akadémia Vied, Jazykovedný Ústav.

[*Historical dictionary of the Slovak language.*] A short historical dictionary that usefully extends the information offered by the *Slovník slovenského jazyka* (**1413**). Each entry gives a gloss followed by a source reference, either a scholarly work (list, vol. 5 pp. 43–65) or an original author (no list or bibliography of these) with first recorded dating. Important for tracing and dating changes in meaning. I have seen only vol. 1, covering **A–J**.

1411.

Ivor Ripka, Ferdinand Buffa [and others], *Slovník slovenských nárecí*.
Bratislava: Veda, 1980– .
Slovenská Akadémia Vied, Jazykovedný Ústav L'udovíta Stúra.

[*Dictionary of Slovak dialects.*]

1412.

Slovník cudzích slov: A–Z. Bratislava: Slovenské Pedagogické Nakladatel'stvo, 1979. 944 pp.
By Mária Ivanová-Salingová, Zuzana Maníková.

[Dictionary of foreign words.]

1413.

Slovník slovenského jazyka. Bratislava: Vydavateľstvo Slovenskej Akadémie Vied, 1959–68. 6 vols.
Chief editor: Stefan Peciar.

[Dictionary of the Slovak language.] A very large-scale dictionary of modern usage with example phrases and some attributed quotations from literature, but no precise citations.

Vol. 6 is a supplement containing additions to the main alphabet, pp. 7–124; personal names, pp. 127–51; place names in Czechoslovakia, pp. 153–254; foreign place names, pp. 255–305; a history of the work, pp. 319–23; corrections, pp. 324–31. Abbreviations, general and of quoted authors, vol. 6 pp. 311–17.

1414.

Veľký rusko–slovenský slovník. Bratislava, 1960–70. 4 vols.
[Big Russian–Slovak dictionary.]

1415.

Veľký slovensko–ruský slovník. Bratislava, 1979– .

[Big Slovak–Russian dictionary.] This and its twin (above) make up the largest available two-way bilingual dictionary of Slovak.

SLOVENE

Slovene is the SLAVONIC language of Slovenia, once a constituent part of Yugoslavia, now an independent republic. It has two million speakers.

There is plenty of evidence of early Slovene in the dictionary of Church Slavonic by Miklošič (**1163**).

Slovene alphabetical order

a/á b c č d e f g h i/í j k l m n o/ó p r s š t u/ú v z ž

1416.

France Bezlaj, *Etimološki slovar slovenskega jezika*. Ljubljana: Slovenska Akademija Znanosti in Umetnosti, Inštitut za Slovenski Jezik, 1976– .

[Etymological dictionary of the Slovene language.] A useful concise etymological dictionary with discussion of changes of meaning, references to other etymological dictionaries, and cognates in other Slavonic and Indo-European languages. Perhaps now complete; I have seen only the first two volumes, covering **A–O**.

1417.

Anton Grad, Henry Leeming, *Slovensko–angleški slovar = Slovene–English dictionary*. Ljubljana: DZS, 1993. 827 pp. 86–341–0984–4.
Slovarji DZS.

A brief-entry dictionary.

1418.

Anton Grad, Ružena Skerlj, Nada Vitorovič, *Veliki anglesko–slovenski slovar.*
Ljubljana: Državna Založba Slovenije, 1978. 1377 pp.

[*Big English–Slovene dictionary.*] A concise bilingual dictionary into Slovene. There are also abridged editions. A much larger new English–Slovene dictionary is now in preparation, commissioned by the same publisher, compiled by Simon Krik and others.

1419.

Stanislaus Hafner, Erich Prunc, editors, *Thesaurus der slowenischen Volkssprache in Kärnten.* Vienna: Verlag der Österreichischen Akademie der Wissenschaften, 1982– .

Schriften der Balkankommission, Linguistische Abteilung. Sonderpublikation.
Accompanied by: Schlüssel zum 'Thesaurus der slowenischen Volkssprache in Kärnten'. 111 pp. [Key.]

[*Dictionary of the Slovene dialects of Carinthia.*] Bibliography: key, pp. 93–101.

1420.

Slovar slovenskega knjiznega jezika. Ljubljana: DZS, 1994. 1714 pp. New edn. 86–341–1111–3.

Edited by Anton Bajec and others. Slovenska Akademija Znanosti in Umetnosti, Znanstvenoraziskovalni Center, Institut za Slovenski Jezik.
1st edn: Ljubljana: Slovenska Akademija Znanosti in Umetnosti, Institut za Slovenski Jezik, 1970–91. 5 vols.

[*Dictionary of the Slovene literary language.*] A large-scale dictionary of modern usage. The new one-volume edition is lightly revised and incorporates in the main alphabet the supplementary entries that appeared in vol. 5 of the first edition. There are plenty of example phrases but no attributed quotations.

1421.

Marko Snoj, *Slovenski etimoloski slovar.* Ljubljana: Mladinska Knjiga, 1997. 900 pp. 86–11–14772–3.

[*Slovene etymological dictionary.*] A good one-volume etymological dictionary. The index, pp. 771–900, helps in finding compound words but is otherwise supererogatory.

SOMALI

Somali is a CUSHITIC language, and thus a member of the Afroasiatic family. It is the national language of Somalia, and has five and a half million speakers. There has been some experiment with new alphabets, but for most purposes the Latin alphabet is used.

1422.

R. C. Abraham, *Somali–English dictionary.* London: University of London Press, 1964. 332 pp.

Companion work: R. C. Abraham, *English–Somali dictionary.* London: University of London Press, 1967. 208 pp.

SORBIAN

Sorbian is one of the more obscure of SLAVONIC LANGUAGES, with 100,000 speakers in eastern Germany. The language takes two distinct regional forms, Upper and Lower Sorbian. There was frequent discrimination against the use of Sorbian until the Communist takeover in 1945. After that date the situation was reversed and Sorbian was favoured.

Upper Sorbian alphabetical order

a b c č d dź e ě f g h ch i j k ł l m n ń o ó p r ř s š t ć u w y z ź

1423.

Filip Jakubaš, *Hornjoserbsko–němski słownik* = *Obersorbisch–deutsches Wörterbuch*. Bautzen: Domowina, 1954. 543 pp.

[*Upper Sorbian–German dictionary.*] A brief-entry dictionary. Headwords are keyed to the numbered tables 1–106 of the morphological sketch of Upper Sorbian on pp. 1–50.

1424.

Helmut Jentsch, Siegfried Mischalk, Irene Sěrak, *Deutsch–obersorbisches Wörterbuch* = Helmut Jenč, Frido Michałk, Irena Sěrakowa, *Němsko–hornjoserbski słownik*. Bautzen: Domowina, 1987–91. 2 vols.

Begun by Rudolf Jentsch (Jenč). Edited by the Institut für Sorbische Volksforschung in Bautzen der Akademie der Wissenschaften der DDR.

[*German–Upper Sorbian dictionary.*] A concise bilingual dictionary.

1425.

Ernst Mucke, *Wörterbuch der nieder-wendischen Sprache und ihrer Dialekte* = Эрнестъ Мука, *Словарь нижне-лужицкаго языка и его нарѣчій* = Ernst Muka, *Słownik dolnoserbskeje rěcy a jeje narěcow* = Arnošt Muka, *Slovnik dolnolužického jazyka a jeho náreči*. St Petersburg; Prague: Verlag der Russischen und Cechischen Akademie der Wissenschaften, 1911–28. 3 vols.

[*Dictionary of the Lower Sorbian language and its dialects.*] A large-scale dictionary, with glosses in German and Russian (and some Czech and Polish equivalents) and supplying taxonomic names for flora and fauna. There are occasional citations of literary sources, notably the Lower Sorbian translation of the Bible. Vol. 3 (244 pp.) is a supplementary volume including glossaries of personal names, place names and field names.

1426.

H. Schuster-Sewc, *Historisch-etymologisches Wörterbuch der ober- und niedersorbischen Sprache*. Bautzen: Domowina, 1978–89. 4 vols [24 parts; 1888 pp.]. 3–7420–0013–6.

[*Historical and etymological dictionary of the Upper and Lower Sorbian language.*]
An important full etymological dictionary, with citation of Sorbian sources and with cognates in neighbouring languages and dialects (thus important also for Polish and Czech). Headwords are given for both Upper and Lower Sorbian forms, with cross-references.

Supplement, pp. 1820–35; scholarly bibliography, pp. 1845–66; bibliography of Sorbian textual sorces, pp. 1867–78; general abbreviations, pp. 1879–86.

SOTHO

Northern and Southern Sotho, Bantu languages and thus members of the NIGER-CONGO family, are spoken in South Africa and Lesotho (where Southern Sotho is the national language). There are about seven and a half million speakers.

1427.
A. Mabille, H. Dieterlen, *Southern Sotho–English dictionary*. Morija: Morija Sesuto Book Depot, 1950. 445 pp. 'Reclassified, revised and enlarged by R. A. Paroz.'

1428.
D. Ziervogel, *Groot Noord-Sotho-woordeboek*. Pretoria: van Schaik, 1975. 1536 pp.

SOUTH ARABIAN LANGUAGES

In southern Arabia some SEMITIC dialects, not closely related to Arabic, seem likely to represent a modern form of the language known from ancient inscriptions as SABAEAN.

1429.
T. M. Johnstone, *Ḥarsūsi lexicon and English–Ḥarsūsi word-list*. London: Oxford University Press, 1977. 181 pp.

'Ḥarsūsi is spoken by a limited number of people who live to the north of the Dhofar province of Oman [and] is now disappearing fast ...' Johnstone's comparative research on the South Arabian languages is in evidence in this scholarly volume, with numerous parallel forms cited from Soqotri, Mehri and others, as well as Omani Arabic. Latin script is used throughout, but the arrangement is the traditional Semitic one under consonantal roots. Index of English meanings, pp. 153–81.

1430.
T. M. Johnstone, *Jibbāli lexicon*. Oxford: Oxford University Press, 1981.
Followed by: T. M. Johnstone, *Mehri Lexicon and English-Mehri word-list*. London: School of Oriental and African Studies, 1987. With an index of the English definitions in the *Jibbali lexicon*, compiled by G. Rex Smith.

SPANISH

Spanish is the most widely spoken of the ROMANCE LANGUAGES, with 225 million speakers in Spain, the Central and South American countries, and elsewhere. It is sometimes called Castilian, a term which emphasises the origins of standard Spanish in the language of the medieval kingdom of Castile, and tends to exclude not only the regional dialects of Spain but also the multiple national standards of Latin America.

Mozarabic is the little-known language of medieval southern Spain when that part of the country was under Arabic domination. JUDEZMO is an offshoot of Spanish, spoken by the Sephardi Jewish communities expelled from the Iberian peninsula in 1492.

In addition to the etymological dictionaries listed below (**1466**, **1467**), note that Arabic words in Mozarabic and in Spanish are dealt with by Steiger (**1258**). Malkiel (**1469**) provides a useful survey of Spanish dictionaries.

Traditional Spanish alphabetical order

a b c ch d e f g h i j k l ll m n ñ o p q r s t u v x y z

This alphabetical order is no longer 'official', but it is found in most of the dictionaries listed here. Under the new standard, ch and ll are no longer to be treated as separate letters.

Historical dictionaries

1431.

Rufino José Cuervo, *Diccionario de construcción y régimen de la lengua castellana*. Paris: Roger, Chernoviz; Bogotá: Instituto Caro y Cuervo, 1886–1987. Vols 1–3.

Vols 1–2, **A–D**: Paris, 1886–93 [922 + 1348 pp.]. – Reprinted with a new preface: Bogotá, 1953–4
Vol. 3 parts 1–21, **E–Extremo**: Bogotá, 1959–87. Note also: *Thesaurus: boletino del Instituto Caro y Cuervo* (1945–), a periodical in which preliminary versions of some articles from the dictionary have been published.
See also: José Álvaro Porto Dapena, *Elementos de lexicografía: el Diccionario de construcción y régimen de R. J. Cuervo*. Bogotá: Instituto Caro y Cuervo, 1980. 457 pp. (*Publicaciones del Instituto Caro y Cuervo*, 55.)

[*Syntactical and morphological dictionary of the Spanish language.*] Long articles with numerous brief quotations set off by «». The major entries become a forest of meanings, invented examples and attributed quotations, ineffectively laid out. Still, for most of **A** to **E**, this is the best dictionary of Spanish that there is. I have seen no new parts since 1987.

Cuervo (Bogotá 1844–Paris 1911) died leaving the unpublished text of **E–Empero** and notes for some entries up to **Librar**. On his work see Félix Restrepo in *Thesaurus* vol. 1 (1945) pp. 429–32.

1432.

Diccionario histórico de la lengua española. Madrid: Real Academia Española, 1964– .

Planned by Julio Casares. Edited by Vicente García de Diego, Rafael Lapesa Melgar and others. Real Academia Española, Seminario de Lexicografía.

Replaces a 1st edn of which only 2 vols (**A—C**) were published, 1933–6.

[*Historical dictionary of the Spanish language.*] The intention is to cover the whole history of Spanish from its recorded beginnings in the early Middle Ages – and to include Latin American standards and dialects, Mozarabic and JUDEZMO. This dictionary is closely modelled on the *Oxford English dictionary* (**360**), with generous, relatively brief, dated quotations, often divided into three paragraphs for 'medieval', 'early modern 1500–1700', 'modern'; the presence of the third paragraph acts as confirmation that a corresponding entry is to be found in the Academy's *Diccionario de la lengua española* (**1434**). Quotations are marked off with ¶. Sometimes there is in addition, at the head of entries, a historical comment on changes in usage, with citations of linguistic and grammatical works.

This exemplary work has so far covered **A–Aonio**, the latest published part being vol. 3 no. 1 (1993): at the current rate of progress, completion may be expected in 480 years.

1433.

Martín Alonso Pedraz, *Enciclopedia del idioma: diccionario histórico y moderno de la lengua española (siglos XII al XX)*. Madrid: Aguilar, 1958. 3 vols [4258 pp.].

[*Dictionary of the idiom: a historical and modern dictionary of the Spanish language, twelfth to twentieth centuries.*] Generally a brief-entry dictionary, with imprecise definitions – but for selected words it gives precise references to source texts, though these are sometimes merely older dictionaries. No quotations.

The modern standard

1434.

Diccionario de la lengua española. Madrid, 1992. 1515 pp. 84–239–4399–2.
Real Academia Española.
1st edn: *Diccionario de la lengua española (diccionario de autoridades)*. Madrid, 1726–39. 6 vols. – Reprint of 1st edn: Madrid: Gredos, 1963. 6 vols in 3.
20th edn 1987. 2 vols.
Additions and corrections to each edition are published in *Boletín de la Real Academia Española* (1914–).

[*Dictionary of the Spanish language.*] A prescriptive dictionary which takes account of Latin American usage: even the earliest edition included many Americanisms. This first edition was a fine piece of work, ahead of its time, supplying a good range of literary quotations, with verse set line for line.

1435.

Tana de Gámez, editor-in-chief, *Simon and Schuster's international dictionary English/Spanish Spanish/English = Diccionario internacional Simon and Schuster inglés/español español/inglés*. New York: Simon and Schuster, 1973. 1605 pp. 0–671–21507–8.

A brief-entry bilingual dictionary giving American English pronunciations, in the International Phonetic Alphabet, for English headwords. Taxonomic names are given as glosses for some (but not all) Spanish plant and animal terms. For a comparison of Spanish/English bilingual dictionaries see **1470**.

1436.

Ramón García-Pelayo y Gross, editor, *Gran diccionario español–inglés = English–Spanish dictionary, unabridged edition.* Paris: Larousse, 1993. 718 + 804 pp. 'New edn by Larousse staff.' 2–03–451351–7.

Older version: *Larousse gran diccionario español–inglés.* 1983.

A brief-entry bilingual dictionary. Generous coverage of American Spanish (*AMER* after headword) and of American English (*US* after headword or preceding gloss).

1437.

Aniceto de Pagés, José Herrás, *Gran diccionario de la lengua castellana, autorizado con ejemplos de buenos escritores antiguos y modernos.* Barcelona [1901–31]. 5 vols.

[*Big dictionary of the Spanish language, supported by quotations from the best authors, classical and modern.*]

1438.

Vox: diccionario actual de la lengua española. Madrid, 1990. [6th edn] by Manuel Alvar Ezquerra.

1st edn, by Samuel Gili Gaya: 1945. – 4th edn: 1980. – New [5th] edn: *Vox, diccionario general ilustrado de la lengua española.* Barcelona, 1987. 1178 pp.

[*Vox: current dictionary of the Spanish language.*] A well-planned one-volume brief-entry dictionary.

1439.

Elías Zerolo [and others], *Diccionario enciclopédico de la lengua castellana.* Paris: Garnier [1895]. 3 vols in 4. 'New edition.'

[*Encyclopaedic dictionary of the Spanish language.*] A very large-scale dictionary of modern usage, with some quotations from literature illustrating the general vocabulary, but no quotations for technical terms. 'Supplement' of corrections and additions, vol. 2 pp. 1079–82, perhaps incorporated in the new vol. 3 (see below). Rhyming dictionary, by Juan Peñalver, vol. 2 final pages 1–119.

The new edition is a reprint of an older one, with a new volume 3 (in two physical volumes), a supplement largely of scientific terminology and with new encyclopaedic entries for names of people and places. There are few if any attributed quotations in vol. 3.

Older periods

Medieval

1440.

Martín Alonso [Pedraz], *Diccionario medieval español, desde las Glosas Emilianenses y Silenses (s. X) hasta el siglo XV.* Salamanca, 1986. 2 vols [1635 pp.]. 84–7299–169–5.

[*Medieval Spanish dictionary, from the early glosses (tenth century) to the fifteenth century.*] A handy concise historical dictionary with very brief quotations, marked off by «», in generous number in vol. 1, which covers **A–C**. In vol. 2 (**Ch–Z**) the quotations are cut down. Bibliography, vol. 1 pp. lix–lxxx; abbreviations, pp. lxxx–lxxxiii.

1441.

R. S. Boggs, Lloyd Kasten, Hayward Keniston, H. B. Richardson, *Tentative dictionary of medieval Spanish*. Chapel Hill, 1946. 2 vols [537 pp.].

Supersedes: Victor R. B. Oelschläger, *A medieval Spanish word-list*. Madison, Wisconsin, 1940.

Brief-entry bilingual dictionary with tentative datings.

1442.

Américo Castro, *Glosarios latino–españoles de la Edad Media*. Madrid, 1936. 378 pp.

Revista de filología española, supplement 22.

Reprinted: Madrid: Consejo Superior de Investigaciones Científicas, 1991. (*Biblioteca de filología hispánica*, 3.)

See the extensive review by Leo Spitzer in *Modern language notes* vol. 53 (1938) pp. 122–46.

[*Latin–Spanish glossaries of the Middle Ages.*] An edition of the manuscript glossaries followed by an alphabetical dictionary (under Latin or Latinate forms) with important etymological notes, pp. 149–314 (addenda, pp. 363–76) and with a Spanish index, pp. 315–48.

1443.

Bodo Müller, *Diccionario del español medieval*. Heidelberg, 1987– .

Sammlung romanischer Elementar- und Handbücher. 3. Reihe, Wörterbücher. Heidelberger Akademie der Wissenschaften.

[*Dictionary of medieval Spanish.*] A really big dictionary, consisting almost entirely of a collection of quotations, barren of discussion and somewhat greedy of paper. References are mechanically given to other major Spanish dictionaries: these references are useful particularly when the medieval word is no longer used in the same form. Preliminary bibliography, vol. 1 pp. viii–xliv, with a supplement in part 11.

The dictionary has so far reached vol. 2 part 16 and covers **A–Aguardar**.

Early modern

1444.

Peter Boyd-Bowman, *Léxico hispanoamericano del siglo XVI*. London: Tamesis, 1971. 0–900411–28–7.

[*Spanish American glossary of the sixteenth century.*] A collection of quotations, mostly from manuscripts, arranged under keywords. Each quotation is preceded by a geographical and date annotation in brackets (see the list of geographical abbreviations, pp. ix–x) and followed by a source reference, in brackets again (see list of sources, pp. xvii–xxii).

1445.

Samuel Gili Gaya, *Tesoro lexicográfico (1492–1726)*. Madrid, 1947–57. Vol. 1 [1005 pp.; no more published].

[*Lexicographical treasury, 1492–1726.*] There is no other work quite like this republication, in alphabetical order, of the entries from all the main Spanish dictionaries, monolingual and bilingual, published between 1492 and 1726: it runs up to, but excludes, the first edition of the *Diccionario de la lengua española* (which has in any case been reprinted in full, see **1434**). It is in no sense original, but is a handy compilation, often very informative on grammarians' opinions and on older usage.

Regional forms

1446.

Günther Haensch, Reinhold Werner, editors, *Nuevo diccionario de americanismos*. Santafé de Bogotá, 1993– .

Vol. 1: *Nuevo diccionario de colombianismos*. 1993.
Vol. 2: Claudio Chuchuy, Laura Hlavacka de Bouzo, *Nuevo diccionario de argentinismos*. 1993. 708 pp.
Vol. 3: Ursula Kühl de Mones, *Nuevo diccionario de uruguayismos*. 1993.

[*New dictionary of Americanisms.*] Publication is planned in national volumes. The undertaking has been referred to as "Proyecto de Augsburgo". It was to be accompanied by a *Bibliografía de inventarios lexicográficos del español de América* [*Bibliography of word-lists of the Spanish of America*].

I have seen vol. 2, Argentina, which makes enthusiastic use of geometrical symbols. Abbreviations are used to distinguish local dialects. Taxonomic names are given for flora and fauna. Synonyms, including standard Castilian equivalents, are added in square brackets. Castilian index of meanings, pp. 635–94, followed by indexes of botanical and zoological names. Bibliography, pp. xlix–lxvii.

Vols 1 and 3, for Colombia and Uruguay, are also available.

1447.

Isaias Lerner, *Arcaísmos léxicos del español de América*. Madrid: Insula, 1974. 275 pp. 84–7185–115–6.

[*Lexical archaisms of American Spanish.*] A glossary of words still in use in American standards or dialects but dropped from modern standard Castilian. Discursive entries, packed with citations of dictionaries and other sources. Bibliography, pp. 241–74.

1448.

Augusto Malaret, *Diccionario de americanismos*. Buenos Aires: Emecé, 1946. 835 pp. 3rd edn.

1st edn: Mayagüez, 1925. – Followed by a booklet of corrections: *Fe de erratas de mi Diccionario de americanismos*. 1926.
2nd edn: San Juan de Puerto Rico, 1931. – Supplements to this were published in *Boletín de la Academia Argentina de Letras* and in *Boletín de la Academia Chilena de la Lengua*.

[*Dictionary of Americanisms.*] A brief-entry dictionary with careful enumeration of local usages for each Latin American state.

Malaret's first work was *Diccionario de provincialismos de Puerto Rico* (San Juan de Puerto Rico: Sociedades Españolas, 1917), which appeared in a second edition as *Vocabulario de Puerto Rico* (1937).

1449.
Marcos Augusto Morínigo, *Diccionario del español de América*. Madrid, 1993.

First published as: *Diccionario manual de americanismos*. Buenos Aires: Muchnik, 1966. 738 pp. This was reprinted as: *Diccionario de americanismos*. Barcelona, 1985.

[*Dictionary of the Spanish of America.*] The first edition includes a long, useful bibliography, pp. 693–738 – but there are no references to it in the text. On the new edition see the review article by Werner (**1472**).

1450.
Alfredo N. Neves, *Diccionario de americanismos*. Buenos Aires: Sopena Argentina, 1975. '2nd edn.'

1st edn: 1973.

[*Dictionary of Americanisms.*]

1451.
Francisco J. Santamaría, *Diccionario general de americanismos*. Mexico: Robredo, 1942[–1943]. 3 vols.

[*General dictionary of Americanisms.*] A brief-entry dictionary of Latin American usage, with examples. Taxonomic names are given for flora and fauna. There are a few very long articles with quotations, including the one for **Vos** 'you'.

Supplement, vol. 3 pp. 329–43; enormous index of Latin taxonomic names, pp. 347–633; bibliography, pp. 635–75.

1452.
María Schwauss, *Lateinamerikanisches Sprachgut. 1: Wörterbuch der regionalen Umgangssprache in Lateinamerika, Amerikaspanisch–Deutsch, mit einer Liste der Indiostämme*. Leipzig, 1986. 2nd edn.

1st edn: 1977.
See the review by Reinhold Werner in *Lebende Sprachen* vol. 33 (1988) pp. 43–4.

[*Latin American vocabulary, 1. Spanish–German dictionary of the regional colloquial speech of Latin America, with a list of Indian peoples.*]

Canary Islands

1453.
Cristóbal Corrales Zumbado [and others], *Tesoro lexicográfico del español de Canarias*. Canarias: Viceconsejería de Educación, 1995. 3 vols [2822 pp.]. 2nd edn.

1st edn: 1992?

[*Lexicographical guide to the Spanish of the Canaries.*] A very useful full glossary, with examples and quotations, compiled from existing dictionaries and other printed sources, of the special vocabulary of Canary Islands Spanish dialects. The new edition has been extensively revised.

Chile

1454.

Rodolfo Lenz, *Diccionario etimológico de las voces chilenas derivadas de lenguas indígenas americanas*. 1979. New edn by M. Ferreccio Podestí.

1st edn: *Diccionario etimolójico de las voces chilenas derivadas de lenguas indíjenas americanas.*Santiago de Chile: Cervantes, 1904–10. 2 vols [938 pp.]. (*Anales de la Universidad de Chile, anexo.*)

[*Etymological dictionary of Chilean words derived from native American languages.*] I have not seen the new edition.

1455.

Felix Morales Pettorino [and others], *Diccionario ejemplificado de chilenismos*. Valparaiso: Academia Superior de Ciencias Pedagógicas de Valparaiso, 1984–7. 4 vols [4913 pp.]

Preceded by an *Estudio preliminar*: Santiago de Chile, 1983. 150 pp.

[*Dictionary of Chilenisms, with examples.*] With quotations from sources, and references to scholarly literature.

Cuba

1456.

Esteban Rodríguez Herrera, *Léxico mayor de Cuba*. Havana: Lex, 1958–9. 2 vols.

[*Big Cuban dictionary.*] An enjoyable, informal dictionary of Cubanisms. Many words are illustrated by quotations (no datings). Bibliography, pp. 1–5. List of reviews of vol. 1, vol. 2 pp. 658–74.

Mexico

1457.

Juan M. Lope Blanch, *Léxico del habla culta de México*. Mexico, 1978. 586 pp.

[*Dictionary of the educated speech of Mexico.*]

1458.

Francisco J. Santamaria, *Diccionario de mejicanismos*. Mexico: Porrua, 1983. 1207 pp. 2nd edn.

1st edn: 1959. 1197 pp.

[*Dictionary of Mexicanisms.*] A concise dictionary of usage, notable for its generous inclusion of quotations (though not for every word). Some are drawn from literature, others from grammatical works and from other dictionaries. References to dictionaries of other Latin American countries. On pp. xi–xxiv of the first edition (I have not seen the second) there is a discussion of earlier publications on and dictionaries of Latin American Spanish. A landmark work.

Peru

1459.

Juan de Arona, *Diccionario de peruanismos*. Lima, 1975. Edited by Estuardo Núñez.

(*Biblioteca peruana*, 48–9.) First published: Lima, 1883.

    [*Dictionary of Peruanisms.*] The author's real name was Pedro Paz Soldán y Unánue.

Spain

1460.

Antonio Alcalá Venceslada, *Vocabulario andaluz*. Madrid: Gredos. 676 pp.

Biblioteca románica hispánica, ser. 5, diccionarios, 8.

    [*Andalusian dictionary.*] I have only seen a 1980 reprint.

1461.

Rafael Andolz, *Diccionario aragones aragones–castellano castellano–aragones*. Zaragoza: Libreria General, 1977. 422 pp. 84–7078–024–7.

    [*Aragonese dictionary, Aragonese–Castilian Castilian–Aragonese.*] A brief-entry illustrated dictionary with careful notation of local dialect differences (abbreviations for these, pp. xi–xiii) for which the Castilian–Aragonese section can serve as a thesaurus.

1462.

José María Iribarren, *Vocabulario navarro*. Pamplona: Comunidad Foral de Navarra, Departamento de Educación y Cultura, Institución Principe de Viana, 1984. 564 pp. New edition by Ricardo Ollaquindia.

    [*Navarrese dictionary.*]

United States

1463.

Roberto A. Galván, Richard V. Teschner, *El diccionario del español chicano = The dictionary of Chicano Spanish*. Lincolnwood, Illinois: National Textbook Co., 1989. 145 pp. [3rd edn?] 0–8325–9634–5.

    A brief, lively dictionary of usages that differ from standard Spanish. List of proverbs and sayings, pp. 125–36.

Uruguay

1464.

Daniel Granada, *Vocabulario rioplatense razonado*. Montevideo, 1957. 2 vols.

Colección de clásicos uruguayos, 25–6.

1st edn: Montevideo, 1889. 314 pp. With an introduction by A. Magariños Cervantes. – 2nd edn: 1890. 409 pp. New introduction by D. J. Valera.

    [*Explanatory dictionary of Uruguayan Spanish.*]

Venezuela

1465.

Maria Josefina Tejera: *Diccionario de venezolanismos*. Caracas, 1983– .
[*Dictionary of Venezuelanisms.*] Vol. 1, covering **A–I**, runs to 549 pages.

Etymological dictionaries

1466.

Vicente García de Diego, *Diccionario etimológico español e hispánico*. Madrid [1955?]. 1069 pp.

[*Spanish and Hispanic etymological dictionary.*] Part 1 is an alphabetical list of modern words, functioning as an index to part 2, a series of word histories. 'Hispanic' means that the dictionary aims to cover Catalan and Portuguese as well as Spanish.

1467.

Joan Corominas, *Diccionario crítico etimológico castellano e hispánico*.
Madrid: Gredos, 1980–91. 6 vols. New edn. 84–249–1362–0.

With the assistance of José A. Pascual. *Biblioteca románica hispánica, V: diccionarios*, 7.
1st edn: Juan Corominas: *Diccionario crítico etimológico de la lengua castellana*. Bern: Francke, 1954–7. Also published: Madrid: Gredos, 1954–7. 4 vols. (*Biblioteca románica hispánica, V: diccionarios etimológicos.*) – See the long reviews by Joseph E. Gillet in *Hispanic review* vol. 26 (1958) pp. 261–95, and by Leo Spitzer in *Modern language notes* vol. 71–4 (1956–9). 'Overextended and slightly verbose' (Malkiel, **9**, repetitively). Abridged version: Juan Corominas: *Breve diccionario etimológico de la lengua castellana*. 1974. 3rd edn. (*Biblioteca románica hispánica, V: diccionarios, 2.*) – 1st edn: 1961. 2nd edn: 1967.

[*Critical Castilian and Spanish etymological dictionary.*] This extensive work is important not only for Spanish but also for Portuguese, Catalan, Galician and other Romance languages too, being the fullest complete etymological dictionary that exists for any of them. Very important and useful index of cited forms, all languages in one alphabet, vol. 6 pp. 149–1047. The first edition had separate language indexes, particularly copious for Catalan and Portuguese.

The abridged edition gives datings and brief word histories with Romance cognates. It is generous in cross-references for derived forms.

Other works of interest

1468.

L. F. Lara, R. H. Chande, 'Base estadística del Diccionario del Español de México' in *Nueva revista de filología hispánica* vol. 23 (1974) p. 260ff.

1469.

Yakov Malkiel, 'Distinctive features in lexicography: a typological approach to dictionaries, exemplified with Spanish' in *Romance philology* vol. 12 (1959) pp. 366–99 and vol. 13 pp. 111–55.

1470.

Elizabeth Miller, 'Five English–Spanish/Spanish–English dictionaries' in *Reference services review* (Summer 1983) pp. 35–8.

1471.

Homero Serís, *Bibliografía de la lingüística española*. Bogotá, 1964. 981 pp.
Publicaciones del Instituto Caro y Cuervo, 19.

1472.

Reinhold Werner, 'Neuere Wörterbücher des Spanischen in Amerika: was ist neu an ihnen?' in *Lebende Sprachen* vol. 41 no. 3 (1996) pp. 98–112.

SUMERIAN

An extinct language of Iraq, and one of the two oldest of all languages of which records exist (the other being Egyptian). Sumerian ceased to be spoken well over two thousand years ago, and has no known relatives.

1473.

Hermann Behrens, *Glossar zu den altsumerischen Bau- und Weihinschriften*. Wiesbaden: Steiner, 1983. 424 pp.
Freiburger altorientalische Studien, 6.
   [*Glossary of the old Sumerian building and dedication inscriptions.*]

1474.

Anton Deimel, editor, *Šumerisches Lexikon*. Rome: Pontificium Institutum Biblicum, 1927–50. 4 parts in 8 vols.
1. Teil: P. Deimel, P. Gössmann, *Šumerische, akkadische und hethitische Lautwerte nach Keilschriftzeichen und Alphabet*. 1947. 194 + 46* pp. 3rd edn. The second pagination is an alphabetical index of transliterated forms. – 1st edn [issued as Heft 1]: P. Deimel, *Vollständiges Syllabar (S⁴) mit dem wichtigsten Zeichenformen*. 1925. 184 pp.
2. Teil [issued as Heft 2–17]: *Vollständige Ideogramm-Sammlung*. 1927–33. 4 vols [1144 pp.]. This is the main dictionary, following the order of signs already set out in Teil 1, with references to source texts. Supplement, pp. 1116–44.
3. Teil, vol. 1: A. Deimel, *Šumerisch–Akkadisches Glossar*. 1934. 212 pp.
3. Teil, vol. 2: A. Deimel, *Akkadisch–Šumerisches Glossar*. 1937. 480 pp. Includes German glosses for each word, and multiple Sumerian equivalents where available.
4. Teil: A. Deimel, editor, *Pantheon babylonicum oder Keischriftkatalog der babyl. Gn*. 1950. 226 pp. A list of divine names, in transliteration, in character order. German/Latin index of star and constellation names, pp. 222–6.
Note also: Anton Deimel, *Šumerische Grammatik*. Rome: Verlag des Päpstl. Bibelinstituts, 1939. 284 + 16* + (120) pp. The last pagination is a glossary, in essence an abridgment of part 1 and part 3 vol. 2 of the *Lexikon*.

   [*Sumerian dictionary*.] The whole work is reproduced from Deimel's careful calligraphy. In part 2 his German handwriting, though pretty, is not easy on the modern eye.

1475.

Barbara Hübner, Albert Reizammer, *Inim Kiengi I: deutsch–sumerisches Glossar*. Marktredwitz: Reizammer, 1993– . 'Enlarged edition.'
1st edn: *Inim Kiengi: deutsch–sumerisches Glossar*. 1984. 280 pp.

[*German–Sumerian glossary.*] In three columns, in dreadful typescript. The third column gives references to scholarly literature, numbered. These numbers key to the table of reference numbers at the front of each volume. The enlarged edition is to be in three volumes: I have not seen the third.

1476.

Barbara Hübner, Albert Reizammer, *Inim Kiengi II: sumerisch–deutsches Glossar*. Marktredwitz: Reizammer, 1985–6. 2 vols [1229 pp.]

[*Sumerian–German glossary.*] Reproduced from typescript.

1477.

Ake W. Sjöberg, *The Sumerian dictionary of the University Museum of the University of Pennsylvania*. Philadelphia, 1984– .
See review articles by Joachim Krecher in *Zeitschrift für Assyriologie* vol. 73 (1988) pp. 241–75; by Piotr Steinkeller in *Journal of Near Eastern studies* vol. 46 (1987) pp. 55–9.

Vol. 2 has appeared.

SUNDANESE

An AUSTRONESIAN language of the island of Sunda in Indonesia. There are 27 million speakers. The language was formerly written in kawi (Javanese) script, but Latin is now used.

1478.

F. S. Eringa, *Soendaas–Nederlands woordenboek*. Dordrecht: Foris, 1984. 846 pp. 90–6765–056–0.
Edited in collaboration with A. A. Fokker. Koninklijk Instituut voor Taal-, Land- en Volkenkunde.

[*Sundanese–Dutch dictionary.*] Based on a manuscript by R. A. Kern, begun before 1950. The Sundanese is in Latin script.

1479.

Kamus umum basa Sunda. Bandung: Tarate, 1975. 568 pp.

[*Popular dictionary of Sundanese.*] A monolingual dictionary with about 17,000 entries. The fourth printing, 1985, contains a 7–page addendum.

1480.

H. J. Oosting, *Nederduitsch–Soendasch woordenboek*. Amsterdam: Müller, 1887. 390 pp.

[*Dutch–Sundanese dictionary.*]

1481.

H. J. Oosting, *Soendasch–Nederduitsch woordenboek*. Batavia: Ogilvie, 1879. 874 pp.

Followed by: *Supplement*. Amsterdam: Muller, 1882. 206 + xxi pp.

[*Sundanese–Dutch dictionary.*] Headwords and examples are in kawi script throughout, with no transliteration.

SWAHILI

One of the Bantu languages of the NIGER-CONGO family, and strongly influenced by Arabic, Swahili is probably the most widely spoken indigenous African language. Swahili is an official or national language of Tanzania, Kenya and Uganda. It has perhaps only four million speakers as a first language, but many millions more use it as a second or third language.

On the way that Swahili dictionaries deal with derivatives, compounds and prefixes, a fundamental issue, see Bwenge's paper (**1488**), with its comments on Madan's, Johnson's and Rechenbach's Swahili–English dictionaries.

1482.

Frederick Johnson, editor, *A standard English–Swahili dictionary, founded on Madan's English–Swahili dictionary*. Oxford: Oxford University Press, 1939. 635 pp.

By the Inter-Territorial Language Committee of the East African Dependencies.

Preceding work: A. C. Madan, *English–Swahili dictionary*. Oxford: Clarendon Press, 1894. 415 pp. – 2nd edn: 1902. 462 pp.

A concise bilingual dictionary with room for variant forms and for example phrases.

1483.

Frederick Johnson, editor, *A standard Swahili–English dictionary, founded on Madan's Swahili–English dictionary*. Oxford: Oxford University Press, 1939. 548 pp. [0–19–864403–5.]

By the Inter-Territorial Language Committee for the East African Dependencies.

Preceding work: A. C. Madan, *Swahili–English dictionary*. Oxford: Clarendon Press, 1903. 442 pp.

The brief etymological notes often cite the original Arabic forms of loanwords.

1484.

Jan Knappert, *Proverbs from the Lamu Archipelago and the central Kenya coast*. Berlin: Reimer, 1986. 127 pp. 3–496–00839–3.

Language and dialect atlas of Kenya, supplement 6.

1485.

Charles W. Rechenbach, *Swahili–English dictionary*. Washington: Catholic University of America Press, 1967. 641 pp.

Assisted by Angelica Wanjinu Gesuga and others.

A brief-entry bilingual dictionary.

1486.

Ch. Sacleux, *Dictionnaire swahili–français*. Paris: Institut d'Ethnologie, 1939. 1114 pp.

[*Swahili–French dictionary.*] A discursive dictionary with some historical and etymological information, especially for Arabic loanwords. 'Although the official dialect, the ki-Ungudya of Zanzibar, has taken precedence in the layout of articles, each dialect has been given its place in the alphabetical order.' There is indeed detailed information on dialect variation (survey of dialects, pp. 7–14). Some quotations, especially of verse and of proverbs and sayings: quotations are given in Swahili and French.

1487.

TUKI English–Swahili dictionary. Dar es Salaam: Institute of Kiswahili Research, University of Dar es Salaam, 1996. 883 pp.

A concise dictionary intended for Swahili-speaking users, claiming more than 50,000 entries. TUKI is the Institute's Swahili name, Taasisi ya Uchungusi wa Kiswahili.

Other works of interest

1488.

Charles Bwenge, 'Lexicographical treatment of affixational morphology: a case study of four Swahili dictionaries' in Gregory James, editor, *Lexicographers and their works* (Exeter: University of Exeter, 1989) pp. 5–17.

SWEDISH

One of the Scandinavian languages, and thus a GERMANIC language and a member of the Indo-European family. Swedish, the national language of Sweden, has nine million speakers.

Sigurd (**1502**) provides a survey of Swedish dictionaries.

Historical dictionaries

1489.

Ordbok öfver svenska språket utgifven af Svenska Akademien. Lund: Gleerup, 1893– .

Accompanied by: *Källförtecking: supplement*. Lund: Lindstedt, 1975. 206 columns. New edn. – Earlier edn: 1939. 296 columns.

Note also: Carl-Erik Lundbladh, *Handledning till Svenska Akademiens ordbok*. Stockholm: Norstedts, 1992. 94 pp. 91–1–915681–2. [*Guide to the Swedish Academy's dictionary.*] – S. Ekbo, 'Reflections on some kinds of information given in historical dictionaries' in W. Pijnenburg, F. de Tollenaere, editors, *Proceedings of the Second International Round Table Conference on Historical Lexicography* (Dordrecht: Foris, 1980) pp. 303–19.

A large-scale historical dictionary, often known as *SAOB* ('Svenska Akademiens ordbok'). Later volumes are much more hospitable, with a larger number both of quotations and of citations, all of which are dated. Swedish is fertile in compounds: all recorded compounds are listed (filed at the first element, with cross-references at the second element) and all get at least one citation, but few quotations are wasted on the more specialised compounds.

The supplement contains a list of abbreviations and a bibliography of source texts.

The modern standard

1490.

Olof Östergren, *Nusvensk ordbok*. Stockholm: Wahlström & Widstrand, 1915–72. 10 vols [127 parts].

[*Modern Swedish dictionary.*] A very large-scale dictionary of the modern literary language, supported by numerous brief quotations which are attributed to named authors, and sometimes dated, but without precise references. List of sources, vol. 10 columns 715–886; guide to the dictionary, with a brief history, columns 887–902.

1491.

Stora engelsk–svenska ordboken = A comprehensive English–Swedish dictionary. [Stockholm:] Esselte Studium, 1980. 1071 pp. 91–24–29824–7.
Edited by Rudolph Santesson, Bo Svensén, Vincent Petti and others.

A large-scale brief-entry dictionary.

1492.

Stora svensk–engelska ordboken = A comprehensive Swedish–English dictionary. [Stockholm:] Esselte Studium, 1988. 1111 pp. 91–24–33425–1.
Edited by Vincent Petti.

A large-scale brief-entry dictionary.

Older periods

1493.

F. A. Dahlgren, *Glossarium öfver föråldrade eller ovanliga ord och talesätt i svenska språket från och med 1500–talets andra årtionde*. Lund: Gleerup, 1914–16. 1044 pp.
Preface by Evald Ljunggren. Reprinted 1961.

[*Glossary of old and rare words and expressions in the Swedish language.*] A concise dictionary in which most entries are supported by quotations from literature. List of sources, pp. xi–xxiii.

1494.

K. F. Söderwall, *Ordbok öfver svenska medeltids-språket*. Lund: Berling, 1884–1918. 2 vols in 3.
K. F. Söderwall, K. G. Ljunggren, E. Wessén: *Supplement*. 1925–73. 2 vols [35 parts; 1149 pp.].

[*Dictionary of the medieval Swedish language.*] A concise historical dictionary with numerous lengthy quotations from medieval literature. List of abbreviations inside cover of each unbound issue. Corrections and additions, vol. 2 pp. 1187–1341, with a second list on pp. 1342–7.

Regional forms

Finland and Estonia

1495.

Olav Ahlbäck, [Peter Slotte,] *Ordbok över Finlands svenska folkmål.* Helsingfors: Forskningscentralen för de Inhemska Språken, 1976– . 951-46-2345-2.

[*Dictionary of the Swedish dialects of Finland.*] A dictionary based on oral collections. Headwords are in standard Swedish, with pronunciations and examples usually given in a phonetic script. So far two volumes have appeared, covering **A–Hux flux**.

1496.

Hermann Vendell, *Ordbok över de östsvenska dialekterna.* Helsinki, 1904–7.

[*Dictionary of the East Swedish dialects.*] Covers the Swedish dialects of Finland and also Estonia, where the language is now no longer spoken.

Sweden

1497.

Lars Levander, Stig Björklund, [Kristina Hagren,] *Ordbok över folkmålen i övre Dalarna = Dictionary of dialects of Upper Dalecarlia.* Stockholm: Almqvist & Wiksell, 1961– .

Skrifter utgivna genom Dialekt- och Folkminnesarkivet i Uppsala, ser. D, 1.

A dictionary of a group of dialects of central Sweden that show many archaic features. The work is based mainly on oral collections by Levander and others. A phonetic script is used (concordance with the International Phonetic Alphabet, vol. 1 pp. 20–21). Abbreviations, vol. 1 pp. 22–6. Headwords are in standard Swedish; glosses in both Swedish and English.

The dictionary is planned in five volumes, with illustrations to appear in the last. So far it covers **A–Sno** in 34 published parts.

1498.

Ordbok över Sveriges dialekter. N.p.: Arkivet för Ordbok över Sveriges Dialekter, 1991– .

Editors-in-chief: Vidar Reinhammar, Gunnar Nyström.

[*Dictionary of the dialects of Sweden.*] Based on oral collections. Headwords are in Swedish. The dictionary uses a very complex phonetic alphabet, unexplained here (but luckily Levander provides a table, **1497**, pp. 20-21). Map of local dialects on back cover of part 2.

So far only two parts have appeared, covering **A–Arsa** in 160 pages.

1499.

Johan Ernst Rietz, *Svenskt dialekt-lexikon eller ordbok öfver svenska allmogespråket*. Lund: Gleerup, 1867. 859 pp.

Corrected reissue: 1877.

Erik Abrahamson, *Svenskt dialekt-lexikon eller ordbok öfver svenska allmogespråket, III: register och rättelser*. Uppsala: Lundequist, 1955. 380 pp.

[*Swedish dialect lexicon or dictionary of the Swedish colloquial.*] A very concise dictionary of colloquial and dialect Swedish as recorded in written literature. Some references to sources: abbreviations for these, pp. x–xvi.

Abrahamson's *Register och rättelser* [*Index and corrections*] is labelled vol. 3, though it does not appear from the copies I have seen that the original work was intended to be in two volumes. It consists mainly of a modern Swedish index of meanings, with some additions and corrections to the original entries interfiled.

Etymological dictionaries

1500.

Elof Hellqvist, *Svensk etymologisk ordbok*. Lund: Gleerup, 1935–9. 2 vols [1484 pp.] 2nd edn.

1st edn: 1920–22. – The '3rd edn', 1948, is a reprint of the second.

[*Swedish etymological dictionary.*] Abbreviations, pp. 1474–84.

1501.

Einar Odhner, *Etymologisk ordlista: våra ords ursprung och betydelse*. Stockholm: Liber, 1967. Revised edn.

First published as: *Vad betyder orden? etymologisk ordlista*. 1952.

[*Etymological dictionary: every word's origin and meaning.*] Not seen.

Other works of interest

1502.

B. Sigurd, *Svenska ordböcker*. Lund: Liber, 1981.

1st edn: 1968.

SYRIAC

Syriac is the name used for the forms of classical and medieval ARAMAIC that were written in the distinctive Syriac script, shown here in its slightly different eastern and western forms.

The Syriac alphabet

ܐ ܒ ܓ ܕ ܗ ܘ ܙ ܚ ܛ ܝ ܟ ܠ ܡ ܢ ܣ ܥ ܦ ܨ ܩ ܪ ܫ ܬ

’ b g d h w z ḥ ṭ y k l m n s ‘ p ṣ q r š t

ܬ ܫ ܪ ܩ ܨ ܦ ܥ ܣ ܢ ܡ ܠ ܟ ܝ ܛ ܚ ܙ ܘ ܗ ܕ ܓ ܒ ܐ

1503.

Louis Costaz, *Dictionnaire syriaque–français = Syriac–English dictionary = Qamus Siryani `Arabi*. Beyrouth: Imprimerie Catholique [1963]. 421 pp.

1504.

E. S. Drower, R. Macuch, *A Mandaic dictionary*. Oxford: Clarendon Press, 1963. 491 pp.

Deals with both the medieval and the modern forms of this Aramaic language of southern Iraq. 'A palaeolithic ancestor, asked why he had made a stone axe, might have replied that he had often wanted such an implement, and our dictionary has grown out of our needs in much the same casual way.' Headwords are in Latin transliteration, but arranged in the Mandaic alphabetical order of consonants. Basic verbs, entered under triliteral root forms, are interfiled with the rest: at these root entries, brief sub-entries or cross-references are given to the derived forms, for which full entries appear in alphabetical order. The headwords are followed by cognates in classical Syriac, Hebrew, Arabic, Akkadian, Greek, etc., as appropriate. Quotations are in Latin transliteration, with English translations and usually (but not always – see p. v) precise references.

Macuch also published a *Handbook of classical and modern Mandaic* (Berlin, 1965).

1505.

R. Payne Smith, editor, *Thesaurus Syriacus*. Oxford: e typographeo Clarendoniano, 1868–1901. 2 vols [10 parts in 11; 4516 columns].

Includes materials collected by S. M. Quatremère, G. H. Bernstein and others.

J. P. Margoliouth, *Supplement to the Thesaurus Syriacus of R. Payne Smith, S. T. P.* Oxford: Clarendon Press, 1927. 345 pp. Margoliouth, Smith's daughter, based this supplement partly on her father's notes. Abbreviations of source titles, pp. ix–xvii.

Abridged edn: Jessie Payne Smith (Mrs Margoliouth), editor, *A compendious Syriac dictionary: founded upon the Thesaurus Syriacus of Robert Payne Smith*. Oxford: Clarendon Press, 1896–1903. 626 pp.

A large-scale Syriac–Latin dictionary of classical Syriac, with generous citations and quotations, many but not all accompanied by Latin translations. Uses Syriac script. Full discussion of meanings, in Latin, but no etymologies except that the source of Greek and Latin loanwords in indicated. Many of the texts excerpted are Biblical and theological translations from Greek. Abbreviations of source titles, vol. 1 pp. iii–v.

The abridged edition has no citations, but may be useful sometimes as it is in simple alphabetical order.

TAGALOG

Tagalog is the AUSTRONESIAN language that has become the national language of the Philippines. It has about 11 million speakers as a first language, and is used by many millions more. The names Pilipino and Filipino have been used for Tagalog in its national role.

The modern standard

1506.

Leo James English, *Tagalog–English dictionary*. Manila: Congregation of the Most Holy Redeemer, 1986. 1583 pp. 971–91055–0–X.

10th printing: Metro Manila: National Book Store, 1995. 971–08–4357–5.

A comprehensive modern dictionary with numerous phrases and example sentences. The origin of loanwords is indicated. English loanwords are given in Tagalog spellings in the main alphabet, with the English spellings (which are often used in Tagalog) in an initial appendix.

1507.

Leo James English, *English–Tagalog dictionary*. Manila: National Book Store, 1977.

1st edn: Manila: Department of Education, 1965. 1211 pp.

Many example phrases.

1508.

José Villa Panganiban, *Diksyunaryo-tesauro Pilipino–Ingles*. Quezon City: Manlapaz, 1973. 1027 pp.

[*Pilipino–English dictionary-thesaurus.*] A remarkably hospitable and endlessly enjoyable work offering not only English glosses but also synonyms in other Philippine languages; sub-entries for phrases and compound words. Notes on origin of loanwords. 'Begun as a curiosity venture in 1935 by studying the *Artes y reglas* and *Vocabularios* on different Philippine ethnic groups written by Spanish missionaries.'

1509.

Jose Villa Panganiban, *Tesauro diksiyunaryo ingles–pilipino*. San Juan Rizal, 1966. 1363 pp.

[*English–Pilipino dictionary-thesaurus.*] An enormous roneoed volume, with over 25,000 entries.

1510.

Vito C. Santos, *Vicassan's Pilipino–English dictionary*. Manila: National Book Store, 1983. 2675 pp.

Vicassan is the author's 'popular name'. This dictionary tends to give prefixed forms a separate entry, and thus is simpler in use than Panganiban's *Diksyunaryo-tesauro Pilipino–Ingles* (above) which groups them under base forms.

1511.
Vito C. Santos, Luningning E. Santos, *New Vicassan's English–Pilipino dictionary*. Pasig, Metro Manila: Anvil Publishing, 1995. 1603 pp. 971–27–0349–5.

The English is that of the Philippines, sometimes appreciably different from other standards, e.g. *he bared his intention to run for reelection*. This is by far the best available dictionary into Tagalog.

Etymological dictionaries

1512.
R. David Zorc, *Core etymological dictionary of Filipino*. Manila, 1979.
Linguistic Society of the Philippines. *Publications*, 12–14.

TAI LANGUAGES

This language family of south east Asia was once thought to be a branch of the Sino-Tibetan languages. It now seems more likely that Tai languages belong to the AUSTRO-TAI family first proposed by Paul Benedict.

Tai languages with separate entries in this book are: AHOM, LANNA (with Khün and Lü), LAO, SHAN, THAI.

Somewhat distinct from all these, though still unmistakably related, are the Kam-Sui Languages of southern China: see **1514** for these.

1513.
Fang Kuei Li, *A handbook of comparative Tai*. Honolulu: University Press of Hawaii, 1977.

1514.
Fang-Kuei Li, 'The Tai and the Kam-Sui languages' in *Lingua* vol. 14 (1965) pp. 148–79.

A short comparative vocabulary (325 entries) of three Sui dialects, Mak and T'en.

TAMIL

Tamil is the DRAVIDIAN language of the Indian state of Tamilnadu, also spoken by an important minority in Sri Lanka and by a diaspora community whose largest communities are in Malaysia, Singapore and Vietnam. There are 52 million speakers in total.

It is written in its own script, which (unlike other Indic scripts) cannot be used for writing Sanskrit.

The Tamil alphabet

அ ஆ இ ஈ உ ஊ எ ஏ ஐ ஒ ஓ ஔ   க ங ச ஞ ட ண த ந ப ம ய ர ல வ ழ ள ற ன

a ā i ī u ū e ē ai o ō au   k ṅ c ñ ṭ ṇ t n p m y r l v ẓ ḷ r ṉ

BASED ON A FONT BY VIJAY K. PATEL

1515.

A. Chidambaranatha Chettiar, *English–Tamil dictionary*. Madras: University of Madras, 1963–5.

1516.

Louis Marie Mousset, Louis Savinien Dupuis, *Dictionnaire tamoul–français*. Pondichéry, 1938–41. 2 vols. 3rd edn.

1st edn: 1855–62. – 2nd edn: 1895. – Reprint of 2nd edn: New Delhi: Asian Educational Services, 1981.

[*Tamil–French dictionary*.]

1517.

Tamil lexicon. Madras: Diocesan Press, 1924–36. 6 vols [3944 pp.].

Followed by: *Supplement*. 1938–9. 3 parts [423 pp.].

Published under the authority of the University of Madras.

On this dictionary, its predecessors, and the need for further work see S. Agesthialingom, N. Kumaraswami Raja, 'Dictionary making in the Tamil region' in Misra (**10**).

A concise historical dictionary. Headwords are in Tamil and Latin scripts followed by brief etymology. Glosses in English and Tamil, with, in most cases, one or more precise references to literary sources, sometimes with a quotation.

Preliminaries, pp. i–cv, were included with vol. 6 part 5. They include a history of the dictionary and a survey of earlier Tamil lexicography, pp. xxv–xliii; the plan of the dictionary; general abbreviations, pp. lxi–lxiii; abbreviations for scholarly literature, pp. lxiv–lxvi; list of sources with abbreviations, pp. lxix–cv.

Other works of interest

1518.

Ayyadurai Dhamotharan, *Tamil dictionaries: a bibliography*. Wiesbaden: Steiner, 1978. 185 pp. 3–515–03005–0.

Beiträge zur Südasienforschung, 50.

1519.

Gregory James, 'Landmarks in the development of modern Tamil lexicography' in Gregory James, editor, *Lexicographers and their works* (Exeter: University of Exeter, 1989) pp. 117–48.

TANGUT

Tangut or Hsihsia is an extinct language of the SINO-TIBETAN family.

The Hsihsia kingdom was founded in AD 990 on the great bend of the Yellow River just south of the Ordos Desert. A unique script was devised for its language in 1037. 'It is perhaps the most complicated system ever invented by a human mind ... Only a small fraction of characters has been read; of others, the meaning only is known, but not the phonetic value' (Laufer, **1521**). Genghis Khan died in 1226/7 while besieging the Hsihsia capital. In his memory, his son Kublai massacred the Hsihsia, and the language became extinct.

1520.

Luc Kwanten, editor, *The timely pearl: a 12th century Tangut–Chinese glossary*. Bloomington: Research Institute for Asian Studies, Indiana University, 1982. Vol. 1 [265 pp.]. 0–933070–10–1.
Indiana University Uralic and Altaic series, 142.

Vol. 1 deals with 'the Chinese glosses'.

1521.

Berthold Laufer, 'The Si-hia language' in *T'oung pao* vol. 17 (1916) pp. 1–126.

'Laufer numbers and analyses over 200 words, with comparisons in a vast number of languages; and concludes that the language undoubtedly belongs to the Tibeto-Burman sub-family' (Luce, **1397**, p. 99).

1522.

N. A. Nevskii, *Tangutskaya filologiya: issledovaniya i slovar'*. Moscow: Izdatel'stvo Vostochnoi Literatury, 1960. 2 vols.

[*Tangut philology: a study and dictionary.*] Not seen.

TASMANIAN LANGUAGES

All too little is known of the Tasmanian languages, whose speakers were exterminated by European colonists in the course of the nineteenth century. They are not known to be related to Australian or to any other languages: see, however, the study by Greenberg (**1185**).

1523.

N. J. B. Plomley, *A word-list of the Tasmanian aboriginal languages*. Hobart, 1976. 486 pp.

A full compilation of available information on Tasmanian language vocabularies.

1524.

W. Schmidt, *Die tasmanischen Sprachen*. Utrecht: Spectrum, 1952.

[The Tasmanian languages.] On pp. 227–460 a reproduction of the word-lists compiled in the nineteenth century, in a single connected sequence under German terms or concepts, with sources indicated. Schmidt deduces five dialects: north-east, mid-east, south-east form one group; west and north form another. Not all linguists agree with this grouping.

TATAR

A TURKIC language of Russia, with six million speakers.

Tatar alphabetical order

а б в г д е ж з и й к л м н о п р с т у ф х ц ч ш щ ъ ы ь э ю я ә ө ү җ ң һ

1525.
Ф. А. Ганиев, *Русско–татарский словарь = Русча–татарча сузлек* [F. A. Ganiev, editor, *Russko–tatarskii slovar'*]. Moscow: Russkii Yazyk, 1984. 740 pp.
  [Tatar–Russian dictionary.] 47,000 entries.

1526.
К. З. Хәмзин, М. И. Мәхмүтов, Г. Ш. Сәйфуллин, *Гарәпчә–татарча–русча алынмалар сузлеге = Арабско–татарско–русский словарь заимствований* [K. Z. Khamzin, M. I. Makhmütov, G. Sh. Saifullin, *Garapcha–tatarcha–ryscha alynmalar süzlege*]. Kazan: Tatarstan, 1965. 854 pp.
  An Arabic–Tatar–Russian dictionary of Arabic loanwords in Tatar literature.

1527.
Татар теленең диалектологик сузлеге = Диалектологический словарь татарского языка [*Tatar teleneng dialektologik süzlege*]. Kazan: Tatarstan, 1969. 643 pp.
  [Dialect dictionary of the Tatar language.] In Tatar, with Russian glosses in brackets.

1528.
Татарско–русский словарь = Татарча–русча сузлек [*Tatarsko–russkii slovar'*]. Moscow: Sovetskaya Entsiklopediya, 1966. 863 pp.
Edited by Golovkina O. V. and others.
  [Tatar–Russian dictionary.] 38,000 entries.

TELUGU

One of the DRAVIDIAN LANGUAGES, Telugu is the state language of Andhra Pradesh and one of the official languages of India. It has 45 million speakers.

A Telugu dialect dictionary (*Māṇḍalika vṛttipadakōśam*) is appearing in subject sections: the first, Agriculture, is by Bhadriraju Krishnamurti.

Telugu script: the consonant characters

కఖగఘ చఛజఝ టఠడఢణ తథదధన పఫబభమ యరలవ శషసహళ

k kh g gh   c ch j jh   ṭ ṭh ḍ ḍh ṇ   t th d dh n   p ph b bh m   y r l v   ś ṣ s h ḷ

Telugu script is very similar to that of Kannada. As with other descendants of the Brahmi script, a consonant is combined with a following vowel in each symbol.

1529.

C. P. Brown, *A dictionary of mixed Telugu*. Madras, 1854. 131 pp.

A dictionary of loanwords from Arabic, English and other non-Indian languages.

1530.

C. P. Brown, *Telugu–English dictionary*. Madras, 1903. 1416 pp. Revised by M. Venkata Ratnam, W. H. Campbell, K. Veeresalingam.

1st edn: C. P. Brown, *A dictionary, Telugu–English*. Madras, 1852. 1303 pp.

A pioneering work, dealing with both classical and spoken Telugu, but flawed by its unusual alphabetical order in which the four stops at each point of articulation (e.g. **k kh g gh**) are interfiled.

1531.

El. Cakradhararavu, chief editor, *Telugu vyutpatti kōśam*. Visakhapattanam: Andhra Yunivarsiti Pressu, 1978–95. 9 vols in 8.

Andhra Yuniversiti siris, 138 [etc.].

[*Telugu etymological dictionary.*] Entirely in Telugu (with taxonomic names in Latin) and one of the best reasons I know for learning Telugu.

1532.

J. P. L. Gwynn, *A Telugu–English dictionary*. Delhi: Oxford University Press, 1991. 569 pp.

Assisted by J. Venkateswara Sastry.

A brief-entry bilingual dictionary of the modern language. Headwords are in Telugu script and the author's non-standard transliteration.

1533.

G. N. Reddy, editor, *English–Telugu dictionary*. Hyderabad: Telugu Akademi, 1978. 1312 pp.

A concise bilingual dictionary with many set phrases and brief examples.

1534.

B. Sitaramacaryulu, *Sabdaratnakaramu*. Madras, 1885. 868 pp.

[*Treasury of words.*] A concise monolingual dictionary with special attention to classical Telugu: quotations from about 100 sources.

THAI

Thai, once better known as Siamese, is the national language of Thailand and the best known of the TAI LANGUAGES. It has perhaps 25 million speakers in central and southern Thailand.

The Thai alphabet

กขฃคฅฆง จฉชซฌญ ฎฏฐฑฒณ ดตถทธน

k kh kh kh kh kh ng　c ch ch s ch y　d t th th th n　d t th th th n

บปผฝพฟภม ยรฤลฦว ศษสหฬอฮ

b p ph f ph f ph m　y r rl r w　s s h l a h

Many of the above consonant symbols appear to duplicate one another: they are used for borrowed Pali and Sanskrit words, and to help in representing tone distinctions.

There are 25 vowel signs. To exemplify them, all 25 are written here in conjunction with the consonant ก k. One has to be able to recognise the vowel signs that are placed to the left of the relevant consonant, since they are counted after the consonant in determining alphabetical order.

กะ กิ กึ กุ เกะ แกะ โกะ เกาะ เกอะ กำ ใก ไก เกา กา กี กี กู เก แก โก กอ กัว เกีย เกือ เกอ

1535.

Mary R. Haas, *Thai–English student's dictionary*. Stanford: Stanford University Press, 1964. 638 pp. 0–8047–0567–4.

Clear printing from typescript: about 12,000 entries, covering the modern spoken and written language. Adopts the spelling of the Royal Institute dictionary, **1539**, and adds phonetic transcriptions. Includes place names and abbreviations. Preliminaries: alphabetical order, p. x; Brief description of Thai, pp. xi–xxii.

1536.

George Bradley McFarland, *Thai–English dictionary*. Bangkok, 1941. 1019 + 39 pp.

Reprinted: Stanford: Stanford University Press, 1944 (the so-called 'second edition'); and later reprints.

About 20,000 entries, with examples. Published after its author's death and, no doubt for this reason, open to criticism for some inaccuracies. The glosses for Sankrit and Pali loanwords are said to be unreliable, while the phonetic transcriptions, given after each headword, are imperfect, as is indicated in the foreword to the Stanford reprints.

Appendices (39 pp.): the thousand commonest Thai words; scientific Latin–Thai glossaries of names of birds, fishes, flora, shells, snakes.

1537.

มานิตมานิตเจริญ *พจนานุกรมไทย*. [Manit Manitcharoen, *Photchananukrom Thai*.] Bangkok: Eksilapakan, 2514 [1971]. 1600 pp.

Cover title in English: *The most up-to-date Thai dictionary.*

1st edn: 1961. 2nd edn: 1964. 1571 pp.

[*Thai dictionary.*] Third edition of a medium-sized monolingual dictionary, a work much indebted to the Royal Institute dictionary (**1539**) but including many additional technical terms and foreign loanwords. Scientific Latin, and sometimes English, glosses are added in defining technical terms.

1538.

D. J. B. Pallegoix, *Dictionnaire siamois français anglais* = *Siamese French English dictionary*. Bangkok: Catholic Mission, 1896. 1165 pp. Revised by J. L. Vey.

1st edn: D. J. B. Pallegoix, *Dictionarium linguae thai sive siamensis, interpretatione latina, gallica et anglica illustratum.* Paris: in Typographeo Imperatorio, 1854. 897 pp. – Reprint of the 1st edn: Farnborough: Gregg, 1972. 0–576–03340–5.

[*Thai–French–English dictionary.*] In four columns, the second giving romanized Thai with tone markings. Grammatical introduction, in French, English and Thai, on preliminary pages 1–69. The first edition had a fifth column giving Latin glosses.

1539.

พจนานุกรมฉบับราชบัณฑิตยสถาน. [*Photchananukrom chabap Ratchabandit Sathan.*] Bangkok: Ratchabandit Sathan, 2525 [1982]. 996 pp. New edn. 974–8122–69–7.

Frequently reprinted.

1st edn: 2493 [1950]. 1053 pp.

[*Royal Institute dictionary.*] A monolingual Thai dictionary initially compiled over the period 1932–50. It aimed to prescribe a standard spelling (and the result is indeed generally accepted as the official standard) but to describe historical and existing usage as to pronunciation and meaning. Additionally, the pronunciation of each word is given in a phonologically normalised Thai script. Includes scientific Latin glosses for botanical and zoological terms.

1540.

So. Sethaputra, *New model English–Thai dictionary*. Bangkok: So. Sethaputra, 1961. 2 vols [1598 pp.]. 3rd edn.

1st edn: 1940. 2nd edn: 1952. 1722 + 129 pp.

A concise bilingual dictionary, principally for Thai users, with many examples.

1541.

So. Sethaputra, *New model Thai–English dictionary*. Bangkok: Thai Watana Panich, 1972. 2 vols [1072 pp.]. 2nd edn.

1st edn: 1965.

Notable (like its widely-distributed abridged relatives) for very clear discursive explanations of usage. About 12,000 entries, with many examples.

TIBETAN

One of the SINO-TIBETAN LANGUAGES, Tibetan has about seven million speakers in Tibet and adjacent Chinese provinces, in Bhutan, India and Nepal. It is one of the classical languages of Buddhism.

The Tibetan script

ཀ ཁ ག ང ཅ ཆ ཇ ཉ ཏ ཐ ད ན པ ཕ བ མ ཙ ཚ ཛ ཝ ཤ ཟ འ ཡ ར ལ ཤ ས ཧ

k kh g ng c ch j ny t th d n p ph b m ts tsh dz w sh z ' y r l ś s h a

Tibetan script is a descendant of the Brahmi script of ancient India. As in others, consonants are combined with a following vowel to make a single character. The five vowel signs are shown here with the character ཨ a:

ཨ ཨི ཨུ ཨེ ཨོ

a   i   u   e   o

The modern standard

1542.

Stuart Buck, *Tibetan–English dictionary with supplement.* Washington: Catholic University of America Press, 1969. 833 pp.

Note the review by R. A. Miller in *Language* vol. 46 (1970) pp. 975–80.

A dictionary of modern written Tibetan as it appears in Chinese publications.

1543.

Tanpi Gyaltshan Dhongthog, *The new light English–Tibetan dictionary.* Dharmsala: Library of Tibetan Works and Archives, 1973. 523 pp.

A brief-entry dictionary intended for Tibetan-speaking users.

1544.

Melvyn C. Goldstein, *English–Tibetan dictionary of modern Tibetan.* Berkeley: University of California Press, 1984. 600 pp. 0–520–06140–3.

1545.

Melvyn C. Goldstein, editor, *Tibetan–English dictionary of modern Tibetan.* Kathmandu: Ratna Pustak Bhandar, 1975. 1234 pp.

Bibliotheca Himalayica, 2nd series, 9.

The '2nd edn' of 1978 (reprinted: New York, 1987) has the same pagination. I have not compared the two.

Older periods

1546.

Sarat Chandra Das, *A Tibetan–English dictionary with Sanskrit synonyms.*
Alipore: West Bengal Government Press, 1902. 1353 pp.

Revised by Graham Sandberg and A. William Heyde.
Many reprints in India and Japan.

Tibetan entries, and sub-entries for compound words, are given both in script and in transliteration; example phrases are in script only, and are not translated. Aims to deal with both classical and nineteenth century literary Tibetan. Sanskrit equivalents are often given for religious and philosophical terms. Authors and works are sometimes cited (abbreviations, pp. xxvii–xxxii), but there are few precise references to texts. This is the best available dictionary for the reader of Tibetan literature.

Classical Tibetan

1547.

Alexander Csoma de Körös, *Essay towards a dictionary, Tibetan and English.*
Calcutta, 1834.

Revised German version: Isaac Jacob Schmidt, *Tibetisch–deutsches Wörterbuch, nebst deutschem Wortregister.* St Petersburg, 1841. 784 pp. [*Tibetan–German dictionary with a German index.*]
For those who can read it, the following, entirely in Tibetan, is a facsimile publication of Csoma's sources for some technical terminology: *Tibetan compendia written for Csoma de Koros by the lamas of Zans-dkar. Manuscripts in the Library of the Hungarian Academy of Sciences*, ed. J. Terjek. New Delhi: Mrs Sharada Rani, 1976. 373 columns. Sata-pitaka series, 231. Texts deal with logic, Buddhism, medicine, chronology, astronomy, grammar, metrics, dramaturgy, lexicography and poetics.

1548.

Auguste Desgodins, *Dictionnaire thibétain–latin–français.* Hong Kong, 1899.
1091 pp.

1549.

Lokesh Chandra, *Tibetan–Sanskrit dictionary, based on a close comparative study of Sanskrit originals and Tibetan translations of several texts.* New Delhi: International Institute of Indian Culture, 1958–61. 12 vols.

Sata-pitaka series, 3. *Bhota-pitaka*, 1.
See reviews by J. W. de Jong in *Indo-Iranian journal* vol. 4 (1960) pp. 73–4; by C. Vogel in *Indo-Iranian journal* vol. 14 (1972) p. 206.

Nineteenth century

1550.

H. A. Jäschke, *A Tibetan–English dictionary with special reference to the prevailing dialects, to which is added an English–Tibetan vocabulary.* London: Trübner, 1881. 671 pp.

Reprints include: London: Routledge, 1990. 0–415–05897–X.

'A new and thoroughly revised edition of a Tibetan–German dictionary, which appeared in a lithographed form between the years 1871 and 1876.' Jäschke includes literary as well as colloquial vocabulary, citing Csoma and Schmidt (**1547**) for words he had not encountered himself; but, according to Sarat Chandra Das (**1546**), he was unaware in general of 'modern', i.e. nineteenth century, Tibetan literature. Headwords are in Tibetan script and in transliteration; compounds and phrases are given in transliteration only.

English–Tibetan section, pp. 611–68.

Other works of interest

1551.
W. Simon, 'Tibetan lexicography and etymological research' in *Transactions of the Philological Society* (1964) pp. 85–107.

TIGRE

Tigre is a minority SEMITIC language of northern Ethiopia.

1552.
Enno Littmann, Maria Höfner, *Wörterbuch der Tigre-Sprache: Tigre–Deutsch–Englisch*. Wiesbaden: Steiner, 1956–62.

   [*Dictionary of the Tigre language: Tigre–German–English.*]

TIGRINYA

Tigrinya is one of the SEMITIC LANGUAGES. With about three and a half million speakers, it is the major language of Eritrea. Like AMHARIC, it is normally written in Ethiopic script.

1553.
Dictionary English–Tigrigna–Arabic. Rome: Research and Information Centre on Eritrea, 1985. 718 pp.
Eritrean People's Liberation Front.

   In three columns, in alphabetical order of the English headwords. The Tigrinya and Arabic columns are wider and more detailed and discursive than the English.

TIV

A regional NIGER-CONGO language of Nigeria, Tiv has one and a half million speakers.

1554.
R. C. Abraham, *A dictionary of the Tiv language*. London: Crown Agents for the Colonies, 1940. 331 pp.
Earlier version in R. C. Abraham, *The grammar of Tiv*. Kaduna: Government Printer, 1933. 97 + 213 pp.

Abraham's orthography is much more complex than the standard, which was that of the Dutch Reformed Mission. Words are filed under first consonant (e.g. **akara** under **k**).

TOCHARIAN

Tocharian represents a separate branch of the INDO-EUROPEAN LANGUAGES, once spoken on the Silk Road that linking China with central Asia – thus far to the east of the traditional locations of all the other languages of the family. The language became extinct several hundred years ago, and has been deciphered from texts discovered in the course of the twentieth century. Two very different dialects, 'Tocharian A' and 'Tocharian B', have been distinguished.

1555.
Albert J. van Windekens, *Lexique étymologique des dialectes tokhariens.*
Louvain: Muséon, 1941. 217 pp.
Bibliothèque du Muséon, 11.
[*Etymological dictionary of the Tocharian dialects.*]

TONGAN

An AUSTRONESIAN language, Tongan has 130,000 speakers in the island kingdom of Tonga in the western Pacific.

1556.
C. Maxwell Churchward, *Tongan dictionary (Tongan–English and English–Tongan).* London: Oxford University Press, 1959. 836 pp.
The Tongan–English section is the larger (pp. 1–574). There is a separate appendix listing loanwords. List of sources cited, p. xxv.

TONTEMBOAN

A minority AUSTRONESIAN language of northern Sulawesi.

1557.
J. Alb. T. Schwartz, *Tontemboansch–Nederlandsch woordenboek met Nederlandsch–Tontemboansch register.* The Hague, 1908. 690 pp.
[*Tontemboan Dutch dictionary with Dutch index.*]

TORAJA

An AUSTRONESIAN language of southern Sulawesi, with half a million speakers.

1558.

J. Tammu, H. van der Veen, *Kamus Toradja–Indonesia*. Rantepao: Jajasan Perguruan Kristen Toradja, 1972. 692 pp.

[*Toradja–Bahasa Indonesia dictionary.*] About 10,000 entries. A reworking of van der Veen's material (**1559**).

1559.

H. van der Veen, *Tae' (Zuid-Toradjasch)–Nederlandsch woordenboek met register Nederlandsch–Tae'*. The Hague, 1940. 930 pp.

[*Tae' (South Toradja)–Dutch dictionary with Dutch–Tae' index.*] Includes a short grammatical introduction.

TSWANA

Tswana is a Bantu language (and thus a member of the NIGER-CONGO family) spoken in Botswana and South Africa by four and a half million people.

1560.

Z. I. Matumo, *Setswana English Setswana dictionary*. Gaborone: Macmillan Botswana, 1993. 647 pp. 4th edn.

1st edn: 1875. – 2nd edn: 1895. – 3rd edn: 1925.

1561.

J. W. Snyman, editor, *Dikisinare ya Setswana–English–Afrikaans = Setswana–English–Afrikaans dictionary*. Pretoria: Via Africa, 1990. 527 pp. 0–7994–1218–X.

TURKIC LANGUAGES

The Turkic family includes the following languages that have entries in this book: AZERI, BASHKIR, CHUVASH, KARACHAI-BALKAR, KAZAKH, KHAZAR, KYRGYZ, TATAR, TURKISH, TURKMEN, UIGUR, UZBEK, YAKUT. Gagauz is dealt with in this book at TURKISH. Karakalpak is dealt with at KAZAKH.

Many scholars refer to the whole family of languages, or to most members of it, as 'Turkish' rather than 'Turkic'. In particular, 'Old Turkish' is in effect the ancestral form of most of these languages: in this book pre-thirteenth century Turkish is covered here at 'Turkic languages', not at TURKISH.

For Turkic loanwords in other languages see Miklosich (**18**).

1562.

Gerard Clauson, *An etymological dictionary of pre-thirteenth century Turkish*. Oxford: Clarendon Press, 1972. 989 pp.

An index was published separately: Szeged, 1981. 2 vols [342 + 261 pp.].

Deals with the Turkic vocabulary before the intrusion of great numbers of loanwords from Arabic, Persian and other languages. The early languages or dialects covered are 'Türkü, Uyğur, including Uyğur-A, Old Kırğız, Xākāni, Oğuz, Kipçak' and others. Quotations are given from literature to establish word meanings (source texts, pp. xiii–xxvi). Derivatives and cognates in the modern Turkic languages (see introduction, pp. xxvi–xxix, on these).

The 'alphabetical order' and arrangement are unique: see explanations on pp. x–xii. General abbreviations, pp. xxxiii–xxxviii.

1563.

Древнетюрский словарь [*Drevnetyurskii slovar'*]. Leningrad: Nauka, 1969. 676 pp.

Edited by V. M. Nadelyaev, D. M. Nasilov, E. R. Tenishev, A. M. Shcherbak. Akademiya Nauk SSSR, Institut Yazykoznaniya.

[*Old Turkish dictionary.*] A concise historical dictionary with Russian glosses, covering Turkish dialects from the seventh to the thirteenth century. Headwords are in the Latin alphabet, with some cross-references for variant forms. The headword is followed by etymologies for loanwords, often using Arabic and occasionally Chinese script. Then quotations are given from text sources, often quite lengthy, with precise references (list of sources, pp. xxi–xxxviii) and with Russian translations.

Table of old Turkic alphabets, pp. xv–xviii.

1564.

W. Radloff, *Versuch eines Wörterbuches der Türk-Dialecte*. St Petersburg: Glasunoff, 1888–1911. 4 vols.

A. v. Gabain, W. Veenker, *"Radloff" Index der deutschen Bedeutungen*. Wiesbaden: Otto Harrassowitz, 1969. Vol. 1. (*Veröffentlichungen der Societas Uralo-Altaica*, 1.) [*Index to German meanings in Radloff.*]

[*Preliminary dictionary of the Turkish dialects.*] A fundamental comparative dictionary of Turkic languages. Headwords are in a phonetic script based on Cyrillic, followed in square brackets by notes on dialect origin and the actual forms found if varying. Radloff makes use of numerous scripts, Arabic, Armenian, Mongolian, Hebrew, Syriac and Greek among others, to record these forms. Russian and German glosses are given, with example phrases; textual sources are cited.

Radloff's alphabetical order is extravagantly individual: it starts out conforming to what is set out on p. ii of vol. 1, but soon takes on a life of its own. Fortunately von Gabain and Veenker's index refers to page numbers, not to headwords.

1565.

Martti Räsänen, *Versuch eines etymologischen Wörterbuchs der Türksprachen*. Helsinki: Suomalais-Ugrilainen Seura, 1969–71. 2 vols.

Lexica Societatis Fenno-Ugricae, 17.

[*Towards an etymological dictionary of the Turkic languages.*] Entries are under reconstructed forms if available. Vol. 2 (136 pp.), compiled by István Kecskeméti, consists of word indexes: table of contents for these on last page.

1566.

Е. В. Севортян, *Этимологический словарь тюркских языков* [E. V. Sevortyan, *Etymologicheskii slovar' tyurkskikh yazykov*]. Moscow: Nauka, 1974– .

[*Etymological dictionary of Turkic languages.*] A very full etymological dictionary. Headwords are usually given at a recorded Old Turkish form, in a phonetic script based on Cyrillic. Entries include all variant forms that are recorded, in Turkic and other related and adjacent languages, either in Arabic or Latin script as recorded or in the phonetic script, with citations of textual sources. Then meanings are given in detail. Finally, preceded by ◊, there is a paragraph of etymological discussion, with references to the scholarly literature.

So far four volumes have appeared, the first dealing with the vowels; vols 2 to 4 cover the consonants from *Б* to *Й*.

Other works of interest

1567.

Gyula Moravcsik, *Byzantino–Turcica*. Berlin: Akademie-Verlag, 1958. 2 vols. 2nd edn.

Berliner byzantinische Arbeiten, 10–11. – 1st edn: Budapest, 1942–3.

Vol. 2 pp. 51–350 consists of a dictionary, 'Evidence of Turkic languages in Byzantine sources', with headwords in Greek script. Turkish index, pp. 365–76.

TURKISH

Turkish is the best known of the TURKIC LANGUAGES, with 50 million speakers. It is the national language of Turkey, and it is increasingly influential among the Turkic-speaking states (formerly Soviet republics) of Central Asia.

Pre-thirteenth century Turkish is dealt with in this book under TURKIC LANGUAGES. Note Miklosich (**18**) on Turkish words in European languages.

The Turkish alphabet

By a 1928 decree of Mustafa Kemal Atatürk, Turkish exchanged its old Arabic script for a new Latin alphabet of 29 letters.

A B C Ç D E F G Ğ H I İ J K L M N O Ö P R S Ş T U Ü V Y Z

a b c ç d e f g ğ h ı i j k l m n o ö p r s ş t u ü v y z

Historical dictionaries

1568.

XIII. yüzyıldan beri Türkiye Türkçesiyle yazılmış kitaplardan toplanan tanıklariyle tarama sözlüğü. Ankara: Türk Tarih Kurumu Basimevi, 1963–77. 8 vols.

Editors, Ömer Asim Aksoy, Dehri Dilçin. *Türk Dil Kurumu yayinlari*, 212.

Brief glosses are followed by long quotations from classical Turkish literature of the thirteenth to nineteenth centuries. List of sources, vol. 1 pp. x–lxxxiv; chronology of sources, pp. lxxxv–xci.

The main alphabetical sequence occupies vols 1–6. Vol. 7, *Ekler*, is a dictionary of suffixes. Vol. 8, *Dizin*, is a modern Turkish index of meanings.

The modern standard

1569.

Fahir Iz, H. C. Hony, A. D. Alderson, *The Oxford Turkish dictionary*. Oxford: Oxford University Press, 1992. 526 + 619 pp. 0–19–864190–7.

A reprint of the following two works in one volume:

A. D. Alderson, Fahir Iz, *The Oxford Turkish English dictionary*. Oxford: Clarendon Press, 1984. 526 pp. 3rd edn. 0–19–864124–9. (1st edn: H.C. Hony, Fahir Iz, *A Turkish–English dictionary*, 1947. – 2nd edn: 1957.)

A. D. Alderson, Fahir Iz, *The Oxford English–Turkish dictionary*. 1978. 619 pp. 2nd edn. 0–19–864123–0.

A brief-entry dictionary.

1570.

Karl Steuerwald, *Türkisch–deutsches Wörterbuch = Türkçe–Almanca sözlük*. Wiesbaden: Harrassowitz, 1972. 1057 pp. 3–447–01375–3.

[*Turkish–German dictionary.*] A large-scale brief-entry bilingual dictionary, much better and fuller than any current Turkish–English one.

Older periods

1571.

James W. Redhouse, *A Turkish and English lexicon, shewing in English the signification of the Turkish terms*. Constantinople: Boyajian, 1884–90. 8 parts [2224 pp.].

'Published for the American Mission.'

Headwords are in Arabic script, which was at that time the standard script for Turkish, followed by a Latin transliteration. A brief-entry dictionary rich in the vocabulary of classical Turkish literature.

Regional forms

1572.

G. A. Gaydarci [and others], *Gagauz Türkçesinin sözlügü*. Ankara : Kültür Bakanligi, 1991. 284 pp. 975–17–0840–0.

Kültür Bakanligi yayinlari, 1294. *Türk dünyasi edebiyati dizisi*, 16. Alternate title: *Gagauz sözlügü*.
Earlier version: Г. А. Гаидаржи, *Гагаузско–русско–молдавский словарь = Дикционар гэгэуз–рус–молдовенеск = Гагаузча–русча–молдованжа лафлык* [G. A. Gaidarzhi and others, *Gagauzsko–russko–moldavskii slovar'*]. Moscow: Sovetskaya Entsiklopediya, 1973. 664 pp. Edited by N. A. Baskakov.

[*Dictionary of Gagauz Turkish.*] Gagauz, generally regarded as a separate language, is an offshoot of Turkish spoken in southern Moldova and in smaller enclaves in

Romania and Bulgaria. The original dictionary offered glosses in Russian and Moldavian (Romanian); the new version has glosses in Turkish.

Foreign words

1573.

Robert Dankoff, *Armenian loanwords in Turkish*. Wiesbaden: Harrassowitz, 1995. 217 pp. 3–447–03640–0.

Turcologica, 21.

In alphabetical order under the Armenian original forms, in Armenian script. Turkish index, pp. 195–214. Note on Turkish loanwords in Armenian, pp. 215–7.

1574.

Henry Kahane, Renée Kahane, Andreas Tietze, *The Lingua Franca in the Levant: Turkish nautical terms of Italian and Greek origin*. Urbana: University of Illinois Press, 1958.

These Italian and Greek loanwords in Turkish are seen as evidence of the use of the Lingua Franca, the Romance-based mixed language of the medieval Mediterranean.

1575.

Gustav Meyer, *Türkische Studien, I: Die griechischen und romanischen Bestandteile im Wortschatz des Osmanisch-Türkischen*. Vienna, 1893. 96 pp.

Sitzungsberichte der philosophisch-historischen Klasse der Kaiserlichen Akademie der Wissenschaften, vol. 128 part 1.

[*Turkish studies, 1: the Greek and Romance components of the Osmanli Turkish vocabulary.*] Arranged in semantic groups. Turkish headwords appear in Arabic script, which was at that time the standard script for Turkish, and in Roman transliteration. Addenda, pp. 88–93; bibliography, pp. 94–6.

TURKMEN

The TURKIC LANGUAGE that is the national language of Turkmenistan, once a Soviet republic, now independent. Turkmen has four million speakers.

The Cyrillic alphabet for Turkmen

а б в г д е ё ж җ з и й к л м н ң о ө п р с т у ү ф х ц ч ш щ ъ ы ь э э ю я

1576.

Б. Чарыяров, С. Алтаев, *Большой русско—туркменский словарь* = *Улы русча-түркменче сөзлук* [B. Charyyarov, S. Altaev, *Bol'shoi russko–turkmenskii slovar'*]. Moscow: Russkii Yazyk, 1986–7. 2 vols.

Akademiya Nauk Turkmenskoi SSR, Institut Yazyka i Literatury.

[*Big Russian–Turkmen dictionary.*] 77,000 entries.

1577.

Н. А. Баскаков, Б. А. Каррыев, М. Я. Хамзаев, *Туркменско–русский словарь* = *Туркменче-русча сөзлук* [N. A. Baskakov, B. A. Karryev, M. Ya. Khamzaev, *Turkmensko–russkii slovar'*]. Moscow: Sovetskaya Entsiklopediya, 1968. 832 pp.

[*Turkmen–Russian dictionary.*] 40,000 entries.

UDMURT

Udmurt or Votyak is a URALIC language of Russia, with 550,000 speakers.

Udmurt alphabetical order

а б в г д е ё ж ӝ з ӟ и й й к л м н о ӧ п р с т у ф х ц ч ӵ ш щ ъ ы ь э ю я

1578.

В. И. Алатырев, *Этимологический словарь удмуртского языка: буквы А, Б* [V. I. Alatyrev, *Etimologicheskii slovar' udmurtskogo yazyka: bukvy A, B*]. Izhevsk, 1988. 240 pp.
Edited by V. M. Vakhrushev, S. V. Sokolov.

[*Etymological dictionary of the Udmurt language: letters A and B.*]

1579.

Munkácsi Bernát, editor, *Lexicon linguae Votiacorum* = *A Votják nyelv szótára.* Budapest, 1890–96. 4 parts [836 pp.].

[*Dictionary of the language of the Votyaks.*] Glosses in Hungarian and German. German index, pp. 759–836. For the alphabetical order, which is unique, see p. xv.

1580.

Pirkko Suihkonen, chief editor, *Udmurt–English–Finnish dictionary, with a basic grammar of Udmurt.* Helsinki: Suomalais-Ugrilainen Seura, 1995. 326 pp. 951–9403–79–5.
Bibinur Zagulyayeva and Galina Tronina, co-editors.
Lexica Societatis Fenno-Ugricae, 24.

The dictionary, on pp. 17–264, is in cut-down three-column format. The Udmurt is in a phonetic script. Entries are keyed to the tables of word forms in the grammar, which is on pp. 267–324.

1581.

В. М. Вахрушев, *Удмуртско-русский словарь* = *Удмурт-ӟуч словарь* [V. M. Vakhrushev, editor, *Udmurtsko–russkii slovar'*]. Moscow: Russkii Yazyk, 1983. 590 pp.
Authors, A. S. Belov and others. Nauchno-Issledovatel'skii Institut pri Sovete Ministrov Udmurtskoi ASSR.

[*Udmurt–Russian dictionary.*] A brief-entry bilingual dictionary; about 35,000 entries.

UGARITIC

A SEMITIC language of the second millennium BC, known from clay tablets found in the remains of the city of Ugarit on the Syrian coast. As with other early Semitic languages, the ancient script records consonants only. There is a standard transliteration, and Ugaritic scholars have a standard alphabetical order, too, which is not the one that is familiar to the rest of us:

ʾ b g d ð h w z ḥ ḫ ṭ z y k l m n s ʿ ġ p ṣ q r š t θ

1582.

Joseph Aistleitner, *Wörterbuch der ugaritischen Sprache*. Berlin, 1967. 364 pp. 3rd edn, by Otto Eißfeldt.

The '4th edn', 1974, is a reprint of the third.

1st edn: 1963. – 2nd edn: 1965.

Berichte über die Verhandlungen der Sächsischen Akademie der Wissenschaften in Leipzig, philologisch-historische Klasse, vol. 106 part 3.

[*Dictionary of the Ugaritic language.*] A concise dictionary which gives a brief German gloss followed by all available citations from the texts, sometimes quoting illustrative phrases. The Ugaritic is in consonantal transliteration. The second and third editions have supplementary bibliographies in their preliminary pages: some corrections and additions have been made to the text.

1583.

John Huehnergard, *Ugaritic vocabulary in syllabic transcription*. Atlanta: Scholars Press, 1987. 374 pp.

Harvard Semitic studies, 32.

This modest but fundamental work aims to contribute to the phonetics – specifically the vocalisation – of Ugaritic. It takes the form of a dictionary (pp. 103–94) with proposed pronunciation, supporting evidence, and discussion.

1584.

G. del Olmo Lete, J. Sanmartín, *Diccionario de la lengua ugarítica*. Barcelona: Ausa, 1996– .

Aula orientalis, supplementa, 7.

[*Dictionary of the Ugaritic language.*] Detailed entries with Spanish glosses and full references to the scholarly literature, followed by further paragraphs giving citations of Ugaritic texts. The first volume (250 pp.) covers ʾ–L, which is half the alphabet.

UIGUR

Uigur is a TURKIC LANGUAGE of eastern China, with nearly seven million speakers: they are one of the largest of Chinese minorities. It is normally written in a form of Arabic script.

1585.

Э. Н. Наджип, *Уйгурско–русский словарь* [*Uigursko–russkii slovar'*].
Moscow: Sovetskaya Entsiklopediya, 1968. 828 pp.

[*Uigur–Russian dictionary.*] In Arabic script with Cyrillic phonetic transcription.

1586.

Klaus Röhrborn, *Uigurisches Wörterbuch: Sprachmaterial der vorislamischen türkischen Texte aus Zentralasien.* Wiesbaden: Steiner, 1977– .

[*Uigur dictionary: linguistic material of the pre-Islamic Turkish texts from Central Asia.*] A detailed dictionary, in Latin transliteration (but with some use of Chinese script), with many quotations and citations. Glosses in German. With part 5 (1994) the dictionary extends to 372 pages and covers **A–ämgäklig**.

1587.

Henry G. Schwarz, *An Uyghur–English dictionary.* Bellingham, Washington, 1992. 1083 pp.

Center for East Asian Studies, Western Washington University. *East Asian research aids & translations*, 3.

1588.

Uigursko–kitaisko–russkii slovar'. Beijing, 1953.

[*Uigur–Chinese–Russian dictionary.*] Not seen.

UKRAINIAN

A SLAVONIC language with 45 million speakers in Ukraine, Russia and some other former Soviet countries. There is also a large Ukrainian minority in Canada. Ukrainian is written in a variant of the Cyrillic alphabet that is used for Russian.

Ukrainian alphabetical order

а б в г ґ д е є ж з и і ї й к л м н о п р с т у ф х ц ч ш щ ь ю я

Historical dictionaries

1589.

Словник української мови [*Slovnyk ukraïns'koï movy*]. Kiev, 1970–80 . 11 vols.

Edited by I. K. Bilodid and others.

[*Dictionary of the Ukrainian language.*] A historical dictionary of the modern language from the eighteenth century to modern times Glosses are followed by quotations from texts (in sloping face) with precise references. Variant meanings are separated by // and are sometimes set out in numbered paragraphs. Supplement (*Додатки*), vol. 11 pp. 663–99.

Arrangement is on the basis of the then current orthography, naturally: one emigré reviewer refers severely to the 'confiscation of the letter G and of all the words commencing with it' (J. B. Rudnyckyj in *Wörterbücher*, **12**, col. 2332: compare next entry). Actually the words are all there, filed under **Г**.

Classified bibliography of sources, vol. 1 pp. xii–xxvii. Note that there is no single alphabetical list of abbreviations.

The modern standard

1590.

C. H. Andrusyshen, J. N. Krett, *Ukrainian–English dictionary* = *Українсько-англійський словник*. Toronto: University of Toronto Press, 1955. 1163 pp.

Assisted by H. V. Andrusyshen. Published for the University of Saskatchewan.

A dictionary of modern written Ukrainian: the vocabulary is drawn from texts including 'belletristic, scholarly, scientific, journalistic, and even those with dialectal coloring'. Claims 95,000 entries. Based on the old 1928 orthography, which differs slightly from what was current in the contemporary Soviet Union (but it is apparently now being revived in independent Ukraine). Explanation of spelling differences, pp. xi–xii; the main one is the presence of a letter **Г** 'g' distinct from **Г** 'h'.

Older periods

1591.

Словник староукраїнської мови xiv-xvcт. [*Slovnyk staroukraïns'koï movy XIV–XVst.*]. Kiev: Naukova Dumka, 1977–8. 2 vols [630 + 592 pp.].

Edited by L. L. Humets'ka, I. M. Kernits'kii. Akademiya Nauk Ukraïns'koï RSR, Instytut Suspil'nykh Nauk.

[*Dictionary of the Old Ukrainian language, fourteenth–fifteenth centuries.*] A historical dictionary of the Old Ukrainian (or, many would say, Middle Ukrainian) written language. Often no glosses are provided, simply the quotations from early Ukrainian texts – and not only Ukrainian, sometimes also Polish and Church Slavonic if they contain Ukrainian forms. Brief etymologies are provided for loanwords. A final paragraph, headed *Форми*, gives variant forms and spellings. Sources and bibliography, vol. 1 pp. 19–56.

1592.

Словник української мови XVI—першої половини XVIIст. [*Slovnyk ukraïns'koi movy XVI–pershoi polovyny XVII st.*]. Kiev: Naukova Dumka, 1983. 156 pp.

Edited by D. H. Hrynchyshyn. Akademiya Nauk Ukraïns'koï RSR, Instytut Suspil'nykh Nauk.

[*Dictionary of the Ukrainian language, sixteenth–first half of seventeenth century.*] Not a finished dictionary but a collection of experimental entries.

Etymological dictionaries

1593.

Етимологічнии словник української мови [*Etymolohichnyi slovnyk ukraïns'koï movy*]. Kiev: Naukova Dumka, 1982– .
Chief editor, O. S. Mel'nychuk. Akademiya Nauk Ukraïns'koï RSR, Instytut Movoznavstva.

[*Etymological dictionary of the Ukrainian language.*] A large-scale etymological dictionary providing some cognates from other Slavonic languages. Little attention to dating; many references to other etymological dictionaries (bibliography, vol. 1 pp. 17–35).

The latest volume seems to be vol. 3 (1989); coverage is now **A–M**. Seven volumes are planned.

1594.

J. B. Rudnyckyj, *An etymological dictionary of the Ukrainian language.* Winnipeg, Ottawa, 1962–82. 2 vols [968 + 1129 pp.].

URALIC LANGUAGES

The Uralic language family of northern Asia and northern Europe includes the following languages with entries in this book: ESTONIAN, FINNISH, HUNGARIAN, KHANTY, KOMI, LIVONIAN, MANSI, MARI, MORDVIN, SAMI, SAMOYEDIC LANGUAGES, UDMURT.

Some scholars have considered it linked with TURKIC, MONGOLIAN and other languages in a wider grouping called 'Ural-Altaic'. Others trace links between Uralic and INDO-EUROPEAN LANGUAGES.

Comparative dictionaries

1595.

Björn Collinder, *Fenno-Ugric vocabulary: an etymological dictionary of the Uralic languages.* Uppsala: Almqvist & Wiksell, 1977. 217 pp. 2nd edition.
1st edn: 1955.
The first edn was later counted as: *A handbook of the Uralic languages*, part 1. Part 2 was *Survey of the Uralic languages* (1957); part 3 was *Comparative grammar of the Uralic languages* (1960).

Arranged in two main sequences, the first for words that can be traced to proto-Uralic (because they are found both in Finno-Ugric and in Samoyedic languages); the second for proto-Finno-Ugric words that cannot be traced further back. Then follows a list of Indo-European loanwords; then an appendix of 72 items, already included in the first two lists, that have apparent cognates in Altaic languages (Turkic, Tungusic, Mongolian, Korean). There are separate indexes of cited forms from individual languages.

1596.

Otto Donner, *Vergleichendes Wörterbuch der Finnisch-Ugrischen Sprachen.* Helsinki, 1874–88. 3 vols.

[*Comparative dictionary of the Finno-Ugric languages.*]

1597.

Károly Rédei, editor, *Uralisches etymologisches Wörterbuch*. Wiesbaden: Harrassowitz, 1986–8.

[*Uralic etymological dictionary.*]

Other works of interest

1598.

Juha Janhunen, 'Uralaisen kantakielen sanastosta = Über den Wortschatz des proto-Uralischen' in *Journal de la Société Finno-Ougrienne* vol. 77 (1981) pp. 219–74.

1599.

Denis Sinor, editor, *The Uralic languages: description, history and foreign influences*. Leiden: Brill, 1988. 841 pp. 90–04–07741–3.

UZBEK

Uzbek, a TURKIC language of central Asia, was once (in the form known as Chagatai) the vehicle of a literature written in Arabic script. The Cyrillic alphabet was used under Soviet rule, but independent Uzbekistan has adopted the Latin alphabet. There are 16 million speakers.

The Chagatai alphabet

ي و ه ن م ل گ ک ق ف غ ع ظ ط ض ص ش س ژ ز ر ذ د چ ج ح خ ج ث ت پ ب ا

a b p t ṣ j ḥ kh č d z̲ r z ž s š ṣ ż ṭ z̧ ' gh f q k g l m n h v y

In the Arabic script as used for Chagatai, the two semivowel signs (the last two letters of the alphabet) were also used for vowels: و *v* served for *o u ö ü*; ي *y* served for *i ı*.

The Cyrillic alphabet for Uzbek

а б в г д е ё ж з и й к л м н о п р с т у ф х ц ч ш э ю я ӯ қ ғ ҳ

1600.

Қўшжонов М. Қ., *Русча–ўзбекча луғат* = Кошчанов М. К., *Русско–узбекский словарь* [Qöshzhonov M. K., *Ruscha–Özbekcha lughat*]. Toshkent: Uzbek Sovet Entsiklopedyasi Bosh, 1983– .

Edited by Kushjonov M. K. and others.

[*Russian–Uzbek dictionary.*] Vol. 1 covers **A–O**. I have not seen the second volume, which would complete the set.

1601.

С. Ф. Акабиров, З. М. Магруфов, А. Т. Ходжаханов, *Узбекско—русский словарь* [S. F. Akabirov, Z. M. Magrufov, A. T. Khodzhakhanov, *Uzbeksko–russkii slovar'*]. Moscow, 1959. 839 pp.

[*Uzbek–Russian dictionary.*] Index in Arabic script, pp. 731–839.

VEGLIOTE

Vegliote or Dalmatian became extinct at the beginning of this century. It was a ROMANCE language of the eastern coast of the Adriatic.

1602.

M. Bartoli, *Das Dalmatische: altromanische Sprachreste von Veglia bis Ragusa und ihre Stellung in der Apennino-balkanischen Romania.* Vienna, 1906. 2 vols.

[*Dalmatian: remains of Old Romance from Veglia to Ragusa and their classification within Italian-Balkan Romance.*] Bartoli worked with the last known speaker of Vegliote. The language was recorded just in time – but the fact that this speaker had lost his teeth may have affected the phonetic interpretation.

VIETNAMESE

Vietnamese or Annamese, the national language of Vietnam, is an AUSTROASIATIC language of the Viet-Muong group, with 55 million speakers.

In the Latin alphabet as used for Vietnamese, the following are counted as single letters:

A Ă Â B C Ch D Đ E Ê G Gi H I K Kh L M N
Ng Nh O Ô Ơ P Ph Q R S T Th Tr U Ư V X Y

Historical dictionaries

1603.

Diễn-Hương, *Thành ngữ điển tích.* Saigon: Khai-Trí, 1969. 536 pp. 3rd edn.

Cover title: *Từ-điển thành-ngữ điển-tích.*

1st edn: Saigon: Tác Gia, 1949. 2 vols. – 2nd edn: 1961. 503 pp.

[*Classical literary Vietnamese.*] A dictionary-encyclopaedia, strong on phrases and idioms, with relevant literary examples. Also includes many proper names. Entries for poets include specimens of their work.

1604.

Paul Schneider, *Dictionnaire historique des idéogrammes vietnamiens.* Nice: Université de Nice-Sophia Antipolis, Unité de Recherches Interdisciplinaires sur l'Asie du Sud-Est, Madagascar et les Iles de l'Océan Indien, 1992. 914 pp. 2–909592–00–6.

[*Historical dictionary of Vietnamese ideograms.*] Reproduced from typescript, with Chinese characters inserted by hand. A working paper rather than a finished dictionary, intended to cover the history of the vocabulary from the fourteenth to the twentieth century, but without references to sources. Bibliography, pp. 2–4.

The modern standard

1605.

К. М. Аликанов, В. В. Иванов, И. А. Мальханова, *Русско–Вьетнамский словарь* = K. M. Alikanôp, V. V. Ivanôp, I. A. Malkhanôva, *Từ-điển Nga Việt.* Moscow: Russkii Yazyk, 1977. 2 vols [648 + 704 pp.].

[*Russian–Vietnamese dictionary.*] One of the biggest bilingual dictionaries of Vietnamese. Generous with near-synonyms but short on exemplification.

1606.

Bùi Phung, *Từ điển Việt Anh* = *Vietnamese English dictionary: 95000 words.* Hanoi: Hanoi University Press, 1993. 1710 pp.

Replaces a briefer dictionary: Bùi Phung, *Từ-điển Việt–Anh* = *Vietnamese–English dictionary*. Hanoi: Hanoi University Press, 1977 [1978 on cover]. 1322 pp.
2nd edn: 1986. 992 pp. 3rd edn: 1992. 1139 pp. '55,000 words.'

Concentrates on contemporary Vietnamese, but also deals with archaic words, foreign loanwords and slang.

1607.

Lê Khả Kế [and others], *Từ điển Pháp–Việt* = *Dictionnaire français-vietnamien.* Hanoi: Agence de Coopération Culturelle et Technique, 1981. 1276 pp.

Comité des Sciences Sociales de la République Socialiste du Vietnam.

[*French–Vietnamese dictionary.*] A beautifully printed modern dictionary with a good selection of examples, synonyms, phrases and other semantic help. There were no French on the editorial committee; but for all that the vocabulary is fairly well chosen and up to date.

1608.

Lê-Văn-Đức, Lê-Ngọc-Trụ, *Từ điển Việt-nam.* Saigon: Khai Trí, 1970. 2 vols.

Cover title: *Việt-nam từ điển.*

[*Vietnamese dictionary.*] A useful monolingual dictionary of Vietnamese, complicated in its arrangement. Each volume contains three separately paginated sequences on different-coloured paper: general vocabulary, proverbs and idioms, places and persons.

1609.

Dinh-Hoa Nguyen, *NTC's Vietnamese–English dictionary*. Lincolnwood, Illinois: NTC, 1995. 0–8442–8356–8.

Earliest version: Nguyen-Dinh-Hoa: *Vietnamese–English vocabulary*. Washington, 1955.
Succeeded by: Nguyen-Dinh-Hoa, *Vietnamese–English dictionary*. Saigon: Binh-Minh, 1959. 568 pp. – This was reprinted as: *Hoa's Vietnamese–English dictionary*. Rutland: Tuttle, 1966. 0–8048–0618–7.
Succeeded by: Nguyễn Dình Hoà, *Vietnamese–English student dictionary*. Saigon: Vietnamese-American Association, 1967. 675 pp. – Reprinted: Carbondale: Southern Illinois University Press; Amsterdam: Feffer and Simons, 1971. 0–8093–0476–7.

A concise, practical dictionary, benefiting from the author's expertise in English. He was Professor at the University of Saigon and Cultural Counsellor at the Vietnamese Embassy in Washington.

The author's earliest dictionary, 1955, was a typescript teaching glossary (9000 entries) compiled at Columbia University. His 1959 dictionary has about 20,000 entries, with some guidance on usage. Includes pronunciation guide (International Phonetic Alphabet) for north, central and south Vietnam. Formerly much used in the US Armed Forces. The latest, 1995, version is a reprint of the 1967 one, with a considerable supplement of new words (pp. 679–728).

1610.

Từ điển Anh Việt. Hanoi: Khoa Học Xã Hội, 1975. 1959 pp.

Ủy Ban Khoa Học Xã Hội Việt Nam, Viện Ngôn Ngữ Học.
Unacknowledged reprint: Dang The Binh and others: *Từ điển Anh–Việt hiện đại = Modern English–Vietnamese dictionary*. Glendale, California: Dainamco, n.d.

[*English–Vietnamese dictionary.*] A large-scale dictionary of 65,000 headwords, including translations for many English phrases. The compilers are all Vietnamese, and a serious defect is the inclusion of many practically unknown English words (e.g. 'defervescence') and the omission of many current and technical terms.

The older period

1611.

Đào Duy-Anh, *Pháp–Việt từ điển chú thêm chữ Hán = Dictionnaire français–vietnamien*. Saigon: Truòng-Thi, 1957. 1958 pp.

2nd edn: Paris, 1950. 1st edn: 1936.

[*French–Vietnamese dictionary, with nôm characters for Chinese terms.*] Latest version of a big dictionary which retains its usefulness for older vocabulary: its strongest feature is the offering of precise Vietnamese renderings of French terms and phrases.

1612.

Eugène Gouin, *Dictionnaire vietnamien–chinois–français*. Saigon: Imprimerie d'Extrême-Orient, 1947.

[*Vietnamese–Chinese–French dictionary.*] Vietnamese headwords are in the French rather than the Vietnamese alphabetical order. The dictionary is arranged under monosyllabic 'words' or morphemes, with numbered sub-headings for distinct meanings. These are followed by sub–entries for multisyllabic words and compounds, with references back to the numbered sub-headings. This is a very comprehensive dictionary, but with only brief definitions and little exemplification. 'Chinese' is here only in the sense that nôm characters are given for forms of Chinese origin: there is a 40–page index of Chinese characters but no French index.

1613.

Gustave Hue, *Từ điển Việt–Họa–Pháp = Dictionnaire Vietnamien–Chinois–Français*. Saigon: Librairie Khai Trí, 1971. 1199 pp.

[*Vietnamese–Chinese–French dictionary.*] Seven pages of corrections at end.

1614.

Nguyễn Quang Xỹ, Vũ Van Kính, *Từ-điển chữ nôm*. Saigon: Bô Giáo-Dục, Trung-Tâm Học-Liệu Xuất Bản, 1971.

[*Nôm to quôc-ngu dictionary.*] Contains 10,000 headwords. Index, in nôm (Chinese) script, in character order (i.e. by number of strokes), pp. 3–102; alphabetical dictionary, including brief 'etymological' notes on nôm characters, pp. 105–860.

Foreign words

1615.

Đào Duy Anh, *Hiêu dinh-han man tu Hán Việt từ điển*. Saigon: Trường Thị, 1957. 605 pp.

1st edn: 1932. 2nd edn: 1936. 3rd edn: Paris, 1951.

[*Concise Sino-Vietnamese dictionary.*] Latest printing of a specialised dictionary of the Chinese element in Vietnamese, giving Chinese characters, translations and explanations in everyday Vietnamese.

1616.

Hoàng Văn Hành [and others], *Từ điển yếu tố Hán Việt thông dụng = Dictionary of Sino-Vietnamese everyday usage elements*. Hanoi: Khoa Học Xã Hội, 1991. 492 pp.

Intended to highlight the elements that are shared among Vietnamese, Chinese and Japanese. About 3500 entries, filed under Vietnamese spelling. Entries give Chinese character, 'international' pronunciation, Peking pronunciation, Japanese pronunciation, English gloss, then Vietnamese meanings in full.

WA LANGUAGES

This group of AUSTROASIATIC LANGUAGES has well over a million speakers in mountainous regions of Burma, Yunnan and Thailand, centring on the 'golden triangle' where much of the world's opium is produced. There is no full dictionary.

1617.

G. Diffloth, 'The Wa languages' in *Linguistics of the Tibeto-Burman area* vol. 5 no. 2 (1980) pp. 1–182.

A brief comparative vocabulary in tabular form, with references to earlier sources.

1618.

V. Mitani, 'A short vocabulary of Lawa' in *Tōnan Ajia kenkyū* vol. 10 no. 1 (1972) pp. 131–68.

WELSH

One of the CELTIC LANGUAGES, Welsh was the language of the independent principality of Wales which fell to English rule in 1282. Determined resistance has led to the gradual easing of official discrimination against Welsh in the last half-century. There are perhaps half a million speakers.

Users of Welsh dictionaries need to be aware of the very different shapes that words can assume because of initial mutations. For example, the word for 'cat', a loanword from English, appears as *cath* in dictionaries but will also be found in texts spelt *chath*, *gath* and *nghath*.

Welsh alphabetical order

a b c ch d dd e f ff g h i j l ll m n o p r rh s t th u w y

Historical dictionaries

1619.

D. Silvan Evans, *Geiriadur Cymraeg = A dictionary of the Welsh language.* Carmarthen: Spurrell, 1887–1906. Parts 1–5 [1884 pp.; no more published].

Brief glosses in English are followed (for major entries) by quotations from literature, neatly laid out with verse set line for line. Although now superseded by the University of Wales dictionary (**1620**) Evans's remains useful for its quotations. It covers only **A–Engwyn**.

1620.

Geiriadur Prifysgol Cymru = A dictionary of the Welsh language. Cardiff: Gwasg Prifysgol Cymru, 1950– .
Edited by R. J. Thomas, [Gareth A. Bevan].

[*The University of Wales dictionary.*] An extremely concise historical dictionary. Major entries are allowed numerous brief quotations from the texts, early and modern: these are dated, and give precise references (see list of sources at head of each volume). Less favoured entries are allowed just a dating, without explicit references or quotations. The work is in Welsh, but with glosses also in English; the general abbreviations are explained in both languages in each volume.

Publication has reached part 47 (p. 2996), midway through vol. 3. Coverage is **A–Rhadus**.

The modern standard

1621.

Bruce Griffiths, Dafydd Glyn Jones, *The Welsh Academy English–Welsh dictionary*. Cardiff: University of Wales Press, 1995. 1710 pp. 0–7083–1186–5.

A major bilingual dictionary, far better than anything that has gone before. Taxonomic names as well as Welsh glosses are given for flora and fauna. How to use the dictionary, pp. ix–xii; the morphology of the Welsh language, pp. xx–lxxix.

1622.

W. Owen Pughe, *Geiriadur cenhedlaethol Cymraeg a Saesneg = A national dictionary of the Welsh language, with English and Welsh equivalents*. Denbigh: T. Gee, 1871–2. 2 vols [21 parts]. 3rd edn, enlarged by Robert John Pryse.
The title page of vol. 1 is incorrectly dated MDCCCLXVI [1866].
1st edn: London: E. Williams, 1803. – 2nd edn: Denbigh, 1832.

A concise bilingual dictionary with many set phrases: still the largest complete Welsh–English dictionary. Very brief etymologies or derivations in brackets.

Older periods

1623.

J. Lloyd-Jones, *Geirfa barddoniaeth gynnar Gymraeg*. Cardiff: Gwasg Prifysgol Cymru, 1931–63. Vols 1–2 [no more published].

[*Vocabulary of Old Welsh poetry.*] A dictionary of the language of early Welsh poetic texts, amounting to a fairly full concordance of the older literature. There are great numbers of precise citations; relatively few, but long, quotations. Full attention is given to variant forms and spellings. The dictionary is entirely in Welsh.

It was essentially a one-man work, and publication ceased on the author's death: the two published volumes cover **A–Heilic**.

XHOSA

One of the Bantu languages, and thus a member of the NIGER-CONGO family, Xhosa has nearly seven million speakers in South Africa, making them the second largest language group in the country after speakers of ZULU.

1624.

Albert Kropf, *A Kafir–English dictionary*. Lovedale: Lovedale Mission, 1915. 525 pp.

1625.

A. Fischer, *English–Xhosa dictionary*. Cape Town: Oxford University Press, 1985. 738 pp. 0–19–570290–5.

YAKUT

Yakut is the TURKIC language of eastern Siberia, with 30,000 speakers.

1626.

Otto Böhtlingk, *Über die Sprache der Jakuten*. St Petersburg, 1851. 54 + 400 + 180 pp.
Part 1: Introduction, Yakut text, Yakut grammar. Part 2: Yakut–German dictionary.

[*On the language of the Yakuts.*] This was, writes Krueger (**1627**), 'the original and classic work on the Yakut language, written by a famous Sanskritist with the aid of a bilingual informant'.

1627.

John R. Krueger, *Yakut manual*. Bloomington: Indiana University, 1962. 389 pp.
Indiana University publications, Graduate School, Uralic and Altaic series, 21. American Council of Learned Societies, Research and studies in Uralic and Altaic languages, project no. 63.
Fuller title facing title page: *Yakut manual: area handbook, grammar, graded reader and glossary.*

Includes a Yakut–English glossary in the modern Cyrillic orthography (pp. 316–80) and a text and analysis of K. P. J. von Strahlenberg's Yakut vocabulary from his *Das nord- und ostliche Theil von Europa und Asia* (Stockholm, 1730), the earliest word-list of the language.

1628.

Э. К. Пекарскій, *Словарь якутскаго языка* [E. K. Pekarskii, *Slovar' yakutskago yazyka*]. St Petersburg, 1881–1930. 3 vols [13 parts; 3858 columns].
Reprint: Leningrad: Akademiya Nauk SSSR, 1958–9.
On Pekarskii's work see: E. I. Okoneshnikov, *E. K. Pekarskii kak leksikograf.* Novosibirsk: Nauka, 1982. 140 pp. [*E. K. Pekarskii as a lexicographer.*]

[*Dictionary of the Yakut language.*] 'Professor Fred Adelman secured for me on a trip to the Soviet Union the last available copy of Pekarskii's huge, three-volume Yakut dictionary, and, what is more, laboriously brought it to me as 30 lbs of overweight luggage on his air ticket' (Krueger, **1627**).

YAO

With MIAO, Yao is one of the two dialect groups in the Miao-Yao language family of southern China. It is now believed to be a member of the wider grouping of AUSTRO-TAI LANGUAGES. There are nearly a million speakers.

1629.

Sylvia J. Lombard, Herbert C. Purnell Jr, *Yao–English dictionary*. Ithaca: Cornell University, Department of Asian Studies, 1968. 363 pp.
Southeast Asia Program. *Data paper*, 69. *Linguistics series*, 2.

Uses material gathered between 1952 and 1966 during residence in Yao villages in Chiengrai province and visits to refugee groups in Laos and South Vietnam. In Latin script: on the transcription see pp. x–xv.

Appendices: numbers, pp. 317–20; kinship terms, pp. 321–7; proverbs and idioms, pp. 335–9; and others. Substantial addenda, pp. 345–63.

YIDDISH

Yiddish is a GERMANIC language and thus a member of the Indo-European family. It is a variant of medieval German, spoken until the Second World War in many Jewish communities scattered across central and eastern Europe. Millions of Yiddish speakers were killed in the early 1940s. There are now perhaps two million speakers. Discouraged in Israel, where Hebrew is preferred, Yiddish is now in decline. Significant Yiddish-speaking communities remain in several European and American cities, notably New York.

See Wander (**566**) for Yiddish proverbs.

Yiddish alphabets

א אָ בּ ג ד ה וּ ז ט י יִ כּ לּ מּ נּ סּ עּ פּ פֿ צּ ק ר שּׁ תּ וּ ו שׁ יי ייִ וי

a o b g d h u z t i y kh l m n s e p f ts k r sh t v zh tsh ey ay oy

Yiddish is most often written in Hebrew script; the standard romanisation, given in this table, is also used.

1630.

Judah A. Joffe, Yudel Mark, editors in chief, *Great dictionary of the Yiddish language* = גרויסער ווערטערבוך פֿון דער יידישער שפּראַך. New York: Yiddish Dictionary Committee, 1961– .

A large-scale historical dictionary, entirely in Yiddish (in Hebrew script). Brief glosses are followed by long quotations from texts.

To be complete in 12 volumes: the last I know of is vol. 4 (1990). Coverage has not reached beyond א, the first letter of the alphabet – but in a Yiddish dictionary one third of all entries begin with א.

1631.

М. А. Шапиро, И. Г. Спивак, М. Я. Шульман, *Русско—еврейский (идиш) словарь* [M. A. Shapiro, I. G. Spivak, M. Ya. Shul'man, editors, *Russko-evreiskii (idish) slovar'*] = רוסיש-יידישער ווערטערבוך. Moscow: Russkii Yazyk, 1984. 720 pp. [5–200–00427–6.]
Authors: R. Ya. Lerner and others.

[*Russian–Yiddish dictionary.*] The largest bilingual dictionary into Yiddish. Where the spelling is not phonetic (as with Hebrew words), the Yiddish is pointed to assist with pronunciation.

1632.

Alexander Harkavy, *Yiddish–English–Hebrew dictionary*. New York, 1928. 583 pp. 2nd edn.

Reprinted with an introduction by Dovid Katz: New York: Yivo Institute for Jewish Research, 1988. 0–8052–4027–6.

1st edn: 1925. 530 pp. – Earlier version: Alexander Harkavy, *A dictionary of the Yiddish language, with a treatise on Yiddish reading, orthography and dialectal variations* = ייִדיש-ענגלישעס ווערטערבוך. New York: Harkavy, 1898. 351 pp. – Companion work: Alexander Harkavy, *Complete English–Jewish dictionary*. New York, 1891. 359 pp.

A brief-entry dictionary with many short notes of historical and ethnographical interest (as emphasised by Katz in his important introduction to the 1988 reprint). It includes numerous nineteenth century loanwords from German that were then current in spoken and written Yiddish, many of them no longer familiar.

The 1898 publication is a bilingual Yiddish–English dictionary. Harkavy also published an English–Yiddish dictionary in 1891. His greatest work, the encyclopaedic *Yidisher folks-verterbukh*, remains in manuscript.

1633.

Uriel Weinreich, *Modern English–Yiddish, Yiddish–English dictionary*. New York: Yivo Institute for Jewish Research, 1968. 789 pp.

A brief-entry two-way dictionary, intended mainly for English speakers, by an eminent historian of Yiddish. Where Yiddish spelling is not phonetic, as with Hebrew words, pronunciation is indicated in Latin script (explanations, pp. xx–xxv). 'Grammatical analysis of Yiddish vocabulary,' pp. xxvi–xxxvii.

YORUBA

Yoruba is one of the four major languages of Nigeria (with Hausa, Igbo and English), and a member of the NIGER-CONGO family. There are 20 million speakers, including some in Benin.

1634.

R. C. Abraham, *Dictionary of modern Yoruba*. London: Oxford University Press, 1958. 776 pp.

A Yoruba–English dictionary which claims, with the compiler's accustomed modesty, to cover 'every aspect of Yoruba civilization' and to include 'countless idioms, current phrases, proverbs and riddles'. Very useful illustrations of plants and animals at end, preceded by a list giving taxonomic names.

ZULU

Zulu speakers are the largest language community in South Africa: there are nearly nine million of them. Zulu is a Bantu language, a member of the NIGER-CONGO family, closely related to its neighbour Xhosa.

1635.

C. M. Doke, D. M. Malcolm, J. M. A. Sikakana, *English–Zulu dictionary*. Johannesburg: Witwatersrand University Press, 1958. 572 pp.

Reprints incorporate a short Zulu–English dictionary (342 pp.). [0–8549–4010–3.]

1636.

C. M. Doke, B. W. Vilakazi, *Zulu–English dictionary*. Johannesburg: Witwatersrand University Press, 1953. 918 pp. Reprint of the 1st edn with a supplement. [0–8549–4027–8.]

1st edn: 1948. 903 pp.

1637.

J. W. Colenso, *Zulu–English dictionary*. Durban: Vause, Slatter, 1905. 728 pp. 4th edn, revised by Harriette Emily Colenso.

1st edn: Pietermaritzburg: Davis, 1861. 552 pp. – 'New edn:' Durban: Davis, 1884. 672 pp.

INDEX

This is an index of personal names and of the titles of dictionaries. In general, organisations, series titles, article titles, and titles of books which are not dictionaries, are not indexed. All references are to entry numbers.

INDEX